Frommer's

Walt Disney World® & Orlando with Kids

3rd Edition

by Laura Lea Miller

Here's what the critics say about Frommer's:

"Amazingly easy to use. Very portable, very complete."

—*Booklist*

"Detailed, accurate, and easy-to-read information for all price ranges."
—*Glamour Magazine*

"Hotel information is close to encyclopedic."

—*Des Moines Sunday Register*

"Frommer's Guides have a way of giving you a real feel for a place."
—*Knight Ridder Newspapers*

WILEY

Wiley Publishing, Inc.

Published by:

Wiley Publishing, Inc.

111 River St.
Hoboken, NJ 07030-5774

ISBN: 978-0-470-13471-9
Editors: Leslie Shen and Cate Latting
Production Editor: Lindsay Conner
Cartographer: Elizabeth Puhl
Photo Editor: Richard Fox
Production by Wiley Indianapolis Composition Services

For information on our other products and services or to obtain technical support, please
contact our Customer Care Department within the U.S. at 800/762-2974, outside the
U.S. at 317/572-3993 or fax 317/572-4002.

Wiley also publishes its books in a variety of electronic formats. Some content that
appears in print may not be available in electronic formats.

Manufactured in the United States of America

5   4   3   2   1

Contents

8   Orlando for Active Families   302

9   Shopping for the Whole Family   311

10 Entertainment for the Whole Family   323

11 Side Trips from Orlando   340

Appendix: Useful Toll-Free Numbers & Websites   358

Index   360

List of Maps

Acknowledgments

Thanks to Amy Voss of the Orlando/Orange County Convention & Visitors Bureau; Gary Buchanan and Dave Herbst over at Walt Disney World; Rhonda Murphy and Jennifer Hodges at Universal Orlando; Jackie Wilson at SeaWorld; as well as the marketing and PR reps at the countless hotels, resorts, and smaller attractions who have all been so incredibly helpful, making my travels—and my life—so very much easier.

A big thanks to my five children—Ryan, Austin, Nicolas, Hailey, and Davis—who happily offer their opinions on just about everything. Their endless energy and enthusiasm is invaluable when tackling the theme parks time after time.

My agent, Julie Hill, whose encouragement and enthusiasm are more appreciated than she'll ever know, is a blessing.

—Laura Lea Miller

About the Author

Laura Lea Miller is a freelance writer based in Orchard Park, New York. This snowbird has gladly flown south to warmer weather to spend countless hours scouring Central Florida's many theme parks, hotels, resorts, and restaurants over the years—both with and without her five children. A family-travel expert who focuses on Central Florida, Laura continues to religiously make an annual pilgrimage (or four or five) to the Land the Mouse Built, to ensure she can check out all of Orlando's latest and greatest offerings and provide you with the most up-to-date insider information. She's written several other Orlando and Florida books, including *Frommer's Walt Disney World & Orlando* and *Walt Disney World & Orlando For Dummies,* and has contributed to *Frommer's Florida.*

An Invitation to the Reader

In researching this book, we discovered many wonderful places—hotels, restaurants, shops, and more. We're sure you'll find others. Please tell us about them, so we can share the information with your fellow travelers in upcoming editions. If you were disappointed with a recommendation, we'd love to know that, too. Please write to:

Frommer's Walt Disney World & Orlando with Kids, 3rd Edition
Wiley Publishing, Inc. • 111 River St. • Hoboken, NJ 07030-5774

An Additional Note

Please be advised that travel information is subject to change at any time—and this is especially true of prices. We therefore suggest that you write or call ahead for confirmation when making your travel plans. The author, editors, and publisher cannot be held responsible for the experiences of readers while traveling. Your safety is important to us, however, so we encourage you to stay alert and be aware of your surroundings. Keep a close eye on cameras, purses, and wallets, all favorite targets of thieves and pickpockets.

Other Great Guides for Your Trip:

Frommer's Florida
Frommer's Walt Disney World & Orlando
Frommer's Irreverent Guide to Walt Disney World
The Unofficial Guide to Walt Disney World
The Unofficial Disney Companion
Beyond Disney: The Unofficial Guide

Frommer's Star Ratings, Icons & Abbreviations

Every hotel, restaurant, and attraction listing in this guide has been ranked for quality, value, service, amenities, and special features using a **star-rating system.** In country, state, and regional guides, we also rate towns and regions to help you narrow down your choices and budget your time accordingly. Hotels and restaurants are rated on a scale of zero (recommended) to three stars (exceptional). Attractions, shopping, nightlife, towns, and regions are rated according to the following scale: zero stars (recommended), one star (highly recommended), two stars (very highly recommended), and three stars (must-see).

In addition to the star-rating system, we also use **six feature icons** that point you to the great deals, in-the-know advice, and unique experiences that separate travelers from tourists. Throughout the book, look for:

Finds	Special finds—those places only insiders know about
Fun Fact	Fun facts—details that make travelers more informed and their trips more fun
Moments	Special moments—those experiences that memories are made of
Overrated	Places or experiences not worth your time or money
Tips	Insider tips—great ways to save time and money
Value	Great values—where to get the best deals

The following **abbreviations** are used for credit cards:

AE	American Express	DISC	Discover	V	Visa
DC	Diners Club	MC	MasterCard		

Frommers.com

Now that you have this guidebook, to help you plan a great trip, visit our website at **www. frommers.com** for additional travel information on more than 3,600 destinations. We update features regularly, to give you instant access to the most current trip-planning information available. At Frommers.com, you'll find scoops on the best airfares, lodging rates, and car rental bargains. You can even book your travel online through our reliable travel booking partners. Other popular features include:

- Online updates of our most popular guidebooks
- Vacation sweepstakes and contest giveaways
- Newsletters highlighting the hottest travel trends
- Online travel message boards with featured travel discussions

How to Feel Like an Orlando Family

In my house, and undoubtedly in many others, the mere mention of Walt Disney World and Orlando can cause little eyes to sparkle and smiles to appear, a phenomenon often accompanied by the spontaneous outbreak of jumping and dancing about the room. If there is any doubt at all that a trip to Orlando is worth the effort, I need only see the wonder, amazement, and excitement in the faces of my five kids, not to mention the tens of thousands of other kids I see when visiting Orlando. It simply confirms what I've known for a long time: that this is truly a magical place where children and families are the real VIPs.

Orlando businesses roll out the red carpet to children of all ages and their families. The city tempts you with special child check-in desks, kids' menus, character meet-and-greets, and an array of unique attractions (with slightly lower admission prices for those 3 to 9 years old). Some hotels and resorts have special programs for youngsters—and, in a few cases, teenagers—giving them their own space to hang out with their peers. A handful offer rooms with cartoon-character or action-hero themes. And almost every one of them lets kids ages 17 and under stay free with paying adults.

Thank Walter Elias Disney and his wannabes for that.

Uncle Walt laid the foundation for what in the past 3 decades has become America's *number-one vacation destination* for the young and young at heart.

Until Disney's heirs opened the gates to the Magic Kingdom in 1971, water-skiing and alligator-wrestling shows were the only attractions in town. Nowadays, the Kingdom That Walt Built tempts you with four major theme parks; two water parks; a dozen or so smaller attractions; an entertainment, shopping, and dining district; tens of thousands of hotel rooms (including timeshares—or what's called the Disney Vacation Club); scores of restaurants; and a cruise line all its own (with two—soon to be four—cruise ships). Universal Orlando adds two theme parks, three luxury hotels, and an entertainment district to the mix, while SeaWorld tosses in three more parks. The smaller fry ante up 80 or so lesser attractions, an avalanche of restaurants, and enough hotel rooms to boost Central Florida's total population to more than 114,000.

Of course, all of that comes with a price—and you're the one paying.

A typical family of four spends about $300 a day for admission, parking, a fast-food lunch, and two small souvenirs. That's not taking into account your hotel room, meals other than lunch, transportation (both to and from Orlando as well as to and from the parks, if need be), and other miscellaneous expenses and incidentals.

There's also an intangible price to pay: anxiety. There are so many things to see and do that even a 2-week stay and very deep pockets won't allow you the time to

Orlando Area Theme Parks

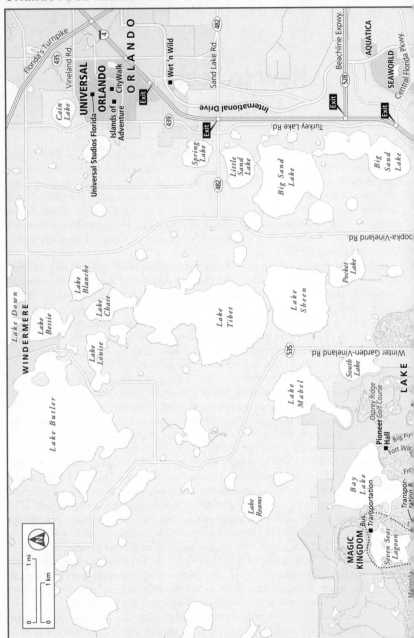

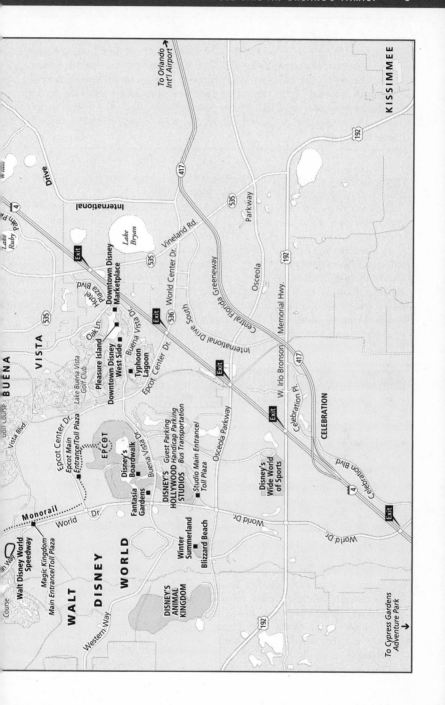

Fun Fact **By the Numbers**

With tourism once again on the rise, Central Florida finds itself hosting a staggering number of visitors. While individual parks don't release specific figures, *TEA (Themed Entertainment Association)*, in association with *Economic Research Associates*, estimates theme-park attendance and releases the reports annually. Its figures show that Disney parks welcome around 49 million visitors annually; Universal's two parks, about 12 million; and SeaWorld chips in another 6 million.

experience all of the parks and attractions. That completely unravels a good many travelers and can leave the unwary family feeling frazzled.

But don't panic—not yet, anyway. Over the years, I've explored and re-explored the parks with (and without) my five kids in tow, dined at Orlando's restaurants, and scoped out the area's best resorts and hotels just so I can give you the inside track. With this book, you'll have the tools to plan ahead, ensuring that all members of your family will have a good time. There's more than enough information here to make you a savvy shopper. My job: to make your family vacation easy to arrange and as enjoyable as possible, so you'll be able to relax and have fun while you're here. At the same time, I give plenty of options to make your vacation affordable. I've noted some of the best deals around, along with a handful of ways to maximize your fun while keeping your expenses to a minimum. And Orlando tourism gurus will make sure your family has a steady stream of new things to see and do each and every time you visit.

1 Frommer's Favorite Orlando Family Experiences

From Cinderella Castle to Space Mountain, everybody loves the Magic Kingdom, but here are plenty of other things to explore at Disney, Universal, SeaWorld, and in the greater Orlando area (see chapters 6 and 7 for details):

- **Go Globe Trotting at Epcot:** This is a great stop if your kids are old enough to have inquiring minds. You can travel around the world at the World Showcase pavilions, explore the all-new Seas with Nemo & Friends, blast off riding Mission: Space, get your thrills on Test Track, fly through the skies aboard Soarin', and glimpse the future at Innoventions. And what better way to cap your day than watching the **IllumiNations** fireworks show? See the "Epcot" section, beginning on p. 207.

- **Get Behind the Scenes at Disney's Hollywood Studios:** This park has plenty to offer both tots and teens. Ariel, Belle, and Bear in the Big Blue House come alive on stage, entrancing the younger set, while kids over 8 won't want to miss the thrills of the Tower of Terror and the Rock 'n' Roller Coaster. The whole family should see the Light, Motors, Action! Extreme Stunt Show, where stunt-car secrets are revealed. Get shrunk to the size of a toy and play along the midway on Toy Story Mania!; watch your favorite Disney-Pixar characters come to life in the all-new Block Party Bash parade; and catch Wildcat fever when you sing, dance, and cheer 'em on at the High School Musical 2: School's Out! street show. End the day with Fantasmic!, the fireworks, live-action, and laser-lights show. See the "Disney's Hollywood Studios" section, beginning on p. 226.

- **Catch a Wave at Typhoon Lagoon & Blizzard Beach:** Sandy beaches to sink your toes in and waterslides that range from terrifying to toddler-friendly—the entire family will have fun at these Disney water parks. You can even hang ten before park opening at Typhoon Lagoon: Surf lessons are offered twice weekly. See the "Disney Water Parks" section, beginning on p. 246.

- **Co-Pilot the WDW Monorail:** If there's no one but the pilot aboard, ask to sit up front, and you and your kids can pretend to drive Disney's monorail. Your best chance is if you board at the Grand Floridian, Contemporary, or Polynesian resorts, where the crowds are thinner than at the transportation center. Don't try this at park opening and closing times.

- **Experience Universal Orlando:** Universal Studios Florida and its sister park, Islands of Adventure, combine cutting-edge, high-tech special effects with edgy and amazing creativity. Not-to-be-missed attractions include the new Simpsons ride, Fear Factor Live, Terminator 2: 3-D Battle Across Time, Revenge of the Mummy, Men in Black Alien Attack, Jimmy Neutron's Nicktoon Blast, Shrek 4-D, Dueling Dragons, the Incredible Hulk Coaster, the Amazing Adventures of Spider-Man, and Dudley Do-Right's Ripsaw Falls. You'll have a tough time tearing the younger ones away from A Day in the Park with Barney, Curious George Goes to Town, Fievel's Playland, Caro-Seuss-el, and Camp Jurassic. And look for the highly anticipated Wizarding World of Harry Potter (a park-within-a-park) to make its debut in late 2009. See the "Universal Studios Florida" (p. 255) and "Islands of Adventure" (p. 270) sections.

- **Explore Eco-Edutainment at Sea-World, Discovery Cove & Aquatica:** The Journey to Atlantis and Kraken rides give SeaWorld a little zip, and the expansion of Shamu's Happy Harbor adds a little zing, but it's the hands-on encounters with sea critters, spectacular shows, and up-close viewing of the animals from polar bears to killer whales (kids of all ages will be entranced) that you should come for here. Its younger sister, Discovery Cove, gives you a chance to swim with dolphins and other undersea inhabitants (alas, currently at a cost of $249–$279). SeaWorld's newest sibling, Aquatica, takes undersea adventure one step further: The eco-themed water park is filled with slides and rides featuring up-close animal encounters and aquatic edutainment. See the "SeaWorld" section, beginning on p. 285.

- **Go Wild at Gatorland:** Located between Orlando and Kissimmee, this throwback park is a great way to spend a half day at less than a third of the price of the major theme parks. In addition to the animal exhibits, make sure to catch Gator Jumparoo, a signature show since the park opened in 1949. Gator Wrestlin' is worth a look, too. Other options include a children's water playground, an aviary, and a train ride through the park. If you have money to spare, and your kids are over 12, they (or you) can be a Trainer for a Day—definitely a once-in-a-lifetime experience. See p. 296.

- **Star-Gaze at the Orlando Science Center:** The center's planetarium is only part of the fun. Your heirs can dabble in Weird Science, 123 Math Avenue, KidsTown, and lots more at this popular downtown attraction. See p. 301.

Moments   Chills & Thrills

For parents and older children (who meet the mandatory height requirements) looking for the ups and downs of a good ride, here are the top stomach-churners and G-force generators in Orlando:

- **Incredible Hulk Coaster** (Islands of Adventure): Blast from 0 to 40 mph in 2 seconds, spin upside down, and endure seven rollovers and two plummets on this glow-in-the-dark roller coaster. See p. 278.
- **Rock 'n' Roller Coaster** (Disney's Hollywood Studios): You'll launch from 0 to 60 mph in 2.8 seconds and go into the first inversion as 120 speakers in your "stretch limo" mainline Aerosmith at (yeeeow!) 32,000 watts. See p. 234.
- **Dueling Dragons** (Islands of Adventure): Your legs dangle as you ride through five inversions at 55 to 60 mph and—get this—come within 12 inches of the other roller coaster three times. See p. 281.
- **Summit Plummet** (Blizzard Beach): This one starts from a 120-foot-high perch and turns into the world's fastest body slide—a test of your courage and swimsuit, as it has you moving sans vehicle at 60 mph. See p. 250.
- **The Twilight Zone Tower of Terror** (Disney's Hollywood Studios): The free-fall experiences are more than thrilling—they're also scary (even one of the ride's designers is too scared to go on it). Once your legs stop shaking, *some* of you will want to ride again. See p. 235.
- **Expedition Everest** (Disney's Animal Kingdom): Disney's latest contribution to the thrill-ride category takes you on a hair-raising expedition through the Himalayas. You'll career through twisted tracks and tight turns—and even make an 80-foot drop before ending up face to face with the legendary Yeti.
- **The Amazing Adventures of Spider-Man** (Islands of Adventure): 3-D doesn't get any better than this ride, which has you twisting, spinning, and soaring before a simulated 400-foot drop that feels awfully real. See p. 277.
- **Mission: Space** (Epcot): If you're claustrophobic or prone to motion sickness, stay clear of this ride, which simulates an actual liftoff (and the accompanying G-force) and gets the seal of approval from the NASA astronauts who helped design it. See p. 215.
- **Kraken** (SeaWorld): This floorless, open-sided coaster uses speed (up to 65 mph), steep climbs, deep drops, and seven loops to create a stomach-churning ride that lasts far too long for some folks. See p. 290.
- **Revenge of the Mummy** (Universal Studios): In shadowy darkness, you'll plunge forward, propel backward, twist and turn, start and stop without warning—all while flames and fireballs fly past you and creepy skeletal creatures give chase. See p. 266.

2 Best Hotel Bets

- **Most Family-Friendly Hotels:** All Disney properties cater to families, with special menus for kids, video arcades, free transportation to the parks, extensive recreational facilities, and, in some cases, character meals and kids' clubs. Camping at woodsy **Fort Wilderness** (© 407/934-7639; p. 105) makes for a unique and fun-filled family experience. If bunk beds, bubbling springs in the lobby, and a gushing geyser sound good, check into the **Wilderness Lodge** (© 407/934-7639; p. 99). Set sail for the **Yacht Club** and **Beach Club** (© 407/934-7639; p. 96, 87), where the sand-bottom pool and pirate-ship play area are just part of the seaside charm. The African savanna serves as a backdrop for the **Animal Kingdom Lodge** (© 407/934-7369; p. 98).

  Beyond the House of Mouse, the **Nickelodeon Family Suites** (© 877/387-5437; p. 115), **Holiday Inn Main Gate East** (© 888/465-4329; p. 120), **Holiday Inn SunSpree Resort Lake Buena Vista** (© 800/366-6299; p. 114), and **Seralago Hotel & Suites Main Gate East** (© 407/396-4488; p. 121) offer kids' suites, kids' clubs, activities, and more. See chapter 4 for more family-friendly accommodations.

- **Best Moderately Priced Hotels:** For Southern charm, head to the French Quarter and Riverside areas in **Disney's Port Orleans Resort** (© 407/934-7639; p. 102); the pool in the French Quarter has a water slide that curves out of a dragon's mouth. In the free world, the **Hilton in the Walt Disney World Resort** (© 407/827-4000; p. 108) is the only official resort on Hotel Plaza Boulevard to offer Disney's Extra Magic Hours option. Other pluses include two pools and spacious junior suites—and it's located just across from Downtown Disney. Nearby, the **Staybridge Suites Lake Buena Vista** (© 407/238-0777; p. 116) has room to spare, with oversize one- and two-bedroom suites. Full kitchens, free breakfasts, weekday receptions, and helpful services, including grocery delivery, are all part of the deal here. A second location on International Drive (© 407/352-2400; p. 126) offers much the same. The **Marriott Village at Lake Buena Vista,** which includes a Courtyard, SpringHill Suites, and Fairfield Inn & Suites (© 407/938-9001; p. 113), offers an array of accommodations to fit families (including themed family suites), conveniences like microwaves and fridges (in select rooms), pools and play areas, and plenty of nearby dining options—all just down the road from Downtown Disney.

- **Best Value/Deal:** That's easy: **Disney's All-Star Movies Resort** (© 407/934-7639; p. 103), **All-Star Music Resort** (© 407/934-7639; p. 103), **All-Star Sports Resort** (© 407/934-7639; p. 104), and **Pop Century Resort** (© 407/934-7639; p. 105). If you're going to stay on WDW property, you can't beat them, though they would be significantly overpriced outside the realm. The **Best Western Lakeside** (© 407/396-2222; p. 119) has three pools, miniature golf, a convenience store, free shuttles to area theme parks, and a kids-eat-free program. Plenty of restaurants are right nearby, and Disney is only 2 miles away. The **Comfort Suites Maingate East** (© 407/397-7848; p. 119) offers plenty of freebies including breakfast, shuttles to all theme parks, and high-speed

Internet access. From this all-suite hotel, it's only a short walk to shops, restaurants, and miniature golf, plus Disney is only minutes away.

- **Best Budget Motel:** The **Comfort Suites Maingate** (© 407/390-9888; p. 120) is modern, clean, and comfortable, with a location and price that are hard to beat. Restaurants and shops are steps away and Disney's just 2 miles down the road.

- **Best Spa for Kids:** That's not a typo. The **Nickelodeon Family Suites** (© 877/387-5437; p. 115) started something good with its Kids' Spa, with services such as manicures and temporary tattooing. The resort also has a lounge where parents can spend a little time on their own. At the Mandara Spa in the **Portofino Bay Hotel at Universal Orlando** (© 800/235-6397; p. 122), teens can choose from a menu of special services just for them.

- **Best Kids' Programs:** The Wizard of Diz has dandy kids' clubs at select resorts, but some really good ones can be found beyond Disney's doorstep, too. The top picks beyond Mickey's boundaries include Camp Gator at the **Hyatt Regency Grand Cypress** (© 800/233-1234; p. 111), Ritz-Kids at the **Ritz-Carlton** (© 800/241-3333; p. 112), La Petite Academy at **Gaylord Palms** (© 877/677-9352; p. 110), Camp Holiday at **Holiday Inn SunSpree** (© 800/366-6299; p. 114), Kids Crew at the **Ginn Reunion Resort** (© 888/418-9611; p. 118), Camp Lil' Rock at the **Hard Rock Hotel at Universal Orlando** (© 407/503-2236; p. 125), the Mariner's Club at the **Royal Pacific Resort at Universal Orlando** (© 407/503-3235; p. 125), and Campo Portofino at the **Portofino Bay Hotel at Universal Orlando** (© 407/503-1200; p. 122). You can find more details in chapter 4, "Family-Friendly Accommodations."

- **Tops for Tots & Toddlers:** Watch your kids' faces light up when larger-than-life raccoon mascots Max and Maxine show up to tuck them in at **Holiday Inn SunSpree Resort Lake Buena Vista** (© 800/366-6299; p. 114). Of course, it's hard to beat the **Nickelodeon Family Suites** (© 407/387-5437; p. 115), with its water-park-style pools, themed kids' suites, and character breakfasts. Kids from tots to tweens will go crazy for this one.

- **Tops for Teens:** I've yet to find a mainstream hotel that comes close to the activities offered in **Aloft** and **The Stack,** the teen clubs aboard the **Disney Cruise Line** ships *Wonder* and *Magic* (© 800/951-3532; p. 56). Activities include karaoke, a Hawaiian pool party, and improv. Inland, head over to the **Hard Rock Hotel at Universal Orlando** (© 407/503-2000; p. 125), with its sandy beach, way-cool underwater sound system, and hip rock-star decor.

- **Best Location:** Disney's **Grand Floridian Resort & Spa** (© 407/934-7639; p. 92), **Polynesian Resort** (© 407/934-7639; p. 94), and **Contemporary Resort** (© 407/934-7639; p. 92) not only offer waterfront access to Seven Seas Lagoon and Bay Lake, but they're also right on the WDW monorail, providing quick and easy access to the parks. The **Portofino Bay Hotel** (© 407/503-1000; p. 122), **Hard Rock Hotel** (© 407/503-2000; p. 125), and **Royal Pacific Resort** (© 407/503-3000; p. 125) are within walking distance of Universal's parks and CityWalk, with boat service available as well.

- **Best Views:** The whole family can watch the Magic Kingdom's Wishes

---

Fun Fact Room Roulette

If you wanted to stay one night in every guest room at the hotels and resorts currently on Walt Disney World property, it would take you well over 72 years to get the job done.

---

fireworks display from the comfort of your room if you book one on an upper floor on the west side of **Disney's Contemporary Resort** (© 407/ 934-7639; p. 92). From boardwalk-side rooms at **Disney's BoardWalk Inn & Villas** (© 407/934-7639; p. 90), you can catch the fireworks during Epcot's IllumiNations. And you have a front-row seat for the action at SeaWorld from the upper-east-side floors at the **Renaissance Orlando Resort at SeaWorld** (© 800/327-6677; p. 126).

- **Best Family Pools:** Arguably the best pool in O-Town is at the **Hyatt Regency Grand Cypress Resort** (© 800/233-1234; p. 111). It's a half-acre, lagoonlike pool that flows through rock grottoes, is spanned by a rope bridge, and has 12 waterfalls

and two steep water slides. The Lazy River at the **JW Marriott** (© 800/ 241-3333; p. 113) finishes a very close second. It's a 24,000-square-foot stream winding through small waterfalls and rock formations. At Disney, squish your toes in the sand-bottom pool of Stormalong Bay at **Disney's Yacht Club Resort** (© 407/ 934-7639; p. 96) and **Beach Club Resort** (© 407/934-7639; p. 87)— though most WDW resorts have fabulous pools, this one's a stand-out. The newest addition to the list is the **Nickelodeon Family Suites** (© 407/ 387-5437; p. 115). Thanks to its two water-park–style pools, complete with slides, flumes, squirters, fountains, and more, the action here is almost unending.

3 Best Dining Bets

While Orlando can't compete with U.S. destinations such as New York or San Francisco, it has everything from fast-food eateries that will satisfy your kids to five-star fine dining for a more adult palate. Look for more details on these and other eateries in chapter 5, "Family-Friendly Dining."

- **Best Character Meal:** Hands down, it doesn't get any better than **Chef Mickey's** (© 407/939-3463) breakfasts and dinners at Disney's Contemporary Resort. These events feature their respective namesake and other characters, but a word of warning: They draw up to *1,600 guests* at each meal! See p. 171.

- **Best Kids' Menu Variety:** When it comes to the deepest menu for young tastebuds, **Pastamore Ristorante,** at Universal's CityWalk (© 407/363-8000; p. 162), and the **Rainforest Cafe,** at Downtown Disney (© 407/ 827-8500; p. 157), each give kids a choice of 10 entrees.
- **Best Offbeat Kids' Menu:** With a menu that offers crispy chicken, shrimp tempura, and barbecued pork or beef—each served with shrimp chips and lo mein noodles—it's hard to beat the **Ming Court** (© 407/351-9988) in this category. See p. 164.
- **Best Burgers:** From cheeseburgers in paradise to Cuban meatloaf survival

Tips   Orlando's Best Websites

Given Orlando's enormous popularity, it should come as no surprise that hundreds of websites are devoted to it. These sites have information about everything from WDW history to getting around town.

There are several sites written by Disney fans, employees, and self-proclaimed experts. A favorite, **www.hiddenmickeys.org**, is about **Hidden Mickeys,** a park tradition. These subtle images can be found scattered throughout the realm, though they are sometimes in the eye, or imagination, of the beholder (see "Find the Hidden Mickeys," p. 232, to learn more). **Deb's Unofficial Walt Disney World Information Guide (www.allearsnet. com)** offers tons of family info on hotels, restaurants, attractions, and more. Definitely take a look at Disney's official site, **www.disneyworld.com**, if you're planning a pilgrimage to the Land of the Mouse. The newest addition to the wireless waves, **www.travel-insights.com**, is filled with information for families, including travel tips and insider advice on everything Disney, as well as Orlando's kid-friendliest hotels, hot spots, restaurants, and attractions (including Universal Orlando and SeaWorld).

If a trip to Universal Orlando's theme parks or CityWalk is on your dance card, stop at **www.universalorlando.com**. You can check out the attractions, order tickets, make reservations, and find out about special events. Fish fans can get in the know about SeaWorld at **www.seaworld.com**, Discovery Cove at **www.discoverycove.com**, and Aquatica at **www.aquatica byseaworld.com**.

For general information about the city, accommodations, dining, nightlife, or special events, head to the Orlando/Orange County Convention & Visitors Bureau website at **www.orlandoinfo.com**. The *Orlando Weekly* site, **www.orlandoweekly.com**, offers reviews and recommendations for arts, movies, music, restaurants, and more from Orlando's premier alternative weekly. Other great options include the online version of the local newspaper, at **www.orlandosentinal.com**, as well as the *Sentinel*-produced site **www.go2orlando.com**. Both feature information on upcoming events, area attractions, restaurant reviews, and local nightlife.

sandwiches, **Jimmy Buffett's Margaritaville,** at Universal's CityWalk (© **407/224-2155**), has some of the juiciest and most unusual burgers in town. See p. 161.

- **Best Outdoor Eating:** Kids can get into the festive jungle atmosphere while digging into their own wild menu at the **Rainforest Cafe,** at Downtown Disney (© **407/827-8500;** p. 149), which offers indoor dining in an outdoor atmosphere.

The terrace at **Artist Point** (© **407/939-3463;** p. 151), the premier restaurant at Disney's Wilderness Lodge, overlooks a lake, waterfall, and scenery evocative of America's national parks. And the **Rose & Crown,** at Epcot (© **407/939-3463;** p. 140), delivers a front-row seat for the IllumiNations fireworks display.

- **Best Value:** At **Romano's Macaroni Grill** (© **407/239-6676**), the ambience and northern Italian cuisine score very high, and prices are low, low, low. See p. 159.

- **Best Spot for a Parents' Night Out:** Dinners don't get much more romantic than those at the Victorian-style **Victoria & Albert's,** at Disney's Grand Floridian Resort (© 407/939-3463). The meal, which comprises seven courses, is served in an opulent and very intimate atmosphere by none other than Victoria & Albert. See p. 151.

- **Best Barbecue:** Hands down, follow your nose to **Bubbalou's Bodacious BBQ** (© 407/628-1212) after catching a whiff of the tangy hickory smoke. It tastes as good as it smells. See p. 169.

- **Best Italian Cuisine:** I have to give the nod to **Pacino's Italian Ristorante,** in Kissimmee (© 407/396-8022). It has great food and a moderately priced menu. See p. 168.

- **Most Entertaining Restaurant:** It's hard to contain yourself when the corny jokes and lively music kick into gear at the **Hoop-Dee-Doo Musical Revue,** at Disney's Fort Wilderness Resort (© 407/939-3463; p. 324). Outside of Disney's dinner shows, the **Whispering Canyon Café,** at Disney's Wilderness Lodge (© 407/939-3463; p. 152), ensures a stompin' good time with its kid-friendly activities and wild Western theme.

- **Best Steakhouse:** At the **Yachtsman Steakhouse,** at Disney's Yacht Club Resort (© 407/939-3463), the aged steaks, chops, and seafood are grilled over a wood fire. See p. 151.

- **Best Breakfast:** Disney character breakfasts certainly get the nod if you have children under 10 in tow. But it's hard to beat the buffet at **Boma,** in Disney's Animal Kingdom Lodge (© 407/938-3000). See p. 152.

- **Most Kid-Friendly Service:** The kids-eat-free program at the **Nickelodeon Family Suites** (© 877/387-5437) makes it a winner. Up to four kids per family, ages 5 and under (the real VIPs at this hotel), eat at select on-site eateries for free when accompanied by at least one paying adult. See p. 115.

- **Best Late-Night Dining:** The trendy **B-Line Diner,** at the Peabody Orlando (© 407/345-4460), is open around the clock for eclectic fare ranging from steaks to falafel sandwiches to grits and eggs. You and your kids won't be able to resist the desserts. See p. 163.

- **Best Spot to Celebrate with Kids:** The chefs at **Mikado Japanese Steakhouse,** in the Marriott Orlando World Center (© 407/239-4200; p. 166), entertain by slicing and dicing your meal. It makes for a fun and entertaining evening out. For a lively yet laid-back celebration, head to **Jimmy Buffett's Margaritaville,** at Universal's CityWalk (© 407/224-2155; p. 161). If you're celebrating sans kids (or with teens, not tots), **Emeril's,** at CityWalk (© 407/224-2424; p. 160), and **Todd English's Bluezoo,** at the WDW Dolphin (© 407/934-1111; p. 154), are both great choices for a high-end special occasion.

- **Best Special Sunday Brunch:** The **House of Blues,** at Disney's West Side (© 407/934-2583), has a down-home gospel brunch featuring live foot-stomping music and an array of vittles that includes greens, red beans and rice, jambalaya, gumbo, and more. The entertainment makes it a certifiable winner. Reservations aren't accepted for parties under six, so arrive early for the 10:30am or 1pm show. See p. 158.

2

Planning a Family Trip to Walt Disney World & Orlando

Within minutes of choosing Orlando as your vacation destination, panic often sets in as you're confronted with a seemingly endless selection of hotels, restaurants, attractions, and package plans to choose from. Talk about overload! With so much information to sift through, an anxiety attack is inevitable if you don't do a little advance planning. That's why I've filled this chapter with things travelers with kids in tow need to know before they go. In addition to the information you'll find in the following pages, plenty more helpful tips can be found in chapters 4 through 7—those covering the area's best hotels, restaurants, theme parks, and smaller attractions.

1 Visitor Information & Maps

The moment you've decided that Orlando is your destination, immediately contact the **Orlando/Orange County Convention & Visitors Bureau** (aka the Orlando CVB) and its visitor center, at 8723 International Dr., Suite 101, Orlando, FL 32819 (℃ **407/363-5872** or 800/551-0181; www.orlandoinfo. com). Staffers can answer questions, assist with reservations, help find discounts, and send you maps and brochures, such as the *Official Vacation Guide,* the *Unexpected Orlando* guide, and the *Orlando Holiday Guide.* The free packet should arrive within 3 weeks and include the **Orlando Magicard,** which is good for $500 in discounts on rooms, car rentals, attractions, and more. By calling the Official Travel Counselors (℃ **800/551-0181**), available Monday through Friday from 8am to 5pm, you can book vacation packages, buy discounted attraction tickets, and get plenty of planning tips.

The Orlando CVB's website also includes information on special vacation packages specifically designed for families and has a list of hundreds of family-appropriate things to see and do in Orlando.

For information on **Walt Disney World,** write to Walt Disney World, Box 10000, Lake Buena Vista, FL 32830-1000; call ℃ **407/934-7639** or 407/824-4321; or go online to **www.disneyworld. com**. You can view the planning kit online or have one sent to your home that also includes a vacation DVD and planning CD. The website is filled with photos, theme-park maps, current ticket prices, customized driving directions, park hours on specific days, ride and show information (including scheduled rehab dates), detailed descriptions of WDW dining options, information on special events, indoor and outdoor recreation options, the Disney Cruise Line, an online booking service, and much, much more.

For information on **Universal Studios Florida, CityWalk,** and **Islands of Adventure,** call ℃ **800/837-2273** or 407/363-8000; write to Universal Orlando, 1000 Universal Studios Plaza,

Visitor Information Abroad

There are several **Orlando Tourism Offices** outside the United States. You can get information from the following sources:

- **Argentina** ✆ 001-407-363-5872, www.orlandoinfo.com/espanol
- **Belgium** ✆ 001-407-363-5872, www.orlandoinfo.com/global
- **Brazil** ✆ 0800-770-6752, www.orlandoinfo.com/portugues
- **Canada** ✆ 1-800-646-2079, www.orlandoinfo.com/canada
- **France** ✆ 001-407-363-5872, www.orlandoinfo.com/francais
- **Germany** ✆ 0800-1007325, www.orlandoinfo.com/de
- **Italy** ✆ 01-407-363-5872, www.orlandoinfo.com/italiano
- **Japan** ✆ 81-3-5251-8671, www.orlandoinfo.com/japan
- **Latin America** ✆ 001-407-363-5872, www.orlandoinfo.com/global
- **Mexico** ✆ 0800-777-6752, www.orlandoinfo.com/espanol
- **Portugal** ✆ 407-363-5872, www.orlandoinfo.com/portugues
- **Spain** ✆ 001-407-363-5872, www.orlandoinfo.com/espanol
- **United Kingdom** ✆ 0800-018-6760, www.orlandoinfo.com/uk

Orlando, FL 32819; or visit www.universalorlando.com.

For information on **SeaWorld,** call ✆ **407/351-3600** or visit www.seaworld.com. For **Discovery Cove** information, call ✆ **877/4-DISCOVERY** or 407/370-1280, or visit www.discoverycove.com.

Both the sites for Universal Orlando, **www.universalorlando.com**, and Sea-World, **www.seaworld.com**, offer ride descriptions, ticket prices, some restaurant menus, and more, including information beyond the theme parks. While greatly improved over the last few years to include far more information, they still lack the thoroughness of the Disney site.

The **Kissimmee Convention & Visitors Bureau,** 1925 E. Irlo Bronson Memorial Hwy., Kissimmee, FL 34744 (✆ **800/333-5477** or 407/847-5000; www.floridakiss.com), can also provide maps, brochures, coupons, and a planning kit that details accommodations and attractions.

For information on Orlando's **International Drive** area, call ✆ **866/243-7483** or go to www.internationaldriveorlando.com. The phone reps have information on hotels, restaurants, attractions, shops, and the I-Ride Trolley. The website features more than 50 ways to have fun, many of them suitable for families with kids.

For information on all of Florida's family-friendly offerings, go to **www.visitflorida.com**, the state's official vacation-planning site. There's tons of great information online, but if you request planning materials, you can customize your order to include only the publications you're interested in. Just a few of the choices include *The Official Florida Vacation Guide, Florida's Map, Play FLA Golf, Florida Bicycle Trails,* and the *Florida Camping Directory.* Additional guides such as *Family Getaways, Beach Getaways, History & Cultural Getaways,* and *Boating Getaways,* among others, are available online in electronic form.

For more online advice, **Deb's Unofficial Walt Disney World Information Guide** (www.allearsnet.com) is an excellent source of family fun and arguably the best unofficial Disney guide on the Internet, though at times it isn't entirely objective. Disney doesn't own it, but it's run and written mainly by diehard Disney

Destination WDW & Orlando: Pre-Departure Checklist

- Along with the Mouse, Orlando's biggest draw is its climate. And though it may seem obvious, a word of caution is warranted regarding Florida's most natural and abundant commodity: the sun, which is hotter and stronger than in most other parts of the country and, as such, requires that you take some extra precautions. One of the most important survival rules of an Orlando vacation: **Use sunscreen!** Pour on one with an SPF rating of at least 30 or higher (50 is preferable), especially on kids. Florida's sun can deliver a dangerous burn, or even sun poisoning, year-round (even more quickly when you're in or near the water)—a souvenir I guarantee you do not want to take home with you. The sun can pack a powerful punch even on a cloudy day, so don't leave the sunscreen and hats behind. Remember to reapply sunscreen throughout the day; one application when you're sweating in the parks or playing in the pools will not protect you for very long. Many sunscreens are now available in a spray (best for your body) as well as a solid stick (best for faces, ears, and lips), making them quick and easy to apply (and reapply), especially if your kids are squirmy or can't stand messy lotions. You can also protect yourself and your kids by wearing wide-brimmed hats, airy clothes, and sunglasses. If you have a stroller with you, a light blanket draped over the top will help to protect infants or sleeping toddlers from the sun's rays. Also remember to drink plenty of fluids throughout the day to prevent dehydration, and have your kids do the same, even if they say they aren't thirsty. And remember—*children need protection* as much as or more than you do, and they may not recognize the symptoms of a burn, or of dehydration, until it's too late, so it's up to you to do it for them. Last but certainly not least, don't forget to pack a pair or two of comfortable, worn-in walking shoes for those days spent pounding the theme-park pavement.

- **Advance Dining Reservations** (*©* **407/939-3463**), which let you stake a claim to a table up to 180 days in advance, are a necessity at any sit-down Disney restaurant—especially those serving character meals or a dinner show. To avoid disappointment, call as soon as possible to make your reservations, as some of the more popular restaurants and dinner shows get booked within hours—sometimes even minutes (no kidding)—of when the time tables are released (7am EST).

fans, so you have to factor out (or in, if you prefer) their exuberance while digesting the many valuable tips this guide offers. The no-nonsense, text-driven site includes comprehensive insider information on tickets, detailed restaurant menus, the scoop on the Disney Cruise Line, and more. There are pages specifically aimed at parents of infants and toddlers, 5- to 11-year-olds, expectant moms, and families bringing one or more of their children's friends.

If you're looking for the best tips and insider information on saving some cash

- **Be flexible.** Many families come with their hearts set on (and days planned around) specific attractions, hotels, or restaurants. But not all dreams come true, even at Disney. Disney has reduced park hours, limited the days certain shows are staged, and temporarily closed hotels, restaurants, and attractions for rehab during slower weeks (or months) throughout the year. Other theme parks have taken similar steps. Before you promise the kids anything, make sure your dreams can come true by calling or checking websites beforehand. Note that even in the best of times, rides break down or have to be shut for routine maintenance (though you don't get a break on ticket prices when your favorite rides or shows are dark). Some of the websites listed earlier in this chapter have updated "rehab" schedules. The parks can adjust hours not only seasonally, but also weekly—even daily—so check the schedule when you arrive so you'll know about last-minute changes or closings.

- **Pack your camera,** extra batteries (and a charger, if they're rechargeable), and enough film or memory cards before you go. If you packed film in your checked baggage, consider investing in protective pouches to shield film from airport X-rays. If you must buy film or other supplies, try a local Wal-Mart or Walgreens for better prices (and selection) than you'll find at the parks and resorts.

- **Bring your ID cards,** including AAA and AARP cards, student IDs, the Orlando Magicard, and so on: Producing them will help save a few dollars along the way. Speaking of identification, a photo ID is a necessity at the airports, among other places, so keep it handy.

- **Don't forget your prescription medicines,** as well as the phone numbers of your doctor, pediatrician, and insurance company (along with your insurance card). Pack these items in your carry-on, not in your checked baggage where they may become lost or separated from you. Also bring an extra pair of glasses and/or contact lenses.

- **Leave a copy of your itinerary with someone at home,** and keep an extra copy for yourself (in a safe place other than your wallet or handbag). Be sure it includes your hotel, car, and airline information, as well as any reservation or confirmation numbers for park admission, shows, or restaurants.

on your Disney vacation, go to **www.mousesavers.com**, which lists discount and reservation codes for the Disney resorts, as well as special discounts and offers of its own.

Another site chock full of information on Central Florida, reaching from the Gulf Coast to the Space Coast (with an in-depth look at WDW, Universal, SeaWorld, and Orlando's many offerings), is **www.travel-insights.com**. Written specifically with families in mind, it includes tons of insider tips, details on dining, and the scoop on the area's kid-friendliest attractions and accommodations, with plenty more for parents, including how to survive a family vacation in Central Florida with your sanity intact.

The city's newspaper, the *Orlando Sentinel,* produces an online version at **www.orlandosentinel.com**, with a variety of entertainment information. And **www.go2orlando.com** focuses on attractions, accommodations, restaurants, discounts, and more.

2 Entry Requirements

PASSPORTS
For information on how to get a passport, go to **"Passports"** in the **"Fast Facts"** section at the end of chapter 3—the websites listed provide downloadable passport applications as well as the current fees for processing passport applications. For an up-to-date, country-by-country listing of passport requirements around the world, go to the "Foreign Entry Requirement" Web page of the U.S. State Department at **http://travel.state.gov**. International visitors can obtain a visa application at the same website. *Note:* Children are required to present a passport when entering the United States at airports. More information on obtaining a passport for a minor can be found at http://travel.state.gov.

VISAS
For specifics on how to get a visa, go to **"Visas"** in the **"Fast Facts"** section at the end of chapter 3.

The U.S. State Department has a **Visa Waiver Program (VWP)** allowing citizens of the following countries (at press time) to enter the United States without a visa for stays of up to 90 days: Andorra, Australia, Austria, Belgium, Brunei, Denmark, Finland, France, Germany, Iceland, Ireland, Italy, Japan, Liechtenstein, Luxembourg, Monaco, the Netherlands, New Zealand, Norway, Portugal, San Marino, Singapore, Slovenia, Spain, Sweden, Switzerland, and the United Kingdom. Canadian citizens may enter the United States without visas; they will need to show passports and proof of residence,

however. *Note:* Any passport issued on or after October 26, 2006, by a VWP country must be an **e-Passport** for VWP travelers to be eligible to enter the U.S. without a visa. Citizens of these nations also need to present a round-trip air or cruise ticket upon arrival. These e-Passports contain computer chips capable of storing biometric information, such as the required digital photograph of the holder. (You can identify an e-Passport by the symbol on the bottom center cover of your passport.) If your passport doesn't have this feature, you can still travel without a visa if it is a valid passport issued before October 26, 2005, and includes a machine-readable zone, or between October 26, 2005, and October 25, 2006, and includes a digital photograph. For more information, go to **www.travel.state.gov/visa**.

Citizens of all other countries must have (1) a valid passport that expires at least 6 months later than the scheduled end of their visit to the United States, and (2) a tourist visa, which may be obtained without charge from any U.S. consulate.

As of January 2004, many international visitors traveling on visas to the United States will be photographed and fingerprinted on arrival at Customs in airports and on cruise ships in a program created by the Department of Homeland Security called **US-VISIT.** Exempt from the extra scrutiny are visitors entering by land or those that don't require a visa for short-term visits. For more information, go to the Homeland Security website at **www.dhs.gov/dhspublic**.

U.S. Entry: Passport Required

New regulations issued by the Homeland Security Department now require virtually every air traveler entering the U.S. to show a passport—and future regulations will cover land and sea entry as well. As of January 23, 2007, all persons, including U.S. citizens, traveling by air between the United States and Canada, Mexico, Central and South America, the Caribbean, and Bermuda are required to present a valid passport. As of January 31, 2008, all U.S. and Canadian citizens traveling by land or sea between the United States and Canada, Mexico, Bermuda, and the Caribbean must present either a WHTI-compliant document or a government-issued ID. Stricter regulations requiring either a valid passport or passport card for those traveling by land or sea between countries (including by ferry) are expected to take effect at a date yet to be determined.

MEDICAL REQUIREMENTS

Unless you're arriving from an area known to be suffering from an epidemic (particularly cholera or yellow fever), inoculations or vaccinations are not required for entry into the United States. If you have a medical condition that requires **syringe-administered medications,** carry a valid signed prescription from your physician; syringes in carry-on baggage will be inspected. Insulin in any form should have the proper pharmaceutical documentation. If you have a disease that requires treatment with **narcotics,** you should also carry documented proof with you—smuggling narcotics aboard a plane carries severe penalties in the U.S.

For **HIV-positive visitors,** requirements for entering the United States are somewhat vague and change frequently. For up-to-the-minute information, contact **AIDSinfo** (© **800/448-0440** or 301/519-6616 outside the U.S.; www.aids info.nih.gov) or the **Gay Men's Health Crisis** (© **212/367-1000;** www.gmhc. org).

CUSTOMS

For information on what you can bring into and take out of Orlando, go to **"Customs"** in the **"Fast Facts"** section at the end of chapter 3.

3 When to Go

Orlando is the theme-park capital of the world, and you could almost argue that there really is no off season here, though the busiest seasons are whenever kids are out of school: late May to just past Labor Day, long holiday weekends, winter holidays (mid-Dec–early Jan), and especially spring break (late Mar–Apr). Keep in mind that kids in other hemispheres follow a completely different schedule. Obviously, an Orlando—and most especially a Disney—vacation is most enjoyable when the crowds are at their thinnest and the weather is the most temperate.

Hotel rooms (likely the largest chunk of your vacation bill) are also priced lower (albeit slightly) during the off season, though don't expect that period to follow the traditional winter/summer patterns of most areas.

Peak-season rates can go into effect during large conventions and special events. Even something as remote as Bike Week in Daytona Beach (about an hour by car northeast) can raise prices, even during the off season. These kinds of events will especially affect the moderately

Tips   Weather Wise

It's not uncommon for the skies to open up on Orlando, even when the day begins with the sun ablaze. Florida is well known for its afternoon downpours, so don't be too concerned; storms don't usually last too long. Most people simply run for temporary cover and then resume their activities when the rain slows to a drizzle or stops altogether. It is wise, however, to bring along some type of rain gear, as storms can spring up rather quickly. A small fold-up umbrella can protect you until you can get to shelter. If you forget your gear, rain ponchos can be purchased throughout the parks for about $6 for a child size or $8 for an adult size. The child-size poncho also happens to cover the average stroller quite well, protecting camera equipment and souvenirs—not to mention the child sitting inside it.

Don't let a rainy afternoon spoil your fun. Crowds are dramatically thinner on these days, and there are plenty of indoor attractions to enjoy, particularly at Epcot, Disney's Hollywood Studios, and Universal Studios Florida. The flip side, of course, is that many of the outdoor rides at Disney, Universal, and SeaWorld are temporarily closed during downpours and lightning storms.

priced hotels and resorts located off Walt Disney World.

Best times: The week after Labor Day until the week before Thanksgiving when the kids have just returned to school, the week after Thanksgiving until mid-December, and the 6 weeks before and after school spring vacations (which generally occur around Easter).

Worst times: The absolute worst time of year to visit is during spring break—usually the 2 weeks prior to and after Easter. The crowds are unbelievable; the lines are unbearable (my kids have waited upward of 2 hours to hop on some of the most popular attractions); waiting times at local restaurants can lead to starvation; and traffic—particularly on International Drive—will give you an unbelievable headache. The December holidays and summer, when out-of-state visitors take advantage of school breaks and many locals bring their families to the parks (taking advantage of Florida resident discount months, which usually fall in May and Nov), can also prove a challenge.

Packed parking lots and long lines are the norm the week before and after Christmas, and the summer brings with it oppressive heat and humidity. You may have noticed that the best times to avoid crowds happen to coincide with the times your kids will likely be in class. While I don't usually advocate skipping school, I strongly advise you to *seriously consider pulling your kids out* for a few days around an off-season weekend to avoid long lines. (You may be able to keep them in their schools' good graces by asking teachers to let them write a report on an educational element of the vacation. Epcot, SeaWorld, and the Orlando Museum of Science offer the most in the way of educational exhibits.) Even during these periods, though, the number of international visitors guarantees you won't be alone.

Note: If you're taking advantage of a land/cruise package (see "Disney Cruise Packages," later in this chapter), make sure you take into account the Florida hurricane season, which runs from around June 1 to November 30 (when the majority of Central Florida's afternoon downpours tend to occur). Inland, the worst is usually only sheets of rain and enough wind to wipe the smile right off your face. That said, the summer of 2004 (when three hurricanes passed through the area) was a noticeable reminder that worse can happen, and 2005 brought with it what seemed like an endless number of storms, extending the rainy season well beyond the normal timeline. While 2006 was relatively quiet weather-wise, tornados touched down and devastated areas just north of Orlando in 2007. If you are on the coastal areas or at sea, you will likely be at the point where the storms hit their hardest, making them extremely dangerous. Also, don't take tornadoes and lightning—two particularly active summer curses—too lightly. Central Florida is the lightning capital of the United States, and short but intense electrical storms aren't uncommon in summer (young kids may be frightened, but I've seen teens absolutely enthralled by the natural electric show). Just make sure all observing is done from a safe place.

Central Florida Average Temperatures

	Jan	Feb	Mar	Apr	May	June	July	Aug	Sept	Oct	Nov	Dec
High °F	71.7	72.9	78.3	83.6	88.3	90.6	91.7	91.6	89.7	84.4	78.2	73.1
°C	22.0	22.7	25.7	28.7	31.3	32.5	33.2	33.1	32.0	29.1	25.7	22.8
Low °F	49.3	50.0	55.3	60.3	66.2	71.2	73.0	73.4	72.5	65.4	56.8	50.9
°C	9.6	10.0	12.5	15.7	19.0	21.8	22.7	23.0	22.5	18.6	13.8	10.5

KIDS' FAVORITE ORLANDO EVENTS

For an exhaustive list of events beyond those listed here, check http://events.frommers.com, where you'll find a searchable, up-to-the-minute roster of what's happening in cities all over the world.

January

Capital One Florida Citrus Bowl. New Year's kicks off with this football game in downtown Orlando. It pits the second-ranked teams from the Southeastern and Big Ten conferences against each other. If your family's sports-crazy, this is a good place to go. Tickets run $65 before November 1, $75 thereafter. For info, call ✆ **800/ 297-2695** or 407/423-2476; for tickets, call Ticketmaster (✆ **877/803-7073** or 407/839-3900) or visit www. fcsports.com. A free downtown parade is held a few days before the game and features marching bands and floats. Most kids will find it entertaining. January 1.

Walt Disney World Marathon. About 90% of the 16,000 runners finish this 26.2-mile "sprint" through the resort area and parks. It's open to anyone over 18 years of age, including runners with disabilities as long as they are able to maintain the 16-minute mile pacing requirements. If you are unable to do so, you'll be picked up and transported to the finish line. The registration fee is $105 and includes race entry, a T-shirt, a medal, and other extras for those who finish—along with souvenirs for all who enter. The registration deadline is usually in early November, and preregistration is required. There's also a half-marathon ($95), Goofy's Race and a Half Challenge (includes registration for both marathons; $195), and a Family Fun Run that includes shorter races for adults and kids ($30 if postmarked by Dec 26, $35 after that; $5 per child for kids' races). Call ✆ **407/939-7810** or go to www.disneysports.com. Early January.

Disney's Pirate & Princess Party. The Magic Kingdom's newest after-hours event is held on select nights beginning in late January and ending in March (plus select dates in Aug). Pirates and princesses of all ages can head out on a quest for treasure, filling their booty bags with beads and chocolate doubloons—just look for the Xs on your treasure map. Party the night away at pirate coves and royal courts, where you'll find plenty of live interactive entertainment such as Captain Jack's Pirate Tutorial, Jasmine's Royal Guard Recruitment, and Sebastian's Undersea Dance Party. The highlights of the evening include Disney's Enchanted Adventures Parade and the Magic, Music, and Mayhem fireworks spectacular. A separate admission ticket is required ($39 adults, $33 kids 3–9; add $7 per ticket if purchased the day of the event). I highly recommend purchasing tickets well in advance for any of Disney's after-hours events. For information, call ⓒ **407/934-7639** or visit www.disneyworld.com.

SeaWorld BBQ Fest. Spanning two weekends (beginning in late Jan and ending in early Feb), SeaWorld sets out a sumptuous barbecue spread to accompany a series of country-music concerts. The concerts are included with park admission, but if you're hankering for a mouth-watering meal you'll have to pay extra. For information, call ⓒ **800/428-8368** or go to www.seaworld.com. February

Silver Spurs Rodeo. Real yippee-i-o cowboys compete in calf roping, bull riding, barrel racing, and more. The rodeo is a celebration of the area's rural roots and a nice escape from the more typical tourist traps. If you've got a little cowboy (or girl), it's sure to be a treat. For a root'n toot'n good time, head to the Silver Spurs Arena, 1875 E.

Irlo Bronson Memorial Hwy. (U.S. 192), Kissimmee. Tickets run $15. Call ⓒ **407/677-6336** or visit www. silverspursrodeo.com for details. Second weekend in February (and 3 days in June).

Houston Astros. Here's another event for the sports-minded family. The Astros train at Osceola County Stadium, 1000 Bill Beck Blvd., Kissimmee. Tickets are $17 and $20. Get them through Ticketmaster (ⓒ **877/803-7073** or 407/839-3900). For information, check out www.astros.com. Late February to mid-March.

March

Atlanta Braves. The Braves have been holding spring training at Disney's Wide World of Sports complex since 1998. There are 16 games during the 1-month season, and they usually offer a much more up-close experience than young fans will get at a major-league ballpark. Tickets run $14 to $23. To purchase tickets, call Ticketmaster (ⓒ **877/803-7073** or 407/839-3900). For information, call ⓒ **407/939-4326** or check out www.disneysports.com. The team arrives in mid-February; games begin in early March.

Viva La Musica. This celebration of Latin culture and music is held annually at SeaWorld. Festivities include concerts, food, and crafts displays throughout the park. There is no extra charge to join in the fun, which happens on two successive weekends in the beginning of March. For more information and exact dates, call ⓒ **800/423-8368** or head to www.seaworld.com. Early March.

Florida Film Festival. The Enzian Theater has been showcasing American independent and foreign films for more than a decade. This 10-day festival, sponsored in part by Universal

Orlando, usually features a selection of family-friendly films that you and your kids might not otherwise get a chance to see, and some of the films presented are made by teenage students. If your child is a budding director, it's worth attending. This was named one of the top 10 such events in the world by *The Ultimate Film Festival Survival Guide.* Call ✆ **407/629-8587** or visit www.floridafilmfestival.com. Late March to early April.

April

Epcot International Flower & Garden Festival. This 6-week-long event showcases colorful gardens, topiary characters, floral displays, speakers, seminars, and a concert series. Children will likely be entertained by the whimsical topiaries, the kids' garden (including a family-friendly hedge-style maze), Kids' Day, and animal and insect demonstrations (where ladybugs and butterflies get released). The festival is free with regular park admission ($71 adults, $60 kids 3–9). For information, call ✆ **407/934-7639** or visit www.disneyworld.com. Late April to mid-June.

May

Orlando International Fringe Festival. More than 100 diverse acts from around the world participate in this eclectic event, held for 10 days in May at various venues in downtown Orlando. Everything performed on outdoor stages, from sword swallowing to *Hamlet,* is available free to Fringe attendees after they purchase a festival button for about $6. There's also a special **Kids Fringe** during the festival's two weekends. Events include storytelling and theater performances. Tickets for indoor events vary, but most are under $10. Call ✆ **407/648-0077** or visit www.orlandofringe.org. Mid-May.

Star Wars Weekends. Every year, WDW features a fan-fest full of activities for *Star Wars* fanatics at Disney's Hollywood Studios. Characters, as well as a handful of *Star Wars* actors, are on hand for up-close meet-and-greets. Games, parades, and special entertainment top off the festivities. The celebrations are included with park admission ($71 adults, $60 kids 3–9). Call ✆ **407/934-7639** or go to www.disneyworld.com to find out more. Five consecutive weekends beginning in May.

June

Silver Spurs Rodeo. See the entry under "February," above.

July

Independence Day. Disney adds an extra sparkle to its fireworks displays at the parks, which stay open later than usual. Call ✆ **407/934-7639** or visit www.disneyworld.com for details. SeaWorld (✆ **407/351-3600;** www.seaworld.com) features a dazzling fireworks display as well. Downtown Orlando has a free fireworks display at Lake Eola Park; for information, call ✆ **407/246-2827.** Other fireworks events are listed in the local newspaper, the *Orlando Sentinel.* July 4.

Tampa Bay Buccaneers. The NFL's Tampa Bay Bucs run their training camp at Disney's Wide World of Sports. For information, call ✆ **407/939-4236** or go to www.buccaneers.com. Late July through August.

September

Night of Joy. The Magic Kingdom hosts this festival of contemporary-Christian music featuring top artists. It's very popular, so get tickets early. Performers also make a free appearance at Long's Christian Bookstore in College Park, about 20 minutes north of Disney. Admission to the concert is $40 for

1 night (7:30pm–12:30am), $68 for 2 nights. Use of Magic Kingdom attractions is included. For concert details, call ☎ 407/934-7639; for information on the Long's appearance, call ☎ 407/422-6934. First weekend (Thurs–Sun) in September.

Universal has gone head to head with Disney on this one, scheduling its **Rock the Universe** concert the same weekend (☎ 866/788-4636). Big-name Christian bands and speakers headline the event. Tickets (which include admission to the parks after 4pm) cost $38 for 1 night or $62 for both nights of the event. A package including both nights of celebration, as well as 3 full days of admission to the parks (Fri–Sun), runs $91.

Epcot International Food & Wine Festival. Here's your chance to sip and savor the food and beverages of 26 cultures. More than 100 wineries from across the United States participate. Events include wine tastings for adults, seminars, dinners, concerts, and celebrity-chef cooking demonstrations. Tickets for the dinner-and-concert series or wine tastings are $35 to $175, including gratuity; signature dinners and vertical wine tastings are $60 to $195. The party's not just for adults; kids get their own activities as well. In 2007, kid-friendly options included the Pearville Fair with fun and games and a big-top coloring tent; the chance for children ages 4 to 10 to bake their own Toll House cookies through the Junior Chef program at the Land Pavilion; storytelling presented by the state of Oklahoma; and a Kidcot scavenger hunt. The event also features 26 food-and-wine marketplaces where appetizer-size portions of dishes ranging from pizza to octopus on purple potato salad sell for under $6 each (a fun way to introduce your kids to exotic cuisines). Entrance to the festival is included in park admission

($71 adults, $60 kids 3–9). Call ☎ 407/939-3378 or check out www.disneyworld.com for details. Generally from mid-September to early November.

October

Orlando Magic. The local NBA team plays half of its 82-game regular season between October and April at the Amway Arena, 600 W. Amelia St. Ticket prices range from $10 to $115. Single-game tickets can be hard to come by the day of the game. Call ☎ 407/916-2400 for details; call ☎ 866/448-7849 or 407/839-3900 for tickets. Online, go to www.nba.com/magic.

Halloween Horror Nights. Universal's Islands of Adventure transforms its grounds for 20 or more nights into haunted attractions with live bands, a psychopath's maze, special shows, and hundreds of ghouls and goblins roaming the streets. The parks essentially close at dusk, reopening in a new, macabre form from 7pm to midnight or later. Adult admission ($71) is charged for this event. *Note:* This is far too intense for children and is definitely geared to grown-ups, as the liquor flows quite freely and the frightfulness is *truly* that. Call ☎ 800/837-2273 or visit www.universalorlando.com. Late September to early November.

Mickey's Not-So-Scary Halloween Party. Disney World invites you to join Mickey and his pals for a far-from-frightening time. In this one, you can come in costume and trick-or-treat through the Magic Kingdom from 7pm to midnight on any of 15 or so nights in October (you'll get bags and can collect candy from characters in set areas in the park). The alcohol-free party includes parades, live music, and storytelling. The climax is a bewitching fireworks spectacular. This is your best

Halloween bet if you have young kids. A separate admission fee is charged ($39 adults, $33 kids 3–9; add $7 if purchased the day of the event). Tickets go on sale at the end of April and nearly always sell out. Call ☎ **407/ 934-7639** or visit www.disneyworld. com.

SeaWorld's Halloween Spooktacular. Halloween festivities, all part of your regular park admission, include parades, special not-so-spooky shows, concerts, costumed characters (including favorite *Sesame Street* characters thanks to a new partnership), and tricks and treats. A special trick-or-treat family sleepover for families with kids in grades K through 5 is available on 4 select nights ($78 per person; $113 with park admission). For more details, call ☎ **407/351-3600** or visit www.seaworld.com or www.seaworld spooktacular.com. Weekends throughout October.

November

ABC Super Soap Weekend. For fans of ABC's daytime soaps, this is a don't-miss event. Soap celebs are on hand for parades, parties, Q&As, music, and more in this weekend catering to fans and fanatics alike. If you and your older kids are soap-happy, you'll be in heaven. The events are included with Disney's Hollywood Studios admission ($71 adults, $60 kids 3–9). For details and the exact dates, call ☎ **407/397- 6808** or visit www.disneyworld.com.

Festival of the Masters. One of the largest art shows in the South takes place at Downtown Disney Marketplace, featuring over 150 top artists, photographers, and craftspeople—all winners of juried shows throughout the country. You can listen to the music of the jazz festival or enjoy one of the many family activities, all for free. Call ☎ **407/934-7639** or visit www.disneyworld.com. Second weekend in November.

Osborne Family Spectacle of Dancing Lights. This classic holiday tradition has returned by popular demand after being closed for renovations in 2004 and 2005. Lighting up the nights and dancing through the streets at Disney's Hollywood Studios are millions of sparkling bulbs acquired from a family whose Christmas-lights collection got a bit too bright for their neighbors (see "Star Light, Star Bright," in this section). For information, call ☎ **407/934-7639** or visit www.disneyworld.com. November to early January.

Jack Hanna Animal Adventure at Sea-World. For one weekend, renowned animal expert and TV host Jack Hanna shows off some of his unusual animals in a special show that's included in park admission ($65 adults, $54 kids 3–9). Call ☎ **407/351-3600** or visit www. seaworld.com for details.

December

Christmas at Walt Disney World. During the holiday festivities, Main Street in the Magic Kingdom is lavishly decked out with twinkling lights and Christmas holly; all the while, carolers greet visitors throughout the park. Epcot, Hollywood Studios, and Animal Kingdom also offer special embellishments and entertainment throughout the season, and the Disney resorts are adorned with towering Christmas trees, wreaths, boughs, and bows.

Some holiday highlights include **Mickey's Very Merry Christmas Party,** an after-hours (7pm–midnight) ticketed event ($41 adults, $34 kids 3–9; add $7 if purchased the day of the event). This takes place on selected nights at the Magic Kingdom and features a festive parade, fireworks, special

Fun Fact **Star Light, Star Bright**

The Osborne family of Arkansas built a collection of more than 3 million Christmas lights. It was so bright that neighbors complained and eventually went to court in what became a nationally known battle. Disney came to the rescue and, in 1995, moved the entire display to Orlando, adding another 2 million or so bulbs. After being closed for a few years, the December extravaganza has returned at a new location with more sparkle than ever (thanks to swirling snow flurries and a new dancing-lights display choreographed to festive holiday music). This awesome family favorite is a must-see; there are few displays (if any) on the planet like it.

shows, and admission to a handful of rides. Also included are complimentary cookies and hot cocoa.

Holidays Around the World and the **Candlelight Procession** at Epcot feature hundreds of carolers, storytellers from a host of international countries, celebrity narrators telling the Christmas story, a 450-voice choir, and a 50-piece orchestra in a very moving display. A tree-lighting ceremony, visits from Santa (as well as France's Pere Noel and Italy's La Befana), and the Lights of Winter light show will entertain the kids as well. The event is included with park admission ($71 adults, $60 kids 3–9).

Call ℂ **407/824-4321** or go to www.disneyworld.com for details on all of the above. The holiday fun lasts from mid-December to early January.

Macy's Holiday Parade at Universal Studios Florida. That's not a typo! Universal and Macy's (the latter a tenant at the Mall at Millenia, p. 319) teamed up for the first time in December 2002 to offer a smaller version of Macy's Thanksgiving Day Parade. It features several of the floats and gigantic balloons from the original New York City parade. Park admission is required ($71 adults, $60 kids 3–9). For information, call ℂ **407/363-8000** or visit www.universalorlando.com. Mid-December to early January.

Grinchmas at Islands of Adventure. The famous Seussian Scrooge, the Grinch, spreads his own brand of grumpy holiday cheer. Seuss Landing is transformed into Whoville for the holidays, with "Whos" running all about to create a festive mood. Families can explore the Grinch's lair, see a holiday-themed show, and attend a tree-lighting ceremony. All the fun is included in park admission ($71 adults, $60 kids 3–9). Late November to early January. For information, call ℂ **407/363-8000** or visit www.universalorlando.com.

SeaWorld's Holiday Celebration. Festivities include visits from Santa, Christmas carolers, a colorful holiday-themed fountain show, fireworks, and snow flurries. All the fun is included with park admission ($65 adults, $54 kids 3–9). In addition, a special 1-night **Frosty & Friends Sleepover** ($75 per person) and a special holiday-themed **Makahiki Christmas Luau** ($46 adults, $30 kids 3–9) are offered as well. Advance reservations are suggested. For information, call ℂ **800/428-8368** or go to www.seaworld.com. Late November through December.

Walt Disney World New Year's Eve Celebration. For 1 night a year, the Magic Kingdom is open until the wee hours for a massive fireworks explosion, a very kid-friendly event. Other New Year's festivities in WDW include a big (and pricey) bash at Pleasure Island (geared to older teens and young adults) featuring music headliners, a special Hoop-Dee-Doo Musical Revue at Fort Wilderness, and guest performances by well-known musical groups at Disney's Hollywood Studios and Epcot. Call ✆ **407/934-7639** for details or visit **www.disneyworld.com**. December 31.

4 What to Pack

You're going to be spending a lot of time on your feet and most likely in the heat, so it's important to pack comfortable clothes and footwear. Brand-new shoes may look great, but chances are that if they're not worn in, your feet will pay the price. You won't need anything dressy unless you are going to an upscale restaurant or attending a special event that requires it. Assume that the weather will be warm to downright hot, so make shorts and lightweight clothing a priority, but also remember to bring layers if you're coming December through February (it can get downright cold at times). Check the local weather forecast just before you go to see if jackets, or even mittens, may be necessary. Bring a sweater or sweatshirt no matter what the time of year, as the air-conditioning inside can be brutal—especially on the kids.

Don't forget to bring sunglasses, a hat, a bathing suit, and cover-up if you're coming in spring, summer, or fall; plenty of socks (Band-Aids and moleskin, too, to prevent blisters); and your camera.

Pack a small tote bag filled with toys, puzzles, games, and activities to keep your kids busy on the plane or in the car.

If you're flying, be sure to pack a supply of hard candies or chewing gum for older kids, or a bottle or sippy cup for tinier tots, to help them deal with the pressure they may feel in their ears during takeoff and landing.

If you're traveling with a toddler or baby, a lightweight and reasonably priced stroller, with a hood and storage space, is a good way to keep little ones from pooping out at the parks—and keep them dry in the rain and shaded from the sun. You can rent them at the parks if you don't want to schlep yours from home. Be aware, however, that while the park versions have improved over the years, they generally aren't appropriate for infants or even particularly good for kids under 2. Most are constructed of hard plastic, making them uncomfortable; they don't recline (a necessary function, if you have younger children); and storage space is at a minimum.

Most restaurants can supply a highchair or booster seat, but this is where having your own stroller may come in handy. Nearly every hotel will have cribs available (though of varying quality). The

---

⟮Tips⟯ Leave That Baby Gear at Home

There's no reason to schlep like a Sherpa: Rental gear for tiny tots and toddlers—including strollers and cribs, swings and car seats, and even beach supplies—are all available by the day or by the week through local companies such as **Baby's Away** (✆ **888/923-9030** or 407/932-0189; www.babiesaway.com) and **All About Kids** (✆ **800/728-6506** or 407/812-9300; www.all-about-kids.com). The bonus: Both companies deliver your gear right to your hotel and pick it up before you leave.

websites **www.babyage.com** and **www. amazon.com** both offer a good selection of travel-related gear if you can't find what you need at your local baby store, Target, or Wal-Mart.

You won't need to cart your entire supply of diapers, wipes, formula, and food—you can find familiar brands of supplies at Walgreens drugstores in the area, as well as Publix and Gooding's grocery stores. Just remember to bring enough to tide you over until you can get to a store. Powder and rash creams should be added to the list as well: Orlando's heat and humidity can wreak havoc on baby bottoms, even if your kids aren't generally susceptible to problems. And don't forget the sunscreen and hats!

As for older kids, keep them to one bag apiece, and invest in suitcases or duffle bags with wheels (you don't want to be lugging their luggage in addition to your own). Kids are usually happy with one or two pairs of shoes (sneakers or sturdier styles of sport sandals), jeans, shorts, and T-shirts, or whatever's fashionable at the moment. Pack a sweatshirt or sweater no matter when you're traveling, and include a jacket in cooler months.

Backpacks for all kids over 5 are great for stowing unused jackets, books, pens, paper, souvenirs, sunscreen, a baseball cap, water bottle, map, and sunglasses.

5 Getting There

BY PLANE
Orlando International Airport (© 407/825-2001;   www.orlandoairports.net) offers direct or nonstop service from 60 U.S. cities and two dozen international destinations, serving more than 30 million passengers each year. Rated one of the top airports in the country, it's a thoroughly modern and user-friendly facility with tons of restaurants, shops, a 446-room on-site Hyatt Regency hotel, and centrally located information kiosks.

Delta Air Lines (© 800/221-1212; www.delta.com) has recaptured the top spot, claiming nearly 20% of the flights to and from Orlando International Airport. It offers service from roughly 150 cities. Other carriers include **AeroMexico** (© 800/237-6639; www.aeromexico. com), **Air Canada** (© 888/247-2262; www.aircanada.ca), **American Airlines** (© 800/433-7300; www.americanair. com), **British Airways** (© 800/247-9297; www.british-airways.com), **Continental Airlines** (© 800/525-0280; www. continental.com), **Iberia** (© 800/772-4642 in the U.S.; www.iberia.com), **Icelandair** (© 800/223-5500 in the U.S. or 020/7874-1000 in the U.K.; www.ice landair.com), **Northwest Airlines** (© 800/225-2525; www.nwa.com), **Southwest Airlines** (© 800/435-9792; www.south west.com), **United Airlines** (© 800/241-6522; www.united.com), **US Airways** (© 800/428-4322; www.usairways.com), and **Virgin Atlantic** (© 800/862-8621; www.virgin-atlantic.com).

Several so-called no-frills airlines (those offering lower fares but providing few or no amenities) fly to Orlando. These include **JetBlue Airways** (© 800/538-2583; www.jetblue.com), which has personal video screens offering 24 TV channels (a big plus for those traveling with kids); **Spirit Airlines** (© 800/772-7117; www.spiritair.com); and **Ted** (© 800/225-5833; www.flyted.com), United's younger sibling.

Overseas visitors can take advantage of the **APEX** (Advance Purchase Excursion) reductions offered by all major U.S. and European carriers. In addition, some large airlines offer transatlantic or transpacific passengers special discount tickets under the name **Visit USA,** which allows mostly one-way travel from one

> ## (Tips) **Stuck on You**
>
> Your tween or teen just got his or her first set of contact lenses and is probably very attached to them. But if your kids wear those lenses on a plane, they could possibly become too attached. The air in an airplane cabin is especially dry and depletes the moisture in the eyes. If your kids aren't careful, their contact lenses (or yours, for that matter) could get vacuum-sealed onto their eyes. And I doubt you want your first sightseeing experience in Orlando to be an emergency room. Your best bet is for everyone to ditch the lenses for the plane ride, but if that isn't possible, make sure all lens wearers put in lots of rewetting drops over the course of the plane ride.

U.S. destination to another at very low prices. Unavailable in the U.S., these discount tickets must be purchased abroad in conjunction with your international fare. This system is the easiest, fastest, cheapest way to see the country.

For a comprehensive list of major airlines that fly into Orlando, see the appendix, "Useful Toll-Free Numbers & Websites."

FLYING FOR LESS: TIPS FOR GETTING THE BEST AIRFARE

- Passengers who can book their ticket either **long in advance or at the last minute,** or who **fly midweek** or **at less-trafficked hours** may pay a fraction of the full fare. If your schedule is flexible, say so, and ask if you can secure a cheaper fare by changing your flight plans.
- Search **the Internet** for cheap fares. The most popular online travel agencies are **Travelocity.com** (www.travelocity.co.uk), **Expedia.com** (www.expedia.co.uk and www.expedia.ca), and **Orbitz.com.** Other websites for booking airline tickets online include **Cheapflights.com, SmarterTravel.com, Priceline.com,** and **Opodo** (www.opodo.co.uk). Meta search sites (which find and then direct you to airline and hotel websites for booking) include **Sidestep.com** and **Kayak.com**—the

latter includes fares for budget carriers like JetBlue and Spirit as well as the major airlines. **Site59.com** is a great source for last-minute flights and getaways. In addition, most **airlines** offer online-only fares that even their phone agents know nothing about. British travelers should check **Flights International** (© 0800/018-7050; www.flights-international.com) for deals on flights all over the world.

- There's no shortage of discounted and promotional fares to Florida. The months of November, December, and January (excluding holidays) often bring **fare wars,** when airlines lower prices on their most popular routes. Watch local newspapers for **promotional specials,** too, and check airline websites. Also keep an eye on price fluctuations and deals at websites such as **Airfarewatchdog.com** and **Farecast.com.**
- No-frills airlines have reduced their price advantage, but some **charter flights** still go to Florida, especially during the winter season and particularly from Canada. They often cost less than regularly scheduled flights, but they're very complicated. It's best to go to a good travel agent and ask him or her to find one for you.
- Join frequent-flier clubs. Frequent-flier membership doesn't cost a cent,

but it does entitle you to free tickets or upgrades when you amass the airline's required number of frequent-flier points. You don't even have to fly to earn points; frequent-flier credit cards can earn you thousands of miles for doing your everyday shopping. But keep in mind that award seats are limited, seats on popular routes are hard to snag, and more and more major airlines are cutting their expiration periods for mileage points—so check your airline's frequent-flier program so you don't lose your miles before you use them. *Tip:* Award seats are offered almost a year in advance, but seats also open up at the last minute, so if your travel plans are flexible, you may strike gold. To play the frequent-flier game to your best advantage, consult the community bulletin boards on FlyerTalk (www.flyertalk.com) or go to Randy Petersen's Inside Flyer (www.insideflyer.com). Petersen and friends review all the programs in detail and post regular updates on changes in policies and trends.

ARRIVING AT THE AIRPORT

IMMIGRATION & CUSTOMS CLEARANCE Foreign visitors arriving by air, no matter what the port of entry, should cultivate patience and resignation before setting foot on U.S. soil. U.S. airports have considerably beefed up security clearances in the years since the terrorist attacks of 9/11, and clearing Customs and Immigration can take as long as 2 hours, especially on summer

---

Tips Getting through the Airport

- Arrive at the airport at least 1 hour before a domestic flight and 2 hours before an international flight. You can check the average wait times at your airport by going to the TSA **Security Checkpoint Wait Times** website (waittime/tsa.dhs.gov).
- Know what you can carry on and what you can't. For the latest updates on items you are prohibited to bring in carry-on luggage, go to **www.tsa.gov/travelers/airtravel**.
- Beat the ticket-counter lines by using the self-service electronic ticket kiosks at the airport or even printing out your boarding pass at home from the airline website. Using curbside check-in is also a smart way to avoid lines.
- Bring a current, government-issued photo ID such as a driver's license or passport. Children under 18 do not need government-issued photo IDs for flights within the U.S., but they do need passports for international flights to most countries.
- Help speed up security before you're screened. Remove jackets, shoes, belt buckles, heavy jewelry, and watches and place them either in your carry-on luggage or the security bins provided. Place keys, coins, cellphones, and pagers in a security bin. If you have metallic body parts, carry a note from your doctor. When possible, pack liquids in checked baggage.
- Use a TSA-approved lock for your checked luggage. Look for Travel Sentry certified locks at luggage or travel shops and Brookstone stores (or online at www.brookstone.com).

> **Tips   Don't Schlep It—Ship It**
>
> If ease of travel is your main concern, and money is no object, consider shipping your luggage, baby gear, and sports equipment. Specialists in door-to-door luggage delivery include **Virtual Bellhop** (www.virtualbellhop.com), **SkyCap International** (www.skycapinternational.com), **Luggage Express** (www.usxpluggageexpress.com), and **Sports Express** (www.sportsexpress.com).
>
> The same advice follows for souvenirs. Why drag them back in an over-stuffed bag that may exceed the airline's size or weight limits and incur a penalty fee? Many a UPS store can be found throughout Orlando, and most resorts will help with shipping arrangements for a fee. It's more economical to ship via FedEx, DHL, or UPS than to pay the airline's excessive overage fees.

weekends, so be sure to carry this guidebook or something else to read. According to Orlando International Airport's website, the average time between deplaning and leaving the airport for an international visitor is 46 minutes.

People traveling by air from Canada, Bermuda, and certain Caribbean countries can sometimes clear Customs and Immigration at the point of departure, which is much faster.

GETTING INTO TOWN FROM THE AIRPORT

Orlando International is 25 miles east of Walt Disney World and 20 miles south of downtown. At rush hour (7–9am and 4–6pm), the drive can be a torturous hour or more; at other times, it's about 30 to 40 minutes, depending on your destination.

BY SHUTTLE & CAR SERVICE   The **Mears Transportation Group** (© 407/423-5566; www.mearstransportation.com) runs vans that shuttle passengers from the airport's ground level to the Disney resorts and official hotels, as well as most other Orlando properties. These air-conditioned vehicles operate around the clock, departing every 15 to 25 minutes in both directions. Rates vary by destination. Round-trip fare for adults is $31 ($20 for kids 4–11) between the airport and International Drive, $43 ($34 for kids 4–11) for Walt Disney World/Lake Buena Vista

or West U.S. 192. Children 3 and under ride free.

Quicksilver Tours & Transportation (© 888/GOTOWDW or 407/299-1434; www.quicksilver-tours.com) is more personal. Its folks greet you at baggage claim with a sign bearing your name. Rates are only slightly higher than what Mears charges, but they're coming for you—and they're going only to *your* resort. The big bonus is a free 30-minute grocery stop, and there's no extra charge for car seats and boosters. Prices run from $115 to $125, depending on whether you want a town car or a van and, of course, on where you're going.

Tiffany Towncar (© 888/838-2161 or 407/370-2196; www.tiffanytowncar.com) offers a $120 round-trip rate for up to five people in a van from Orlando International to I-Drive, Universal, Disney, and U.S. 192. Drivers will meet you right at baggage claim; a free 30-minute grocery stop is included with the service. Booster and car seats area available upon request (at no charge).

Disney's **Magical Express** began operating in 2005 and is slated to run through at least 2011. This complimentary service is available to WDW resort guests flying on select airlines to Orlando International. If you use the service, Disney will pick up your bags from the airport and deliver them right to your room without

Flying with Film & Video

Never pack film—exposed or unexposed—in checked bags, because the new, more powerful scanners in U.S. airports can fog film. The film you carry with you can be damaged by scanners as well. X-ray damage is cumulative; the faster the film, and the more times you put it through a scanner, the more likely the damage. Film under 800 ASA is usually safe for up to five scans. If you're taking your film through additional scans, U.S. regulations permit you to demand hand inspections. In international airports, you're at the mercy of airport officials. On international flights, store your film in transparent baggies, so you can remove it easily before you go through scanners. Keep in mind that airports are not the only places where your camera may be scanned: Highly trafficked attractions are X-raying visitors' bags with increasing frequency.

Most photo supply stores sell protective pouches designed to block damaging X-rays. The pouches fit both film and loaded cameras. They should protect your film in checked baggage, but they also may raise alarms and result in a hand inspection.

You'll have little to worry about if you are traveling with **digital cameras.** Unlike film, which is sensitive to light, the digital camera and storage cards are not affected by airport X-rays, according to Nikon.

Carry-on scanners will not damage **videotape** in video cameras, but the magnetic fields emitted by the walk-through security gateways and hand-held inspection wands will. Always place your loaded camcorder on the screening conveyor belt or have it hand-inspected. Be sure your batteries are charged, as you may be required to turn the device on to ensure that it's what it appears to be.

your having to lift a finger. Attach the special luggage tags Disney will send you, check your bags at your departure city, and, when you get to Orlando, bypass baggage claim altogether and head straight for the special Magical Express bus that will transport you to your Disney resort. Your luggage will be delivered to your room after you arrive at your resort. The service saves both time and money; it must be booked at least 10 days in advance of your arrival through your travel agent or through Disney (© **407/ 934-7639;** www.disneyworld.com).

BY RENTAL CAR   All major car-rental agencies are located at or near the airport; see "Getting Around," in chapter 3, and

the appendix, "Useful Toll-Free Numbers & Websites," for more information about car rentals.

To get from the airport to the attractions, take the **North** exit out of the airport to **Highway 528 West.** Follow signs to **I-4;** it takes about 30 to 40 minutes to get to Disney World if the traffic isn't too heavy (double or worse in rush hour or when there's an accident). When you get to I-4, follow the signs **west** toward the attractions.

Note: It's always a good idea when you make reservations to ask about transportation options between the airport and your hotel. Also be sure to ask how far you have to travel to pick up and drop off a rental car. Some lots are miles from the airport, adding to the time you'll spend waiting in line and catching shuttles.

BY CAR

Orlando is 436 miles from Atlanta, 1,312 miles from Boston, 1,120 miles from Chicago, 1,009 miles from Cleveland, 1,170 miles from Dallas, 1,114 miles from Detroit, 1,088 miles from New York City, and 1,282 miles from Toronto.

From Atlanta, take I-75 south to the Florida Turnpike to I-4 west. From points northeast, take I-95 south to Daytona Beach and I-4 west. **AAA** (© **800/222-1134;** www.aaa.com) and some other auto-club members should call their local offices for maps and optimum driving directions.

For information on car rentals, see "Getting Around," in chapter 3.

BY TRAIN

Amtrak (© **800/872-7245;** www.amtrak. com) operates train service to stations at 1400 Sligh Blvd. in downtown Orlando (23 miles from Walt Disney World) and 111 Dakin Ave. in Kissimmee (15 miles from WDW). There are also stops in Winter Park, 10 miles north of downtown Orlando, at 150 W. Morse Blvd.; and in Sanford, 23 miles northeast of Orlando, at 800 Persimmon Ave., which is also the end terminal for the Auto Train (see below).

FARES   As with airline fares, you can sometimes get discounts if you book far in advance. There may be some restrictions on travel dates for discounted fares, mostly around very busy holiday times. Amtrak also offers money-saving packages—including accommodations (some at WDW resorts), car rentals, tours, and train fare. Call © **800/321-8684** for details.

The good news for families is that up to two children ages 2 to 15 can ride for half fare with a paying adult; one child under 2 rides for free with an accompanying

adult. The discounts apply year-round and on all trains except the Acela.

International visitors can buy a **USA Rail Pass,** good for 5, 15, or 30 days of unlimited travel. In 2007, prices for a 15-day adult pass were $389 off peak, $499 peak. For visitors spending time only on the East Coast of the U.S., prices in 2007 for a 15-day adult East pass were $329 off peak, $369 peak. The pass is available online or through many overseas travel agents. With a foreign passport, you can also buy passes at some Amtrak offices in the United States, including locations in San Francisco, Los Angeles, Chicago, New York, Miami, Boston, and Washington, D.C. Reservations are generally required and should be made as early as possible. Regional rail passes are also available.

AUTO TRAIN   This option offers the convenience of bringing your car to Florida without having to drive it all the way. It begins in Lorton, Virginia—about a 4-hour drive from New York, a 2-hour drive from Philadelphia—and ends at Sanford, 23 miles northeast of Orlando. (There are no stops in between.) Reserve early for the lowest prices. Fares average $760 ($1,200 with a berth) for two passengers and an auto. Call © **800/872-7245** for details.

BY BUS

Bus travel is often the most economical form of public transit for short hops between U.S. cities, but it's certainly not an option for everyone (particularly when Amtrak, which is far more luxurious, offers similar rates). **Greyhound** (© **800/231-2222;** www.greyhound.com) is the sole nationwide bus line. International visitors can obtain information about the **Greyhound North American Discovery Pass.** The pass can be obtained from foreign travel agents or through (www. discoverypass.com) for unlimited travel and stopovers in the U.S. and Canada. In

2007, passes were priced as follow: 7 days ($283), 15 days ($415), 30 days ($522), and 60 days ($645). Special rates are available for seniors, students, and children.

6 Tips on Flying with Children

Most airlines require that an infant be 2 weeks old to travel. American and Continental require that the child be 7 days old. Alaska lets babies fly as soon as they're born. Bring a birth certificate for your newborn.

The practice of allowing children younger than 2 to ride for free on a parent's lap is still in effect; however, a new rule proposed by the FAA would require all children under 40 pounds to have their own tickets and be secured in a child safety seat, so be sure to double-check the rules when you book your flight.

Most major American airlines offer discounted infant tickets for children 2 or younger to make it more affordable for you to reserve a separate adjacent seat for your baby (and his safety seat).

If a seat adjacent to yours is available, your lap child can sit there free of charge. When you check in, ask if the flight is crowded. If it isn't, explain your situation to the agent, and ask if you can reserve two seats—or simply move to two empty adjacent seats once the plane is boarded. You might want to shop around before you buy your ticket and deliberately book a flight that's not very busy (though that's often difficult, given the destination). Ask the reservationist which flights tend to be most full, and avoid those if possible. Only one extra child is allowed in each row, however, due to the limited number of oxygen masks.

On international journeys, children can't ride free on parents' laps. On flights overseas, a lap fare usually costs 10% of the parent's ticket. Children under the airline's age limit (which ranges from 11–15) can purchase international fares at 50% to 75% of the lowest coach fare in certain markets. Some of the foreign carriers make even greater allowances for children.

Note: Children riding for free will usually not be granted any baggage allowance.

Very few airlines offer child meals anymore, so come prepared with formula, juice, snacks, and sandwiches if you're flying around mealtime. Another option is to eat at one of the airport's fast-food joints—or get a meal to go, and bring it along for the ride. If your kids drink only milk, grab a few extra cartons at the airport, as oftentimes I've found the airlines run out in flight. All major airlines except Alaska and Southwest will warm bottles on request.

Tips Unplugged

If you or your kids are flying with a cold or sinus problems, use a decongestant an hour before takeoff and landing to minimize pressure buildup in the inner ear. It's difficult for kids to make their ears pop, and they can have an especially tough time with pressure in their ears. Takeoff and landing can be particularly painful—even dangerous—for a child with congested sinuses. Nursing and/or sucking on a bottle or pacifier, or a sippy cup of a favorite drink, will help alleviate pressure in your infant or toddler. A cough drop or hard candy should work for older kids (don't give these to younger ones, who might choke on them if there's turbulence).

In-Flight Fun for Kids

With one of these children's game books on board, even the longest plane ride will go faster.

The Everything Kids Travel Activity Book
by Erik A Hanson & Jeanne Hanson
Retail price: $6.95
Ages 4 to 8
This book is full of entertaining educational games to help your kids while away the miles.

Brain Quest for the Car: 1100 Questions and Answers All About America
by Sharon Gold
Retail price: $11
Ages 7 to 12
This book features cards with questions about American geography, culture, and customs.

Vacation Fun Mad Libs: World's Greatest Party Game
by Roger Price
Retail price: $4
Ages 8 and up
As suggested by the title, this book is chock-full of Mad Libs. Your kids will want to keep playing even after you've touched down.

Additional sanity savers include **The Everything Kids' Activity Book: Games to Play, Songs to Sing, Fun Stuff to Do—Guaranteed to Keep You Busy the Whole Ride!** (Adams Media Corporation, $6.95); **Miles of Smiles: 101 Great Car Games** (Carousel Press, $8.95); **Miles of Smiles: Travel Games & Quizzes To Go** (American Girl Library, $9.95); **Travel Wise with Children: 101 Games & Ideas to Make Family Travel Fun for Everyone** (Gramercy, $9.95); *Are We There Yet* (Backseat Books, $3.95); and *Kids Travel: A Backseat Survival Guide* (Klutz, $20). This last one's even endorsed by the Save the Parents' Sanity foundation.

CHILD SEATS: THEY'RE A MUST

According to *Consumer Reports Travel Letter,* the National Transportation Safety Board says that since 1991, the deaths of five children and injuries to four could have been prevented had the children been sitting in restraint systems during their flights. Even in the event of moderate turbulence, children sitting on a parent's lap can be thrust forward and injured. When you consider that a commercial aircraft hits a significant amount of turbulence at least once a day on average, you'd do well to think about investing a few extra dollars for a separate airline ticket and safety seat for your child.

The FAA recommends that children under 20 pounds ride in a rear-facing child-restraint system; those who weigh 20 to 40 pounds should sit in a forward-facing child-restraint system. Children over 40 pounds should sit in a regular seat and wear a seat belt.

All child seats manufactured after 1985 are certified for airline use, but make sure your car seat will fit in an airline seat—it must be less than 16 inches wide. You may not use booster seats, seatless vests, or harness systems. Safety seats must be placed in window seats—except in exit rows, where they are prohibited, so as not to block the passage of other travelers in the case of an emergency.

The airlines themselves should carry child safety seats on board. Unfortunately, most don't. To make matters worse, overzealous flight attendants have been known to try to keep safety seats off planes. One traveler recounts in the November 2001 issue of *Consumer Reports Travel Letter* how a Southwest attendant attempted to block use of a seat because the red label certifying it as safe for airline use had flaked off. That traveler won her case by bringing the owner's manual and appealing to the pilot; you should do the same.

If you can't afford the expense of a separate ticket, book your seat toward the back of the plane at a time when air travel is likely to be slowest—and the seat next to you will be more likely to be empty. The reservationist should also be able to recommend the best (meaning the least busy) time for you to fly.

EASING AIR TRAVEL WITH THE TOTS IN TOW

Several books on the market offer tips to help you travel with kids. *Trouble-Free Travel with Children—Over 700 Helpful Hints for Parents on the Go* (Book Peddlers, $9.95) is full of good general advice that can apply to travel anywhere. Other reliable tomes, with a worldwide focus, are *Adventuring with Children* (Avalon House Travel Series, $15) and *Lonely Planet Travel with Children* (Lonely Planet Publications, $10).

- **Reserve a seat in the bulkhead row.** You'll have more legroom, and your children will be able to spread out and play on the floor underfoot.

- **Check your luggage,** and limit family members to one backpack or bag for which they are responsible. This will make life much simpler.

- **Have a long talk with your children** before you depart for your trip. If they've never flown before, explain to them what to expect. If they're old enough, you may even want to describe how flying works, assuring them, if necessary, that air travel is safe. Explain to your kids the importance of good behavior in the air (and in the airport)—how the crew depends upon their being quiet and staying in their seats during the trip to fly safely.

- **Ask the flight attendant if the plane has special safety equipment for children.** Make a member of the crew aware of any medical problems your children have that could manifest during flight.

- **Be sure you've slept sufficiently** for your trip. If you fall asleep in the air, and your child manages to break away, there are all sorts of perilous predicaments he or she could get into. It's dangerous for a child to be crawling or walking around the cabin unaccompanied by an adult.

- **Be sure your child's seat belt remains fastened properly,** and try to reserve the seat closest to the aisle for yourself. This will make it harder for your children to wander off—in case, for instance, you're taking the red-eye or a long flight overseas, and you do happen to nod off. You will also protect your child from jostling passersby and falling objects—in the rare but entirely possible instance that an overhead bin pops open.

- **Try to sit near the lavatory,** though not so close that your children are jostled by the crowds that tend to gather there.

Travel in the Age of Bankruptcy

Airlines go bankrupt, so protect yourself by **buying your tickets with a credit card.** The Fair Credit Billing Act guarantees that you can get your money back from the credit card company if a travel supplier goes under (and if you request the refund within 60 days of the bankruptcy). **Travel insurance** can also help, but make sure it covers against "carrier default" for your specific travel provider. And be aware that if a U.S. airline goes bust mid-trip, a 2001 federal law requires other carriers to take you to your destination (albeit on a space-available basis) for a fee of no more than $25, provided you rebook within 60 days of the cancellation.

- **Pack clean, self-containing compact toys** in each child's bag. Electronic games can interfere with the aircraft navigational system, and their noisiness, however lulling to children's ears, will surely not win the favor of your adult neighbors. That said, if you're clear about the rules with regard to their use ahead of time, they can easily keep kids busy for hours. Magnetic checkers sets and other such travel games are a great distraction, as are coloring books, crayons, and card games such as Go Fish.

  By all means, don't leave home without a favorite blanket or stuffed animal—especially if it's your child's best friend at bedtime. It might also come in handy if the going gets rough, and kids need something comforting to cuddle.

- **Pack age-appropriate extras** in the bag of the responsible adult (you, for example)—this means a deck of cards, postcards, pens, an address book, extra bottles, bibs, pacifiers, diapers, and chewing gum to help relieve any ear-pressure problems. A package of wipes is also handy. With an infant on board, you'll likely need a change of clothes for him or her and quite possibly for yourself.

- **Bring some snacks**—you'll certainly be grateful to yourself later for packing rolled dried fruit, graham crackers, fishy crackers, or pretzels. Gingersnaps actually help curb mild cases of motion sickness. If you have a mini collapsible cooler, you can bring along yogurt (drinkable or in tubes) and cheese cubes, too. And don't forget to stash a few resealable plastic baggies in your bag. They'll prove invaluable for storing everything from half-eaten crackers and fruit to checkers pieces and Matchbox cars (not to mention the occasional dirty diaper).

- **Offer juice or cookies** to keep kids distracted during takeoff and landing—often the scariest parts of flight for a child—and to help their little ears pop as cabin air pressure shifts rapidly. Juice (paper cartons travel best) will also keep them swallowing and help them stay properly hydrated.

- **Don't forget bottles and extra milk or formula** (bottled water, too, if you use the powdered type) if your children are very young, as these are unavailable on most aircraft. Many airlines prohibit flight attendants from preparing formula, so plan on mixing it yourself unless you bring along a travel-size can of ready-to-feed formula.

7 Money & Costs

It's always advisable to bring money in a variety of forms on a vacation: a mix of cash, credit cards, and traveler's checks. You should also exchange enough petty cash to cover airport incidentals, tipping, and transportation to your hotel before you leave home, or withdraw money upon arrival at an airport ATM.

ATMS

Nationwide, the easiest and best way to get cash away from home is from an ATM (automated teller machine), sometimes referred to as a "cash machine" or "cashpoint." The **Cirrus** (© 800/424-7787; www.mastercard.com) and **PLUS** (© 800/843-7587; www.visa.com) networks span the country; you can find them even in remote regions. Go to your bank card's website to find ATM locations at your destination. Be sure you know your daily withdrawal limit before you depart.

Note: Many banks impose a fee every time you use a card at another bank's ATM, and that fee is often higher for international transactions (up to $5 or more) than for domestic ones (where they're rarely more than $2). In addition, the bank from which you withdraw cash may charge its own fee. To compare banks' ATM fees within the U.S., use **www.bankrate.com**. (Visitors from outside the U.S. should also find out whether their bank assesses a 1%–3% fee on charges incurred abroad.)

ATMs inside the Disney theme parks are on Main Street in the Magic Kingdom and at the entrances to Epcot, Disney's Hollywood Studios, and Disney's Animal Kingdom. They're also at Pleasure Island, in Downtown Disney Marketplace, at Disney resorts, and at the Crossroads Shopping Center.

At Universal Studios Florida, Islands of Adventure, and SeaWorld, you can find ATMs near Guest Services.

Inside the entrances of most of the parks, you'll find maps listing all ATMs. If this isn't the case when you visit, look for them at Guest Relations or Guest Services near the entrances or at most shops.

Outside the parks, you can find ATMs in most malls, grocery stores, drugstores, and some convenience stores, such as 7-Eleven and Circle K.

Be *very* careful when using ATMs; the Land of Mickey can lull you into a false sense of security. Goofy and Pluto won't mug you, but some of their estranged neighbors might. Cuddly critters aside, this is a big city, and its crime rate is the same as that of others. Even in seemingly safe places, when entering your PIN, make sure you shield the keyboard from others in line. And if you're using a drive-through, keep your doors locked.

CREDIT CARDS & DEBIT CARDS

Credit cards are the most widely used form of payment in the United States: **Visa** (Barclaycard in Britain), **MasterCard** (EuroCard in Europe, Access in Britain, Chargex in Canada), **American Express, Diners Club,** and **Discover.** They also provide a convenient record of

---

(*Tips* Online Ticketing

The Big Three all offer online booking of tickets, hotel rooms, vacation packages, and more. Disney's official deals can be found at **www.disneyworld.com**, Universal Orlando's offers at **www.universalorlando.com**, and SeaWorld's specials at **www.seaworld.com**. All offer Web-only discounts and specials with added savings if you purchase ahead of time and online.

What Things Cost in Orlando	US$	UK£
Taxi from airport to Walt Disney World (up to 4 people)	50.00	25.00
Shuttle from the airport to Walt Disney World (2 adults, 2 kids)	94.00–108.00	47.00–54.00
Double room at Disney's Grand Floridian Resort & Spa (very expensive)	375.00–710.00	187.50–355.00
Double room at Disney's Caribbean Beach Resort (moderate)	145.00–225.00	72.50–112.50
Double room at Staybridge Suites Lake Buena Vista (moderate)	159.00–299.00	79.50–149.50
Double room at Disney's All-Star Music Resort (inexpensive)	82.00–141.00	41.00–70.50
All-you-can-eat dinner buffet at a Disney theme park restaurant (adult/child)	29.00/14.00	14.50/7.00
Child's meal at most theme-park restaurants	7.00	3.50
Chef Mickey's character breakfast at Disney's Contemporary Resort (adult/child)	19.00/11.00	9.50/5.50
Huggies Pull-Ups, 21 count, at Walgreens	16.00	8.00
2.5-ounce jar of baby-food entree at Publix	1.29	.65
Tube of sunblock in the theme parks	12.00	6.00
Evening movie tickets at AMC Pleasure Island (adult/child)	9.50/6.50	4.75/3.25
4-Day Magic Your Way Park Hopper ticket to Walt Disney World (adult/child)	257.00/223.00	128.50/111.50
1-day, 1-park ticket to Walt Disney World (adult/child)	71.00/60.00	35.50/30.00
Parking at WDW (car)	11.00	5.50
1-day, 1-park ticket to Universal Orlando (adult/child)	71.00/60.00	35.50/30.00
Parking at Universal Orlando (car)	11.00	5.50
1-day, 1-park ticket to Sea World (adult/child)	65.00/54.00	32.50/27.00
Parking at SeaWorld	10.00	5.00
Admission to Orlando Science Center (adult/child)	15.00/10.00	7.50/5.00

all your expenses, and offer relatively good exchange rates. You can withdraw cash advances from your credit cards at banks or ATMs, but high fees make credit-card cash advances a pricey way to get cash.

It's highly recommended that you travel with at least one major credit card. You must have a credit card to rent a car, and hotels and airlines usually require a credit card imprint as a deposit against expenses.

Disney parks, resorts, shops, and restaurants (though not most snack carts) accept all of the aforementioned major credit cards. Additionally, the WDW and Universal resorts will let you charge purchases made in their respective park shops and restaurants to your hotel room, but you have to settle up when you check out. Be sure, however, to keep track of your spending as you go along so you won't be surprised when you get the total bill.

There are a handful of stores and restaurants that do not take credit cards, so be sure to ask in advance. Most businesses display a sticker near their entrance to let you know which cards they accept. (*Note:* Businesses may require a minimum purchase, usually around $10, to use a credit card.)

ATM cards with major credit card backing, known as **debit cards,** are now a commonly acceptable form of payment in most stores and restaurants. Debit cards draw money directly from your checking account. Some stores enable you to receive cash back on your debit-card purchases as well. The same is true at most U.S. post offices.

DISNEY DOLLARS

You can also buy Disney dollars (currency with images of Mickey, Minnie, ships from the Pirates of the Caribbean, and so on) in $1, $5, and $10 denominations. They're good at WDW shops, restaurants, and resorts, as well as Disney stores everywhere. But I don't recommend buying them because you'll have to cash in leftover bills for real currency upon leaving WDW, which means still another line, or keep them as a souvenir (which could be a rather expensive souvenir at that). Also, watch out if you have a refund coming. Some things, such as strollers, wheelchairs, and lockers, require a security deposit, and Disney staffers will frequently dole out Disney dollars for refunds. If you don't want Mickey money,

just let them know, and they'll be happy to give you cash instead.

TRAVELER'S CHECKS

Though credit and debit cards are more often used, traveler's checks are still widely accepted in the U.S. Foreign visitors should make sure that traveler's checks are denominated in U.S. dollars; foreign-currency checks are often difficult to exchange. (Keep in mind that some places won't take traveler's checks at all, though that's rare in tourist-friendly Orlando.)

You can buy traveler's checks at most banks. Most are offered in denominations of $20, $50, $100, $500, and sometimes $1,000. Generally, you'll pay a service charge ranging from 1% to 4%.

The most popular traveler's checks are offered by **American Express** (② 800/807-6233; ② 800/221-7282 for card holders—this number accepts collect calls, offers service in several foreign languages, and exempts Amex gold and platinum cardholders from the 1% fee.); **Visa** (② 800/732-1322)—AAA members can obtain Visa checks for a $9.95 fee (for checks up to $1,500) at most AAA offices or by calling ② 866/339-3378; and **MasterCard** (② 800/223-9920).

Be sure to keep a copy of the serial numbers of your traveler's checks separate from your checks themselves, in the event that they are stolen or lost. You'll get a refund faster if you know the numbers.

Another option is the new **prepaid traveler's check cards,** reloadable cards that work much like debit cards but aren't linked to your checking account. The **American Express Travelers Cheque Card,** for example, requires a minimum deposit ($300), sets a maximum balance ($2,750), and has a one-time issuance fee of $15. You can withdraw money from an ATM ($2.50 per transaction, not including bank fees), and the funds can be purchased in dollars, euros, or pounds. If you lose the card, your available funds will be refunded within 24 hours.

You can cash traveler's or personal checks of $25 or less (drawn on U.S. banks, if you have a driver's license or passport and a major credit card) and exchange foreign currency at **SunTrust Bank,** 1675 Buena Vista Dr. (© **407/ 828-6106**), across from Downtown Disney Marketplace. The bank also has an ATM. It's open weekdays from 9am to 4pm and until 6pm on Thursday.

8 Travel Insurance

Check your existing insurance policies and credit card coverage before you buy travel insurance. You may already be covered for lost luggage, canceled tickets, or medical expenses.

The cost of travel insurance varies widely, depending on the cost and length of your trip, your age and health, and the type of trip you're taking, but expect to pay between 5% and 8% of the vacation itself. You can get estimates from various providers through **InsureMyTrip.com**. Enter your trip cost and dates, your age, and other information, for prices from more than a dozen companies.

For **U.K. citizens,** insurance is always advisable when traveling in the States. Travelers or families who make more than one trip abroad per year may find an annual travel insurance policy works out cheaper. Check **www.moneysupermarket. com**, which compares prices across a wide range of providers for single- and multi-trip policies.

Most big travel agents offer their own insurance and will probably try to sell you their package when you book a holiday. Think before you sign. **Britain's Consumers' Association** recommends that you insist on seeing the policy and reading the fine print before buying travel insurance. **The Association of British Insurers** (© **020/7600-3333**; www.abi. org.uk) gives advice by phone and publishes *Holiday Insurance,* a free guide to policy provisions and prices. You might also shop around for better deals: Try **Columbus Direct** (© **0870/033-9988**; www.columbusdirect.net).

TRIP-CANCELLATION INSURANCE

Trip-cancellation insurance will help retrieve your money if you have to back out of a trip or depart early, or if your travel supplier goes bankrupt. Trip cancellation traditionally covers such events as sickness, natural disasters, and State Department advisories (which aren't likely to happen in Orlando). The latest news in trip-cancellation insurance is the availability of expanded **hurricane** coverage and the **"any-reason"** cancellation coverage—which costs more but covers cancellations made for any reason. You won't get back 100% of your prepaid trip cost, but you'll be refunded a substantial portion. **TravelSafe** (© **888/885-7233**; www.travelsafe.com) offers both types of coverage. Expedia also offers any-reason cancellation coverage for its air-hotel packages.

For details, contact one of the following recommended insurers: **Access America** (© 866/807-3982; www.access america.com), **Travel Guard International** (© 800/826-4919; www.travel guard.com), **Travel Insured International** (© 800/243-3174; www.travel insured.com), and **Travelex Insurance Services** (© 888/457-4602; www.travelex-insurance.com).

MEDICAL INSURANCE

Although it's not required of travelers, health insurance is highly recommended. Most health insurance policies cover you if you get sick away from home—but check your coverage before you leave.

International visitors should note that unlike many European countries, the United States does not usually offer free or low-cost medical care to its citizens or visitors. Doctors and hospitals are expensive, and in most cases will require advance payment or proof of coverage before they render their services. Good policies will cover the costs of an accident, repatriation, or death. Packages such as **Europ Assistance's "Worldwide Healthcare Plan"** are sold by European automobile clubs and travel agencies at attractive rates. **Worldwide Assistance Services, Inc.** (© **800/777-8710;** www. worldwideassistance.com) is the agent for Europe Assistance in the United States.

Though lack of health insurance may prevent you from being admitted to a hospital in nonemergencies, don't worry about being left on a street corner to die: The American way is to fix you now and bill the living daylights out of you later.

If you're ever hospitalized more than 150 miles from home, **Medjet-Assist** (© **800/527-7478;** www.medjet assistance.com) will pick you up and fly you to the hospital of your choice in a medically equipped and staffed aircraft 24 hours day, 7 days a week. Annual memberships are $225 individual, $350 family; you can also purchase short-term memberships.

Canadians should check with their provincial health plan office or call **Health Canada** (© **866/225-0709;** www.hc-sc.gc.ca) to find out the extent of their coverage and what documentation and receipts they must take home in case they are treated in the United States.

LOST-LUGGAGE INSURANCE
On flights within the U.S., checked baggage is covered up to $2,500 per ticketed passenger. On flights outside the U.S. (and on U.S. portions of international trips), baggage coverage is limited to approximately $9.05 per pound, up to approximately $635 per checked bag. If you plan to check items more valuable than what's covered by the standard liability, see if your homeowner's policy covers your valuables, get baggage insurance as part of your comprehensive travel-insurance package, or buy Travel Guard's "BagTrak" product.

If your luggage is lost, immediately file a lost-luggage claim at the airport, detailing the luggage contents. Most airlines require that you report delayed, damaged, or lost baggage within 4 hours of arrival. The airlines are required to deliver luggage, once found, directly to your house or destination free of charge.

9 Health

STAYING HEALTHY
Limit your family's exposure to Florida's strong sun, especially during the first few days of your trip and, thereafter, during the hours of 11am to 2pm, when the sun is at its strongest. Use a sunscreen with the highest sun-protection factor (SPF) available (especially for children), and apply it liberally. If you have children under a year old, check with your pediatrician before applying a sunscreen; some ingredients may not be appropriate for infants.

You should also bring along some moleskin and plenty of Band-Aids. This will help with the inevitable blisters brought on by the day's activities.

WHAT TO DO IF YOU GET SICK AWAY FROM HOME
If you get sick or are injured, there are basic first-aid centers in all Orlando theme parks. **Doctors** and **dentists, emergency numbers, hospitals,** and **pharmacies** are listed under "Fast Facts," at the end of chapter 3.

If you suffer from a chronic illness, consult your doctor before your departure. Pack **prescription medications** in your carry-on luggage, and carry them in their original containers, with pharmacy labels—otherwise they won't make it through airport security. Visitors from outside the U.S. should carry generic names of prescription drugs. For U.S. travelers, most reliable health-care plans provide coverage if you get sick away from home. Foreign visitors may have to pay all medical costs upfront and be reimbursed later. See "Medical Insurance," under "Travel Insurance," above.

10 Safety

Walt Disney World and Orlando are safe in general, and the theme parks are even safer—but crime free, they're not. You can take some general precautions to minimize your chances of being the victim of a crime.

STAYING SAFE

Although Florida's tourist zones are generally safe, foreign visitors should note that U.S. urban areas tend to be less safe than those in Europe or Japan. You should always stay alert. This is particularly true of large American cities. If you're in doubt about which neighborhoods are safe, don't hesitate to make inquiries with the hotel front desk staff or the local tourist office.

Avoid deserted areas, especially at night, and don't go into public parks after dark unless there's a concert or similar occasion that will attract a crowd.

Avoid carrying valuables with you on the street, and keep expensive cameras or electronic equipment bagged or covered when not in use. If you're using a map, try to consult it inconspicuously—better yet, study it before leaving your room. Hold your pocketbook—or sling the strap across your chest—and put your billfold in an inside pocket. In theaters, restaurants, and other public places, keep possessions in sight.

Always lock your room door; don't assume that once you're inside the hotel, you are automatically safe and no longer need to be aware of your surroundings. Hotels are open to the public, and in a large hotel, security may not be able to screen everyone who enters.

KEEPING KIDS SAFE

There is one major safety issue when traveling with kids that usually comes up a lot more frequently in Orlando than it does in other destinations (though it's fortunately not common): the Lost Child.

Theme parks are hives of activity, and it's easy for you or your child to get distracted or confused; the next thing you know, Junior is missing. The good news is that the theme parks know this, and if it has to happen, better it happen here than in a lot of other places. So do not panic, no matter how inclined you may be to do so.

If a child turns up missing, report it immediately to the closest park employee. They are all trained to deal with lost kids—and to spot little lambs who've apparently gone astray from their flock. After making your report, find out where lost children are brought (there are usually one or two central locations in each park) and head directly there. Odds are your little wanderers are either already there or will arrive shortly.

The best way to prevent any of this from happening is to take a few preventive steps:

- **Dress young kids in easily identifiable clothing** so you don't lose them in a crowd.
- **Always set up a meeting spot** for your kids to head to, should you all get separated. Pick a place that's central, specific, and easily located (saying "I'll

meet you at Cinderella Castle" rather than "I'll meet you at the entrance to Cinderella's Royal Table" is a recipe for disaster).

- **Hold on tight to young kids** (even carry them or secure them in the stroller if possible) when exiting the park at closing time, at parades, and when leaving shows. It's very easy to get separated when you're smack in the middle of a massive wave of people. I'm not a huge fan of toddler harnesses, but in this case, I make an exception.
- **Sew or affix a name tag to your child's clothing** (though not in a place it can be read casually) with your child's first name, your cellphone number, and a contact number at home. The minute you get into the park, show your kids the distinctive name tags that the theme-park employees wear, and tell them to report to one of them if they get lost.
- **Don't assume that rides or restrooms have a single exit.** Always give a specific place for your child to meet you. Otherwise, you may end up in two different spots . . . and at least one of you will panic.

DRIVING SAFETY

Driving safety is important, too, and carjacking is not unprecedented. Question your rental agency about personal safety, and ask for a traveler-safety brochure when you pick up your car. Obtain written directions—or a map with the route clearly marked—from the agency showing how to get to your destination. (Many agencies now offer the option of renting a cellphone for the duration of your car rental; check with the rental agent when you pick up the car. Otherwise, contact **InTouch USA** at ✆ **800/ 872-7626** or www.intouchusa.com for short-term cellphone rental.) If possible, arrive and depart during daylight hours.

If you drive off a highway and end up in a dodgy-looking neighborhood, leave the area as quickly as possible. If you have an accident, even on the highway, stay in your car with the doors locked until you assess the situation or until the police arrive. If you're bumped from behind on the street or are involved in a minor accident with no injuries, and the situation appears to be suspicious, motion to the other driver to follow you. Never get out of your car in such situations. Go directly to the nearest police precinct, well-lit service station, or 24-hour store.

Park in well-lit and well-traveled areas whenever possible. Always keep your car doors locked, whether the vehicle is attended or unattended. Never leave any packages or valuables in sight. If someone attempts to rob you or steal your car, don't try to resist the thief/carjacker. Report the incident to the police department immediately by calling ✆ **911.**

11 Words of Wisdom on Family Travel

If you have trouble getting your kids out of the house in the morning, dragging them thousands of miles away may seem like an insurmountable challenge. But family travel can be immensely rewarding, giving you new ways of seeing the world through smaller pairs of eyes.

No city in the world is geared more to family travel than Orlando. In addition to theme parks, its recreational facilities provide loads of opportunities for family fun. Most restaurants have low-priced ($4–$9) children's menus (if not, the appetizer menu works well), plus fun distractions such as placemats to color or games to play while younger diners wait for their food. Many hotels have supervised children's activity centers (see chapter 4, "Family-Friendly Accommodations," for details).

Keep an eye out for discount coupons for meals and attractions. The Calendar section in Friday's *Orlando Sentinel* newspaper often contains coupons and good deals. Many restaurants, especially those in tourist areas, offer great discounts that are yours for the clipping. Check the information you receive from the Orlando/Orange County Convention & Visitors Bureau (see "Visitor Information & Maps," earlier in this chapter), including free or cheap things to do. Many hotel lobbies have free coupon books available, too.

Most major theme parks offer parent-swap programs in which one parent rides while the other waits in a designated area along with the kids too young or too nervous to ride. Then parents switch places, and the parent who was waiting can ride without having to return to the end of the line. Inquire at Guest Services or Guest Relations, near the park entrances, or ask the ride attendant.

Here are more suggestions for making traveling with children easier:

- **Are your kids old enough?** Do you really want to bring an infant or toddler to the parks? If you plan on visiting Disney several times as your children grow, the best age for a first visit to Disney is just about 3 years old. Why? Because the kids are old enough to walk around and enjoy the sights and sounds, and a good deal of the rides and shows as well. The thrill rides would most likely frighten them, but most inappropriate rides for the tiny-tot set have height restrictions that prevent any unfortunate mistakes. If, however, this trip is going to be a one-time occasion, I recommend waiting until your child is between 7 and 10. They'll still be able to appreciate the magic and wonder of the experience but won't have reached the stage where all they'll want is chills and thrills.

Some of the characters walking about may make young kids a bit nervous, though most will run right up to Donald or Mickey and give him a big hug. Younger children may need a nap just when you want to see a show or hop on a ride, but if you have kids, this is nothing new to you. When you plan your day's activities, be sure to account for these necessary breaks.

Will your whole family be able to enjoy the experiences that Disney and the other parks have to offer? This is something you will have to decide. My five kids range in age from 6 to 14, and we have traveled with just about every age combination you can think of. On our first family trip to WDW, my oldest was 5, and his two younger siblings were ages 3 and 1. While the 1-year-old has absolutely no recollection of the trip, he was thoroughly amused by the sights and sounds everywhere we went. The 3- and 5-year-olds (now 12 and 14) still remember plenty. You'll need to take into account your kids' stamina, interest, and tolerance levels before you decide whether to make the trip and when planning your daily itineraries. My kids could go well into the evening inside the parks, but many other children can't, so it may take you longer to cover a park (it took me 2–3 days to tour Magic Kingdom when my youngest was 2). My 8-year-old nephew (now 12) was petrified by some of the rides in the parks, and even my own kids, who'll try almost anything once and have never been wary of rides, completely freak out at attractions involving sensory effects. It may be repetitious, but I'll say it again: Know your own child before deciding whether he or she is ready for this sort of trip. Not every child will fall in love with Disney

Tips **The Royal Treatment**

Geared to those who have no time to plan but plenty of money to spend, **Michael's VIPs (www.michaelsvips.com)** is a professional service that will take care of all the tedious itinerary planning, but also provides personalized and private tours through attractions in and around Orlando. The price tag hovers around $100 per hour (plus a 20% gratuity), with the average guest paying roughly $3,500 per vacation for this VIP experience. Every detail is prearranged, and your private tour guide ensures that you'll never have to think or make decisions as you explore the sights. Due to Michael's extensive background knowledge of the area's attractions (he's a former Walt Disney World VIP host, where he was in charge of selecting and planning every attraction, dining, and activity choice while escorting world-famous celebs, athletes, execs, and their families through the resort), you'll experience minimal waiting times and maximum fun!

Don't have time to plan your vacation itinerary or your days at the parks? The **TourGuideMIKE Automated Vacation Planner** may be just what you need. Simply fill out the detailed questionnaire at **www.tourguidemike. com** (a charge of $22 applies); then, based on the information you provide, you'll get your own customized website to use to plan and tailor your itinerary. The best part: The site offers sample park tours and seasonal crowd charts to help you out.

World at first sight, and it's a rather large expense to incur if Junior's going to be frightened, sleepy, or cranky throughout the entire trip.

• **Plan ahead.** Make reservations for character breakfasts at Disney (see chapter 5, "Family-Friendly Dining") as soon as possible. Disney now accepts them up to 180 days in advance, and many are booked only minutes after the 180-day window opens, so mark your calendar to call (it can be as early as 7am EST). Also, in any park, check the daily schedule for character appearances (all the major ones post them on maps or boards near the entrances); kids love meeting their favorite characters and it's often the highlight of their day. (Be wary, however, of promising them specific characters, as schedules and character lineups can change.)

Advance planning will help you avoid running after every character you see.

The latest craze is collecting character autographs. The lines however, can be excruciatingly long, so you may want to pick and choose just a couple of favorite characters to do this with. Take my advice: Buy an autograph book and some Disney stickers (to decorate it) at home instead of paying theme-park prices—but if you forget, they can be found throughout the parks.

• **Pack the essential gear.** Although your home may be toddler-proof, hotels aren't. Bring outlet covers and whatever else is necessary to prevent an accident from occurring in your room. Most hotels have cribs available; however, they are usually limited in number and sometimes of questionable quality. Some hotels have bedrails available as well.

Locals can spot tourists by their bright-red sunburns. *Both parents and kids should bring and use sunscreen with an SPF rating of at least 30 (preferably 50).* If you do forget it, it's available at convenience stores, drugstores, some theme-park shops, and the resorts. Young children should be slathered, even if they're in a stroller. Be sure to pack a wide-brim hat for infants and toddlers. Adults and children alike should also drink plenty of water to avoid dehydration.

- **Research accommodations.** Kids under 12 and, in many cases, those as old as 17 stay free in their parent's room in most hotels, but to be certain, ask when you book your room. Most hotels have pools and other recreational facilities that will give you a little no-extra-cost downtime. If you want to skip a rental car and aren't staying at Disney, consider International Drive and Lake Buena Vista. Many hotels offer family discounts; some have "kids eat free" programs; and some provide free or moderate-cost shuttles to the major attractions. International Drive also has the I-Ride Trolley, which travels the length of the road, making numerous stops along the way.

- **Set ground rules.** Establish firm rules before leaving home regarding things such as bedtime and souvenirs. It's easy to get off track as you get caught up in the excitement of Orlando, but don't allow your vacation to seize control of your better judgment. Having the kids earn their own money or at least allotting a specific prearranged amount for them to spend works wonders. Making them part of your decisions also works wonders. They'll be far more accommodating and cooperative when they understand that everyone in the family gets a say in the plan for the day

and that they will eventually get to do something or go somewhere that they want to.

- **Be safe at the parks.** Getting lost is all too easy in a place as strange and overwhelming as the theme parks. For adults (yes, they get lost, too) and older kids, arrange a lost-and-found meeting place before you arrive in the park, and if you become separated, head there immediately. Make sure your kids know to find a staff member (point out the special name tags employees wear) to help them. Attach a name tag with the child's first name and your cellphone (or hotel) number to the inside of younger kids' T-shirts, and tell them to find a park employee (and only a park employee) immediately and show them the tag if they become lost.

- **Read the signs that post height restrictions,** if any, or identify those rides that may unsettle youngsters. Save yourself and your kids some grief before you get in line and are disappointed. (The ride listings in chapters 6 and 7 note any minimum heights, as do the guide maps you can get at the parks.) A bad experience— whether it be a dark, scary section of a ride; the loop-de-loop of a roller coaster; or too dramatic a drop—can cause your child long-lasting anxiety. It can also put a damper on things for the rest of your day (and possibly even your vacation).

I've explained to my older boys that if they hear adults screaming, that's a pretty good indication that a ride is not the best choice for them. With younger kids, you have to be steadfast in your decisions, though most height restrictions will keep those who really shouldn't be riding at bay. With the older ones . . . well, you may have to indulge them a bit and let them ride just one; they likely

Tips Kids Come First—or Do They?

Southwest Airlines, like Delta Air Lines, has stopped allowing families with children to board first on its Orlando (and other) flights. They believe that it's more fair to other passengers and often better for the kids, who won't be cooped up as long (they, of course, are not the ones hauling the baby gear, folding the stroller, or fastening in the car seat). Most other airlines, however, still allow pre-boarding for those traveling with tinier tots (usually under the age of 3 or 4) in tow.

won't make the same mistake twice. Note that once you get past the height restriction, age is not always as much of a deciding factor when it comes to rides as one might think. It really depends on your children's experiences and their personalities. I've seen 5-year-olds squeal with glee on rides that I can't even stomach; on the other hand, I've observed kids as old as 8 or 10 walk out of some of the attractions with touchy-feely sensory effects practically in tears.

- **Take a break.** The Disney parks, Universal Orlando, and SeaWorld have fabulous interactive play areas, offering both parents and young kids a break. By all means take advantage of them. They allow kids to expend some of their pent-up energy after having to wait in lines and not wander far from Mom and Dad all day long. They offer a nice break for you, too (if you can sit down to watch them, that is). Note that many of these kid zones are filled with water squirters and shallow pools, and most of the parks feature a fair number of water-related attractions, so getting wet is practically inevitable—at least for the kids. It's advisable to bring along a change of clothes or even a bathing suit. You can rent a locker ($7 or less) for storing the spares until you need them. During the summer, the Florida humidity is enough to keep you feeling soggy, so you may

appreciate the change of clothing even if you don't go near any water.

- **Schedule showtimes.** Plan on an indoor air-conditioned show two or three times a day, especially midafternoons in summer. You may even get your littlest tykes to nap in the darkened theater. For all shows, arrive at least 20 minutes early to get the better seats, but not so early that the kids are tired of waiting (most waits are outside in the heat at Disney, while Universal has covered queue areas at most attractions).
- **Have a stash for snack times.** When dreaming of your vacation, you probably don't envision hours spent standing in lines, waiting and waiting. It helps to store some lightweight snacks in a backpack, or in the stroller if you have one, especially when traveling with small children. This may save you some headaches, as kids get hungriest just when you are farthest from food. It will also be much healthier and will certainly save you money, as the parks' prices are quite high.
- **Bring your own stroller.** While you will have to haul it to and from the car and on and off trams, trains, or monorails at Disney, having your own stroller can be a tremendous help. It will be with you when you need it— say, back in the hotel room as a highchair or for an infant in a restaurant when a highchair is inappropriate.

Remember to bring the right stroller, too. It should be lightweight, easy to fold and unfold with one hand, have a canopy, be able to recline for naps, and have plenty of storage space. The parks offer stroller rentals for around $10, but these are often hard and uncomfortable. They do not recline and have little or no storage space. And they are absolutely inappropriate for infants and very young toddlers. They are good, however, if you have older kids who may just need an occasional break from walking. For infants and small toddlers, you may want to bring a snuggly sling or backpack-type carrier for use in traveling to and from parking lots and while you're standing in line for attractions.

• **Read up.** I've listed some additional tips for tackling the theme parks in chapter 6, "What Kids Like to See & Do in Walt Disney World." *The Unofficial Guide to Walt Disney World* is another good source of information, as is *Frommer's Walt Disney World.* Recommended websites include **Family Travel Forum** (www.familytravel forum.com), a comprehensive site that offers customized trip planning; **Family Travel Network** (www.family travelnetwork.com), an online magazine providing travel tips; and **Travel-WithYourKids.com** (www.travelwith yourkids.com), a comprehensive site written by parents for parents offering sound advice for long-distance and international travel with children.

12 Specialized Travel Resources

FOR TRAVELERS WITH DISABILITIES

There's no reason for anyone with disabilities to miss most of the fun that Orlando and the theme parks have to offer—as long as you engage in a little advance planning. Whether autistic, wheelchair-bound, or hearing-impaired, everyone comes to Orlando, and all are accommodated to the best of each park's ability.

ACCOMMODATIONS

Every hotel and motel in Florida is required by law to have a special room or rooms equipped for wheelchair users. A few have wheel-in showers. **Disney's Coronado Springs Resort** (© 407/934-7639 or 407/939-1000; www.disney world.com) has 99 rooms designed to accommodate guests with disabilities. **Disney's Polynesian** and **Grand Floridian** resorts are both particularly well suited to guests who use wheelchairs, as their location on the monorail system makes travel to the Magic Kingdom and Epcot a bit easier. For other information

about special Disney rooms, call © 407/939-7807. Make your needs known when booking reservations.

If you don't mind staying 15 minutes from Disney, **Yvonne's Property Management** (© 877/714-1144 or 863/424-0795; www.villasinorlando.com) is a rental agent for, among other things, some handicapped-accessible homes that have multiple bedrooms, multiple bathrooms with accessible showers, full kitchens, and pools outfitted with lifts. Most cost less than $300 a night and are located in Davenport.

Medical Travel Inc. (© 800/778-7953; www.medicaltravel.org) is another source of rentals, scooters and vans, and medical equipment, and can satisfy other needs of disabled travelers (including those with terminal illnesses) and their families.

Some hotels also have special **hypoallergenic rooms** for those with severe allergies or asthma. These rooms usually offer special ventilation systems, pillows, toiletries, and so on. Ask about this when

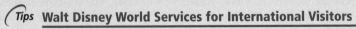

Tips Walt Disney World Services for International Visitors

Disney welcomes millions of international guests every year and offers a phone service that provides information in many languages (✆ **407/824-2222**). Here are other services available in Disney theme parks and resorts:

- **Ears to the World** are personal translator units that translate over 25 of Disney's shows and attractions into French, German, Japanese, Portuguese, and Spanish. They're available at Guest Relations just inside the Magic Kingdom, Epcot, Disney's Hollywood Studios, and Disney's Animal Kingdom.
- Detailed **guidebooks** and **maps** to the four major parks are available in French, German, Japanese, Portuguese, and Spanish at the five International Information Centers (marked by an "i" on handout guide maps) in the theme parks and Downtown Disney.
- **Menus** in French, German, Japanese, Portuguese, and Spanish are available at all theme-park restaurants that offer table or counter service.
- Over 7,000 theme-park **employees who speak a foreign language** sport a gold badge with the flag of that country on their name tag.
- **Resort phones** are equipped with software that expedites international calls by allowing guests to dial directly to international destinations. All public phones provide instructions in French, German, Japanese, and Portuguese. International calling cards can be found in vending machines just inside the main entrances of the four major theme parks.
- There's also online help at **www.disneyworld.com**. Once you're on the website, go to the bottom of the screen and click "International Sites."
- **Currency exchange** of up to $100 is available at Guest Relations in each of the four major theme parks and all WDW resorts. Note, however, that you won't get the best rate if you do so; it's better to withdraw cash from an ATM.

booking your hotel if this is an issue for you or your child.

TRANSPORTATION

Public buses in Orlando have hydraulic lifts and restraining belts for wheelchairs. They serve Universal Orlando, SeaWorld, the shopping areas, and downtown Orlando. If you're staying at Disney, most shuttle buses in the WDW Transportation System can accommodate wheelchairs.

If you need to rent a wheelchair or electric scooter for your visit, **Walker Medical & Mobility Products** (✆ **888/726-6837** or 407/518-6000; www.walker mobility.com) offers delivery to your

room, and there's a model for guests who weigh up to 375 pounds. These products fit into Disney's transports and monorails, as well as rental cars. **CARE Medical Equipment** (✆ **800/741-2282** or 407/856-2273; www.caremedicalequipment. com) offers similar services.

Amtrak (✆ **800/872-7245**; www. amtrak.com) provides redcap service, wheelchair assistance, and special seats if given 72 hours' notice. Travelers with disabilities are entitled to a 15% discount off the lowest available adult coach fare. Documentation from a doctor or an ID card proving your disability is required.

Amtrak also provides wheelchair-accessible sleeping accommodations on long-distance trains. Service dogs are permitted aboard and travel free. TDD/TTY service is available at ℂ **800/523-6590,** or you can write to P.O. Box 7717, Itasca, IL 60143.

INSIDE THE THEME PARKS

Many attractions at the parks, especially the newer ones, are designed to be accessible to a wide variety of guests. People with wheelchairs and their parties are often given preferential treatment so they can avoid lines.

Available assistance is outlined in the guide maps you get as you enter the parks. All of the theme parks offer parking close to the entrances for those with disabilities. Let the parking attendant know your needs, and you'll be directed to the appropriate spot. Wheelchair and electric-cart rentals are available at most major attractions. If you bring your own, keep in mind that wheelchairs wider than 24½ inches may be difficult to navigate through some attractions. And crowds may make it tough for any guest.

AT DISNEY WORLD   Disney's many services are detailed in each theme park's *Guidebook for Guests with Disabilities.* You can pick one up at Guest Relations near the front entrance of each park, or access it online at **www.disneyworld. com**. You can also call ℂ **407/934-7639** or 407/824-2222 for answers to any questions regarding special needs. Examples of services are as follows:

- Almost all Disney resorts have rooms for those with disabilities.
- Braille guidebooks, cassette tapes, and portable tape players are available

at City Hall in the Magic Kingdom and Guest Relations in the other parks (a $25 refundable deposit is required).

- Service animals are allowed in all parks and on some rides.
- All parks have special parking lots near the entrances for those with disabilities.
- Assisted-listening devices are available to amplify the audio at selected attractions at WDW parks. Also, at some attractions, hearing-impaired guests can use handheld wireless receivers that allow them to read captions about the attractions. Both services are free but require a $25 refundable deposit.
- Wheelchairs and electric carts can be rented at all parks.
- Downtown Disney West Side, with crowded shops and bars, may be a bit difficult to navigate in a wheelchair. The movie theater is, however, wheelchair accessible.
- For information about Telecommunications Devices for the Deaf (TDDs) or sign-language interpreters at Disney World live shows, call ℂ **407/827-5141** (TDD/TTY). You can usually get an ASL interpreter at several events and attractions if you call no later than 2 weeks in advance.

On a final note, if you or your child has a life-threatening food allergy (or even just a bad one), Disney will try to accommodate your needs so your family can have a meal at the park. Your best bet is to do this at a sit-down restaurant. When making your Advance Dining Reservations (p. 130), inform the reservations agent that the allergy is an issue.

ⓘ *Tips* **Don't Forget the 407**

Local calls in Orlando require that you dial the area code—**407**—followed by the seven-digit local number, even when you're calling just across the street.

When you get to the restaurant, ask to speak to a chef about your particular concern. You may end up having to pay a full adult price for your child if his or her dish doesn't appear on the kids' menu, but you won't pay extra to have it specially prepared. *Warning:* If your child has a peanut allergy, forget about eating any Asian food in the parks—it's made with peanut oil. If you have doubts about what's in a dish, just ask; most restaurants carry an ingredient list.

AT UNIVERSAL ORLANDO Those with disabilities should go to Guest Services, located just inside the main entrances of the Universal parks, for a *Rider's Guide for Rider Safety & Guests with Disabilities,* a TDD, or other special assistance. Wheelchair and electric-cart rentals are available at the entrance of each park. Universal also provides audio descriptions on cassette for visually impaired guests and has sign-language guides and scripts for its shows. Advance notice of 1 to 2 weeks is required; call © **888/519-4899** (TTY) or 407/224-5929 (voice) for details. You can also get information online at **www.universalorlando.com**. From the main page, click either Islands of Adventure or Universal Studios Florida, and then scroll down the left side to the ADA page.

All Universal Orlando resorts offer rooms for those with mobility impairments. Note, however, that if you or your child has severe pet allergies, pets are accepted at all the Universal resorts, too.

AT SEAWORLD The park has a guide for guests with disabilities, although most of its attractions are easily accessible to those in wheelchairs. SeaWorld also provides a Braille guide for the visually impaired and a very brief synopsis of its shows for the hearing-impaired. Sign-language interpreting services are available at no charge, but must be reserved by calling © **407/363-2414** at least a week in advance of your visit. Assisted-listening devices are available at select attractions for a $20 refundable deposit. For information, call © **407/351-3600** or check out the park's website at **www.seaworld.com** to see the accessibility guide.

OTHER RESOURCES

Organizations that offer a vast range of resources and assistance to disabled travelers include **MossRehab** (© **800/CALL-MOSS;** www.mossresourcenet.org), the **American Foundation for the Blind (AFB)** (© **800/232-5463;** www.afb.org), and **SATH (Society for Accessible Travel & Hospitality)** (© **212/447-7284;** www.sath.org). **AirAmbulanceCard.com** is now partnered with SATH and allows you to preselect topnotch hospitals in case of an emergency.

Access-Able Travel Source (© **303/232-2979;** www.access-able.com) offers a comprehensive database on travel agents from around the world with experience in accessible travel; destination-specific access information; and links to such resources as service animals, equipment rentals, and access guides.

For comprehensive information on accessibility in Florida, **WheelchairsOnTheGo.com** covers everything from ground transportation to medical-equipment rentals, accommodations, attractions, and plenty more.

Many travel agencies offer customized tours and itineraries for travelers with disabilities. Among them are **Flying Wheels Travel** (© **507/451-5005;** www.flyingwheelstravel.com) and **Accessible Journeys** (© **800/846-4537** or 610/521-0339; www.disabilitytravel.com).

Flying with Disability (www.flying-with-disability.org) is a comprehensive information source on airplane travel. **Avis Rent a Car** (© **888/879-4273**) has an "Avis Access" program that offers services for customers with special travel needs. These include specially outfitted vehicles with swivel seats, spinner knobs, and hand controls; mobility scooter rentals; and accessible bus service. Be sure to reserve well in advance.

Also check out the quarterly magazine *Emerging Horizons* (www.emerging horizons.com), available by subscription ($17 year U.S.; $22 outside U.S).

The "Accessible Travel" link at **Mobility-Advisor.com** (www.mobility-advisor. com) offers a variety of travel resources to disabled persons.

British travelers should contact **Holiday Care** (© 0845/124-9971 in UK only; www.holidaycare.org.uk) to access a wide range of travel information and resources for disabled and elderly people.

FOR GRANDPARENTS

Many family vacations now include several generations, and traveling with the grandkids to Orlando will provide a host of memorable experiences at both ends of the age spectrum.

Mention you're a senior when you make reservations. Several hotels offer discounts for seniors (Loews, which runs Universal Orlando's resorts, even offers a special package to grandparents traveling with their grandkids). In most cities, people over 60 qualify for reduced admission to theaters, museums, and other attractions; discounts at select restaurants; and reduced fares on public buses.

You can order a copy of the *Mature Traveler Guide,* which contains local discounts mainly on rooms but also on attractions and activities, from the Orlando/Orange County Convention & Visitors Bureau, 8723 International Dr., Suite 101, Orlando, FL 32819 (© 800/643-9492 or 800/551-0181; www. orlandoinfo.com).

Members of **AARP,** 601 E St. NW, Washington, DC 20049 (© 888/687-2277; www.aarp.org), get discounts on hotels, airfares, and car rentals. AARP offers members a wide range of benefits, including *AARP: The Magazine* and a monthly newsletter. Anyone over 50 can join.

Recommended publications offering travel resources and discounts for seniors include: the quarterly magazine *Travel 50 & Beyond* (www.travel50andbeyond. com) and the bestselling paperback *Unbelievably Good Deals and Great Adventures That You Absolutely Can't Get Unless You're Over 50 2005–2006, 16th Edition* (McGraw-Hill), by Joann Rattner Heilman.

FOR SINGLE PARENTS

Single parents face unique challenges when they travel with their children. **Parents without Partners** (© 561/391-8833; www.parentswithoutpartners.org) provides links to numerous single-parent resources. Single mom Brenda Elwell's website, **www.singleparenttravel.net**, is full of advice garnered from traveling around the world with her two children.

FOR GAY & LESBIAN FAMILIES

The popularity of Orlando with gay and lesbian travelers, including families, parallels the growing number of same-sex households in the area. **Gay, Lesbian & Bisexual Community Services of Central Florida,** 934 N. Mills Ave., Orlando, FL 32803 (© 407/228-8272; www. glbcc.org), is a great source of information on Central Florida. Welcome packets usually include the latest issue of the *Triangle,* a quarterly newsletter dedicated to gay and lesbian issues, and a calendar of events pertaining to the gay and lesbian community. Though not a tourist-specific packet, it includes information and ads for local gay and lesbian clubs.

In the **Company of Women** (© 407/331-3466; www.companyofwomen.com) and **Gay Orlando Network** (www. gayorlando.com) are two other local resources.

The **International Gay and Lesbian Travel Association (IGLTA)** (© 800/448-8550 or 954/776-2626; www.iglta. org) is the trade association for the gay

Tips The Peripatetic Pet

It is illegal in Florida to leave your pet inside a parked car, windows rolled down or not. The sweltering heat can easily kill an animal in only a few minutes. All the major theme parks have kennel facilities; use them.

Make sure your pet is wearing a name tag with the name and phone number of a contact person who can take the call if your pet gets lost while you're away from home. Better yet, the American Kennel Club has an affiliated nonprofit **Companion Animal Recovery** service, in which a veterinarian embeds a microchip in your pet so that it can be identified—collar or not—should it get lost and end up in a shelter or veterinary office. The service is open to all pets, not just dogs, and has an excellent track record. For more information, check out **www.akccar.org**.

and lesbian travel industry. It offers an online directory of gay- and lesbian-friendly travel businesses and tour operators.

Many agencies offer tours and travel itineraries specifically for gay and lesbian travelers. San Francisco–based **Now, Voyager** (© **800/255-6951;** www.now voyager.com) offers worldwide trips and cruises. **Olivia** (© **800/631-6277;** www. olivia.com) offers lesbian cruises and resort vacations.

Gay.com Travel (© **800/929-2268** or 415/644-8044; www.gay.com/travel or www.outandabout.com) is an excellent online successor to the popular *Out & About* print magazine. It provides regularly updated information about gay-owned, gay-oriented, and gay-friendly lodging, dining, sightseeing, nightlife, and shopping establishments in destinations worldwide. British travelers should click on the "Travel" link at **www.uk.gay. com** for advice and gay-friendly trip ideas. The Canadian website **GayTraveler** (www.gaytraveler.ca) offers ideas and advice for gay travel all over the world.

FOR VEGETARIAN TRAVELERS

Happy Cow's Vegetarian Guide to Restaurants & Health Food Stores (www.happycow.net) has a restaurant guide with more than 6,000 restaurants

in 100 countries. VegDining.com also lists vegetarian restaurants (with profiles) around the world. Vegetarian Vacations (www.vegetarian-vacations.com) offers vegetarian tours and itineraries.

TRAVELING WITH PETS

Many of us wouldn't dream of going on a family vacation without our pets. And more and more lodgings and restaurants are pet-friendly. Policies vary, however, so call ahead to find out the rules.

None of the Disney resorts (with the exception of the Fort Wilderness Resort & Campground) allows animals to stay on the premises (service dogs are the exception) or have their own kennels, but resort guests are welcome to board their animals overnight in kennel facilities at the Transportation and Ticket Center. If you require boarding only during the day, kennels are located at all four Disney parks. Universal Orlando and SeaWorld will board small animals during the day only.

Universal's three Loews-run resorts do allow pets on site. In fact, "Loews Loves Pets" is a program that caters to pets and their families by offering such pet-friendly amenities as food, leashes, bedding, toys, and more. Pet walking, pet pagers, and door hangers to let the resort staff know that there is a pet in the room are also available. All Motel 6 motels accept pets as well.

An excellent resource is **www.pets welcome.com**, which dispenses medical tips, names of animal-friendly lodgings and campgrounds, and lists of kennels and veterinarians. Also check out **www. dogfriendly.com**, which features links to Orlando accommodations, eateries, attractions, and parks that welcome canine companions.

If you plan to fly with your pet, the FAA has compiled a list of all requirements for transporting live animals at **air consumer.ost.dot.gov**. Click the "Travel Tips & Publications" link on the home page; then select "Traveling with Animals." You may be able to carry your pet on board a plane if it's small enough to put inside a carrier that can slip under the seat. Pets usually count as one piece of carry-on luggage. Note that summer may not be the best time to fly with your pet: Many airlines will not check pets as baggage in the hot summer months. The ASPCA discourages travelers from checking pets as luggage at any time, as storage conditions on planes are loosely monitored, and fatal accidents are not unprecedented. Your other option is to ship your pet with a professional carrier, which can be expensive. Ask your veterinarian whether you should sedate your pet on a plane ride or give it anti-nausea medication. Never give your pet sedatives used by humans.

13 Staying Connected

TELEPHONES

Generally, hotel surcharges on long-distance and local calls are astronomical, so you're better off using your **cellphone** or a **public pay telephone.** Many convenience stores and packaging services sell **prepaid calling cards** in denominations up to $50; for international visitors these can be the least expensive way to call home. Many public pay phones at airports now accept American Express, MasterCard, and Visa credit cards. **Local calls** made from pay phones in most locales cost either 25¢ or 35¢ (no pennies, please).

Most long-distance and international calls can be dialed directly from any phone. **For calls within the United States and to Canada,** dial 1 followed by the area code and the seven-digit number. **For other international calls,** dial 011 followed by the country code, city code, and the number you are calling.

Calls to area codes **800, 888, 877,** and **866** are toll-free. However, calls to area codes **700** and **900** (chat lines, bulletin boards, "dating" services, and so on) can be very expensive—usually a charge of 95¢ to $3 or more per minute, and they sometimes have minimum charges that can run as high as $15 or more.

For **reversed-charge or collect calls,** and for person-to-person calls, dial the number 0 then the area code and number; an operator will come on the line, and you should specify whether you are calling collect, person-to-person, or both. If your operator-assisted call is international, ask for the overseas operator.

For **local directory assistance** ("information"), dial 411; for long-distance information, dial 1, then the appropriate area code and 555-1212.

CELLPHONES

Just because your cellphone works at home doesn't mean it'll work everywhere in the U.S. (thanks to our nation's fragmented cellphone system). It's a good bet that your phone will work in major cities, but take a look at your wireless company's coverage map on its website before heading out; T-Mobile, Sprint, and Nextel are particularly weak in rural areas. If you need to stay in touch at a destination where you know your phone won't work,

Online Traveler's Toolbox

Veteran travelers usually carry some essential items to make their trips easier. Following is a selection of handy online tools to bookmark and use.

- **Airplane Food** (www.airlinemeals.net)
- **Airplane Seating** (www.seatguru.com and www.airlinequality.com)
- **Foreign Languages for Travelers** (www.travlang.com)
- **Maps** (www.mapquest.com)
- **Time and Date** (www.timeanddate.com)
- **Universal Currency Converter** (www.xe.com/ucc)
- **Visa ATM Locator** (www.visa.com), **MasterCard ATM Locator** (www. mastercard.com)
- **Weather** (www.intellicast.com; and www.weather.com)

rent a phone that does from **InTouch USA** (© **800/872-7626**; www.intouch global.com) or a rental-car location, but be aware that you'll pay $1 a minute or more for airtime.

If you're not from the U.S., you'll be appalled at the poor reach of our **GSM (Global System for Mobile Communications) wireless network,** which is used by much of the rest of the world. Your phone will probably work in most major U.S. cities; it definitely won't work in many rural areas. To see where GSM phones work in the U.S., check out www. tmobile.com/coverage/national_popup. asp. And you may or may not be able to send SMS (text messaging) home.

VOICE-OVER INTERNET PROTOCOL (VOIP)

If you have web access while traveling, you might consider a broadband-based telephone service (in technical terms, **Voice over Internet protocol,** or **VoIP**) such as Skype (www.skype.com) or Vonage (www.vonage.com), which allows you to make free international calls if you use their services from your laptop or in a cybercafe. The people you're calling must also use the service for it to work; check the sites for details.

INTERNET/E-MAIL WITHOUT YOUR OWN COMPUTER

To find cybercafes in your destination check **www.cybercaptive.com** and **www. cybercafe.com**.

Most major airports have **Internet kiosks** that provide basic Web access for a per-minute fee that's usually higher than cybercafe prices. Check out copy shops like **Kinko's** (FedEx Kinkos), which offers computer stations with fully loaded software (as well as Wi-Fi).

WITH YOUR OWN COMPUTER

More and more hotels, resorts, airports, cafes, and retailers are going Wi-Fi (wireless fidelity), becoming "hotspots" that offer free high-speed Wi-Fi access or charge a small fee for usage. Wi-Fi is also found in campgrounds, RV parks, and even entire towns. Most laptops sold today have built-in wireless capability. To find public Wi-Fi hotspots at your destination, go to **www.jiwire.com**; its Hotspot Finder holds the world's largest directory of public wireless hotspots.

For dial-up access, most business-class hotels in the U.S. offer dataports for laptop modems, and a few thousand hotels in the U.S. and Europe now offer free high-speed Internet access.

Wherever you go, bring a **connection kit** of the right power and phone adapters, a spare phone cord, and a spare Ethernet network cable—or find out whether your hotel supplies them to guests.

For information on electrical currency conversions, see "Electricity," in the "Fast Facts" section at the end of chapter 3.

14 Package Deals for Families

The number and diversity of package tours to Orlando is staggering—you can save money if you're willing to do the research. Start by looking in the travel section of your local Sunday newspaper and checking the ads in the back of travel magazines such as *Arthur Frommer's Budget Travel Magazine, Travel + Leisure,* and *Condé Nast Traveler.* Stop at a sizable travel agency and pick up brochures from several companies. Go over them at home, and compare offerings to find the optimum package for your trip.

For **Walt Disney World** packages, you should obtain the vacation-planning DVD from Disney (see "Visitor Information & Maps," at the beginning of this chapter) or go to www.disneyworld.com for online information. The array of choices can include airfare, accommodations on or off Disney property, theme-park passes, a rental car, meals, a Disney cruise, and/or a stay at Disney's beach resorts in Vero Beach or Hilton Head, South Carolina. Some packages are tied to a season, while others are for special-interest vacationers, including golfers, honeymooners, and spa aficionados. For more information on Disney vacation packages, call © **407/939-7675.** Just be sure to press the reservations agent for the best possible deal.

Although not on the same scale as Disney's options, the packages offered by **Universal Vacations** (© **800/711-0080;** www.univacations.com) have improved greatly with the addition of the Islands of Adventure theme park, the CityWalk

Frommers.com: The Complete Travel Resource

It should go without saying, but we highly recommend **Frommers.com,** voted Best Travel Site by *PC Magazine.* We think you'll find our expert advice and tips; independent reviews of hotels, restaurants, attractions, and preferred shopping and nightlife venues; vacation giveaways; and an online booking tool indispensable before, during, and after your travels. We publish the complete contents of over 128 travel guides in our **Destinations** section covering nearly 3,600 places worldwide to help you plan your trip. Each weekday, we publish original articles reporting on **Deals and News** via our free **Frommers.com Newsletter** to help you save time and money and travel smarter. We're betting you'll find our new **Events** listings (http://events.frommers.com) an invaluable resource; it's an up-to-the-minute roster of what's happening in cities everywhere—including concerts, festivals, lectures, and more. We've also added weekly **Podcasts, interactive maps,** and hundreds of new images across the site. Check out our **Travel Talk** area featuring **Message Boards** where you can join in conversations with thousands of fellow Frommer's travelers and post your trip report once you return.

> **Tips   A Magical Gathering**
>
> Disney's **Magical Gatherings** program caters to large families or groups traveling together, offering online trip-planning tools to help you put together a vacation with extended family. Large groups of eight or more people (ages 3 or above) traveling together to Walt Disney World—**Grand Gatherings,** as Disney calls them—also get free assistance from a Disney trip planner, who will help you get hotel rooms, make dining reservations, plan recreation, schedule golf tee times, and put together special event and attractions options (these extras will cost you) that appeal to all age groups and that are not available to individuals and smaller families. These options (which can be reserved at least 90 days in advance) may include special character breakfasts, safari outings at Animal Kingdom, an international dining experience at Epcot, and a fireworks cruise on the Seven Seas Lagoon.
>
> If you're interested, call © **407/934-7639** or go to **www.disneyworld. com/magicalgatherings** and request a Magical Gathering Vacation Planning Kit or an interactive DVD. You can ask for specialized planning brochures for groups that include preschoolers, with information on attractions for younger children, child-care options, and tips for a well-planned vacation with preschool-age kids.

entertainment district, and Universal's Loews-run hotels. Options include lodging (both on site and off), VIP access to Universal's theme parks, and discounts to other non-Disney attractions. Some packages include round-trip airfare.

SeaWorld (© **800/557-4268;** www. seaworldvacations.com) also offers packages that include rooms from a choice of SeaWorld-area hotels, car rental, and tickets to SeaWorld.

Another good source of package deals is the airlines themselves. Major airlines offering Orlando packages include **American Airlines Vacations** (© 800/321-2121; www.aavacations.com), **Continental Airlines Vacations** (© 800/301-3800; www.covacations.com), **Delta**

Vacations (© 800/221-6666; www.delta vacations.com), and **United Vacations** (© 888/854-3899; www.unitedvacations. com). Packages can include airfare, accommodations, rental car or round-trip airport transfers, unlimited admission to Disney (or other) parks, and other special features. In packages that feature WDW and Universal Studios resorts, you will receive all the advantages given to guests of these properties. Prices vary widely, depending on the resort you choose, your departure point, and the time of year.

Several big **online travel agencies**—Expedia, Travelocity, Orbitz, Site59, and Lastminute.com—also do a brisk business in packages. If a packager won't tell you where it's based, don't fly with that company.

15 Disney Cruise Packages

There's hardly a Florida tourist market that WDW hasn't tried to tap. Ocean-going vacations are no exception. The

Disney Cruise Line (© **800/951-3532;** www.disneycruise.com) launched the *Magic* and *Wonder* in 1998 and 1999, respectively, and has plans to launch two more ships in 2011 and 2012.

The *Magic* is Art Deco in style, with Mickey in the three-level lobby and a *Beauty and the Beast* mural in its top restaurant, Lumiere's. The *Wonder* has Art Nouveau decor. Ariel commands its lobby, and its featured eatery, Triton's, sports a mural from *The Little Mermaid.*

Subtle differences aside, these are nearly identical twins. Both are 83,000 tons, with 12 decks, 875 cabins, and room for 2,400 guests. There are some adults-only areas; however, both ships have extensive kids' and teens' programs that take up almost an entire deck. They're broken into four age groups: the **Flounder's Reef Nursery,** for ages 3 months to 3 years; **Disney's Oceaneer Club,** for ages 3 to 7; **Disney's Oceaneer Lab,** for ages 8 to 12; and **Aloft** (on the *Wonder*) and **The Stack** (on the *Magic*), for ages 13 to 17. **Ocean Quest** (on the Magic) is the newest addition, filled with activities for almost every age: video games, plasma TVs, and a simulator that allows kids to steer the ship in and out of ports of call.

Restaurants, shows, and other onboard activities are extremely family-oriented. One of the line's unique features is a dine-around option that lets you move among main restaurants (each ship has four) from night to night while keeping the same servers.

Something new: Visitors to Castaway Cay get the chance to participate in a hands-on stingray encounter, which includes a brief history and biology lesson, in addition to an in-the-water interaction with the rays.

The 3-night voyages visit Nassau and Castaway Cay, Disney's own private island; 4-day voyages add Freeport. There are also 7-night Eastern Caribbean (St. Thomas, St. Maarten, St. John, and Castaway Cay) and 7-night Western Caribbean (Key West, Grand Cayman, Cozumel, and Castaway Cay) itineraries. Special 10- and 14-day Caribbean cruises as well as 10-, 11-, and 14-day (transatlantic) Mediterranean cruises are offered as well; call for details and rates.

Seven-night Land & Sea packages include 3 or 4 days afloat, with the rest of the week at a WDW resort. Prices at press time ranged from $939 to $5,399 for adults, $399 to $2,199 for kids 3 to 12, and $189 for kids under 3 (infants under 12 weeks are not allowed aboard ship), depending on your choice of stateroom and resort. Packages are available that add round-trip air and unlimited admission to the WDW parks, Pleasure Island, and

---

ⓘ Tips Ask Before You Go

Before you invest in a package deal or an escorted tour:

- Always ask about the **cancellation policy.** Can you get your money back? Is there a deposit required?
- Ask about the **accommodations choices and prices** for each. Then look up the hotels' reviews in a Frommer's guide and check their rates online for your specific dates of travel. Also find out what types of rooms are offered.
- Discuss what is included in the **price** (transportation, meals, tips, airport transfers, and more).
- Finally, look for **hidden expenses.** Ask whether airport departure fees and taxes, for example, are included in the total cost—they rarely are.

> **Tips Avoid the Ups and Downs**
>
> Nothing spoils a cruise like a storm—or worse. In the first case, consider avoid-
> ing hurricane season altogether (June 1 to Nov 30, though the peak is July to
> mid-Oct). Unpredictable storms can both spoil your fun and upset the strongest
> of stomachs. Pack a few motion-sickness pills or patches, just in case.
>
> Speaking of spoiling a cruise, several cruise ships, including the Disney *Magic*,
> have had outbreaks of a virus that caused stomach flu–like symptoms in the
> past. This is no ill reflection on any one line: Cruise ships are closed environ-
> ments, and sometimes a passenger brings the illness on board. For an online rat-
> ing by the **Centers for Disease Control**, go to www.cdc.gov/travel/cruiships.htm.
> Note, however, that the site is often weeks out of date.

other Disney attractions. Cruise-only options for 3 nights are $429 to $2,999 for adults, $229 to $1,099 for kids 3 to 12, and $149 for those under 3; 4-night cruises are $499 to $3,999 for adults, $329 to $1,199 for kids 3 to 12, and $149 for kids under 3. Disney's 7-night cruises sell for $849 to $5,399 for adults, $399 to $2,199 for kids 3 to 12, and $189 for kids under 3.

The 10- and 11-night Mediterranean cruises out of Barcelona, Spain, aboard the *Disney Magic* feature stops in such ports of call as Naples, Italy, and Marseilles, France, among others. Also included are two 14-day transatlantic itineraries (to Barcelona from Cape Canaveral and vice versa). These itiner-aries are limited, so advance bookings are suggested. Rates range from $1,399 to $6,699 per person based on double occu-pancy. For more information on Euro-pean cruises, call ✆ **888/325-2500.**

With the exception of select West Coast and Mediterranean itineraries, cruises depart from Port Canaveral, which is about an hour east of Orlando by car. If you buy a Land & Sea package, transportation to and from Orlando is included. You can get discounted fares if you book well in advance and go during non-peak periods; in addition, specials or "Magic Rates" run periodically.

For more information, call Disney Cruise Line or check out its very informa-tive website, which also allows you to plan and reserve shore excursions before you go. Another good source of detailed informa-tion on both cruising and the Disney line is *Frommer's Cruises & Ports of Call.*

16 Show & Tell: Getting the Kids Interested in Orlando

In most cases, you won't have to do much to get your child interested in Orlando. It will be more a case of trying to restrain the obvious enthusiasm your youngsters will display at the idea of meeting Mickey and the gang or riding the Incredible Hulk Coaster. That said, involving your kids in the planning of your vacation will certainly help prevent any disappoint-ments and will make them feel as though they're contributing to the experience.

Before you leave (I recommend at least 3–4 months), ask the folks at Disney to send you its vacation-planning DVD, which should be of interest to most of the family. You can get it by writing to Walt Disney World, Box 10000, Lake Buena Vista, FL 32830-1000; calling ✆ **407/ 934-7639** or 407/824-4321; or going to www.disneyworld.com. Your little ones will no doubt enjoy watching the video, and you can gauge their reactions to certain rides, characters, and attractions. This is also a good time to explain to young kids about height and weight restrictions that may keep them from riding a few attractions so you can avoid disappointment later on.

You might want to buy your younger children an autograph book before leaving so they can get character autographs in the parks. This is a wildly popular activity and a good souvenir to bring back from Orlando.

Break out some Disney classic films before you go to get your kids in the mood. No matter what your child's age, you'll find something appropriate for them, be it the 2007 hit film *Pirates of the Caribbean: At World's End,* for tweens and teens, or the enchanting *Cinderella,* for your little ones. Another good choice is *Disneyland Sing Along Songs* (even if it was filmed at Disneyland instead of Disney World), as it introduces tinier tots to the parks, rides, and characters they'll encounter on your trip.

On the book front, kids (and even adults) will enjoy *Popping Up Around Walt Disney World* (Disney Editions, 2004). This colorful and detailed pop-up book offers an illustrative tour through the world of Disney. It takes readers through the parks, details some of the attractions, and tosses in a bit of trivia, too. *Hidden Mickeys, 2nd Edition: A Field Guide to Walt Disney World's Best Kept Secrets* (Intrepid Traveler, 2005) is filled with trivia and, of course, those Hidden Mickeys—including tips on where and how to look for them.

Videos and documentaries on African animals and aquatic life, as well as age-appropriate books, will prepare your kids for the sights and sounds they'll experience at Disney's Animal Kingdom and SeaWorld. Similarly, books and videos on the different cultures represented in the World Showcase will give your kids a rudimentary introduction to the countries they'll walk though at Epcot.

If you're visiting Universal's parks, you can watch **Nickelodeon** with your young kids and read them *The Cat in the Hat.* They'll be charmed when they actually get to ride through the story at Islands of Adventure. Older kids and teens might appreciate a selection of classic **Marvel comic books,** or perhaps could be induced to watch some of the films and TV shows that many of Universal's rides are based on, including *Shrek, The Mummy Returns, The Simpsons, Men in Black, Twister,* and *Jurassic Park,* among others.

3

Getting to Know
Walt Disney World & Orlando

Orlando didn't become a favorite destination for families until just around 37 years ago. It was only after a magical man and a mouse named Mickey moved to town, after the Magic Kingdom opened its gates for the first time, that families first took notice.

Walt Disney started something back then—something big. He blazed a pioneering trail that over the last 37 years or so has spawned a deluge of development. I don't think even he could have predicted what was to come. Disney may not be the exact center of the Orlando universe, but it's a close call. Walt Disney World has grown to include four major theme parks; a large three-part shopping, dining, and entertainment district; 23 resorts and timeshare properties; 10 partner hotels; two full-fledged water parks; a cruise line; and loads more. Those are Disney's ways of trying to keep you, your kids, and your tourist dollars from straying to Universal Orlando, SeaWorld, or its other competitors. They are good at it, too. Although WDW is easy enough to navigate once you get your bearings, it's so sprawled out, you might just hesitate to leave.

But all that unrelenting cheerfulness, days of $2.50 sodas, and the musk of sweaty patrons make it a small world, after all. Besides, you're cheating yourself if you don't spend some time away from

Walt Disney's world, especially if you have tweens and teens, for whom Universal Orlando (and its thrill rides) is a major mecca, or aquarium-lovers of any age, who will find SeaWorld a wonderfully relaxed place to visit. And don't overlook some of the less frazzling things to do with your kids in O-Town, including, among others, the Orlando Science Center. I'll let you know all about the area's layout and what's where in the first section of this chapter.

The good news is that getting around the major tourist areas of Orlando is relatively easy if you have a car, if you're a decent navigator, and if traffic is cooperating. If you plan on staying only in Walt Disney World, you can even make do without the car (the pros and cons of using Disney's own transportation network are listed later on). The major attractions are all centered on large interstates or highways, and the city has done its utmost best to make sure that your family (and its tourist dollars) won't get lost on the way to your chosen destination. Disney's taken efficiency a step further, creating a new private roadway—the result of which is less congestion along I-4 and a more direct route to WDW. And if you do get lost, you'll find a ton of roadside billboards on most major thoroughfares that will lead you right to the city's biggest attractions.

1 Orientation

VISITOR INFORMATION

Once you're in town, you can stop at the visitor center run by the **Orlando/Orange County Convention & Visitors Bureau,** 8723 International Dr., Suite 101, Orlando (© **407/363-5872;** www.orlandoinfo.com). Folks working at the bureau will answer questions and give you maps, brochures, and coupons good for discounts or freebies. It's worth a visit even if you take my advice in chapter 2 and send for them before arriving. The bureau sells discount tickets to several attractions (savings on single-day passes to Universal and SeaWorld are $3 or less; Disney's 3-day or longer passes are discounted $4 to $15; and savings on passes to Cirque du Soleil, DisneyQuest, and Pleasure Island run $3 to $7). Its multilingual staff will also make dinner reservations and hotel referrals for you. Open daily from 8am to 7pm except on Christmas. From I-4, take Exit 74A east 2 blocks, turn south on International Drive, and go 1 mile. The center is on the left, at I-Drive and Austrian Row.

The **Kissimmee Convention & Visitors Bureau** is located at 1925 E. Irlo Bronson Memorial Hwy./U.S. 192, Kissimmee (© **800/333-5477** or 407/847-5000; www.floridakiss.com). It's open Monday through Friday from 8am to 5pm and offers maps, brochures, and coupons. From I-4, take Exit 64A/U.S. 192 east about 12 miles to Bill Beck Boulevard; then go left into the parking lot.

If you're driving into town from the north on I-75 and looking for the **Disney Welcome Center** in Ocala, you'll find that the center has closed. You'll have to wait until you get to Orlando and head to the visitor centers listed above or your hotel concierge for tickets, maps, and other area information.

Finally, nearly all hotel lobbies and many restaurants, highway rest stops, and attractions have racks containing brochures for various activities. These often include discount coupons.

INFORMATION (& MORE) AT THE AIRPORT

Orlando's theme-park fun starts almost from the minute you get off the plane at Orlando International Airport.

The airport has two Disney shops. The **Magic of Disney** (© **407/825-2370** or 407/825-2360) is in the main terminal, third level, right behind the Northwest Airlines ticket desk. **Disney Earport** (© **407/825-2339**) is in the main terminal, across from the Hyatt Regency. They sell WDW multiday tickets, make dinner-show and hotel reservations at Disney resorts, and provide brochures and assistance. They're open daily, usually from 7am to 9 or 10pm, but don't plan on making many purchases at the airport stores unless you're on your way home and find you've forgotten to buy that must-have Mickey for the kid who's watering your plants while you're gone. Chances are you'll find a far better selection and (possibly) cheaper prices elsewhere in town.

The **Universal Studios Stores** (© **407/825-2473**), usually open daily from 7am to 9pm, sell park tickets at two locations: Airside A, main terminal, and Airside B, Delta-side before security, both on the third level. The **SeaWorld Stores** (© **407/825-2642** or 407/825-2414), at Airside A and B, are open from 7am to 10pm. **Kennedy Space Center** (© **407/825-3170** or 407/825-3245) has locations in both the East and West halls, open from 6am to 9pm. Even the **Ron Jon Surf Shop** (© **407/825-2217**) has an airport outpost. For a complete list of airport stores and services, including hours and phone numbers, check out **www.orlandoairports.net** (click on the "Passenger Terminal" link and then "Shops & Services").

CITY LAYOUT

Orlando's major artery is Interstate 4, or **I-4.** This runs across Florida from Tampa to Daytona Beach. Exits from I-4 take you to all the Disney properties, Universal, Sea-World, International Drive, U.S. 192, Kissimmee, Lake Buena Vista, and downtown Orlando. Most are well marked, but construction is common, and exit numbers can change. For the latest exit numbers, see **www.myflorida.com**; for additional traffic and construction information, see **www.expresswayauthority.com**. If you get directions by exit number, always ask the name of the road, too, to avoid getting lost. Note that the road in question is often a traffic-laden nightmare loathed by locals. (Cell-phone users can dial ℂ **511** to get a report of I-4 delays.)

The **Florida Turnpike**, a toll road, crosses I-4 and links with I-75 to the north and Miami to the south. **U.S. 192/Irlo Bronson Memorial Highway** is an east–west artery that reaches from Kissimmee to U.S. 27, crossing I-4 near World Drive, the main Disney entrance road. Construction in and around where U.S. 192 and I-4 cross creates backups as bad as the ones on I-4 during rush hour (7–9am and 4–6pm daily). Farther north, the **Beachline Expressway** (Hwy. 528), also a toll road, goes east from I-4 past Orlando International Airport to Cape Canaveral and Kennedy Space Center. The **East–West Expressway** (also known as Hwy. 408) is a toll road that can be helpful in bypassing surface traffic in the downtown area.

If you're jockeying between Disney and Universal, one of the lesser traffic evils is **Apopka–Vineland Road.** It tends to be less cluttered than I-4 or International Drive. Follow it north from Lake Buena Vista and the northeast side of WDW to Sand Lake Road; then go right to Turkey Lake Road and left to Universal. Another option would be to take Apopka–Vineland Road; turn right onto Palm Parkway, which then turns into Turkey Lake Road; and follow it to the Universal entrance.

I-4 and Highway 535 border **Walt Disney World** to the east (the latter is also a northern boundary), while U.S. 192/Irlo Bronson Memorial Highway borders it to the south. World Drive is WDW's main north–south artery. Epcot Center Drive (Hwy. 536/the south end of International Dr.) and Buena Vista Drive cut across the complex in a more or less east–west direction; the two roads cross at Bonnet Creek Parkway. Despite a reasonably good highway system and explicit signs, it's easy to get lost or miss a turn here. Don't panic or pull across several lanes of traffic to make an exit, especially once you're on Disney property. All roads lead to the parks, and you'll soon find another sign directing you to the same place. It may take a bit longer, but Goofy will still be there.

Note: If you're going to be driving around town, I highly recommend getting a good, detailed map of the area. The map the Orlando/Orange County Convention & Visitors Bureau sends in its visitor packet (p. 12) and offers at its visitor center is one of the best. Tourist magazines such as *See Orlando, Travelhost,* and *Where Orlando,* many of which you'll find right at your hotel, have good maps as well.

ORLANDO NEIGHBORHOODS IN BRIEF

Walt Disney World   The empire—its big and little parks, resorts, restaurants, shops, and assorted trimmings—is scattered across 40 square miles. To put it in better perspective, it's roughly the size of San Francisco.

The surprising thing to some folks: WDW isn't really in Orlando at all. It's actually southwest of the city proper, off I-4, in Lake Buena Vista. The convenience of staying here, however, comes at a price, with rooms running

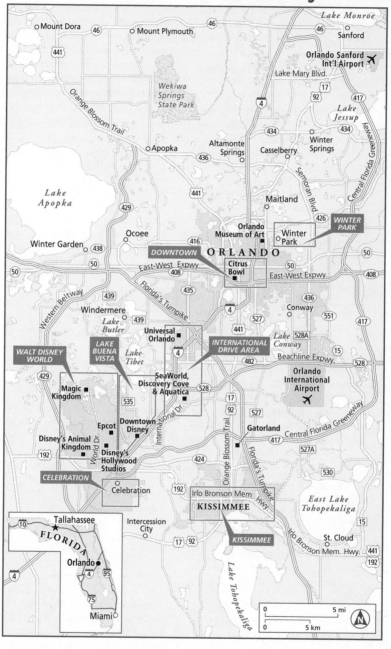

almost twice what they do in nearby Kissimmee. For kids (and some adults), however, this is the Promised Land.

Lake Buena Vista   This is Disney's next-door neighbor. It's where you'll find the "official" (though not Disney-owned) hotels situated along Hotel Plaza Boulevard. It's close to Downtown Disney and Pleasure Island, and is a good spot for families who appreciate the perks of staying at an official Disney hotel but not the hefty prices of staying on the parks' doorstep. This charming area has manicured lawns, tree-lined thoroughfares, and free transportation throughout the realm.

Downtown Disney   This is more Disney dessert than an actual neighborhood, though it's certainly large enough to be distinguished as one. Simply put, it's what WDW has taken to calling its two nighttime entertainment areas, Pleasure Island and Disney's West Side, as well as its shopping district, the Downtown Disney Marketplace. The area is filled with clubs, entertainment venues, uniquely themed restaurants, and interesting shops. You can dance the night away, shop till you drop, or tempt your taste buds—all in the space of a single afternoon or evening. Pleasure Island is geared to adults; the West Side best suited for older kids, teens, and parents; and the Marketplace is appropriate for everyone. If you have tinier tots in tow, however, the afternoon may be a better time to survey this territory.

Celebration   Driving through this quaint little town, filled with gingerbread-trimmed houses and apartments, some with white picket fences and shade trees in the front yard, you may find yourself musing about the Disneyesque perfection found in this 4,900-acre community. It should come as no surprise that Disney had a hand in its creation—experts as they are at creating the perfect version of almost anything. The Market Street area's charming collection of shops, restaurants, and even its own small hotel is reminiscent of a bygone era—and a perfectly upscale version at that.

Kissimmee   This once-sleepy city is closer to Disney than Orlando. It's just a few miles from Mickey and has some of the least expensive offerings in the area. Brought back to life by a multi-million-dollar "Rebeautivacation" project, U.S. 192, Kissimmee's main tourist strip, now sports extrawide sidewalks, colorful (and plentiful) street lamps, landscaping, and location markers. Even the roadway itself has been improved to handle traffic more easily and safely. Kissimmee is lined practically end to end with a variety of budget and moderate resorts and hotels, most of which cater to families (though a few more upscale options have started to spring up), a plenitude of casual restaurants, and a handful of minor attractions.

International Drive Area (Hwy. 536)   Known as **I-Drive,** this busy tourist zone is home to more than 100 resorts and hotels, countless restaurants, attractions both big and small, shopping, entertainment, and even its own transportation system—the I-Ride Trolley. It's home to the Orange County Convention Center and offers easy access to Universal Orlando and SeaWorld. The areas north of Sand Lake Road are by far the most congested, filled to capacity with T-shirt shops, tourist traps, resorts, restaurants, and attractions. If you head south, toward the intersection at S.R. 528 (aka the Beachline Expwy.), it's still chock full of restaurants and hotels, but the landscaping is far more appealing, and tree-lined walkways offer a more pleasant place to walk. The driving, however, is still slow going at best.

Downtown Orlando Orlando is actually much smaller than most major U.S. cities but has a charm all its own. The downtown area is northeast of Walt Disney World on I-4. It's far less congested with tourists than the theme-park zones. Parents in need of a night off will appreciate the array of upscale restaurants and nightclubs, along with theaters, museums, and more. Families will find the very visitor-friendly Orlando Science Center a fun and unique place to spend an afternoon. Shopping is plentiful, but it's the adults in the family who will appreciate the dozens of antiques shops that line Antiques Row.

Winter Park Those who make the effort to get up to Winter Park, located just north of downtown (Orlando, that is), will enjoy its upscale ambience and quaint Southern charm. The town's biggest draw is Park Avenue, with its upscale shops and restaurants set along tree-lined cobblestone streets. This part of the suburbs is a great adult getaway and a good place to relax and escape the WDW, Universal, and I-Drive crowds. It's not, however, a good place to take the kids.

2 Getting Around

In a city that thrives on its attractions, you won't find it difficult to get around—especially if you have a car. Don't count on public transportation to get you where you want to go—not quickly or efficiently, anyway. If you're traveling outside the tourist areas, avoid the 7-to-9am and 4-to-6pm rush whenever possible. Commuter traffic creates difficulties in any city, but here, it's further complicated (and congested) by tourist traffic. And don't expect weekends to be any better; the locals who run the hotels, restaurants, and attractions still have to get to work, making commuter traffic a 7-days-a-week dilemma. Most of the parks don't open until 9am or so, and they usually stay open at least until dusk, so you won't miss much by leaving a little later. (The exception is Disney's Animal Kingdom, where the animals move around early in the day and then seek shelter and shade when the sun comes out.)

The good news if you are driving is that road signs have become more accurate than they were a few years back. But to make sure you're heading the right way, follow the directions I supply for the various attractions and hotels later in this book. Also, call your destination and ask whether new construction or other temporary roadblocks might be in your way.

Some hotels offer transportation to and from the theme parks and other tourist destinations; however, you'll need to check with your hotel to find out just which parks it goes to and whether it charges for the service. If your hotel does charge for shuttle service, by the time you add up the cost of transporting your family (and consider that you'll be at the mercy of your shuttle's schedule—not always the one your kids will adhere to), you're often better off renting a car.

International Drive has two alternative means of transportation: walking and taking the I-Ride Trolley, though I don't at all recommend the former with kids in tow. Even with plenty of sidewalks, crossing this extremely busy road is a dangerous proposition. Drivers are often more interested in getting to where they're going than to any pedestrian daring to cross in front of them. The **I-Ride Trolley** (© **407/248-9590** or 407/354-5656; www.iridetrolley.com) is a much safer bet. It makes 85 stops between the Prime Outlets on the north end of the drive and the Premium Outlets to the south. The Main Line trolley runs every 20 minutes, from 8am to 10:30pm, and costs $1 for adults and 25¢ for seniors; kids under 12 ride free with a paying adult. *Exact change is required.* There's an unlimited 1-day pass available for $3 per person. For those of you staying on I-Drive, 3-, 5-, 7-, and 14-day passes are also available at a substantial savings. This is a great way to avoid I-Drive's bumper-to-bumper driving.

BY DISNEY TRANSPORTATION SYSTEM

If you're going to stay at WDW and spend a majority of your time visiting its parks and attractions, using Disney's own, rather extensive transportation network is an option you should consider.

Guests at Disney resorts and "official" hotels get unlimited transportation via bus, monorail, ferry, and water taxi to all Disney's major parks throughout the day and well into the evening. There's also service to other Disney and official hotels, Downtown Disney, Typhoon Lagoon, Blizzard Beach, Pleasure Island, and other resort areas. If, however, you want to venture beyond Disney boundaries (say, to Universal or Sea-World), you'll have to pay extra.

The system has several advantages—the biggest of which is that it's free. This can save you on car rental, insurance, and gas (which nowadays can mean big bucks). The cost of parking at the theme parks ($11 a day at the bigger parks) doesn't count as real savings because Disney resort guests can park for free, but you can avoid the lines at the lots. Another big advantage is the ability to split up and head off in different directions. One parent can head back to the room with younger kids in need of a nap, while the other can hang back with the older kids (unless they're old enough to strike out on their own) and play at the parks.

The disadvantages? There are some serious ones. The system can be slow as molasses, and you're at the mercy of Disney's schedule. There are times when you have to take a ferry to catch a bus to get on the monorail to reach your hotel. The system makes a complete circuit, but it's not necessarily the most direct path to your destination. It can take an hour or more to get somewhere that's right across the lagoon from you. This is especially true if you stay at the outlying Disney resorts, such as Fort Wilderness. Even with recent improvements, it's still slow going.

Another problem: If you're staying at Disney's value or moderate resorts, and you've got little kids in tow, be advised that you're going to have to hike quite a bit from the theme-park exit to the bus stops that will get you back to your hotel. Even exhausted adults won't relish the walk at the end of a tiring day, and it'll be that much worse if you're carrying a day's worth of souvenirs, a diaper bag, a camera bag, and a tired toddler. Buses to these and other resorts can also get crowded, and the last thing tired and cranky kids will want to do is get packed in like sardines and remain standing for what could be a long ride.

And finally, without a car, you may find yourself at Mickey's mercy, spending all your time (and money) in Mickeyville.

The best rule when using Disney transportation: Ask the driver or someone at your hotel's front desk to help you take the most direct route or the easiest one for your children. Keep asking questions along the way. Unlike missing a highway exit, missing a bus stop means your toddler may be old enough to vote before you arrive at your destination. If you have time before locking in your trip, use the maps in this book to find the attractions you want to visit and their proximity to the various WDW resorts. You can also check them out at www.disneyworld.com.

BY CAR

To rent or not to rent—that's the question. If you're going to stay happily immersed in everything Disney, or if you're going to stick to International Drive or Universal, you might do just as well without your own wheels. ***But remember:*** You'll become a virtual prisoner unless you rent a car at least a few days during your stay. In Disney's case, the least expensive properties, the All-Star resorts, are among the farthest from the Disney parks. Waits between buses can be considerable—if not unendurable, especially with kids.

During peak hours in the busy seasons, or even on an average day at park closing, you may have trouble getting a seat on the bus, something to keep in mind. Also, if you're hauling a stroller, consider the frustration factor of loading and unloading it, along with all your other kiddie paraphernalia, on and off buses, ferries, and trams. (Renting strollers in the parks will alleviate this problem.)

A car may drastically cut the commute time between the parks and those hotels not directly on the monorail routes, so decide how much your time is worth and what the car will cost, and make sure to factor in the $11-per-day theme-park parking charge (but not if you're a Disney resort guest; parking is free if you stay at a Disney hotel).

In general, if you're going to spend all of your time at Disney, and you're laid-back enough to go with the flow of traffic within the transportation network, there's no sense in renting a car that will sit in the parking lot. This is especially true if you're staying at one of the Disney resorts on the monorail system. But if you're staying a week or more, you'll probably want a car for at least a day or two to venture beyond the traditional tourist areas. You can discover downtown Orlando, visit museums, tour the Space Coast, or head to the Gulf Coast. Trust me: You and your kids will need a good dose of reality after spending a few days in Mickey madness.

If you are going to be spending the majority of your vacation outside the House of Mouse, a car is an absolute necessity (unless you plan on staying solely within the bounds of Universal Orlando for your entire trip). While there are plenty of transportation options, such as shuttles, trolleys, and taxis, using them every time you venture outside your hotel can't be done without losing your sanity (and lots of cash); don't even think of doing it!

RENTING A CAR

All of the major car-rental companies are represented in Orlando and maintain desks at or near the airport (see the appendix, "Useful Toll-Free Numbers & Websites," for contact information). When you're planning your trip, poring over all those brochures, or searching through cyberspace, keep your eye out for discounts on car rentals. If you're using a travel agent, ask whether a discount is included in any packages. It also can't hurt to simply ask for the best rate available. Be advised that city and state rental taxes and surcharges (often not included in a quoted rate) can add almost 25% to your bill, so make sure to ask if taxes are included in any quotes that you get.

If you're visiting from abroad and plan to rent a car in the United States, keep in mind that foreign driver's licenses are usually recognized in the U.S., but you should get an international one if your home license is not in English. You will also need a major credit card and must be at least 25 years old. Some companies rent to younger people but add a daily surcharge, which can run as high as $20 per day or more.

Note: Under Florida law, children under the age of 4 must ride in a car seat; children over 4 but under 6 must either ride in a car seat or wear a safety belt. Most agencies in Orlando also rent car seats; just remember to ask for one when you reserve your car. They generally charge between $9 and $12 per day per seat. If you're vacationing for

Tips Fun While Driving

Alamo Rent A Car has a **"Fun For Kids"** page on its website (www.alamo.com) that features printable quizzes, word games, and more to keep your kids happy while on a car trip. Several of the items on the page are Disney-related, making it even more appropriate for an Orlando car trip.

more than a few days or have more than one child requiring a seat, you may want to consider bringing along your own. Be sure to ask for a seat that's the correct size for your child; an infant shouldn't be put in a seat that's too large or a toddler in a seat that's too small. Most major car-rental websites provide excellent information on choosing the proper seat restraints for your kids; two of the best are run by Avis (www.avis.com) and Hertz (www.hertz.com).

All children over age 4 and under age 16 must wear seat belts—even in the back seat. It's recommended that kids sit in the back seat, especially if the car you're driving has airbags. Infants and toddlers should *never* be placed in a car seat in the front of your vehicle.

GETTING A GOOD DEAL

Car-rental rates vary even more than airline fares. The price you pay will depend on the size of the car, where and when you pick it up and drop it off, the length of the rental period, where and how far you drive it, whether you purchase insurance, and a host of other factors. A few key questions could save you hundreds of dollars:

- Are weekend rates lower than weekday rates? Ask whether the rate is the same for pickup Friday morning, for instance, as it is for Thursday night.
- Is a weekly rate cheaper than the daily rate? Even if you need the car for only 4 days, it may be cheaper to keep it for 5 or even 7.
- Does the agency assess a drop-off charge if you don't return the car to the same location where you picked it up? Is it cheaper to pick up the car at the airport compared with a downtown location?
- Are special promotional rates available? If you see an advertised price in your local newspaper, be sure to ask for that specific rate; otherwise, you may be charged the standard cost. Terms change constantly, and reservations agents are notorious for not mentioning available discounts unless you ask.
- Are discounts available for members of AARP, AAA, frequent-flier programs, or trade unions? If you belong to any of these organizations, you may be entitled to discounts of up to 30%.
- How much tax will be added to the rental bill? Local tax? State tax?
- What is the cost of adding an additional driver's name to the contract?
- How many free miles are included in the price? Free mileage is often negotiable, depending on the length of your rental.
- How much does the rental company charge to refill your gas tank if you return with the tank less than full? Though most rental companies claim that these prices are "competitive," fuel is almost always cheaper in town. Try to allow enough time to refuel the car yourself before returning it.

Some companies offer refueling packages, in which you pay for an entire tank of gas upfront. The price is usually fairly competitive with local gas prices, but you don't get credit for any gas remaining in the tank. If a stop at a gas station on the way to the airport will make you miss your plane, by all means take advantage of the fuel-purchase option; otherwise, skip it.

Many packages are available that include airfare, accommodations, and a rental car with unlimited mileage. Compare these prices with the cost of booking airline tickets and renting a car separately to see whether these offers are good deals. See "Package Deals for Families," in chapter 2, for details on packages and where to find them. Also check out **Breezenet.com,** which offers domestic car-rental discounts with some of the most competitive rates around.

CAR-RENTAL INSURANCE

Before you drive off in a rental car, be sure that you're insured. Hasty assumptions about your personal auto insurance or a rental agency's additional coverage could end up costing you tens of thousands of dollars—even if you are involved in an accident that clearly was the fault of another driver.

If you already hold a **private auto insurance** policy, you are most likely covered in the United States for loss of or damage to a rental car and liability in case of injury to any other party involved in an accident. Be sure to find out whether you are covered in the area you are visiting, whether your policy extends to all people who will be driving the rental car, how much liability is covered in case an outside party is injured in an accident, and whether the type of vehicle you are renting is included under your contract. (Rental trucks, sport-utility vehicles, and luxury vehicles such as the Jaguar may not be covered.) There is also another area: "loss," as in "loss of income," as in the loss of the income that rental car would have made for the rental-car company. Many insurers don't cover this.

Most **major credit cards** provide some degree of coverage as well—provided that they were used to pay for the rental. Terms vary widely, however, so be sure to call your credit card company before you rent.

If you are uninsured, your credit card may provide primary coverage as long as you decline the rental agency's insurance. This means that the credit card will cover damage or theft of a rental car for the full cost of the vehicle. If you already have insurance, your credit card may provide secondary coverage—which basically covers your deductible. *Credit cards will not cover liability* or the cost of injury to an outside party and/or damage to an outside party's vehicle. Bear in mind that each credit card company has its own peculiarities; call your own credit card company for details before relying on a card for coverage. If you do not hold an insurance policy, you may seriously want to consider purchasing **additional liability insurance** from your rental company. Be sure to check the terms, however: Some rental agencies cover liability only if the renter is not at fault; even then, the rental company's obligation varies from state to state.

The basic insurance coverage offered by most car-rental companies, known as the **Loss/Damage Waiver (LDW)** or **Collision Damage Waiver (CDW),** can cost as much as $20 per day or more. The former should cover everything, including loss. It usually covers the full value of the vehicle with no deductible if an outside party causes an accident or other damage to the rental car. In all states but California, you probably will be covered in case of theft as well. Liability coverage varies according to the company policy and state law, but the minimum is usually at least $15,000. If you are at fault in an accident, however, you will be covered for the full replacement value of the car but not for liability. Most rental companies will require a police report in order to process any claims you file, but your private insurer will not be notified of the

Tips **Look Both Ways**

I don't recommend foot travel anywhere in Orlando, but occasionally, you'll have to walk across a parking lot or street. *Be careful.* In 2002, Orlando was named the most dangerous large city in the country for pedestrians by the Mean Streets study. Subsequent years haven't raised the safety level all that much. Wide roads designed to move traffic quickly and a shortage of sidewalks, streetlights, and crosswalks are to blame. So stay close to your kids, and keep a wary eye on traffic.

accident. Check your own policies and credit cards before you shell out money on this extra insurance, as you may already be covered.

BY BUS

Stops for the **LYNX** bus system, operated by the Central Florida Regional Transportation Authority (© **407/841-2279;** www.golynx.com), are marked with a paw print. LYNX will get you to Disney, Universal, and I-Drive ($1.50 adults, 75¢ kids 8–18), but it's slow and generally not tourist-friendly. I can't recommend using it, especially if you've got toddlers and younger children with you.

Mears Transportation (© **407/423-5566;** www.mearstransportation.com) runs buses to attractions such as Kennedy Space Center, Universal Orlando, SeaWorld, and Busch Gardens in Tampa, among others. Its service is the largest in the area, and with good reason. Rates vary based on where you are going and where you are coming from, so call ahead for the particulars. Many area hotels use Mears for their shuttle service to the parks and attractions.

BY TAXI

Taxis line up in front of major hotels and a few smaller properties. Your front desk will be happy to hail one for you, too. You can also call **Yellow Cab** (© **407/699-9999**) or **Ace Metro** (© **407/855-0564**). Rates average $2.50 for the first mile (but can run as high as $3.25 or more) and average $1.75 per mile thereafter, though sometimes you can get a flat rate. In general, cabs are economical only if you have four or five people aboard. You could actually rent your own car (depending on the model) for the price of just a few taxi rides.

Note: Under Florida law, children under the age of 4 must ride in car seats in all vehicles, including taxis. For a taxi ride, you'll need to bring your own seat, making this mode of travel inconvenient for families whose kids require a seat.

FAST FACTS: Walt Disney World & Orlando

American Express There's an office at 7618 Sand Lake Rd. (© **407/264-0104**).

Area Codes Because of its growth spurt, Orlando has had to go to 10-digit dialing. If you're making a local call in Orlando's 407 area-code region, even across the street, *you must dial the 407 area code,* followed by the number you wish to call, for a total of 10 digits.

ATM Networks See "Money & Costs," p. 36.

Automobile Organizations Auto clubs will supply maps, suggested routes, guidebooks, accident and bail-bond insurance, and emergency road service. The **American Automobile Association (AAA)** (© 800/222-4357; http://travel.aaa.com) is the major auto club in the United States. The cost of joining (depending on the level of coverage) runs from $50 to $104 for singles or $82 to $171 for two members, but if you're a member of a foreign auto club, you may be able to enjoy free AAA service in America—inquire about AAA reciprocity before you leave. AAA is actually an organization of regional auto clubs, so look under "AAA Automobile Club" in the White Pages of the telephone directory. AAA has a nationwide emergency road service telephone number (© 800/AAA-HELP).

Babysitters Several Orlando hotels, including all of Disney's resorts, offer babysitting, usually from an outside service such as **Kids Nite Out** (© 800/ 696-8105 or 407/828-0920; www.kidsniteout.com) or **All About Kids** (© 800/ 728-6506 or 407/812-9300; www.all-about-kids.com). In-room rates usually run between $10 and $15 per hour for the first child and $2 to $3 per additional child, per hour. A premium fee of $2 per hour (not per child) is often added for services provided during unusually early or late hours. A transportation fee of approximately $10 is often charged as well. Several resorts offer child-care facilities with counselor-supervised activity programs right on the premises, with rates that run per child per hour or, in some cases, on a set schedule. The Disney resorts' programs (© 407/939-3463)—offered at Disney's Animal Kingdom Lodge, Beach Club, BoardWalk, Contemporary, Grand Floridian, Polynesian, and Wilderness Lodge resorts—offer supervised activities, entertainment, and meals. They're open to kids 4 to 12 (who must be toilet-trained), run from 4:30 or 5pm to midnight, and cost $11 per child per hour, often with a meal included. Reservations are highly recommended for Disney's kids' clubs and are often required for outside child-care services.

Business Hours Most theme parks open at 9am and stay open until at least 6 or 7pm (sometimes as late as 9pm, 10pm, or even midnight during summer and holidays). Business offices are generally Monday through Friday from 9am to 5pm. Banks are open Monday through Friday from 9am to 4pm or later and sometimes Saturday mornings as well. Stores typically open between 9 and 10am and close between 5 and 6pm from Monday through Saturday. Stores in shopping complexes and malls tend to stay open later, until about 9pm daily, and many malls and larger department stores stay open on Sundays as well.

Camera Repair **Colonial Photo**, 634 N. Mills Ave., in downtown Orlando (© **407/841-1485**), repairs most 35mm and some digital brands.

Car Rentals See "Getting Around," p. 65.

Cashpoints See "Money & Costs," p. 36.

Currency & Currency Exchange The most common bills are the $1 (a "buck"), $5, $10, and $20 denominations. There are also $2 bills (seldom encountered), $50 bills, and $100 bills (the last two are usually not welcome as payment for small purchases).

Coins come in seven denominations: 1¢ (1 cent, or a penny); 5¢ (5 cents, or a nickel); 10¢ (10 cents, or a dime); 25¢ (25 cents, or a quarter); 50¢ (50 cents, or a half dollar); the gold-colored Sacagawea coin, worth $1; and the rare silver dollar.

The "foreign-exchange bureaus" so common in Europe are rare even at airports in the United States and nonexistent outside major cities. It's best not to change foreign money (or traveler's checks denominated in a currency other than U.S. dollars) at a small-town bank or even a branch in a big city. In fact, leave any currency other than U.S. dollars at home; it may prove a greater nuisance to you than it's worth. You can exchange foreign currency at **Guest Relations** windows at all four Disney parks, at **City Hall** in the Magic Kingdom, and at **Earth Station** at Epcot. Currency can also be exchanged at Walt Disney World resorts and at the **SunBank** across from Downtown Disney Marketplace. There are also currency exchanges at **Guest Services** at Universal Orlando and Sea-World.

For additional currency information, see "Money & Costs," p. 36.

Customs **What You Can Bring Into the U.S.** Every visitor more than 21 years of age may bring in, free of duty, the following: (1) 1 liter of wine or hard liquor; (2) 200 cigarettes, 100 cigars (but not from Cuba), or 3 pounds of smoking tobacco; and (3) $100 worth of gifts. These exemptions are offered to travelers who spend at least 72 hours in the United States and who have not claimed them within the preceding 6 months. It is altogether forbidden to bring into the country foodstuffs (particularly fruit, cooked meats, and canned goods) and plants (vegetables, seeds, tropical plants, and the like). Foreign tourists may carry in or out up to $10,000 in U.S. or foreign currency with no formalities; larger sums must be declared to U.S. Customs on entering or leaving, which includes filing form CM 4790. For details regarding U.S. Customs and Border Protection, consult your nearest U.S. embassy or consulate, or **U.S. Customs** (© 202/927-1770; www.customs.ustreas.gov).

What You Can Take Home from the U.S.:

Australian Citizens: A helpful brochure available from Australian consulates or Customs offices is *Know Before You Go.* For more information, call the **Australian Customs Service** at © 1300/363-263, or log on to www.customs.gov.au.

Canadian Citizens: For a clear summary of Canadian rules, write for the booklet *I Declare,* issued by the **Canada Border Services Agency** (© 800/461-9999 in Canada, or 204/983-3500; www.cbsa-asfc.gc.ca).

New Zealand Citizens: Most questions are answered in a free pamphlet available at New Zealand consulates and Customs offices: *New Zealand Customs Guide for Travellers, Notice no. 4.* For information, contact **New Zealand Customs,** The Customhouse, 17–21 Whitmore St., Box 2218, Wellington (© 04/473-6099 or 0800/428-786; www.customs.govt.nz).

U.K. Citizens: For information, contact **HM Customs & Excise** at © 0845/010-9000 (from outside the U.K., 020/8929-0152), or consult their website at www.hmce.gov.uk.

Doctors & Dentists There are basic first-aid centers in all of the theme parks. The **Poison Control Center** (© 800/282-3171) runs a 24-hour, toll-free number.

Doctors on Call Service (© 407/399-3627) makes house and room calls in most of the Orlando area (including the Disney resorts). **Centra Care** has several walk-in clinics listed in the Yellow Pages, including ones on Turkey Lake Road, near Universal (© 407/351-6682); at Lake Buena Vista, near Disney (© 407/934-2273); and on U.S. 192 (W. Irlo Bronson Hwy.), in the Formosa Gardens shopping center (© 407/397-7032). The **Medical Concierge** (© 407/648-5252; www.themedicalconcierge.com) makes house calls to hotel rooms, has a walk-in clinic (listed in the Yellow Pages), arranges for emergency dental appointments, and rents medical equipment.

To find a dentist, contact **Dental Referral Service** (© 800/235-4111; www.dentalreferral.com), which can tell you the nearest dentist who meets your needs. Check the Yellow Pages for local 24-hour emergency services.

Drinking Laws The legal age for purchase and consumption of alcoholic beverages is 21; proof of age is required and often requested at bars, nightclubs, and restaurants, so it's always a good idea to bring ID when you go out. Beer and wine can often be purchased in supermarkets.

Do not carry open containers of alcohol in your car or any public area that isn't zoned for alcohol consumption. The police can fine you on the spot. And nothing will ruin your trip faster than getting a citation for DUI ("driving under the influence"), so don't even think about driving while intoxicated.

Electricity Like Canada, the United States uses 110 to 120 volts AC (60 cycles), compared with 220 to 240 volts AC (50 cycles) in most of Europe, Australia, and New Zealand. Downward converters that change 220–240 volts to 110–120 volts are difficult to find in the United States, so bring one with you.

Embassies & Consulates All embassies are located in the nation's capital, Washington, D.C. Some consulates are located in major U.S. cities, and most nations have a mission to the United Nations in New York City. If your country isn't listed below, call for directory information in Washington, D.C. (© 202/555-1212), or log on to **www.embassy.org/embassies**.

The embassy of **Australia** is at 1601 Massachusetts Ave. NW, Washington, DC 20036 (© 202/797-3000; www.austemb.org). There are consulates in New York, Honolulu, Houston, Los Angeles, and San Francisco.

The embassy of **Canada** is at 501 Pennsylvania Ave. NW, Washington, DC 20001 (© 202/682-1740; www.canadianembassy.org). Other Canadian consulates are in Buffalo (New York), Detroit, Los Angeles, New York, and Seattle.

The embassy of **Ireland** is at 2234 Massachusetts Ave. NW, Washington, DC 20008 (© 202/462-3939; www.irelandemb.org). Irish consulates are located in Boston, Chicago, New York, San Francisco, and other cities. See the website for a complete listing.

The embassy of **New Zealand** is at 37 Observatory Circle NW, Washington, DC 20008 (© 202/328-4800; www.nzemb.org). New Zealand consulates are located in Los Angeles, Salt Lake City, San Francisco, and Seattle.

The embassy of the **United Kingdom** is at 3100 Massachusetts Ave. NW, Washington, DC 20008 (© 202/588-7800; www.britainusa.com). Other British consulates are in Atlanta, Boston, Chicago, Cleveland, Houston, Los Angeles, New York, San Francisco, and Seattle.

Emergencies Call ℂ **911** to report a fire, call the police, or get an ambulance anywhere in the United States. This is a toll-free call. (No coins are required at public telephones.)

The Florida Tourism Industry Marketing Corporation, the state tourism-promotions board, sponsors a **help line** (ℂ **800/647-9284**) with operators who speak **over 100 languages.** This source can provide general directions and assist with lost travel papers and credit cards, minor medical emergencies, accidents, money transfers, airline confirmations, and much more.

Gasoline (Petrol) At press time, in the U.S., the cost of gasoline (also known as gas, but never petrol), is abnormally high ($2.98 a gallon in Orlando) and fluctuating drastically. Taxes are already included in the printed price. One U.S. gallon equals 3.8 liters or .85 imperial gallons. Fill-up locations are known as gas or service stations.

Holidays Banks, government offices, post offices, and many stores, restaurants, and museums are closed on the following legal national holidays: January 1 (New Year's Day), the third Monday in January (Martin Luther King, Jr., Day), the third Monday in February (Presidents' Day), the last Monday in May (Memorial Day), July 4 (Independence Day), the first Monday in September (Labor Day), the second Monday in October (Columbus Day), November 11 (Veterans' Day/Armistice Day), the fourth Thursday in November (Thanksgiving Day), and December 25 (Christmas). The Tuesday after the first Monday in November is Election Day, a federal government holiday in presidential-election years (held every 4 years, and next in 2008 and 2012).

Hospitals **Sand Lake Hospital,** 9400 Turkey Lake Rd. (ℂ **407/351-8550**), is about 2 miles south of Sand Lake Road. From the WDW area, take I-4 east to the Sand Lake Road exit and make a left on Turkey Lake Road. The hospital is 2 miles up on your right. To avoid the highway, take Palm Parkway (off Apopka–Vineland near Hotel Plaza Blvd.); it turns into Turkey Lake Road. The hospital is 2 miles up on your left. **Celebration Health,** 400 Celebration Place (ℂ **407/303-4000**), is located in the near-Disney town of Celebration. From I-4, take the U.S. 192 exit. At the first light, turn right onto Celebration Avenue. At the first stop sign, take another right. *Note:* Be sure to check with your health-care provider or insurance carrier regarding regulations for medical care outside your home area.

Internet Access You'll find a few local cybercafes listed at **www.cybercaptive.com** or **www.cybercafe.com.** Most hotels and resorts provide some form of Internet access, whether via WebTV, a dataport, Wi-Fi, or a business center; charges vary.

Legal Aid If you are "pulled over" for a minor infraction (such as speeding), never attempt to pay the fine directly to a police officer; this could be construed as attempted bribery, a much more serious crime. Pay fines to the clerk of the court (ℂ **407/836-6000** in Orlando; ℂ **407/343-3530** in Kissimmee). If accused of a more serious offense, say and do nothing before consulting a lawyer. Here the burden is on the state to prove a person's guilt beyond a reasonable doubt, and everyone has the right to remain silent, whether he or she is suspected of a crime or actually arrested. Once arrested, a person can make one telephone call to a party of his or her choice. International visitors should call their embassy or consulate.

Libraries Orange County has 14 libraries (www.ocls.lib.fl.us), including the downtown **Orlando Public Library,** 101 E. Central Blvd. (© **407/835-7323**), and **South Creek Library,** 1702 Deerfield Blvd. (© **407/858-4779**).

Lost & Found Be sure to tell all of your credit card companies the minute you discover your wallet has been lost or stolen and file a report at the nearest police precinct. Your credit card company or insurer may require a police report number or record of the loss. Most credit card companies have an emergency toll-free number to call if your card is lost or stolen; they may be able to wire you a cash advance immediately or deliver an emergency credit card in a day or two. Visa's U.S. emergency number is © **800/847-2911** or 410/581-9994. American Express cardholders and traveler's check holders should call © **800/221-7282.** MasterCard holders should call © **800/307-7309** or 636/722-7111. For other credit cards, call the toll-free number directory at © **800/555-1212.**

If you need emergency cash over the weekend when all banks and American Express offices are closed, you can have money wired to you via **Western Union** (© **800/325-6000;** www.westernunion.com).

Lost Children Every theme park has a designated spot for adults to be reunited with lost children (or lost spouses). Ask where it is when you enter (or consult the free park-guide map), and instruct your children to ask park personnel (not a stranger) to take them there if they get separated from you. Point out what park personnel look like, including how to recognize their badges. *Young children under 7 should wear name tags* (concealed inside their clothing) that include parents' names and contact numbers both in Orlando and back home.

Mail Starting in May 2008, domestic postage rates will increse to 27¢ for a postcard and 42¢ for a letter. For international mail, a first-class letter of up to 1 ounce will cost 94¢ (72¢ to Canada and Mexico); a first-class postcard costs the same as a letter. For more information, go to **www.usps.com** and click on "Calculate Postage."

If you aren't sure what your address will be in the United States, mail can be sent to you, in your name, c/o General Delivery at the main post office of the city or region where you expect to be. The post office nearest Disney and Universal is at 10450 Turkey Lake Rd., in Orlando (© **800/275-8777**). The zip code is 32819. The addressee must pick up mail in person and must produce proof of identity (driver's license, passport, etc.). Most post offices will hold your mail for up to 1 month, and are open Monday to Friday from 8am to 6pm, Saturday from 9am to 3pm.

Always include zip codes when mailing items in the U.S. If you don't know your zip code, visit www.usps.com/zip4.

Maps AAA is an excellent source of free maps if you are a member (or someone you know is). The Orlando/Orange County Convention & Visitors Bureau is another. You can pick up a copy of its official visitor map in most hotel lobbies. You can also buy decent maps for $5 or less at the bookstore in the Orlando International Airport and at most convenience and discount stores.

Measurements See the chart on the inside front cover of this book for details on converting metric measurements to U.S. equivalents.

Newspapers & Magazines The *Orlando Sentinel* is the major local newspaper. The Friday edition includes extensive entertainment and dining listings, as does the website, **www.orlandosentinel.com**. *Orlando Weekly* is a free alternative paper with entertainment and art listings focused on events outside tourist areas.

Passports **For residents of Australia:** You can pick up an application from your local post office or any branch of Passports Australia, but you must schedule an interview at the passport office to present your application materials. Call the **Australian Passport Information Service** at ℂ **13 12 32,** or visit the government website at www.passports.gov.au.

For residents of Canada: Passport applications are available at travel agencies throughout Canada or from the central **Passport Office,** Department of Foreign Affairs and International Trade, Ottawa, ON K1A 0G3 (ℂ **800/567-6868;** www.ppt.gc.ca). *Note:* Canadian children who travel must have their own passport. However, if you hold a valid Canadian passport issued before December 11, 2001, that bears the name of your child, the passport remains valid for you and your child until it expires.

For residents of Ireland: You can apply for a 10-year passport at the **Passport Office,** Setanta Centre, Molesworth Street, Dublin 2 (ℂ **01/671-1633;** www.irl-gov.ie/iveagh). Those under age 18 and over 65 must apply for a 3-year passport. You can also apply at 1A South Mall, Cork (ℂ **021/272-525**), or at most main post offices.

For residents of New Zealand: You can pick up a passport application at any New Zealand Passports Office or download it from the website. Contact the **Passports Office** at ℂ **0800/225-050** in New Zealand or 04/474-8100, or log on to www.passports.govt.nz.

For residents of the United Kingdom: To pick up an application for a standard 10-year passport (5-yr. passport for children under 16), visit your nearest passport office, major post office, or travel agency; contact the **United Kingdom Passport Service** at ℂ **0870/521-0410;** or go to its website at www.ukpa.gov.uk.

Pharmacies There's a **Walgreens** 24-hour pharmacy at 7650 W. Sand Lake Rd. (ℂ **407/345-9497**). You can find several additional locations (many open 24 hours) near Disney, Universal Orlando, and in Kissimmee by going to **www.walgreens.com**. Numerous other pharmacies in and around Orlando, including those inside local grocery stores, are listed in the Yellow Pages.

Post Office The post office most convenient to both Disney and Universal is at 10450 Turkey Lake Rd. (ℂ **800/275-8777**). It's open Monday through Friday from 9am to 5pm, Saturday from 9am to noon. A smaller location, closer to Disney, is at 12133 Apopka–Vineland Rd. (S.R. 535) in Lake Buena Vista, just up the street from Hotel Plaza Boulevard (ℂ **800/275-8777**). If all you need to do is buy stamps and mail letters, you can do so at most hotels.

Radio Local stations include 101.1 FM (rock), 94.5 FM (R&B), 89.9 FM (jazz), 90.7 FM (classical), 92.3 FM (country), 580 AM (news), and 990 AM (Radio Disney).

Safety Just because Minnie, Mickey, Donald, and Goofy all live here doesn't mean that a few more seedy characters aren't lurking about as well. Even in the most magical place on earth, you shouldn't let your guard down; Orlando has a crime rate that's comparable with that of other large U.S. cities (and the tourist districts are no exception). Stay alert, remain aware of your surroundings, and keep your valuables out of sight. Most hotels are equipped with in-room safes or offer the use of a safety deposit box at the front desk, just for that purpose. Keep a close eye on your valuables when you're in public places like restaurants, theaters, and even airport terminals. Renting a locker is always preferable to leaving your valuables in the trunk of your car, even in the theme-park lots. Avoid carrying large amounts of cash in a backpack or fanny pack, which could be easily accessed while you're standing in line for a ride or show. And don't leave valuables unattended under a stroller; that's pretty much asking for them to be stolen.

If you're renting a car, carefully read the safety instructions provided by the rental company. Never stop for any reason in a suspicious, poorly lighted, or unpopulated area, and remember that children should never ride in the front seat of a car equipped with airbags. See "Driving Safety" (p. 42) for more information.

One safety issue that often comes up when families visit Orlando is that of lost kids—not only at the parks, but at the hotels, too (and it happens a lot more than most people think). If you and your family have a safety plan in place ahead of time, you'll save lots of heartache and worry. For more on this topic, see "Keeping Kids Safe" (p. 41).

Smoking   Heavy smokers have it rough in Florida: Smoking is banned in public buildings, sports arenas, elevators, theaters, banks, lobbies, restaurants, offices, stores, bed-and-breakfasts, many small hotels, and bars. Inside the theme parks and at the WDW resorts, you can smoke only in designated outdoor areas.

Taxes   The United States has no value-added tax (VAT) or other indirect tax at the national level. Every state, county, and city may levy its own local tax on all purchases, including hotel and restaurant checks and airline tickets. These taxes will not appear on price tags. In Florida, purchases are taxed at a rate of 6.5% to 7% (depending on the county you happen to be in) on all goods, with the exception of most edible grocery-store items and medicines. Hotels add another 2% to 5% in resort taxes to your bill, so the total tax on accommodations can run up to 12%.

Telegraph, Telex & Fax   **Telegraph and telex services** are provided primarily by Western Union. You can telegraph money, or have it telegraphed to you, very quickly by calling ⓒ **800/325-6000,** but this service can cost as much as 15 to 20 percent of the amount sent.

Most hotels have **fax machines** available for guest use (be sure to ask about the charge to use it). Many hotel rooms are even wired for guests' fax machines. A less expensive way to send and receive faxes may be at stores such as **The UPS Store** (formerly Mail Boxes Etc.).

Time   The continental United States is divided into **four time zones:** Eastern Standard Time (EST), Central Standard Time (CST), Mountain Standard Time (MST), and Pacific Standard Time (PST). Alaska and Hawaii have their own zones. For example, when it's 9am in Los Angeles (PST), it's 7am in Honolulu (HST),10am in Denver (MST), 11am in Chicago (CST), noon in New York City (EST), 5pm in London (GMT), and 2am the next day in Sydney.

Daylight saving time is in effect from 2am on the second Sunday in March to 2am on the first Sunday in November, except in Arizona, Hawaii, the U.S. Virgin Islands, and Puerto Rico. Daylight saving time moves the clock 1 hour ahead of standard time.

Tipping Tips are a very important part of certain workers' income, so it's necessary to leave appropriate gratuities. (Tipping is certainly not compulsory if the service is poor!) In hotels, tip **bellhops** at least $1 per bag ($2–$3 if you have a lot of luggage) and tip the **chamber staff** $1 to $2 per day (more if you've left a disaster area for him or her to clean up). Tip the **doorman** or **concierge** only if he or she has provided you with some specific service (for example, calling a cab for you or obtaining difficult-to-get theater tickets). Tip the **valet-parking attendant** $1 every time you get your car.

In restaurants, bars, and nightclubs, tip **service staff** 15% to 20% of the check, tip **bartenders** 10% to 15%, tip **checkroom attendants** $1 per garment, and tip **valet-parking attendants** $1 per vehicle.

As for other service personnel, tip **cab drivers** 15% of the fare; tip **skycaps** at airports at least $1 per bag ($2–$3 if you have a lot of luggage); and tip **hairdressers** and **barbers** 15% to 20%.

Toilets You won't find public toilets or restrooms on the streets in most U.S. cities, but they can be found in hotel lobbies, bars, restaurants, museums, department stores, railway and bus stations, and service stations. Large hotels and fast-food restaurants are probably the best bet for clean facilities. Restaurants and bars in resorts or heavily visited areas may reserve their restrooms for patrons. Some establishments display a notice indicating this. You can ignore this sign or, better yet, avoid arguments by paying for a cup of coffee or a soft drink, which will qualify you as a patron.

Visas For information about U.S. visas, go to **http://travel.state.gov** and click on "Visas." Or go to one of the following websites:

Australian citizens can obtain up-to-date visa information from the **U.S. Embassy Canberra,** Moonah Place, Yarralumla, ACT 2600 (© **02/6214-5600**), or by checking the U.S. Diplomatic Mission's website at http://usembassy-australia.state.gov/consular.

British subjects can obtain up-to-date visa information by calling the **U.S. Embassy Visa Information Line** (© **0891/200-290**) or by visiting the "Visas to the U.S." section of the American Embassy London's website at www.usembassy.org.uk.

Irish citizens can obtain up-to-date visa information through the **Embassy of the USA Dublin,** 42 Elgin Rd., Dublin 4, Ireland (© **353/1-668-8777**), or by checking the "Consular Services" section of the website at http://dublin.usembassy.gov.

Citizens of **New Zealand** can obtain up-to-date visa information by contacting the **U.S. Embassy New Zealand,** 29 Fitzherbert Terrace, Thorndon, Wellington (© **644/472-2068**), or get the information directly from the website at http://wellington.usembassy.gov.

Family-Friendly Accommodations

Unquestionably, families and kids are the real VIPs in Central Florida, which has nearly 114,000 rooms, including scores of places located in or near the hottest tourist spots: Walt Disney World, Universal Orlando, SeaWorld, and all of International Drive. Many of these places allow kids 17 and under to stay free with paying adults—and some even offer free meals or perks for preteens, rolling out the red carpet in a variety of ways!

Beautifully landscaped grounds are the rule at properties within WDW, neighboring Lake Buena Vista, Universal Orlando, and on the southern portions of I-Drive. But heavier traffic and, at times, higher prices come with those trimmings. Visitors looking for an inexpensive or moderately priced motel would do well to check out the options in Kissimmee and, to a lesser degree, on the northern end of International Drive. No matter your budget or

tolerance for crowds, there's most definitely something for everyone in Orlando.

Once you've decided on dates for your Orlando vacation, make sure to book your accommodations as soon as is possible, especially if you want to stay at Disney or Universal. Advance reservations are a necessity if you're hoping to find moderate or preferred rooms in these areas—especially during peak seasons or around a holiday. In addition to the individual listings in this chapter, there are several places where you'll find discounts on rooms. HotelKingdom.com (© 877/766-6787 or 407/294-9600; www.hotelkingdom.com) is just one good source for bargains. Others include the Orlando/Orange County Convention & Visitors Bureau (© 800/643-9492; www.orlandoinfo.com) and the Kissimmee Convention & Visitors Bureau (© 800/333-5477; www.floridakiss.com).

1 Choosing Your Orlando Hotel

There seemed to be no end to Orlando's hotel boom a while back—about 4,000 new rooms were added every year through 2000. Then, in the years that followed, far fewer rooms were added. However, tourism is once again on the rise, and so too are the number of rooms in and around Orlando. Disney alone lays claim to 33 resorts, timeshares, and "official" hotels, three of them added within the last few years (with more on the way), for a total just over 31,000 rooms, including 784 campsites at Fort Wilderness. That's roughly 25% of the area's entire roster.

Orlando's tourism-based economy is showing signs of yet another growth spurt. Two major properties—the Ritz-Carlton and neighboring JW Marriott (known collectively as the Orlando Grande Lakes)—opened in mid-2003, and others, including the Omni Orlando Resort and the Reunion Resort & Club of Orlando, followed soon after. Plans for the next few years look to be headed in the same direction, as a handful of large-scale luxury resorts (including a joint venture between Disney and the Four Seasons) are scheduled to open, with several other smaller-scale properties just on the horizon.

In this section, I'll give you the tools to choose the ideal hotel for your family vacation in Orlando. I discuss options for saving money on room rates, outline the amenities at Orlando hotels that most appeal to families, give details on discount hotel packages, and—most important of all when looking for a hotel in Orlando—list the pros and cons of staying at a Walt Disney World resort.

SAVING MONEY ON HOTEL RATES

All of the prices cited in the following pages are what are called "rack rates." That means they're the typical prices listed in hotel brochures or that hotel reservations agents give over the phone. *Don't pay them!* You can almost always negotiate a better price by purchasing package deals; by assuring the agents they can do better; or by mentioning that you belong to one of several organizations that receive a discount, such as AARP, AAA, or a labor union. The Orlando Magicard can save you plenty of cash as well (see p. 12 for more on this cost-saving option). Even the type of credit card you use could get you a 5% to 10% discount at some of the larger chains. Any discount you get will help ease the impact of local resort taxes, which aren't included in the quoted rates. *These taxes will add 11% to 12% to your bill, depending on where you're staying.*

The **average, undiscounted hotel rate** for the Orlando area is currently about $101 per night double, and that rate in good times climbs about 5% a year. The lowest rates at WDW are at the Pop Century and three All-Star resorts, which, depending on the season, can run from $82 to $141. They're pricier than comparable rooms in the outside world, but though they are small and basic, they are still Disney-owned and offer the same on-property advantages as Disney's more expensive resorts.

In 2008, WDW's value seasons or lowest rates are generally available from January 1 to February 13, August 3 to October 1, and November 30 to December 18. Regular-season rates are available from March 30 to May 21 and October 2 to November 29. Summer rates (at Disney's moderate and value resorts only) apply from May 22 through August 2. Peak rates apply from February 14 to March 29, with holiday rates from December 19 to December 31. While the actual dates will shift a little (and will also change depending on the level of hotel you choose), the same general time periods should apply in 2009; however, it's best to double-check when you make your reservations, as holiday dates, which pretty much regulate the "seasons," can change from year to year. *Note:* Disney now charges by the individual night, not by the season your vacation started in. For instance, if the first three days of your vacation fall during the regular season and the remainder of your vacation during the peak season, you will be charged the regular rate for the first three nights and the peak rate for the remaining nights—no longer will you be able to reap the benefits of paying the lower rate should your vacation dates fall in more than one season. When you book your reservation, Disney will provide only a total room rate for your stay, so be sure to ask for a nightly breakdown if the amount is different than expected.

If you're not renting a car or staying at a Walt Disney World or Universal resort, be sure to ask when booking your room if the hotel or motel offers **transportation to the theme parks** and, if so, whether there's a charge. (You'll find this in my listings, but things sometimes change.) Some hotels and motels offer free service with their own shuttles. Others use Mears Transportation (see "Getting Around," in chapter 3). Rates can be $15 or more per person round-trip (some hotels make these arrangements for you; others require you to do it). On the other hand, if you have a car, expect to pay $11 a day to park it at Disney or Universal, $10 at SeaWorld.

If you stay at a WDW resort or one of Disney's "official" hotels, transportation is complimentary within WDW. For more information on this and the other advantages (and disadvantages) of staying at Disney properties, see "The Perks & Downsides of Staying with Mickey," later in this chapter.

In or out of Walt Disney World, if you book your hotel as part of a **package deal** (see "Package Deals for Families" for details), you'll likely enjoy some kind of savings. Call the **Walt Disney Travel Company** (© 407/939-7675 for packages, © 407/939-7429 for rooms only) or head online to **www.disneyworld.com** to book resort packages or hotel rooms at WDW.

Outside Disney, you'll probably be quoted a better price than the rack rates contained in the following listings; even then, try to bargain further to ensure you get the best deal possible. Ask about discounts for students, government employees, seniors, military, firefighters, police, AFL–CIO, corporate clients, AARP or AAA, holders of the Orlando Magicard, and even frequent-traveler programs (whether you have hotel or airline membership). Special Internet-only discounts and packages may be featured on hotel websites, especially those of the larger chains, and many hotels are teaming up with the airlines, offering discounted package deals. No matter where you end up staying, always ask again when you arrive if there are any additional discounts or promotions available. But never come to Orlando without a reservation: Taking chances on your negotiating skills is one thing; taking chances on room availability is quite another. Orlando is a year-round destination, with a heavy convention and business trade, and international vacationers flock here during periods when domestic travelers don't. If you come without a reservation, you may find yourself extremely disappointed—or completely out of luck.

HOTEL RATES IN THIS CHAPTER

The hotels listed in this chapter are categorized by location and price. As you might expect, many of the inexpensive properties are the farthest from the action and/or have the most spartan of all accommodations.

Keep in mind, however, that this isn't one of the world's best bargain destinations. Unlike other Florida tourist areas, there are very few under-$60 motels that meet the standards demanded for listing in this book. That's why I've raised the price bar. The accommodations in the **inexpensive** category charge an average of less than $90 per night for a double room. Those offering rooms for $90 to $180 are in the **moderate** category; rooms for $181 to $250 are listed as **expensive;** and anything over $250 is **very expensive.** Any included extras (such as breakfast) are listed for each property. Note that Orlando has peak and off seasons, often with complicated boundaries. Even remote events such as Bike Week in Daytona Beach or the International Sweet Potato Growers convention in Orlando can raise rates. These events especially affect moderately priced properties outside WDW.

The rack rates listed are for a per-night double room, unless otherwise noted, and don't include hotel taxes of 11% to 12%. Also, most Orlando hotels and motels let **kids under 12 (and usually under 18) stay free** with a parent or guardian if you don't exceed maximum room occupancy. But to be safe, verify when booking your room.

Value Staying for Less

Although many folks participate in the airlines' frequent-flier programs, not many take advantage of the major hotel chains' frequent-stay clubs. Even if you don't stay in a hotel for more than your yearly vacation, you may be able to realize savings by joining its program.

Like the airlines' schemes, some hotels let you build points for staying at a participating property, dining in its restaurant, or using another partner service. Although programs vary, points can be traded for free nights; discounted rates; special perks; and, in some cases, frequent-flier miles. And the price to join is right—it's free. Simply joining a hotel club may make you immediately eligible for discounts; give you express check-in and checkout privileges; and provide free breakfasts, local calls, or morning newspapers. And there's no reason you can't join more than one.

Here are a few frequent-stay programs that offer perks to travelers:

- **Choice-Hotels International Choice Privileges** (© 888/770-6800; www. guestprivileges.com) covers Sleep, Quality, Comfort, Clarion, Cambria, and Mainstay properties. Participants receive perks such as express check-in, special rates, room upgrades based on availability, extended checkout times, and free local calls and newspapers.

- **Hilton Honors Worldwide** (© 800/548-8690; www.hiltonhhonors.com) covers Hilton, Conrad, DoubleTree, Embassy Suites, Hampton Inn, and Homewood Suites properties. It offers expedited check-in, a dedicated reservations line, late checkout, and a free daily newspaper.

- **Hyatt Hotel's Gold Passport** (© 800/304-9288; www.goldpassport.com) gives its members a private reservations line, express check-in, complimentary newspapers, and access to the hotel's fitness center. You'll also receive special offers and discounted rates from select Hyatt properties including Hyatt Hotels and Suites, Hyatt Place, and Hyatt Summerfield Suites.

- **Six Continents Hotels Priority Club** (© 800/272-9273; www.priorityclub. com) covers the Inter-Continental, Crowne Plaza, Holiday Inn, Staybridge Suites, Candlewood Suites, and Hotel Indigo properties. Priority Club members get express check-in, access to discounted rates at select hotels, and other perks. Freebies vary according to hotel, but often include breakfast, local phone calls, and/or parking.

Other frequent-stay programs include **Starwood Preferred Guest** (© 888/625-4988; www.spg.com), **Marriott Rewards** (© 801/468-4000; www.marriottrewards.com), and **Loews First** (© 800/563-9712; www. loews-first.com).

RESERVATIONS SERVICES

Many of the hotels listed under "Places to Stay in the Kissimmee Area," later in this chapter, can be booked through the **Kissimmee Convention & Visitors Bureau** (© 800/333-5477; www.floridakiss.com). The same goes for Orlando and the **Orlando/Orange County Convention & Visitors Bureau** (© 800/643-9492; www.orlandoinfo.com).

Florida Hotel Network (© 800/293-2419; www.floridahotels.com), **Central Reservation Service** (© 800/555-7555 or 407/740-6442; www.crshotels.com), and **Hotels.com** (© 800/246-8357; www.hotels.com) are other services that can help with hotel bookings and other kinds of reservations in Central Florida.

You can book Walt Disney World hotels directly by visiting **www.disney world.com** or by calling © 407/939-7675 for vacation packages, © 407/939-7429 for room reservations only, or © 407/934-7639 for central reservations. Universal Orlando properties can be booked by visiting **www.universalorlando.com** or by calling © 800/837-2273 or 407/363-8000.

HOTEL AMENITIES FOR FAMILIES

In the "Amenities" sections of the accommodations listings that follow, I mention **concierge levels** where available. In these hotels within a hotel, guests pay more to enjoy a luxurious private lounge (sometimes with great views), free continental or full breakfasts, hot and cold hors d'oeuvres served at cocktail hour, and/or late-night cordials and pastries. Rooms are usually on higher floors, and guests are pampered with special services (including private registration and checkout, a personal concierge, and nightly bed turndown) and amenities (upgraded toiletries, bathroom scales, terry robes, hair dryers, and more). The free food may make these rooms more economical for families than one might otherwise think (especially if you're staying in a hotel where breakfast isn't included in the rate). Ask for specifics when you reserve.

You'll also find counselor-supervised **child-care** or **activity centers** at some hotels. Very popular in Orlando, these can be marvelous, creatively run facilities that may offer movies, video games, arts and crafts, storytelling, puppet shows, indoor and outdoor activities, and more. Some provide meals and/or have beds where a child can sleep while you're out on the town. Check individual hotel listings for these facilities.

THE PERKS & DOWNSIDES OF STAYING WITH MICKEY

The decision on whether to bunk with the Mouse is one of the first you'll have to make when planning an Orlando vacation, and you'll probably get a strong pro-WDW argument from any younger kids in your family. In the sections "Places to Stay in Walt Disney World" and "'Official' Hotels in Lake Buena Vista," later in this chapter, you'll find information on the hotels, villas, timeshares, and campsites that are owned by Disney or are "official" hotels—those that are privately owned but have earned Disney's seal of approval. All 33, including the new Saratoga Springs Resort & Spa, are in WDW or nearby Lake Buena Vista.

In addition to their proximity to the theme parks, there are other **advantages** to staying at a Disney property or one of the "official" hotels. The following amenities are included at all Disney resorts, and *some* are offered by the "official" hotels, but make sure to ask when booking:

- The **Extra Magic Hours** (see the box "The Early Bird . . ." in this section).
- Free transportation for guests and their baggage from Orlando International Airport (and back again) via Disney's **Magical Express.** Not only does the service get Disney resort guests to their hotels, but it also delivers their baggage straight from the plane to their room, allowing them to bypass airport baggage claim altogether. As an added bonus, guests can check their luggage and print their boarding passes (when traveling on select airlines) for their return trip before even leaving their resort, allowing them to skip the lines at the airport. This complimentary service is slated to continue through at least December 2011.

- Unlimited **free transportation** on the Walt Disney World Transportation System's buses, monorails, ferries, and water taxis to and from the four WDW parks, from 2 hours prior to opening until 2 hours after closing. Free transportation is also provided to and from Downtown Disney West Side and Pleasure Island, Downtown Disney Marketplace, Typhoon Lagoon, Blizzard Beach, and the WDW resorts. Three of them—the Polynesian, Grand Floridian, and Contemporary resorts—are on the Disney monorail system. This service can save money you might otherwise spend on a rental car, parking (note, however, that parking is free if you're a Disney resort guest), and shuttles. It also means you're guaranteed admission to all the parks, even during peak times, when parking lots sometimes fill to capacity.
- Reduced-price **children's menus** in many resort (and park) restaurants.
- **Character meals**—at breakfast, lunch, and/or dinner—at select restaurants.
- TVs equipped with the Disney Channel, **nightly bedtime stories** (Channel 22, 7–10pm, audio only), and WDW information stations.
- A **lobby concierge** (replacing the Guest Services desk) where you can buy tickets to all Disney parks and attractions and get information on everything Disney without standing in long lines at the parks.
- Playing privileges; preferred **tee times;** and, in some cases, free transportation to Disney golf courses (see "Hitting the Links," in chapter 8).
- Some of the best **swimming pools** in Orlando. WDW has recently built new ones or remodeled old ones as zero-entry or zero-grade pools, meaning that there's a gradual slope into the water on at least one side rather than only a step down. These include pools at the Grand Floridian, Animal Kingdom, and Polynesian resorts.
- Mears Transportation **shuttle service** (see "Getting There" in chapter 2) for trips to non-Disney parks and attractions (fees vary), including the **Kennedy Space Center** (see chapter 11).
- On-premises Alamo **car rental** (there are also car-rental desks at the Walt Disney World Swan and Dolphin, but not at the other "official" hotels).
- Disney's **refillable-mug program,** which lets you buy—for around $12—a bottomless mug for soda, coffee, tea, and/or cocoa at its resorts. The offer is for the length of your stay, but it isn't transferable to the theme parks, and you can use it only at the property at which it is bought.
- The **Disney Dining Plan,** which allows you two meals and one snack per day per person (for the length of your stay) for one discounted price. The **Disney Deluxe Dining Plan** allows you three meals and two snacks per day per person. Over 100 select eateries in the parks and at the resorts participate.
- **Central billing,** which allows guests to "charge" all (or most) of their purchases (including meals) made anywhere inside WDW to their room. In many cases, purchases made inside the theme parks can be delivered to your resort at no extra charge.

Tips **Tight Squeeze**

An average hotel or motel room in Orlando has 325 to 400 square feet of space, with two beds that sleep up to four people. While hardly a castle, most travelers find that adequate for a short stay. For those requiring a bit more space, I've made a special note in the listings where rooms are substantially larger (or smaller) than the average.

Tips The Early Bird . . .

Disney World's **Extra Magic Hours** allow resort guests lots of extra time at the theme parks. Each day, one of the four major theme parks opens 1 hour early or remains open up to 3 hours late—but only for WDW resort guests, making for a more relaxing and less-crowded experience. Even Disney's two water parks are included in the lineup. Not all the rides and attractions run during these special periods; however, the best ones usually are open, along with a handful of restaurants and shops. You can pick up a copy of the current week's Extra Magic Hours schedule at your WDW resort. A complete list of what rides are running, which shops are open, and which restaurants are serving is available at the parks.

Keep in mind that there is a catch: If you hold a ticket with a park-hopper option, you're good to go. If, however, you hold a ticket without the hopper option, the ticket must be for admission to the park that's participating. Say you have a ticket to the Magic Kingdom without the hopper option. If Epcot is the park participating in the Extra Magic Hour that day, you'll find yourself checking out what's on TV that night instead of playing at the park.

But there are also **disadvantages** to entering Mickey's boudoir:

- That free **Magical Express** service to and from the airport isn't without its faults. Luggage delivery may at times take up to several hours, leaving you with only the clothes on your back (and whatever you packed in your carry-on). And departure shuttles (from your resort to the airport) are scheduled several hours in advance of your flight (thanks in part to the numerous resort stops they make before getting on their way), ensuring that you'll wait at the airport far longer than you would otherwise.

- The complimentary **Walt Disney World Transportation System** can be *excruciatingly* slow. At times, you have to take a ferry to catch a bus to get on the monorail to reach your hotel. It can take an eternity (sometimes an hour or more) to get to where you need to go—even if it's just across the lagoon (and even with recent improvements). And to add insult to injury, most resort bus stops are a considerable hike from the park entrances. So as you drag your kids and lug all their gear, your family's aching feet will have to wait a bit longer before they can really rest. Keep this in mind if there are fidgety kids or adults in your party.

- The WDW resorts charge **20% to 30% higher rates** than those at comparable hotels and motels away from the parks.

- Without a car or another means to get off the property, you'll be resigned either to paying WDW's higher prices or paying for a shuttle to get to Orlando's other offerings.

- Mickey, MICKEY, MICKEY . . . eek! Even the Mouse can get old after a few days unless you take a break. (Admittedly, your kids will have far less a problem with this issue than you likely will.) And if you don't spend a little time away from Mickey's monarchy, you'll miss out on the real Florida and the array of other great parks, restaurants, shops, and activities Orlando has to offer.

WDW CENTRAL RESERVATIONS OFFICE & WALT DISNEY TRAVEL COMPANY

To book a room or package at Disney's resorts, campgrounds, and "official" hotels, contact the **Central Reservations Office (CRO),** P.O. Box 10000, Lake Buena Vista, FL 32830-1000 (℃ **407/934-7639**).

CRO can recommend accommodations suited to your budget and needs, such as a location near a particular park, one with supervised child care, or a pool large enough to swim laps. It can even recommend rooms at a particular resort that are closer to the pools or food courts. But the folks who answer the phones usually don't volunteer information about a better deal or a special—*unless you ask.*

Be sure to inquire about Disney's numerous package plans, which can include meals, tickets, recreation, and other features. The right package can save you money and time, but having a comprehensive game plan first is helpful in order to calculate the cost of your vacation in advance. This is especially true if you're traveling with more than one child; the cost per person will usually drop considerably with the right package deal.

CRO can also give you information about various theme-park ticket options, the airlines, and car rentals. It can also make dinner-show reservations for you at the resort of your choice.

OTHER SOURCES FOR HOTEL PACKAGES

In addition to the Disney sources above, there are several travel companies that offer WDW packages, including **AAA** (℃ **800/732-1991**; www.aaa.com) and **American Express Vacations** (℃ **800/346-3607**; www.travel.americanexpress.com). Almost all the major airlines offer vacation packages to Orlando, including **Delta Vacations** (℃ **800/872-7786**; www.deltavacations.com), **American Airlines Vacations** (℃ **800/ 321-2121**; www.aavacations.com), **Northwest Airlines WorldVacations** (℃ **800/ 225-2525**; www.nwaworldvacations.com), and **Continental Airlines Vacations** (℃ **800/301-3800**; www.coolvacations.com). Give each a call, ask for brochures, and compare offerings to find the best package for you. See "Package Deals for Families," in chapter 2, for more information on packages.

On a slightly smaller scale than Disney, **Universal Orlando** and **SeaWorld** both offer several packages that can include resort stays (Universal includes its official resorts as well as a few off-site resorts, while SeaWorld teams up with only off-site resorts), VIP access to the parks, discounts to other Orlando attractions, and cruises. One major Universal resort perk that Disney simply can't provide (given the sheer number of its hotels) is **Universal Express** (p. 254) access to most major rides in the Universal theme parks and priority seating at select Universal restaurants. This is a big

---

⟨Tips Special Treatment

AAA (℃ **800/732-1991**; www.aaa.com) members can take advantage of special lodging programs at select WDW resorts and preferred parking at the theme parks if they purchase one of the AAA Disney vacation packages or pre-purchase their park tickets at participating AAA locations (these cannot be purchased at the parks!). The AAA Hospitality Desk located right inside the Magic Kingdom's Town Square provides basic member services.

plus for families with kids from tots to teens whose patience level hovers near zero. Airfare and car rentals are also available. For Universal, you can book a package by visiting **www.universalstudiosvacations.com** or by calling ℂ **888/322-5537** or 407/224-7000. For SeaWorld, call ℂ **800/557-4268** or surf the Internet to **www.sea worldvacations.com**.

2 Places to Stay in Walt Disney World

The resorts in this section are Disney-owned or "official" Disney hotels that offer many of the same perks. All are on the Walt Disney World Transportation System, which means those of you who don't mind being entombed in Mouseville can likely do without a car.

If you decide Disney is your destination, come up with a short list of preferred places to stay; then call the WDW **Central Reservations Office** (ℂ **407/934-7639**) for rates. Web wanderers can get tons of information at **www.disneyworld.com**.

If you come by car, you will see big signs along all the major roads on Disney property, pointing the way to the various resorts. You'll find these hotels listed on the "Walt Disney World & Lake Buena Vista Accommodations" map (p. 88).

Pets are not allowed in WDW hotels, but if you can't resist bringing along Fido or Fluffy, you can board your dog or cat during the day or overnight at the **pet kennels** located at the Transportation and Ticket Center on Seven Seas Drive (near Disney's Polynesian Resort) and near the entrance to Fort Wilderness Resort & Campground. The cost is $13 per night for resort guests, $15 for guests of other hotels. At Fort Wilderness, Fluffy is also welcome to bunk with you if you're staying at a designated campsite. Day-only accommodations ($10 per day) are offered at kennels just outside the Entrance Plaza at Epcot (the only location offering walking services) and at the entrances to Disney's Hollywood Studios and Disney's Animal Kingdom.

Prices in the following listings reflect the ranges available at each resort when this guide was published. Rates vary depending on season and room location, but the numbers should help you determine which places best fit your budget.

Kid's Night Out (ℂ **407/827-5444,** or 407/828-0920 via Disney) provides **babysitting services** at all Disney resorts. The **supervised kids' clubs** listed at the Animal Kingdom, Beach Club, Grand Floridian, Polynesian, and Wilderness Lodge resorts are open to guests of any WDW resort. Disney advises parents to reserve spots for their kids in the clubs well in advance by calling ℂ **407/WDW-DINE** (reservations can be made up to 60 days in advance). Participants must be between 4 and 12 years old and toilet trained. The programs run daily from 4 or 4:30pm until midnight. Dinner is included. The cost runs $11 per child per hour.

Note: Free portable **cribs** are available at WDW resorts, at no extra charge, but **rollaway beds** aren't. If you're carrying medications or other kid stuff that needs to be kept cool, **refrigerators** are complimentary at Disney's deluxe and moderate resorts, and can be rented at the value resorts for $10 per day, plus tax.

VERY EXPENSIVE

Disney's Beach Club Resort ★★★   This property re-creates the grand turn-of-the-20th-century Victorian seaside resorts of Cape Cod and has a more casual ambience than its sister, the Yacht Club (detailed below), with which it shares restaurants, shops, and numerous recreational activities. Striped and floral wicker furnishings, seashells, and beach umbrellas adorn the hotel's casual interior. The Beach Club is

Walt Disney World & Lake Buena Vista Accommodations

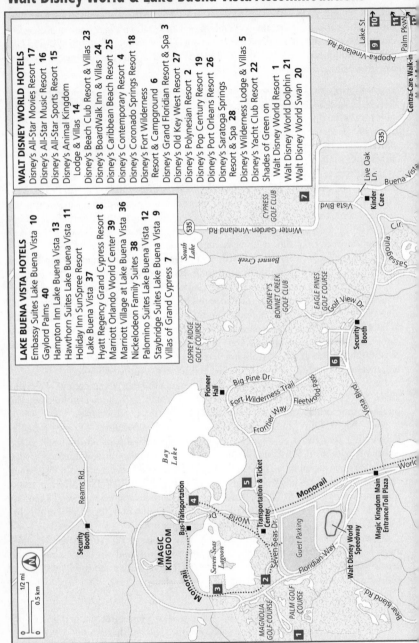

WALT DISNEY WORLD HOTELS

Disney's All-Star Movies Resort 17
Disney's All-Star Music Resort 16
Disney's All-Star Sports Resort 15
Disney's Animal Kingdom
 Lodge & Villas 14
Disney's Beach Club Resort & Villas 23
Disney's BoardWalk Inn & Villas 24
Disney's Caribbean Beach Resort 25
Disney's Contemporary Resort 4
Disney's Coronado Springs Resort 18
Disney's Fort Wilderness
 Resort & Campground 6
Disney's Grand Floridian Resort & Spa 3
Disney's Old Key West Resort 27
Disney's Polynesian Resort 2
Disney's Pop Century Resort 19
Disney's Port Orleans Resort 26
Disney's Saratoga Springs
 Resort & Spa 28
Disney's Wilderness Lodge & Villas 5
Disney's Yacht Club Resort 22
Shades of Green on
 Walt Disney World Resort 1
Walt Disney World Dolphin 21
Walt Disney World Swan 20

LAKE BUENA VISTA HOTELS

Embassy Suites Lake Buena Vista 10
Gaylord Palms 40
Hampton Inn Lake Buena Vista 13
Hawthorn Suites Lake Buena Vista 11
Holiday Inn SunSpree Resort
 Lake Buena Vista 37
Hyatt Regency Grand Cypress Resort 8
Marriott Orlando World Center 39
Marriott Village at Lake Buena Vista 36
Nickelodeon Family Suites 38
Palomino Suites Lake Buena Vista 12
Staybridge Suites Lake Buena Vista 9
Villas of Grand Cypress 7

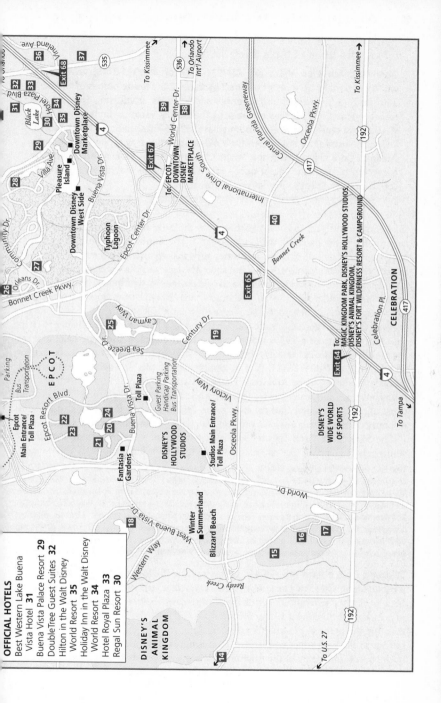

OFFICIAL HOTELS

Best Western Lake Buena
Vista Hotel **31**
Buena Vista Palace Resort **29**
DoubleTree Guest Suites **32**
Hilton in the Walt Disney
World Resort **35**
Holiday Inn in the Walt Disney
World Resort **34**
Hotel Royal Plaza **33**
Regal Sun Resort **30**

Tips   The Beach Club's Baby Sister

Disney's **Beach Club Villas** (© **407/934-7639** or 407/934-2175; www.disney
world.com) make up a resort inspired by Cape May seaside homes of the early
20th century, with clapboard exteriors and intricate wood trim. The 280-unit
resort, opened in 2002, is a member of the Disney Vacation Club, which rents
studios and one- and two-bedroom villas ($325–$490 studios, $435–$1,140 villas) to mainstream guests when their owners are not staying on the property.
Amenities are shared with the Yacht Club and Beach Club resorts, with the
exception of the Villas' quiet pool—which is accessible only to villa guests. It,
too, is close to Epcot's International Gateway.

close enough to Epcot to allow you to walk to the park, though most guests prefer to
take the ferry (the parks are workout enough!). The shipwreck at Stormalong Bay (a
huge free-form swimming pool and water park that sprawls over 3 acres) invites you
to explore its decks, climb around, and slide 230 feet into the water waiting below. It
includes a stretch of sandy beach, sand-bottom pools, whirlpools, and waterslides
(including a toddler slide, so no one misses out). Room views range from the pool
(more expensive) to the parking lot. Some units have balconies.

Note: Both the Beach Club and the Yacht Club (see below) offer the chance to charter a reproduction of a 1930s mahogany runabout to cruise **Crescent Lake** and see
Epcot's **IllumiNations** fireworks display ($220–$275, plus tax, for up to 12 people for
45-min.; © **407/824-2621**). A new option, specifically for ages 4 to 10 (potty
trained, of course), is the **Albatross Treasure Cruise** ($28 per child), which has kids
following clues and searching for treasure while listening to the Legend of the Albatross. Lunch is included, and the kids get to split the booty. Reservations are highly
recommended, as the cruise sails only on Mondays, Wednesdays, and Fridays.

The **Sandcastle Club** features activities, entertainment, a meal, and a snack for
youngsters ($11 per hr. per child; ages 4–12; 4:30pm–midnight).

1800 Epcot Resorts Blvd. (off Buena Vista Dr.; P.O. Box 10000), Lake Buena Vista, FL 32830-0100. © **407/934-7639**
or 407/934-8000. Fax 407/934-3850. www.disneyworld.com. 583 units. $325–$710 double; $445–$2,400 concierge;
$560–$2,400 suite. Extra person $25. Children 17 and under stay free in parent's room. Rollaway beds not available;
cribs free. AE, DC, DISC, MC, V. Free self-parking; valet parking $10. Take I-4 east to Exit 67, Hwy. 536/Epcot Center
Dr. Follow signs to WDW, then to the resort. Pets $13 a night. **Amenities:** 2 restaurants; grill; 4 lounges; 2 outdoor
heated pools; kids' pool; 2 lighted tennis courts; Jacuzzi; watersports equipment; children's club; arcade; playground;
WDW Transportation System, transportation for a fee to non-Disney theme parks; business center; salon; 24-hr. room
service; babysitting; laundry; nonsmoking rooms. *In room:* A/C, TV, dataport, Wi-Fi, minibar, fridge, hair dryer, iron, safe.

Disney's BoardWalk Inn 🎈🎈🎈   Disney's plush 1940s-style "seaside" resort, set on
45 acres along Crescent Lake, near Epcot, is worth a visit even if you don't stay here.
It's a great place to recapture a little bit of yesterday, whether that means kicking back
in a rocker overlooking a village green or prowling the shops, restaurants, and clubs
that line the property's ¼-mile BoardWalk. After the sun goes down, the BoardWalk
springs to life with street performers, food vendors, and midway games, reminiscent
of the hustle and bustle of the Atlantic City boardwalk in its heyday. *Note:* The activity on Disney's BoardWalk reaches well into the late-evening hours, as does the noise,
which carries to the rooms overlooking it.

Some of the Cape Cod–style rooms have balconies; the corner units offer a bit more
space. At night, the rooms overlooking the BoardWalk, mostly those in the center,

enjoy a view of Epcot's fireworks display. The priciest rooms overlook the BoardWalk or pool; the less expensive ones overlook the parking lot but are sheltered from the BoardWalk noise (good if your family is full of light sleepers). Hang on to your swimsuit if you hit the pool's famous—or infamous, depending on how you look at it—**200-foot "keister coaster" waterslide,** which is very popular with kids. (Tinier tots will appreciate the spraying elephant fountains.) The Inn isn't necessarily the best place for those with really young kids, though you'll see plenty of them here. Families with older kids and teens (who will like the posh surroundings, the Coney Island atmosphere of the BoardWalk, and the ESPN club) will do just fine.

Note: There is no kids' club at this hotel, so if you want to hit the BoardWalk's clubs after dark, you can hire an in-room babysitter or have the kids head to the facilities at the Beach Club (keep in mind that the kids' club is open only until midnight).

2101 N. Epcot Resorts Blvd. (off Buena Vista Dr.; P.O. Box 10000), Lake Buena Vista, FL 32830-1000. © **407/ 934-7639** or 407/939-5100. Fax 407/934-5150. www.disneyworld.com. 378 units. $325–$600 double; $455–$2,629 concierge; $610–$2,620 suite. Extra person $25. Children 17 and under stay free in parent's room. Rollaway beds not available, cribs free. AE, DC, DISC, MC, V. Free self-parking, valet parking $10. Take I-4 east to Exit 67, Hwy. 536/Epcot Center Dr. Follow signs to WDW, then to the resort. Pets $13 a night. **Amenities:** 4 restaurants; groceries; grill; 2 lounges; 3 clubs; 3 outdoor heated pools; kids' pool; 2 lighted tennis courts; croquet; health club; children's activity center; 2 arcades; playground; concierge; WDW Transportation System, transportation to non-Disney parks for a fee; business center; shopping arcade; 24-hr. room service; babysitting; laundry; nonsmoking rooms; concierge-level rooms. *In room:* A/C, TV, dataport, Wi-Fi, fridge, hair dryer, iron, safe.

Disney's BoardWalk Villas ★★★
Located on the same site as the BoardWalk Inn, the villas are an out-of-the-mainstream option that may make sense for larger families or those traveling in groups. Sold as timeshares, they're also rented to traditional tourists. Accommodations range from standard-size studios to one-, two-, and three-bedroom villas (the latter with 2,100 sq. ft. and beds for 12). Most have a balcony or patio and the same trimmings as the BoardWalk Inn, above. (They also share amenities.) Studios have kitchenettes, while villas have full kitchens, a fabulous feature for those who want to prepare food or formula for the kids. The service is first-rate; the location near Epcot is convenient; and the spacious villas are just the ticket for larger families or families traveling together.

2101 N. Epcot Resorts Blvd. (off Buena Vista Dr.; P.O. Box 10000), Lake Buena Vista, FL 32830-1000. © **407/934-7639** or 407/939-5100. Fax 407/934-5150. www.disneyworld.com. 520 units. $325–$490 studio; $435–$2,155 villa. Extra person $25. Children 17 and under stay free in parent's room. Rollaway beds not available, cribs free. AE, DC, DISC, MC, V. Free self-parking, valet parking $10. Take I-4 east to Exit 67, Hwy. 536/Epcot Center Dr. Follow signs to WDW, then to the resort. Pets $13 a night. **Amenities:** 4 restaurants; groceries; grill; 2 lounges; 3 clubs; 2 outdoor heated pools; kids' pool; 2 lighted tennis courts; croquet; health club; Jacuzzi; children's activity center; 2 arcades; playground; concierge; WDW Transportation System, transportation to non-Disney parks for a fee; business center; shopping arcade; 24-hr. room service; babysitting; laundry; nonsmoking rooms. *In room:* A/C, TV, dataport, Wi-Fi, kitchenette or full kitchen, fridge, coffeemaker, hair dryer, iron, safe, microwave.

⸤Tips⸥ Sink Space

Disney's resort rooms have notoriously cramped bathrooms (shutting the door with one person standing inside can require the skills of a contortionist). Bathing kids will be something of a challenge as well. The good news: Most rooms sport double sinks, usually set in a small dressing area outside the bathroom. (All-Star resorts however, have only singles.) So while you may bang your shin on the shower, you won't have to wait in line to brush your teeth.

Disney's Contemporary Resort ✮✮   If location is one of your priorities, it's hard to beat this Disney resort, which is right beside the Magic Kingdom and one of only three resorts on the **monorail** system (the Grand Floridian and Polynesian are the others). The Contemporary offers great views of the Magic Kingdom and Seven Seas Lagoon from its west side and Bay Lake on its east. This 15-story, concrete A-frame dates to WDW's infancy, and a complete renovation in 1999 was only the first phase of its restoration process, which has once again resumed. The result will bring the resort in line with the others in the same class and category (hence the upgraded star rating from previous years).

In 2006, guest rooms were completely redecorated to reflect an upscale-Asian-retro-yet-contemporary flair. While it sounds complicated, it looks amazing! The decor will definitely appeal to adults (the flatscreen TVs are fabulous, and the new color scheme is very appealing), and with kids in tow, you'll appreciate the rounded corners, kid-proof locks on the sliding doors (remember how high up you are here), and breakables placed high above a little one's reach. On the plus side, the rooms can fit up to five people instead of the usual four (though space will be tight). In 2007, additional renovations included major improvements to the Concourse (the resort's main shopping and dining area, located on the fourth floor) and the demolition of the North Garden Wing (though no official word has been released regarding the newly created space). In 2008, a new full-service restaurant, the Wave, is slated to open, and a quick-service on-the-go eatery will replace the Concourse Steakhouse. The pool, while less spectacular than most others at WDW, is quite large and sports a wading pool for toddlers and a small sandy beach just off to the left. Other kids' facilities include a playground with a good-size sandbox and a pretty decent arcade.

There's plenty for kids here, including **Chef Mickey's** (p. 171), but the modern upscale theme makes it a better choice for families with children of at least school age. Riding the monorail through the resort—yes, it goes straight *through*—is something kids of all ages will find very cool. If you do bunk here, request an upper-floor or Tower room for the best views and a tad more quiet; the lower-floor rooms are more exposed to public areas and the monorail.

4600 N. World Dr. (P.O. Box 10000), Lake Buena Vista, FL 32830-1000. © **407/934-7639** or 407/824-1000. Fax 407/824-3539. www.disneyworld.com. 1,008 units. $270–$500 double; $515–$2,755 concierge; $885–$2,755 suite. Extra person $25. Children 17 and under stay free in parent's room. Rollaway beds not available, cribs free. AE, DC, DISC, MC, V. Free self-parking, valet parking $10. Take I-4 east to Exit 67, Hwy. 536/Epcot Center Dr. Follow signs to WDW, then to the resort. Pets $13 a night. **Amenities:** 3 restaurants (contemporary, New American, buffet); food court; 2 lounges; outdoor heated pool; kids' pool; fitness center; Jacuzzi; watersports equipment; kids' club; arcade; playground; concierge; WDW Transportation System, transportation to non-Disney parks for a fee; business center; salon; 24-hr. room service; babysitting; laundry; nonsmoking rooms; concierge-level rooms. *In room:* A/C, TV, dataport, Wi-Fi, fridge, hair dryer, iron, safe.

Disney's Grand Floridian Resort & Spa ✮✮✮ *Moments*   From the moment you step into the opulent, five-story, domed lobby of this Victorian-themed resort, you'll feel as if you've slipped back to an era that started in the late 19th century and lasted through the Roaring '20s. Close to the Magic Kingdom, the property is one of three on the **monorail** system. While a romantic choice for couples, especially honeymooners, who like luxuriating in the first-class spa and health club—one of the best in WDW—those with tots in tow should fear not. It's a surprisingly appropriate place for families (no matter what age), thanks to its numerous amenities and special options for kids.

Moments A Piece of Yesterday, Today

The *Grand 1*, the Grand Floridian's luxurious 52-foot yacht, is available for hire for up to 18 passengers. It cruises Seven Seas Lagoon and Bay Lake, where in the mornings you can catch a glimpse of the spouting geyser at Disney's Wilderness Lodge, and in the evenings you can watch as the Magic Kingdom's Wishes fireworks display sparkles in the sky above. Voyages run $450 per hour, including the charter fee, captain, and deckhand. Private dining and butler service are available at an additional cost. Call © 407/824-2682 for details.

The inviting Victorian-style rooms overlook the garden, pool, courtyard, or Seven Seas Lagoon. The standard rooms are large enough to fit five; the dormer and Lodge Tower rooms can fit only four. Cribs, highchairs, and playpens are free of charge to guests, though you may have trouble fitting them in your room all at once. If you ask in advance, your kids will even find child-size bathrobes waiting for them in your room.

The main pool here is nice enough, but it's the newer kids' pool that will grab your attention. Off to the side, in its own area near the stretch of sandy beach, lifeguards stand watch as kids splash in the waterfalls, slide down the rocky waterslide, or sink their toes in the sand. A zero entry makes it easy for younger kids to get in on the fun, though they may be more amused with the nearby dancing water. A neat little shop sells towels, swimsuits, beach toys, and so much more. Kids can get their hair wrapped or make chalk drawings on the concrete. A snack bar with a pretty good menu is also close by.

The **Mouseketeer Clubhouse** features activities, entertainment, a meal, and a snack ($11 per hr. per child; 2-hr. minimum; ages 4–12; 4:30pm–midnight). Older children might enjoy a chance to partake of a formal afternoon tea, which costs between $5.95 and $26 (depending on your choice of tea) per person (an a la carte menu is available as well) and is served in the Garden View Lounge from 3 to 6pm (be sure to call © **407/WDW-DINE** to reserve a spot well in advance).

If you prefer the royal treatment, the **Princess Tea Party** may be more your style. Most days (schedules vary, so call ahead), you and your little princess can enjoy tea for two, princess cakes, and a personal visit from Princess Aurora (aka Sleeping Beauty). Girls ages 3 to 11 receive a My Disney Doll dressed to match Aurora, along with their very own ribbon tiara, silver link bracelet, scrapbook set, and more. Most little girls come in costume—as their favorite princess, of course—as this is a dressy affair. This extravagant experience has a price tag to match, at $225 for one child and one adult. An additional adult pays $75, while an extra child pays $150.

In addition to other special activities, the hotel offers a trio of **Grand Adventure** programs for young children. On Disney's **Pirate Cruise Adventure,** potty-trained children ages 4 to 10 depart from the Grand Floridian Marina to visit exotic "ports of call," where they follow clues and collect buried treasure. Most kids will have a jolly good time. It's offered Monday, Wednesday, and Thursday from 9:30 to 11:30am; the $28 price tag includes lunch. For information on the **Wonderland Tea Party** and **Grand Adventures in Cooking,** the resort's two culinary-themed programs, see "Cooking for Kids" (p. 152).

4401 Floridian Way (P.O. Box 10000), Lake Buena Vista, FL 32830-1000. © **407/934-7639** or 407/824-3000. Fax 407/824-3186. www.disneyworld.com. 867 units. $375–$710 double; $505–$2,795 concierge; $670–$2,795 suite. Extra person $25. Children 17 and under stay free in parent's room. Rollaway beds not available, cribs free. AE, DC,

DISC, MC, V. Free self-parking, valet parking $10. Take I-4 east to Exit 67, Hwy. 536/Epcot Center Dr. Follow signs to WDW, then to the resort. Pets $13 a night. **Amenities:** 5 restaurants; grill; 3 lounges; 2 outdoor heated pools; beach area; kids' pool; 2 lighted tennis courts; health club; spa; watersports equipment; children's center; arcade; playground; concierge; car-rental desk; WDW Transportation System, transportation to non-Disney parks for a fee; business center; shopping arcade; salon; 24-hr. room service; babysitting; laundry; nonsmoking rooms; concierge-level rooms. *In room:* A/C, TV, dataport, Wi-Fi, minibar, fridge, hair dryer, iron, safe.

Disney's Old Key West Resort ★★★   An understated theme (at least by Disney standards) makes the Old Key West a good choice for those who prefer palms and pastels over Peter Pan and princesses. The sheer size of this resort, however, means that Disney transportation can be slow going at times; a rental car may be in order here.

Located between Epcot and Downtown Disney West Side, this resort offers some of the quietest, homiest rooms on WDW property. Architecturally mirroring Key West at the turn of the 20th century, Old Key West is affiliated with the Disney Vacation Club—Disney's version of a timeshare—but the units are rented to visitors when not being used by owners. The 156-acre complex has tree-lined brick walkways edged by white picket fences. A tremendous sandcastle, a waterslide hidden inside, now keeps the giant pail and shovel (good for climbing on) company in the pool area. With a sandy beach, bike and boat rentals, an activity room full of games, an arcade, movie rentals, playgrounds, pools, and numerous other recreational activities, you may have difficulty finding time for the parks. All accommodations sport balconies or patios, and all have kitchens or kitchenettes. The extra space and the kitchen facilities make this a good bet for large families. The villas also have whirlpool tubs and can sleep up to eight (in a two-bedroom villa) or 12 (in a grand villa, which measures 2,202 sq. ft.). There's no child care available on the premises, but you can use the kids' clubs at other Disney resorts. A variety of unique activities for both kids and adults is scheduled daily.

1510 N. Cove Rd. (off Community Dr.; P.O. Box 10000), Lake Buena Vista, FL 32830-1000. ✆ **407/934-7639** or 407/827-7700. Fax 407/827-7710. www.disneyworld.com. 761 units. $285–$410 studio; $380–$875 1- and 2-bedroom villa; $1,170–$1,645 grand villa. Call for rates for extra adults. Children 17 and under stay free in parent's room. Rollaway beds not available, cribs free. AE, DC, DISC, MC, V. Free self-parking. Take I-4 east to Exit 67, Hwy. 536/Epcot Center Dr. Follow signs to WDW, then to the resort. Pets $13 a night. **Amenities:** Restaurant (American); groceries; 4 outdoor heated pools; kids' pool with sand playground; 3 tennis courts (2 lighted); Jacuzzi; sauna; watersports equipment; 2 game rooms; scheduled daily activities; WDW Transportation System, transportation to non-Disney parks for a fee; massage; babysitting; laundry; nonsmoking rooms. *In room:* A/C, TV, dataport, kitchen (villa) or kitchenette (studio), fridge, microwave, coffeemaker, hair dryer.

Disney's Polynesian Resort ★★   Just south of the Magic Kingdom, the 25-acre Polynesian Resort bears some similarity to the South Pacific (torchlit walkways, the distant sound of beating drums, tropical foliage, luaus, and waterfalls), but there's no denying this is Disney World, thanks to Mickey's minions scurrying hither and yon. (And the **monorail,** which stops here, is a dead giveaway as well.) The extensive play areas, themed swimming pools, character dining, and dinner show make it a good

---

Tips **Don't Be Left Fuming: Disney's Gone Smoke-Free**

As of June 1, 2007, Disney Resorts became smoke-free. Smoking is now banned at all of the Disney-owned and -operated resorts—that means it's prohibited in guest rooms, indoor public areas, and on balconies, as well as in other public areas. Those wishing to light up will have to head outdoors to one of only a few select designated smoking areas.

Tips Surfing the Net in Walt Disney World

All WDW resorts have high-speed Internet access; some even offer Wi-Fi capability. To get access, there's a charge of $10, good for a 24-hour period (starting the minute you sign up). Depending on how often you need (or want) to use the service, you can cut costs a bit by signing up late enough in the morning that you can check your e-mail or surf the Web on two separate days while paying for only one 24-hour period.

choice for those traveling with kids (who usually find the resort agreeably exotic). The Volcano pool, featuring a waterslide, underwater jets, and nearby dancing water, is a major hit with children, though it can get crowded. Small watercraft can be rented nearby as well. The beach is lined with canvas cabanas, hammocks, and big swings overlooking the 200-acre lagoon.

Extensive renovations include a reconfigured lobby, though it still includes all the same great shops and eateries, with some new additions tossed in. Still reflective of the islands, the accommodations now feature muted earth-tone colors and stylish new space-conscious furnishings that allow for additional room, so you can really spread out and relax. Upgraded amenities, including flatscreen TVs and small refrigerators, give the place a far more upscale feel than before. Most units (spread across three-story "longhouses") sleep up to five. If your kids are young and don't have much stamina, you might want to request a room close to the Great Ceremonial House, where the resort's restaurants, shops, and monorail station are located. Some rooms offer child-pleasing views of Cinderella Castle (for a price, of course), so request your desired view when making your reservation.

Kids who enroll in the **Neverland Club** get activities, entertainment, movies, free video games, a meal, and a snack ($11 per hr. per child; ages 4–12; 4pm–midnight). Advance reservations for the kids' club are an absolute must and can be made by calling ✆ **407/WDW-DINE.**

Also check out the reviews of the family-friendly **Spirit of Aloha Dinner Show** (p. 324) and **'Ohana** (p. 155).

600 Seven Seas Dr. (P.O. Box 10000), Lake Buena Vista, FL 32830-1000. ✆ **407/934-7639** or 407/824-2000. Fax 407/824-3174. www.disneyworld.com. 853 units. $340–$690 double; $480–$2,810 concierge; $590–$2,810 suite. Extra person $25. Children 17 and under stay free in parent's room. Rollaway beds not available, cribs free. AE, DC, DISC, MC, V. Free self-parking, valet parking $10. Take I-4 east to Exit 67, Hwy. 536/Epcot Center Dr. Follow signs to WDW, then to the resort. Pets $13 a night. **Amenities:** Restaurant (Pacific Rim); cafe; 2 lounges; 2 outdoor heated pools; kids' pool; beach; watersports equipment; children's club; arcade; playground; concierge; WDW Transportation System; transportation to non-Disney parks for a fee; shopping arcade; 24-hr. room service; babysitting; laundry; non-smoking rooms; concierge-level rooms. *In room:* A/C, TV, dataport, fridge, hair dryer, iron, safe.

Disney's Saratoga Springs Resort & Spa ✿

The first phase of this Disney Vacation Club resort opened back in May 2004, its second phase in 2005, and its third in 2007, bringing the room count to a staggering 828—making it the largest Vacation Club resort to date. The property transports guests back in time to the heyday of upstate New York's 19th-century resorts. It resembles—with a little imagination—the resort town of Saratoga Springs, thus you'll find lavish gardens, Victorian architecture, and bubbling springs. The main pool brings to mind its namesake's natural springs, with "healing" waters spilling over the rocky landscaping. The renowned spa offers an array of services and treatments meant to invoke the healing powers of Saratoga's springs themselves. Accommodations resemble those of the other Disney Vacation Club properties (the grand villas stand out, however, as they're slightly more impressive than their predecessors), making the resort a good choice for larger families or families traveling together. Units range from studios that sleep 4 to grand villas that sleep up to 12. Families with older children and teens will appreciate the location, a stone's throw from Downtown Disney (and only a short ferry ride across the lake) and all of its offerings. Getting to the parks, however, will require a bit more effort.

1960 Broadway St., Lake Buena Vista, FL 32830. ✆ **407/827-1100** or 407/934-3400. Fax 407/827-1151. www.disney world.com. 828 units. $285–$410 studio; $380–$1,645 villa. Extra person no charge. Children 17 and under stay free in parent's room. Rollaway beds not available, cribs free. AE, DC, DISC, MC, V. Free self-parking. Take I-4 east to Exit 68, Hwy. 535/Apopka–Vineland Rd., turn left onto Hotel Plaza Blvd., turn right onto Buena Vista Dr., follow signs to the resort. Pets $13 a night. **Amenities:** Restaurant; lounge; themed heated pool; kids' interactive pool area; golf; tennis; health club; spa; biking; boating; playground; arcade; WDW Transportation System, transportation to non-Disney parks for a fee; limited room service; babysitting; laundry; barbecue areas; limited grocery delivery; nonsmoking rooms. *In room:* A/C, TV, dataport, VCR (villas), full kitchen (villas), kitchenette (studios), fridge, microwave, hair dryer, iron, safe, washer/dryer (villas).

Disney's Yacht Club Resort 🐟🐟🐟   This resort is a cut above its sister, the Beach Club (see above), thanks to better rooms, views, service, and ambience. It's also geared more to adults and families with older children, given its far more upscale atmosphere, though young kids are catered to (this is Disney, after all). Epcot is a 10- to 15-minute walk from the front door, but you can save your energy for the parks by using the water taxi to the World Showcase's International Gateway. The theme is a turn-of-the-20th-century New England yacht club, and the atmosphere is posh, with fine leather furnishings, antique glass chandeliers, and brass accents adorning the lobby. The Yacht Club shares Stormalong Bay, a huge free-form, sand-bottom swimming pool and water park, with the Beach Club. It features a 230-foot waterslide, cleverly hidden within a shipwreck, and a special kids' pool area, 2 to 3 feet deep, for little ones.

Accommodations sleep up to five people, and most have balconies; views run from asphalt to Crescent Lake and the gardens. You would, however, have to be a contortionist to see the lake from some of the "water-view" rooms, so if this is a must, make sure that you request one with a direct view.

Note: The Yacht Club offers specialty cruises on **Crescent Lake,** including an **Illumi-Nations** fireworks excursion ($220–$275, plus tax, for 45 min.; ✆ **407/939-7529** or 407/939-2329). Older kids will likely enjoy the experience. A new option, specifically for kids 4 to 10 (who must be potty trained), is the **Albatross Treasure Cruise** ($28 per child). Kids follow clues and search for treasure while listening to the Legend of the Albatross. Lunch is included, and the kids get to split the booty. Reservations are highly recommended, as the cruise sails only on Mondays, Wednesdays, and Fridays.

There's no kids' club at the hotel, though guests can park their little ones at the Sandcastle Club at the Beach Club Resort next door.

1700 Epcot Resorts Blvd. (off Buena Vista Dr.; P.O. Box 10000), Lake Buena Vista, FL 32830-1000. ✆ **407/934-7639** or 407/934-7000. Fax 407/924-3450. www.disneyworld.com. 621 units. $325–$560 double; $445–$2,385 concierge; $590–$2,385 suite. Extra person $25. Children 17 and under stay free in parent's room. Rollaway beds not available, cribs free. AE, DC, DISC, MC, V. Free self-parking, valet parking $10. Take I-4 east to Exit 67, Hwy. 536/Epcot Center Dr. Follow signs to WDW, then to the resort. Pets $13 per night. **Amenities:** 2 restaurants; grill; lounge; 2 outdoor heated pools; kids' pool; 2 lighted tennis courts; Jacuzzi; watersports equipment; croquet; arcade; playground; concierge; WDW Transportation System, transportation to non-Disney parks for a fee; business center; shopping arcade; salon; 24-hr. room service; babysitting; laundry; nonsmoking rooms; concierge-level rooms. *In room:* A/C, TV, dataport, Wi-Fi, minibar, fridge, coffeemaker, iron, safe.

Walt Disney World Dolphin ✪✪   Most kids love the whimsical touch of architect Michael Graves, who designed this Starwood resort and its sister, the Walt Disney World Swan (below). The Dolphin centers on a 27-story pyramid with two 11-story wings that are crowned by 56-foot twin dolphin sculptures that look more like the whale in *Pinocchio*. It's close to Epcot, next to Disney's BoardWalk, and right across the street from the Fantasia Gardens miniature golf courses. The resort's free-form sculpted grotto pool, with waterfalls, waterslide, rope bridge, and three secluded whirlpools, sprawls across 2 acres between the Dolphin and the Swan. It's a major hit with the young set.

Public areas are now far more avant-garde thanks to a recent (and complete) redesign that includes dramatic lighting, earth-tone color schemes, and chic upscale furnishings. Guest rooms, which offer views of the grounds and parts of Mickey's World, were all completely refurbished in 2004 to include 27-inch TVs and new decor. Corner units have a little more space. If traveling with small children, parents can request a free safety kit with outlet covers and nightlights. Unlike at the Disney-owned resorts, you can get a rollaway bed here, though space will be somewhat tight. You can also rent a fridge ($12 per night) or use the available minibar (for a $20 charge . . . ouch!). The good news is that the hotel's hefty resort fee has been abolished.

On check-in, young guests get a **Kids Passport** that entitles them to a free ice-cream cone or cup at the Dolphin Fountain or Splash Terrace restaurant after they have collected five stamps from various parts of the hotel, including restaurants, shops, and other facilities. Another nice touch for kids is the **Straight A Club;** if your child shows a report card filled with all As, he or she gets a Straight A cap (and, when they wear the cap, a free ice cream at the ice-cream parlor and a 20% discount on kids' meals at resort restaurants).

Kids enrolled in the supervised **Camp Dolphin** enjoy arts and crafts, movies, a video arcade, and dinner ($10 per hr. per child; ages 4–12; 5:30pm–midnight). Be sure to reserve a space well in advance by calling ✆ **407/934-4241.** Parents wishing to dine at Shula's Steak House, Todd English's Bluezoo, or II Mulino New York Trattoria without the kids along, or who wish to relax and enjoy services offered at the spa, are allowed up to two free hours of time at Camp Dolphin for their kids (one child admitted per adult entree or spa service purchased). The Dolphin and Swan also share a beach on Crescent Lake, the new Mandara Spa (with special programs designed specifically for teens), and a Body by Jake health club.

1500 Epcot Resorts Blvd. (off Buena Vista Dr.; P.O. Box 22653), Lake Buena Vista, FL 32830-2653. ✆ **888/828-8850** or 407/934-4000. Fax 407/934-4099. www.swananddolphin.com or www.disneyworld.com. 1,509 units. $369–$529 double; $785–$1,525 suite. Extra person $25. Children 17 and under stay free in parent's room. Rollaway beds

---

(Tips) When a WDW Property Is Not a WDW Property

There are nine "official" Disney hotels that aren't owned by Mickey's stock-holders. But there are a couple of asterisks. Walt Disney World Swan and Walt Disney World Dolphin have Uncle Walt's name, and they're on mainstream WDW resort property, but they're not Disney-owned resorts, so we consider them "officials." The good news for you: You can get discounted room rates and other special offers at the Swan and Dolphin that you won't get at a Disney-owned resort.

$25/night, cribs free. AE, DC, DISC, MC, V. Self-parking $9, valet parking $16. Take I-4 east to Exit 67, Hwy. 536/Epcot Center Dr. Follow signs to WDW, then to the resort. Pets $13 a night. **Amenities:** 9 restaurants; grill; 2 lounges; 4 outdoor heated pools; 4 lighted tennis courts; health club; spa; watersports equipment; children's center; 2 game rooms; playground; concierge; car-rental desk; WDW Transportation System, transportation to non-Disney parks for a fee; shopping arcade; salon; 24-hr. room service; massage; babysitting; laundry; nonsmoking rooms; concierge-level rooms. *In room:* A/C, TV, Nintendo, dataport, minibar, hair dryer, iron, safe.

Walt Disney World Swan 🎭🎭   Not to be outdone by the huge dolphins at its sister property, this high-rise Starwood resort is topped with dual 45-foot swan statues and seashell fountains. It offers a good location—close to Epcot, Fantasia Gardens, and Disney BoardWalk's dining and nightlife—and a chance to be in the WDW mainstream without being quite so overwhelmed by mouse decor. It shares a beach, 3-acre pool area, health club, spa, a number of restaurants, and other trimmings with the Dolphin (see above). Note that the beach next to the pool offers a great view of Epcot's IllumiNations fireworks.

As with the Dolphin, the Swan's lobby now sports a more modern decor—upscale and chic, no longer sugary sweet. Major renovations in 2004 included an upgrade of all guest rooms, which now sport Starwood's famous "Heavenly Beds" (the perfect thing to come home to after a busy day in the parks). Rooms here are just a tad smaller than those at the Dolphin. If you're traveling with young kids, ask at check-in for a safety kit, which includes outlet covers and a nightlight. Alas, though the Swan and the Dolphin have ditched the awful resort fee, they still levy a hefty refrigerator rental charge (don't use the minibar to store necessary medications; it's not cold enough!).

Kids staying at the Swan can enroll in the supervised Camp Dolphin program next door at the Dolphin and are eligible for the Kids Passport and Straight A programs as well.

1200 Epcot Resorts Blvd. (off Buena Vista Dr.; P.O. Box 22786), Lake Buena Vista, FL 32830-2786. ℂ **888/828-8850** or 407/934-3000. Fax 407/934-4499. www.swandolphin.com or www.disneyworld.com. 758 units. $369–$529 double; $995–$1,770 suite. Extra person $25. Children 17 and under stay free in parent's room. Rollaway beds $25/night, cribs free. AE, DC, DISC, MC, V. Self-parking $9, valet parking $16. Take I-4 east to Exit 67, Hwy. 536/Epcot Center Dr. Follow signs to WDW, then to the resort. Pets $13 a night. **Amenities:** 9 restaurants; grill; 2 lounges; 4 outdoor heated pools; 4 lighted tennis courts; health club; watersports equipment; children's center; 2 game rooms; playground; concierge; car-rental desk; WDW Transportation System, transportation to non-Disney parks for a fee; shopping arcade; salon; 24-hr. room service; massage; babysitting; laundry; nonsmoking rooms; concierge-level rooms. *In room:* A/C, TV, Nintendo, dataport, minibar, hair dryer, iron, safe.

EXPENSIVE

Disney's Animal Kingdom Lodge 🎭🎭🎭   This resort has the feel of an African game-reserve lodge, complete with thatched roof, tremendous mud fireplace, and ornate shield chandeliers. Not surprisingly, this is the closest you can stay to Animal Kingdom, but almost everything else on WDW property is quite a distance away. Location aside, this is a great place for families, who will appreciate not only the resort's more exotic inhabitants, but also the unique array of kids' activities (a lot of them quite educational, including nightly storytelling by the fire, sing-alongs, and more).

Rooms at the lodge follow a traditional *kraal* (horseshoe) design that gives patient guests a view of the birds, giraffes, gazelles, and other African animals that graze on the 30-acre savanna. Most kids—and adults, for that matter—will find the notion of waking up to a giraffe outside their window quite cool. (Not all rooms have savanna views—which cost a bit more—but the scenery is available at no extra charge through the large floor-to-ceiling windows in the lobby, and from the trail behind the pool.) Typical rooms are slightly smaller than those at Disney's other "deluxe" resorts, but the distinctive theme and spectacular surroundings are unparalleled, making a stay here well worth the slightly tighter squeeze. "Mosquito netting" curtains, balconies, and other neat details in the decor continue the theme throughout the rooms, and all come with animal-identification checklists (so your kids can keep track of their sightings). If you do get a room overlooking the savanna, be sure that your children understand that dropping food and other items off the balconies to the animals is strictly *verboten*. For those staying in concierge-level rooms, venturing beyond the main path of the savanna is allowed if you're one of the lucky few to sign up for an exclusive guided excursion of Kilimanjaro Safaris (at Disney's Animal Kingdom) and provided you are willing to pay a bit more for the privilege.

The 9,000-square-foot pool has a waterslide, a wading area for young children, and a good view of the savanna. **Simba's Clubhouse,** the kids' program, offers activities, entertainment, a meal, and a snack ($11 per hr. per child; ages 4–12; 4:30pm–midnight). Call © **407/WDW-DINE** well in advance to reserve a space for your child. **Bush Camp,** now available to guests staying at any of the official WDW resorts, allows kids 6 to 14 an opportunity to learn about African culture through a variety of unique activities (including games, arts and crafts, and more). There's even a chance to safari out on the savanna. The program is offered Saturdays from 1 to 4pm and costs $70 per child, of which $20 will be donated to the Wildlife Conservation Fund. Reservations and a credit card deposit are required; call © **407/WDW-PLAY.** There are also daily **Junior Researcher** (animal familiarization) and **Junior Chef of the Day** programs, along with a long list of activities that are free for children staying at the lodge. The resort's programs and activities are generally geared to children ages 4 to 12; if you're interested, ask for details at check-in. All in all, this is the best of the Disney properties when it comes to providing both an educational and an entertaining environment for kids.

At press time, construction of the **Villas at Disney's Animal Kingdom Lodge** were well underway, with the fifth and sixth floors of the existing resort already converted to Vacation Club Villas. Additional villas are being built adjacent to the existing lodge, a project slated for completion in 2009. The expansion is said to include a new full-service restaurant, themed pool and water-play island, retail shops, and recreational facilities.

Warning: Because of animal-safety issues, the resort doesn't allow balloons of any sort into the rooms. You will be forced to check yours upon entry and won't get it back until departure, so to avoid upsetting little ones, do yourself a favor and don't buy one for them at the theme parks.

2901 Osceola Pkwy., Bay Lake, FL 32830. © **407/934-7639** or 407/938-3000. Fax 407/939-4799. www.disney world.com. 1,293 units. $225–$475 double; $335–$2,820 concierge; $705–$2,820 suite; $265–$560 studio; $375–$2,155 villa. Extra person $25. Children 17 and under stay free in parent's room. Rollaway beds not available, cribs free. AE, DC, DISC, MC, V. Free self-parking, valet parking $10. Take I-4 east to Exit 67, Hwy. 536/Epcot Center Dr. Follow signs to WDW, then to the resort. Pets $13 a night. **Amenities:** 2 restaurants (African, American); lounge; outdoor heated pool; kids' pool; health club; children's center; arcade; playground; concierge; WDW Transportation System, transportation to non-Disney parks for a fee; shopping arcade; limited room service; babysitting; laundry; nonsmoking rooms; concierge-level rooms. *In room:* A/C, TV, dataport, fridge, hair dryer, iron, safe.

Disney's Wilderness Lodge ⭐⭐⭐   The geyser out back, the mammoth stone hearth in the lobby, and bunk beds for the kids are just a few reasons this resort is a family favorite. The building looks like a rustic national park lodge, in part because it's patterned after the one at Yellowstone. Surrounded by 56 acres of oaks and pines, it offers a remote, woodsy setting that can be a plus but also a drawback: It's more difficult to access other areas via the WDW Transportation System, because the bus and water taxi are the only ways to get in and out (unless you have a car, which I would recommend if you're staying here).

The comfy rooms offer two queen beds or a queen and a set of bunk beds (which have side rails). The deluxe rooms are an especially good deal for families, as they have a seating area with a pullout couch, TV, and refrigerator that's separated from the main bedroom by French doors—perfect if parents want a little privacy after the kids are in bed. If a view is important, ask for a room that looks out onto the woods.

The aforementioned geyser "blows" periodically throughout the day and is a hit with kids. The lodge also has an immense swimming area, fed by a thundering waterfall whose water flows in from the "hot springs" in the lobby (though the waterslide here is one of the shortest). The kids' program, **Cub's Den,** includes activities, entertainment, movies, video games, a meal, and a snack ($11 per hr. per child; ages 4–12; 4:30pm–midnight). Call ✆ **407/WDW-DINE** for advance reservations, which are strongly suggested.

The 181 units at the **Villas at Disney's Wilderness Lodge** were added in 2000. This is another Disney Vacation Club timeshare property (others include the Board-Walk Villas, the Villas at Disney's Animal Kingdom, Old Key West, and Saratoga Springs) that rents vacant rooms, usually to larger groups and families. It offers a more upscale experience, although you get less kitchen space here than in Old Key West. The one- and two-bedroom villas have 727 and 1,080 square feet, respectively.

Note: If you have a budding engineer in your party, check out **Wonders of the Lodge,** a free tour touting the resort's architecture, offered Wednesday through Saturday at 9am. Most kids, however, will probably find it boring. The lodge does offer a special family option that both kids and adults will enjoy: the **Flag Family** program. If you're selected, the entire family can traipse up to the Wilderness Lodge's roof in the morning (times vary, so ask) and raise the American flag that flies over the resort. You'll get a picture, a certificate, and a fabulous view. If you're interested, ask at the front desk upon check-in.

901 W. Timberline Dr. (on the southwest shore of Bay Lake just east of the Magic Kingdom; P.O. Box 10000), Lake Buena Vista, FL 32830-1000. ✆ 407/934-7639 or 407/938-4300. Fax 407/824-3232. www.disneyworld.com. 909 units. $225–$710 lodge; $315–$1,120 villa; $385–$1,330 concierge; $405–$1,330 suite. Extra person $25. Children 17 and under stay free in parent's room. Rollaway beds not available; cribs free. AE, DC, DISC, MC, V. Free self-parking, valet parking $10. Take I-4 east to Exit 67, Hwy. 536/Epcot Center Dr. Follow signs to WDW, then to the resort. Pets $13 a night. **Amenities:** 3 restaurants; 2 lounges; outdoor heated pool; kids' pool; 2 Jacuzzis; watersports equipment; children's center; arcade; playground; WDW Transportation System, transportation to non-Disney parks for a fee; limited room service; babysitting; laundry; nonsmoking rooms; concierge-level rooms. *In room:* A/C, TV, dataport, fridge, hair dryer, iron, safe.

MODERATE

Note: None of the moderate resorts has particularly good connections to the WDW Transportation System. Worse, the stops for the buses to the resorts outside the theme parks can be a long, long, long hike away from the main exits. If you opt to stay at one of these resorts, and you're lugging around young kids and the usual paraphernalia that goes along with them, I strongly suggest that you opt for a rental car.

Disney's Caribbean Beach Resort 🐾🐾   With its moderate pricing scheme and recreational activities, the Caribbean Beach is a great choice for families who don't need a lot of frills or amenities. The rooms are spread across five villages (all moderate WDW resorts have a similar general layout) of pastel buildings, each named for the islands of Aruba, Barbados, Jamaica, Martinique, and Trinidad (north and south). The lush tropical greenery adds a touch of island atmosphere. Parrot Cay, the resort's

---

Tips A Friendly Reminder

If you have a package delivered to your WDW resort from one of the WDW shops, it might be delivered directly to your room but also might get sent to your hotel's gift shop. If your package goes to the gift shop, a friendly reminder will be left via the telephone messaging service, stating that your package has arrived and is ready to be picked up.

---

main pool area and playground, is themed as an old Spanish-style fort, complete with water cannons, waterslides, and waterfalls—a popular spot with kids.

A new cruise option, specifically for kids 4 to 10 (they must be potty trained), is Disney's **Caribbean Pirate Adventure** ($28 per child). Kids will sail the high seas in search of pirate treasure as the captain regales the tale of Old Port Royale. Lunch is included. Reservations are highly recommended, as the cruise sails from the Caribbean ports on Sundays and Tuesdays only.

Note: The resort's restaurants and shops are located in the central Old Port Royale complex, quite a hike from most rooms; those in the Martinique and Trinidad North areas are closest. The nearest park is Disney's Hollywood Studios, but it can take 45 minutes to get there if you use the WDW Transportation System.

900 Cayman Way (off Buena Vista Dr.; P.O. Box 10000), Lake Buena Vista, FL 32830-1000. ℂ 407/934-7639 or 407/934-3400. Fax 407/934-3288. www.disneyworld.com. 2,112 units. $145–$225 double. Extra person $15. Children 17 and under stay free in parent's room. Rollaway beds not available; cribs free. AE, DC, DISC, MC, V. Free self-parking. Take I-4 east to Exit 67, Hwy. 536/Epcot Center Dr. Follow signs to WDW, then to the resort. Pets $13 a night. **Amenities:** Restaurant; food court; large outdoor heated pool; 6 smaller pools in the villages; kids' pool; Jacuzzi; watersports equipment; arcade; 3 playgrounds; WDW Transportation System, transportation to non-Disney parks for a fee; limited room service; babysitting; laundry; nonsmoking rooms. *In room:* A/C, TV, dataport, fridge, hair dryer, iron, safe.

Disney's Coronado Springs Resort ✿   Here's another clone of the Disney moderate class. The American Southwestern theme carries through four- and five-story hacienda-style buildings in shades of pink and desert-sand stucco, with terra-cotta tile roofs and shaded courtyards, all of which surrounds a 15-acre lake. As with most WDW properties, it has an above-par pool, in this case inspired by the Maya ruins of Mexico, featuring a tremendous Maya temple with cascading water and a twisting waterslide (watch out for the spitting jaguar). The children's pool has a spouting fountain. Keeping with the theme (which most kids adore), the playground has an archaeological dig site. Because this is a convention resort, you'll find extras including a barber and beauty shop, a variety of suites, and Wi-Fi access, among others.

Guest rooms are identical in size to those in the Caribbean Beach Resort; don't expect to fit more than one person into the bathroom at a time. Accommodations nearest the central public area, pool, and lobby tend to be noisier, but if you avoid them, you'll have a longer hike to the food court (one of the better ones in WDW) and shops. If a member of your party requires mobility-friendly accommodations, keep in mind that there are 99 such rooms at this resort. The nearest park is Disney's Animal Kingdom, but the Coronado is at the southwest corner of WDW and a good distance from much of the action.

1000 Buena Vista Dr. (near All-Star resorts and Blizzard Beach), Lake Buena Vista, FL 32830. ℂ **407/934-7639** or 407/939-1000. Fax 407/939-1003. www.disneyworld.com. 1,967 units. $145–$235 double; $340–$1,245 suite. Extra person $15. Children 17 and under stay free in parent's room. Rollaway beds not available; cribs free. AE, DC, DISC, MC, V. Free self-parking. Take I-4 east to Exit 67, Hwy. 536/Epcot Center Dr. Follow signs to WDW, then to the resort.

Pets $13 a night. **Amenities:** Restaurant; grill/food court; 2 lounges; 4 outdoor heated pools; kids' pool; health club; Jacuzzi; sauna; watersports equipment; 2 arcades; playground; WDW Transportation System, transportation to non-Disney parks for a fee; business center; salon; limited room service; massage; babysitting; laundry; nonsmoking rooms; rooms for those w/limited mobility. *In room:* A/C, TV, dataport, fridge, hair dryer, iron, safe.

Disney's Port Orleans Resort ✫✫ *(Value)*   One of my favorite choices for families, Port Orleans has the best location (just east of Epcot and Disney's Hollywood Studios), landscaping, and, perhaps, the coziest atmosphere of the resorts in this class. This Southern-style property is really a combination of two distinct resorts: the French Quarter and Riverside. The French Quarter offers magnolia trees, wrought-iron railings, cobblestone streets, and an idealistic vision of New Orleans's famous French Quarter. Riverside transports you back to Louisiana's Mississippi River towns, its accommodations housed in buildings resembling grand plantation homes and the "rustic" wooden shacks of the bayou.

Overall, Port Orleans offers some romantic spots and is relatively quiet, making it popular with couples, though the pools, playgrounds, and wide array of activities make it a hit with families as well. The recently refurbished Doubloon Lagoon pool in the French Quarter is a family favorite, with a waterslide that curves out of a sea serpent's mouth before entering the pool. The guest rooms and bathrooms (equivalent to all rooms at Disney's moderate resorts) are somewhat of a tight fit for four, though the Alligator Bayou rooms have a trundle bed that allows for an extra child, and the vanity areas now have privacy curtains. *Note:* All 1,080 rooms on the French Quarter side underwent a top-to-bottom refurbishment in 2004. The 2,048 rooms in Riverside were renovated in phases throughout 2005.

A new cruise option, specifically for kids 4 to 10 (they must be potty trained), is Disney's **Bayou Pirate Adventure** ($28 per child). Sailing along the river, kids will follow clues and search for treasure while listening to tales of the pirate captain John Lafitte. Lunch is included. Reservations are highly recommended, as the cruise sails from the Riverside Marina on Sundays, Tuesdays, and Thursdays only.

2201 Orleans Dr. (off Bonnet Creek Pkwy.; P.O. Box 10000), Lake Buena Vista, FL 32830-1000. ✆ **407/934-7639,** 407/934-5000 (French Quarter), or 407/934-6000 (Riverside). Fax 407/934-5353 (French Quarter) or 407/934-5777 (Riverside). www.disneyworld.com. 3,056 units. $145–$225 double. Extra person $15. Children 17 and under stay free in parent's room. Rollaway beds not available, cribs free. AE, DC, DISC, MC, V. Free self-parking. Take I-4 east to Exit 67, Hwy. 536/Epcot Center Dr. Follow signs to WDW, then to the individual resorts. Pets $13 a night. **Amenities:** Restaurant (American); food court; lounge; 2 outdoor heated pools; 2 kids' pools; Jacuzzi; watersports equipment; arcade; playground; WDW Transportation System, transportation to non-Disney parks for a fee; limited room service; babysitting; laundry; nonsmoking rooms. *In room:* A/C, TV, fridge, hair dryer, iron, safe.

Shades of Green on Walt Disney World Resort ✫ *(Value)*   Shades of Green, nestled among three of Disney's golf courses near the Magic Kingdom, is open only to folks in the military and their spouses, military retirees and widows, 100% disabled veterans, and Medal of Honor recipients. If you qualify, don't think of staying anywhere else; it's the best bargain on WDW soil. And it's even better now, thanks to a $92-million renovation that was completed in 2004, nearly doubling the room capacity of the resort, and adding fully ADA-compliant rooms with wide doorways and roll-in showers. In addition to the new rooms and suites (which sleep up to eight people), the existing rooms were completely overhauled. All of the large rooms offer TVs with wireless keyboards (access to the Internet is offered for a fee), balconies or patios, and pool or golf-course views. Transportation—though slow—is available to all the Disney parks and attractions.

1950 W. Magnolia Dr. (across from the Polynesian Resort). © **888/593-2242** or 407/824-3400. Fax 407/824-3665. www.shadesofgreen.org. 587 units. $89–$129 double (based on military rank); $250–$275 6- to 8-person suite (regardless of rank). Extra person $15. Children 17 and under stay free in parent's room. Rollaway beds not available, cribs $5/night. AE, DC, DISC, MC, V. Take I-4 east to Exit 67, Hwy. 536/Epcot Center Dr. Follow signs to WDW, then to the resort. Pets $13 a night. **Amenities:** 2 restaurants (American, Italian); 2 lounges; 2 heated outdoor pools; kids' pool; 2 lighted tennis courts; arcade; playground; activities desk; WDW Transportation System, transportation to non-Disney parks for a fee; babysitting; laundry; nonsmoking rooms; rooms for those w/limited mobility. *In room:* A/C, TV, fridge, coffeemaker, hair dryer, iron, safe.

INEXPENSIVE

Note: All of Disney's value resorts are out of the way and offer less-than-ideal transportation connections. If you and your brood stay at one of them, I strongly recommend renting a car.

Disney's All-Star Movies Resort   Most kids love the larger-than-life themes at the three All-Star resorts; however, it can be Disney overload for many adults. Movies such as *Toy Story, 101 Dalmatians,* and *Fantasia* live on in a very big (and I mean BIG) way at this family-friendly resort. Gigantic larger-than-life characters such as Buzz Lightyear, Pongo, and even Mickey himself mark this property's buildings, and the pools are themed after *The Mighty Ducks* and *Fantasia* (both usually noisy and crowded—a theme that carries throughout the resort). However, they add the only Disney flair to what is essentially a no-frills budget motel with basic, tiny (only 260 sq. ft.) rooms. Think old-school roadside motels, back when all you expected was a clean bed and a bathroom. The soundproofing leaves something to be desired, especially with the number of children staying here. Like its two siblings (listed below), the All-Star Movies Resort is pretty isolated in WDW's southwest corner. If, like the White Rabbit, you're often "late for a very important date," renting a car is a far better choice than relying on the Disney Transportation System.

1991 W. Buena Vista Dr., Lake Buena Vista, FL 32830-1000. © **407/934-7639** or 407/939-7000. Fax 407/939-7111. www.disneyworld.com. 1,900 units. $82–$141 double. Extra person $10. Children 17 and under stay free in parent's room. Rollaway beds not available, cribs free. AE, DC, DISC, MC, V. Free self-parking. Take I-4 east to Exit 67, Hwy. 536/Epcot Center Dr. Follow signs to WDW, then to the resort. Pets $13 a night. **Amenities:** Food court; lounge; 2 outdoor heated pools; kids' pool; arcade; playground; WDW Transportation System, transportation to non-Disney parks for a fee; limited room service; babysitting; laundry; nonsmoking rooms. *In room:* A/C, TV, dataport, fridge ($10 a night), safe.

Disney's All-Star Music Resort   Giant trombones and musical motifs from jazz and calypso to rock and Broadway are the only giveaways that this is the All-Star Music Resort—and the only thing to differentiate it from the other All-Star resorts. In keeping with the theme, the main pools are shaped like a guitar and a grand piano (quieter and better for older kids). While the extra frills of the other Disney resorts

---

Tips **Value in the Eyes of the Beholder**

Disney's All-Star resorts charge a "preferred room" rate, but don't expect much for the top rate of $141. Guests who book it are paying for location: Preferred rooms are closer to the pools, food court, and/or transportation. If you've got a rental car or don't mind walking, don't bother paying extra; some of the quietest rooms at the All-Stars are the standard ones.

---

won't be found at the All-Stars, these places do have a significant perk: They're the least expensive (by a large margin) of all the Disney properties. There is, however, a good reason for the substantial savings—the guest rooms and bathrooms are tiny. But most people don't come to WDW to lounge in their rooms, so if you're only going to be here to sleep, the cramped quarters may not be so bad. The closest parks are Blizzard Beach and Animal Kingdom, which you can reach (not necessarily in an expedient manner) via the WDW Transportation System. *Note:* Disney is home to a ton of sporting and cheerleading championships as well as a slew of other kids' events—and all the participants usually get housed at the All-Stars, making for an especially noisy environment. For (relative) quiet, ask for a room on the third floor of a building.

Tip: Larger families with smaller budgets can still stay at the Mouse's house thanks to a recent room redesign. The rehab brought with it the addition of larger, more comfortable **family suites.** At 550 square feet, each suite sleeps up to six and features two bathrooms, a kitchenette, a separate bedroom and living area, and upgraded amenities including flatscreen TVs.

1801 W. Buena Vista Dr. (at World Dr. and Osceola Pkwy.; P.O. Box 10000), Lake Buena Vista, FL 32830-1000.
© 407/934-7639 or 407/939-6000. Fax 407/939-7222. www.disneyworld.com. 1,920 units. $82–$141 double; $179–$285 family suite. Extra person $10. Children 17 and under stay free in parent's room. Rollaway beds not available, cribs free. AE, DC, DISC, MC, V. Free self-parking. Take I-4 east to Exit 67, Hwy. 536/Epcot Center Dr. Follow signs to WDW, then the resort. Pets $13 a night. **Amenities:** Food court; lounge; 2 outdoor heated pools; kids' pool; arcade; playground; WDW Transportation System, transportation to non-Disney parks for a fee; limited room service; babysitting; laundry; nonsmoking rooms. *In room:* A/C, TV, dataport, fridge ($10 a night), safe.

Disney's All-Star Sports Resort   It's an instant replay of the other All-Star resorts (listed above), including the tight quarters (if you aren't a team player, the togetherness may cause frayed tempers after a while), but your kids, especially young ones, probably won't mind (on the contrary—sports-crazed kids love it). Rooms here are in buildings designed around football, baseball, basketball, tennis, and surfing motifs. For instance, the turquoise surf buildings have waves along the roof, surfboards mounted on exterior walls, and pink fish swimming along balcony railings. Again, if your threshold for visual overload is low, you may need to visit a sanatorium once you've left this la-la land. Kids will have plenty of fun cooling off at the two themed pools (Surfboard Bay and the Grand Slam). Note that unlike the other Disney resorts, the inexpensive ones don't provide towels at the pool, so you'll have to use the ones in your room.

One last warning: The rates and themes tempt lots of families with little kids, and the noise level can get very high, so if you're looking for a quiet vacation, steer clear of these resorts.

1701 W. Buena Vista Dr. (at World Dr. and Osceola Pkwy.; P.O. Box 10000), Lake Buena Vista, FL 32830-1000.
© 407/934-7639 or 407/939-5000. Fax 407/939-7333. www.disneyworld.com. 1,920 units. $82–$141 double. Extra person $10. Children 17 and under stay free in parent's room. Rollaway beds not available, cribs free. AE, DC, DISC, MC, V. Free parking. Take I-4 east to Exit 67, Hwy. 536/Epcot Center Dr. Follow signs to WDW, then to the resort. Pets $13 a night. **Amenities:** Food court; lounge; 2 outdoor heated pools; kids' pool; arcade; playground; WDW Transportation System, transportation to non-Disney parks for a fee; limited room service; babysitting; laundry; nonsmoking rooms. *In room:* A/C, TV, dataport, fridge ($10 a night), safe.

Fun Fact **By the Numbers**

If you add up all the Dalmatians residing at the All-Star Movies resort—including the puppies, Pongo, and Perdita—there are actually 101 Dalmatians.

Fun Fact Sizing Things Up

Disney's Pop Century Resort sports a gigantic Big Wheel in its 1970s courtyard. If an actual child were to ride it, proportionally, he or she would have to weigh approximately 800 pounds.

Disney's Pop Century Resort   The newest of WDW's inexpensive—or, as Mickey calls them, value-class resorts—debuted in 2003 (opening in stages, with some yet to open). Gigantic memorabilia representing the hottest fads of decades past—from Duncan Yo-Yos and the Rubik's Cube to flower power and eight-tracks—mark the exteriors of the Pop Century's buildings. Another clone of the All-Star school (though a slight step up because the rooms are newer and the furniture a tad nicer), you won't get a lot of frills, but the price is right for travelers on a budget. A family of four could, with a bit of effort, squeeze into the small, basic rooms. The resort is divided into decades, starting with the Legendary Years of the 1900s to 1940s (alas, there is no projected date for completion of this phase) and the Classic Years of the 1950s to 1990s (the only section currently operating). The **six pools** range in theme from a crossword puzzle to a soda bottle to a bowling pin and a computer. The resort is closest to the Wide World of Sports Complex (p. 251) but a bit of a ride from everything else (yes, you should definitely rent a car).

1050 Century Dr. (P.O. Box 10000), Lake Buena Vista, FL 32830-1000. © **407/934-7639** or 407/938-4000. Fax 407/938-4040. www.disneyworld.com. 5,760 units. $82–$141 double. Extra person $10. Children 17 and under stay free in parent's room. Rollaway beds not available, cribs free. AE, DC, DISC, MC, V. Free parking. Take I-4 east to Exit 67, Hwy. 536/Epcot Center Dr. Follow signs to WDW, then to the resort. Pets $13 a night. **Amenities:** Food court; lounge; 6 outdoor heated pools; kids' pool; arcade; playground; WDW Transportation System, transportation to non-Disney parks for a fee; limited room service; babysitting; laundry; nonsmoking rooms. *In room:* A/C, TV, dataport, fridge ($10 a night), safe.

A DISNEY CAMPGROUND

Disney's Fort Wilderness Resort & Campground ✦   Why not take the kids camping? Pine and cypress trees, lakes, and streams surround this woodsy 780-acre resort, which offers a host of unique recreational opportunities for the whole family. It's close to the Magic Kingdom but quite a distance from everything else, though if you're a true outdoors type, you may want to be sheltered from some of the Mickey make-believe. There are 784 campsites for RVs, pull-behind campers, and tents (with 110/220-volt outlets, outdoor cooking grills, and comfort areas with showers and restrooms). Some sites are open to **pets**—at an additional cost of $5 per site, not per pet, which is cheaper than using the WDW resort kennel, where you pay $13 per pet. The 408 wilderness cabins (actually mobile homes with an outdoor deck and grill) offer full kitchens and 504 square feet, enough for six people once you pull down the Murphy beds (there's also a set of bunk beds for kids).

Nearby Pioneer Hall is home to the popular **Hoop-Dee-Doo Musical Revue** (p. 324). The resort also has a nightly campfire sing-along where kids can roast marshmallows (you'll have to buy them or bring along your own); sing songs with Chip N' Dale; and then sit back, relax, and watch a favorite Disney flick in the outdoor theater. Pony rides at the petting farm and horse-drawn wagon and horseback rides offer a different kind of thrill than you'll find at the theme parks, especially for younger kids.

103520 N. Fort Wilderness Trail (P.O. Box 10000), Lake Buena Vista, FL 32830-1000. © **407/934-7639** or 407/824-2900. Fax 407/824-3508. www.disneyworld.com. 784 campsites, 408 wilderness cabins. $41–$96 campsite double; $249–$365 wilderness cabin double. Extra person $2 at campsites, $5 in cabins. Children 17 and under stay free w/parent. Rollaway beds not available, cribs free. AE, DC, DISC, MC, V. Free self-parking. Take I-4 east to Exit 67, Hwy. 536/Epcot Center Dr. Follow signs to WDW, then to the resort. **Amenities:** 2 restaurants (American); grill; lounge; 2 outdoor heated pools; kids' pool; 2 lighted tennis courts; watersports equipment; outdoor activities (fishing, horseback and pony rides, hayrides, campfire programs); 2 game rooms; playground; WDW Transportation System, transportation to non-Disney parks for a fee; babysitting; laundry; nonsmoking cabins. *In room:* A/C, TV/VCR, dataport, kitchen, fridge, coffeemaker, outdoor grill, hair dryer (all in cabins only).

3 "Official" Hotels in Lake Buena Vista

These resorts, designated "official" Disney hotels, are located on or around Hotel Plaza Boulevard, at the northeast corner of WDW. They're near Downtown Disney Marketplace, Downtown Disney West Side, and Pleasure Island. The boulevard has enough greenery to make it a nominee for Main Street, U.S.A.

Guests at these hotels enjoy some WDW privileges (see "The Perks & Downsides of Staying with Mickey," earlier in this chapter), including free bus service to the parks and the ability to purchase theme-park tickets right at the resort, but make sure when booking to ask which privileges you get, as they vary from hotel to hotel and year to year. Their locations spare you from some of the pixie dust, but the boulevard's high-speed traffic is frustrating, as it's the main thoroughfare between Downtown Disney and the free world. Also note that the Walt Disney World Dolphin and Walt Disney World Swan (listed in the previous section) should be considered the eighth and ninth "official" hotels, as they're not owned by Disney. The difference is that they're still on the mainstream property.

Another perk of the "official" hotels is that they generally have less relentless Disney themes, although some do offer character breakfasts a few days each week (call the reservations line for details and schedules). They're often much cheaper than equivalent accommodations at the Mouse's house and are usually a step above the moderate Disney-owned resorts. Almost all of these resorts have kiddie pools, in-room electronic games (for an extra fee), and arcades or other activities for children.

You can make reservations for all of the following properties through the **Central Reservations Office** (© **407/934-7639**) or through the hotel numbers included in the listings. To ensure that you get the best rates, call each hotel or its parent chain (or check the websites) to see if specials are available.

You'll find all these hotels located on the "Walt Disney World & Lake Buena Vista Accommodations" map (p. 88).

Tips Getting Away

If you want to enjoy the amenities and service of a Disney resort but can't do without some beach time, the Disney Vacation Club offers the option of renting a room just 2 hours south of WDW at its **Vero Beach Resort** (© **407/ 939-7775**; www.dvcresorts.com), directly on the Atlantic, with sand, surf, and all the Disney trimmings. Studios, standard rooms, one- and two-bedroom villas, and three-bedroom cottages are all available, ranging from about $175 to $1,125 per night. You will need to arrange your own transportation.

Tips **Add-Ons & Extras**

Several of the properties in this chapter add "resort fees" to their daily room rates. That's part of an unfortunate but growing hotel trend of charging for services that used to be included in the rates, such as use of the pool; admission to the health club; or in-room coffee, phone calls, or safes. Ask if your hotel charges such a fee when you reserve so you don't get blindsided at checkout.

EXPENSIVE

Buena Vista Palace Resort ★★   Previously known as the Wyndham Palace Resort & Spa, this hotel is still the most upscale of the Hotel Plaza Boulevard–area properties and is popular with leisure travelers, though businesspeople make up 75% of its clientele. For that reason, some of the best rates are offered in July and August, contrary to the mainstream tourist resorts. Thanks to a $45-million makeover, the hotel's spacious and recently redesigned accommodations now feature 32-inch flatscreen TVs, wired and wireless Internet access, and very comfy new bedding. Many of the upscale business-standard rooms have balconies or patios; kids will probably prefer the in-room game system over the views, but you should still ask for a room above the fifth floor with a "recreation view," facing the pools on Recreation Island, Downtown Disney, and, in the distance, Disney's Hollywood Studios' Tower of Terror. (The "Epcot view" rooms offer views of the IllumiNations fireworks but little else.) The resort is known for its spacious fitness center and full-service European-style spa (with massage, wraps, steam room, sauna, salon, fitness center, and more), which are open to the public. One of the pools is situated partially indoors, providing cover from sun and rain.

1900 Buena Vista Dr. (just north of Hotel Plaza Blvd.; P.O. Box 22206), Lake Buena Vista, FL 32830. © **800/996-3426** or 407/827-2727. Fax 407/827-6034. www.buenavistapalace.com. 1,014 units. $119–$309 double; $219–$450 suite. Resort fee $12. Extra person $20. Children 17 and under stay free in parent's room. Rollaway beds $20/night, cribs free. AE, DC, DISC, MC, V. Free self-parking, valet parking $15. From I-4, take Exit 68, Hwy. 535/Apopka–Vineland Rd., north to Hotel Plaza Blvd. and go left. At 3rd light, turn right onto Buena Vista Dr. It's the 1st hotel on the right. **Amenities:** 3 restaurants (Continental, steak); 2 lounges; 3 outdoor heated pools; kids' pool; 3 lighted tennis courts; half basketball court; sand volleyball court; spa; Jacuzzi; sauna; children's center; arcade; playground; concierge; complimentary bus service to WDW parks, transportation for a fee to non-Disney parks; salon; 24-hr. room service; massage; babysitting; laundry; nonsmoking rooms; concierge-level rooms. *In room:* A/C, TV w/game system and pay movies, dataport, Wi-Fi, minibar, coffeemaker, hair dryer, iron.

MODERATE

Best Western Lake Buena Vista Hotel ★ *Value*   This 12-acre lakefront hotel is reasonably modern, with nicer rooms and public areas than you might find in other properties within the chain. Tropical-themed rooms, all with balconies, are located in an 18-story tower. Accommodations here are definitely a step above and larger than the rooms in Disney's moderate category. The views improve from the eighth floor and up, and those on the west side have a better chance of seeing something Disney. The tropical pool here is decent and has a separate wading area for little ones.

You can reserve an oversize room with a sleeper sofa (about 20% larger) or a WDW fireworks-view room for a few dollars more a night. ***Note:*** It definitely pays to surf the corporate website at www.bestwestern.com, which sometimes offers great deals and special rates for this hotel.

2000 Hotel Plaza Blvd. (between Buena Vista Dr. and Apopka–Vineland Rd./Hwy. 535), Lake Buena Vista, FL 32830. *C* **800/348-3765** or 407/828-2424. Fax 407/828-8933. www.orlandoresorthotel.com. 325 units. $79–$239 standard for up to 4; $299–$399 suite. Resort fee $6.95. Children 17 and under stay free in parent's room. Rollaway beds $10/night, cribs free. AE, DC, DISC, MC, V. Free self-parking. From I-4, take Exit 68, Hwy. 535/Apopka–Vineland Rd., north to Hotel Plaza Blvd., and go left. It's the 1st hotel on the right. **Amenities:** Restaurant (American); grill; outdoor heated pool; kids' pool; arcade; playground; Guest Services desks; complimentary bus service to WDW parks, transportation for a fee to non-Disney parks; limited room service; babysitting; laundry; nonsmoking rooms. *In room:* A/C, TV w/pay movies, game system, Wi-Fi, coffeemaker, hair dryer, iron, safe.

DoubleTree Guest Suites ✮✮ Children have their own check-in desk and theater, and they even get a gift upon arrival at this hotel, the best of the "official" hotels for families traveling with little ones. (Don't forget that everyone gets a tasty chocolate-chip cookie as a bonus!) Adults may find some of the public areas lacking in personality, though the hand-painted mural that spans the lobby and large aviary are nice touches. All the accommodations in this seven-story hotel are two-room suites that offer 643 square feet—large by most standards—with refrigerators, microwaves, and space for up to six to catch some zzzzs. The large pool offers lush landscaping and a children's wading area. This is the easternmost of the "officials," which means that it's farthest from the other Disney action but closest to (even within walking distance of) the shops, restaurants, and activities located in the Crossroads Shopping Center or along Apopka–Vineland Road.

2305 Hotel Plaza Blvd. (just west of Apopka–Vineland Rd./Hwy. 535), Lake Buena Vista, FL 32830. *C* **800/222-8733** or 407/934-1000. Fax 407/934-1015. www.doubletreeguestsuites.com. 229 units. $99–$309 double. Extra person $20. Rollaway beds $10/night, cribs free. Children 17 and under stay free in parent's room. AE, DC, DISC, MC, V. Free self-parking. **Amenities:** Restaurant; 2 lounges; outdoor heated pool; kids' pool; 2 lighted tennis courts; volleyball; playground; arcade; kids' theater; Disney Store; concierge; car-rental desk; complimentary bus service to WDW parks, transportation for a fee to non-Disney parks; limited room service; laundry service. *In room:* A/C, TV w/pay movies, video games (fee), dataport, fridge, microwave, coffeemaker, hair dryer, iron, safe.

Hilton in the Walt Disney World Resort ✮✮ This upscale resort welcomes many a Disney vacationer, even though business travelers constitute the bulk of its clientele. Its major claim to fame: It's the only official resort on Hotel Plaza Boulevard to offer guests Disney's Extra Magic Hour option (see p. 203 for details). The lobby boasts a somewhat nautical flair (though evidence of contemporary touches are apparent), and its public areas reflect a New England theme, sporting shingles, weathered-wood exteriors, and seafaring touches. The accommodations have an upscale Shaker-style decor and offer plenty of space in which to relax and unwind. Junior suites are especially spacious and can sleep up to six—a perfect choice for families. Rooms on the north and west sides of floors 6 though 10 offer a view of Downtown Disney (just a short walk away) and, in the distance, the Magic Kingdom fireworks. On-site dining options are both numerous and varied, ensuring that everyone in the family will find something to please their palate—there's even a Disney character breakfast on Sundays. The resort's recreational options include a generous pool area (with two pools, a children's pool, and plenty of space to soak up the sun) and a game room for kids.

1751 Hotel Plaza Blvd. (just east of Buena Vista Dr.), Lake Buena Vista, FL 32830. *C* **800/782-4414** or 407/827-4000. Fax 407/827-3890. www.hilton.com. 814 units. $199–$299 double; $359–$1,500 suite. Extra person $20. Children 17 and under stay free in parent's room. Rollaway beds $15/night, cribs and highchairs free. AE, DC, DISC, MC, V. Free self-parking, valet parking $12. **Amenities:** 4 restaurants; deli; minimarket; 3 lounges; 2 outdoor heated pools; kids' pool; fitness center; Jacuzzi; arcade; concierge; car-rental desk; complimentary bus to WDW parks, transportation for a fee to non-Disney parks; business center; Disney Store; shopping arcade; salon; 24-hr. room service; babysitting; laundry service; concierge-level rooms; ATM. *In room:* A/C, TV w/pay movies and games, dataport, Wi-Fi, minibar, coffeemaker, hair dryer, iron, safe.

Holiday Inn in the Walt Disney World Resort *Value*   This former Courtyard by Marriott suffered extensive damage during the summer hurricanes of 2004, an unfortunate happenstance given that the hotel had just undergone a $6-million face-lift prior to the storms. At press time, the resort (and website) remains closed, its official status unknown.

1805 Hotel Plaza Blvd. (between Lake Buena Vista Dr. and Apopka–Vineland Rd./Hwy. 535), Lake Buena Vista, FL 32830. © **800/223-9930** or 407/828-8888. Fax 407/827-4623. www.downtowndisneyhotels.com, www.holiday innwdw.com, or www.hiorlando.com.

Hotel Royal Plaza *⚲*   The Plaza is one of the boulevard's originals, but renovations over its 25 years (including a recent multimillion-dollar makeover) have kept it in quite good shape. A favorite with the budget-minded, its hallmark is a friendly staff (some of whom have been there since the hotel opened) and excellent service. The nicely outfitted rooms, now sporting new decor and furnishings (pullout sofas, plasma TVs, and premium amenities now standard in every room), are a good size, with enough space for five. Poolside rooms have balconies and patios; the tower rooms have separate sitting areas, and some offer whirlpool tubs in the bathrooms. If you want a view from up high, ask for a room facing west and toward WDW; the south and east sides keep a watchful eye on I-4 traffic. The inner courtyard offers a quiet escape where you can sit by the pool and soak up the Florida sunshine surrounded by scattered palm trees. *Note:* Though the pool area is inviting, situated in the landscaped courtyard and hidden away from the bustling roadway nearby, there are no kiddie pool or play areas here, so families with tinier tots might want to look elsewhere.

1905 Hotel Plaza Blvd. (between Buena Vista Dr. and Apopka–Vineland Rd./Hwy. 535), Lake Buena Vista, FL 32830. © **800/248-7890** or 407/828-2828. Fax 407/827-6338. www.royalplaza.com. 394 units. $99–$189 double; $189–$669 suite. Resort fee $8. Extra person $15. Children 17 and under stay free in parent's room. Rollaway beds not available, cribs free. AE, DC, DISC, MC, V. Free self-parking, valet parking $12. From I-4, take Exit 68, Hwy. 535/ Apopka–Vineland Rd., north to Hotel Plaza Blvd., and go left. It's the 2nd hotel on the left. **Amenities:** 2 restaurants; lounge; outdoor heated pool; 4 lighted tennis courts; fitness center; Jacuzzi; Guest Services desk; car-rental desk; complimentary bus service to WDW parks, transportation for a fee to non-Disney parks; room service; laundry; nonsmoking rooms. *In room:* A/C, TV w/pay movies and games, dataport, Wi-Fi, minibar, coffeemaker, hair dryer, iron, safe.

Regal Sun Resort   At press time, the former Grosvenor Resort had just completed a major transformation (and a much needed one at that, since for years the rooms had been a hit-or-miss proposition). Thanks to millions in renovations, all of its guest rooms and suites now sport upgraded bedding, carpeting, lighting, and furnishings. Public areas, including the lobby, restaurants, and recreational areas (and the pool) received an overhaul as well. This lakeside resort, located within walking distance of Downtown Disney, is popular with budget-conscious travelers thanks to the availability of package rates and special offers. Ask for a Tower Room on the west side (floors 9–19) for a limited view of Lake Buena Vista. A Saturday-night mystery dinner theater ($40 adults, $11 kids 3–9) is held in the Lake View Restaurant for an entertaining evening away from Disney. A character breakfast is also offered Tuesday, Thursday, and Saturday mornings.

1850 Hotel Plaza Blvd. (just east of Buena Vista Dr.), Lake Buena Vista, FL 32830. © **800/624-4109** or 407/ 828-4444. Fax 407/828-8192. www.regalsunresort.com. 626 units. $89–$299 double. Resort fee $10. Extra person $15. Children 17 and under stay free in parent's room. Rollaway beds $19/night, cribs free. AE, DC, DISC, MC, V. Free self-parking, valet parking $12. **Amenities:** 2 restaurants; 3 lounges; 2 outdoor heated pools; 2 lighted tennis courts; fitness center; playground; concierge; business center; complimentary bus service to WDW parks, transportation for a fee to non-Disney parks; babysitting; laundry service. *In room:* A/C, TV w/pay movies and games, dataport, Wi-Fi, fridge, coffeemaker, hair dryer, iron, safe.

4 Other Lake Buena Vista–Area Hotels

The hotels in this section are within a few minutes' drive of the Disney parks (and you'll need a rental car if you stay at them). They offer great location, but not the Disney-related privileges given to guests in the "official" hotels, such as the official Disney Transportation System and character breakfasts. On the flip side, because you're not paying for those privileges, hotels in this category are generally a shade less expensive for comparable rooms and services (though there are exceptions, of course).

Most of these hotels are listed on the "Walt Disney World & Lake Buena Vista Accommodations" map (p. 88); the Grande Lakes hotels can be found on the "International Drive Area Accommodations" map (p. 123).

VERY EXPENSIVE

Gaylord Palms ★★★   This Central Florida star may be a convention center, but it appeals to family vacationers, too, and it's not your run-of-the-mill resort. It could be considered a destination unto itself, offering its own entertainment, fabulous dining, shops, and recreational facilities. The 4½-acre octagonal Grand Atrium, topped by a glass dome, surrounds a miniature version of the Castillo de San Marcos, the old fort at St. Augustine. Waterfalls, lush foliage, and a rocky landscape complete the feel. Kids of all ages will likely find it worth exploring and definitely impressive—especially when they learn that humans aren't the only inhabitants of the Gaylord Palms. **"The Best of Florida LIVE"** is an ongoing exhibition that includes Gator Springs, where 15 juvenile alligators (you can actually feed them by hand) and 30 species of turtles lurk in the swamps; **Sawgrass Place** is home to four species of Florida snakes and baby alligators (known as grunts); tarpon, redfish, and snook swim about a coral reef in **Key West's 161,000-gallon indoor ocean;** and the waterways in the eerily foggy **Everglades** are filled with bluefish, tilapia, gar, catfish, pickerel, largemouth bass, and oscars.

The resort and its rooms are divided into themes: Emerald Bay, a 362-room hotel within the hotel, has an elegant air; St. Augustine captures the essence of America's oldest city; Key West delivers the laid-back ambience of Florida's southernmost city; and the Everglades uses a misty swamp, snarling faux gator, fiber-optic fireflies, and tin-roofed shanties to muster a wild-and-woolly air. The rooms are spacious, beautifully decorated, and well appointed (the soundproofing, though, could be a bit better); each has its own balcony as well. The kids' Marine Activity pool features a huge eight-legged octopus waterslide, and cabanas at the adult pool have Internet access. The service is impeccable, yet it's also extremely friendly and welcoming—not standoffish, as is the case at many other resorts of this class.

An entirely new adult recreation complex recently opened, featuring a large croquet lawn; beach volleyball court; bocce court; shuffleboard court; and the Green, a 9-hole, lighted putting green. And if you need to unwind further, try the 20,000-square-foot branch of the famous **Canyon Ranch Spa.**

The 4,000-square-foot branch of **La Petite Academy** (*©* **407/586-2505**), a member of the well-known child-care chain, is available only to resort guests ($10 per hr. per child; no minimum; ages 3–14). It offers a ton of LEGO fun; a karaoke stage; an art studio; and Sega, PlayStation, and Nintendo games.

6000 Osceola Pkwy., Kissimmee, FL 34747. *©* **877/677-9352** or 407/586-0000. Fax 407/239-4822. www.gaylord palms.com. 1,406 units. $239–$439 double; $655–$2,700 suite. Resort fee $10. Extra person $20. Kids under 18 stay free in parent's room. Rollaway beds $30/night; cribs free. AE, DC, DISC, MC, V. Self-parking $12, valet parking $18.

Amenities: 5 restaurants; 4 lounges; golf (nearby); 2 outdoor heated pools; fitness center; spa; supervised children's center; concierge; tour desk; car-rental desk; free transportation to Disney parks, transportation to non-Disney parks for a fee; business center; shopping arcade; salon; room service; massage; babysitting; dry cleaning; concierge-level rooms. *In room:* A/C, TV w/pay movies and video games, in-room computer system, coffeemaker, hair dryer, iron, safe.

Hyatt Regency Grand Cypress Resort ★★★ *(Finds)*

This resort is a favorite of families seeking an upscale experience without Mickey Mouse extras. The lobby has lush foliage and several colorful birds, including a **macaw** that waves to passersby and naturally attracts youthful attention. The 18-story atrium has inner and outer glass elevators (take the kids for a ride on the outers for a panoramic rush). The rooms are large and comfortable, and rollaways, cribs, bed rails, highchairs, and refrigerators are all available upon request. Accommodations on the west side, from floors 7 and up, have a distant view of Cinderella Castle and the Magic Kingdom fireworks.

The Hyatt gets my vote for **Orlando's coolest pool,** a half-acre, 800,000-gallon extravaganza with caves, grottoes, 12 waterfalls, a couple of waterslides, and a swinging rope bridge. A nearby sandy beach surrounds the 21-acre lake, where canoes and paddleboats are available for rent. Adults and kids will love it! The Hyatt shares a golf club and academy, racquet club, and equestrian center (kids' lessons are available) with its sister, the **Villas of Grand Cypress** (✆ **800/835-7377** or 407/239-4700; www.grandcypress.com).

Younger kids (ages 5–12) can enjoy supervised play and recreation—including boating, swimming, arts and crafts, video games, and horse-related activities—at **Camp Gator** (fees apply; lunch or dinner available at an additional cost).

1 Grand Cypress Blvd., Orlando, FL 32836. ✆ **800/233-1234** or 407/239-1234. Fax 407/239-3800. www.hyattgrand cypress.com. 750 units. $215–$499 double; $599–$5,750 suite. Optional $13 daily resort fee (includes health club, free local calls, daily newspaper, and in-room coffee). Extra person $25. Children 18 and under stay free in parent's room. Rollaway beds and cribs free. AE, DC, DISC, MC, V. Free self-parking, valet parking $12. **Amenities:** 4 restaurants; 4 lounges; large heated outdoor pool; 45 holes of golf; 12 tennis courts (5 lighted); health club; 2 racquetball courts; spa; watersports equipment; children's center; arcade; concierge; car-rental desk; free Disney shuttle, transportation to non-Disney parks for a fee; store; salon; 24-hr. room service; in-room massage; babysitting; laundry service; concierge-level rooms; equestrian center. *In room:* A/C, TV w/pay movies and games, dataport, minibar, hair dryer, iron, safe.

Marriott Orlando World Center ★★ *(Finds)*

Often mistakenly overlooked by families, the World Center Marriott offers not only beautifully appointed rooms, but also an array of fun and unique recreational activities for kids of all ages. Surprisingly, and somewhat unexpectedly, this resort is one of a very few that caters to both the business traveler and families—and does it rather impressively. The lobby's centerpiece is a 28-story tower fronted by flowers and fountains. The large, comfortable, and beautifully

---

Tips Coolest Pools

My favorite hotel splash zone in Orlando is the Hyatt Regency Grand Cypress Resort's half-acre, **800,000-gallon swimming pool,** which has caves, grottoes, waterfalls, and a 45-foot waterslide. The runner-up is the JW Marriott's **Lazy River,** a reasonably shallow, slow-current journey around the beautifully landscaped Grande Lakes property. Other cool pools include the water park–like pools (there are two) at the **Nickelodeon Family Suites,** with flumes, fountains, water guns, and more; and **Stormalong Bay,** which is shared by Disney's Beach and Yacht Club resorts. The über-cool pool at **Universal's Hard Rock Hotel,** with underwater sound system, waterslide, and nearby beach, is a contender, too.

decorated rooms sleep four, and the higher poolside floors offer views of Disney. For a large-scale resort, it is remarkably easy to get around, as it is not spread out so much as up. The largest of its five pools has waterslides and waterfalls surrounded by plenty of space to relax among the palm trees and tropical plants. There's plenty of dining right on the property, ranging from counter-service casual to fine dining, including the **Mikado Japanese Steakhouse** (p. 166). The location, only 2 miles from the Disney parks, is a fabulous plus. The resort often offers deals and discounts that are especially family friendly; past deals have included a great two-room package, as well as special packages with the parks (most notably with Disney, SeaWorld, and Discovery Cove).

8701 World Center Dr. (on Hwy. 536 between I-4 and Hwy. 535), Orlando, FL 32821. © **800/621-0638** or 407/239-4200. Fax 407/238-8777. www.worldsbestvacation.com or www.marriottworldcenter.com. 2,111 units. $189–$329 for up to 5; $750–$1,600 suite. Children 17 and under stay free in parent's room. Rollaway beds and cribs free. AE, DC, DISC, MC, V. Self-parking $7, valet parking $18. **Amenities:** 4 restaurants; 2 lounges; 3 heated outdoor pools; heated indoor pool; kids' pool; 18-hole golf course; 8 lighted tennis courts; health club; spa; whirlpool; sauna; concierge; car-rental desk; transportation to all theme parks for a fee; business center; salon; 24-hr. room service; massage; babysitting; laundry service. *In room:* A/C, TV w/pay movies and games, dataport, Wi-Fi, minibar, coffeemaker, hair dryer, iron, safe.

Ritz-Carlton Orlando, Grande Lakes 🐾🐾🐾 Orlando's destination for deep-pocketed travelers opened in 2003, part of a 500-acre complex that also includes a JW Marriott (see below). The posh resort's many kid-friendly options make it an attractive choice for families with plenty of extra cash. The grounds are beautiful; the entrance and lobby area have the feel of an Italian palazzo; and kids get their own separate check-in desk and welcome kit.

All units come with a balcony and two sinks, hand-painted Italian furniture, and plenty of room to move around in. (Kids won't mind zoning out in front of the 27-in. flatscreen TV.) The hotel will provide highchairs, cribs, rollaways, and strollers on request (some for an extra fee). If you call in advance, the staff will childproof the electrical outlets in your room and remove alcoholic drinks from the minibar. Kids Suites feature a separate but adjoining room, impeccably decorated and including twin trundle beds, a closet stocked with games, a TV with video-game system, separate bathroom, pint-size table and chairs, and milk and cookies waiting upon arrival. Rooms on the west side, especially on floors 6 through 14, offer a distant view of SeaWorld and its brief nighttime fireworks, as well as the resort's pool, golf course, waterways, and woodlands. In addition to the pools at the Ritz, guests can enjoy those at the JW Marriott, including the **Lazy River.** Additionally, the resort has a 40,000-square-foot full-service spa.

The **Ritz-Kids** program has two options: supervised open playtime at an hourly rate ($17 per hr. per child, including snacks and beverages; lunch and/or dinner available upon request at an extra charge; no minimum; ages 5–12; noon–10pm) and a supervised evening camp ($80 for the first child, $75 each additional child, dinner included; no minimum; ages 5–12; 4–10pm). Activities include playground play, arts and crafts, swimming, nature walks, Frisbee games, junior tennis, croquet, dance parties, and plenty more. There's a nanny service available as well (simply contact the concierge to make arrangements).

4012 Central Florida Pkwy. (at intersection with John Young Pkwy.), Orlando, FL 32837. © **800/241-3333,** 800/576-5760, or 407/206-2400. Fax 407/206-2401. www.grandelakes.com. 584 units. $229–$399 double; $599–$5,000 suite. Extra person $30. Children 17 and under stay free in parent's room. Rollaway beds $15/night; cribs free. AE, DC, DISC, MC, V. Self-parking $12, valet parking $19. From I-4, take Exit 72, Hwy. 528/Beachline Expwy.

east to the John Young Pkwy., then south to Central Florida Pkwy. **Amenities:** 3 restaurants; cafe; snack bar; 2 lounges; outdoor heated pool; kids' pool; 18 holes of golf; 3 tennis courts (lighted); spa; health club; children's center; arcade; playground; concierge; free transportation to Universal and SeaWorld, transportation to Disney parks for a fee; business center; car-rental desk; salon; 24-hr. room service; babysitting; nonsmoking rooms, concierge-level rooms. *In room:* A/C, TV, dataport, minibar, iron, safe.

EXPENSIVE

JW Marriott Orlando, Grande Lakes ✹✹   This less-expensive sister of the Ritz-Carlton Orlando (see above) is another smoke-free resort with one of the niftiest pools in Orlando, the 24,000-square-foot **Lazy River** pool that takes you on a slow, winding, tropical journey through rock formations and small waterfalls (depth 3–5 ft.). Standard rooms at the Moorish-theme resort are on par with those in Disney's moderate class and are kept in tiptop condition. Those on the west side, especially on floors 6 through 26, offer a distant view of SeaWorld and its brief nighttime fireworks, as well as the resort's pool, golf course, waterways, and woodlands. The playground has a sandbox where young kids like to hang out. JW junior guests are eligible for the **Ritz Kids** program at the neighboring Ritz-Carlton. Additionally, the two properties share pool, spa, golf, and tennis amenities.

4040 Central Florida Pkwy. (at intersection with John Young Pkwy.), Orlando, FL 32837. ✆ **800/241-3333,** 800/576-5750, or 407/206-2300. Fax 407/206-2301. www.grandelakes.com. 1,000 units. $189–$369 double; $299–$4,000 suite. Extra person $25. Children 17 and under stay free in parent's room. Rollaway beds $15/night, cribs free. AE, DC, DISC, MC, V. Self-parking $12, valet parking $19. From I-4, take Exit 72, Hwy. 528/Beachline Expwy. east to the John Young Pkwy., then south to Central Florida Pkwy. **Amenities:** 3 restaurants (Italian, French, American); cafe; lounge; 2 outdoor heated pools; kids' pool; 18 holes of golf; 3 tennis courts (lighted); spa; health club; children's center; arcade; playground; concierge; free transportation to Universal and SeaWorld, transportation to Disney parks for a fee; business center; car-rental desk; salon; 24-hr. room service; babysitting; nonsmoking rooms. *In room:* A/C, TV, dataport, minibar, coffeemaker, hair dryer, iron, safe.

Tips **Marriott Montage**

The December 2000 christening of **Marriott Village at Lake Buena Vista,** 8623 Vineland Ave., Orlando (✆ **877/682-8552** or 407/938-9001; www.marriottvillage. com), brought together three of the flagship's properties in a cluster just east of Lake Buena Vista, 3 miles from WDW. The resort includes a 400-unit **SpringHill Suites** ($85–$135 double); a 312-unit **Courtyard by Marriott** ($85–$135 double); and a 388-unit **Fairfield Inn & Suites** that has 48 Hawaiian-themed family suites with bunk beds, flatscreen TVs, and video games ($70–$125 double). Children under 17 stay free in a parent's room; an extra person pays an additional $10. All units have fridges and high-speed Internet access (for a fee).

All properties have adults' and kids' pools, whirlpools, fitness centers, kids' clubs, and car-rental and Guest Services desks. All offer transportation for a fee ($5–$15 per person per day) to Disney and non-Disney parks. There are three family-friendly restaurants within walking distance, as well as an array of snack-style eateries located right in the village. Downtown Disney is just minutes away. To get here from I-4, take Exit 68, Highway 535/Apopka–Vineland Road, head south to Vineland, and go left a half-mile to the village. Self-parking is free.

MODERATE

Embassy Suites Lake Buena Vista 🔆   Set near the end of Palm Parkway, just off Apopka–Vineland, this fun and welcoming all-suite resort is close to all the action of Downtown Disney and the surrounding area, yet remains a quiet retreat. Each suite sleeps five and includes a separate living area (with a pullout sofa) and sleeping quarters. The roomy accommodations make it a great choice for families. Some of the other perks here include a complimentary cooked-to-order breakfast and a daily manager's reception.

8100 Lake Avenue, Orlando, FL 32836. ℂ **800/257-8483**, or 407/239-1144. Fax 407/238-0230. www.embassy suiteslbv.com. 333 units. $119–$229 for up to 5. Extra person $15. Rates include full breakfast. AE, DC, DISC, MC, V. Free self-parking, valet parking $7. Pets accepted. **Amenities:** Restaurant; cafe; lounge; indoor and outdoor heated pools; kids' pool and play area; whirlpool; sauna; fitness center; tennis court; basketball court; business center; high-speed Internet access; laundry service; room service; free shuttle to Disney parks. *In room:* A/C, TV w/pay movies, dataport, fridge, microwave, safe, hairdryer, iron.

Hawthorn Suites Lake Buena Vista 🔆 (Value)   One of the most appealing features of this relatively young property is a floor plan that allows separation of kids and adults, giving Mom and Dad some (relative) private time. Its 500-square-foot standard rooms have four areas: a living room with a sleeper sofa, chair, and TV; bedroom with recliner and TV; full kitchen with dining table for four; and bathroom with vanity. Two-bedroom units are also available. The extras here are a big plus for families, too. The Hawthorn offers a free American breakfast buffet daily, and a social hour (hors d'oeuvres, beverages, and snacks) Monday through Thursday. The pool is small, but it's downright restful compared with those at some other hotels. The atmosphere is friendly; the service is good; it offers a complimentary grocery-shopping service; and it's just 3 minutes from Hotel Plaza Boulevard. All in all, this is an excellent value choice, especially for those on a budget.

8303 Palm Pkwy., Orlando, FL 32836. ℂ **800/527-1133** or 407/597-5000. Fax 407/597-6000. www.hawthorn.com. 120 units. $99–$169 for up to 6 (8 in a 2-bedroom suite). Rates include full breakfast. Rollaway beds $10/night; cribs free. AE, DC, DISC, MC, V. Free self-parking. **Amenities:** Outdoor heated pool; exercise room; basketball court; Jacuzzi; free shuttle to Disney parks, transportation to non-Disney parks for a fee; laundry service. *In room:* A/C, TV w/pay movies, dataport, kitchen, fridge, microwave, coffeemaker, hair dryer, iron.

Holiday Inn SunSpree Resort Lake Buena Vista 🔆🔆   Just a mile from the Disney parks, this is another hotel that caters to kids big time. They get their own check-in desk, a welcome from raccoon mascots Max and Maxine (who will tuck them in at night for a nominal fee if you make a reservation), and a bag filled with goodies. The hotel's 231 KidSuites have beds for up to six (bunk beds are placed in a separate sleeping area, which also has Nintendo video games) and themes (a jail, a fort, a space

---

(Tips) Special Delivery

Gooding's Supermarkets (ℂ **407/827-1200**; www.goodings.com) offers grocery delivery service to theme-park area hotels in Lake Buena Vista, Disney, Celebration, I-Drive, and Kissimmee. There is a $50 minimum, plus a $20 service charge. You can order groceries (but no alcohol) online up to 48 hours before your requested delivery date; delivery hours are 4 to 7pm. This is a great option if you're staying in a hotel room with kitchen facilities, or if you have kids and want to stock up on snacks and supplies.

capsule, and more). Child-safety kits and outlet covers are provided upon request. If you like sleeping in, ask for a room that doesn't face the pool area (a delightful spot that's very popular with the young set). All suites have kitchenettes.

Camp Holiday offers kids activities such as games, movies, arts and crafts, magic shows, and karaoke ($5 per hr. per child; no minimum; ages 4–12; 11am–10pm). Parents get a beeper so they can be reached if necessary. Free movies are also shown daily in the Castle Theater. Note that kids under 12 eat free when accompanied by adults, though it isn't fine dining.

13351 Apopka–Vineland Rd./Hwy. 535 (between Hwy. 536 and I-4), Lake Buena Vista, FL 32821. (C) **800/366-6299** or 407/239-4500. Fax 407/239-7713. www.kidsuites.com. 507 units. $89–$129 standard for up to 4; $119–$179 Kid-Suite. Children 17 and under stay free in parent's room. Rollaway beds $10/night, cribs free. AE, DISC, MC, V. Free self-parking. Pets under 25 lbs. $40. **Amenities:** Restaurant; food court; minimart; outdoor heated pool; kids' pool; fitness center; Jacuzzi; playground; supervised children's center; family activities; children's movie theater; arcade; Guest Services desk; free shuttle to Disney parks, transportation to non-Disney parks for a fee; limited room service; laundry service. *In room:* A/C, TV, dataport, fridge, microwave, coffeemaker, hair dryer, iron, safe.

Nickelodeon Family Suites ★★ *Finds* *Kids*   This all-suite property, and first-ever Nickelodeon-branded resort, is one of the best properties in the Orlando area for families. Its two-bedroom suites feature mini kitchenettes, a pullout sofa in the living area, and a second bedroom for the kids with either bunk or twin beds. Recent upgrades include flatscreen TVs and more space-conscious furniture. Three-bedroom suites offer plenty of space and include a sitting area, separate dining area, second full bathroom, and full-size kitchen—the decor is more modern and chic than in smaller suites. The lobby and the Mall (where you'll find the various restaurants, arcade, shops, and nightly entertainment) are all themed with Nickelodeon colors and characters. The resort's two pool areas are veritable water parks, with extensive multilevel waterslides, flumes, climbing nets, and water jets. Activities are scheduled poolside, and there are also a wide variety of recreational options, including a small miniature golf course, playgrounds, and play areas. A daily character breakfast is offered in addition to the hotel's regular breakfast buffet; at the latter, up to four kids eat free with paying adults. There's even a spa that caters to kids!

14500 Continental Gateway (off Hwy. 536), Lake Buena Vista, FL 32821. (C) **877/387-5437**, 407/387-5437, or 866/GO2-NICK. Fax 407/387-1489. www.nickhotel.com. 800 units. $169–$1,050 suite. Children 17 and under stay free in parent's room. Rollaway beds not available, cribs free. AE, DC, DISC, MC, V. Free self-parking. **Amenities:** Restaurant; lounge; several fast-food counters; minimarket; 2 water-park pools; miniature golf course; fitness center; 2 Jacuzzis; 3 outdoor Ping-Pong tables; 2 shuffleboard courts; game room; complimentary recreation center for ages 4–12; tour desk; free shuttle to Disney and non-Disney parks; coin-op washers and dryers. *In room:* A/C, TV w/pay movies and VCR (some w/Nintendo), dataport, full kitchen (select suites), fridge, microwave, coffeemaker, hair dryer, iron, safe.

Palomino Suites Lake Buena Vista ★   These moderately priced suites are less than 2 miles from WDW, located near Downtown Disney. This hotel is a good choice if you want a little home-style comfort and the chance to perform do-it-yourself stuff in the fully equipped kitchen. The two-bedroom suites sleep up to eight and offer plenty of room to rest and relax. A complimentary expanded continental breakfast and free Internet access are a few of the perks you'll enjoy when staying here.

8200 Palm Pkwy. (off S. Apopka–Vineland Rd./Hwy. 535), Orlando, FL 32836. (C) **800/936-9412** or 407/465-8200. Fax 407/465-0200. www.palominosuites.com. 123 units. $80–$249 double. Extra person $15. Rates include continental breakfast. Children 18 and under stay free in parent's room. Rollaway beds not available, cribs free. AE, DC, DISC, MC, V. Free self-parking. **Amenities:** Pool; exercise room; Jacuzzi; game room; Guest Services desk; free shuttle to Disney parks, transportation to non-Disney parks for a fee; laundry; safe-deposit boxes. *In room:* A/C, TV/VCR w/pay movies, dataport, kitchen, fridge, microwave, coffeemaker, hair dryer, iron.

Tips **Don't Worry: Dinners Delivered**

For those of you who can't stand the thought of heading out to dinner after a long day at the parks, **Take Out Express** is a restaurant delivery service that will bring dinner to you from 4:30 to 11pm daily. Simply check out its list of participating area restaurants and order from the menu, and your meal will be on its way. There is a charge of $5 per restaurant (you can order from more than just one), and a minimum order of $15 per restaurant is required. Don't forget to tip. Call ℂ **407/352-1170** to order or get more information.

Staybridge Suites Lake Buena Vista 𝒢𝒢   This chain hotel is located just off Apopka–Vineland, close to the action of Downtown Disney and the theme parks, as well as many restaurants. An excellent choice for families, this hotel's room sizes, prices, and friendly staff are three more good reasons to stay here. The one- and two-bedroom suites can sleep up to eight and come with full kitchens; some two-bedroom suites have two bathrooms. The separate living areas are large and comfortable, especially when compared with those in other all-suite hotels. A unique plus is the complimentary grocery shopping service: You can check off items on the list and drop it off at the front desk, and your items will be delivered to you later—even if you are not in your room. Prices run about 50¢ to $1.50 higher than those you'll find at the supermarket, but the convenience factor makes the expense worth it for time-strapped families.

8751 Suiteside Dr., Orlando, FL 32836. ℂ **800/866-4549** or 407/238-0777. Fax 407/238-2640. www.sborlando.com or www.ichotelsgroup.com. 150 units. $159–$299. Children 17 and under stay free in parent's room. Rates include continental breakfast. Rollaway beds not available, cribs free. AE, DC, DISC, MC, V. **Amenities:** Deli; convenience store; outdoor heated pool; kids' pool; 24-hr. exercise room; Jacuzzi; 24-hr. game room; free shuttle to Disney parks; Guest Services desk; 24-hr. laundry service; nonsmoking rooms; suites for those w/limited mobility; complimentary grocery service. *In room:* A/C, TV/VCR, kitchen, dataport, hair dryer, iron, safe.

INEXPENSIVE

Hampton Inn Lake Buena Vista   Location rules at this modern property, only 1 mile from the entrance to Hotel Plaza Boulevard on the northeast corner of WDW. It's not fancy, but the price is right, and there are lots of nearby places to eat, shop, and play thanks to its location just down the road from Downtown Disney. Microwaves and fridges are available upon request. Some connecting rooms (useful for larger families) are available, and the perks include free continental breakfast. While the pool is nothing special (and is pretty small), it'll cool you off when you need it.

8150 Palm Pkwy., Orlando, FL 32836. ℂ **800/370-9259** or 407/465-8150. Fax 407/465-0150. www.hamptoninn lbv.com. 147 units. $89–$149 for up to 4. Extra person $10. Rates include continental breakfast. Children 17 and under stay free in parent's room. Rollaway beds $10/night, cribs free. AE, DC, DISC, MC, V. Free self-parking. From I-4, take Exit 68, Hwy. 535/Apopka–Vineland Rd., east to Palm Pkwy., then right ¼ mile to hotel. **Amenities:** Outdoor heated pool; Jacuzzi; Guest Services desk; free shuttle to Disney parks, transportation to non-Disney parks for a fee; nonsmoking rooms. *In room:* A/C, TV w/pay movies, dataport, coffeemaker, hair dryer, iron.

5 Places to Stay in the Kissimmee Area

This stretch of highway (U.S. 192, also known as Irlo Bronson Memorial Hwy.) is within close proximity of the Disney parks. Over the past few years, a revitalization of the area has added such features as extrawide sidewalks, streetlamps, highway markers, and widened roads to make it a more friendly and appealing destination to stay

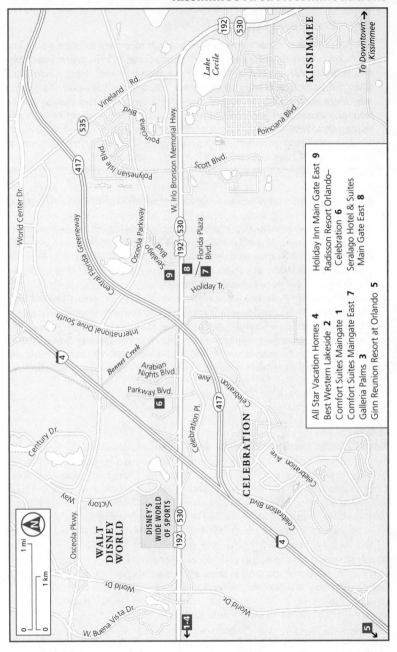

Holiday Inn Main Gate East 9
Radisson Resort Orlando–
Celebration 6
Seralago Hotel & Suites
Main Gate East 8

All Star Vacation Homes 4
Best Western Lakeside 2
Comfort Suites Maingate 1
Comfort Suites Maingate East 7
Galleria Palms 3
Ginn Reunion Resort at Orlando 5

(*Tips* **Prime Real Estate**

The **Four Seasons,** in partnership with Disney, is scheduled to open a new luxury resort, complete with its own 18-hole golf course, in 2010. Other future Disney projects include the addition of an entirely new resort community, projected to include between 4,000 and 5,000 rooms in the value and moderate range, along with shops and restaurants. The new community will be located just outside the Disney gateway at the western edge of the Mouse's house. And these are just the tip of the iceberg on the Orlando expansion front—several high-end destination properties and resort communities are set to open around town over the next few years. Stay tuned.

and play. Traffic here can nevertheless be frustrating, especially when you're trying to cross the street.

Budget hotels and restaurants abound, though a few higher-priced luxury resorts are starting to appear a bit off the main drag. While Disney is close by, Universal and SeaWorld are not; they are a good 20-minute (or more) ride away. If you don't have a car, Mears Transportation (see "Getting Around," in chapter 3) can take you there for about $15 to $20 per person, per day, round-trip.

In addition to the hotels reviewed below, the **DoubleTree Resort Orlando Villas at Maingate,** 4787 W. Irlo Bronson Hwy. (*©* **407/397-0555;** www.doubletree.com), offers spacious one-, two-, and three-bedroom town-house accommodations with kitchens that are great for families and larger groups. The **Quality Suites Maingate East,** 5876 W. Irlo Bronson Hwy. (*©* **800/848-4148** or 407/396-8040; www.choice hotels.com), offers suites with separate bedroom and living areas, plus fully stocked kitchens.

You'll find these hotels and motels listed on the "Kissimmee Area Accommodations" map (p. 117).

EXPENSIVE

Ginn Reunion Resort at Orlando ⭐⭐⭐   This luxury resort community is still in its early phases, with a completion date set for some 8 years into the future. Currently, a luxury condominium, several different villas, and a variety of vacation homes are open (all available for rent to visitors). Several of the spectacular villas feature a rather unique layout, with bedrooms located on the ground level, and the main living area and additional bedrooms on the second level (making it less likely you'll have to drag your luggage up a flight of stairs). Most villas have private patios or balconies; some of the vacation homes have their own private pools. Recent additions include an extensive on-site water park (in addition to other pools located throughout the property), a colonial-style spa, and a third championship golf course. A kids' program offering a variety of supervised activities started up in 2006. The downside: The Ginn is a bit further from the attractions, restaurants, and other activities than other resorts—and it charges an exorbitantly high "gratuity" fee.

1000 Reunion Way, Reunion, FL 34747. *©* **888/418-9611** or 407/662-1000. Fax 407/662-1111. www.reunionresort. com. Eventually 8,000 units. $279–$689 condo; $295–$535 villa; $425–$945 home. Gratuity fee of 9.6% assessed on total bill. Rollaway beds and cribs free. Free self-parking. **Amenities:** Numerous pools; water park; 3 golf courses; kids' program. *In room:* A/C, TV w/pay movies, DVD/CD player, dataport, fully stocked kitchen, fridge, microwave, coffeemaker, hair dryer, iron, safe, washer/dryer.

MODERATE

Comfort Suites Maingate East ⚔ *(Value*   Set back from the main drag, this fairly new and welcoming hotel is one of the nicest in the area. The lobby and accommodations—consisting of studio and one-bedroom suites—are bright and inviting. The main pool and the children's pool, with an umbrella fountain to keep everyone cool, are open around the clock. For entertainment, Old Town (a small-scale shopping, dining, and entertainment complex) is next door, and a great miniature golf course is located just in front·of the property. It's also one of the few resorts to offer free shuttle service to all major theme parks.

2775 Florida Plaza Blvd., Kissimmee, FL 34746. © **888/782-9772** or 407/397-7848. Fax 407/396-7045. www.comfort suitesfl.com. 198 units. $69–$175 double. Extra person $10. Rates include continental breakfast. Children 17 and under stay free in parent's room. Rollaway beds not available, cribs free. AE, DC, DISC, MC, V. Free self-parking. **Amenities:** Outdoor heated pool; kids' pool; fitness center; game room; concierge; free shuttle to Disney, Universal, and SeaWorld parks; business center; laundry service. *In room:* A/C, TV, dataport, refrigerator, microwave, coffeemaker, hair dryer, iron, safe.

Radisson Resort Orlando–Celebration ⚔   Located 1½ miles from Disney, this 20-acre property was last renovated in 2001 and has standard motel-style rooms (two double beds or a king), with views ranging from the pool or courtyard to the parking lot. Aside from the reasonable prices and location, its offerings include a dining program that lets kids 10 and under eat free with paying adults. The main pool—with waterfalls, a waterslide, a wading pool for young kids, and a location set back from the main drag—are part of what makes this property so inviting. It's also one of the few resorts to offer free shuttle service to all major parks.

2900 Parkway Blvd., Kissimmee, FL 34747. © **800/333-3333** or 407/396-7000. Fax 407/396-6792. www.radisson parkway.com. 718 units. $69–$175 for up to 5. Rollaway beds $12/night, cribs free. AE, DC, DISC, MC, V. Free self-parking. From I-4, take Exit 64A/U.S. 192 east to 1st light, Parkway Blvd., then left. **Amenities:** 2 outdoor heated pools; kids' pool; 2 lighted tennis courts; exercise room; arcade; playground; free shuttle to Disney, Universal, and Sea-World parks; limited room service; babysitting; laundry; nonsmoking rooms. *In room:* A/C, TV w/movies, dataport, minibar, coffeemaker, hair dryer, iron, safe.

INEXPENSIVE

The accommodations listed below may at times lack a lot of the kid-friendly amenities, but they help stretch a family budget. Most are within a few miles of Disney, have rooms in the 300-square-foot range, and arrange transportation to the parks. Many sell attractions tickets, but *be careful:* Some folks land at the parks with invalid tickets or waste a half day or more listening to a timeshare pitch to get 30% to 40% off the regular price (single-day Disney-park tickets are $52 for adults, $42 for kids 3–9). If a discount is more than $2 to $5 per ticket, it's probably too good to be true. Stick to buying tickets through the parks, or accept the modest discounts offered by such groups as AAA, AARP, and the visitor information centers listed in chapter 2.

Best Western Lakeside ⚔⚔ *(Kids* *(Value*   Recent renovations have ensured that this Best Western (formerly the La Quinta Inn Lakeside) remains in tip-top shape. Just up the road from the Disney entrance, the 24-acre resort looks deceptively small when you first pull up (most of the accommodations are hidden behind the lobby area), but amenities include numerous recreational options (pools, playgrounds, and so on), a food court, a good-sized convenience store, and a bountiful breakfast. Rooms are standard in size and offerings, but are nicely decorated and comfortably sleep four. Other pluses include an evening child-care facility (for a fee), free transportation to all major theme parks, free high-speed or Wi-Fi Internet in select rooms, free Wi-Fi in the lobby and eateries, a general store, and three casual on-site dining options.

7769 Irlo Bronson Memorial Hwy. (U.S. 192), Kissimmee, FL 34747. © **800/531-5900** or 407/396-2222. Fax 407/396-7087. www.bestwesternlakeside.com. 651 units. $59–$129 double. Extra person $10. Rates include continental breakfast. Children 17 and under stay free in parent's room. Rollaway beds $10/night, cribs free. Discount packages available. Small pets accepted ($25 fee). AE, DC, DISC, MC, V. Free self-parking. **Amenities:** 2 restaurants; food court; 3 outdoor heated pools; 2 kids' pools; small miniature golf course; 2 tennis courts; exercise room; Jacuzzi; playgrounds; kids' activities; Guest Services desk; free bus to Disney, Universal, and SeaWorld parks; laundry service. *In room:* A/C, TV w/pay movies and PlayStation, dataport, fridge, coffeemaker, hair dryer, iron, safe.

Comfort Suites Maingate *(Value)*   Just across the street from the Best Western Lakeside (see above) and up the road from WDW, this clean, comfortable choice has kept itself modern and in good shape. The "suites" have a small dividing wall slightly separating the living area from the sleeping quarters, but the illusion of privacy is there. Accommodations are a bit bigger than most and can squeeze in up to six. A bit of tropical landscaping gives the place an inviting atmosphere and shelters guests from busy U.S. 192. At least 10 restaurants and a small shopping plaza are within walking distance, and there's a miniature golf course right across the street.

7888 W. Irlo Bronson Memorial Hwy. (U.S. 192), Kissimmee, FL 34747. © **888/390-9888** or 407/390-9888. Fax 407/390-0981. www.kisscomfortsuite.com. 150 units. $59–$250. Rates include continental breakfast. Children 17 and under stay free in parent's room. Rollaway beds not available, cribs free. AE, DC, DISC, MC, V. Free self-parking. **Amenities:** Bar; outdoor heated pool; kids' pool; Jacuzzi; arcade; car-rental/Guest Services desk; free shuttle to Disney, Universal, SeaWorld, and Wet 'n Wild parks; laundry service. *In room:* A/C, TV, dataport, coffeemaker, fridge, microwave, hair dryer, iron, safe.

Galleria Palms *(F)*   Just 1½ miles west of WDW, this relatively new hotel is not only welcoming, but also a good choice for the budget-conscious vacationer. The rooms are nicely decorated and sport a modern upscale look, but are a bit on the small side, making them a snug fit for four. The property is well maintained and provides a bit beyond the basics with good taste—frills include flatscreen TVs, pillowtop mattresses, and rainshower showerheads. There's no restaurant, but a free breakfast is served in the lobby, and there are more than enough dining choices just a minute or two away to keep you and the kids from going hungry.

3000 Maingate Lane, Kissimmee, FL 34747. © **800/936-9417** or 407/396-5457. Fax 407/396-8989. www.galleria palmsorlando.com. 104 units. $69–$149 double. Extra person $10. Rates include continental breakfast. Children 17 and under stay free in parent's room. Rollaway beds $10/night, cribs free. AE, DC, DISC, MC, V. Free self-parking. **Amenities:** Outdoor heated pool; concierge; free shuttle to Disney, Universal, and SeaWorld parks. *In room:* A/C, TV w/pay movies, dataport, high-speed internet access, fridge, microwave, coffeemaker, iron.

Holiday Inn Main Gate East *(F) (Kids) (Value)*   This newly re-created Holiday Inn, formerly the Travelodge Main Gate, has been given the Mouse's "Good Neighbor" stamp of approval. An extensive redesign brought with it an all-new updated contemporary look both inside and out, an inviting pool with a waterslide and rocky waterfall, and all the hallmark amenities associated with this family-friendly chain. Younger guests will appreciate the children's theater, playground, and roomy Kid Suites, while parents will appreciate the "Kids Eat Free" program.

5711 W. Irlo Bronson Memorial Hwy., Kissimmee, FL 34747. © **888/890-0242** or 407/396-4222. Fax 407/396-0570. www.holidayinn.com. 445 units. $69–$239 double. Rollaway beds $10/night, cribs free. AE, DC, DISC, MC, V. Free self-parking. From I-4, take Exit 64A/U.S. 192, follow it 5 miles, and look for hotel on the left. **Amenities:** Outdoor heated pool; fitness center; game room; Guest Services desk; car-rental desk; free shuttle to Disney parks, transportation to non-Disney parks for a fee; business center; nonsmoking rooms. *In room:* A/C, TV, dataport, fridge, microwave, coffeemaker, iron.

(Tips) Homes Away from Home

Some families, especially those who like all the comforts of home or are traveling in groups of five or more, bypass motels in favor of rental condos or homes. Rates vary widely, depending on quality and location, and some may require at least a 2- or 3-night minimum. A lot of these properties are 5 to 15 miles from the theme parks and offer no transportation, so having a car is a necessity.

On the plus side, most have two to six bedrooms and a pullout couch, two or more bathrooms, a full kitchen, multiple TVs and phones, and irons. Some have washers and dryers. Homes often have their own private screen-enclosed pool, while condos have a common one.

On the minus side, they can be lacking in services. Most don't have daily maid service, and restaurants can be as far away as the parks. (That's another reason you'll need a car.) And unless a condo or home is in a gated community, don't expect on-site security. Some properties offer dinnerware, utensils, and salt and pepper shakers; check when you book, as amenities vary widely.

All Star Vacation Homes (© 888/249-1779 or 407-997-0733; www.allstar vacationhomes.com) is one of the area's best home and condo rental outfits, with a wide variety of properties to choose from—all of them within a 4-mile radius of Disney. Do check its website; you will be able to see the exact home you are renting, as opposed to a "typical" room. Other popular players include **Holiday Villas** (© 800/344-3959; www.holidayvillas.com), **Summer Bay Resort** (© 888/742-1100; www.summerbayresort.com), **LikiTiki Village** (© 407/239-5000), **Bahama Bay Resort** (© 888/782-9722), and **Cypress Point Orlando** (© 407/597-2700). Rates generally range from about $109 to $529 per night, or $750 to $3,600 per week.

Seralago Hotel & Suites Main Gate East (★★ (Kids (Value   Location (it's just down the road from Disney) and price are just some of the draws at this former Holiday Inn. The revamped hotel sports new colors but still features themed KidSuites with separate sleeping areas for your tots, as well as standard rooms and regular two-room suites. The rooms provide a reasonable amount of space for a family of five, with the two-room suites sleeping up to eight. There are plenty of recreational activities, from swimming to tennis, and the hotel's movie theater shows free family films nightly. There's also a family-friendly food court, and kids 12 and under eat free (two kids per paying adult) in the hotel's cafe.

5678 Irlo Bronson Memorial Hwy. (U.S. 192), Kissimmee, FL 34746. © **800/366-5437** or 407/396-4488. Fax 407/396-8915. www.seralagohotel.com. 614 units. $69–$119 double. Extra person $10. Children 18 and under stay free in parent's room. Rollaway beds $10/night; cribs free. AE, DC, DISC, MC, V. Free self-parking. **Amenities:** Restaurant; food court; convenience store; lounge; 2 outdoor heated pools; toddler pool; 2 tennis courts; exercise room; basketball; volleyball; Jacuzzi; playground; arcade; Guest Services desk; free shuttle to Disney parks, transportation to non-Disney parks for a fee; limited room service; laundry service; small movie theater. *In room:* A/C, TV/VCR, video games, fridge, microwave, coffeemaker, hair dryer, iron.

6 Places to Stay in the International Drive Area

The hotels and resorts listed here are 7 to 10 miles north of Walt Disney World (via I-4) and 1 to 5 miles from Universal Orlando and SeaWorld. The advantages of staying on I-Drive: It's a destination unto itself, filled with accommodations, restaurants, and small attractions; it has its own inexpensive trolley service (see "Getting Around," in chapter 3); and it's centrally located for those who want to visit Disney, Universal, SeaWorld, *and* the downtown area. The disadvantages: The north end of I-Drive is badly congested; the shops, motels, eateries, and attractions along this stretch can be tacky; and some of the motels and hotels don't offer free transportation to the parks (the going rate is $6–$15 round-trip).

You'll find these places located on the "International Drive Area Accommodations" map (p. 123).

VERY EXPENSIVE

Loews Portofino Bay Hotel at Universal Orlando ★★★ *(Finds* Universal Orlando's premier hotel is as grand as Disney's Grand Floridian (p. 92). It's a replica of Portofino, Italy, with a harbor and canals on which boats travel to the theme parks. The old-world ambience is carried throughout the public areas, restaurants, and rooms by a staff that tries hard to match the friendliness of the Peabody (see below).

A recent multimillion-dollar makeover revamped the already-beautiful rooms and suites (all 750 of them) to be more reflective of the Mediterranean-seaside theme. The entire decor is warmer, as the colors now run to shades of green and cream accented with darker jewel tones—noticeable in the upholstery, carpeting, bedding, and curtains throughout. The drawbacks: There are stairs everywhere you turn, making it difficult if not impossible to maneuver with tinier tots or with strollers, and the sheer size of the resort can make it difficult to find your way around.

Guest rooms are large and luxurious, with sleeping space for up to five and beds made up with Egyptian-woven sheets. The pillows are so soft that you'll want to take them home. (Alas, they're too big for your suitcase, so ask the resort how to order one.) Kid's Suites have a private bedroom with a king bed and a separate room with two small beds, a beanbag chair, TV, VCR, and CD player (your young ones will love their pint-size bathrobes). Hypoallergenic rooms are also available.

The Loews hotel chain, which manages the property, is known for its child-friendly programs (including a special program for grandparents traveling with their grandchildren; call the hotel for details). **Campo Portofino** is a supervised children's activity and game center ($12 per hr. per child; no minimum; ages 4–14; 5pm–midnight). **Kids Kloset** loans things such as games, books, car seats, potty seats, and other items to visiting families. The resort also supplies pagers for teens, giving them some freedom without being completely out of touch with their parents. Mom and Dad can relax while the kids are otherwise occupied at the resort's privately run **Mandara Spa** (www.mandaraspa.com), which features a state-of-the-art fitness center and full-service spa (including specialized treatments for teens). Like many of the Disney properties, the Portofino doesn't just have swimming pools; its beach pool has a fort with a waterslide (the villa pool offers several cabanas). To entertain guests in the evenings, **Musica Della Notte** (Music of the Night) has become a permanent addition to the Harbor Piazza. Guests can enjoy the music of strolling musicians performing opera, "popera," and popular music as they sit, relax, and take in the sunset. Parents will likely appreciate this more than their kids do.

International Drive Area Accommodations

DoubleTree Castle Hotel **10**

DoubleTree Hotel at the Entrance to Universal Orlando **1**

Embassy Suites Orlando–International Drive South **8**

Hard Rock Hotel at Universal Orlando Resort **4**

Hyatt Place Orlando/Universal **2**

JW Marriott Orlando, Grande Lakes **14**

La Quinta Inn & Suites Orlando Convention Center **9**

Loews Portofino Bay Hotel at Universal Orlando **3**

Loews Royal Pacific Resort at Universal Orlando **5**

Peabody Orlando **12**

Ramada Convention Center **6**

Renaissance Orlando Resort at SeaWorld **13**

Ritz-Carlton Orlando, Grande Lakes **14**

SpringHill Suites Orlando Convention Center **11**

Staybridge Suites International Drive **7**

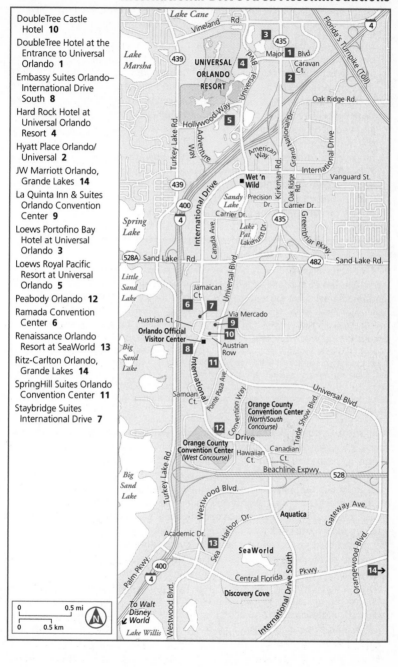

(*Tips*   **Smaller Homes Away from Home**

Several area timeshare resorts rent rooms or apartments to visitors when their owners aren't using them. The **Disney Vacation Club** (© 407/939-7775; www.dvcresorts.com) offers studios and one- to two-bedroom apartments at its time-share resorts. Some have small fridges and microwaves; others have full kitchens. Rates start at about $305 and can run up to $2,090 per night. Outside Disney World, rack rates begin at around $189 (and go up from there) for one- and two-bedroom apartments with kitchens. As with hotel rooms, you can get major discounts (as low as $79 a night) for these properties if you do your homework. An especially nice choice is the **Sheraton Vistana Resort** (© 866/208-0003; www.starwoodvo.com). Another good place to look is the **Marriott Vacation Club** (© 800/845-5279; www.vacationclub.com).

One minor caveat: Because each unit that's rented is individually owned, quality can at times vary, so be sure to specify your exact requirements when booking.

One of the biggest pluses: Guests get **Universal Express** access to most rides at Universal Studios Florida and Islands of Adventure, as well as seating privileges at shows and restaurants. It's a big advantage if you have fidgety children or impatient teens.

5601 Universal Blvd., Orlando, FL 32819. © 800/235-6397 or 407/503-1000. Fax 407/224-7118. www.loewshotels.com/hotels/orlando. 750 units. $269–$499 double; $519–$2,500 suite or villa. Extra person $25. Children 17 and under stay free in parent's room. Rollaway beds $25/night, cribs free. AE, DC, DISC, MC, V. Self-parking $12, valet parking $18. Pets accepted (no fee, though deposit required). **Amenities:** 4 restaurants; deli; 3 lounges; 2 outdoor heated pools (1 for concierge-level and suite guests only); kids' pool; bocce courts (concierge-level and suite guests only); fitness center; spa; watercraft rentals; playground; supervised children's center; arcade; concierge; tour desk; free water-taxi transportation to Universal Orlando parks, free shuttle to SeaWorld, transportation to WDW parks for a fee; business center; shopping arcade; 24-hr. room service; babysitting; laundry service; concierge-level rooms. *In room:* A/C, TV, hair dryer, iron, safe.

Peabody Orlando ☆☆ *Moments*   Kids and fun-loving adults flock to this hotel's main lobby, where five mallards march from the elevators into a fountain daily at 11am, accompanied by John Philip Sousa's "King Cotton March" and their own red-coated duck master (see p. 299 for more on the ducks). That's just one of the magnets at a grand hotel that has one of the friendliest staffs in Central Florida.

That said, though it's a favorite, the Peabody is primarily a business and convention hotel, and usually sees lots of kids only during school-vacation times, when parents coming to town for work tend to bring their offspring along. This isn't the best choice for the mainstream vacationer, but if you want to stay on I-Drive and do end up here, your kids certainly won't suffer. It's classy without being stuffy, and if your budget allows the splurge, you won't be disappointed. Rooms are large and comfortable (sleeping up to five), tastefully decorated, and very well appointed. West-side rooms (floor 6 and up) offer a distant view of Disney fireworks. The kids' pool has a mini waterfall, and there are tennis courts for sports-oriented youngsters.

Tip: Your best chance at getting a deal is in July and August, when the convention trade falls flat and occupancy drops to as low as 20%.

9801 International Dr. (between Beachline Expwy. and Sand Lake Rd.), Orlando, FL 32819. © 800/732-2639 or 407/352-4000. Fax 407/354-1424. www.peabodyorlando.com. 891 units. $184–$425 standard room for up to 3; $550–$1,775 suite. Extra person $15. Children 17 and under stay free in parent's room. Rollaway beds $15/night, cribs free. AE, DC, DISC, MC, V. Free self-parking, valet parking $17. **Amenities:** 3 restaurants; deli; 3 lounges; outdoor heated pool; kids' pool; 4 lighted tennis courts, instruction available (fee); fitness center; spa; Jacuzzi; game room; concierge; Guest Services desk; shuttle to WDW and other parks for a fee; business center; shopping arcade; 24-hr. room service; concierge-level rooms. *In room:* A/C, TV, dataport, minibar, hair dryer.

EXPENSIVE

Hard Rock Hotel at Universal Orlando Resort ★★   You can't get any closer than this to Universal Studios at Universal Orlando. This California mission–style resort with a rock-'n'-roll theme opened in 2001 with rates a level lower than its Universal sister property, the Portofino (see above). Compared to its Universal siblings, the atmosphere here is bit more casual and kid friendly, though still with an air of sophistication. The collection of rock memorabilia scattered throughout the public areas is impressive. The pool area, however, takes center stage: A tremendous oasis of palm trees, rocky landscaping, and waterslides surrounds a large free-form pool whose most unique feature is a first-rate underwater sound system. It's outfitted with 12 underwater speakers that make sure you don't miss a beat.

The accommodations and amenities at the Hard Rock are a cut above those at some of Disney's comparable properties, even the Animal Kingdom Lodge (p. 98). Thanks to a recent multimillion-dollar renovation, rooms now have flatscreen TVs, MP3 docking stations, and upgraded bedding, while the decor remains sophisticated and modern. Unfortunately, though the rooms are fairly soundproof, a few notes seep through the walls, so you may want to ask for one that's away from the lobby area if you have light sleepers. All units here sleep four quite comfortably. Though the bathrooms aren't big, there are (like at the Disney resorts) separate dressing areas with a sink. The Lil' Rock Suites have a separate room with two small beds, a TV, and a separate bathroom. Like the Portofino, the best views here are on the "bay" side, overlooking the piazza.

Camp Lil' Rock is a supervised children's activity and game center ($12 per hr. per child; no minimum; ages 4–14; 5pm–midnight). Kids' amenity bags are available on request. The hotel also offers a special package for grandparents traveling with their grandkids.

There is a Hard Rock Cafe several hundred yards from the hotel, but the resort has two of its own restaurants on the property. As with the Portofino, staying here means **Universal Express** access to almost every ride at Universal Studios Florida and Islands of Adventure, plus seating privileges for shows and restaurants. It's a huge plus if you're here during a busy season.

5800 Universal Blvd., Orlando, FL 32819. © **800/232-7827** or 407/503-2000. Fax 407/224-7118. www.loewshotels. com/hotels/orlando. 650 units. $239–$479 double; $479–$2,020 suite. Extra person $25. Children 17 and under stay free in parent's room. Rollaway beds $25/night; cribs free. AE, DC, DISC, MC, V. Self-parking $12, valet parking $18. Pets accepted (no fee, though deposit required). **Amenities:** 3 restaurants; grill; 2 lounges; outdoor heated pool; kids' pool; fitness center; playground; kids' club; arcade; concierge; free water-taxi transportation to Universal Studios, Islands of Adventure, and CityWalk; free shuttle to SeaWorld; transportation to WDW parks for a fee; shopping arcade; 24-hr. room service; babysitting; laundry service. *In room:* A/C, TV, video games (fee), minibar, fridge (select rooms), microwave (select rooms), hair dryer, iron, safe, CD player, DVD player (fee), high-speed Internet access (fee).

Loews Royal Pacific Resort at Universal Orlando ★★ *Value*   The third of Universal Orlando's three resorts has an open-air courtyard with an exquisite orchid garden, palm trees, waterfalls, and lagoons. The abandoned floatplane (a scene that reminds more than a few people of *Gilligan's Island*) makes a great backdrop. The Royal Pacific doesn't quite succeed at creating a Polynesian paradise (you can hear the screams of riders on the Hulk Coaster from the pool area), but it's definitely the best Universal resort in the theme department.

The rooms, smaller than those at other Universal resorts, are decorated with wood accents and intricate carvings, but are quite plain when lined up against those in comparable Disney resorts. The public areas (whether inside or out), however, are impressive and well worth exploring. The lagoon pool complex—the largest in Orlando—has a beach and play area that's very popular with the young set. Kids will likely enjoy the free water-taxi ride that goes from all of Universal's resorts to its theme parks (though it's admittedly slow). The addition of the **Wantilan Luau Pavilion** ensures that the weekly luau is held rain or shine (see p. 327 for details).

The **Mariner's Club** is a supervised children's activity and game center ($12 per hr. per child; no minimum; ages 4–14; 5–11pm). And, of course, the biggest plus: Guests get **Universal Express** access to almost every ride at Universal Studios Florida and Islands of Adventure, along with seating privileges for shows and restaurants. The big minus: The self-parking lot is a hike from the hotel, and you have to pay $12 for the privilege.

6300 Hollywood Way, Orlando, FL 32819. ✆ **800/232-7827** or 407/503-3000. Fax 407/503-3202. www.loewshotels. com/hotels/orlando. 1,000 units. $209–$429 double; $339–$1,950 suite. Extra person $20. Children 17 and under stay free in parent's room. Rollaway beds $25/night, cribs free. AE, DC, DISC, MC, V. Self-parking $12, valet parking $18. From I-4, take Exit 75B, Kirkman Rd./Hwy. 435, and follow the signs to Universal. Pets accepted (no fee, though deposit required). **Amenities:** 2 restaurants (Asian-Polynesian, American); 3 lounges; outdoor heated pool; kids' pool; sauna; Jacuzzi; kids' club; arcade; concierge; free water-taxi transportation to Universal Studios, Islands of Adventure, and CityWalk; free shuttle to SeaWorld; transportation to WDW parks for a fee; babysitting; nonsmoking rooms. *In room:* A/C, TV, dataport, hair dryer, iron, safe.

Renaissance Orlando Resort at SeaWorld 🎭🎭

Large rooms, good service, and a thoroughly chic interior (gone are the gardens, cascading waterfalls, koi pond, and free-flight aviary) are this hotel's calling cards. While it doesn't have much in the way of kids' amenities, its most valuable feature is a location that's perfect if you're going to Universal, SeaWorld (right across the street), and, to a lesser degree, the second-tier I-Drive attractions. The beautifully decorated (now trendier) rooms, all recently renovated, are oversized and offer plenty of space to spread out and relax. The resort also sports a health club, spa, and sauna (an extensive expansion of which was just completed); plus an inviting Mediterranean-style pool area with an Olympic-size pool, two whirlpools, and a children's wading pool. There are two restaurants, along with plenty of others nearby on I-Drive. Transportation to the parks is available for a fee, though most guests can easily walk to SeaWorld.

6677 Sea Harbor Dr., Orlando, FL 32821. ✆ **800/327-6677** or 407/351-5555. Fax 407/351-1991. www.renaissance hotels.com. 778 units. $149–$329 double. Extra person no charge. Children 17 and under stay free in parent's room. Rollaway beds and cribs free. AE, DC, DISC, MC, V. Self-parking $8, valet parking $12. **Amenities:** 2 restaurants; lounges; outdoor heated pool; kids' pool; golf privileges (fee); 4 lighted tennis courts, available instruction (fee); health club; basketball; volleyball; spa; 2 Jacuzzis; sauna; playground; arcade; concierge; tour desk; car-rental desk; transportation to all parks for a fee; business center; shopping arcade; salon; 24-hr. room service; massage; babysitting; laundry service. *In room:* A/C, TV w/pay movies and games, dataport, minibar, fridge (select rooms), hair dryer, safe.

Staybridge Suites International Drive 🎭

Like its Lake Buena Vista cousin (reviewed on p. 116), this hotel is friendly, well run, and neat as a pin, attracting both families and business travelers. The rates and the spacious one- and two-bedroom suites (the latter 550 sq. ft., with beds for eight) are two of its biggest draws; there's also a supervised child-care center. Courtyard rooms have balconies. The property is across the street from the Square (I-Drive's newest shopping village), a slew of restaurants, and just up the road from the newly renovated Pointe Orlando and all its offerings. An expanded continental breakfast is included in the daily rate.

I-Drive Alternatives

If you're having trouble finding a room during peak season, try the 1,052-unit **Wyndham Orlando Resort,** 8001 International Dr. ((C) **800/WYNDHAM** or 407/ 351-2420; www.wyndham.com), an impeccably landscaped property that features numerous pools, playgrounds, and a kids' club for children 4 to 12. The 1,338-unit **Caribe Royale,** 8101 World Center Dr. ((C) **800/823-8300** or 407/238-8000; www.cariberoyale.com), offers spacious and newly remodeled one-bedroom suites (with kitchenettes) and two-bedroom villas (with Jacuzzis and full kitchens). The pool has cascading waterfalls and a 75-foot waterslide; a playground is nearby; and the service is tops.

8480 International Dr., Orlando, FL 32819. (C) **800/866-4549** or 407/352-2400. Fax 407/352-4631. www.sborlando. com or www.ichotelsgroup.com. 150 units. $159–$299 double. Rates include continental breakfast. Rollaway beds and cribs free. AE, DC, DISC, MC, V. **Amenities:** Deli; convenience store; outdoor heated pool; kids' pool; 24-hr. exercise room; Jacuzzi; 24-hr. game room; free shuttle to Disney parks; Guest Services desk; 24-hr. laundry service; nonsmoking rooms; suites for those w/limited mobility; complimentary grocery service. *In room:* A/C, TV/VCR, kitchen, dataport, hair dryer, iron, safe.

MODERATE

DoubleTree Castle Hotel   Built on a medieval-castle theme, this nine-story I-Drive property is entertaining from the moment you enter. Topped with spiraling turrets and two rooftop terraces, the castle is painted in pink, lavender, and gold shades, and adorned in public areas with art, antique dolls, weaponry from around the world, and unusual timepieces. Renaissance music adds to the theme. As if that weren't enough, you get DoubleTree's famous chocolate-chip cookies upon check-in. Rooms are standard motel style, with two queen beds or one king bed. The circular pool is equipped with fountains for extra fun. The hotel sometimes shows family films on a poolside screen on weekends.

8629 International Dr., Orlando, FL 32819. (C) **800/952-2785** or 407/345-1511. Fax 407/248-8181. www.doubletree castle.com. 216 units. $89–$219 double; $139–$269 suite. Extra person $10. Children 17 and under stay free in parent's room. Rollaway beds $15/night, cribs free. AE, DC, DISC, MC, V. Free self-parking. From I-4, take Exit 74A, Sand Lake Rd./Hwy. 482, go east to International Dr., then south to Austrian Row. **Amenities:** Restaurant (tapas); cafe; 2 lounges; outdoor heated pool; exercise room; arcade; Guest Services desk; free transportation to Disney, Universal, and SeaWorld parks; limited room service; laundry; nonsmoking rooms. *In room:* A/C, TV w/PlayStation, dataport, fridge, coffeemaker, hair dryer, iron, safe.

DoubleTree Hotel at the Entrance to Universal Orlando (F)   Location alone (right across the street from Universal Orlando) earns this hotel a star. Built for the convention trade, this former Radisson was recently renovated and features reasonably nice rooms. Stay here and save over the Portofino Bay, Hard Rock, and Royal Pacific hotels (reviewed above). Rooms on the west side, floors 6 through 18, offer views of the Universal parks and CityWalk. DoubleTree's famous chocolate-chip cookies are complimentary upon check-in (though you may want to buy some to take home, because they're *that* good).

5780 Major Blvd., Orlando, FL 32819. (C) **800/333-3333** or 407/351-1000. Fax 407/363-0106. www.doubletree orlando.com. 742 units. $99–$229 double. Extra person $20. Children 17 and under stay free in parent's room. Rollaway beds $20/night, cribs free. AE, DC, DISC, MC, V. Free self-parking. **Amenities:** 3 restaurants; grill; lounge; outdoor heated pool; kids' pool; exercise room; Jacuzzi; arcade; free transportation to Universal and SeaWorld parks; transportation for a fee to Disney/airport; car-rental desk; salon; limited room service. *In room:* A/C, TV w/pay movies, dataport, coffeemaker, hair dryer, iron.

Embassy Suites Orlando–International Drive South ★ This is another hotel with a run-of-the-mill exterior hiding an impressive interior atrium highlighted by brick and wrought-iron accents, palm trees, and lush foliage. Eight floors of suites surround the atrium, some with balconies overlooking the courtyard. Suites are fairly spacious, with separate living and sleeping areas. This is one of the few hotels to offer both indoor and outdoor pools. Another big advantage: the proximity to I-Drive's nightlife, restaurants, and shops. Recent renovations have kept the property in good condition. A complimentary cooked-to-order breakfast and evening reception are a few of the perks here. Transportation to Disney is free.

8978 International Dr., Orlando, FL 32819. ℂ 800/EMBASSY or 407/352-1400. Fax 407/363-1120. www.embassy suitesorlando.com. 244 units. $129–$289 for up to 6. Extra person $10. Rates include full breakfast. Rollaway beds $15/night; cribs free. AE, DC, DISC, MC, V. Free self-parking, valet parking $8. **Amenities:** Restaurant; lounge; 2 heated pools (1 indoor, 1 outdoor); toddler pool; fitness center; game room; Guest Services desk; free transportation to Disney; 24-hour business center; room service; laundry service. *In room:* A/C, TV w/pay movies, dataport, fridge, microwave, coffeemaker, hair dryer, iron.

Hyatt Place Orlando/Universal Major renovations have transformed this former Amerisuites into a modern and stylish property. A newly redesigned lobby now sports a cafe, TV den, and e-room with a chic and upscale decor. Self-service check-in and checkout kiosks offer an efficient alternative to standing in line at the front desk, and the spacious guest rooms feature all-new comfy bedding, sleeper sofas, and 42-inch flatscreen TVs. Complimentary high-speed Wi-Fi, available throughout the hotel, keeps you connected without costing you a bundle. A free continental breakfast is part of the package, but for those with heartier appetites, hot breakfast entrees are available (they cost extra), as are 24-hour made-to-order entrees and snacks. If your goal is to be very close to the Universal theme parks without having to pay the heftier rates that come with staying on park property, this is the place for you.

5895 Caravan Court, Orlando, FL 32819. ℂ 800/993-6506 or 407/351-0627. Fax: 407/331-3317. www.hyatt place.com. 151 units. $109–$239 double. Rates include free continental breakfast. Children 17 and under stay free in parent's room. Rollaway beds not available, cribs free. AE, DC, DISC, MC, V. Free self-parking. **Amenities:** Pool; 24-hr. exercise room. *In room:* A/C, TV w/pay movies and games, dataport, fridge, coffeemaker, hair dryer, iron, safe.

La Quinta Inn & Suites Orlando Convention Center ★ Opened in 1998, this is one of a handful of upscale, moderately priced motels on Universal Boulevard, which runs parallel to (but isn't as congested as) I-Drive. The hotel is aimed at business travelers, but this is Orlando, so families traveling with kids are welcomed with open arms. King rooms are designed for extended stays and come with a fridge and a microwave. There's also a limited number of two-room suites with separate living and sleeping areas.

8504 Universal Blvd., Orlando, FL 32819. ℂ 800/531-5900 or 407/345-1365. Fax 407/345-5586. www.laquinta. com. 184 units. $95–$165 double; $129–$179 suite. Extra person $6. Rates include continental breakfast. Rollaway beds not available, cribs free. Children 18 and under stay free in parent's room. AE, DC, DISC, MC, V. Free self-parking. Take I-4 to the Sand Lake Rd./Hwy. 482 exit, go east toward Universal, then right. Small pets accepted. **Amenities:** Outdoor heated pool; exercise room; Jacuzzi; transportation to all theme parks for a fee; laundry. *In room:* A/C, TV w/pay movies and games, dataport, high-speed Internet access (some rooms), fridge (some rooms), microwave (some rooms), coffeemaker, hair dryer, iron.

SpringHill Suites Orlando Convention Center *Value* This property offers guests a chance to stay near but not in the middle of the I-Drive crowds and traffic. Clean, very spacious suites (about 700 sq. ft., with beds for five and a separate living area), reasonable rates, and a handful of perks (like a complimentary breakfast buffet and high-speed Internet) make this all-suite property worth considering.

8840 Universal Blvd., Orlando, FL 32819. © 888/287-9400 or 407/345-9073. Fax 407/345-9075. www.springhill suites.com. 167 units. $129–$199 double. Extra person $10. Rates include hot breakfast buffet. Rollaway beds and cribs free. Children 17 and under stay free in parent's room. AE, DC, DISC, MC, V. Free self-parking. **Amenities:** Outdoor heated pool; exercise room; Jacuzzi; concierge; free transportation to the WDW parks; transportation to Universal and SeaWorld for a fee; business center; laundry service. *In room:* A/C, TV w/pay movies, dataport, high-speed Internet access, minifridge, microwave, coffeemaker, hair dryer, iron.

INEXPENSIVE

Ramada Convention Center ⚡ *Value*   If you're looking for I-Drive's best value, it's hard to beat this one. This Ramada combines a quiet location off the main drag; down-to-earth rates; perks that include free high-speed Internet and a complimentary breakfast buffet; and a clean, modern motel in one package. It's one of the best in this category, and arguably a half step ahead of the La Quinta in the previous category. The rooms are very comfortable, the staff is friendly, and there are a number of restaurants within walking distance of the hotel.

8342 Jamaican Court (off International Dr. between the Beachline Expwy. and Sand Lake Rd.), Orlando, FL 32819. © 800/272-6232 or 407/363-1944. Fax 407/363-1944. www.ramada-idrive.com. 135 units. $69–$84 for up to 4. Children 17 and under stay free in parents' room. Rates include continental breakfast. Rollaway beds and cribs free. AE, DC, DISC, MC, V. Free self-parking. **Amenities:** Outdoor heated pool; Guest Services desk; transportation to the parks for a fee; laundry service. *In room:* A/C, TV w/pay movies, dataport, high-speed Internet access, coffeemaker, hair dryer, safe.

5

Family-Friendly Dining

If you're a fast-food fan, you'll find hundreds of choices here, thanks to Orlando's 30-something years of growth as a family destination. Themed and theme-park restaurants, only a rung or two higher on the culinary scale, aren't far behind in the numbers. While the local dining scene doesn't compare to that of foodie havens such as New York, San Francisco, and Las Vegas, in fairness, more than a few of Orlando's 5,000-plus restaurants can easily go head to head with the competition. (Disbelievers should grab a chair at **Emeril's** at CityWalk or **Victoria & Albert's** at Disney's Grand Floridian Resort & Spa, to name a couple.)

Because most Central Florida visitors spend much of their time at Disney or Universal, I focus most of my energy there, but I won't leave out worthwhile restaurants beyond the parks' boundaries. In this chapter, you'll also find a sampling of what's cooking along International Drive and visit a fair share of other dining rooms that have benefited from the culinary infusion created by the attractions.

Keep in mind that most moderate to inexpensive restaurants have **kids' menus** (generally $4–$9, often including a beverage and fries), and many offer distractions, such as coloring books and mazes, to keep your little tykes busy until the food arrives. I'll make a note of those

available at press time, but offerings may change, so ask when reserving a table. You'll also want to pay attention to the places that offer **character meals** (see the listings later in this chapter)—an experience most kids, or parents, won't want to miss.

If you go to a place that caters to kids, expect the noise level to be high. They don't take a vacation from squeals of joy or fits of temper, so you shouldn't expect to, either. On the plus side, if it's your kids who tend to turn up the volume, it's far more likely that their antics will go unnoticed when there are others around doing the very same thing.

Also note that the higher the meal costs, the less likely you'll be in the same dining room as a lot of little ones. So if you're hankering to rekindle the romance, or are simply in need of a night off, let the kids crash at the hotel's supervised activity center or make arrangements for in-room child care (see chapter 4), and reserve a table for two at one of the area's better bistros. (They're easy to spot—they're often the ones without kids' menus.)

For online information about area restaurants, visit **www.disneyworld. com**, **www.universalorlando.com**, **www. orlandoinfo.com**, or the websites in the listings that follow.

ADVANCE DINING RESERVATIONS AT WDW RESTAURANTS

At Walt Disney World, an Advance Dining Reservation (formally known as Priority Seating) is like a regular reservation, but less precise. It means you get the next table available after you arrive, but a table isn't kept empty while the eatery waits for you to show. Therefore, you will probably wait 15 to 30 minutes even if you arrive on time. You can make Advance Dining Reservations 180 days ahead of time for most full-service restaurants in the Magic Kingdom, Epcot, Disney's Hollywood Studios, Disney's Animal Kingdom, the Disney resorts, and Downtown Disney. Advance Dining Reservations can also be made for character meals (later in this chapter) and dinner shows (a notable change from the previous time frame of 2 years). To make arrangements, call © **407/939-3463,** or 407/939-7707 for groups of eight or more. You'll get a confirmation number, which you should bring with you. Disney's dinner shows (p. 323), however, require full payment in advance, and cancellations must be made at least 48 hours prior to the time of the show to avoid penalties.

Note: Since the Advance Dining Reservations phone number was instituted in 1994, it has become much more difficult to obtain a table as a walk-in at the resorts' more popular restaurants. I *strongly* advise you to call as far ahead as possible, especially if you're traveling during the peak seasons, considering a character meal, or intending to dine at a dinner show. It wouldn't hurt to mark your calendar and enter the phone number into your speed dial, either. Amazingly, some restaurants can book up quite literally within only a minute or two of the phone lines opening (at 7am) on that 180th day out.

If you don't book your meals in advance, you can take your chances by making your Advance Dining Reservations arrangements once you have arrived in the parks—just stop by one of the following places:

- **In the Magic Kingdom:** Guest Relations in City Hall (on Main Street, U.S.A.) or directly at your desired restaurant.
- **In Epcot:** Guest Relations to the east of Spaceship Earth, near Innoventions, or directly at your desired restaurant.
- **In Disney's Hollywood Studios:** Guest Relations near Hollywood Junction or directly at your desired restaurant.
- **In Disney's Animal Kingdom:** Guest Relations near the entrance. You can also arrange for Advance Dining Reservations at the Rainforest Cafe located here, but this is a *very* popular place, so the sooner you call, the better.

Also, keep these restaurant facts in mind:

- As of July 1, 2003, *all* Florida restaurants and bars that serve food are **smoke-free.**
- The Magic Kingdom (including its restaurants) serves no **alcoholic beverages,** but liquor is available at Disney's Animal Kingdom, Epcot, and Disney's Hollywood Studios restaurants and elsewhere in the WDW complex.
- All sit-down restaurants in Walt Disney World take the following **credit cards:** American Express, Diners Club, Discover, MasterCard, Visa, and Disney Visa.
- Unless otherwise noted, restaurants in the parks **require park admission.**
- Guests at Disney resorts and official properties can make restaurant **reservations** through Guest Services or concierge desks.
- Nearly all WDW restaurants with sit-down or counter service offer **kids' menus** with items ranging from $4 to $9, though in a few cases they can reach to $12. Some include a beverage and fries.

A NOTE ABOUT PRICES

The prices for adult meals at Orlando restaurants—except those inside the theme parks and other attractions—are no more exorbitant than you'd find anywhere else. Restaurants in this chapter are organized first by location and second by price range,

---

> **Tips How Early Can You Book It?**
>
> At press time, Advance Dining Reservations could be made up to 180 days in advance for all character meals and for restaurants at the Disney resorts and theme parks, including a meal at Victoria & Albert's or one of Disney's dinner shows (including the Hoop-Dee-Doo Musical Revue, Spirit of Aloha, and Mickey's Backyard BBQ). In addition, WDW resort guests can make Advance Dining Reservations for up to 10 days' worth of meals all at once (even if it extends beyond the 180-day window)—a huge timesaver. For arrangements, call ℰ **407/939-3463.**

---

which reflects the cost of an average entree per person. Restaurants in the **inexpensive** category charge $10 or less for an entree; those in the **moderate** category charge $11 to $20; **expensive** restaurants will set you back $21 to $30; and **very expensive** restaurants will top that, sometimes by a large margin.

One last note: The restaurants in this chapter occasionally change menus (and sometimes more than just occasionally), so items described here may not be on offer when you visit. And as entrees vary, so do prices.

That said, it's time to divide and conquer.

1 Restaurants by Cuisine

AFRICAN

Boma 🍴🍴🍴 (Disney's Animal Kingdom Lodge, $$$, p. 152)

Jiko—The Cooking Place 🍴 (Disney's Animal Kingdom Lodge, $$$, p. 153)

AMERICAN

B-Line Diner (International Drive Area, $$, p. 163)

Cinderella's Royal Table 🍴 (Magic Kingdom, $$$, p. 143)

Columbia Harbour House 🍴 (Magic Kingdom, $, p. 146)

Cosmic Ray's Starlight Café (Magic Kingdom, $, p. 146)

ESPN Club 🍴 (Disney's BoardWalk, $$, p. 155)

50's Prime Time Café (Disney's Hollywood Studios, $$, p. 147)

Hard Rock Cafe (Universal Orlando, $$, p. 161)

Hollywood Brown Derby (Disney's Hollywood Studios, $$$, p. 147)

Liberty Tree Tavern 🍴 (Magic Kingdom, $$, p. 143)

Panera Bread 🍴 (Downtown, $$, p. 168)

Pecos Bill Café 🍴 (Magic Kingdom, $, p. 146)

Planet Hollywood (Pleasure Island, $$, p. 157)

Plaza Restaurant (Magic Kingdom, $, p. 146)

Sci-Fi Dine-In Theater Restaurant (Disney's Hollywood Studios, $$, p. 148)

Tusker House (Disney's Animal Kingdom, $, p. 149)

BARBECUE

Bubbalou's Bodacious BBQ 🍴 (Winter Park, $, p. 169)

BRAZILIAN

Texas de Brazil 🍴 (International Drive Area, $$$$, p. 163)

BRITISH

Rose & Crown Pub & Dining Room (Epcot, $$, p. 140)

BRUNCH

House of Blues ✪ (Disney's West Side, $$$, p. 158)

CALIFORNIA

California Grill ✪✪✪ (Disney's Contemporary Resort, $$$, p. 152)

Rainforest Cafe ✪ (Disney's Animal Kingdom & Downtown Disney Marketplace, $$, p. 149 and p. 157)

Wolfgang Puck Grand Café ✪ (Disney's West Side, $$, p. 158)

CANADIAN

Le Cellier Steakhouse (Epcot, $$, p. 140)

CARIBBEAN

Bahama Breeze ✪ (International Drive Area, $$, p. 163)

Jimmy Buffett's Margaritaville (Universal's CityWalk, $$, p. 161)

CHARACTER MEALS

Akershus Royal Banquet Hall (Epcot, $$, p. 139)

Backstage at Believe–Dine with Shamu (SeaWorld, $$, p. 172)

Cape May Café (Disney's Beach Club Resort, $$, p. 155)

Chef Mickey's ✪✪ (Disney's Contemporary Resort, $$, p. 171)

Cinderella's Royal Table ✪ (Magic Kingdom, $$, p. 143)

Confisco Grill (Islands of Adventure, $$, p. 172)

Crystal Palace Buffet ✪ (Magic Kingdom, $$, p. 172)

Donald's Safari Breakfast (Disney's Animal Kingdom, $$, p. 172)

Garden Grill ✪ (Epcot, $$, p. 172)

Liberty Tree Tavern (Magic Kingdom, $$, p. 143)

1900 Park Fare ✪ (Disney's Grand Floridian Resort & Spa, $$, p. 172)

'Ohana Character Breakfast (Disney's Polynesian Resort, $$, p. 173)

Princess Storybook Dining (Epcot, $$, p. 173)

CHINESE

Lotus Blossom Café (Epcot, $, p. 142)

Ming Court ✪ (International Drive Area, $$, p. 164)

Nine Dragons (Epcot, $$, p. 140)

CUBAN

Bongos Cuban Café (Disney's West Side, $$, p. 158)

Rolando's ✪ (Casselberry, $$, p. 168)

FOOD COURT

Sunshine Seasons in the Land (Epcot, $, p. 142)

FRENCH

Bistro de Paris (Epcot, $$$$, p. 135)

Chefs de France (Epcot, $$$, p. 136)

Citricos ✪ (Disney's Grand Floridian Resort & Spa, $$$$, p. 150)

GERMAN

Biergarten (Epcot, $$, p. 139)

Sommerfest (Epcot, $, p. 142)

INTERNATIONAL

Café Tu Tu Tango ✪✪ (International Drive Area, $$, p. 164)

Victoria & Albert's ✪✪✪ (Disney's Grand Floridian Resort & Spa, $$$$, p. 151)

ITALIAN

Bice ✪ (Loews Portofino Bay Hotel, $$$$, p. 160)

Carrabba's ✪ (Kissimmee, $$, p. 166)

Mama Melrose's Ristorante Italiano (Disney's Hollywood Studios, $$, p. 148)

Pacino's Italian Ristorante ✪ (Kissimmee, $$, p. 168)

Pastamore Ristorante ✚ (Universal's CityWalk, $$, p. 162)

Portobello Yacht Club ✚ (Pleasure Island, $$$, p. 156)

Romano's Macaroni Grill ✚ (Lake Buena Vista, $, p. 159)

Tony's Town Square Restaurant (Magic Kingdom, $$$, p. 143)

Tutto Italia (Epcot, $$$, p. 139)

JAPANESE

Mikado Japanese Steakhouse ✚ (Marriott Orlando World Center, $$$, p. 166)

Teppan Edo (Epcot, $$$, p. 138)

Tokyo Dining (Epcot, $$$, p. 138)

Yakitori House (Epcot, $, p. 142)

MEXICAN

Cantina de San Angel (Epcot, $, p. 141)

San Angel Inn ✚ (Epcot, $$, p. 141)

MISSISSIPPI DELTA

House of Blues (Disney's West Side, $$, p. 158)

MOROCCAN

Marrakesh ✚ (Epcot, $$$, p. 138)

NEW ORLEANS

Boatwright's Dining Hall (Disney's Port Orleans Resort, $$, p. 154)

Emeril's ✚✚ (Universal's CityWalk, $$$$, p. 160)

NORWEGIAN

Akershus Royal Banquet Hall (Epcot, $$, p. 139)

Kringla Bakeri og Kafe (Epcot, $, p. 142)

PACIFIC RIM

'Ohana ✚ (Disney's Polynesian Resort, $$, p. 155)

Tchoup Chop ✚✚ (Loews Royal Pacific Resort at Universal, $$$, p. 161)

PIZZA

Toy Story Pizza Planet (Disney's Hollywood Studios, $, p. 148)

SEAFOOD

Artist Point ✚ (Disney's Wilderness Lodge, $$$, p. 151)

Cape May Café (Disney's Beach Club Resort, $$, p. 155)

Columbia Harbour House ✚ (Magic Kingdom, $, p. 146)

Coral Reef ✚ (Epcot, $$$, p. 136)

Crab House (Lake Buena Vista, $$, p. 159)

Crabby Bill's ✚ (Kissimmee, $$, p. 168)

Fishbones (International Drive Area, $$, p. 164)

Flying Fish Café (Disney's Board-Walk, $$$, p. 153)

Fulton's Crab House ✚ (Downtown Disney Marketplace, $$$$, p. 157)

The Palm (Universal's Hard Rock Hotel, $$$$, p. 160)

Todd English's Bluezoo ✚✚ (WDW Dolphin, $$$, p. 154)

Yachtsman Steakhouse ✚ (Disney's Yacht Club Resort, $$$$, p. 151)

SOUTHWESTERN

Logan's Roadhouse (Kissimmee, $, p. 169)

STEAKS/CHOPS

Artist Point ✚ (Disney's Wilderness Lodge, $$$, p. 151)

The Palm (Universal's Hard Rock Hotel, $$$$, p. 160)

Yachtsman Steakhouse ✚ (Disney's Yacht Club Resort, $$$$, p. 151)

TAPAS

Café Tu Tu Tango ✚✚ (International Drive Area, $$, p. 164)

Spoodles (Disney's BoardWalk, $$$, p. 154)

2 Places to Dine in Walt Disney World

From fast food on the fly to fine-dining establishments, there are literally hundreds of restaurants scattered throughout Walt Disney World, including those at the theme parks (Epcot, Magic Kingdom, Disney's Hollywood Studios, and Disney's Animal Kingdom), the Disney resorts, and the "official" hotels. And those totals don't include the eateries located throughout the Downtown Disney areas of Pleasure Island, West Side, and the Marketplace, some of which are listed in the Lake Buena Vista section later in this chapter. As a general rule, the food at Disney is decent enough, though only a small handful of the restaurants would truly qualify as gourmet. Portions are generally large, practically ensuring that you'll never walk away hungry, though prices match portion sizes accordingly. Be prepared to spend a rather hefty amount each day for just a few meals, a snack, and a drink (or two). Families may find sharing a good option, especially if you have very young children who tend not to eat so much when on the go. For those unwilling to share, sit-down and counter-service eateries, at least in the theme parks, do offer pint-size platters in the $4-to-$9 range. Another option is to order a la carte, but don't expect to see this listed as an option on the restaurant menus—you have to ask.

Note: All Disney sit-down restaurants have highchairs and booster seats.

IN EPCOT

The world is at your feet at Epcot—quite literally, in fact. In addition to the eateries found at Future World, the World Showcase features several ethnic cuisines from around the globe, all served in some rather impressive settings. Though dining at one of the World Showcase pavilions is a traditional part of the Epcot experience, many of the following establishments are rather overpriced when compared to an equivalent restaurant beyond the park's boundaries. Unless your budget is unlimited, you may want to consider the more casual counter-service eateries located throughout the park and save the sit-down service for somewhere else. These informal dining spots don't require reservations (for details, check the Epcot guide map that you can pick up upon entering the park) and often go overlooked; they usually offer **kids' meals** for ages 3 to 9. If you simply can't resist a more formal meal, try the full-service restaurants at lunch, when the price for a meal is much lower. Almost all the establishments listed here serve lunch and dinner daily (hours vary with park operating hours), and unless otherwise noted, they offer children's meals. All but one or two require theme-park admission and the $11 parking fee, too. These restaurants are located on the "Epcot Dining" map (p. 137).

Note: Because the clientele at even the fanciest Epcot World Showcase restaurant comes directly from the park, you don't have to dress up for dinner. An **Advance Dining Reservation** (p. 130) is crucial if you want to dine at a specific table-service restaurant in Epcot; call © **407/939-3463** far ahead of time.

VERY EXPENSIVE

Bistro de Paris TRADITIONAL FRENCH   Located above Chefs de France (see below), this pricey bistro offers an intimate and elegant atmosphere overlooking the streets of Paris a-la-Epcot just below. The occasionally changing menu might include grilled veal chops with chanterelles, rack of lamb with a mustard crust, sun-dried-tomato risotto and eggplant caviar, or seared scallops with porcini mushrooms. It's definitely not a good choice for families, though if Mom and Dad have the night off

> **Tips** **The Disney Dining Plan**
>
> The **Disney Dining Plan**—an option available to Disney resort guests—can save you plenty when dining at the parks. It gives you one counter-service meal, one table-service meal, and one snack per person, per night of your stay, including taxes and tips. You can use your meals in any order you wish. The program participants include over 120 establishments throughout WDW, including resort restaurants, select character dining, dinner shows, and "signature" restaurants (though these may "cost" more than one of your allotted meals, so be sure to ask). Call ✆ **407/934-7639** or visit **www.disneyworld.com** for details.

(the kids with a sitter), by all means indulge. The restaurant has a respectable list of French wines.

France Pavilion, World Showcase. ✆ 407/939-3463. www.disneyworld.com. No kids' menu. Advance Dining Reservations strongly recommended. Main courses $28–$37 dinner. Tasting menu $70, w/wine pairing $100. AE, DC, DISC, MC, V. Daily 5pm–1 hr. before park closes. Parking $11.

EXPENSIVE

Chefs de France TRADITIONAL FRENCH   Focusing on nouvelle cuisine, Les Chefs de France is one of the most expensive restaurants at Epcot, but not without good reason. An eye-catching, domed-glass exterior hides an Art Nouveau interior filled with candelabra and glass-and-brass partitions, offering an intimate setting. You can credit three internationally acclaimed chefs—Paul Bocuse, Roger Verge, and Gaston LeNotre—with the menu here, which combines fresh Florida ingredients and a good dose of French imports. Light sauces (when compared with more traditional French cooking, that is) complement such tasty entrees as grilled tenderloin of beef with a black-pepper sauce, potato gratin, and green beans, or roasted perch with lobster mousse, potato scales on sautéed fennel, and a lobster reduction. Throw in a substantial wine list, plus desserts and pastries that are among the best in the World. The service, however, can get a bit lackluster when the restaurant is busy. Older kids would fare well, though most children will likely prefer to head elsewhere.

France Pavilion, World Showcase. ✆ 407/939-3463. www.disneyworld.com. Kids' menu w/activities, highchairs, boosters. Advance Dining Reservations strongly recommended. Main courses $8–$20 lunch, $17–$30 dinner; kids $7–$8. AE, DC, DISC, MC, V. Daily noon–3:30pm and 5pm–1 hr. before park closes. Parking $11.

Coral Reef ⊛ SEAFOOD   We've seen both kids and adults mesmerized by the Reef's **5.6-million-gallon aquarium.** Mood is half the fun here as Disney denizens swim to "La Mer" and other classical music. Tiered seating, mainly in semicircular booths, allow everyone a good view. Diners get fish-identifier sheets with labeled pictures so they can put names on the faces swimming by their tables. This is one of the most popular restaurants in all of the parks, especially with kids. The menu features fresh seafood, including grilled mahimahi, grilled tilapia, and seared salmon. A selection of landlubber fare is on offer as well. Wine is available by the glass.

Living Seas Pavilion, Future World. ✆ 407/939-3463. www.disneyworld.com. Kids' menu w/activities, highchairs, boosters. Advance Dining Reservations recommended. Main courses $12–$22 lunch, $16–$32 dinner; kids $7–$8. AE, DC, DISC, MC, V. Daily 11:30am–3pm and 4:30–8pm. Parking $11.

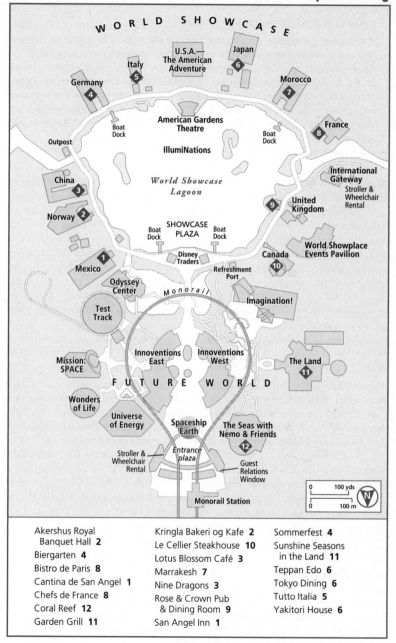

Akershus Royal Banquet Hall **2**	Kringla Bakeri og Kafe **2**	Sommerfest **4**
Biergarten **4**	Le Cellier Steakhouse **10**	Sunshine Seasons in the Land **11**
Bistro de Paris **8**	Lotus Blossom Café **3**	Teppan Edo **6**
Cantina de San Angel **1**	Marrakesh **7**	Tokyo Dining **6**
Chefs de France **8**	Nine Dragons **3**	Tutto Italia **5**
Coral Reef **12**	Rose & Crown Pub & Dining Room **9**	Yakitori House **6**
Garden Grill **11**	San Angel Inn **1**	

> **Fun Fact   Just Desserts**
>
> Playing with your food usually isn't appropriate, but WDW features plenty of places where kids can create their own decadent and delightful desserts. At the **California Grill** (p. 152), kids can make Ms. Ice Cream Head with vanilla ice cream and candy. At **Le Cellier** (p. 140), in Epcot's Canada Pavilion, chocolate mousse is rolled in cookie crumbs, then decorated with cookie antlers and candy for the face to make a "moose." Troll cookies with candy eyes and cotton-candy hair are the treat of choice at the **Akershus Royal Banquet Hall** (p. 139), in the Norway Pavilion.

Marrakesh ⭐ *(Finds)* MOROCCAN   Marrakesh exemplifies the spirit of Epcot more than any other restaurant. Mosaic tiles, latticed shutters, a painted ceiling, and exquisitely carved faux-ivory archways frame the dining area. Unfortunately, many guests shy away, mistakenly thinking the cuisine's too exotic—but don't be put off. Belly dancers entertain while your eyes feast on options including marinated beef and chicken kabobs; braised chicken with green olives, garlic, and lemon; and a medley of seafood, chicken, and lamb. Most entrees come with the national dish, couscous. If you can't decide what you want, sampler platters allow a taste of everything. On the kids' side, the choices are chicken tenders, Moroccan pasta, burgers, or vegetable couscous. Older kids will likely find the atmosphere to their taste. There's a small selection of wine and beer for the adults in the family.

Morocco Pavilion, World Showcase. ℭ **407/939-3463**. www.disneyworld.com. Kids' menu w/activities, highchairs, boosters. Advance Dining Reservations strongly recommended. Main courses $17–$21 lunch, $20–$32 dinner; prix fixe $25–$40; kids $6–$7. AE, DC, DISC, MC, V. Daily noon–park closing. Parking $11.

Teppan Edo JAPANESE   Once the Mitsukoshi Teppanyaki Dining Room, Teppan Edo, thanks to a complete redesign, now features a chic upscale interior. The experience, however, remains the same. If you've been to a Japanese steakhouse *(teppanyaki)*, you know the drill: Diners sit around grill tables while expert chefs rapidly dice, slice, stir-fry, and sometimes launch the food onto your plate with amazing skill. The theatrics should keep your kids' attention riveted. Entrees include chicken, steak, shrimp, scallops, or a combination. A small selection of sushi is available as well. Kids can order grilled chicken, shrimp, veggies, or a combo. As at Tokyo Dining (see below), Kirin beer, plum wine, and sake are served. The atmosphere is lively, and the noise level is generally high, so no worries with little ones here.

Japan Pavilion, World Showcase. ℭ **407/939-3463**. www.disneyworld.com. Kids' menu w/activities, highchairs, boosters. Advance Dining Reservations strongly recommended. Main courses $15–$28 lunch, $15–$28 dinner; kids $9–$10. AE, DC, DISC, MC, V. Daily 11am–1 hr. before park closes. Parking $11.

Tokyo Dining JAPANESE   After a recent overhaul (and a new name), this eatery now seats 140 (a substantial increase over the previous intimate setting for 25). A central stage of sorts allows diners to watch as chefs expertly roll and wrap nearly 50 varieties of sashimi and sushi. You'll enjoy the tempura-battered shrimp, chicken, scallops, or beef. A new kids' menu features shrimp and chicken tempura, chicken teriyaki, and vegetable croquettes. The atmosphere and main menu, however, make this a better bet for those with tweens and teens. For Mom and Dad, Tokyo Dining also features steaks and seafood, boasts six varieties of sake, and serves Kirin beer, plum wine, and a handful of specialty drinks.

Japan Pavilion, World Showcase. ℂ **407/939-3463**. www.disneyworld.com. Kids' menu w/activities, highchairs, boosters. Advance Dining Reservations recommended. Main courses $9–$14 lunch, $13–$25 dinner. AE, DC, DISC, MC, V. Daily 11am–1 hr. before park closes. Parking $11.

Tutto Italia ITALIAN   Replacing L'Originale Alfredo di Roma, albeit only temporarily, this inviting eatery features a menu filled with Italian specialties such as bucattini pasta with prosciutto, peas, and Parmesan; roasted chicken with lemon, herbs, and hot peppers; and fennel-roasted pork loin with an orange-zest/parsley gremolata—all dished out from an open kitchen. Kids can choose penne with pomodoro sauce, spaghetti with meatballs, a ham and cheese panino, or pizzetta with mozzarella and tomatoes. The wine list, filled with Italian choices, is reasonably extensive. The dining-room noise level can be quite high, so if you want a quieter meal, ask for a seat out on the veranda—a most pleasant choice in the evenings. A permanent restaurant is slated to open in late 2008.

Italy Pavilion, World Showcase. ℂ **407/939-3463**. www.disneyworld.com. Kids' menu w/activities, highchairs, boosters. Advance Dining Reservations strongly recommended. Main courses $19–$28 lunch, $24–$36 dinner; family-style lunch $40 adults, $15 kids 3–9; family-style dinner $59 adults, $19 kids; kids $9. AE, DC, DISC, MC, V. Daily noon–park closing. Parking $11.

MODERATE

Akershus Royal Banquet Hall NORWEGIAN   This restaurant, set inside a re-created 14th-century castle, now features Princess Storybook character meals all day long. And you can sample from an all-you-can-eat feast of traditional Norwegian fare, making it a relative bargain for big eaters. It is also reasonably good food, though some diners may find it difficult to adapt to Scandinavian tastes. An impressive smorgasbord of hot and cold dishes, including baked salmon with spicy mustard, pasta with garden vegetables, venison stew, and *kjottkaker* (a traditional Norwegian dish), are among the choices. Disney princesses (excluding Cinderella) are the biggest draw for kids—they make their way around the hall as you dine, stopping at each table to say hello.

Note: The character meals take place at breakfast, lunch, and dinner. The popular Princess breakfast (p. 173) includes mostly American fare, but the lunch and dinner buffets feature a sampling of Norwegian cuisine along with kid-friendly favorites, such as grilled chicken, ravioli, pasta and meatballs, hot dogs, and a turkey-and-cheese roll.

Norway Pavilion, World Showcase. ℂ **407/939-3463**. www.disneyworld.com. Kids' menu w/activities, highchairs, boosters. Advance Dining Reservations required. Character breakfast $23 adults, $13 kids; character lunch $25 adults, $14 kids; character dinner $29 adults, $14 kids. AE, DC, DISC, MC, V. Daily 8:30–10:10am, 11:40am–2:50pm, and 4:20–8:40pm. Parking $11.

Biergarten GERMAN   The festive Biergarten feels like a Bavarian village at Oktoberfest. A working waterwheel and geranium-filled flower boxes adorn the Tudor-style

---

⧏Tips Fill 'er Up

Got a family full of thirsty kids? Guests ages 9 and under can now get free refills on drinks when dining at Disney's sit-down restaurants. Milk, juice, soda pop, and bottled water are all included, but specialty drinks are not—you'll have to pay extra for those.

houses that line the dining area. An oompah band entertains with its accordions and cowbells, and guests are encouraged to dance and sing along. The all-you-can-eat buffet is filled with Bavarian fare (sausages, pork schnitzel, sauerbraten, spaetzle, and sauerkraut), as well as roasted chicken, roasted pork, and salmon. Though there's no kids' menu, the extensive buffet should satisfy even picky eaters. Beck's and Kirschwasser—served in immense steins—are on tap for adults.

Germany Pavilion, World Showcase. ⑦ 407/939-3463. www.disneyworld.com. Advance Dining Reservations strongly recommended. Lunch buffet $20 adults, $11 kids; dinner buffet $24 adults, $12 kids. AE, DC, DISC, MC, V. Daily noon–3:45pm and 4pm–park closing. Parking $11.

Le Cellier Steakhouse CANADIAN   The restaurant's French Gothic facade and steeply pitched copper roofs lend it a castlelike ambience. The lantern-lit dining room resembles a wine cellar, where you'll sit in tapestry-upholstered chairs under vaulted stone arches. If you're in the mood for steak, this is the right place; offerings include the usual range of cuts, such as filet mignon and New York strip. Other options are seared king salmon, sautéed shrimp and bay scallops, and squash ravioli. The lunch menu also has lighter fare, such as sandwiches and salads. Kids can choose pizza, beef and tomato macaroni, a 6-ounce steak, or a hot dog. Wash down your meal with a Canadian wine (ice wines are a good after-dinner treat for adults) or a Canadian beer.

Canada Pavilion, World Showcase. ⑦ 407/939-3463. www.disneyworld.com. Kids' menu w/activities, highchairs, boosters. Advance Dining Reservations strongly recommended. Main courses $12–$25 lunch, $18–$30 dinner; kids $7–$9. AE, DC, DISC, MC, V. Daily noon–park closing. Parking $11.

Nine Dragons CHINESE   When it comes to decor, Nine Dragons shines, with carved-rosewood furnishings and a dragon-motif ceiling. Some windows overlook the lagoon. But the food doesn't match the ornate surroundings. Main courses feature Mandarin, Shanghai, Cantonese, and Szechuan cuisines, but portions are small. The dishes include spicy beef stir-fried with scallions and bell peppers; steamed orange roughy with a five-flavor sauce; and a casserole of shrimp and scallops sautéed with scallions and tofu. Two- and four-person sampler plates offer a bit of everything for sharing. Kids' choices (finicky eaters, beware) are sweet-and-sour chicken, pot stickers, spring rolls, and fried rice. You can order Chinese or California wines with your meal.

Note: The Nine Dragons is slated to close in early 2008 to make way for an all-new dining experience, which will include an exhibition kitchen featuring five separate cooking stations that allow for interaction with the chefs as they prepare your meal. An opening date is scheduled for late the same year.

China Pavilion, World Showcase. ⑦ 407/939-3463. www.disneyworld.com. Kids' menu w/activities, highchairs, boosters. Advance Dining Reservations strongly recommended. Main courses $13–$20 lunch, $18–$30 dinner; sampler plates $44 for 2, $60 for 4; kids $6–$10. AE, DC, DISC, MC, V. Daily 11:30am–park closing. Parking $11.

Rose & Crown Pub & Dining Room BRITISH   Visitors from the U.K. flock to this spot, with its dark-oak wainscoting, beamed Tudor ceilings, and a belly-up bar where English folk music and the occasionally saucy server entertain as you feast your eyes on a short but traditional menu. It beckons with fish and chips wrapped in newspaper (kids love 'em), bangers and mash, a Stilton cheese and fruit plate, and the best of the bunch, an English-pie sampler. Offerings for younger guests include mac and cheese, pizza, bangers and mash, and cottage pie. Wash your meal down with a pint of Irish lager, Bass Ale, or Guinness Stout.

> ⟨*Tips*⟩ **Special Tastes**
>
> When it comes to eating at Disney, just because something's not on the menu doesn't mean it's not available. Looking for kosher food? Worried WDW can't entertain your vegetarian taste buds? What about low-sodium, low-sugar, or fat-free diets? Disney can usually handle lifestyle diets as well as special dietary requirements (allergies, lactose intolerance) at any of its full-service restaurants, as long as guests provide advance notice—3 days is suggested to accommodate special dietary needs, while at least 24 hours is necessary for lifestyle diets. This holds true for other dining requests, too. If you're headed to one of the resort's restaurants and know your kids may have a tough time with the menu, chicken nuggets and other kid-friendly items can be requested in advance. Make special requests when you book your Advance Dining Reservations (℃ **407/939-3463**) or, if you're staying at a Disney resort, by stopping by the lobby concierge desk.

Note: The outdoor tables (weather permitting) offer a fantastic view of Illumi-Nations (p. 225). These seats are first come, first served, so ask the hostess when you arrive if a patio table is available. *Tip:* If you're in a hurry, grab some tasty cod and chips to-go at the **Yorkshire County Fish Shop,** a quick-service kiosk next to the pub.

United Kingdom Pavilion, World Showcase. ℃ 407/939-3463. www.disneyworld.com. Kids' menu w/activities, highchairs, boosters. Advance Dining Reservations available for dining room, but not for pub. Main courses $16–$19 lunch, $17–$30 dinner; kids $7–$8. AE, DC, DISC, MC, V. Daily 11am–1 hr. before park closes. Parking $11.

San Angel Inn ⟨✦⟩ MEXICAN   It's always night at the San Angel, where you can feast on some of the best south-of-the-border cuisine in all of the parks. Candlelit tables set the mood, and the menu delivers reasonably authentic food. The atmosphere is more romantic than family oriented, and it's probably better for older kids rather than little ones (though you'll see them anyway). You'll hear the occasional rumble of a volcano and the sounds of distant songbirds as you dine on the top-selling *mole poblano* (chicken with more than 20 spices, carrots, and a hint of chocolate). Mahimahi, chicken tenders with pasta, and chicken quesadillas fill out the kids' menu.

Note: Parents may appreciate the new tequila bar (adjacent to the restaurant) as well as the expansion of the restaurant itself, including an all-new menu. The changes are slated to be in place by mid-2008.

Mexico Pavilion, World Showcase. ℃ 407/939-3463. www.disneyworld.com. Kids' menu w/activities, highchairs, boosters. Advance Dining Reservations strongly recommended. Main courses $12–$18 lunch, $18–$24 dinner; kids $7–$8. AE, DC, DISC, MC, V. Daily 11:30am–park closing. Parking $11.

INEXPENSIVE

Cantina de San Angel MEXICAN   Counter-service eateries are the most common places to grab a bite—and are probably the best bet for families with young kids who can't sit still. The Cantina serves up nachos, burritos, quesadillas, tacos, and churros. The patio overlooks the lagoon, and umbrellas shade you from the sun. *Note:* An expanded seating area and new menu are slated to debut in late 2008.

Mexico Pavilion, World Showcase. ℃ 407/939-3463. www.disneyworld.com. Advance Dining Reservations not available. Meals $7–$8. AE, DC, DISC, MC, V. Daily 11:30am–1 hr. before park closes. Parking $11.

Kringla Bakeri og Kafe NORWEGIAN   The lunch-pail crowd loves this cafe/bakery. Grab-and-go options include a plate of smoked salmon and scrambled eggs, smoked ham and Jarlsberg cheese sandwiches, and tempting pastries, cakes, cookies, and waffles with strawberry preserves. Sit in the small, open-air seating area (just beyond the door, adjacent to the Stave Church). Alas, the nearby Viking Ship, once a place where kids could work off excess energy, is now only for show. Wine is sold by the glass.

Norway Pavilion, World Showcase. ☎ **407/939-3463.** www.disneyworld.com. Advance Dining Reservations not available. Sandwiches and salads $4–$10; pastries $3–$6. AE, DC, DISC, MC, V. Daily 11am–park closing. Parking $11.

Lotus Blossom Café CHINESE   If you're in a hurry but still in the mood for some good Chinese, this recently refurbished open-air cafe offers familiar favorites. Expect veggie stir-fry, beef noodle soup, sesame chicken salad, and eggrolls that are slightly above fast-food quality. The outdoor covered seating is refreshing. Chinese beer and wine are available.

China Pavilion, World Showcase. ☎ **407/939-3463.** www.disneyworld.com. Advance Dining Reservations not available. Meals $4–$8. AE, DC, DISC, MC, V. Daily 11am–park closing. Parking $11.

Sommerfest GERMAN   At the rear of the Germany Pavilion, this outdoor eatery's quick-bite menu includes bratwurst and frankfurter sandwiches with sauerkraut. There is no specific menu for kids, making it a poor choice for very young children, although the school-age set and older kids should be fine. Black Forest cake and apple strudel sweeten the deal.

Germany Pavilion, World Showcase. ☎ **407/939-3463.** Advance Dining Reservations not available. All items under $7. AE, DC, DISC, MC, V. Daily 11am–park closing. Parking $11.

Sunshine Seasons in the Land (Value) FOOD COURT   The food isn't gourmet, but of all the cafeterias and counter-service stops in Disney World, the recently renovated Sunshine Seasons (with an impressionistic decor more reflective of the Land Pavilion's theme) offers the most diversity. It's especially good if you're traveling with kids who possess finicky (and varied) palates. There's the Asian Wok (stir-fry and barbecue), a wood-fired grill (salmon and flatbreads), a sandwich shop (Black Forest ham, salami, Cuban), a soup-and-salad counter (with veggies from the Land's own gardens), and a bakery. In addition to the main menu, each station offers a single kids' item— mac and cheese, grilled chicken, sweet-and-sour chicken. Wine by the glass, a frosty draft, and bottled beer are available.

Land Pavilion, Future World. ☎ **407/939-3463.** www.disneyworld.com. Advance Dining Reservations not available. Meals $7–$10; kids $4. AE, DC, DISC, MC, V. Daily 9am–8pm. Parking $11.

Yakitori House JAPANESE   Resembling the teahouse of the Imperial Summer Palace, this very small eatery offers teriyaki chicken and beef, tempura, sushi, salads, and Japanese curry. The food is reasonably good, though portions are smaller than at many other Disney restaurants. Teriyaki chicken is the only kid-specific item on the menu. There's seating both indoors and out, but no matter where you dine, you'll overlook tranquil Japanese gardens and a gentle waterfall.

Japan Pavilion, World Showcase. ☎ **407/939-3463.** www.disneyworld.com. Advance Dining Reservations not available. Meals $6–$8; kids $4. AE, DC, DISC, MC, V. Daily 11am–park closing. Parking $11.

IN THE MAGIC KINGDOM

In addition to the places mentioned below, there are plenty of fast-food outlets in the park. You may find, however, that a quiet sit-down meal is an essential way to get away from the madness. And remember: Magic Kingdom restaurants *don't serve alcohol*, so the adults in your party will have to go elsewhere if they want a drink with their meal.

These restaurants are located on the "Walt Disney World & Lake Buena Vista Dining" map (p. 144). See also "The Magic Kingdom" map (p. 188).

EXPENSIVE

Cinderella's Royal Table ⭐ AMERICAN   You'll be greeted by handmaidens before making your way inside this royal restaurant—by far the most popular place to dine in the Magic Kingdom. Those who enter are usually swept off their feet as they're transported back to a time when medieval kings and queens reigned—a feeling that's helped along by the Gothic interior, which includes leaded-glass windows, stone floors, and beamed ceilings. The servers treat you like a lord or lady (I'm not kidding; that's how they'll address you).

The restaurant underwent changes to its lineup in 2006 and now features only character meals, with decent but expensive food. Breakfast remains an all-you-can-eat buffet, while lunch and dinner offer a selection of appetizers, entrees, and desserts. Cinderella and a few other princesses are on hand during breakfast and lunch; the Fairy Godmother does hostess duty at the royal dinner (a souvenir photo package is included with your meal).

Note: Because of its location and ambience, a meal here is sought by everyone from little girls who dream of Prince Charming to romantics seeking a more intimate meal. The problem: This is actually one of the smallest dining rooms in Disney World, making Advance Dining Reservations a must. It may very well take several calls (and a lot of flexibility on your part) to ensure a spot. And thanks to a new policy, payment (via credit card) for your meal is required in full at the time of booking (no exceptions!). Slightly higher holiday pricing (add $2 per meal) is in effect during Thanksgiving week and from mid-December through the first week of January.

Cinderella Castle, Fantasyland. © **407/939-3463.** www.disneyworld.com. Advance Dining Reservations required. Character breakfast (p. 171) $33 adults, $23 kids 3–9; character lunch $36 adults, $24 kids; character dinner $41 adults, $26 kids. AE, DC, DISC, MC, V. Daily 8–11:15am, noon–3pm, and 4pm–1 hr. before park closes. Parking $11.

Tony's Town Square Restaurant ITALIAN   Inspired by the cafe in *Lady and the Tramp,* Tony's dishes up pastas and pizzas in a pleasant, if somewhat harried, dining room with etched glass and ornate gingerbread trim. Original animation cels from the movie (including the film's famous spaghetti smooch) line the walls. Lunch includes sandwiches, salads, and pizzas, along with such entrees as pasta primavera, spaghetti and meatballs, and the catch of the day. Evening fare might include chicken Florentine, seafood in a spicy tomato sauce, or a New York strip steak. Tony's has one of the kid-friendliest menus in the kingdom and is a top spot for families with young children. Additional seating is available in a sunny, plant-filled solarium.

Main Street. © **407/939-3463.** www.disneyworld.com. Kids' menu w/activities, highchairs, boosters. Advance Dining Reservations strongly recommended. Main courses $11–$15 lunch, $20–$26 dinner; kids $7–$8. AE, DC, DISC, MC, V. Daily 11am–park closing. Parking $11.

MODERATE

Liberty Tree Tavern ⭐ AMERICAN   Soak up the historic ambience in this replica of an 18th-century Colonial pub, with oak-plank floors and a brick fireplace hung with copper pots. Lunch includes sandwiches, seafood (such as cured salmon and crab cakes), salads, soups, burgers, and pot roast. The nightly character dinner (a family favorite; see p. 172) is a set family-style meal that includes roast turkey, carved beef, smoked pork,

Walt Disney World & Lake Buena Vista Dining

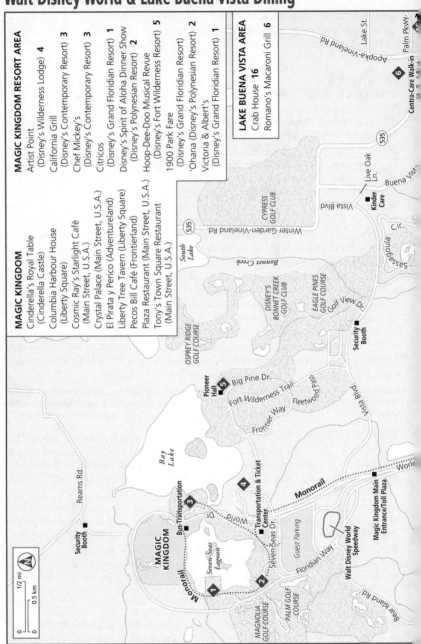

MAGIC KINGDOM

Cinderella's Royal Table (Cinderella Castle)
Columbia Harbour House (Liberty Square)
Cosmic Ray's Starlight Café (Main Street, U.S.A.)
Crystal Palace (Main Street, U.S.A.)
El Pirata y Perico (Adventureland)
Liberty Tree Tavern (Liberty Square)
Pecos Bill Café (Frontierland)
Plaza Restaurant (Main Street, U.S.A.)
Tony's Town Square Restaurant (Main Street, U.S.A.)

MAGIC KINGDOM RESORT AREA

Artist Point (Disney's Wilderness Lodge) **4**
California Grill (Disney's Contemporary Resort) **3**
Chef Mickey's (Disney's Contemporary Resort) **3**
Citricos (Disney's Grand Floridian Resort) **1**
Disney's Spirit of Aloha Dinner Show (Disney's Polynesian Resort) **2**
Hoop-Dee-Doo Musical Revue (Disney's Fort Wilderness Resort) **5**
1900 Park Fare (Disney's Grand Floridian Resort)
'Ohana (Disney's Polynesian Resort) **2**
Victoria & Albert's (Disney's Grand Floridian Resort) **1**

LAKE BUENA VISTA AREA

Crab House **16**
Romano's Macaroni Grill **6**

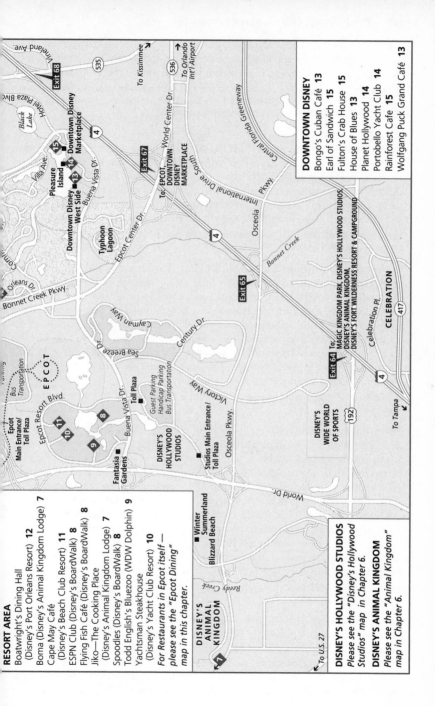

RESORT AREA

Boatwright's Dining Hall
(Disney's Port Orleans Resort) **12**

Boma (Disney's Animal Kingdom Lodge) **7**

Cape May Café
(Disney's Beach Club Resort) **11**

ESPN Club (Disney's BoardWalk) **8**

Flying Fish Café (Disney's BoardWalk) **8**

Jiko—The Cooking Place
(Disney's Animal Kingdom Lodge) **7**

Spoodles (Disney's BoardWalk) **8**

Todd English's Bluezoo (WDW Dolphin) **9**

Yachtsman Steakhouse
(Disney's Yacht Club Resort) **10**

*For Restaurants in Epcot itself —
please see the "Epcot Dining"
map in this chapter.*

DISNEY'S HOLLYWOOD STUDIOS
*Please see the "Disney's Hollywood
Studios" map in Chapter 6.*

DISNEY'S ANIMAL KINGDOM
*Please see the "Animal Kingdom"
map in Chapter 6.*

DOWNTOWN DISNEY

Bongo's Cuban Café **13**

Earl of Sandwich **15**

Fulton's Crab House **15**

House of Blues **13**

Planet Hollywood **14**

Portobello Yacht Club **14**

Rainforest Cafe **15**

Wolfgang Puck Grand Café **13**

mashed potatoes, stuffing, and mac and cheese—along with apple crisp and vanilla ice cream. While the fare's not all that interesting, it is appropriate to the setting. Kids' fare includes mac and cheese, sliced turkey, beef and tomato macaroni, and pizza.

Liberty Square. ℂ 407/939-3463. www.disneyworld.com. Kids' menu w/activities, highchairs, boosters. Advance Dining Reservations recommended. Main courses $11–$16 lunch, $7–$8 kids; character dinner $28 adults, $13 kids. AE, DC, DISC, MC, V. Daily 11:30am–3pm and 4pm–park closing. Parking $11.

INEXPENSIVE

Columbia Harbour House ⋆ AMERICAN/SEAFOOD   This small eatery often goes overlooked because of its size—it has only a handful of cozy little rooms, all nautically themed—but it does offer some rather decent light fare. Battered fish and shrimp (far meatier than most), sandwiches, clam chowder, tasty ham, hummus, tuna sandwiches, and fruit are among the items listed on the menu. Kids can choose mac and cheese or chicken, though they may find the main menu to their liking as well.

Liberty Square. ℂ 407/939-3643. www.disneyworld.com. All items $6–$8; kids $4. AE, DC, DISC, MC, V. Daily 11am–park closing. Parking $11.

Cosmic Ray's Starlight Café AMERICAN   The largest of the park's fast-food spots, this cafe features an appropriately huge menu. Three separate counters, similar to a food court, serve a variety of chicken options (whole- or half-rotisserie, dark meat, white meat, fried or grilled), ribs, sandwiches, burgers, hot dogs, veggie wraps, soups, and salads. The casual atmosphere and varied menu make Ray's a great choice for those with kids. Do note, however, that you may have to wait in more than one line here, as each station offers a different selection. The large dining area fills up quickly, and the noise level is generally high. *Tip:* Kosher meals are available here for direct purchase (though they're not particularly noteworthy).

Tomorrowland. ℂ 407/939-3463. www.disneyworld.com. All items $7–$14. AE, DC, DISC, MC, V. Daily 11am–park closing. Parking $11.

Pecos Bill Café ⋆ AMERICAN   Set in an old-time saloon with heavy chandeliers and a golden-stucco interior, this sit-and-go fast-food joint serves up burgers, hot dogs, salads, a barbecue-pork sandwich, and a great Southwestern chicken wrap. Kids can choose chilled chicken or a mini-hot-dog meal. Portions are large, as are the prices. The good location—between Frontierland and Adventureland—means that those traveling clockwise through the park will probably hit the area just in time for lunch. It can get very crowded at peak times, though there is quite a bit of indoor and outdoor seating.

Tip: If your cravings run more toward Mexican food, head through the indoor seating area in the back to the seasonal **El Pirata y Perico,** a covered outdoor snack spot featuring tacos, empanadas, chips, and taco salad (all under $6). It's located in Adventureland, just across from Pirates of the Caribbean.

Frontierland. ℂ 407/939-3643. www.disneyworld.com. All items $6–$8; kids $4. AE, DC, DISC, MC, V. Daily 11am–park closing. Parking $11.

Plaza Restaurant AMERICAN   The sundaes, banana splits, and other ice-cream creations—arguably the best in WDW—at this 19th-century–inspired restaurant draw more folks than anywhere else, especially during the dog days of summer. The Plaza also has tasty, if expensive, sandwiches (turkey, Reuben, vegetarian, tuna, burgers) that come with fries or potato salad. On the kids' side, choices range from a grilled cheese, PB&J, or turkey sandwich to grilled chicken on a stick. You can eat inside the Art Nouveau dining room or on a veranda overlooking Cinderella Castle.

On Again, Off Again . . . On Again

The Plaza Pavilion in Magic Kingdom's Tomorrowland was transformed in 2005 into **Tomorrowland Terrace Noodle Station.** Its menu includes chicken and beef dishes, egg rolls, and other Asian-themed cuisine. This is one of the nicest and largest outdoor seating areas in the park; you can sit out in the fresh air even as you get a respite from the sun—and there's a great view of the gardens, water-ways, and Cinderella Castle. If you've picked up a sweet treat on Main Street and can't find a place to sit down, this is the perfect spot—it's often overlooked by visitors. *Note:* The Noodle Station has been closed sporadically, so check your guide map to see if it's open when you're visiting. All items are $6 to $8.

Main Street. 𝒞 **407/939-3463.** www.disneyworld.com. Kids' menu w/activities, highchairs, boosters. Advance Dining Reservations recommended. Meals $10–$11; kids $8; ice cream $3–$6. AE, DC, DISC, MC, V. Daily 11am–park closing. Parking $11.

IN DISNEY'S HOLLYWOOD STUDIOS

Some of the most uniquely themed eateries in all of WDW can be found in this park. That, however, also makes them some of the most difficult to get into, so Advance Dining Reservations are a must at any of the full-service restaurants in the park. Those listed below are the best of the bunch.

They're located on two maps, "Walt Disney World & Lake Buena Vista Dining" (p. 144) and "Disney's Hollywood Studios Theme Park" (p. 227).

EXPENSIVE

Hollywood Brown Derby AMERICAN   This elegant restaurant is modeled after the famed Los Angeles celebrity haunt. It features some of the finest food and the fanciest surroundings in the park—along with some of the highest prices. White linens, chandeliers, and potted palms add to the upscale atmosphere, and over 1,500 caricatures of its most famous patrons over the years line the walls, including those of Lucille Ball, Bette Davis, and Clark Gable. Owner Bob Cobb created the original restaurant's signature Cobb salad in the 1930s. (It's so popular that this Derby serves over 31,000 of them a year.) Most kids won't be interested in that option, but hot dogs, grilled chicken, tempura grouper strips, grilled cheese, or beef and tomato macaroni should tempt them. Dinner entrees include pan-fired grouper with balsamic roasted asparagus, sesame-seared ahi tuna, and roasted pork rib chop with smoked cheese tomato fondue. The signature dessert, grapefruit cake with cream-cheese icing, is the perfect way to end your meal (there are ice-cream options for younger tastes). The Derby has a full bar and a modest selection of California wines. If you're looking for a more sophisticated edge with kid-friendly options, this is the place (though older kids will likely fare best).

Hollywood Blvd. 𝒞 **407/939-3463.** www.disneyworld.com. Kids' menu w/activities, highchairs, boosters. Advance Dining Reservations strongly recommended. Main courses $12–$22 lunch, $18–$30 dinner; kids $5–$7. Fantasmic Dinner Package $44 adults, $12 kids. AE, DC, DISC, MC, V. Daily 11:30am–park closing. Parking $11.

MODERATE

50's Prime Time Café AMERICAN   Ever wanted to go back to when life was simpler? This homey cafe looks like a 1950s kitchen, complete with Formica counters and black-and-white TVs showing clips from classics such as *My Little Margie.* The servers add to the fun, greeting diners with lines like, "Hi, Sis; I'll go tell Mom you're home," and they may threaten to withhold dessert if you don't eat all your food. Kids love it—and they adore seeing their parents admonished for dinner-table infractions. The entrees—fried chicken, meatloaf, pot roast, and open-faced sandwiches—aren't quite as good as Mom's, but taste decent nonetheless. The kids' fare (grilled fish, grilled chicken, meatloaf, hot dogs, chicken nuggets, mac and cheese) is always a hit. The s'mores and sundaes are worth the wait. Beer and specialty drinks (including a mean margarita) are served.

Near the Indiana Jones Stunt Spectacular. ℂ 407/939-3463. www.disneyworld.com. Kids' menu w/activities, highchairs, boosters. Advance Dining Reservations strongly recommended. Main courses $11–$17 lunch, $13–$20 dinner; kids $8. AE, DC, DISC, MC, V. Daily 11am–park closing. Parking $11.

Mama Melrose's Ristorante Italiano ITALIAN Set along the simulated New York street, this large warehouse-style neighborhood eatery is filled with red-checked tablecloths, wood floors, and vinyl booths. The best adult bets are the wood-fired flatbreads (grilled pepperoni, four-cheese, portobello, and others for $12–$13). The bambino menu features pasta, pizza, and chicken Parmesan.

Near the Backlot Tour. ℂ 407/939-3463. www.disneyworld.com. Kids' menu w/activities, highchairs, boosters. Advance Dining Reservations strongly recommended. Main courses $12–$18 lunch, $12–$24 dinner; kids $5. Fantasmic Dinner Package $33 adults, $12 kids. AE, DC, DISC, MC, V. Daily 11:30am–park closing. Parking $11.

Sci-Fi Dine-In Theater Restaurant AMERICAN This restaurant's simulated night sky is filled with fiber-optic stars that twinkle overhead as you sit in a chrome "convertible" watching a giant screen showing '50s and '60s sci-fi flicks, zany newsreels, cartoons, and B horror-movie clips. Fun-loving carhops deliver free popcorn along with your meal. The menu features such items as Attack of the Killer Club Sandwich, the Beach Party Panic, and Red Planet (translation: sandwiches, ribs, burgers, seafood, pasta, steak, and salads). Kids will love the drinks served with souvenir glow-in-the-dark ice cubes. The food is average; it's the atmosphere that keeps the crowds coming. *Note:* The dining room here is fairly dark, and the clips, though pretty harmless, could scare a very young child.

Near Indiana Jones Epic Stunt Spectacular. ℂ 407/939-3463. www.disneyworld.com. Kids' menu w/activities, highchairs, boosters. Advance Dining Reservations strongly recommended. Main courses $11–$19 lunch, $11–$19 dinner; kids $8. AE, DC, DISC, MC, V. Daily 11am–park closing. Parking $11.

INEXPENSIVE
Toy Story Pizza Planet PIZZA The menu here is far from original, but will satisfy some of the younger (and pickier) eaters in your family with pizza, salad, and

---

Tips **Disney's Hollywood Dining Alternative**

If you forgot to make Advance Dining Reservations or couldn't get a table at your chosen restaurant, try the Sci-Fi Dine-In Theater Restaurant's next-door neighbor, the **ABC Commissary**. While not a themed restaurant per se, it offers one of the most diverse menus in the park, with items such as Cuban sandwiches, vegetable noodle stir-fry, tabbouleh wraps, fish and chips, curry chicken, burgers, and rather good desserts. Most items cost $6 to $8. Plainer than most Disney eateries, it really resembles a commissary, and TVs lining the walls play commercials for the latest and greatest shows running on Disney-owned ABC.

Tips A Balancing Act

Well-balanced kids' meals are a new menu standard at WDW's restaurants. In an effort to encourage healthier eating habits, kids' meals (for ages 3–9) now include nutritious side dishes and beverages instead of the usual suspects (most notably fries and soda). In addition to an entree of their choice, kids can pick low-fat milk, 100% fruit juice, or water to drink, plus a side of unsweetened applesauce, baby carrots, or fresh fruit. Fries and soda, while still available, are upon request only.

---

desserts. It's a big favorite with kids, thanks to the arcade games located just next door: Avoid it if you don't want to spend the afternoon trying to pull littler ones away, or else remember to bring plenty of change.

In the Muppet Courtyard. ☎ 407/939-3463. www.disneyworld.com. Advance Dining Reservations not available. All meals $6–$9. AE, DC, DISC, MC, V. Daily 10:30am–park closing. Parking $11.

IN DISNEY'S ANIMAL KINGDOM

There are few restaurants in the newest of Disney's parks, and most that exist are counter-service or grab-and-go places (though decent ones, at that). In my opinion, only two are worth listing below.

Note: At press time, a new (and much needed) restaurant, **Yak & Yeti,** was nearing completion. Its exotic atmosphere and location near Expedition Everest give the impression that you're dining amid the foothills of the Himalayas. Both sit-down and counter-service areas with Pan-Asian cuisine will be available. See map p. 237.

MODERATE
Rainforest Cafe ✯ CALIFORNIA   Expect California fare with an island spin at this Rainforest and its cousin, listed on p. 157. Menu offerings tend to be tasty and somewhat creative. That said, the cafe, like other Disney restaurants, falls on the pricier side. Fun dishes include Mogambo Shrimp (sautéed in olive oil and served with penne), Rumble in the Jungle Turkey Wrap (with romaine, tomatoes, and bacon), Maya's Mixed Grill (ribs, chicken, and shrimp). Tables situated among the dining room's vines and generally inanimate animals are usually packed; that's partly due to the lack of other full-service options at Animal Kingdom, but also because of the real popularity of this loud and lively establishment. Beer, wine, and other alcoholic concoctions are served.

Just outside Disney's Animal Kingdom entrance. *Admission to park not required* (though there is an entrance from inside the park, too). ☎ 407/938-9100. www.rainforestcafe.com. Kids' menu w/activities, highchairs, boosters. Advance Dining Reservations strongly recommended. Main courses $11–$40 (most under $25) lunch and dinner; kids $7. AE, DC, DISC, MC, V. Daily 8am–11pm. Parking $11.

INEXPENSIVE
Tusker House AMERICAN   The thatched-roof Tusker House in Harambe Village features a buffet of options with a bit of culinary flair. Thanks to a recent overhaul, this eatery now does a character breakfast (Donald's Safari Breakfast with Donald, Mickey, and Goofy), while a buffet (sans the characters) replaces the previous a la carte menu at lunch and dinner.

In Africa, near entrance. ☎ 407/939-3463. www.disneyworld.com. Advance Dining Reservations highly recommended for breakfast. Character breakfast $19 adults, $11 kids 3–9; lunch $19 adults, $11 kids; dinner $34 adults, $13 kids. AE, DC, DISC, MC, V. Daily 8–10:30am and 11:30am–park closing. Parking $11.

Tips More Kid Cuisine . . .

Here are a few more places in the Disney resorts and parks to find food that might tickle younger tastes. Many of these are walk-up or casual eateries that don't require Advance Dining Reservations, though you should consider making them at Big River Grille & Brewing Works, Cap'n Jacks, Grand Floridian Café, Kona Café, and Narcoossee's by calling ✆ **407/939-3463.**

- **Big River Grille & Brewing Works,** Disney's BoardWalk: grilled cheese, burgers, hot dogs, PB&J, mac and cheese ($4–$5).
- **Cap'n Jacks,** Downtown Disney: grilled chicken sandwich, mac and cheese, hot dogs, PB&J ($7–$8).
- **Flame Tree Barbecue,** Disney's Animal Kingdom: hot dogs, baked chicken wings ($4).
- **Grand Floridian Café,** Grand Floridian Resort & Spa: pizza, PB&J, miniburgers, chicken strips, and penne pasta ($5.50), plus beef filet, fish filet, and grilled chicken ($11).
- **Kona Café,** Polynesian Resort: chicken fingers, pasta, grilled cheese, PB&J, burgers, hot dogs ($5.50).
- **Lottawatta Lodge,** Blizzard Beach: chicken strips, fish and chips, turkey sandwich, pizza, burgers, hot dogs ($7–$8).
- **Narcoossee's,** Grand Floridian Resort & Spa: grilled fish, fish filet, petite filet, mac and cheese, chicken fingers, pasta marinara or pasta with butter, burgers ($6–$13).
- **Pecos Bill Café,** Magic Kingdom: chicken nuggets, salad with chicken ($4).
- **Pinocchio Village Haus,** Magic Kingdom: mac and cheese, PB&J ($7–$8).
- **Pizzafari,** Disney's Animal Kingdom: cheese quesadilla, PB&J ($4).
- **Plaza Pavilion,** Magic Kingdom: grilled chicken strips, chef salad, miniburgers, grilled cheese, turkey sandwich, PB&J ($7–$8).
- **Todd English's Bluezoo,** WDW Dolphin: spaghetti, beef tenderloin, fried fish filet, grilled chicken ($7–$12).
- **Toontown Farmers' Market,** Magic Kingdom: fresh fruit ($1–$3.29).
- **Typhoon Tilly's,** Typhoon Lagoon: grilled cheese pretzel, PB&J, burgers, hot dogs ($5–$6).
- **Whispering Canyon Café,** Wilderness Lodge: all-you-can-eat skillet, chicken strips, grilled fish, burgers, mac and cheese ($8).

IN THE WALT DISNEY WORLD RESORTS

Most restaurants listed in this category continue the Disney trend of being above market price. On the flip side, many offer food that's a notch or two better than what you find in the theme parks.

These restaurants are located on the "Walt Disney World & Lake Buena Vista Dining" map (p. 144).

VERY EXPENSIVE

Citricos ⓐ MODERN FRENCH   The perfect spot for a night out without the kids (even if this restaurant does welcome them), the Grand Floridian's number-two restaurant (Victoria & Albert's is number one) offers a menu of French, Alsatian, and Provençal cuisine with California and Florida touches (except when it comes to the kids' menu, which ranges from chicken tenders to grilled tenderloin). The old-world decor includes plenty of wrought-iron railings, mosaic-tile floors, flickering amber lights, and a spectacular show kitchen—all with an upscale artsy feel. The view of the Seven Seas Lagoon and Magic Kingdom fireworks is a bonus. Add a three-course wine pairing for $30.

At Disney's Grand Floridian Resort & Spa, 4401 Floridian Way. ✆ **407/939-3463.** www.disneyworld.com. Kids' menu w/activities, highchairs, boosters. Advance Dining Reservations strongly recommended. Main courses $23–$36; kids $6–$12. AE, DC, DISC, MC, V. Wed–Sun 5:30–10pm.

Victoria & Albert's ★★★ *Finds* INTERNATIONAL   Consider this **adults-only** restaurant (it's definitely not a place for kids) if you have a healthy budget and a desire for an evening without the young 'uns. It's Disney's most elegant restaurant and truly a dining event. The romantic space is crowned by a domed ceiling, and Victorian lamps softly illuminate 20 exquisitely appointed tables. Dinner is next to perfect—if the portions seem small, I dare you to make it through all seven courses. The fare changes nightly, but expect a feast fit for royalty (and costing a royal fortune). You might begin with chilled lobster roll, followed by Iranian Osetra caviar, pheasant consommé, and an entree such as tamari-glazed bluefin tuna over bok choy. English Stilton served with a burgundy-poached pear sets up desserts such as vanilla-bean crème brûlée and Kona chocolate soufflé. You can add a wine pairing to your meal for an extra $60 (an option I recommend).

At Disney's Grand Floridian Resort & Spa, 4401 Floridian Way. ✆ **407/939-3463.** www.disneyworld.com. No kids under 10. Advance Dining Reservations required. Jackets required for men. Not recommended for children. Prix fixe $115 per person, $175 w/wine pairing; $165 Chef's Table, $235 w/wine pairing. AE, DC, DISC, MC, V. 2 dinner seatings daily Sept–June 5:45–6:30pm and 9–9:45pm; 1 dinner seating July–Aug 6:45–8pm. Chef's Table 6pm only. Free self- and validated valet parking.

Yachtsman Steakhouse ★ SEAFOOD/STEAKS/CHOPS   Even by outside-the-park standards, the Yachtsman earns a B+ among steakhouses, and it's a good place to have a special dinner out with the kids. Its grain-fed Western beef is aged, cured, and cut here. You can see the cuts in a glass-enclosed aging room, and the exhibition kitchen provides a tantalizing glimpse of steaks, chops, and seafood being grilled over oak and hickory. Adult options range from an 8-ounce filet to a 12-ounce strip to a belly-busting 24-ounce T-bone. If you're not in the mood for beef, the Yachtsman also serves pan-seared sea bass, free-range chicken, and roasted winter-squash ravioli. The junior menu lists 6-ounce cuts of steak or prime rib, grilled chicken, chicken strips, burgers, hot dogs, and pasta. The decor features knotty-pine beams, plank floors, and leather-and-oak chairs. The staff is very cordial. The Yachtsman has an extensive wine list, though it's not in the same league as the other two contestants in this category.

At Disney's Yacht Club Resort, 1700 Epcot Resorts Blvd. ✆ **407/939-3463.** www.disneyworld.com. Kids' menu w/activities, highchairs, boosters. Advance Dining Reservations recommended. Main courses $21–$80 (most over $25); kids $6–$12. AE, DC, DISC, MC, V. Daily 5:30–10pm. Free self- and valet parking.

EXPENSIVE
Artist Point ★ *Finds* SEAFOOD/STEAKS/CHOPS   Enjoy a grand view of Disney's Wilderness Lodge and rather impressive murals of the Pacific Northwest (your kids can hunt for Hidden Mickeys; see p. 232) as you dine in this two-story restaurant, whose immense windows overlook waterfalls, rocky landscaping, and the resort's

erupting geyser. In keeping with the park-lodge theme, you'll be surrounded by iron chandeliers, wood furnishings, and animal carvings. The seasonal menu might feature the signature cedar-plank-roasted wild king salmon. Kids can dig into grilled chicken, baked salmon, pasta with cheese sauce, or a burger. There's terrace seating in fair weather. Expect a wine list now featuring exclusively Pacific Northwest choices. *Note:* Artist Point has a much more relaxed atmosphere than some of the busier WDW resort restaurants.

Tip: If you're looking for more family-oriented dining at the Wilderness Lodge, try the **Whispering Canyon Café,** where kids can horse-race on broomsticks, everyone gets a-whoopin' and a-hollerin' at dinner, and meals are served family style (though a la carte service is available if you so desire).

At Disney's Wilderness Lodge, 901 W. Timberline Dr. ✆ **407/939-3463.** www.disneyworld.com. Kids' menu w/activities, highchairs, boosters. Advance Dining Reservations recommended. Main courses $21–$49; kids $6–$10. AE, DC, DISC, MC, V. Daily 5:30–10pm. Free self- and valet parking.

Boma 🌟🌟 *Moments* AFRICAN   Boma, in the Animal Kingdom Lodge, is modeled after an African marketplace. There's plenty of open space to roam about, a thatched roof strewn with colorful banners, and large wood tables shaped like tree trunks. The rear overlooks the savanna, offering a pretty good view. The show kitchen and wood-burning grill send delicious aromas wafting throughout the room and fill the dinner buffet with diverse delicacies from more than 50 African nations.

Adventurous diners can expect such treats as Moroccan seafood salad (mussels, scallops, shrimp, and couscous), curried coconut seafood stew, chicken pepper-pot soup, and much more. The watermelon-rind salad is a specialty, but save room for the yummy desserts. The restaurant is set up in sections, each with a chef who can answer your questions about the cuisine. If there's something you particularly like, ask for the recipe; Disney is surprisingly good about sharing its culinary secrets. Kids will appreciate the penne with meatballs, chicken fingers, and large selection of fresh fruit. There's also a breakfast buffet.

At Disney's Animal Kingdom Lodge, 2901 Osceola Pkwy. ✆ **407/939-3463.** www.disneyworld.com. Kids' activities, highchairs, boosters. Advance Dining Reservations strongly recommended. Breakfast buffet $17 adults, $10 kids; dinner buffet $26 adults, $12 kids. AE, DC, DISC, MC, V. Daily 7–11am and 5–10pm. Free self-parking.

California Grill 🌟🌟🌟 CALIFORNIA   Located on the Contemporary Resort's 15th floor, this stunning restaurant offers views of the Magic Kingdom and lagoon below. The interior incorporates Art Deco elements (curved pearwood walls, vivid splashes of color, polished black-granite surfaces), but the focus is an exhibition kitchen with a wood-burning oven and rotisserie. The eclectic menu changes to take advantage of

---

⌒ Fun Fact Cooking for Kids

Disney's Grand Floridian Resort & Spa offers two special cooking programs for children. **Grand Adventures in Cooking** invites up to 12 youngsters, ages 4 to 10, to make dessert in a 2-hour decorating class ($29 per child). The **Wonderland Tea Party** gives kids the same age a 1-hour primer in cupcake decorating—with their fingers! They also feast on heart-shaped PB&Js and sip apple-juice "tea" while they play with Alice and the Mad Hatter ($29 per child). Call ✆ **407/824-3000** or 407/939-3463 for details on both programs.

Tips Pint-Size Portions

If your children are adventurous in the food department but can't handle adult-size portions, several Disney restaurants allow kids to sample dishes geared to adult tastes but served in portion sizes suited to smaller stomachs (and at smaller prices, too). Options include (but are not limited to):

- **Coral Reef,** Epcot: grilled mahimahi ($8).
- **Rose & Crown Pub & Dining Room,** Epcot: bangers and mash, cottage pie ($8).
- **Citricos,** Disney's Grand Floridian Resort: chicken noodle soup ($2), oak-grilled filet of beef ($12).
- **Artist Point,** Disney's Wilderness Lodge: baked salmon with mashed potatoes and veggies ($9).
- **California Grill,** Disney's Contemporary Resort: grilled petit filet with mashed potatoes and veggies ($11).
- **Flying Fish Café,** Disney's BoardWalk: lettuce salad ($3), buttermilk fried flying fish of the day with roasted potatoes and veggies ($8).

fresh market fare, but headliners may include seared day boat scallops with farro-wheat risotto and crustacean butter sauce, or perhaps oak-fired filet of beef with Gruyère–potato pavé. The Grill also has a nice sushi and sashimi menu. Most kids will wrinkle their noses at those choices, but options for youngsters include pizza, mac and cheese, grilled salmon, grilled chicken, and an oak-fired steak. Save this one for a night when your kids are with a babysitter, unless they're old enough to stay up for the fireworks display. The list of California wines complements the meal and views.

Note: It can be tough to get a table, especially on weekends and during Disney fireworks hours, so reserve as far in advance as possible. Also note that this is one of the few WDW restaurants with a dress code; think business casual.

At Disney's Contemporary Resort, 4600 N. World Dr. ✆ 407/939-3463. www.disneyworld.com. Kids' menu w/activities, highchairs, boosters. Advance Dining Reservations recommended. Main courses $25–$35; sushi and sashimi $13–$24; kids $7–$11. AE, DC, DISC, MC, V. Daily 5:30–10pm. Free self-parking.

Flying Fish Café SEAFOOD   Chefs at this boardwalk-inspired restaurant take the stage in a show kitchen that turns out entrees such as potato-wrapped red snapper, coriander-crusted yellowfin tuna, and oak-grilled mahimahi. It's likely none of these will tempt your offspring, but the grilled chicken or steak, fish and chips, or cheese pasta should. Vibrant tile floors, delicate jellyfish-like lighting, and shimmering fish scales create an undersea ambience. A whimsical Ferris wheel and hand-painted murals conjure thoughts of Coney Island. The atmosphere is a bit more upscale than you'd think; this might not be the best place for those too young to sit still. *Note:* If you can't get a table here, ask to sit at the counter—you'll get a great view of the exhibition kitchen.

At Disney's BoardWalk, 2101 N. Epcot Resorts Blvd. ✆ 407/939-3463. www.disneyworld.com. Kids' menu w/activities, highchairs, boosters. Advance Dining Reservations strongly recommended. Main courses $23–$38; kids $6–$12. AE, DC, DISC, MC, V. Daily 5:30–10pm. Free self-parking.

Jiko—The Cooking Place ✿ AFRICAN   The Animal Kingdom Lodge's signature restaurant is a nice diversion from the normal Disney restaurants and a complementary addition to the multicultural dining rooms at Epcot's World Showcase. Jiko's show kitchen turns out a unique menu of international cuisine with African overtones. Dishes might include Durban curry shrimp, maize-crusted Pacific sturgeon, or Chermoula roasted Tanglewood chicken with red-skinned potatoes, preserved lemons, kalamata olives, and roasted garlic. Kids face some usual (grilled cheese, grilled chicken, PB&J, mac and cheese) and unusual (broiled fish, grilled steak) suspects. The wine list features a number of South African vintages.

At Disney's Animal Kingdom Lodge, 2901 Osceola Pkwy. ℂ 407/939-3463. www.disneyworld.com. Kids' menu w/activities, highchairs, boosters. Advance Dining Reservations strongly recommended. Main courses $14–$30; kids $6–$11. AE, DC, DISC, MC, V. Daily 5:30–10pm. Free self-parking.

Spoodles TAPAS Mediterranean flavor and old-world charm are vividly apparent upon entering this lively (read: noisy) family restaurant. Exposed brick, high-beamed ceilings, and warm hues of deep red and golden yellow run throughout the sizeable dining room. An eclectic mix of mismatched lighting and wooden farmhouse furnishings add to the casual, comfortable feel. The large open kitchen raises the noise level a notch or two, as does the pizza kitchen across the room, but that's all part of the appeal. Kids face beef kabobs, cheese pizza, chicken strips, beef and tomato macaroni, or mac and cheese. Adult fare might include oak-grilled salmon with roasted vegetable stew or lemon chicken with saffron orzo. A respectable wine list has recently been added, including tableside sangria presentations. Breakfast is served daily.

Note: Try for a table on the small patio, where you can take in all of the BoardWalk action. During the peak summer season, thanks to Spoodles' location on Disney's BoardWalk, the wait for a table can be long, even with Advance Dining Reservations—so this may not be the best option for famished families.

At Disney's BoardWalk, 2101 N. Epcot Resorts Blvd. ℂ 407/939-3463. www.disneyworld.com. Kids' menu w/activities, highchairs, boosters. Advance Dining Reservations strongly recommended. Breakfast $8–$12; dinner $17–$29. AE, DC, DISC, MC. V. Daily 7am–10pm. Pizza window 5pm–midnight. Valet and free self-parking.

Todd English's Bluezoo ✦✦ SEAFOOD Set inside the WDW Dolphin, this is the hippest, hottest, happeningest place to dine in town. Acclaimed chef Todd English has created an amazing menu of fresh seafood and coastal dishes that are served with flair in an artsy, contemporary setting designed to evoke the ocean. Chefs at work in the show kitchen turn out an amazing flatbread appetizer and melt-in-your-mouth entrees like Cantonese lobster and miso-glazed Chilean sea bass. The portions here are meal-worthy, not miniscule, but prices are still hefty and do not include side dishes. Dress is casual (this is Disney); however, the atmosphere is definitely upscale and caters to adults. It's perfect for an evening out on the town without the kids in tow. *Tip:* The unique bar/lounge has frequent live music or a DJ spinning today's hottest tunes.

At the WDW Dolphin, 1500 Epcot Resort Blvd. ℂ 407/934-1111. www.disneyworld.com. Advance Dining Reservations recommended. Main courses $20–$48. AE, DISC, MC, V. Daily 3:30–11pm. Free self- and validated valet parking.

MODERATE

Boatwright's Dining Hall NEW ORLEANS A family atmosphere (noisy), good food (by Disney standards), and reasonable prices (ditto) make Boatwright's a hit. The jambalaya is sans seafood but is filled with vegetables, chicken, and sausage—all rather spicy and giving it quite a kick. Other dinner items include grilled salmon, slow-roasted prime rib, and penne with shrimp. Boatwright's is modeled after a 19th-century boat factory, complete with the wooden hull of a Louisiana fishing boat suspended from its lofty beamed ceiling. Most kids like the wooden toolboxes on every table; each contains

---

(*Tips* **For Smaller Stomachs**

If your youngsters aren't satisfied with the offerings on the kids' menu (though many feature pint-sized portions of more adult options, along with plenty of familiar favorites), try the appetizer menu. They'll have more to choose from and the price is right. Also ask if half-portions are available; they are generally not advertised, though some restaurants offer them upon request. The same applies when requesting items a la carte: Disney's menus won't always reflect a la carte items, though they are often available if you ask.

---

a salt shaker that doubles as a level, a wood-clamp sugar dispenser, a pepper-grinder-cum-ruler, a jar of unmatched utensils, shop rags (read: napkins), and a little metal pail of crayons. On the food side, they can choose a cheeseburger, chicken strips, or mac and cheese. At breakfast, they can get Mickey Mouse–shaped pancakes!

At Disney's Port Orleans Resort, 2201 Orleans Dr. (407/939-3463. www.disneyworld.com. Kids' menu w/activities, highchairs, boosters. Advance Dining Reservations recommended. Main courses $8–$10 breakfast, $14–$21 dinner; kids $6–$8. AE, DC, DISC, MC, V. Daily 7–11:30am and 5–10pm. Free self-parking.

Cape May Café *Overrated* SEAFOOD   This New England–style clambake offers a selection of oysters, clams, mussels, baked fish, and small peel-and-eat shrimp. Accompaniments include corn on the cob, potatoes, and other veggies. Landlubbers, fear not; the not-so-fishy fare includes pasta, barbecued ribs, and sirloin. The kids' bar has fish nuggets, chicken strips, hot dogs, and mac and cheese. Though the choices are plentiful, this is still a resort-style buffet and nowhere near as fun as an authentic beachside clambake. The casual nautical theme carries into the restaurant from the surrounding Beach Club Resort. A character breakfast buffet is held daily (p. 171).

At Disney's Beach Club Resort, 1800 Epcot Resorts Blvd. (407/939-3463. www.disneyworld.com. Kids' menu w/activities, highchairs, boosters. Advance Dining Reservations strongly recommended. Character breakfast $19 adults, $11 kids 3–9; dinner buffet $26 adults, $12 kids. AE, DC, DISC, MC, V. Daily 7:30–11am and 5:30–9:30pm. Free self- and valet parking.

ESPN Club *R* AMERICAN   For sports enthusiasts, this is *the* place to dine in WDW. Guests are surrounded by monitors showing every possible sporting event and lots of sports-related memorabilia. The restaurant also has a small video arcade. The all-American fare includes "Boo-Yeah" chili, hot wings, burgers, sandwiches, and salads. The service is impeccable; never have I had a waiter so quick on his feet. While the food is quite good, it's really the atmosphere—very entertaining for kids—that draws the crowds.

At Disney's BoardWalk, 2101 N. Epcot Resorts Blvd. (407/939-1177. www.disneyworld.com. Advance Dining Reservations not available. Lunch and dinner $9–$13. AE, DC, MC, V. Mon–Thurs 11:30am–1am, Fri–Sat 11:30am–2am. Free self-parking, valet parking $10.

'Ohana *R* PACIFIC RIM   Its star is earned on the fun front, but the decibel level here can get a bit overwhelming, especially for those in search of a relaxing night out. Inside, you're welcomed as a "cousin," which fits because *'Ohana* means family in Hawaiian. As your food is being prepared over an 18-foot fire pit, the staff keeps your eyes and ears filled with all sorts of shenanigans. The blowing of a conch shell summons a storyteller; coconut races get under way in the center aisle; and you can shed your inhibitions and shake it during the hula lessons. The edibles include a variety of

---

Tips Anyone Hungry?

There are plenty of places in WDW to eat and eat and then eat some more, so plan on heading to these food fests when you're plenty hungry. WDW boasts 10 **all-you-can-eat** restaurants, which is really Disney's polite way of saying feel free to eat absolutely everything in front of you.

Options include **'Ohana** at the Polynesian Resort, **Whispering Canyon** at the Wilderness Lodge, **Boma** at the Animal Kingdom Lodge, **Cape May Café** at the Beach Club Resort, **Tusker House** at the Animal Kingdom, **Crystal Palace** at the Magic Kingdom, **Liberty Tree Tavern** at the Magic Kingdom, **Garden Grill** at Epcot, **Akershus Royal Banquet Hall** at Epcot's Norway, **Hollywood & Vine** at Disney's Hollywood Studios, **Chef Mickey's** at the Contemporary Resort, and **1900 Park Fare** at the Grand Floridian.

---

skewers, including turkey, shrimp, steak, and pork. You'll also find lots of trimmings and a full bar with limited wine selections (tropical alcoholic drinks are available for an added fee). *Tip:* Ask for a seat in the main dining room, or you won't get a good view of the entertainment. *Note:* The daily character breakfast, featuring Mickey, Stitch, and friends, is one of the most popular in WDW (p. 173).

At Disney's Polynesian Resort, 1600 Seven Seas Dr. ☎ 407/939-3463. www.disneyworld.com. Kids' menu w/activities, highchairs, boosters. Advance Dining Reservations strongly encouraged. Character breakfast $19 adults, $11 kids 3–9; dinner $27 adults, $11 kids. AE, DC, DISC, MC, V. Daily 7:30–11am and 5–10pm. Free self- and valet parking.

3 Places to Dine in Lake Buena Vista

In this section, I've listed restaurants located in Downtown Disney and the Lake Buena Vista area. Downtown Disney is 2½ miles from Epcot off Buena Vista Drive. It encompasses the Downtown Disney Marketplace, a very pleasant complex of shops and restaurants on a scenic lagoon; the adjoining Pleasure Island, a nighttime entertainment venue; and Downtown Disney West Side, a slightly more upscale collection of shops, restaurants, Cirque du Soleil (p. 335), and a movie theater. *Note:* Pleasure Island's restaurants don't require admission.

Many of these eateries can be found on the "Walt Disney World & Lake Buena Vista Dining" map (p. 144).

AT PLEASURE ISLAND
EXPENSIVE

Portobello Yacht Club ✿ SOUTHERN ITALIAN   The pizzas here go beyond the routine to include an updated *quattro formaggio* (mozzarella, Gorgonzola, Parmesan, and Fontina cheeses) and *margherita* (plum tomatoes, fresh mozzarella, and basil). But it's the less casual entrees that pack people into this place: You may find a nice salmon *puttanesca* (Alaskan king salmon topped with sauteed tomatoes, garlic, capers, and kalamata olives) or *spaghettini frutti del mare* (pasta with Alaskan king crab, scallops, shrimp, and clams). Sausage pizza, spaghetti, grilled fish, chicken tenders, burgers, and hot dogs will keep kids happy, but the service is geared more to adults, and wait times between courses can be a bit much for little ones. Situated in a gabled Bermuda-style house filled with nautical accents, the Portobello's covered patio overlooks Lake Buena Vista. Its cellar is small but offers a nice selection of wines.

At Pleasure Island, 1650 Buena Vista Dr. ℂ **407/934-8888.** www.levyrestaurants.com. Kids' menu w/activities, high-chairs, boosters. Advance Dining Reservations recommended. Main courses $18–$56; pizzas $9–$11; kids $5–$12. AE, DC, DISC, MC, V. Daily 11:30am–3pm and 5–11pm. Free self-parking.

MODERATE

Planet Hollywood *(Overrated* AMERICAN   Those who flock to this restaurant come for the movie memorabilia and scenery from some of Hollywood's hottest hits, much like those who head to the Hard Rock (a far better choice) to check out its musical montage. Though the atmosphere is fairly neat (including a planetarium-like ceiling), the Planet's servers can cop an attitude, and the food is blasé, including the kids' turkey sandwich, pizza, and chicken fingers. Adults will find the usual suspects: salads, sandwiches, burgers, pasta, steaks, and seafood. Although it's unquestionably popular with families, this is not the best food in WDW; the noise level may be too much for young kids (and their parents); and the lines can get excruciatingly long in peak season.

At Pleasure Island, 1506 Buena Vista Dr. (look for the big globe). ℂ **407/827-7827.** www.planethollywood.com. Kids' menu w/activities, highchairs, boosters. Limited Advance Dining Reservations available. Main courses $11–$23 (most under $16); kids $6–$8. AE, DC, DISC, MC, V. Daily 11am–1am. Free self-parking.

AT DOWNTOWN DISNEY MARKETPLACE

VERY EXPENSIVE

Fulton's Crab House ℱ SEAFOOD   Lobster (Maine and Australian) and crab (king and Dungeness) dominate the menu at this fun and fashionable eatery, housed in a replica of a (permanently moored) 19th-century Mississippi riverboat. It's one of the area's best seafood houses—and your bill will reflect that (one reason this should probably be considered only for a special family splurge, though your kids will like the atmosphere). The menu changes often, with over 50 fresh seafood selections to choose from. The rare seared tuna and blue crab cakes are delicious, and a scattering of Florida seafood includes black grouper and red snapper. Kids can go for land (filet, grilled chicken, chicken tenders, burgers, hot dogs, mac and cheese, spaghetti) or sea (popcorn shrimp, fish and chips). Fulton's wine list is pretty good, too.

At Downtown Disney, 1670 Buena Vista Dr., aboard the riverboat. ℂ **407/934-2628.** www.levyrestaurants.com. Kids' menu w/activities, highchairs, boosters. Advance Dining Reservations strongly recommended. Main courses $13–$52 lunch, $28–$52 dinner; kids $5–$13. AE, DC, DISC, MC, V. Daily 11:30am–4pm and 5–11pm. Free self-parking.

MODERATE

Rainforest Cafe ℱ CALIFORNIA   Don't arrive starving at this twin to the Animal Kingdom's Rainforest Cafe (p. 149) unless you have an Advance Dining Reservation. Without it, waits average 2 hours. The fare and the atmosphere at this kid-pleaser are exactly the same as those at the Animal Kingdom's version.

At Downtown Disney Marketplace, near the smoking volcano. ℂ **407/827-8500.** www.rainforestcafe.com. Kids' menu w/activities, highchairs, boosters. Advance Dining Reservations strongly recommended. Main courses $11–$40

Tips A Blast from the Past

T-Rex: A Prehistoric Family Adventure is coming to Downtown Disney Marketplace in 2008. Run by the same folks who operate the Rainforest Cafe, this all-new interactive eatery will follow the same general idea, but with a very different theme: Think prehistoric and age of the dinosaurs. What pint-sized paleontologist won't love eating here?

lunch and dinner (most under $25); kids $7. AE, DISC, MC, V. Sun–Thurs 11:30am–11pm; Fri–Sat 11:30am–midnight. Free self-parking.

AT DISNEY'S WEST SIDE
MODERATE

Bongos Cuban Café *Overrated* CUBAN   Singer Gloria Estefan and her husband, Emilio, created this eatery with high expectations. Its exterior, with a giant pineapple against the Downtown Disney skyline, is hard to miss. The interior is Art Deco with a Havana flavor. A Desi Arnaz impersonator gets things going every night as the restaurant fills with loud Latin music. Alas, the food isn't great: The *ropa vieja* (shredded beef) is tasty but on the dry side, and the *arroz con pollo* (chicken with yellow rice) would be a highlight if the portion matched the price. The best bet: the sanely priced Cuban sandwich. Kid cuisine includes chicken breast or nuggets, a small steak, and burgers, but I wouldn't take children here unless they're over 10 and like Latin music. For quieter times, try the patio or upstairs lounge.

At Disney's West Side, 1498 Buena Vista Dr. ✆ 407/828-0999. www.bongoscubancafe.com. Kids' menu w/activities, highchairs, boosters. Advance Dining Reservations not available. Main courses $8–$17 lunch, $15–$29 dinner (many under $20); kids $6–$7. AE, DC, DISC, MC, V. Daily 11am–2am. Free self-parking.

House of Blues MISSISSIPPI DELTA   Most folks come for the blues bands and Sunday gospel brunch (very popular with families), a foot-tapping, thigh-slapping affair worth high marks on the entertainment side. The noise level is high, and the atmosphere informal. (The omelets are good, and there are enough fillers—bacon, salads, dessert, and bread—that few leave hungry.) The average food has a New Orleans flavor and includes such offerings as pan-seared voodoo shrimp, gumbo with smoked turkey and shrimp, and Creole jambalaya with andouille sausage. Kids' meals include mac and cheese, chicken tenders, pizza, burgers, and hot dogs. The rustic backwater bayou interior has a Cajun feel and is by far the most interesting in Downtown Disney, filled (literally) with bottle caps and buttons, skeletal etchings, and hand-painted folk art.

At Disney's West Side, 1490 Buena Vista Dr., beneath water tower. ✆ 407/934-2583. www.hob.com. Kids' menu, highchairs, boosters. Advance Dining Reservations not available (except for brunch). Main courses $14–$26; pizza and sandwiches $9–$11; kids $7–$8; brunch $33 adults, $16 children 3–9. AE, DC, DISC, MC, V. Daily 11am–2am; Sun brunch seatings 10:30am and 1pm. Free self-parking.

Wolfgang Puck Grand Café ✦ CALIFORNIA   The wait can be distressing, but the energized atmosphere and eclectic menu make it worth the effort. In the more casual downstairs cafe, you'll see colorful tiles and an eye-catching exhibition kitchen. A favorite stop is the sushi bar, a copper-and-terrazzo masterpiece that delivers some of the best sushi in Orlando. The upstairs, with tables that are available only with Advance Dining Reservations, offers a more refined atmosphere. Its seasonal menu might feature shrimp garganelli sautéed with garlic, shrimp stock, and tomato sauce, and tossed with baby arugula and tomato confit. Desserts are a chocolate lover's dream come true. The lower level can be noisy but is far more kid-friendly, offering gourmet pizza, mini burgers, spaghetti, chicken tenders, and grilled chicken for youngsters. You can eat inside or on the patio. Puck's grab-and-go express restaurant sells sandwiches, pizzas, and desserts.

At Disney's West Side, 1482 Buena Vista Dr. ✆ 407/938-9653. www.wolfgangpuck.com. Kids' menu, highchairs. Reservations recommended for dining room; Advance Dining Reservations for lower level strongly recommended. Main courses $22–$37 upstairs; pizza and sushi $11–$35; kids $6–$7. AE, DC, DISC, MC, V. Daily 11am–1am. Free self-parking.

Tips A Royal Debut

The **Earl of Sandwich,** in Downtown Disney, offers great hot and cold sand-wiches, including French roast beef with cheddar and horseradish sauce, turkey with apple bacon and Swiss, and ham with Brie and dijonaise. Cobb and Chinese chicken salads are available as well. There's some indoor seating, though most diners head for the benches outside. For a quick, light meal at a decent price ($4–$6), this is the place.

ELSEWHERE IN LAKE BUENA VISTA
MODERATE
Crab House SEAFOOD   This casual chain restaurant offers a variety of seafood (and a handful of options for landlubbers) at satisfactory prices. The all-you-can-eat seafood and salad bar is great for those who like variety. The regular menu features fish dishes, Maine lobster, and, of course, crabs—from Alaskan and king to Maryland blue. Fishing gear and lobster traps are spread about the dining room, strands of lights are strewn across exposed ceilings, and brown paper (good for kids to draw on) lines the tables. Outdoor patio and deck seating are available as well.

8496 Palm Pkwy. (just off Apopka–Vineland across and up from Hotel Plaza Blvd.). © 407/239-1888. www.crab houseseafood.com. Reservations not necessary. Main courses $9–$22 lunch, $14–$25 dinner; lobster varies according to market. AE, DC, DISC, MC, V. Daily 11:30am–11pm. Free self-parking. From I-4, take Exit 68 (Hwy. 535), turn right, follow it past the Crossroads to Palm Pkwy., and turn right. The restaurant is back a bit on the right.

INEXPENSIVE
Romano's Macaroni Grill *R* *(Value* NORTHERN ITALIAN   Though it's part of a chain, Romano's has the down-to-earth cheerfulness of a mom-and-pop joint. The laid-back atmosphere and fair prices make it a good place for families. The menu offers thin-crust pizzas topped with such items as barbecued chicken. The grilled chicken portobello is worth the trip, as is the grilled salmon with a teriyaki glaze and spinach orzo pasta. Kids' options include pizza, lasagna, spaghetti, grilled chicken, and corn dogs, and all of them come with a dessert and a drink with free refills! Mom and Dad can get premium wines by the glass.

12148 Apopka–Vineland Rd. (just north of County Rd. 535/Palm Pkwy.). © 407/239-6676. www.macaronigrill.com. Kids' menu w/activities, highchairs, boosters. Main courses $7–$16 lunch, kids $6; $9–$21 dinner (most under $12), kids $8. AE, DC, DISC, MC, V. Sun–Thurs 11am–10pm; Fri–Sat 11am–11pm. Free self-parking. From I-4, take Exit 68, Hwy. 535/ Apopka–Vineland Rd., north; continue straight when Hwy. 535 goes to the right. Romano's is about 2 blocks on the left.

4 Places to Dine in Universal Orlando

Universal Orlando stormed onto the restaurant scene with the opening of its dining and entertainment venue, CityWalk, set between Universal Studios Florida and Islands of Adventure. Two of its restaurants (Emeril's and Tchoup Chop) make our all-star team, while others offer cuisine ranging from respectable light bites to dependable dinners. And, of course, this is theme-park-ville, so family-friendliness is a given at most of the restaurants.

Most of the restaurants below can be found on the "CityWalk" map (p. 337). All of the hotel restaurants listed can be found on the "International Drive Area Dining" map (p. 165).

VERY EXPENSIVE

Bice ⓕ ITALIAN   Universal Orlando's newest resort restaurant, appropriately located in the romantic setting of the Portofino Bay Hotel, replaces the Delfino Riviera. The family-owned restaurant (part of a Milan-based chain) features creative Italian cuisine served in an upscale atmosphere. The extensive menu includes items such as a Belgian endive salad in a light Dijon-mustard dressing with Gorgonzola and toasted walnuts; spaghetti with Maine lobster and cherry tomatoes in a tomato bisque; and veal chops with sautéed mushrooms, potatoes, and spinach. The dining room overlooks the waters along the piazza of the hotel; a table on the patio, if timed right, may allow you to enjoy the music of the strolling performers just below. The decor is elegant, accented by subdued lighting and a beautiful fresco of the Italian countryside. The lounge has a more contemporary and chic feel (though the flatscreen TV above the bar detracts greatly from the ambience). If there's a disappointment to be found at this restaurant, it's the air of aloofness created by the servers and staff. This is another spot best saved for an evening out sans kids.

At the Loews Portofino Bay Hotel, 5601 Universal Studios Blvd. ⓒ **407/503-3463** or 407/503-1415. Reservations recommended. Main courses $16–$44. AE, MC, V. Daily 5:30–10:30pm. Free 3-hr. validated self-parking, valet parking $18. From I-4, take Exit 75B, Kirkman Rd./Hwy. 435, and follow the signs to Universal.

Emeril's ⓕⓕ NEW ORLEANS   It's next to impossible to get reservations for dinner less than 3 or 4 weeks in advance. If you do get in, you'll find the dynamic cuisine is worth the struggle. The Creole-inspired menu might include a grilled double-cut pork chop with caramelized sweet potatoes, or andouille-crusted Texas redfish with a grilled vegetable relish, toasted pecans, and shoestring potatoes. If you want some vino with your meal, no problem: The back half of the building is a glass-walled, 12,000-bottle, aboveground wine cellar. Prices at Emeril's are high enough that the restaurant can afford tons of legroom between tables and an assortment of pricey abstract paintings on the walls.

Emeril Lagasse originally had few offerings penciled in for kids (in keeping with the adult atmosphere of his restaurants outside Florida), but quickly adjusted his menu to suit Orlando's family atmosphere. Now your children can feast on filet, fried shrimp, cheese tortellini, chicken tenders, or wood-oven pizza. He's also gone on record to say that parents introducing their kids to fine dining shouldn't make it a chore, but rather emphasize the special nature of the occasion. And that's exactly what this meal should be for your kids—a special treat (though I would leave younger ones with a sitter).

Note: At lunch, prices are lower, the menu lists many entrees served at dinner, it's easier to get a reservation, and the dress code is more casual. Jackets are recommended for gents at dinner, although that goes against the grain after a long day in the parks.

At CityWalk, 6000 Universal Studios Blvd. ⓒ **407/224-2424**. www.emerils.com. Kids' menu w/activities, highchairs, boosters. Reservations necessary. Main courses $18–$28 lunch, $31–$50 dinner; kids $8–$18. Daily 11:30am–2:30pm; Sun–Thurs 5:30–10pm, Fri–Sat 5:30–11pm. AE, DC, DISC, MC, V. Parking $11 (free after 6pm). From I-4, take Exit 75B, Kirkman Rd./Hwy. 435, and follow the signs to Universal.

The Palm SEAFOOD/STEAKS   This upscale restaurant is the 23rd member of a chain started more than 75 years ago in New York. The food is good, though somewhat overpriced. Beef and seafood rule a menu headlined by a 36-ounce prime aged double-cut New York strip steak for two and a 3-pound Nova Scotia lobster. There are, however, plenty of steaks, pasta, seafood, and salads to please every palate. The kids' menu (spaghetti, filet, penne, tortellini, and chicken fingers), while pricey, is often less expensive than what you'll find at Emeril's. The decor leans toward the

---

⌐Tips Another Blockbuster

The **Bubba Gump Shrimp Co.** (www.bubbagump.com or www.universalorlando.
com) is known for its family-friendly atmosphere and diverse menu. This chain
is the latest addition to Universal's CityWalk, taking the place of Decades Cafe
near the CityWalk entrance (across from the Cineplex). Based on the film *Forrest
Gump,* the eatery has a menu likely to please almost every palate (it's not just
for seafood lovers). Spilling over with movie memorabilia, it's the perfect addition to a trip to Universal Studios Florida, a park where the movies come to life.
Main courses are $12 to $19.

---

upscale supper clubs of the '30s and '40s, and the walls are lined with caricatures of
celebrities. Older kids will likely be impressed with the atmosphere, but this isn't the
place to bring little ones.

At the Hard Rock Hotel, 5800 Universal Blvd. ℰ **407/503-7256.** www.thepalm.com. Reservations recommended. Main
courses $20–$52; kids $8–$18. AE, DC, DISC, MC, V. Mon–Thurs 5–10pm, Fri–Sat 5–11pm, Sun 5–9pm. Free 3-hr. validated self-parking, valet parking $18. From I-4, take Exit 75B, Kirkman Rd./Hwy. 435, and follow the signs to Universal.

EXPENSIVE

Tchoup Chop ⭑⭑ PACIFIC RIM   Pronounced "chop chop," the Royal Pacific's
headline restaurant and Emeril Lagasse's second in Orlando is named for the location
of his original restaurant: Tchoupitoulous Street in New Orleans. It's a nice place for
a special night out for the family and a good spot to introduce your kids to the pleasures of fine dining; they'll likely be very taken with the atmosphere. The interior
blends gardens and waterfalls with Batik fabrics, carved wood, and chandeliers. Poly-
nesian- and Asian-influenced dishes may include macadamia-crusted Atlantic salmon
with ginger soy sauce, Polynesian crab cakes, and ahi tuna lettuce wraps. The chefs
solicited opinions from both parents and kids when formulating the kids' menu, so
your offspring will find treats such as tempura chicken nuggets, stir-fried shrimp with
noodles, chicken spring rolls, and burgers.

At Loews Royal Pacific Resort at Universal, 6300 Hollywood Way. ℰ **407/503-2467.** www.emerils.com. Kids' menu
w/activities, highchairs, boosters. Reservations strongly recommended. Main courses $13–$34; kids $8–$12. AE, DC,
DISC, MC, V. Daily 11:30am–2pm; Sun–Thurs 5:30–10pm, Fri–Sat 5:30–11pm. Valet parking $5. From I-4, take Exit
75B, Kirkman Rd./Hwy. 435, and follow the signs to Universal.

MODERATE

Hard Rock Cafe *(Overrated* AMERICAN   The largest Hard Rock Cafe on the planet
features a 1959 pink Cadillac spinning above the bar. With its size, however, comes
that much more noise. Kids love it, but adults shouldn't even think about having a
conversation here. The menu is the same found at Hard Rocks around the world:
burgers, chicken, okay steaks, and fried this-and-that. And, of course, there's a souvenir shop, too. The food is just average American fare; it's the experience that draws
people in. *Note:* The adjacent Hard Rock Live is a huge venue for concerts.

6000 Universal Studios Blvd., near CityWalk. ℰ **407/351-7625.** www.hardrock.com. Kids' menu w/activities, highchairs, boosters. Reservations not accepted. Main courses $9–$23; kids $7. AE, MC, V. Daily 11am–11pm. Parking $11
(free after 6pm). From I-4, take Exit 75B, Kirkman Rd./Hwy. 435, and follow the signs to Universal.

Jimmy Buffett's Margaritaville CARIBBEAN   The laid-back atmosphere may
take you away to paradise, but the noise level after 4pm makes it futile for Parrot

Tips More Kid Cuisine, Part II

Here are a few additional places for your smaller fry to grab a bite in the Universal resorts and parks. You can find additional information online at **www.universalorlando.com**.

- **Confisco Grille,** Islands of Adventure: mac and cheese, cheese pizza, chicken tenders, burgers, ravioli ($6–$8).
- **Finnegan's Bar & Grill,** Universal Studios Florida: grilled cheese, chicken fingers, burgers, mac and cheese, PB&J ($5–$8).
- **Lombard's Seafood Grille,** Universal Studios Florida: chicken fingers, fried fish, burgers, linguine with marinara sauce ($7–$9).
- **Mythos,** Islands of Adventure: chicken fingers, cheese pizza, ravioli, ham-and-cheddar wrap, burgers ($6–$8).
- **NASCAR Sports Grille,** CityWalk: chicken fingers, cheese pizza, spaghetti, burgers, corn dogs ($6).

Heads to talk with their table mates. But most people come to Margaritaville in the evenings to party, not for deep conversation. That said, it should come as no surprise that I recommend bringing kids here for lunch only, before the partying really starts. The back "Porch of Indecision" offers the quietest spot. Despite the cheeseburgers in paradise (yes, they're on the menu), the food has Caribbean leanings and includes a Cuban meatloaf survival sandwich, Creole shrimp marinara, Jimmy's jammin' jambalaya, and corn-and-crab bisque. And while it's not a contender for a critic's-choice award, it's fairly tasty grub. Kids' picks include a small cheeseburger in paradise, mac and cheese, chicken fingers, spaghetti and meatballs, and PB&J. The drinks menu features domestic and imported beer, as well as some unique tropical concoctions.

At CityWalk, 1000 Universal Studios Plaza. © 407/224-2155. www.universalorlando.com. Kids' menu w/activities, highchairs, boosters. Reservations not accepted. Main courses $9–$22 (most under $15); kids $6–$8. AE, DISC, MC, V. Daily 11am–midnight. Parking $11 (free after 6pm). From I-4, take Exit 75B, Kirkman Rd./Hwy. 435, and follow the signs to Universal.

Pastamore Ristorante ⊛ SOUTHERN ITALIAN   This family-style restaurant greets you with display cases brimming with mozzarella and other goodies lurking on the menu. Speaking of menus, Pastamore may have the longest kids' menu in O-Town: chicken parmigiana, chicken fingers, grilled shrimp, filet mignon, fettuccine Alfredo, fried cheese ravioli, spaghetti with tomato sauce, pizza, and burgers. I highly recommend it for families with kids of all ages. On the adult side, the antipasto Amore is a meal unto itself: bruschetta, melon with prosciutto, olives, Italian cold cuts, fresh mozzarella, and more. Also look for such traditional offerings as veal Marsala, shrimp scampi, and lasagna. The food is pretty interesting, and the presentation isn't bad, either. Pastamore has a basic beer and wine menu. You can also eat in the cafe, where a lighter menu (breakfast fare and sandwiches) is served from 8am to 2am.

At CityWalk, 1000 Universal Studios Plaza. © **407/363-8000.** www.universalorlando.com. Kids' menu w/activities, highchairs, boosters. Reservations recommended. Main courses $11–$19; kids $6–$12. AE, DISC, MC, V. Daily 5pm–midnight; cafe 8am–2am. Parking $11 (free after 6pm). From I-4, take Exit 75B, Kirkman Rd./Hwy. 435, and follow the signs to Universal.

5 Places to Dine in the International Drive Area

International Drive has one of the area's larger collections of fast-food joints, but the midsection and southern third also have some of this region's better restaurants. South I-Drive is 10 minutes by car from the Walt Disney World parks.

Most of the restaurants listed here are located on the "International Drive Area Dining" map (p. 165).

VERY EXPENSIVE

Texas de Brazil ⋒ BRAZILIAN   The decor (high ceilings, crimson walls, and abstract art) at this churrascaria is dramatic, but the atmosphere is casual and welcoming. The extensive salad bar is filled with more than 40 varieties of salads, vegetables, and soups. After filling your plate, you head back to your seat, where you'll find a coasterlike disc—one side red, the other green. When you're ready for your main course, just flip your disc to green. Immediately a troop of carvers will show up, offering grilled and roasted meats such as garlic marinated *picanha* (rump steak), Brazillian sausage, and pork ribs. The bacon-wrapped filet is to die for—it simply melts in your mouth. When you've had your fill, just turn your disc back to red. Assorted side dishes (served tableside) are available to complement your meal. A handful of a la carte items, including lobster tail and shrimp cocktail, are available as well (at an additional cost). Drinks and desserts are extra, too.

5259 International Dr. ⓒ 407/355-0355. www.texasdebrazil.com. No kids' menu. Reservations suggested. Fixed-price meals $40; kids 7–12 $20; free for kids 6 and under. AE, MC, V. Sun noon–9:30pm, Mon–Thurs 5–10pm, Fri 11am–3pm and 5–11pm, Sat 4–11pm. Free self parking. From I-4, take Exit 74A, turn right onto Sand Lake Rd., and then left onto International Dr. The restaurant will be on the left.

MODERATE

Bahama Breeze ⋒ CARIBBEAN   This chain restaurant offers a variety of delicious sandwiches and chicken, fish, and pasta entrees with Caribbean twists. Start with the Creole baked goat cheese before moving on to the Cuban sandwich, one of the most authentic around. Kids can dine on chicken fingers, cheese pizza, mac and cheese, or grilled cheese. The atmosphere is island casual, with rich wood and wicker throughout. On a warm evening, ask to sit outside.

Tip: Once famous for its long waits, the restaurant now accepts call-ahead reservations; be sure to make one. *Note:* A second branch is located in Lake Buena Vista at 8735 Vineland Ave., near I-4 (ⓒ **407/938-9010**).

8849 International Dr. ⓒ 407/248-2499. www.bahamabreeze.com. Kids' menu w/activities, highchairs, boosters. Same-day reservations available. Lunch and dinner $9–$25; kids $5–$9. AE, DISC, MC, V. Mon–Fri 4pm–1:30am; Sat noon–1:30am; Sun noon–1am. Free self-parking. From I-4, take Exit 74A and follow I-Drive 1 mile south.

B-Line Diner AMERICAN   Sink into a booth or belly up to the counter at this upscale 1950s-style diner. The bold black-and-white decor has an Art Deco feel thanks to the neon lighting accenting the chrome-lined ceiling. The round-the-clock menu features comfort foods such as chicken potpie, a ham and cheese sandwich on a baguette, and a Floribbean piccata. The kids' menu offers chicken fingers, spaghetti, grilled cheese, and burgers. Just looking at the dessert case could spoil your dinner (the cakes are a major hit with all ages, as are the yummy sundaes and shakes). The portions are hearty, as are the prices. And although this is a diner-style restaurant, it is not particularly kid-friendly, unless your children are exceptionally well behaved.

Value **Self-Service Suppers**

If you're on a budget, consider dining in a night or two and saving a few bucks. Area grocers, many with delis that turn out ready-to-eat treats, include **Albertsons,** near I-Drive (7524 Dr. Phillips Blvd.; ⓒ **407/352-1552;** www.albertsons. com), and **Gooding's,** in Lake Buena Vista (in the Crossroads Shopping Plaza, 12521 Hwy. 535/Apopka–Vineland Ave.; ⓒ **407/827-1200;** www.goodings.com), and along I-Drive (8255 International Dr.; ⓒ **407/352-4215**). You can find more options in the Yellow Pages under "Grocers."

At the Peabody Orlando, 9801 International Dr. ⓒ 407/345-4460. www.peabodyorlando.com. Kids' menu w/activities, highchairs, boosters. Reservations not accepted. Main courses $4–$16 breakfast, $11–$24 lunch and dinner (most under $18); kids $8–$12. AE, DC, DISC, MC, V. Daily 24 hr. Free self- and validated valet parking. From I-4, take Exit 74A, Sand Lake Rd./Hwy. 528, east to International Dr., and then south. The hotel is on the left across from the Convention Center.

Café Tu Tu Tango ⓐⓐ *Finds* INTERNATIONAL/TAPAS This eclectic eatery offers artistic experiences that should keep your children reasonably entertained—there's frequently a painter bringing a canvas to life. The portions here are small, but the tastes are big. The roasted pears on pecan crisps—topped with blue cheese and a balsamic reduction—are a must. The kids' menu has grilled cheese, spaghetti, pizza (they can exercise their creativity by designing their own personal pie), chicken fingers, and corn dogs. The staff is fabulous, and your server will be happy to educate you about the menu. Wine is available by the glass.

8625 International Dr. ⓒ 407/248-2222. www.cafetututango.com. Reservations accepted but not required. Tapas (small plates) $4–$20; kids $3–$9. AE, DC, DISC, MC, V. Sun–Thurs 11:30am–11pm; Fri–Sat 11:30am–2am. Free self-parking. From I-4, take Exit 74A, Sand Lake Rd./Hwy 528, east to International Dr., and then south. The restaurant is on the left.

Fishbones SEAFOOD The fish at this nautically themed restaurant is hand-picked daily to ensure freshness. You can create your own meal by mixing and matching sauces and salsas. If fish isn't your dish, other offerings include rack of lamb, prime rib, and duck. Portions are large; the atmosphere is friendly; and children are catered to with a special menu that includes fried shrimp, fish fingers, burgers, grilled chicken, and pizza.

6707 Sand Lake Rd., off International Dr. ⓒ 407/352-0135. Main courses $13–$40 (most under $25); kids $5–$7. AE, MC, V. Sun–Thurs 5–10:30pm; Fri–Sat 5–11pm. Free self-parking. From I-4, take Exit 74A and go ⅓ mile east on S.R. 482 (Sand Lake Rd.).

Ming Court ⓐ CHINESE Local patronage and a diverse menu make this one of Orlando's most popular Chinese eateries—it was recently included among the top 100 Chinese restaurants in the country by a major restaurant trade publication. The candlelit interior creates a romantic atmosphere, a musician plays classical Chinese music on a *zheng* (a long zither) at dinner, and glass-walled terrace rooms overlook lotus ponds filled with colorful koi.

Start with the duck lettuce cup before moving on to the lightly battered, deep-fried chicken breast; it's got plenty of zip from a delicate lemon–tangerine sauce. If you're in the mood for beef, there's a grilled filet mignon that's seasoned Szechuan style (with toasted onions, garlic, and chili). The mildly innovative menu is extensive, featuring

International Drive Area Dining

Bahama Breeze **7**

Bice (Loews Portofino
 Bay Hotel) **1**

B-Line Diner (Peabody
 Orlando) **10**

Café Tu Tu Tango **6**

Charlie's Lobster
 House **8**

Fishbones **5**

Hard Rock Cafe
 (Hard Rock Hotel) **2**

Ming Court **9**

The Palm
 (Hard Rock Hotel) **2**

Tchoup Chop (Loews
 Royal Pacific Resort) **3**

Texas de Brazil **4**

*For restaurants at
Universal Orlando's
CityWalk, please see
the "CityWalk" map
in chapter 10.*

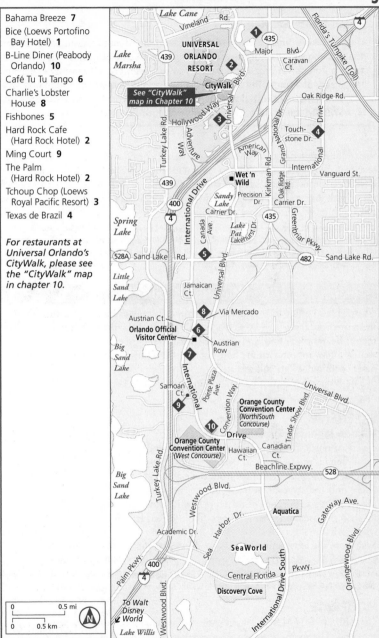

⌐Tips Room Service

If you'd like a break from eating out, several Orlando restaurants are more than willing to come to you. A local service, **Take Out Express,** will deliver food from a number of area restaurants (you can even order from more than one restaurant at a time). The delivery cost runs about $5 per restaurant, with a $15 minimum order per restaurant. Delivery hours are from 4:30 to 11pm daily. Call ℂ **407/352-1170** or go to www.orlandotakeoutexpress.com.

---

the freshest ingredients. Portions are sufficient; there's a moderate wine list; and the service is quite good. The children's menu features a boxed meal with a choice of Oriental-style shrimp, pork, beef, or chicken (and fries!) and comes with a story to read along with dinner. *Tip:* The restaurant's extensive website features lots of information on, and photos of, individual dishes.

9188 International Dr., between Sand Lake Rd. and Beachline Expwy. ℂ 407/351-9988. www.ming-court.com. Reservations recommended. Main courses $7–$13 lunch, $13–$36 dinner; most dim sum items $3–$5. AE, DC, DISC, MC, V. Daily 11am–2:30pm and 4:30–10:30pm. Free self-parking. From I-4, take Exit 74A, Sand Lake Rd./Hwy. 528, east to International Dr., and then south. It's on the right.

6 Places to Dine Elsewhere in Orlando

There's life in other areas, as locals and enterprising visitors discover, though many of them aren't as child-friendly as places near the theme parks and may not have a kids' menu. Below you'll find some family-friendly establishments off the beaten track, as well as a few options that are best reserved for nights out on your own or for special forays with older kids and teens.

The restaurants in this section are located on the "Dining Elsewhere in Orlando" map (p. 167).

EXPENSIVE

Mikado Japanese Steakhouse ⍟ JAPANESE   Compared with other local Japanese steakhouses, Mikado offers a tastier meal and a more intimate atmosphere. The sushi menu is one of the area's best, as is the *teppanyaki*—the chefs slice, dice, and send the chicken, seafood, and beef from their grill right to your plate. Your children will likely find the atmosphere cool, but be aware that the kids' menu is very limited, though pint-size portions of the teppanyaki entrees are available and likely much better than the usual pizza and burgers. Shoji screens lend intimacy to the dining room, where windows overlook rock gardens, reflecting pools, and a palm-fringed pond. Sake from the lounge may be in order for Mom and Dad.

At Marriott Orlando World Center, 8701 World Center Dr. (off Hwy. 536). ℂ 407/239-4200. Reservations recommended. Main courses $16–$37. AE, DC, DISC, MC, V. Daily 6–10pm. Free self- and validated valet parking. From I-4, take Exit 67/Hwy. 536 east to the Marriott Orlando World Center.

MODERATE

Carrabba's ⍟ ITALIAN   Here's yet another chain, but one that serves above-average food. The menu features such specialties as *tagliarini picchi pacchiu* (a fine pasta with crushed tomatoes, garlic, olive oil, and basil served with either chicken or

Dining Elsewhere in Orlando

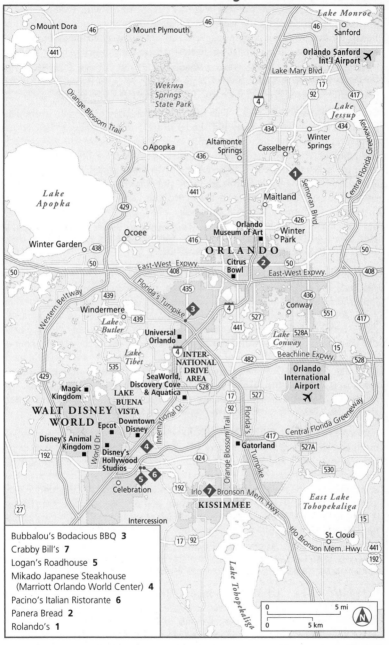

Bubbalou's Bodacious BBQ **3**

Crabby Bill's **7**

Logan's Roadhouse **5**

Mikado Japanese Steakhouse
(Marriott Orlando World Center) **4**

Pacino's Italian Ristorante **6**

Panera Bread **2**

Rolando's **1**

shrimp) and *pollo Rosa Maria* (fire-roasted chicken stuffed with Fontina cheese and prosciutto). Also available are wood-fired pizzas, soups and salads, pastas, and other Italian classics. Kids can choose spaghetti, ravioli, pizza, grilled chicken, or chicken fingers. The atmosphere is casual yet lively—perfect for families.

In the Formosa Gardens Plaza, 7890 W. Irlo Bronson Memorial Hwy. (U.S. 192), Kissimmee. © **407/390-9600.** www. carrabbas.com. Main courses $11–$22 dinner; kids $6–$8. AE, DC, DISC, MC, V. Sun–Thurs 4–10pm; Fri–Sat 4–11pm. Free self-parking. From I-4, take Exit 64 for U.S. 192, continue on, and look for the Formosa Gardens Plaza on the left.

Crabby Bill's ⊛ SEAFOOD   This fun, friendly member of a small Central Florida chain was launched by "Crabby Bill" Loder in 1975 and continues to deliver quality seafood to diners who dig in from family-style tables. In season, the grouper is fresh and fabulous. (I recommend trying it broiled, which keeps it juicy, but you can also order it blackened or fried.) The house specialties—no surprise here—include stone-crab claws (Oct–May) as well as king, snow, and blue crabs. The menu also has a variety of fried, grilled, broiled, and blackened fish. Kids will find burgers, chicken fingers, fried shrimp or fish, mac and cheese, pizza, and grilled chicken.

5030 E. Irlo Bronson Memorial Hwy./U.S. 192 (between Poinciana Blvd. and Vineland Rd.), Kissimmee. © **321/677-0303.** www.crabbybills.com. Reservations not necessary. Main courses $9–$26 (most under $16); sandwiches $4.50–$7; kids $4–$6. AE, DC, DISC, MC, V. Daily 11:30am–10pm.

Pacino's Italian Ristorante ⊛ NORTHERN ITALIAN   The house specialty, veal *osso buco,* is a delicious collision of veal shank, mushrooms, Barolo wine, herbs, and mushrooms. At 32 ounces, the porterhouse steak is a belly-buster, and the house's *frutti di mare* has shrimp, calamari, clams, and scallops heaped on a mound of linguine. Kids get their choice of spaghetti, lasagna, pizza, and chicken tenders. The open two-story interior is filled with exposed brick, wrought-iron accents, and a fiber-optic ceiling that creates the illusion of twinkling stars. The second story offers more intimate seating overlooking the courtyard below. Outdoor patio seating is available.

5795 W. Irlo Bronson Memorial Hwy./U.S. 192, Kissimmee. © **407/396-8022.** www.pacinos.com. Kids' menu w/activities, highchairs, boosters. Reservations recommended. Main courses $8–$32 (most under $20); pizza $9–$12; kids $5–$7. AE, MC, V. Daily 4–10pm. Free self-parking. From I-4, take Exit 64A/U.S. 192 and go east 1 mile.

Panera Bread ⊛ AMERICAN   This trendy cafe/bakery is a great place for a light meal, and its quick growth in the area (there are several locations) attests to its popularity among locals and visitors alike. The menu offers a variety of delicious soups (broccoli cheddar, black bean, and others) and salads (Asian sesame chicken, Caesar, and more). But the real stars are the sandwiches, such as turkey with chipotle mayonnaise, roast beef with creamy horseradish sauce, and portobello and mozzarella panini. A kids' menu satisfies young appetites with deli sandwiches, PB&J, or grilled cheese on white or whole grain.

296 E. Michigan St. © **407/481-9880.** www.panerabread.com. Reservations not accepted. Main courses $7–$14; baked goods $2–$6; kids $4–$6. AE, DISC, MC, V. Mon–Sat 6:30am–9:30pm; Sun 7am–8:30pm. Free self-parking. From I-4, take Exit 80B, U.S. 17/92, go north to Michigan, and then right 1½ miles.

Rolando's ⊛ *Finds* CUBAN   This mom-and-pop restaurant serves large portions of traditional Cuban fare, such as *arroz con pollo* (chicken with yellow rice), *ropa vieja* (shredded beef), and, if you call a few hours or a day in advance, paella. I also recommend Rolando's roast chicken, which is brushed with crushed garlic, white-wine vinegar, cumin, and oregano, and then briefly deep-fried. Kids' options include mac and

---

Value Bargain Buffets

If you spend time on International Drive or U.S. 192/Irlo Bronson Memorial Highway between Kissimmee and Disney, you'll see billboards peddling all-you-can-eat breakfast buffets for $4 to $6. All these spots welcome kids and are a good way to fill your family's tanks early and skip (or at least go easy on) lunch, especially if your day is in the theme parks, where meals are overpriced. Breakfast buffets are served at **Golden Corral,** 8033 International Dr. (© 407/352-6606); **Ponderosa Steak House,** 6362 International Dr. (© 407/352-9343) and 7598 U.S. 192 W. (© 407/396-7721); and **Sizzler Restaurant,** 9142 International Dr. (© 407/351-5369) and 7602 U.S. 192 W. (© 407/397-0997).

---

cheese, a ham-and-cheese sandwich, and chicken fingers. The plain dining room has Formica tables, old photographs of Cuba, and potted philodendrons suspended from the ceiling. There's a very limited beer-and-wine list.

870 E. Hwy. 436/Semoran Blvd., Casselberry. © **407/767-9677.** Kids' menu, highchairs, boosters. Reservations not necessary. Main courses $4–$6 lunch, $8–$18 dinner; kids $4–$5. AE, DC, DISC, MC, V. Mon–Fri 11am–9:30pm; Sat noon–10pm; Sun noon–8:30pm. Free self-parking. From I-4, take Exit 82A, Hwy. 408/East–West Expwy., head east, and make a left on Hwy. 436.

INEXPENSIVE

Bubbalou's Bodacious BBQ *✿ Value* BARBECUE   You can smell the hickory smoke for blocks. This is, hands down, some of the best barbecue you'll find anywhere. If you can eat the night or day away, go for the "Big-Big Pig" platter (beef, sliced pork, and turkey with fixin's). There are also several barbecue baskets, combos, dinners, and sandwiches, as well as side orders ranging from fried pickles and okra to collard greens and black-eyed peas. The uninitiated should stay away from the "Killer" sauce, which can render your taste buds useless, likely for hours. The beans are the perfect side dish. Kids have a choice of barbecued chicken, chicken strips, grilled cheese, burgers, and corn dogs. And there's takeout available if you want to head back to your hotel room.

5818 Conroy Rd. (near Universal Orlando). © **407/423-1212.** www.bubbalous.com. Kids' menu, highchairs, boosters Reservations not accepted. Main courses $4–$15, with larger family sizes available for takeout up to $25. AE, MC, V. Mon–Thurs 10am–9:30pm; Fri–Sat 10am–10:30pm; Sun 11am–9pm. Free self-parking. From I-4, take Exit 75B, head east on Kirkman, and follow your nose; Bubbalou's is at the intersection of Kirkman and Conroy.

Logan's Roadhouse *Kids* SOUTHWESTERN   Set along busy U.S 192 in Kissimmee, this laid-back eatery serves up Southwestern favorites and barbecue. Kick back and relax a spell—and go ahead and throw those peanut shells on the floor (your mom won't yell at you here). Standouts include the San Antonio chicken wrap; mesquite-grilled salmon, chicken, and pork; and barbecued chicken and ribs. You can also get a host of sandwiches, salads, seafood, steaks, burgers, and rib-sticking sides. The casual roadhouse decor, friendly service, and kid-friendly favorites (chicken, burgers, hot dogs, mac and cheese, and steak tips) make this a great choice for families.

5925 W. Irlo Bronson Hwy. (U.S. 192 at the intersection of International Dr. S.), Kissimmee. © **407/390-0500.** www.logansroadhouse.com. Main courses $8–$18; kids $6–$8. AE, DISC, MC, V. Sun–Thurs 11am–10:30pm, Fri–Sat 11am–11:30pm. Free self-parking. Take Exit 64 towards Celebration and follow U.S. 192; the restaurant will be on your left.

Not Just Fries Anymore

Some of you may not be able to go your entire vacation without a trip to McDonald's for a fast-food fix. The good news is that Orlando has a handful of uniquely themed McDonald's unlike any you'll find back home. All of them sport eclectic menus, which, in addition to the usual fare, add (among other items) pizzas, turkey wraps, panini, and crème-brûlée cheesecake.

The 24-hour McDonald's **European Cafe,** 7344 Sand Lake Rd. (© **407/264-0776**), boasts two levels with plenty of glass to allow light to pour in. You won't mistake it for a real European cafe, but cool features include a pool table and arcade games on the second level, plus fabulous views of the sand lakes.

The **Ancient Ruins** branch, at 5401 Altamira Dr. (© **407/345-9477**), is themed on the ancient ruins of Greece, complete with broken columns, stone walls, and frieze-style moldings.

The **Club Safari** location, 2944 S. Kirkman Rd. (© **407/296-6265**), boasts an African safari theme complete with rich wooden fixtures, African masks, crystal chandeliers, and animal prints galore. Animatronic toucan and tiki figures sing jungle jingles, and a 13-foot bronze giraffe and two bronze tigers keep watch.

Chrome shines everywhere you turn at the **Motorcycle McDonald's,** 5400 S. Kirkman Rd. (© **407/352-1526**). Tail pipes, shocks, and various other bike parts adorn the restaurant's walls.

Finally, the **world's largest McDonald's** can be found right at 6875 Sand Lake Rd. (© **407/351-2185**). The location boasts a huge tubular maze with 25,000 feet of twists, turns, sliding, crawling, and jumping space for kids to play in. Another unique feature: You can book hotels and transportation, buy tickets to attractions, and get daily park information, all while enjoying your fries and a Coke (or in this case, maybe a gourmet coffee).

7 Only in Orlando: Dining with Disney Characters

Dining with your favorite costumed characters is a treat for many Disney fans, but it's a truly special occasion for those under age 10. Some of the most beloved movie characters seemingly come to life: shaking hands, hugging, signing autographs, and posing for family photos (most never speak, with the exception of the princesses and a very small handful of others, so forget about conversation). These are *huge* events—it's not uncommon for Chef Mickey's, listed below, to have 1,600 or more guests on a weekend morning—so make your **Advance Dining Reservations** (p.130) as far ahead of time as possible (when you book your room, if not earlier). Don't expect more than just a few moments of one-on-one time, but it's still sure to bring a big smile to your little ones' faces. To make reservations for WDW character meals, call © **407/939-3463.** American Express, Diners Club, Discover, MasterCard, Visa, and the Disney Visa card are accepted at all character meals.

The prices for these meals are much the same, no matter where you're dining (with one exception: Cinderella's Royal Table). Breakfast (most places serve it) runs $19 to $32 for adults and $11 to $22 for children 3 to 9; those that serve dinner charge $28 to $41 for adults and $13 to $28 for kids. The prices vary a bit, though, from location to location.

You'll find all of the restaurants mentioned in this section on the "Walt Disney World & Lake Buena Vista Dining" map (p. 144). For online information, go to **www. disneyworld.com**.

Note: Although the character appearances below are accurate at press time, lineups and booking requirements change frequently (as do menus and prices). I strongly recommend against promising children they will meet a specific character at a meal. And never mention dining with the characters unless your Advance Dining Reservations are confirmed first; character meals book up quickly, and trying to make reservations too late in the game (or worse, attempting to walk in) will most likely result in disappointment. If you have your heart set on meeting a certain character, call to confirm his or her appearance when making your reservations.

Cape May Café   The Cape May Café, a delightful New England–themed dining room, serves lavish buffet breakfasts (eggs, pancakes, bacon, pastries) hosted by **Admiral Goofy** and his crew—**Chip 'n' Dale** and **Pluto** (though characters may vary). Its location at the Beach Club Resort makes it a great way to start the day when you're on your way to nearby Epcot. See also p. 155.

At Disney's Beach Club Resort, 1800 Epcot Resorts Blvd. Breakfast $19 adults, $11 kids. Daily 7:30–11am.

Chef Mickey's 🍴🍴   The whimsical Chef Mickey's offers buffet breakfasts (eggs, bacon, sausage, pancakes, fruit) and dinners (entrees change daily; salad bar, soups, vegetables, ice cream with toppings). Aside from the characters, kids will also enjoy watching the monorail go by overhead as it passes through the Contemporary Resort. **Mickey** and **Minnie** and various pals make their way to every table while meeting and mingling with guests. While this is one of the largest restaurants offering character dining, if you plan on coming here during spring break or around the holidays, it's best to make Advance Dining Reservations well ahead of time.

At Disney's Contemporary Resort, 4600 N. World Dr. Breakfast $19 adults, $11 kids; dinner $28 adults, $13 kids. Daily 7–11:30am and 5–9:30pm.

Cinderella's Royal Table 🍴   Cinderella Castle—the most recognized icon in all of the WDW resort, not to mention the center of the Magic Kingdom—serves character breakfast buffets daily (a variety of breakfast favorites, including scrambled eggs, bacon, Danishes) and recently began serving character lunches and dinners as well (with a choice of appetizer, entree, salad, and dessert from a fixed menu). Princess hosts vary, but **Cinderella** always puts in an appearance; the **Fairy Godmother** joins the celebration for dinner.

Note: This is one of the most popular character meals in the park and the hardest to get into, so *reserve far, far in advance* (reservations are taken 180 days in advance, and you must pay in full at the time you book). To have the best shot at getting in, be flexible about your seating arrangements and dining times, and call Disney exactly at 7am EST on your first date of reservations eligibility (if you aren't sure what date that is, call Disney and they'll help you figure it out). If you get through on your first try (lucky you!), tell the reservations agent you want Cinderella's Royal Table for whatever date you've picked. Don't even think about requesting a specific time—take whatever you can get (most reservations will be gone by 7:15am).

At Cinderella Castle, in the Magic Kingdom. Breakfast $33 adults, $23 kids; lunch $36 adults, $24 kids; dinner $41 adults, $26 kids. Daily 8–10:20am, noon–3pm, and 4pm–park closing. Theme-park admission required.

Tips Other Casts of Characters

Not wanting to feel left out, Universal Orlando and SeaWorld have instituted their own character dining experiences. Like Disney's meals, these are
very popular, so be sure to reserve your spot as far in advance as possible.

At Islands of Adventure, the **Confisco Grille** (✆ **407/224-4012** for information or reservations) is home to a character breakfast buffet where **Spider-
Man, Captain America,** the **Cat in the Hat,** and **Thing 1** and **Thing 2** all join
in on the fun. It runs Thursday through Sunday, from park opening until
10:30am. The cost is $16 for adults, $10 for kids 3 to 9.

At SeaWorld, you can chow down on a buffet lunch right alongside the
killer whales at the daily **Backstage at Believe,** at Shamu Stadium. The cost
is $37 for adults, $19 for children 3 to 9; park admission is required but not
included in the cost.

Crystal Palace Buffet ✿   The prettiest of the Magic Kingdom's restaurants, the
Crystal Palace features a glass exterior that glimmers in sunlight. **Winnie the Pooh**
and pals hold court here throughout the day. The restaurant serves breakfast (eggs,
French toast, pancakes, bacon, and more), lunch, and dinner. The latter features a
long list of hot and cold entrees that usually include some type of poultry, beef,
seafood, an array of veggies, salads, and kid-friendly favorites. The dessert buffet has a
make-your-own-sundae bar.

At Crystal Palace, in the Magic Kingdom. Breakfast $19 adults, $11 kids; lunch $21 adults, $12 kids; dinner $28 adults,
$13 kids. Daily 8–10:30am, 11:30am–3pm, and 4pm–park closing. Theme-park admission required.

Donald's Safari Breakfast ✿   **Donald, Goofy,** and **Pluto** host a buffet breakfast
(eggs, bacon, French toast, and more) in Africa's Tusker House.

In Africa, at Disney's Animal Kingdom. Breakfast $19 adults, $11 kids. Daily 8:30–11:30am. Theme-park admission
required.

Garden Grill ✿   There's a "harvest feast" theme at this revolving restaurant, where
hearty, family-style meals are hosted by **Mickey** and **Chip 'n' Dale.** (Mickey sure gets
around, eh?) Lunch and dinner (chicken, fish, steak, vegetables, potatoes) are served.

In the Land Pavilion, at Epcot. Lunch $21 adults, $12 kids; dinner $28 adults, $13 kids. Daily 11am–3pm and
4:30–park closing. Theme-park admission required.

Liberty Tree Tavern   This Colonial-style 18th-century pub offers character dinners
hosted by **Minnie, Goofy, Pluto,** and **Chip 'n' Dale.** The family-style meals include
salad, roast turkey, ham, flank steak, cornbread, and apple crisp with vanilla ice cream.

At Liberty Square, in the Magic Kingdom. Dinner $28 adults, $13 kids. Daily 4pm–park closing. Theme-park admission required.

1900 Park Fare ✿   The elegant Grand Floridian offers breakfast (eggs, French toast,
bacon, pancakes) and dinner (steak, pork, fish) buffets at the exposition-themed 1900
Park Fare. Big Bertha—a French band organ that plays pipes, drums, bells, cymbals,
castanets, and xylophone—provides the music. **Mary Poppins, Alice in Wonderland,**

and friends appear at breakfast; **Cinderella** and pals show up for Cinderella's Gala Feast at dinner.

At Disney's Grand Floridian Resort & Spa, 4401 Floridian Way. Breakfast $19 adults, $11 kids; dinner $29 adults, $14 kids. Daily 8–11:10am and 4:30–8:20pm.

'Ohana Character Breakfast   Traditional breakfasts (eggs, pancakes, bacon) are prepared in an 18-foot fire pit and served family style. **Mickey, Stitch, Lilo,** and **Pluto** appear, and children are given the chance to parade around with Polynesian musical instruments.

At 'Ohana, in Disney's Polynesian Resort, 1600 Seven Seas Dr. Breakfast $19 adults, $11 kids. Daily 7:30–11am.

Princess Storybook Dining   **Snow White, Jasmine, Ariel, Pocahontas, Belle,** or **Mary Poppins** might show up at any of the character meals offered at Epcot's Norway Pavilion. Breakfast features American fare (scrambled eggs, French toast, sausage, bacon, and potatoes), while family-style lunch and dinner offer Norwegian specialties in addition to traditional American dishes for the kids.

At Akershus Royal Banquet Hall, in Epcot's Norway Pavilion. Breakfast $23 adults, $13 kids; lunch $25 adults, $14 kids; dinner $29 adults, $14 kids. Daily 8:30–10:10am, 11:40am–2:50pm, and 4:20–8:40pm. Theme-park admission required.

6

What Kids Like to See & Do in Walt Disney World

Walt Disney World has grown to include an array of themed resorts, hundreds of restaurants and shops, nightclub venues, smaller attractions, and four major theme parks: the Magic Kingdom, Epcot, Disney's Hollywood Studios, and Disney's Animal Kingdom. And with the economy showing signs of recovery, park attendance is once again on the rise. WDW attracted nearly 46 million paying customers in 2006, according to estimates by a report put out by *TEA Inc.* and *Economic Research Associates*. All four Disney parks make the country's top five in attendance (the remaining park on the list is Disneyland in California). But that should hardly surprise you; they offer a fanciful, self-sufficient vacation where wonderment, human progress, and old-fashioned family fun are the key themes. The Disney Imagineers show off their creative capabilities through spectacular parades and fireworks displays, 3-D and CircleVision films, nerve-racking thrill rides, and adventurous journeys through time and space in addition to maintaining an array of classic time-honored offerings. Though they're expensive, you'll seldom hear people complain about failing to get their money's worth; an evening out at home, including the cost of a babysitter, can add up to almost as much without nearly the same return.

One of the reasons people keep coming back for more is that the rides and shows are periodically updated—and occasionally entirely new ones are added. If something doesn't quite work, Disney usually fixes it (thanks in part to information gathered from park-goers on how well, or poorly, things are working). In addition, Disney likes to shake things up every few years by throwing special (often year-long) celebrations, including its current **Year of a Million Dreams**—which thanks to overwhelming popularity will continue throughout 2008.

There have been changes and additions as Walt Disney World has matured, with new rides and attractions entering the mix. At Disney's Hollywood Studios (formerly Disney–MGM Studios), the kids can cheer on the Wildcats at the **High School Musical 2: School's Out!** street show, train alongside Jedi masters at the **Star Wars Jedi Training Academy,** play their way along the 3-D midway at **Toy Story Mania!,** and join in on the interactive fun at the **Block Party Bash**—the park's newest parade, where Disney-Pixar characters come to life.

Over at the Magic Kingdom, your family can laugh along with Mike Wazowski at **Monsters, Inc. Laugh Floor,** then **Dream Along with Mickey** as the fanciful stage show entrances all who watch, and finally engage in swashbuckling silliness with none other than the great Captain Sparrow himself at **Captain Jack's Pirate Tutorial.** In addition, **Disney's Pirate & Princess Party** has made its debut, joining the likes of

Mickey's Not-So-Scary Halloween Party and Mickey's Very Merry Christmas Party, to become an annual after-hours (and separately ticketed) event.

At Epcot's Seas with Nemo & Friends, guests embark on undersea adventures with familiar finned friends, while at Disney's Animal Kingdom, they can dive into the undersea world of Nemo and friends, entranced by the theatrical production of Finding Nemo–The Musical.

But before I dive into the action, giving you details on these and other exciting experiences, let me take care of some basic business.

1 Essentials

GETTING INFORMATION IN ADVANCE

Before leaving home, call or write to Walt Disney World, Box 10000, Lake Buena Vista, FL 32830-1000 (© 407/934-7639), for a vacation DVD and planning CD, which you can view online as well. Also ask about special events that will be going on during your visit. While I list big-time events under "When to Go," in chapter 2, many other events may be of interest to you.

Once you've arrived in town, the lobby concierge desks in hotels (especially at Disney properties and "official" hotels) have up-to-the-minute information on park happenings. Stop by to ask questions and get literature, including maps and a schedule of park hours and events. If you have questions your hotel's personnel can't answer, call Disney at © 407/824-4321.

You can also get information at City Hall in the Magic Kingdom and at Guest Relations at Epcot, Disney's Hollywood Studios, and Disney's Animal Kingdom.

For online resources, go to www.disneyworld.com, which features regularly updated information on the parks; the Orlando/Orange County Convention & Visitors Bureau site at www.orlandoinfo.com; and www.floridakiss.com, sponsored by the Kissimmee Convention & Visitors Bureau.

GETTING TO WALT DISNEY WORLD BY CAR

The interstate exits to all Disney parks and resorts are well marked. Once you're off I-4, signs will direct you to individual destinations. If you miss your exit, *don't panic.* Simply get off at the next one and turn around. It may take a little more time, but it's safer than cutting across five lanes of traffic to make the off-ramp—or, worse, to risk a fender bender. Drive with extra caution in the attractions area. Disney drivers are divided into two categories: cast members in a hurry to make their shift and tourists in a hurry to get to the fun (and trying to drive while looking at a map). Both can often pull some rather stupid moves. The new WDW Western Beltway, currently under construction, should help alleviate some of the congestion both along I-4 and throughout areas of WDW.

Tips Tighter Security

Guards at the gates at all Disney parks check a variety of carry-ins, including backpacks and large purses. They have also been known to check guests' IDs, so be sure to bring a government-issued photo identification. All this, of course, means it takes a little longer to get to the action.

Upon entering WDW grounds, you can tune your radio to **1030 AM** when you're approaching the Magic Kingdom, or **850 AM** when approaching Epcot, for park information. Tune to **1200 AM** when departing the Magic Kingdom or **910 AM** when departing Epcot. TVs in all Disney resorts and "official" hotels also have park information channels.

PARKING

All WDW lots are tightly controlled; the Disney folks have parking down to a science. You park where they tell you to park—or here comes security. I can't stress enough to **write down your parking place** (lot, row, and space number) on something that you won't lose so you can find your vehicle later. At the end of the day, you'd be surprised at just how many white minivans there are dotting the massive lot. If you think the catchy names will help jar your memory, think again. After a day at the parks, you'll have more characters swimming around in your head than you can count—each sounding all too familiar. The last thing you and your kids will want to do is play a game of "Let's guess where we left the car."

Visitors will likely need to ride the free trams in the massive Magic Kingdom lots (unless you've booked your vacation through AAA and can park up close in the AAA lot), but some folks decide to skip them and walk to the gates at Epcot, Disney's Hollywood Studios, and Disney's Animal Kingdom. Some won't have a choice: Disney has cut tram service to parking areas closest to the entrances to its parks. Guests who can't make the hike can have a driver drop them at special unloading areas outside the entrances. Special lots are available for travelers with disabilities (call ✆ **407/824-4321** for details) right near the entrances as well. If your kids are young, and the tram is available, I recommend you use it; the children are in for enough walking once they're in the parks, and it's best to preserve their energy for the fun stuff. If you do end up walking from your car, be careful! These lots aren't designed for pedestrians. Tourists make for some of the least attentive drivers around—especially when they're in a hurry to get to the park, too.

At press time, parking had just been raised to $11 at the four major WDW parks ($12 for RVs). Disney resort guests do not have to pay for parking.

TICKETS & PASSES

In January 2005, Disney revamped its entire ticketing structure (now called **Magic Your Way**), giving visitors who stay here for a few days far better deals than those who come for just a day. Whereas before you had a limited number of ticket options (a 1-day, one-park ticket or a multiday, multipark pass), the new system allows guests to customize their tickets by first purchasing a base ticket for a set fee and then purchasing add-ons, including a Park Hopper option; a no-expiration option; and the option to include admission to some of Disney's smaller venues, such as Pleasure Island, the water parks, and DisneyQuest (the latter is known as the Water Park Fun & More option).

You can purchase your base tickets for durations running from a single day to several days, with the latter being the most cost effective; the longer you stay, the less you'll pay per day. If you crunch the numbers, tickets good for at least 4 days will cost almost $18 less per day than a single-day ticket would; buy a 6-day ticket, and your per-day price drops by almost 50%. Do note, however, that under the new system, tickets now expire 14 days from the first day of use unless you add on a no-expiration feature (you don't, however, have to use the tickets on consecutive days within that 14-day period).

Walt Disney World Parks & Attractions

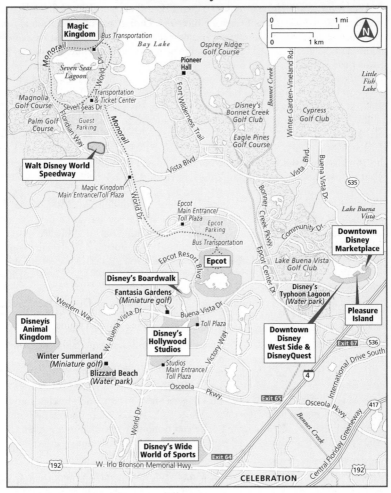

Keep in mind: Unless otherwise noted, the following prices do not include the **sales tax** of 6.5% to 7% (Disney falls in two different counties). Also, **price hikes** are frequent occurrences, so call © **407/824-4321** or go to www.disneyworld.com for the most up-to-the-minute rates. All tickets include unlimited use of the WDW **transportation system.** And bear in mind that Disney considers kids 10 and older adults for pricing purposes, and children under 3 aren't charged admission.

One-day/one-park tickets, for admission to the Magic Kingdom, Epcot, Disney's Hollywood Studios, or Disney's Animal Kingdom, are $71 for adults and $60 for kids ages 3 to 9. Ouch! **Four-day base tickets** (one park per day) are $212 for adults and $178 for kids 3 to 9. **Seven-day base tickets** (one park per day) are $219 for adults (about $31 a day) and $182 for kids 3 to 9 (about $26 a day).

Adding on a **Park Hopper** option to your ticket allows you unlimited admission to the Magic Kingdom, Epcot, Disney's Hollywood Studios, and Disney's Animal Kingdom for the duration of your base ticket. Pricing for the Park Hopper is the same for adults and children and costs $45 above the price of your base ticket (no matter how many days that ticket is valid for). So if you purchase a single-day base ticket, adding the Park Hopper will cost an additional $45 (for a total of $116 for an adult—not very cost effective), but if you purchase a 7-day base ticket, the Park Hopper add-on will still cost you only $45 (for a total of $264—a very good deal).

If you add the **Water Park Fun & More** option to your base ticket, you'll get several admissions to some of WDW's smaller attractions: Blizzard Beach, Typhoon Lagoon, DisneyQuest, Pleasure Island, and Disney's Wide World of Sports. The number of visits allowed depends on the number of days your base ticket is good for: two visits for base tickets covering 1 or 2 days, three visits for a 3-day ticket, four visits for a 4-day ticket, five visits for a 5-day ticket, and so on—the number of visits equaling the number of days your base tickets are good for. This option adds $50 to the cost of your base ticket, and, like the Park Hopper, the longer you stay at Disney, the more cost effective the option becomes. If you plan on visiting only one smaller attraction while at WDW, paying the separate admission fee is cheaper and smarter than opting for the Water Park Fun & More option. If, however, you plan on experiencing at least two of Disney's smaller venues, the Water Park Fun & More option is well worth the added cost.

One-day tickets to Typhoon Lagoon, Blizzard Beach, or **DisneyQuest** are $39 for adults and $33 for children.

One-day tickets to Pleasure Island are $11 for a single-club pass and $22 for a multiclub pass. Because this is primarily an 18-and-over entertainment complex, there's no bargain price for children.

If you're planning an extended stay or going to visit Walt Disney World more than once during the year, **annual passes** ($448–$579 adults, $395–$510 children) are another great option. Florida residents can get a break on park prices by choosing 10% off a 1-day ticket, 50% savings on the Water Parks Fun & More option, or 3- and 4-day park passes for the discounted price and 6 months in which to use them. Residents may also purchase seasonal passes as well as discounted annual passes.

OPERATING HOURS

All of Disney's theme parks are open 365 days a year. Hours of operation vary throughout the year and can be influenced by special events, so it's a good idea to call to check opening and closing times. The **Magic Kingdom** and **Disney's Hollywood Studios** are generally open from 9am to 6 or 7pm, with hours often extended to 9pm and sometimes as late as midnight during major holidays and summer. **Disney's Animal Kingdom** usually opens from 8 or 9am to 5 or 6pm but sometimes closes as late as 7pm.

Epcot's Future World is generally open from 9am to 6 or 7pm and occasionally later. **Epcot's World Showcase** usually opens at 11am or noon and closes at 9pm. Once again, there are extended holiday and summer hours.

Typhoon Lagoon and **Blizzard Beach** are open from 10am to 5pm most of the year (with extended hours during summer and some holidays). Note that during the summer and holiday periods, the water parks can fill up early and close to new visitors, so if you plan on visiting one of them at a busy time of year, do it early or pretty late in the day. In winter, both parks are closed on a rotating basis for maintenance.

2 Making Your Visit More Enjoyable

HOW WE'VE MADE THIS CHAPTER USEFUL TO PARENTS

Before every listing in the major parks, you'll note the **Recommended Ages** entry, which tells which ages will most appreciate that ride or show. Though most families want to do everything, this guideline can be helpful in planning your daily itinerary. In the ride ratings, I also indicate whether a ride will be more enjoyable for kids than for adults, or vice versa. Many, even a couple in the Magic Kingdom, are too intense for young kids, and one bad experience can spook them for a good long time (even beyond your vacation). You'll find any **height** and **health restrictions** noted in the listings, too.

I've also provided a few other yardsticks that will help evaluate the rides for your kids: **Ryan** (age 14), **Austin** (age 12), **Nicolas** (age 10), **Hailey** (age 8), and **Davis** (age 6) have all happily added their two cents to the mix. This bunch have made more than just a few trips to the theme parks right alongside me, and they've provided plenty of pint-size insight and information . . . and a pound's worth of opinions along the way.

BEST TIME OF YEAR TO VISIT

Because of the large number of international visitors, there's really no off season at Disney, but during the winter months, usually mid-January through March, crowds are smaller (except weekends), and though the weather can be unpredictable in January, the rest of the time it's generally mild. The crowds also thin from mid-September until the week before Thanksgiving and in May, before Memorial Day weekend (though weekends can get crowded with locals). *Summer is among the worst times.* The masses throng to the parks. It's also humid and hot, *hot*, HOT. If you can skip a summer visit, you won't have to worry about the possibility of a hurricane (admittedly rare—up until the last few years, anyway) or an electrical storm (an almost-daily occurrence here).

Tip: Summer may be bad, but periods around major holidays are the absolute worst. The 2 weeks on either side of Easter, as well as mid-December through the first weekend in January, are practically intolerable. Admittedly, the festive atmosphere and holiday decor are fun, but if the thought of standing in absurdly long lines and dealing with massive crowds doesn't make you merry, don't even think of coming here to celebrate the season.

⟨Tips⟩ A Tiny Tour Guide

Pal Mickey is a new kind of tour guide: a 10½-inch-tall plush toy with quite a personality. Turn him on, and he'll happily help you tour the parks, letting you know when the parades are about to start, announcing showtimes, and telling you where to find your favorite characters. He shares stories, sings songs, plays games, and spouts off plenty of Disney trivia, too. Designed for 5- to 10-year-olds, Pal Mickey's wireless technology allows him to pick up sound clips from signals located throughout the parks, but he'll also interact with you at the resorts; back home, he'll voice prerecorded facts and jokes. He'll keep kids entertained in those long theme-park lines, and his timesaving tips, including ride height restrictions, can be quite helpful. Pal Mickey costs $65, plus tax. A Spanish version is available as well.

BEST DAYS TO VISIT

The busiest days at all parks are generally Saturday and Sunday. Seven-day guests usually arrive and depart on one of these days, so fewer of them turn the turnstiles, but weekends are when locals and Florida commuters invade. Beyond that, Monday, Thursday, and Saturday are pretty frantic in the Magic Kingdom; Tuesday and Friday are hectic at Epcot; Sunday and Wednesday are crazy at Disney's Hollywood Studios; and Monday, Tuesday, and Wednesday are a zoo at Disney's Animal Kingdom. Crowds tend to thin later in the day, so if you're going to visit during the busy season and have the luxury of the Park Hopper option, you'll bump into fewer guests the later you visit. This also applies to the water parks.

The big attractions at Disney's Animal Kingdom are, clearly, the animals, and the best time to see them is at the opening bell or late in the day, when things are cooler. You'll also get a decent midday glimpse of some of them during the cooler months.

PLANNING YOUR VISIT

How you plan your time at Walt Disney World will depend on a number of factors. These include the ages of any children in your party; what, if anything, you've seen on previous visits; your interests; and whether you're traveling at peak time or off season. Preplanning is always essential. So is choosing age-appropriate activities.

Nothing can spoil a day in the parks more than a child devastated because he or she can't do something that was promised. Before you get to the park, review this book and the suggested ages for children, including **height restrictions.** The WDW staff won't bend the rules despite the pitiful wails of your little ones. *Note:* Many rides that have minimum heights also have enough turbulence to make them unsuitable for folks with neck, back, or heart problems; those prone to motion sickness; and pregnant women.

Unless you're staying for more than a week, you simply can't experience all the rides, shows, and attractions included in this chapter. A ride might last only 3 minutes, but you may have to wait an hour or more just to ride, even if you use FASTPASS (detailed shortly). You'll send yourself and your kids into a tizzy and wear everyone to a frazzle if you try to hit everything. It's far better to follow a relaxed and flexible itinerary, including leisurely meals, breaks, and purely recreational activities, than to make a demanding job out of trying to see and do it all (which, in all honestly, will lead to disappointment and disillusionment in the end). Keep in mind that less is more—especially at Disney.

CREATING AN ITINERARY FOR EACH DAY

Watch the previously mentioned Disney vacation DVD, peruse the planning CD, read the detailed descriptions in this book, and then plan your trip to include those shows and attractions that pique your family's interest and excitement.

Tips The Parent Trap: Switching Places

Many of the attractions at WDW offer a **Rider Swap** program, designed for parents traveling with small children. While one parent rides an attraction, the other stays with the kids not quite ready to handle the experience; then the adults switch places without having to stand in line again. Notify a cast member if you wish to participate when you get in line. Most other Orlando theme parks offer this option, too.

Tips FASTPASS

If lines aren't your thing, well . . . you had better turn back now. Lines are a part of the deal at Disney. But if you're savvy, you can usually avoid the worst of them if you take advantage of Disney's FASTPASS. The free system allows you to wait in a far shorter line at some of the park's most popular attractions. Seems easy enough, right? Well, it is. There is, however, a small price to pay for skipping the big lines. Here's the drill:

Hang onto your ticket stub when you enter, and head to the hottest ride on your list. If it's a FASTPASS attraction (noted in the guide map you get when you enter), you'll see a sign marking the FASTPASS kiosk just near the entrance. Feed your ticket into the ticket-taker. *Note:* Every member of your group must get an individual FASTPASS. Retrieve both your ticket and your FASTPASS slip. Printed on the slip are two times. You can return any time during that 1-hour window and enter the ride (there's a much shorter line for FASTPASS holders). Be sure to keep your slip handy, as you'll need it to get in the right line.

Note #2: Early in the day, your 1-hour window may begin as soon as 40 minutes after you feed the FASTPASS machine, but later in the day, it may be hours later. Initially, Disney allowed you to do this on only one ride at a time. Now your FASTPASS ticket shows a time printed when you can get a second FASTPASS, usually about 2 hours after you got the first one, though it can sometimes be as soon as 45 minutes later, even if you haven't used the first pass yet.

Note #3: Don't think you can fool Disney by feeding your ticket stub in multiple times, figuring you can hit the jackpot for multiple rides or help others in your group who have lost their tickets. These "smart" stubs will reject your attempts by spitting out a coupon that says "Not a valid FASTPASS."

Note #4: FASTPASS slips can run out. If you have your heart set on a ride, and it's peak season, head to your chosen attraction's FASTPASS machine as soon as you can. Tickets for top rides often run out by the early afternoon, sometimes even earlier.

At the same time, consider your loyalties. My younger kids could spend all day in Tomorrowland, spinning around like space rangers with Woody and Buzz Lightyear, but touring Toontown is of far less interest to them. Put the rides featuring your favorite characters, or your kids' favorites, at the top of your list. It's a good idea to make a daily itinerary, putting your choices in some kind of sensible geographical sequence so you're not zigzagging all over the place. Consult the maps in this book, and familiarize yourself in advance with the layout of each park. Also recognize that rides or exhibits nearest an entrance may be busiest when the gates open. That's because a lot of people visit the first thing they see, even if the more popular attractions are deeper into the park.

I repeat this advice: Schedule sit-down shows, recreational activities (a boat ride or a refreshing swim late in the afternoon), and at least some unhurried meals if time permits. This will save you and your kids from exhaustion and aggravation. Breaks in the day will give your family the much-needed opportunity to recharge and rest weary feet. And *be flexible!* The suggested itineraries that follow allow you to see a great deal of the parks as efficiently as possible. If you have the luxury of a multiday pass, you can divide and conquer at a slower pace, and even repeat some favorites.

SUGGESTED ITINERARIES

There are a ton of ways to see the parks; time and budget permitting, it's often better to do it in limited doses. Spending 2 or more days in a park at a casual pace allows you to skip certain rides, saving them for the second day instead of squeezing them all in at once.

That said, I offer suggested itineraries as options for those on a tighter schedule. These itineraries are organized to get the most out of the least amount of time. (Note, though, that using FAST-PASS may require you to double back to a land you've already covered.) I break things into one game plan for families with younger kids and another for those with older kids and teens. With few exceptions (noted later), Disney doesn't have enough true stomach-turning thrill rides to warrant a special itinerary for take-no-prisoners teens and adults. Frankly, the only Orlando park in that class is Universal's Islands of Adventure, which is tackled in chapter 7.

A Day in the Magic Kingdom with Younger Kids

Consider making Advance Dining Reservations for a character meal at **Cinderella's Royal Table** (© 407/ 939-3463), located inside Cinderella Castle. Otherwise consider Advance Dining Reservations at **Tony's Town Square Restaurant** for an Italian treat.

If you have very young kids (preschool to around age 7), go right to the **Walt Disney World Railroad** station on Main Street and hop the next train. Get off at **Mickey's Toontown Fair** to meet Mickey, Minnie, and the gang. Ride the **Barnstormer at Goofy's Wiseacre Farm,** a mini–roller coaster, and explore **Mickey's** and **Minnie's Country Houses.**

If your kids are 8 or older, start the day at **Tomorrowland,** braving **Buzz Lightyear's Space Ranger Spin** (appropriate for any age) and **Space Mountain** (over 8). Little ones under 5 like the **Tomorrowland Indy Speedway** and the **Tomorrowland Transit Authority,** but there's not much else for them here.

Most kids 8 and under will find something that's fun in **Fantasyland,** including **Dumbo the Flying Elephant, Peter Pan's Flight, Mickey's**

PhilharMagic, It's a Small World, The Many Adventures of Winnie the Pooh, Cinderella's Golden Carousel, the **Mad Tea Party,** and the **Dream Along with Mickey** stage show.

Afterward, lunch at **Cosmic Ray's Starlight Cafe** or the **Columbia Harbour House** in Liberty Square.

If you aren't there already, head west to **Liberty Square.** Most kids over 10 will appreciate the Animatronic history lesson in the **Hall of Presidents** show. Before leaving, visit the recently revamped **Haunted Mansion;** then move to Frontierland. **Splash Mountain** and **Big Thunder Mountain Railroad** are best suited for those 8 and older; **Country Bear Jamboree** and **Woody's Cowboy Camp** (an interactive street show of sorts) are fun for the younger set; while **Tom Sawyer Island** allows kids over 7 a great place to run around and parents a well deserved sitdown (unless they're keeping watch over their younger adventurers).

Go to **Adventureland** next. Ride the **Magic Carpets of Aladdin, Pirates of the Caribbean** (right nearby is **Captain Jack's Pirate Tutorial**), and **Jungle Cruise;** then let the kids burn some energy climbing about the **Swiss Family Treehouse.** Younger kids (ages 4–8) will appreciate the liveliness of the **Enchanted Tiki Room.**

Consult the guide map available as you enter the park, and if the **Wishes** fireworks display and **SpectroMagic** are scheduled, be sure to watch them.

A Day in the Magic Kingdom with Older Kids & Teenagers

As mentioned earlier, consider making Advance Dining Reservations at **Cinderella's Royal Table** (© **407/939-3463**) if you're interested in a special character meal; otherwise reserve a spot at **Tony's Town Square Restaurant** for a sit-down dinner.

From Main Street, cut through the center of the park to **Frontierland.** Challenge **Splash Mountain** and then ride **Big Thunder Mountain Railroad.**

Next, go to **Liberty Square** and visit the **Haunted Mansion** and **Hall of Presidents.**

After lunch at **Pecos Bill Café** or **Columbia Harbour House,** cut diagonally through the park, past Cinderella Castle, and into **Tomorrowland** to ride **Space Mountain, Buzz Lightyear's Space Ranger Spin,** and **Astro Orbiter,** and to experience the **Monsters, Inc. Laugh Floor.**

If time permits, head to Adventureland for the **Jungle Cruise** and **Pirates of the Caribbean;** then, if it's scheduled, end the day with the **Wishes** fireworks display.

A Day in Epcot with Younger Kids

Remember to get an Advance Dining Reservation if you want to eat in the park (call © **407/939-3463** before you arrive). For dinner, I suggest **Teppan Edo** in the World Showcase's Japan Pavilion or the **Coral Reef** in the Living Seas. The **Sunshine Seasons** in the Land Pavilion is a good choice for lunch because of its diversity.

While once the least desirable of the parks for young kids, Epcot has added to and improved the number of activities and attractions to keep them entertained. **Future World,** near the front of the park, is the best place to start. Begin your day at the **Seas with Nemo & Friends** to explore the ocean depths, help to find Nemo, and talk turtle at **Turtle Talk with Crush.** If your kids are over the 40-inch minimum, make your way to the **Land Pavilion** for a ride high above California's impressive landscape on **Soarin'** (high-tech interactive games now line the queue, entertaining those waiting to ride).

Next, visit **Innoventions.** On its east side, all but the smallest kids will appreciate today's and tomorrow's high-tech gadgets at the **House of Innoventions** and the **Innoventions Internet Zone.** Building a robot to take home at **Fantastic Plastic Works,** the **Kim Possible Kidcot** stop, and the new **Character Connection** will appeal to younger kids. Over on the west side, kids and adults find it hard to leave **Video Games of Tomorrow.** Those of all ages (even adults) will be mesmerized by the periodic water shows at the **Innoventions Fountain** located in the center.

Break for a late lunch; then head to **Imagination!** and its two great shows: **Journey into Imagination with Figment** and **Honey, I Shrunk the Audience.** Then you're off to the **World Showcase.** The meticulously detailed pavilions of 11 nations surround a big lagoon that you can cross by boat if your feet need a break. Tinier tykes may get bored, but those 5 and up can create cultural crafts to take home at the **Kidcot Fun Stops** along the way.

Norway delivers a history lesson and boat ride to the time of the Vikings aboard the *Maelstrom;* **China** and **Canada** feature fabulous 360-degree movies (China also has the engaging **Dragon Legend Acrobats**);

and the **Germany** exhibit's Biergarten is filled with oompah music (little kids usually love the model train set up right nearby). Also, take in the show, concerts, and displays at **U.S.A.—The American Adventure** before ending your day with **IllumiNations.**

A Day in Epcot with Older Kids & Teenagers

If you want to eat in the park, make an Advance Dining Reservation before you arrive by calling © **407/939-3463.** For dinner, I suggest the **San Angel Inn** in the World Showcase's Mexico exhibit or the **Coral Reef** restaurant in the Living Seas. The **Sunshine Seasons** in the Land is a good family choice for lunch because of its diversity.

Future World, near the front of the park, is the best place to start. Skip the recently revamped **Spaceship Earth,** for now. Save the ride through history till the end of the day—when your feet will appreciate the rest. Go straight to **Mission: Space,** where you can train as the astronauts do. Follow up with next-door-neighbor **Test Track.** Then cut to the west to **Imagination!** for **Honey, I Shrunk the Audience.**

After a late lunch, visit the **Land Pavilion** to ride **Soarin';** then head to **Innoventions.** On its east side, check out the high-tech gadgets at the **House of Innoventions;** then head to the west side for **Video Games of Tomorrow.**

Next, head to the **World Showcase** for a cultural trip around 11 of the world's nations. **Norway** delivers a history lesson and boat ride to the time of the Vikings aboard the *Maelstrom;* **China** and **Canada** feature fabulous 360-degree movies (China also has the engaging **Dragon Legend Acrobats**); don't miss the **Matsuriza** drummers in **Japan.** And the **United Kingdom** offers scheduled interactive comedy with the **World Showcase Players.** Also, take in the show, concerts, and displays at **U.S.A.—The American Adventure** before ending your day by watching **IllumiNations.**

A Day in Disney's Hollywood Studios with Younger Kids

The layout and size of this park make it easier to backtrack from one area to another.

If you want to eat dinner here, make Advance Dining Reservations (© **407/939-3463**) ahead of time. The **Hollywood Brown Derby** is a decent sit-down option but one that's pricey (and slightly stuffy) for families with younger kids. The **Sci-Fi Dine-In Theater Restaurant** and **50's Prime Time Café** are entertaining and appropriate options (but they book up quickly). For lunch, try **Toluca Legs Turkey Co.,** where the smoked turkey legs are one of the best grab-and-go meals in any park (you can also get hot dogs). If your feet are in need of a rest, the **Backlot Express** and **Rosie's All-American Café** offer plenty for pint-sized palates.

Voyage of the Little Mermaid is a must for the young (in years or yearnings); the same goes for **Jim Henson's Muppet*Vision 3-D,** a truly fun show for all ages.

The explosions and noise in the **Indiana Jones Epic Stunt Spectacular!** and the new **Lights, Motors, Action! Extreme Stunt Show** may be too much for tinier tots, but most kids 5 and older will love the action.

Visit the *Honey, I Shrunk the Kids* **Movie Set Adventure;** then make your way along the midway at **Toy Story Mania!** before checking your show schedule for favorites such as **Playhouse Disney–Live on Stage!** (great for little kids), *Beauty and the Beast,* and the new interactive **Block Party**

Bash parade where Disney-Pixar characters come to life. At night, *don't miss* **Fantasmic!** if your kids are 6 and older.

A Day in Disney's Hollywood Studios with Older Kids & Teenagers

Remember to make Advance Dining Reservations (© **407/939-3463**) ahead of time if you want to eat in the park. The **Hollywood Brown Derby** is a decent sit-down option but one that's pricey for families. The **Sci-Fi Dine-In Theater Restaurant** and **50's Prime Time Café** are entertaining options (but they book up quickly). For lunch, consider **Toluca Legs Turkey Co.,** where the smoked turkey legs are one of the best grab-and-go meals in any park (you can also get hot dogs). If you feet are in need of a rest, however, the **ABC Commissary** features a unique and varied menu.

Head directly to the **Twilight Zone Tower of Terror.** It's a high-voltage ride that's not for the young or faint of heart, but adrenaline-crazed kids and teens will keep coming back for more. The same goes for the **Rock 'n' Roller Coaster,** with its incredible takeoff speed, three inversions, and rock music that will blow you (or at least your eardrums) away. Then make your way over to the impressive and high-energy **Lights, Motors, Action! Extreme Stunt Show.**

The park is small, so backtracking isn't as much of a concern here. Consider bypassing attractions that have long lines, saving them for later, or use FASTPASS where you can. **Star Tours** and the **Indiana Jones Epic Stunt Spectacular!** have the longest lines after the thrill rides mentioned above.

Jim Henson's Muppet*Vision 3-D and **Toy Story Mania!** are truly fun for all ages. Afterward, go on the ton-of-fun **Backlot Tour** and check the show schedule to cheer on the Wildcats at

the **High School Musical 2: School's Out!** pep rally.

At night, *don't miss* **Fantasmic!**

A Day in Disney's Animal Kingdom for Kids of All Ages

I'm not breaking this park into separate itineraries for older and younger age groups because there are few things here that can't be done by most kids, no matter how old they are. Instead, I'll suggest age appeal for those attractions that warrant it.

Be here when the gates open, usually around 8 or 9am. (Call © **407/824-4321** to check the time.) This will give you the best chance of seeing the animals, as they're most active in the morning air (the next-best time is late in the afternoon, although some can be seen throughout the day if you come during cooler months). If you want to eat at **Yak & Yeti** or the **Rainforest Cafe,** make Advance Dining Reservations by calling © **407/939-3463.** Fair lunch stops include **Flame Tree Barbecue, Pizzafari,** and the **Tusker House.**

The size of the park (500 acres) means a lot of travel once you pass through the gates. Don't linger in the Oasis area or around the Tree of Life; instead, head directly to the back of the park to be first in line for **Kilimanjaro Safaris.** This will allow your family to see the animals before it gets hot and the lines become monstrous. Work your way back through Africa, visiting **Pangani Forest Exploration Trail** and its lowland gorillas (this may be too long and lifeless for younger kids). Then head to the **Tree of Life** on Discovery Island for **It's Tough to Be a Bug!**

Older kids, teens, and adults should ride **Dinosaur** and **Primeval Whirl** in Dinoland U.S.A., a good choice if you get there before lines form or if you use FASTPASS. Younger kids deserve some time at the **Boneyard** and on

TriceraTop Spin in Dinoland, as well as a trip to **Camp Minnie-Mickey,** on the other side of the park, to meet their favorite characters. Make sure to see the park's (and WDW's) best shows, **Finding Nemo–The Musical** and **Festival of the Lion King.**

Trek through the jungles on the **Maharajah Jungle Trek** in Asia. Older kids and teens will love tackling **Kali River Rapids,** a great way to cool off at the end of the day (and yes, they will get soaked), or meeting up with the yeti on Disney's newest thriller, **Expedition Everest.**

SERVICES & FACILITIES IN THE PARKS

ATMs   Cash machines are available near the entrances to all parks and usually at least one other place inside (see the handout guide map you get when you enter the park). They honor cards from banks using the Cirrus, Honor, and PLUS systems.

Baby Care   All parks have a Baby Care Center that's equipped with private rooms designated for breast-feeding, changing, and feeding, and that sell baby-care basics. All women's restrooms, and some men's, are equipped with changing tables.

Cameras & Film   Film, batteries, disposable cameras, and some digital supplies are sold at various locations in all parks (at much higher prices than those in the free world).

Car Assistance   If you need a battery jump or other assistance, raise the hood of your vehicle and wait for security to arrive.

First Aid   All parks have stations marked on the handout guide maps.

Lost Children   Every park has a designated spot for lost children to be reunited with their families. In the Magic Kingdom, it's City Hall or the Baby Care Center; in Epcot, the Earth Center or the Baby Care Center; in Disney's Hollywood Studios, Guest Relations; and in Disney's Animal Kingdom, Discovery Island. *Children under 7 should wear name tags inside their clothing;* older children and adults should have a prearranged meeting place in case your group gets separated. If that happens, tell the first park employee you see; many employees wear the same type of clothing, and all have special name tags. For more on lost children, see "Traveling Safely with Your Child," in chapter 2.

Package Pickup   Nearly all WDW stores can arrange for purchases to be sent to the front of the park. Allow at least 3 hours for delivery. If you're staying at a Disney resort, you can also have packages purchased by 7pm sent to your hotel room (they will be delivered by noon the next day).

Parking   At press time, Disney charges $11 for car, light-truck, and van parking, and $12 for RVs.

Pet Care   Don't leave yours in a parked car, even with a window cracked open. Cars are death traps in Florida's sun. Only service animals are permitted in the parks, but there are five kennels at WDW (© **407/824-6568;** $10 per day, $13 overnight for resort guests, $15 overnight for those staying elsewhere). The kennels located at the Transportation and Ticket Center in the Magic Kingdom and near the entrance to Fort Wilderness Resort & Campground board animals both during the day as well as overnight. Day-only accommodations are offered at kennels just outside the Entrance Plaza at Epcot (the only location offering walking services) and at the entrances to Disney's Hollywood Studios and Disney's Animal Kingdom. *Proof of vaccination is required.*

Shops   In addition to the ones listed in the following pages, most of Disney's rides have small gift shops featuring souvenirs based on that ride's theme.

Stroller Rental   Strollers are available near all park entrances. The cost for a single is $10 per day, or $8 per day for a length-of-stay rental. A double costs $18 per day, or $16 per day for a length-of-stay rental. *Tip:* Because strollers often have to be parked outside attractions, it's easy to get confused about whose stroller is whose. Attach a brightly colored piece of cloth or some other identifier so that someone doesn't accidentally walk off with your stroller. If it does go astray (and many will), just bring your receipt to the stroller-rental location to get a replacement.

Tip Boards   Each park has at least one tip board that tells visitors the approximate waiting time at all major rides and attractions, showtimes, and parade schedules. In the Magic Kingdom, it's at the end of Main Street on the left as you face the castle; in Epcot, the digital board is in Innoventions Plaza (with a second slated to go up near the Land Pavilion); at Disney's Hollywood Studios, it's at the intersection of Hollywood and Sunset boulevards; and inside Disney's Animal Kingdom, you'll find it just over the bridge to Discovery Island.

Wheelchair Rental   A wheelchair costs $10 per day, or $8 per day for a length-of-stay rental. Electric wheelchairs rent for $35, including a $5 deposit.

3 The Magic Kingdom

America's most popular theme park, the 107-acre Magic Kingdom is filled with over 40 attractions (with new experiences being added almost yearly), unique shops, and themed restaurants. Its centerpiece and most recognizable symbol, Cinderella Castle, forms the hub from which its **seven themed lands** reach out.

ARRIVING   From the immense parking lot, you have to walk to the tram that will take you to the Transportation and Ticket Center, and then wait for a ferry or monorail to take you to the entrance, where you'll have to pass through security for a bag check. All told, the time it takes to get from your car to Main Street, U.S.A., is somewhere

Frommer's Rates the Rides

Because there's so much to do here, I'm shifting from the star-rating system used for hotels and restaurants to one that has a little more range. You'll notice that most of the grades below are *As, Bs,* and *Cs.* That's because Disney designers have done a reasonably good job on the attractions front. But occasionally, my ratings show *Ds* for Duds.

Here's what the **Frommer's Ratings** mean:

A+	=	Your trip wouldn't be complete without it.
A	=	Put it at the top of your to-do list.
B+	=	Make a real effort to see or do it.
B	=	It's fun but not a must-see.
C+	=	A nice diversion; see it if you have time.
C	=	Go if there's no wait and you can walk right in.
D	=	Don't waste your time.

The Magic Kingdom

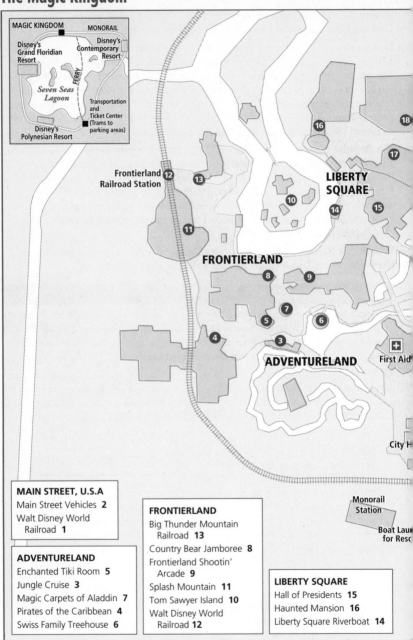

MAGIC KINGDOM **MONORAIL**

Disney's Grand Floridian Resort

Disney's Contemporary Resort

FERRY

Seven Seas Lagoon

Transportation and Ticket Center (Trams to parking areas)

Disney's Polynesian Resort

Frontierland Railroad Station

LIBERTY SQUARE

FRONTIERLAND

ADVENTURELAND

First Aid

City H

Monorail Station

Boat Lau for Reso

MAIN STREET, U.S.A

Main Street Vehicles **2**

Walt Disney World Railroad **1**

ADVENTURELAND

Enchanted Tiki Room **5**

Jungle Cruise **3**

Magic Carpets of Aladdin **7**

Pirates of the Caribbean **4**

Swiss Family Treehouse **6**

FRONTIERLAND

Big Thunder Mountain Railroad **13**

Country Bear Jamboree **8**

Frontierland Shootin' Arcade **9**

Splash Mountain **11**

Tom Sawyer Island **10**

Walt Disney World Railroad **12**

LIBERTY SQUARE

Hall of Presidents **15**

Haunted Mansion **16**

Liberty Square Riverboat **14**

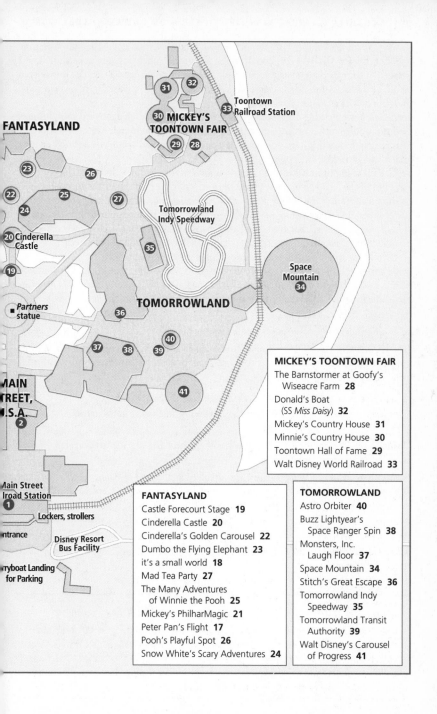

FANTASYLAND

MICKEY'S TOONTOWN FAIR

Toontown Railroad Station

Tomorrowland Indy Speedway

TOMORROWLAND

Space Mountain **34**

■ *Partners* statue

MAIN STREET, U.S.A.

Main Street Railroad Station

Lockers, strollers

Entrance

Disney Resort Bus Facility

Ferryboat Landing for Parking

Cinderella Castle

MICKEY'S TOONTOWN FAIR

The Barnstormer at Goofy's Wiseacre Farm **28**

Donald's Boat (SS *Miss Daisy*) **32**

Mickey's Country House **31**

Minnie's Country House **30**

Toontown Hall of Fame **29**

Walt Disney World Railroad **33**

FANTASYLAND

Castle Forecourt Stage **19**

Cinderella Castle **20**

Cinderella's Golden Carousel **22**

Dumbo the Flying Elephant **23**

it's a small world **18**

Mad Tea Party **27**

The Many Adventures of Winnie the Pooh **25**

Mickey's PhilharMagic **21**

Peter Pan's Flight **17**

Pooh's Playful Spot **26**

Snow White's Scary Adventures **24**

TOMORROWLAND

Astro Orbiter **40**

Buzz Lightyear's Space Ranger Spin **38**

Monsters, Inc. Laugh Floor **37**

Space Mountain **34**

Stitch's Great Escape **36**

Tomorrowland Indy Speedway **35**

Tomorrowland Transit Authority **39**

Walt Disney's Carousel of Progress **41**

around **35 to 45 minutes,** sometimes longer. And that total doesn't include the time spent in lines if you have to stop at Guest Relations, purchase your tickets, or rent a stroller. You'll face the same agony (complicated by escaping crowds) on the way out, so relax. This is one of the most crowded parks, so plan to arrive either an hour before the opening bell or an hour or two after.

Each of the parking lot's sections is named for Disney characters (Goofy, Pluto, Minnie, and so on), and aisles are numbered. I can't stress enough just how important it is to **write down where you parked your vehicle;** you would be amazed at how many cars look just like yours!

The most important thing you can do upon arriving at the park is to pick up a copy (or two) of the Magic Kingdom **guide map** (if you can't find one at the turnstiles, stop at the tunnel under the WDW Railroad, City Hall, or the nearest shop). It provides an array of detailed information about available guest services, restaurants, and attractions. The *Times Guide* (separate from the guide map) will be your key to the daily schedules for showtimes, parades, fireworks, character meet-and-greets, and park hours.

If you have questions, all park employees are very knowledgeable, and City Hall, on your left as you enter, serves as an information center—and, like Mickey's Toontown Fair, a great place to meet costumed characters. Character greeting places are also featured on the map, so make note of them if you have little ones along.

HOURS   The park is open from at least 9am to 6 or 7pm, sometimes later—as late as midnight during major holidays and summer.

TICKET PRICES   Tickets are $71 for adults and $60 for children 3 to 9. Kids under 3 get in free. See "Tickets & Passes," on p. 176, for information on multiday passes and other add-on options.

SERVICES & FACILITIES IN THE MAGIC KINGDOM

Most of the following are noted on the handout guide maps in the park:

ATMs   Cash machines inside the park honor cards from banks on the Cirrus, Honor, and PLUS systems. They can be found near the main entrance, in Frontierland, and in Tomorrowland.

Baby Care   Located next to the Crystal Palace at the end of Main Street, the Baby Care Center is furnished with a nursing room and toddler-size toilets. Disposable diapers, formula, baby food, and pacifiers are sold at a premium (read: bring your own, or pay the price). There are changing tables here, as well as in all women's restrooms and some men's.

Cameras & Film   Film, disposable cameras, and limited digital supplies are available throughout the park.

Tips **76 Trombones . . .**

The **Main Street Family Fun Day Parade** invites guests to join in and march down Main Street right alongside their favorite Disney characters, floats, and marching bands. There's even a pint-sized stroller drill team so that little ones still in strollers (and their parents) can take part in the parade, too. Check the *Times Guide* or the park's tip board for parade times.

⌒Tips A Cut Above

The **Harmony Barber Shop** on Main Street (near the firehouse) is a real working barber shop. It's open daily from 9am to 5pm and gives hundreds of haircuts each week. If your child gets his or her first cut here, Disney throws in bubbles, stickers, and a special set of mouse ears to mark the occasion. Kids 12 and under can get a cut for about $14; cuts for adults cost around $17. To jazz up the experience, kids and adults can add some color to their coif (thanks to a special colored hair gel) for just $5.

First Aid   It's located beside the Crystal Palace next to Baby Care and staffed by registered nurses.

Lockers   Lockers are located in the arcade below the Main Street Railroad Station. The cost is $5, plus a $2 refundable deposit.

Lost Children   Lost children in the Magic Kingdom are usually taken to City Hall or the Baby Care Center. *Children under 7 should wear name tags* inside their clothing.

Package Pickup   Any purchase can be sent to package pickup near City Hall. Allow 3 hours for delivery.

Pet Care   Day boarding is available at the Transportation and Ticket Center for $10 (℅ **407/824-6568**). The center also boards animals overnight ($13 for Disney or official hotel guests, $15 for others). Proof of vaccination is required.

Stroller Rental   The Stroller Shop near the entrance to the Magic Kingdom charges $10 for a single and $18 for a double, with a discounted rate for a length-of-stay rental.

Wheelchair Rental   Go to the gift shop to the left of the ticket booths at the Transportation and Ticket Center, or to the Stroller and Wheelchair Shop inside the main entrance to your right. The cost is $10, or $35 for an electric one, plus a $5 deposit.

MAIN STREET, U.S.A.

Designed to model a turn-of-the-20th-century American street (although it ends in a 13th-c. European castle), this is the gateway to the Kingdom and is filled with shops and on-the-run eateries. Don't dawdle too long on Main Street when you enter; leave it for the end of the day, when you're heading back to your hotel.

Main Street Vehicles
Frommer's Rating: C
Recommended Ages: Mainly nostalgic adults
Ride a horse-drawn trolley, jitney, vintage fire engine, or horseless carriage *only* if you don't mind waiting around. Otherwise, there are far, far better things to see and do throughout the realm.

Walt Disney World Railroad
Frommer's Rating: B
Recommended Ages: All ages
You can board an authentic 1928 steam-powered train for a 15-minute trip clockwise around the perimeter of the park. This is a good way to save wear and tear on your feet *if* you're headed to one of its three stations: the park entrance, Frontierland, and Mickey's Toontown Fair, in that order.

Davis's Rating: "Let's go again . . . can we?" (Of course, he could've just as easily ridden the monorail all day, too.)

ADVENTURELAND

Cross the bridge marked by tikis and torches as the rhythm of beating drums sound in the distance. As you make your way through lush jungle foliage, trees hung with Spanish moss, dense vines, and stands of palm and bamboo, you'll be transported to an exotic locale where swashbuckling adventures await you and your kids.

Enchanted Tiki Room

Frommer's Rating: B for kids, C for adults in need of an amusing break
Recommended Ages: 2–10 and older adults

The large, hexagonal Tiki Room serves up a Polynesian atmosphere, with its thatched roof, bamboo beams, tapa-bark murals, and torches. Inside, guests are entertained by the likes of Iago (from *Aladdin*) and Zazu (from *The Lion King*), as well as an ensemble of boisterous tropical birds (over 200 of them, in fact), along with chanting totem poles and singing flowers that whistle, warble, and tweet. Overall, it's good family fun, but be aware that it's rather loud, and a brief simulated tropical storm, with crackling thunder and flashes of lightning, combined with the multitude of audio and visual effects, may be a bit too overwhelming for very young children.

Jungle Cruise

Frommer's Rating: C+ (B for the foot-weary)
Recommended Ages: 4–adult

It's a nostalgic ride for many an adult, but a yawner for many older kids and teens. You'll sail through the African veldt in the Congo, an Amazon rainforest, and along the Nile in Egypt as your boat captain offers somewhat corny but humorous commentary. You'll encounter dozens of exotic Animatronic animals, ranging from playful elephants to lions, tigers, and alligators as you pass through dense tropical and subtropical foliage (most of it is real). You'll see a Cambodian temple guarded by snakes, a rhino chasing terrified African beaters as they clamor up a totem pole for safety, and a jungle camp taken over by apes. While you're waiting to board, read the prop menu: It includes fricassee of giant stag beetle and barbecued three-toed skink. It's a nice break from the park madness if the line isn't long or you use FASTPASS.

Magic Carpets of Aladdin

Frommer's Rating: A for tykes and parents
Recommended Ages: 2–8

Younger kids will appreciate this ride's gentle ups and downs as they fly through the sky on colorful magic carpets. The view of Agrabah from above is impressive, but be prepared as you make your way around the genie's giant bottle: The spitting camels have pretty good aim, making it likely that you'll get squirted with water (similar to One Fish, Two Fish, Red Fish, Blue Fish at Universal Orlando's Islands of Adventure; see p. 277). If there's a downside here, it's that you may find yourself wishing for shorter lines (though they're not nearly as unbearable as some you'll encounter in Fantasyland).

Pirates of the Caribbean

Frommer's Rating: B+
Recommended Ages: 6–adult

The release of *Pirates of the Caribbean: The Curse of the Black Pearl* and its recent sequels, *Dead Man's Chest* and *At World's End,* has revitalized the popularity of this

---

Tips **One for You . . . One for Me**

Disney's trying out something new: a map made just for preschoolers and their parents. It highlights all of the kid-friendly hot spots, ranging from stroller-rental locations to the Baby Care Center to all restrooms. It also lists which rides are most appropriate and must-sees for the younger set. The map is usually obtainable at the parks' Guest Services desks and at stroller-rental locations.

---

oldie but goodie. They also inspired the recent renovations that now have Jack Sparrow and Barbossa joining the original set of swashbucklers. A tweak in the storyline to better mirror the movies has been added, along with a mix of new and updated special effects. Still, the ride might be a bit scary for kids younger than 5 due to the unexpected yet small waterfall and moments of darkness.

After making your way through dark and dank dungeons, guests board a boat and set sail for a small Caribbean town, its shores teeming with pillaging Animatronic pirates who carouse, chase wenches, and wreak general havoc as Jack and Barbossa race to reach the pirates' treasure. There are plenty of gunfire and cannonballs flying through the air as the marauders battle one another, with you, of course, caught up in the middle. The effects are great, as is the yo-ho-ho music of "A Pirate's Life for Me" that plays in the background (you won't be able to stop yourself from humming along). The bonus here is an immense covered queue area that will protect you and your stroller-bound children from both sun and rain (this ride offers the only covered stroller parking in the park). *Tip:* Nod hello to the parrot (Peglegged Pete) above the entrance plaza, and he may offer you his own greeting.

Note: Right nearby, pirates-to-be can join in on all the interactive fun of **Captain Jack's Pirate Tutorial,** held several times a day. The great captain himself, along with his mate Mack, take on a pint-sized crew of pirates in training, teaching them the art of swordplay and other swashbuckling silliness. Upon completion, the little pirates (picked from the surrounding crowd) are sworn in as official swashbucklers as they say the pirate's oath and become honorary buccaneers and part of Captain Jack's crew—complete with a certificate to take home.

Nicolas's Rating: "The pirates in the movie were better, but the ride is pretty cool. I liked the waterfall part the best." **Davis's** and **Hailey's Rating:** These two couldn't get enough, riding three times before hanging up their pirate hats for the day. The shop at the end of the ride is a favorite spot for all pirates, big and little alike.

Swiss Family Treehouse
Frommer's Rating: C
Recommended Ages: 4–12
This attraction, based on the 1960 Disney movie version of *Swiss Family Robinson,* includes a few more comforts from home than did the original. After climbing its many, many steps, you'll finally reach the treehouse, its rooms filled with mahogany furnishings, decorative accents, and running water. If your kids are nervous about heights, this one's not a good choice; visitors will find themselves walking along a rope-suspended bridge high above the ground, not to mention the climbing that's required to make it up and down all the stairs that lead around this 50-foot banyan tree. The "tree," designed by Disney Imagineers, has 330,000 polyethylene leaves sprouting from a 90-foot span of branches; although it isn't real, it's draped with actual

Tips **A (Baker's) Dozen Suggestions for Fewer Headaches**

1. **Be a leader, not a follower:** Go against the grain—head left toward Adventureland to begin your day (most visitors sprint for Tomorrowland). If you have the luxury of more than a day here, make your way to one or two major attractions early on; then save the others for early on your second day, when crowds are lightest. Pick up a FASTPASS wherever you can. And try to make mealtimes a bit earlier or later than usual—11am or 2pm for lunch and 4 or 7pm for dinner. It can make all the difference in the restaurant lines.

2. **Note your car's location:** That big red Hummer in the next space may not be there when you get out. Write your lot and row number on something with ink that won't run if it gets wet.

3. **Avoid the rush:** I-4 can get horribly crowded at times, so be ready for bumper-to-bumper traffic from 7 to 9am, from 4 to 7pm, and often in between. Check your map for secondary roads and alternative routes, and try to leave the parks a half hour before closing, when crowds disburse in droves.

4. **Be realistic:** You aren't going to be able to do everything in every park (believe me, I've tried). As a group, list three or four "must-do" things each day. Consider splitting up, with each adult taking one or more kids—one heading for the thrill rides; the other for the tamer, tot-friendly attractions. If time allows, you can always backtrack later. Those able to take advantage of Disney's Extra Magic Hours (p. 203) should do so—the crowds will be at their thinnest.

5. **Timing is everything:** I often laugh when I see people racing to make a tram and then gunning for the turnstiles. Relax—the park isn't going anywhere. And rushing just to wait in line seems rather silly, doesn't it? Once inside the park, mix it up a bit; stagger the attraction lines with indoor shows or even breaks on a shady bench.

6. **Call ahead:** If a sit-down dinner in a special restaurant is important to you, be sure to make Advance Dining Reservations (© **407/939-3463**) before your visit.

7. **Set a spending limit:** Kids should know they have a set amount to spend on trinkets (if they do, they generally spend more wisely). You

Spanish moss. It's a good place for kids to work off some excess energy, though things can get crowded up there. *Note:* People with limited mobility, beware; this attraction requires a lot of climbing.

FRONTIERLAND

From Adventureland, step into the wild and woolly past of the American frontier, where Disney cast members are clad in denim and calico; sidewalks are wooden; rough-and-tumble architecture runs to log cabins and rustic saloons; and the landscape is Southwestern scrubby with mesquite, cactus, yucca, and prickly pear.

should, too. Sticking to your budget will be beneficial in the end, but building in a small contingency "fun" fund for emergencies is also a good idea.

8. **Take a break:** If you're staying at a WDW property, spend the midafternoon napping (don't laugh; you may need a nap) or unwinding in the pool. Return to the parks for a few more attractions and the closing shows. (Get your hand stamped when you leave, and you'll be readmitted without charge.)

9. **Dress comfortably:** This may seem like common sense, but judging by the limping, blistered crowds trudging the parks, most people don't understand the immeasurable amount of walking they'll be doing. Wear comfortable, broken-in walking shoes or sneakers; skip the sandals and mules that can easily fall off or cause you to trip.

10. **Don't skimp on the sunscreen:** The Florida sun can be relentless, even in the shade, under the clouds, or in the cooler months. A bad burn can ruin your trip, not to mention your skin. Dress appropriately; wear lightweight, light-colored clothing, and bring along sunglasses and hats (especially for toddlers and infants, even if they'll be in a stroller). Slather on sunscreen with an SPF of at least 30—this is especially important for children. Make sure that you and your kids drink plenty of water to prevent dehydration.

11. **Travel light:** Don't carry large amounts of cash. The Pirates of the Caribbean aren't the only thieves in WDW. There are ATMs in the parks and most resorts if you run short.

12. **Get a little goofy:** Relax, put on those mouse ears, eat that extra piece of fudge, and sing along at the shows. Don't worry about what the cast members think; they've seen it all (and they're dressed pretty goofily, too).

13. **Take measure of your kids:** This guide, park maps, and information boards outside the more adventurous rides list minimum heights. If you know the restrictions early, you can avoid disappointment in the parks. Trust us—WDW won't budge because of sad faces or temper tantrums when your safety is involved.

Big Thunder Mountain Railroad
Frommer's Rating: A
Recommended Ages: 8–adult

This roller coaster earns high marks for what it is: a ride designed for those not quite up to the lunch-losing thrills of Rock 'n' Roller Coaster at Disney's Hollywood Studios (p. 234) or Dueling Dragons and Incredible Hulk Coaster at Islands of Adventure, listed in chapter 7. Think of Big Thunder as Roller Coasters 101. (Survive, and graduate to the next level.) It sports fun hairpin turns and dark descents rather than sudden, steep drops and near collisions. Your runaway train covers 2,780 feet of track and careens through the ribs of a dinosaur, under a thundering waterfall, past spewing

---

Tips Woody's Cowboy Camp

Several times throughout the day, Woody, Jesse, and Bullseye head right through town—**Frontiertown**, that is—rounding up guests along the way. Kids giddyup on wooden horses, making their way through a cowboy obstacle course filled with cacti, mountains, and mineshafts as Bullseye leads the way. For *Toy Story* fans and kiddie cowboys (or cowgirls), this one's a must.

---

geysers, and over a bottomless volcanic pool. Animatronic characters and critters (goats, chickens, donkeys) enhance the scenic backdrop, along with several hundred thousand dollars' worth of authentic antique mining equipment. *Note:* You must be at least 40 inches tall to ride. Disney discourages expectant mothers, people prone to motion sickness, and those with heart, neck, or back problems from riding. It may also be too intense for some kids under 8.

Nicolas's and **Austin's Rating:** *"It's even better at night!!"* (They rode it both during the day and at night, and loved it every time.) **Ryan's Rating:** "It's no kid's ride, that's for sure." (It may not be the Hulk, but it's got plenty of zip just the same. It even thrills a few adults, too!)

Country Bear Jamboree *Finds*
Frommer's Rating: B+
Recommended Ages: 3–adult, but the younger, the better
This is a foot-stomping hoot, though older kids and teens may hate it. Like many of the shows and rides in the Magic Kingdom, it doesn't have a companion in the other parks because it opened when the park did (in 1971!) and dates to a time when entertainment was simpler yet still fun. But it still has the power to bridge the generations (and the A/C is a blessing on hot summer days). The 15-minute show stars a troupe of fiddlin', strummin', and harmonica-playin' bears (audio-Animatronic, of course) belting out lively tunes and woeful love songs. The chubby Trixie, decked out in a satiny skirt, laments lost love as she sings "Tears Will Be the Chaser for Your Wine." Teddi Barra descends from the ceiling in a swing to perform "Heart, We Did All That We Could." In the finale, the cast joins in a rousing singalong.

Frontierland Shootin' Arcade
Frommer's Rating: C
Recommended Ages: 8–adult
Combining state-of-the-art electronics with a traditional shooting-gallery format, this arcade presents an array of targets (slow-moving ore cars, buzzards, and gravediggers) in an 1850s boomtown scenario. Fog creeps across the graveyard, and the setting changes as a calm, starlit night turns stormy with flashes of lightning and claps of thunder. Coyotes howl; bridges creak; and skeletal arms reach out from the grave. If you hit a tombstone, it might spin around and mysteriously change its epitaph. To keep things authentic, newfangled electronic firing mechanisms loaded with infrared bullets are concealed in vintage buffalo rifles. A dollar buys you 35 shots. It's a pretty cool arcade overall, and good for a few minutes of fun for kids over 5, but there are plenty of better ways to spend your time in the Magic Kingdom.

Splash Mountain
Frommer's Rating: A+

Recommended Ages: 8–adult

If you need a quick cooling off, this is the place to go—you and your kids will get wet! Some kids may find it a little intimidating upon inspection, but most have a blast while riding it. Based on Disney's 1946 film *Song of the South,* Splash Mountain takes you flume-style down a flooded mountain, past 26 colorful scenes that include backwoods swamps, bayous, spooky caves, and waterfalls. Riders are caught in the bumbling schemes of Brer Fox and Brer Bear as they chase the ever-wily Brer Rabbit, who, against the advice of Mr. Bluebird, leaves his briar-patch home in search of fortune and the "laughing place." The music from the film forms a delightful audio backdrop. Your hollow-log vehicle twists, turns, and splashes, sometimes plummeting in darkness as the ride leads to a 52-foot, 45-degree, 40-mph splashdown in a briar-filled pond. *Note:* You must be at least 40 inches tall to ride. Expectant mothers, people prone to motion sickness, and those with heart, neck, or back problems shouldn't climb aboard.

Austin's Rating: "Ahhhhhhhhhhhh!!! . . . let's go again!" (sloshing albeit quickly back to the end of the line for yet another go). **Ryan's Rating:** "Are you kidding me? Did you see that drop?" It is, after all, one of the world's longest flume drops—and one of the fastest descents at Disney.

Tom Sawyer Island

Frommer's Rating: C for most, B+ for kids who need to burn any extra energy

Recommended Ages: 4–12

Huck Finn's raft will take you on a 2-minute journey across the Rivers of America to the densely forested Tom Sawyer Island, where kids can explore the narrow passages of Injun Joe's cave (complete with such scary sound effects as whistling wind), a walk-through windmill, a serpentine abandoned mine, and Fort Longhorn. The island's two bridges—one a suspension bridge, the other made of barrels floating on top of the water—create quite a challenge for anyone trying to cross. Maintaining your balance is difficult at best if (or should I say when) the other guests are jumping up and down—but that's half the fun. Narrow, winding dirt paths lined with oaks, pines, and sycamores create an authentic backwoods atmosphere. It's easy to get briefly lost and stumble upon some unexpected adventure, but for younger children, the woods and caves can pose a real problem; toddlers who can't easily find their way back to you or who may get scared by darkness and eerie noises should be watched very carefully.

Aunt Polly's Dockside Inn, which serves up snacks and such, and has outdoor tables on a porch overlooking the river, is the perfect spot for a relaxing lunch after all that running around; as a bonus, it's generally not as crowded as eateries on the mainland. Check the schedule, though; it's open only seasonally.

LIBERTY SQUARE

Pass through Frontierland into this small area, and you'll suddenly find yourself in the middle of Colonial America, standing in front of the Liberty Tree, an immense live oak decorated with 13 lanterns symbolizing the first 13 colonies. The entire area has an 18th-century, early American feel, complete with Federal and Georgian architecture, quaint shops, and flowerbeds bordering manicured lawns. You may even encounter a fife-and-drum corps marching along the cobblestone streets.

Hall of Presidents

Frommer's Rating: B+ for school age and adults

Recommended Ages: 8–adult

American presidents from George Washington to George W. Bush are represented by extremely lifelike audio-Animatronic figures (arguably, the best in WDW). If you look closely, you'll see them fidget and whisper during the performance. The show begins with a film projected on a 180-degree, 70mm screen. It talks about the importance of the Constitution; then the curtain rises on America's leaders, and as each comes into the spotlight, he nods or waves with presidential dignity. Lincoln rises and speaks next, occasionally referring to his notes. In a tribute to Disney thoroughness, painstaking research was done in creating the figures and scenery, with each president's costume reflecting period fashion, fabrics, and tailoring techniques.

Haunted Mansion
Frommer's Rating: A
Recommended Ages: 6–adult
What better way to show off Disney's eye for detailed special effects than through this ride, where "Grim Grinning Ghosts" come out to socialize—or so the ride's theme song goes. Thanks to a recent refurbishment, guests will find even more ghouls and ghosts than ever before. High-tech spectral effects and plenty of all-new sinister silliness have been added as well. The queue here is one of the most amusing in the park, as it winds through a graveyard filled with tombstones whose epitaphs are sure to make you chuckle. Upon entering, you're greeted by a ghostly host, who encloses you in a windowless portrait gallery (are those eyes following you?) where the floor seems to descend (actually, it's the ceiling that's rising), and the room goes dark (the only truly scary moment). Darkness, spooky music, eerie howling, and mysterious screams and rappings enhance its ambience. Your vehicle—err, Doom Buggy—takes you past a ghostly banquet and ball, a graveyard band, a suit of armor that comes alive, cobweb-draped chandeliers, a ghostly talking head in a crystal ball, and more. Keep your eyes on the mirror you pass at the end of your ride, as you'll find another passenger in your buggy . . . boo! The experience is more amusing than terrifying; most children 6 and older will be fine, but those younger (and even some of the older ones) not quite able to differentiate fun from fantasy may not be so amused.

Hailey's Rating: "I was a little scared, but Mom kept reminding me it was all pretend." As fun as it can be for some, the special effects can spook even those you'd least expect. **Davis's Rating:** While he's usually up to the rides with a bit of zip and zing, more so than most others his age, this isn't one he cared to attempt . . . at least not quite yet.

Liberty Square Riverboat (Overrated)
Frommer's Rating: C
Recommended Ages: All ages
An impressive looking steam-powered stern-wheeler aptly named the *Liberty Belle* departs for cruises along the Rivers of America, allowing thrill-ride-weary passengers and tired-out toddlers the chance to rest and relax. As you pass along the shores of Frontierland, the Indian camp, wildlife, and wilderness cabin will make it seem as though you're traveling through the wild and woolly West. Older kids will definitely be bored.

FANTASYLAND
The most fanciful land in the park, Fantasyland features attractions that bring classic Disney characters to life. It is by far the most popular land in the park for young children, who can sail over Merry Ole London and Never Land, ride in a honey pot

through the Hundred-acre Wood, and fly with Dumbo. If your kids are under 8, you'll find yourself spending a lot of your time here.

Cinderella Castle *Moments*
Frommer's Rating: A (for visuals)
Recommended Ages: All ages

There's actually not a lot to do here, but it's the Magic Kingdom's most widely recognized symbol, and I guarantee that you won't be able to pass it by without a look. It's not as though you could miss it anyway: The fairytale castle looms over Main Street, U.S.A., its 189-foot-high Gothic spires taking center stage from the minute you enter the park.

One of the most popular restaurants in the park, **Cinderella's Royal Table** (p. 143), is set inside the castle—along with the **Bibbidi Bobbidi Boutique** (a princess salon of sorts; p. 314) and the spectacular **Cinderella Suite.** The latter was created from a space originally intended as an apartment for Walt and his family, and "re-imagined" for Disney's Year of a Million Dreams celebration slated to run through 2008. Elaborate mosaic murals depict the Cinderella story in the castle's archway, and Disney family coats of arms are displayed over a fireplace. An actress portraying Cinderella, dressed for the ball, often makes appearances in the lobby. The Castle Forecourt Stage features live shows daily, so be sure to check the *Times Guide*'s schedule for **Dream Along with Mickey** (where dreams of adventure and happily-ever-after are played out on stage); the cast of characters includes Mickey, Peter Pan, Captain Hook, and other familiar favorites.

Cinderella's Golden Carousel *Moments*
Frommer's Rating: B+, A for carousel fans
Recommended Ages: All ages

One of the most beautiful attractions at Disney, the Golden Carousel is as enchanting to look at as it is to ride. Built by the Philadelphia Toboggan Co. in 1917, the carousel toured many an amusement park in the Midwest long before Walt bought it and brought it to Orlando 5 years before the Magic Kingdom opened. Disney artisans meticulously refurbished it, adding 18 hand-painted scenes from *Cinderella* on a wooden canopy above the horses. Its organ plays Disney classics such as "When You Wish upon a Star." Adults and kids alike adore riding the ornate horses round and round; there are even a few benches for the littlest tykes in the family. The ride is longer than you might expect, but the lines can get lengthy as well, so check back a bit later if your timing is off the first time around.

Dumbo the Flying Elephant
Frommer's Rating: B+ for young kids and parents
Recommended Ages: 2–6

This is a favorite of the preschool set, a fact that will quickly become apparent when you see the line wrapping around, and around, and around. Much like **Magic Carpets of Aladdin** (p. 192), the miniature Dumbos fly around in a circle, gently rising and dipping as you control them from inside the elephant. If you can stand the brutal lines—much of which can be out in the blazing sun (only a very small area offers cover from the sun and fans for cooling off)—this ride is almost sure to make your little one's day.

It's a Small World
Frommer's Rating: B+ for youngsters and first-timers
Recommended Ages: 2–8

Recently refurbished to spruce up some of its older displays, It's a Small World is one of those rides that you just have to do because it's been there since the beginning; it's a classic (built for the 1964 World's Fair before being transplanted to Disney), and in this day and age, it's nice to see that some things don't change (or at least not too much). Besides, it's a big favorite of younger kids. And as much as some adults pooh-pooh it, I'll bet they come out smiling and singing right along with their kids. If you don't know the song, you will by the end of the ride (and probably ever after), as the hard part is trying to get it *out* of your head. As you sail along, you'll pass through the countries of the world, each filled with appropriately costumed audio-Animatronic dolls greeting you by singing "It's a Small World" in tiny Munchkin voices. The cast of thousands includes Chinese acrobats, Russian kazatski dancers, Indian snake charmers, French cancan girls, and . . . well, you get the picture. To truly experience everything Disney, this one's a must.

Ryan's Rating: "No way! I'm not going on that." (On the other hand, Nicolas, Hailey, and Davis all loved it, mesmerized by the scenery and the song.)

Mad Tea Party
Frommer's Rating: C+
Recommended Ages: 4–adult

Traditional amusement-park ride it may be, but it's still a family favorite—maybe because it is so simple. The mad-tea-party scene in *Alice in Wonderland* was the inspiration for this one, and riders sit in giant pastel teacups set on saucers that careen around a circular platform while the cup, saucer, and platform all spin round and round. Occasionally, the woozy Dormouse pops out of a big central teapot to see just what's going on. Tame as it may appear, this can be a pretty active, even nauseating ride, depending on how much you spin your teacup's wheel. Adolescents seem to consider it a badge of honor if they can turn the unsuspecting adults in their cup green; you have been warned!

Hailey's, Davis's, and **Nicolas's Rating** (in chorus): "Faster, faster . . . let's make Mom turn green!" (They must have read my review. Ugh!)

The Many Adventures of Winnie the Pooh
Frommer's Rating: B
Recommended Ages: 2–8 and their parents

This fun ride features the cute and cuddly little fellow, along with Eeyore, Piglet, and Tigger. You board a golden honey pot and ride through a storybook version of the Hundred-acre Wood, keeping an eye out for Heffalumps, Woozles, Blustery Days, and the Floody Place. Kids, especially those 3 to 5, love it, but prepare yourself for *very, very* long lines if you don't use FASTPASS. *Tip:* Just across the way, **Pooh's Playful Spot** is a toddler-friendly play area complete with a treehouse, honey pots, slides, water fountains, crawl-through logs, and, fortunately, benches for parents in need of a rest while they watch their little ones run about.

Tips Not So Fast

If you're tackling rides with preshows, such as Mickey's PhilharMagic, don't try to be the first one inside. Hang back in the crowd a little, and you may land in the center of the theater, where the seats are better. Folks who rush in are shooed to the theater's far side.

(*Tips* **It Ain't Fair, But . . .**

Disney rides sometimes break down or need routine maintenance that can take them out of commission for a few hours, a day, a week, or sometimes months. Test Track at Epcot, for example, occasionally experiences technical difficulties—and the rain wreaks havoc with the ride. In 2007, the Haunted Mansion at the Magic Kingdom and Spaceship Earth at Epcot closed for months for renovations.

Mickey's PhilharMagic

Frommer's Rating: A+

Recommended Ages: All ages

This 2003 arrival is by far the most amazing 3-D movie production I've ever laid eyes on and a must-see for all ages. Popular Disney characters—including Ariel, Simba, and Aladdin—are brought to 3-D life on a 150-foot screen (the largest wraparound screen on the planet) as they try to help (or, in some cases, hinder) the attempts of Donald Duck to retrieve Mickey's magical sorcerer's hat before the Mouse discovers it's missing. It's the first time the classic Disney characters have ever been rendered in 3-D. Even if you're not a big fan of shows, this is one you should definitely see. Like (but far, far better than) the whimsical **Jim Henson's Muppet*Vision 3-D** (p. 231) at Disney's Hollywood Studios, the show combines music, animated film, puppetry, and special effects that tickle several of the senses. The kids will love the animation and effects, and parents will enjoy the nostalgia factor.

Hailey's Rating: "If this is just a movie, there's no way I'm waiting in this line"—but that was before she became completely entranced, laughing and giggling all the way through the show. After the lights went up, she said, "That was the coolest show I've ever seen" and sheepishly asked, "Can we see it again?"

Peter Pan's Flight

Frommer's Rating: A for kids and parents

Recommended Ages: 3–8

Another of Disney's simple pleasures, this is a classic ride that's fun for the whole family. You'll fly through the sky in your very own ship (much like Captain Hook's), gliding over familiar scenes from the adventures of Peter Pan. Your adventure begins in the Darlings' nursery and includes a flight over an elaborate nighttime cityscape of Merry Ole London before you move on to Never Land. There, you encounter mermaids, Indians, Tick Tock the Croc, the Lost Boys, Princess Tiger Lilly, Tinker Bell, Captain Hook, and Smee, all while listening to the theme, "You Can Fly, You Can Fly, You Can Fly." It's *very* tame fun for the young and young at heart.

Davis's Rating: "Look, look—it's Tinker Bell, and Peter, and the crocodile, and . . ." Well, you get the idea. This one is always a hit with my younger set; the older ones, however, run the other way, especially when they see the never-ending lines for Never Land. This is a ride where using a FASTPASS is definitely in order.

Many, but not all, of the ride rehabs are listed at **www.disneyworld.com**. Both **www.allearsnet.com** and **www.travel-insights.com** list most ride rehabs as well. The moral of the story: Err on the side of caution, and don't make promises to kids about specific rides just in case something happens. Note that refurbishments and technical difficulties are unfortunate but part of the deal; neither Disney nor Universal will discount or refund any tickets when rehabs occur.

Snow White's Scary Adventures
Frommer's Rating: C
Recommended Ages: 4–8

While Disney has changed the ride a bit since it debuted, attempting to make it less scary for the small children for whom it was intended, it still features the wicked witch rather predominantly (though Snow White appears far more often than before). While many of the scenes are pleasant, including such happier moments from the movie as the scenes at the wishing well and Snow White riding away with the prince to live happily ever after, Disney doesn't include the word "Scary" in its title without good reason. This ride still has plenty of scary moments if your child is under 5 (and those any older likely won't even want to ride), so if the lines are long, think about passing this one up.

MICKEY'S TOONTOWN FAIR

Wondering where to find Mickey? Instead of walking about the park, as he did many years ago, the Mouse now holds court in Toontown. The candy-striped **Judge's Tent** and **Toontown Hall of Fame** inside this zone are where kids get a chance to meet many of their favorite Disney characters, including Mickey, Minnie, Donald, Goofy, and Pluto. The entire area (small as it may be) is filled with a whimsical collection of cartoonish attractions geared mostly to those under 6 (making it one of the more crowded spots in the park).

The Barnstormer at Goofy's Wiseacre Farm *Finds*
Frommer's Rating: A for kids and parents
Recommended Ages: 4 and up

This mini–roller coaster is the twin of Woody Woodpecker's Nuthouse Coaster (which it likely inspired) at Universal Studios Florida (p. 268). It's designed to look and feel like a cropduster that flies slightly off course and right through the Goofmeister's barn. The ride has very little in the dip-and-drop department but a little zip on the spin-and-spiral front. *Note:* The 60-second ride has a 35-inch height minimum, and expectant mothers are warned not to ride it.

   Nicolas's Rating: "Wow, that was cool—better than I though it would be!" It even gets squeals from some adults.

Donald's Boat (SS *Miss Daisy*)
Frommer's Rating: B+ for kids
Recommended Ages: 2–8

The good ship *Miss Daisy* offers plenty of interactive fun for kids who enjoy getting wet. Watch out as you make your way around the surrounding "waters," as the leaks squirting from the boat are practically unavoidable—but that's half the fun (you can tell by the little squeals of joy from those who've been doused). *Tip:* The nearby Toon Park (with a 40-in. height *maximum*) is a small covered playground with slides and a small playhouse for dryer adventures. There are also a handful of covered benches for weary parents in need of a momentary break.

Mickey's & Minnie's Country Houses
Frommer's Rating: B for younger kids
Recommended Ages: 2–8

These separate cottages offer a lot of visual fun and a small bit of interactive play for youngsters, but they're usually crowded; the lines flow like molasses. Mickey's place is more for looking than touching, though it does feature a small garden and garage

Value **Extra Magic—Extra Time**

The free **Extra Magic Hour** program allows Disney resort guests (as well as those staying at the WDW Swan, the WDW Dolphin, and the Hilton in the Walt Disney World Resort) some extra playtime in the parks. Under the program, a select number of attractions, shops, and restaurants at one of the four major Disney parks open an hour early on scheduled mornings, and those at another park remain open up to 3 hours after official closing on scheduled evenings. And because only resort guests can participate in the Extra Magic Hour, crowds are almost nonexistent, and lines are much shorter—not to mention that the temperatures are usually a lot more agreeable early in the morning and later in the evening.

To enter a park for the morning Extra Magic Hour, you must present your Disney-resort room key and park ticket. For the evening Extra Magic Hour, your room key, park ticket, and a special wristband (for every member in your group) are required. You can obtain the wristband at the park scheduled to remain open that evening, but no earlier than 1 hour prior to park closing.

Warning: If you hold a ticket with a Park Hopper add-on (see p. 178 for information on Disney ticketing options), you can attend any Extra Magic Hour at any park. But if you hold a base ticket with no park-hopping privileges, you can attend the Extra Magic Hour only at the park where you're spending your day. So if you have only a base ticket, and you go to Epcot that day, you can take advantage of Extra Magic Hours only if they are available at Epcot; you cannot head over to the Magic Kingdom's Extra Magic Hours on the same day. Call © **407/824-4321** or visit **www.disneyworld.com** for details.

playground. Minnie's lets kids play in her kitchen, where popcorn goes wild in a microwave, a cake bakes and then deflates in the oven, and the utensils strike up a symphony of their own.

TOMORROWLAND

Once envisioned to represent the future, this land began to look more like yesteryear thanks to the passing of time. It was later re-envisioned from a '20s and '30s perspective—and is now a galactic, science-fiction–inspired community inhabited by humans, aliens, and robots.

Astro Orbiter
Frommer's Rating: B
Recommended Ages: 6–10
While touted as a tame ride much like the ones you might have ridden when you were a child and the carnival came to town, it does offer a bit of unexpected uneasiness. Its "rockets" are on arms attached to "the center of the galaxy" and move up and down while orbiting the planets, but they also tilt to the side—and when you're on top of the two-story tower, looking down from your perch can make you rather anxious. Because of the ride's limited capacity, the line tends to move at a snail's pace, so unless it's short, skip this one.

Buzz Lightyear's Space Ranger Spin

Frommer's Rating: A+ for kids and parents
Recommended Ages: 3 and up

Recruits stand ready as Buzz Lightyear briefs you on your mission. The evil emperor Zurg is once again up to no good, and Buzz needs your help to save the universe. As you cruise through "space," you'll pass through scenes filled with brightly colored aliens, most of whom are marked with a big "Z," so you know where to shoot. Kids love using the dashboard-mounted laser cannons as they spin through the sky (filled with gigantic toys instead of stars). If they're good shots, they can set off sight-and-sound gags with a direct hit from their lasers (my 6-year-old, however, aims just about everywhere but at the target and still has loads of fun). A display in the car keeps score. This ride uses the same technology as Universal Studios Florida's Men in Black Alien Attack (p. 266), but it's aimed at a younger audience; therefore, it's far tamer.

Davis's, Hailey's, and **Nicolas's Rating:** "To infinity and beyond . . . again! Come on, Mom, again!!!" (It's one of the best rides in the park and fun for the entire family.)

Monsters, Inc. Laugh Floor

Frommer's Rating: B+ for kids and parents
Recommended Ages: 4 and up

Taking its cue from the hit Disney-Pixar film *Monsters, Inc.,* Monster-of-Ceremonies Mike Wazowski, along with a few comedic recruits, tells jokes and pokes fun at audience members, hoping to generate enough laughs to fill the gigantic laugh canister. This new immersive experience is live and unscripted (a guarantee that you'll never see the same show twice); it uses real-time animation, digital projection, sophisticated voice-activated animation, and a cast of talented improv comedians to create the on-screen action. Noticeable time lags detract slightly from the experience, but Disney's still working out some of the kinks. If you think you've got a monstrously funny joke (LOL), text it to the show from your cell (just prior to showtime)—you may find yourself laughing at a joke or two of your own! The phone number is available near the attraction entrance and works only within a very small radius.

Space Mountain

Frommer's Rating: B+
Recommended Ages: 10–adult

This cosmic roller coaster usually has *long* lines (but it has FASTPASS), and most guests find only marginal entertainment value in the preride space-age music and exhibits (meteorites, shooting stars, and space debris whizzing overhead). Once aboard your rocket, you'll climb and dive through the inky, starlit blackness of outer space. The hairpin turns and plunges make it seem as if you're going at breakneck speed, but your car doesn't go any faster than 28 mph. The front seat of the train offers the best bang, but Space Mountain is one of the first generation of modern, dark-side coasters and, therefore, somewhat outdated. If you like dark or semidark thrill rides, you'll be much happier with Rock 'n' Roller Coaster at Disney's Hollywood Studios. *Note:* Riders must be at least 44 inches tall. Also, expectant moms, people prone to motion sickness, and those with heart, neck, or back problems shouldn't climb aboard.

Ryan's Rating: "That was sooooooooo cool!" (In other words, it's a good coming-of-age test for thrill-ride junkies of the near future and those not willing to ride the real biggies.) **Austin's** and **Nicolas's Rating:** Both agreed that it was "one of the best rides at Disney—the dark makes it so amazing."

Stitch's Great Escape (Overrated

Frommer's Rating: C-

Recommended Ages: 5–10

In 2003, the scarier ExtraTERRORestrial Alien Encounter was closed permanently to make way for this newer, (allegedly) more family-friendly attraction. Unfortunately, Disney missed the mark a bit on this one (while rare, it happens). Even though it features the mischievous experiment 626, otherwise known as Stitch—a favorite of many younger kids—the ride isn't really all that child-friendly (at least not for the young set it's aimed at). It's not particularly exciting, either. Upon entering the attraction, guests are briefed on their responsibilities as newly recruited alien prison guards. Suddenly, an alarm sounds; a new prisoner is arriving, and the pandemonium begins (that's the best part of the entire experience). Stitch, after appearing by teleportation, is confined in the middle of the room, but only momentarily; the ride isn't called Stitch's Great Escape for nothing. Guests are seated around the center stage, overhead restraints on their shoulders (slightly uncomfortable unless you're sitting straight up when they are lowered) allowing them to "feel" special sensory effects. It's the attraction's long periods of darkness and silence that make this one inappropriate for younger children—a fact made apparent by some of the screams you'll hear from the audience. Even Stitch fans should skip past this one. ***Note:*** There's a 40-inch height requirement.

Tomorrowland Indy Speedway

Frommer's Rating: B+ for kids; D for tweens, teens, and childless adults

Recommended Ages: 4–10

Younger kids love this ride, especially if they get the chance to drive one of the gas-powered, mini sports cars—though they may need the help of a parent's foot to push down on the gas pedal—for a 4-minute spin around the track. Tweens and teens, however, hate it: Speeds reach a mere 7 mph, which for most is *incredibly* slow, and the steering is atrocious (even I can't control the cars without bumping the rail that it follows). The slow speed seems to work well for young kids (who also think the bumping around is fun). The long lines move even slower than the ride does, so be prepared to wait this one out. ***Note:*** There's a 52-inch height minimum to take a lap without an older rider along with you. This one also carries Disney's warning that expectant mothers and people with heart, neck, or back problems shouldn't climb aboard, likely because of the potential for getting bumped as you try to board or disembark.

Tomorrowland Transit Authority

Frommer's Rating: C, B+ for tired adults or toddlers

Recommended Ages: All ages

After making your way up a moving walkway, you'll spot the futuristic train cars that will take you on a tour of Tomorrowland from high above the ground. The engineless train runs on a track and is powered by electromagnets, creating no pollution, making little noise, and using little power. Narrated by a computer guide named Horack I, TTA offers an overhead view of Tomorrowland, including a brief interior look at Space Mountain. Lines are often nonexistent, as most riders are parents awaiting the return of their children from Space Mountain or those with tired toddlers in need of a brief respite from the activity below. While it packs a small punch at times—thanks to a few tight turns and sections where it quickly speeds up—it's still a tame alternative for toddlers and littler tykes.

Moments   **Where to Find Characters**

Mickey's Toontown Fair was designed as a place where kids can meet and mingle with their favorite characters all day at the Judge's Tent and Toontown Hall
of Fame. Mickey and others are stars in residence. In **Fantasyland,** look for
Ariel's Grotto for daily greetings. **Main Street** (Town Square) and **Adventureland**
(at Pirates of the Caribbean and near Magic Carpets of Aladdin) are other hot
spots. I've occasionally caught a few near the Galaxy Palace Theater in **Tomorrowland** as well. If your child has an autograph book for characters to sign, have
it out and ready with a pen for Goofy to plop down his signature. And have
your camera if you want to capture a picture of your kids with Pluto. Bring lots
of patience: You won't be the only parent waiting for that Kodak moment.

Walt Disney's Carousel of Progress *Overrated*
Frommer's Rating: C
Recommended Ages: 5–10
Open only seasonally, when the crowds are at their peak, the Carousel of Progress
offers more of a respite from the hustle and bustle of the crowds than it does an interesting experience. It debuted at the 1964 World's Fair before Walt decided to include
it in his collection. The ride emigrated from Disneyland to Disney World in 1975 and
was refurbished to its original state just over 10 years ago. The entire show rotates
through scenes illustrating the state of technology from the 1900s to the 1940s. Most
adults find it rather boring, but kids willing to sit still for a few minutes may actually
learn a thing or two.

PARADES, FIREWORKS & MORE

Pick up a guide map (or two) and a *Times Guide* when you enter the park. The latter
includes an **entertainment schedule** that lists all kinds of special goings-on for the
day. These include park hours, restaurant hours, concerts, character encounters, street
shows, holiday events, and the major happenings listed below.

Disney Dreams Come True Parade
Frommer's Rating: B
Recommended Ages: All ages
Known as Share a Dream Come True in a previous life, you'll find that not too much
has really changed. Loads of characters—most atop floats (now sans snowglobes), others alongside—sing, dance, and march their way up Main Street (and into Frontierland) on a daily basis. It's one of the most popular parades in the park and takes place
during the height of the day.

SpectroMagic *Moments*
Frommer's Rating: A
Recommended Ages: All ages
This 20-minute after-dark production combines fiber optics, holographic images,
clouds of liquid nitrogen, old-fashioned twinkling lights, and a soundtrack featuring
classic Disney tunes. Mickey, dressed in an amber-and-purple grand magician's cape,
makes an appearance in a confetti of light. You'll also see the SpectroMen atop the title
float, as well as Chernabog, the monstrous demon of *Fantasia,* who unfolds his 38-foot

wingspan. It takes the electrical equivalent of seven lightning bolts (enough to power a fleet of 2,000 over-the-road trucks) to bring the show to life.

SpectroMagic is held only on a limited number of nights. See your entertainment schedule for availability. When it is held, there are usually two showings: one earlier in the evening and the next one near closing time. If you have little kids, go to the early showing. If you have older kids and teens, the later showing is usually less crowded (and you face shorter ride lines while the first production is going on). No matter which showing you attend, this one is worth having the kids stay up for; it's a memorable experience for the entire family.

Wishes (Moments

Frommer's Rating: A+
Recommended Ages: All ages
This breathtaking 12-minute fireworks display replaced the old **Fantasy in the Sky** fireworks in 2003. The show, narrated by Jiminy Cricket and with background music from several Disney classics, is the story of a wish coming true, and it borrows one element from the old one: Tinker Bell still flies overhead. The fireworks go off nightly during summers and holidays and on some nights (usually Mon and Wed–Sat) the rest of the year. See your entertainment schedule for details. Numerous good views of the action are available, so long as you're standing on the front side of the castle; get too far off to the side or behind the display, and it loses much of its impressive and meticulously choreographed visual effect. Disney hotels close to the park (the Contemporary, Grand Floridian, Polynesian, and Wilderness Lodge) also offer excellent views.

4 Epcot

Epcot is an acronym for Experimental Prototype Community of Tomorrow, and it was Walt Disney's dream for a planned city. Alas, after his death, it became a theme park—Central Florida's second major theme park, which opened in 1982. Its aims are described in a dedication plaque: "May Epcot entertain, inform, and inspire. And, above all . . . instill a new sense of belief and pride in man's ability to shape a world that offers hope to people everywhere."

Ever growing and changing, Epcot occupies 300 vibrantly landscaped acres. If you can spare it, take a little time to stop and smell the roses on your way to and through the two major sections: Future World and World Showcase.

Epcot is so big that hiking the World Showcase end to end (1⅓ miles from the Canada Pavilion on one side to Mexico on the other) can be exhausting (that goes double for your kids). That's why some folks are certain that Epcot stands for "Every Person Comes Out Tired." Depending on how long you intend to linger at each country in World Showcase, this part of the park can be experienced in 1 day. One way to conserve energy is to take the launches across the lagoon from the edge of Future World to Germany or Morocco. But most visitors simply make a leisurely loop, working clockwise or counterclockwise from one side of the World Showcase to the other.

Be sure to pick up the guide map and *Times Guide* (or entertainment schedule) as you enter the park. A large white **K** in a red square denotes the various **Kidcot Fun Stops** throughout the park (including both the World Showcase and Future World). These play and learning stations are for the younger set (geared to ages 4–8) and allow them to create cultural crafts, get autographs, have their Kidcot passports stamped (these are available for purchase in most Epcot stores and make a neat souvenir), and chat with cast members native to those countries. For information, stop by Guest Services in the park.

(*Tips* **Fun for Kids at Epcot**

Epcot, while greatly improved in this department, is the least kid-friendly of the Disney parks (especially for the preschool and toddler set). Recent additions and enhancements, however, ensure that there are still plenty of things for your kids to do.

The stations generally open at 1pm daily (but check the *Times Guide,* as schedules can change).

If you plan to eat lunch or dinner here and haven't already booked Advance Dining Reservations (© **407/939-3463**), you can make them at Guest Services or at the restaurants themselves, many of which are described in chapter 5, "Family-Friendly Dining."

Before you get under way, check the map's schedule and incorporate any shows you want to see into your itinerary.

ARRIVING Unlike Magic Kingdom, much of Epcot's parking lot is close to the gate. Parking sections are named for themes (Harvest, Energy, and so forth), and the aisles are numbered. While some guests are happy to walk to the gate from nearer areas, trams are available, but these days mainly to and from the outer areas. If you're a guest of the Epcot area resorts, including the BoardWalk, the Swan and Dolphin, and the Beach and Yacht clubs, you'll have an easier time of it: Simply hop on the water taxi (one services each of the resorts) and you'll be transported directly to the International Gateway—Epcot's back entrance. If you're feeling energetic, you can even walk.

HOURS Future World is usually open from 9 or 10am to 6 or 7pm but sometimes later during major holidays and the summer. World Showcase doesn't open until 11am or noon, and it usually closes at 9pm (though sometimes later).

TICKET PRICES Ticket are $71 for adults, $60 for children 3 to 9, and free for children under 3. See "Tickets & Passes" (p. 176) for information on multiday passes and add-on options.

SERVICES & FACILITIES IN EPCOT

ATMs The machines here accept cards issued by banks using the Cirrus, Honor, and PLUS systems. They're located at the front of Future World, between Italy and the American Adventure, and near the bridge between World Showcase and Future World.

Baby Care Epcot's Baby Care Center is by the first-aid station near the Odyssey Center in Future World. It's furnished with a nursing room with rocking chairs. Disposable diapers, formula, baby food, and pacifiers are for sale. There are changing tables in all women's restrooms, as well as in some of the men's. Disposable diapers are also available at Guest Relations.

Cameras & Film Film, batteries, Kodak disposable cameras, and limited digital supplies are available throughout the park, including at the Kodak Camera Center at the Entrance Plaza.

First Aid It's located near the Odyssey Center in Future World and staffed by registered nurses.

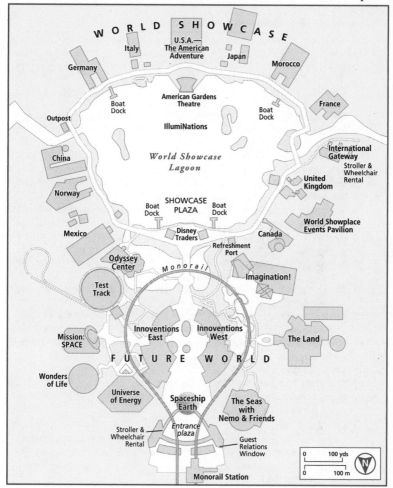

Lockers   Lockers are to the west of Spaceship Earth, outside the Entrance Plaza, and in the Bus Information Center by the bus parking lot. The cost is $5 a day, plus a $2 deposit.

Lost Children   Lost children in Epcot are usually taken to Earth Center or the Baby Care Center, where lost-children logbooks are kept. *Children under 7 should wear name tags* inside their clothing.

Package Pickup   Any purchases can be sent to the Gift Stop near Spaceship Earth. Allow 3 hours for delivery. There's also a package-pickup location at the World Traveler at the International Gateway entrance in the World Showcase.

Parking   It's $11 for cars, pickups, and vans, and $12 for RVs.

Moments Top Orlando Family Attractions

For Very Young Kids:

1. **Turtle Talk with Crush**   Real-time animation allows kids to really talk and interact with Crush as he swims about the virtual on-screen ocean (p. 216).
2. **Caro-Seuss-el**   Cowfish, elephant birds, and other wacky critters inhabit this Islands of Adventure merry-go-round (p. 276).
3. **The Seas with Nemo & Friends**   Nemo has once again gone missing and it's up to you (with the help of a few familiar finned friends) to find him (p. 216).
4. **A Day in the Park with Barney**   The purple dinosaur drives some adults batty, but little Universal Studios guests love him (p. 264).
5. **Jim Henson's Muppet*Vision 3-D**   Don't miss Kermit, Miss Piggy, and the rest of the crew at Disney's Hollywood Studios (p. 231).
6. **Voyage of the Little Mermaid**   Puppets, film, and special effects make for a lively show, also at Disney's Hollywood Studios (p. 236).
7. **If I Ran the Zoo**   Let the little ones play with Seussian creatures at this 19-station, interactive playland at Islands of Adventure (p. 276).
8. **Ketchakiddee Creek**   Disney's Typhoon Lagoon has lots of wet fun for the younger set—and older guests, too (p. 248).
9. **Magic Carpets of Aladdin**   Watch out for spitting camels on this wheel-and-spoke kids' ride in Disney's Magic Kingdom (p. 192).
10. **Cinderella's Golden Carousel**   Built in 1917, this grand old Magic Kingdom carousel delights plenty of adults, too (p. 199).
11. **Mickey's & Minnie's Country Houses**   The utensils and furniture create some surprises inside these houses at Mickey's Toontown Fair in the Magic Kingdom (p. 202).
12. **One Fish, Two Fish, Red Fish, Blue Fish**   Your little ones can fly their funky fish up and down as they spin above ground level at Islands of Adventure's Seuss Landing (p. 277).

For Kids 6–12 & Older:

1. **Expedition Everest–Legend of the Forbidden Mountain**   An up-close encounter with the legendary Yeti will have your hair standing on end on this out-of-control trek through the mysterious Himalayan mountain range (p. 244).
2. **Big Thunder Mountain Railroad**   Hold onto your skivvies, as this runaway train at Disney's Magic Kingdom provides its share of thrills and chills (p. 195).
3. **Popeye & Bluto's Bilge-Rat Barges**   This Islands of Adventure entry is arguably the best faux-whitewater ride in Florida (p. 280).
4/5. **Indiana Jones Epic Stunt Spectacular!/Lights, Motors, Action! Extreme Stunt Show**   Both offer edge-of-your-seat excitement at Disney's Hollywood Studios (p. 231 and 232).
6. **Dudley Do-Right's Ripsaw Falls**   Expect to get wet on this Islands of Adventure log ride that reaches 50 mph (p. 279).
7. **The Barnstormer at Goofy's Wiseacre Farm**   The Magic Kingdom's mini–roller coaster is the fairest of this genre (p. 202).

8. **Woody Woodpecker's Nuthouse Coaster**   But Islands' minicoaster is just half a click behind Goofy's in the fun factor (p. 268).

9. **Jimmy Neutron's Nicktoon Blast**   Help Jimmy battle Yokians and meet SpongeBob and other 'toons at one of Universal Studios Florida's newest attractions (p. 265).

10. **Splash Mountain**   The Magic Kingdom's wettest ride will launch you at 40 mph down a 52-foot, 45-degree slope (p. 196). Made from the same mold is **Jurassic Park River Adventure** at Islands of Adventure, a wild ride that adds hissing dinosaurs to the special effects (p. 280).

11. **Soarin'**   You'll fly high over California's spectacular landscape by hang-glider at this Epcot attraction (p. 215).

12. **Kali River Rapids**   Disney's Animal Kingdom's raft ride isn't quite up to Popeye & Bluto's at Islands, but it's still a ton of wet fun (p. 245).

For Thrill-Seeking Teens & Parents:

1. **Incredible Hulk Coaster**   In Florida, it doesn't get any scarier than this Islands of Adventure rocket ride, which has seven rollovers and two deep drops (p. 278).

2. **Rock 'n' Roller Coaster**   You won't find a faster giddyup-and-go than this 0-to-60-mph, Aerosmith-supported stretch limo at Disney's Hollywood Studios (p. 234).

3. **Dueling Dragons**   Test your courage on one of two coasters that hit speeds of 60 mph and come within 12 inches of each other at Islands of Adventure (p. 281).

4. **Summit Plummet**   Hang onto your swimsuit as you fall 120 feet at 60 mph—sans vehicle!—at this Blizzard Beach water slide (p. 250).

5. **The Twilight Zone Tower of Terror**   If you want to see what it's like to fall in an elevator, yo-yo style, tackle this Disney's Hollywood Studios test of your nerve (p. 235).

6. **The Amazing Adventures of Spider-Man**   Bar none, this Islands of Adventure entry is the best 3-D simulator and action ride east of the Mississippi River (p. 277).

7. **Mission: Space**   Get ready to launch (maybe your lunch) if you climb aboard Epcot's new motion simulator, which NASA astronauts helped design (p. 215).

8. **Kraken**   Speaking of launching, SeaWorld's signature thrill ride is a floorless, open-sided roller coaster that hits 65 mph while making seven loops (p. 290).

9. **Revenge of the Mummy**   Being inside darkened Egyptian tombs with a thousand-year-old mummy screeching "Death is only the beginning!" will make you glad you live in more modern times (p. 266).

10. **Test Track**   Run your six-passenger convertible through a host of tests at this GM-sponsored attraction, which features a 65-mph speed burst on an elevated straightaway (p. 217).

Moments **Behind the Scenes: Special Tours in WDW**

In addition to the greenhouse tour in Epcot's Land Pavilion (p. 214), the WDW parks offer a number of walking tours and learning programs, some of which are suitable for kids. In addition to those listed below, Disney offers DiveQuest, Dolphins in Depth, Mickey's Magical Milestones, the Undiscovered Future World, Wild by Design, Around the World at Epcot, a seasonal Yuletide fantasy tour, and custom guided tours. The tours (and times, days, and prices) are subject to change, and those listed below represent the most popular choices available at press time. It's best to call ahead to Disney's main tour line at © **407/939-8687**, or call © **407/560-4033** for custom guided tours and additional information.

- The **Seas Aqua Tour** at Epcot lends you a wetsuit and takes you on a 2½-hour journey that includes a 30-minute swim in the 5.7-million-gallon Living Seas Aquarium, home to some 65 marine species. The tour includes a souvenir T-shirt, refreshments, and photo. The cost is $100; park admission is not required; and it's open to guests 8 and older (those under 11 must be accompanied by an adult). It's offered daily at 12:30pm.

- The **Family Magic Tour** explores the nooks and crannies of the Magic Kingdom in the form of a 2-hour scavenger hunt; you meet and greet characters at the end. If you have young kids and want to do a special tour, this is the one to take. Children and adults pay $27 per person. You must also buy admission tickets to the park and book in advance. It begins outside City Hall daily at 11:30am (and sometimes at 9:30am, too).

- The **Magic Behind Our Steam Trains Tour** (ages 10 and up) is a fun one for locomotive buffs (Walt himself was one of them). A pair of inveterate conductors gives you insight into the history and present operations of the little engines that could. Tours run Monday, Tuesday, Wednesday, Thursday, and Saturday at 7:30am; the cost is $40 per person, plus park admission.

Several tours are offered only to those age 16 and older. Most of these are aimed at adults (photos are not permitted on these backstage tours, and photo ID is a must). A few that might appeal to teens are:

Pet Care Day accommodations are offered at kennels just outside the Entrance Plaza at Epcot for $10 (© **407/824-6568**). Proof of vaccination is required. Walking service (available only at the Epcot kennel) costs $2.50 per walk. Four other kennels are located in the WDW complex.

Stroller Rental Strollers can be rented from special stands on the east side of the Entrance Plaza and at World Showcase's International Gateway. The cost is $10 for a single and $18 for a double, with a discount available for length-of-stay rentals.

Wheelchair Rental Rent wheelchairs inside the Entrance Plaza to your left, to the right of the ticket booths, and at World Showcase's International Gateway. The cost for regular chairs is $10. Electric wheelchairs cost $35 a day, plus a $5 refundable deposit.

- The 4½-hour **Keys to the Kingdom Tour** provides an orientation to the Magic Kingdom and a glimpse into the high-tech systems behind the magic. It's $60 (park admission required) and is held daily at 8:30, 9:30, and 10am. It's got some interesting insights into the park, and you will get treated to a ride or two, so if your teen is wild about Disney, it's not a bad bet.

- At the top of the price chain ($199) is **Backstage Magic,** a 7-hour, self-propelled bus tour through areas of Epcot, the Magic Kingdom, and Disney's Hollywood Studios that aren't seen by mainstream guests. The 10am weekday tour is limited to 20 people age 16 or older, and you might have trouble getting a date unless you book early. Some will find this overpriced, but if you (or your teen) have a brain that must know how things work, or simply want to know more than your family or friends, you might find it's worth the cost. You'll see WDW mechanics and engineers repairing and building Animatronic beings from attractions such as "It's a Small World." You'll peek over the shoulders of cast members who watch closed-circuit TVs to make sure other visitors are surviving the harrowing rides. And at the Magic Kingdom, you'll venture into the tunnels used for work areas, as well as corridors for the cast to get from one area to the others without fighting tourist crowds. It's not unusual for tour-takers to see Snow White enjoying a Snickers bar, find Cinderella having her locks touched up at an underground salon, or view woodworkers as they restore the hard-maple muscles of the carousel horses. Park admission is *not* required, and lunch is included.

- At Disney's Animal Kingdom, **Backstage Safari** ($65 per person, plus park admission) offers a 3-hour look at the park's veterinary hospital as well as lessons in conservation, animal nutrition, and medicine. It's held Monday, Wednesday, Thursday, and Friday. If your teen dreams of veterinary school, this is a good bet; otherwise, it may be a bit boring for them. *Note:* You won't see many animals.

FUTURE WORLD

Future World is on the front end of Epcot, the first area mainstream guests see after entering the park. Its icon is a huge geosphere known as Spaceship Earth—aka that giant silver golf ball. The focus here is on discovery, scientific achievements, and tomorrow's technologies in areas ranging from energy to undersea exploration. This zone offers two thrill rides that will get the adrenaline pumping in your teens, plus several attractions that will appeal to the small fry in your party.

Imagination!
Frommer's Rating: B+
Recommended Ages: 6–adult

In this pavilion, even the fountains are magical. "Water snakes" arc in the air, offering kids a chance to dare them to "bite." (Little kids love them, and it's a good place for them to work off a little energy and for you to get a great photo.) Figment, the pavilion's much-loved mascot (see below), makes an occasional appearance as well.

The 3-D **Honey, I Shrunk the Audience** show is one of the big attractions here, deserving an **A rating** by itself. Based on the Disney hit film *Honey, I Shrunk the Kids,* its viewers will be terrorized by mice and, once shrunk, by a large cat; then they're given a good shaking by a gigantic 5-year-old. Vibrating seats and creepy tactile effects enhance dramatic 3-D action. Finally, everyone returns to proper size—except the family dog, which creates the final surprise.

Figment, the crazy-but-lovable purple dragon, stars in the **Journey into Imagination** ride. Things begin with an open house at the Imagination Institute, with Dr. Nigel Channing taking you on a tour of labs that demonstrate how the five senses capture and control one's imagination—except that you never get to touch and taste once Figment arrives to prove that it's far, far better to set your imagination free. He invites you to his upside-down house, where a new perspective enhances your imagination. "One Little Spark," an upbeat ditty that debuted when the attraction opened in 1983, has been brought back and incorporated into the ride.

Once you disembark from the ride, head for the **"What If"** labs, where your kids can burn lots of energy while exercising their imagination at a number of interactive stations that allow them to conduct music and experiment with video.

Innoventions East & West
Frommer's Rating: B+ for hungry minds and game junkies
Recommended Ages: 8–adult
Innoventions East, behind Spaceship Earth and to the left as you enter the park, features the **House of Innoventions.** It's a preview of tomorrow's smart house, but many of its products are already on the market (at astronomical prices). Its refrigerator has an Internet-savvy computer that can make your grocery list and place the order. A smart picture frame can store and send photos to other smart frames. And the toilet has a seat warmer, automatic lid opener and closer, and sprayer and blow dryer that eliminate the need for toilet paper if you're worldly. The **Internet Zone** profiles tomorrow's online games for kids, including laser tag with Disney characters, while **Opportunity City** features an online game called Hot Shot Business. An Underwriters Laboratories exhibit, the **Test the Limits Lab,** has six kiosks that let kids and fun-loving adults try out a variety of products. In one, you can pull a rope attached to a hammer that crashes into a TV screen to see if it's shatter resistant. In another, you can push a button that releases a magnet that falls onto a firefighter's helmet.

Across the plaza at **Innoventions West,** crowds flock to **Video Games of Tomorrow,** which has nearly three dozen game stations. **Where's the Fire?,** geared to smaller kids, teaches the basics of fire safety and demonstrates how firefighters fight fires with the help of a pump truck. The younger set will also appreciate the **Kim Possible Kidcot Fun Stop** as well as **Fantastic Plastic Works,** where they can build (and keep) their own tiny robot.

Note: An all-new indoor character meet-and-greet area, aptly named the **Character Connection,** is now located near Innoventions East, behind the Fountainview Cafe.

The Land
Frommer's Rating: B+ for environmentalists and gardeners, C for others
Recommended Ages: 8–adult

Moments **Kids in the Kitchen**

During the Epcot International Food & Wine Festival in the fall, future cooks can take advantage of a free **Junior Chef** program at the Land, which lets kids ages 3 to 10 assist real-life chefs in baking Nestlé Toll House cookies. Your child will get a chef's hat and a couple of cookies to take home (though most can't resist eating them right away). It usually runs about every hour or so. There's no need to reserve a spot; just show up at the Junior Chef storefront in the Sunshine Seasons food court on the first floor about 10 minutes before the program is set to begin.

The largest of Future World's pavilions highlights food and nature. **Living with the Land** is a 13-minute boat ride through three ecological environments (a rainforest, an African desert, and the windswept American plains), each populated by appropriate audio-Animatronic denizens. New farming methods and experiments ranging from hydroponics to plants growing in simulated Martian soil are showcased in real gardens. If you'd like a more serious overview, take the 45-minute **Behind the Seeds** guided walking tour of the growing areas, offered daily. Sign up at the Green Thumb Emporium shop near the entrance to Food Rocks. The cost is $14 for adults and $10 for children 3 to 9. *Note:* It's really geared to children.

Circle of Life combines spectacular live-action footage with animation in a 15-minute motion picture based on *The Lion King*. In this cautionary environmental tale, Timon and Pumbaa are building a monument to the good life called Hakuna Matata Lakeside Village, but their project, as Simba points out, is damaging the savanna for other animals. The message: Everything is connected in the great circle of life.

On the new **Soarin'**, a copy of a popular attraction at Disney's California Adventure theme park, guests are seated in a giant projection-screen dome and then allowed to fly through the sky, 40 feet into the air, over the landscapes of California. This amazing adventure is enhanced by sensory effects as guests are treated to the sights, sounds . . . and smells (think orange blossoms and pine trees) of a dozen locations in California, including the Golden Gate Bridge, the redwood forests, Napa Valley, Yosemite, and more. You really will feel almost as though you're flying through the sky. If you find yourself waiting in a lengthy queue, giant interactive video screens have been added (replacing the landscape images that once lined the walls) to keep you entertained *Note:* The ride carries a 40-inch height minimum. For the best experience, try to get seated in the first row; if you're not sanguine about heights, the third row is the charm.

Mission: Space

Frommer's Rating: A+

Recommended Ages: 10–adult

This $100-million attraction seats up to four riders at a time in a simulated flight to the Red Planet. You'll assume the role of commander, pilot, navigator, or engineer, depending on where you sit, and must complete related jobs vital to the mission (don't worry if you miss your cue; you won't crash). The ride uses a combination of visuals, sound, and centrifugal force to create the illusion of a launch and trip to Mars. Even veteran roller-coaster fanatics who tried the simulator said the sensation mimics a liftoff, as riders are pressed into their seats and the roar and vibration trick the brain during the launch portion of the 4-minute adventure. NASA helped design and tweak this attraction.

Note: Riders must be at least 44 inches tall. Because this is probably one of the most physically intense rides in all of Mickeyville, Disney was prompted to create a less-intense version after numerous guests reportedly experienced various adverse affects. By removing the centrifuge from two of the four simulators, riders can now choose their experience: the original G-force generator or a milder, mellower Mission. If you are prone to motion sickness from spinning, have a low tolerance for loud noises, have stuffy sinuses, or experience severe claustrophobia (it's a pretty tight fit), the mellower Green Team version would definitely be the better choice (or avoid the ride altogether). There's a reason Disney puts motion-sickness bags in each capsule and posts all the warnings. After the door of your pod closes, that's it—there's no escape. You're going to Mars whether you like it or not. If you choose the original (Orange Team) and the experience gets to be too much midtrip, a Disney Imagineer told me that focusing straight ahead can help minimize the effects, and he warned against closing your eyes as that actually *enhances* the ride's intensity. Also, speaking from experience, taller guests may have difficulty seeing the screen the way it was meant to be viewed—and shorter guests may have trouble reaching some of the gear.

Austin's and **Nicolas's Rating:** "That was the coolest ride here—even better than Test Track (see below). Can we go again?" Not until I stop spinning! **Ryan's Rating:** "It was awesome—the whole ride was intense, but awesome," said the kid who has an intense hatred for most roller coasters. He survived, and was even smiling after the (original) ride. Just be aware that this ride (the original version in particular) may be far too intense for those younger than 10.

The Seas with Nemo & Friends
Frommer's Rating: B
Recommended Ages: 3–adult

This "reimagined" pavilion, intent on keeping the kid-set entertained, still contains its signature aquarium filled with 5.7 million gallons of saltwater and coral reefs inhabited by some 4,000 sharks, barracudas, parrotfish, rays, dolphins, and other sea critters. Now, however, instead of exhibits tracing the history of undersea exploration and a 7-minute edu-flick, you pass through a serene undersea set (okay, it's really the queue) before picking up where the blockbuster hit *Finding Nemo* left off. "Clamo-biles" slowly transport guests through the colorful coral reef in search of Nemo—who has once again wandered off from his class field trip with Mr. Ray. Kids will spot several familiar fishes along the way, including Dory, Bruce, Marlin, Squirt, and Crush, who happily join in on the search and (thanks to new animation technology) swim right alongside the aquarium's live inhabitants. The ending is, of course, a happy one, and Nemo is safely reunited with his friends.

The two-level sea base still displays numerous exhibits dealing with various aspects of marine science and technology, and—most important of all—through acrylic windows, you get close-up views of real denizens of the deep, as they swim amidst a tremendous man-made coral reef. Both kids and adults enjoy visiting the rescued manatees (sea cows), which reside on the second level.

Turtle Talk with Crush, an interactive theater presentation, captivates kids' attention, as well as their hearts. In the theater (now slightly larger thanks to a recent refit), adults are seated on benches in the back while children are asked to sit on the floor right in front of the screen (which, for the moment, looks like a giant underwater viewing area). After a brief introduction, Crush, a 152-year-old sea turtle from the film *Finding Nemo,* appears swimming around, chitchatting to himself and, before you know it, with the kids—and I mean really conversing. Through some amazing technology and animation, the talking turtle can "see" the audience, pick out whose question he'd like to answer by describing his or her clothing, and actually respond to his or her questions. Kids (and parents) love it.

Disney has also added a small play area where little ones can expend some of their extra energy. **Bruce's Shark World** features some larger-than-life (albeit animated) sharks to climb on, in, and around.

Note: **Epcot DiveQuest** is a program that enables certified divers ages 10 and up (those ages 10–11 are required to have an adult participate along with them, while those ages 12–17 require a signed waiver) to take part in a 3-hour program that includes a 40-minute dive in the Seas with Nemo & Friends aquarium (bring a swimsuit). The program costs $140. Call © **407/939-8687** for details. Keep in mind, however, that you get more dolphins for your money at **Discovery Cove** (p. 295).

Spaceship Earth *Overrated*
Frommer's Rating: C
Recommended Ages: All ages

Epcot's iconic, silvery geosphere houses an attraction of the same name, a slow-track journey back to the roots of communications. The 15-minute ride begins with Cro-Magnon cave painting and then advances to Egyptian hieroglyphs, the Phoenician and Greek alphabets, the Gutenberg printing press, and the Renaissance. Technologies develop at a rapid pace, through the telegraph, telephone, radio, movies, and TV. It's but a short step to the age of electronic communications. But that's not where it ends: In 2007, in partnership with Siemens, the icon began a lengthy and much needed update (still ongoing even at press time). Scheduled improvements include: an all-new ending allowing riders a sneak peak into the future, thanks in part to the newly installed interactive touch screens aboard each "time machine," enhancements and upgrades to the existing scenes and special effects throughout the attraction, the addition of new scenes, and a hands-on exhibit (located just beyond the exit) featuring games and displays that showcase a variety of innovative future technologies. At the time of this writing, the interactive area is open to guests, but renovations inside are slated for completion in early 2008, with the ride closed down while the improvements are made. Currently, the presentation isn't nearly as engaging as others in the park, but if it's a really hot day, you need time off your feet, or you have time to spare, then by all means sit back, cool off, and enjoy. *Note:* Spaceship Earth is now sans the gigantic arm and wand that once sat high atop the icon's exterior.

Test Track
Frommer's Rating: A+
Recommended Ages: 8–adult

Test Track is a $60-million marvel that combines GM engineering and Disney Imagineering. Most of you will have a blast. The line can be more than an hour long during peak periods, so consider the FASTPASS option (but remember to get one early, before they run out). The last part of the line snakes through displays about corrosion, crash tests, and other things from the GM proving grounds (you can linger long enough to see them even with FASTPASS). The 5-minute ride follows what looks to be an actual highway. It includes braking tests, a hill climb, and tight S-curves in a six-passenger convertible. The left front seat offers the most thrills as the vehicle moves

---

Tips   Visual & Audio Assistance

Free guided-tour audiocassette tapes and players are available at Guest Relations to assist visually impaired guests, and personal translator units are available to amplify the audio at some Epcot attractions (inquire at Earth Station). For more information on WDW services for those with disabilities, see p. 47.

---

through the curves. There's also a 12-second burst of speed that reaches 65 mph on the straightaway (no traffic!).

Note: Riders must be at least 40 inches tall. Expectant mothers, people prone to motion sickness, and those with heart, neck, or back problems shouldn't test the track.

Note #2: This is the only attraction in Epcot that has a single-rider line, which allows singles to fill in vacant spots in select cars. If you're part of a party that doesn't mind splitting up and riding in singles, you can shave off some serious waiting time by taking advantage of this option. FASTPASS offers the same time savings without the break up, but Test Track is in such demand that the last FASTPASS for the *day* is often gone by 11am, so if you don't catch it early enough, the single-rider line will be your only time-saving option.

Note #3: Test Track often experiences technical difficulties. To add insult to injury, it's one of the few rides in Epcot that closes due to inclement weather. If you know a storm's brewing in the afternoon, be sure to head here early in the day.

Nicolas's and **Austin's Rating:** "It's really fast. Let's go again; it's better than when Mom drives!" (Indeed, that last burst provides quite a rush.)

Universe of Energy
Frommer's Rating: B+
Recommended Ages: 6–adult
Sponsored by Exxon, this pavilion has a roof full of solar panels and a goal of bettering your understanding of America's energy problems and potential solutions. Its headline ride, **Ellen's Energy Adventure,** features comedian Ellen DeGeneres being tutored (by Bill Nye the Science Guy) to be a *Jeopardy!* contestant. On a massive screen in Theater I, an animated motion picture depicts the Earth's molten beginnings, its cooling process, and the formation of fossil fuels. You move back in time 275 million years into an eerie, storm-wracked landscape of the Mesozoic Era. Here, giant audio-Animatronic dragonflies, earthquakes, and streams of molten lava threaten you before you enter a steam-filled tunnel deep in the bowels of a volcano. When you emerge, you're in Theater II and the present. In this new setting, which looks like a NASA Mission Control room, a 70mm film projected on a massive 210-foot wraparound screen depicts the challenges of the world's increasing energy demands and the emerging technologies that will help meet them. Your moving seats now return to Theater I, where swirling special effects herald a film about how energy affects our lives. It ends on an upbeat note, with a vision of an energy-abundant future and Ellen as a new *Jeopardy!* champion. *Note:* Most kids enjoy the ride, though younger children may find the dinosaur scenes and parts of the movies rather frightening and too intense to be tolerable.

Wonders of Life
Alas, at press time, this pavilion remains closed with no official word regarding its future status. On Disney's official site, the attractions within the pavilion remain listed

Moments   Water-Fountain Conversations

Many an ordinary item at Disney World has hidden entertainment value. Take a drink at the water fountain in Innoventions Plaza (right next to Mouse Gear) and it may beg you not to drink it dry. No, you haven't gotten too much sun; the fountain actually talks (much to the delight of kids). A few more talking fountains are scattered around Epcot.

The fountains aren't the only items at WDW that will chat you up. I've kibitzed with a walking-and-talking garbage can (named PUSH) in Magic Kingdom and a palm tree (who goes by Wes Palm) at Animal Kingdom. Ask a Disney employee to direct you if you and your kids want to meet one of these conversational contraptions.

Dancing fountains can be found throughout the park as well. Kids love chasing the shooting droplets and spouting streams of water; getting wet is just a bonus. In addition to the large fountain display outside Imagination!, smaller spots can be found to the left of Innoventions and on the way to Mission: Space, as well as near the bridge leading to the World Showcase.

Little kids also love the twinkling lights embedded in the walkway between Innoventions and Mission: Space. And be sure to catch the Innoventions Fountain show, where the waters dance to the beat of recorded music, and are accented by lights and changing colors—it's mesmerizing at any age.

as closed only seasonally. However, save for a brief 3-month engagement in 2006, we have yet to see any real signs of life.

WORLD SHOWCASE

This community of 11 miniaturized nations surrounds the 40-acre World Showcase Lagoon on the park's southern side. All the showcase's countries have authentically indigenous architecture, landscaping, background music, restaurants, and shops. The nations' cultural facets are explored in art exhibits, song and dance performances, and innovative rides, films, and attractions. And all the employees in each pavilion are natives of the country represented.

All pavilions offer some kind of live entertainment throughout the day. Times and performances change, but they're listed in the guide map and the *Times Guide*. World Showcase opens between 11am and noon daily, so there's time for an excursion to Future World if you arrive any earlier.

Note: With the exception of those with an appreciation of world geography and cultures, most young kids will find little of interest here other than a few tame rides and some activities at **Kidcot Fun Stops** (p. 207). There are, however, **regular characters appearances** at the Showcase Plaza (consult the daily schedule for times).

Canada

Frommer's Rating: A
Recommended Ages: 8–adult

Our neighbors to the north are represented by architecture ranging from a mansard-roofed replica of Ottawa's 19th-century French-style Château Laurier (here called

Hôtel du Canada) to a British-influenced stone building modeled after a famous landmark near Niagara Falls.

An Indian village complete with a rough-hewn log trading post and 30-foot replicas of Ojibwa totem poles signifies the culture of the Northwest. The Canadian wilderness is reflected by a rocky mountain, a waterfall cascading into a whitewater stream, and a miniforest of evergreens, stately cedars, maples, and birch trees. Don't miss the stunning floral displays of azaleas, roses, zinnias, chrysanthemums, petunias, and patches of wildflowers inspired by the Butchart Gardens in Victoria, British Columbia.

The pavilion's highlight is *O Canada!*—a dazzling 18-minute, 360-degree CircleVision film, now hosted by Martin Short, that shows Canada's scenic splendor, from the excitement of its cities and diversity of its people to the grandeur of its countryside. Scenes range from the northeastern shores of Newfoundland to the grand redwoods of Cathedral Grove to even the snowcapped mountains of the Kananaskis Valley. If you're looking for foot-tapping live entertainment, **Off Kilter** raises the roof with New Age Celtic music as well as some get-down country music. Days and times vary.

Northwest Mercantile carries sandstone and soapstone carvings, fringed leather vests, duck decoys, moccasins, an array of stuffed animals, Native American dolls, Native American spirit stones, rabbit-skin caps, heavy knitted sweaters, and, of course, maple syrup.

China

Frommer's Rating: A
Recommended Ages: 10–adult
Bounded by a serpentine wall that snakes around its perimeter, the China Pavilion is entered via a triple-arched ceremonial gate inspired by the Temple of Heaven in Beijing, a summer retreat for Chinese emperors. Passing through the gate, you'll see a half-size replica of this ornately embellished red-and-gold circular temple, built in 1420 during the Ming dynasty. Gardens simulate those in Suzhou, with miniature waterfalls, fragrant lotus ponds, and groves of bamboo, corkscrew willows, and weeping mulberry trees.

Reflections of China ✸✸ is a 20-minute movie that explores the culture and landscapes in and around seven Chinese cities. Shot over a 2-month period in 2002, it visits Beijing, Shanghai, and the Great Wall—begun 24 centuries ago!—among other places. **Land of Many Faces** is an exhibit that introduces China's ethnic peoples, and entertainment is provided daily by the amazing and child-pleasing **Dragon Legend Acrobats** ✸✸.

The **Yong Feng Shangdian Shopping Gallery** features silk robes, lacquer and inlaid mother-of-pearl furniture, jade figures, cloisonné vases, brocade pajamas, silk rugs and embroideries, wind chimes, and Chinese clothing. Artisans occasionally demonstrate calligraphy.

Nicolas's and **Austin's Rating:** "Whoa! It looks like the real deal—just smaller!" (Both have been fortunate enough to have traveled to Beijing and Shanghai.)

France

Frommer's Rating: B
Recommended Ages: 8–adult
This pavilion focuses on La Belle Epoque, a period from 1870 to 1910 in which French art, literature, and architecture flourished. It's entered via a replica of the beautiful

cast-iron Pont des Arts footbridge over the Seine, which leads to a park with bleached sycamores, Bradford pear trees, flowering crape myrtle, and sculptured parterre flower gardens inspired by Seurat's painting *A Sunday Afternoon on the Island of La Grande Jatte.* A one-tenth–scale replica of the Eiffel Tower constructed from Gustave Eiffel's original blueprints looms overhead.

The highlight is ***Impressions de France,*** which is definitely more for the older set than for young kids. Shown in a palatial sit-down theater a la Fontainebleau, this 18-minute film is a scenic journey through diverse French landscapes projected on a vast 200-degree wraparound screen and enhanced by the music of French composers. The antics of **Serveur Amusant,** a comedic waiter, and the visual comedy of **Le Mime Roland** delight both children and adults, as do the yummy pastries at **Boulangerie Patisserie.**

The covered arcade has shops selling French prints and original art, cookbooks, wines (there's a tasting counter), French food, Babar books, perfumes, and original letters of famous Frenchmen ranging from Jean Cocteau to Napoleon. Guerlain recently opened a boutique (one of only four in the U.S.) offering a selection of limited-edition fragrances and exclusive Guerlain creations. Another marketplace/tourism center revives the defunct **Les Halles,** where Parisians used to sip onion soup in the wee hours.

Germany
Frommer's Rating: B
Recommended Ages: 8–adult
Enclosed by castle walls and towers, this festive pavilion is centered on a cobblestone *platz* (square), with pots of colorful flowers girding a fountain statue of St. George and the Dragon. An adjacent clock tower is embellished with whimsical glockenspiel figures that herald each hour with quaint melodies. The pavilion's **Biergarten** (p. 139) was inspired by medieval Rothenberg and features a year-round Oktoberfest and its music. And 16th-century facades replicate a merchant's hall in the Black Forest and the town hall in Römerberg Square.

The shops here carry Hummel figurines, crystal, glassware, cookware, Anton Schneider cuckoos, cowbells, Alpine hats, German wines (there's a tasting counter, if Mom or Dad wants to give one a try), specialty foods, toys (German Disneyana, teddy bears, dolls, and puppets), and books. An artisan demonstrates molding and painting Hummel figures; another paints detailed scenes on eggs. Background music runs from oompah bands to Mozart symphonies.

Tip: Model-train enthusiasts and kids enjoy the exquisitely detailed miniature version of a small Bavarian town, complete with working train station. Even the littlest members of your party will be fascinated as they watch the trains dart in and out of tunnels and stations.

Italy
Frommer's Rating: B
Recommended Ages: 10–adult
One of the prettiest World Showcase pavilions, Italy lures visitors over an arched stone footbridge to a replica of Venice's intricately ornamented pink-and-white Doge's Palace. Other architectural highlights include the 83-foot Campanile (bell tower) of St. Mark's Square, Venetian bridges, and a piazza enclosing a version of Bernini's Neptune fountain. A garden wall suggests a backdrop of provincial countryside, and citrus, cypress, pine, and olive trees frame a formal garden. Gondolas are moored on the lagoon.

Finds **Great Buys at Epcot**

Sure, *you* want to be educated about the cultures of the world, but for most families, the two big attractions at the World Showcase are eating and shopping. Dining options are explored in chapter 5, "Family-Friendly Dining." The following list gives you an idea of additional items available for purchase.

If you'd like to check out the amazing scope of Disney merchandise at home, everything from furniture to bath toys, you can order a catalog by calling ② **800/237-5751** or going to **www.disneystore.com**.

• The toys and piñatas draw folks to **Mexico,** and the silver jewelry is beautiful. Choose from a range of merchandise—everything from a simple flowered hair clip to a kidney-shaped stone-and-silver bracelet.

• There are lots of great sweaters available in the shops of **Norway,** and it's really tough to resist the Scandinavian trolls. They're ugly, but you have to love 'em. Your kids will love the LEGOs for sale.

• Discover Disney trading pins and Coca-Cola memorabilia in the shops of **U.S.A.—The American Adventure.**

• Your funky teenager might like the Taquia knit cap, a colorful fezlike chapeau, that's available in **Morocco.** You'll also see a variety of celestial-patterned pottery available in vases and platters, and, for the little princesses, a Jasmine character costume.

• Toy soldiers, British games, candy, and music tapes are popular in the **United Kingdom.** Tennis fans may be interested in the Wimbledon shirts, shorts, and skirts. There's also a nice assortment of rose-patterned tea accessories, Shetland sweaters, tartans, pub accessories, and loads of other stuff from the U.K.

In the street-entertainment department, the seemingly lifeless forms of **Imaginum, A Statue Act,** fascinate visitors young and old daily, while the **Character Masquerade,** featuring traditional Carnevale masks and costumes, will generate enthusiasm as well.

Shops carry cameo and filigree jewelry, Armani figurines, kitchenware, Italian wines and foods, Murano and other Venetian glass, alabaster figurines, and inlaid wooden music boxes.

Japan
Frommer's Rating: A
Recommended Ages: 8–adult
A flaming red *torii* (gate of honor) on the banks of the lagoon and the graceful blue-roofed Goju No To pagoda, inspired by a shrine built at Nara in A.D. 700, welcome you to this pavilion, which focuses on Japan's ancient culture. In a traditional Japanese garden, cedars, yews, bamboo, "cloud-pruned" evergreens, willows, and flowering shrubs frame a contemplative setting of pebbled footpaths, rustic bridges, waterfalls, exquisite rock landscaping, and a pond of golden koi. It's a haven of tranquility in a park that's anything but.

The **Yakitori House** is based on the renowned 16th-century Katsura Imperial Villa in Kyoto, designed as a royal summer residence and considered by many to be the crowning achievement of Japanese architecture. Exhibits ranging from 18th-century Bunraki puppets to samurai armor take place in the moated **White Heron Castle,** a replica of the Shirasagi-Jo, a 17th-century fortress overlooking the city of Himeji. There's also a gallery that puts on temporary exhibits (at press time, it featured a very kid-friendly display of **Japanese Tin Toys**). The drums of **Matsuriza**—one of the best performances in the World Showcase—entertain guests daily (the show is loud, but kids love it).

The **Mitsukoshi Department Store** (Japan's answer to Macy's) is housed in a replica of the Shishinden (Hall of Ceremonies) of the Gosho Imperial Palace, built in Kyoto in A.D. 794, and is popular with kids of all ages. It sells lacquerware, kimonos, kites, fans, dolls in traditional costumes (children love them), Pokémon and Hello Kitty items (ditto), origami books, samurai swords, Japanese Disneyana, bonsai trees, Japanese foods, netsuke carvings, pottery, and modern electronics.

Mexico
Frommer's Rating: A
Recommended Ages: 8–adult

You'll hear the music of marimbas and mariachi bands as you approach Mexico, fronted by a Mayan pyramid modeled on the Aztec temple of Quetzalcoatl (God of Life) and surrounded by dense Yucatán jungle landscaping. Upon entering the pavilion, you'll be in a museum of pre-Columbian art and artifacts.

Down a ramp, a small lagoon is the setting for the **Gran Fiesta Tour Starring the Three Caballeros** (replacing El Rio Del Tiempo). This 8-minute cruise along the Mexican countryside now features Donald Duck, José Carioca, and Panchito (from the 1944 Disney classic *The Three Caballeros*) as they reunite to perform in Mexico City. Donald, however, wanders off to see the sights—leaving José and Panchito to search for him. An animated overlay blends the Caballero characters in with the existing scenery. Along the river route, passengers get a close-up look at the Mayan pyramid and the erupting Popocatepetl volcano. **Mariachi Cobre,** a 12-piece band, plays Tuesdays through Saturdays.

Shops in and around the **Plaza de Los Amigos** (a "moonlit" Mexican *mercado* with a tiered fountain and street lamps) display leather goods, baskets, sombreros, piñatas, pottery, embroidered dresses and blouses, maracas, jewelry, serapes, colorful papier-mâché birds, and blown-glass objects. An artisan occasionally gives demonstrations. The Mexican Tourist Office also provides travel information.

Morocco
Frommer's Rating: A
Recommended Ages: 10–adult

This exotic pavilion has architecture embellished with geometrically patterned tile work, minarets, hand-painted wood ceilings, and brass lighting fixtures. (The king of Morocco took a personal interest in the project and sent royal artisans to help in its construction, and the result is one of the most authentic atmospheres at the World Showcase.) Morocco's landscaping includes a formal garden, citrus and olive trees, date palms, and banana plants. The pavilion is headlined by a replica of the Koutoubia Minaret, the prayer tower of a 12th-century mosque in Marrakech. The Medina (old city), entered via a replica of an arched gateway in Fez, leads to **Fez House** (a traditional Moroccan home) and the narrow, winding streets of the **souk,** a bustling marketplace

---

(Tips) Stay Tuned

Disney hasn't added a new "nation" to World Showcase since Norway became the 11th country in 1988. At one time, the buzz had Spain possibly becoming the 12th, with a pavilion that would blend the city of Toledo with some architectural highlights of Madrid and Barcelona.

---

where all manner of authentic handcrafted merchandise is on display. Here, you can browse or purchase pottery, brassware, hand-knotted Berber or colorful Rabat carpets, ornate silver and camel-bone boxes, straw baskets, and prayer rugs. There are weaving demonstrations periodically during the day. The Medina's rectangular courtyard centers on a replica of the ornately tiled Najjarine Fountain in Fez, the setting for musical entertainment. **Mo'Rockin'** plays Arabian rock music on traditional instruments Tuesday through Saturday.

Treasures of Morocco is a three-times-per-day, 35-minute guided tour (1–5pm) that highlights this country's culture, architecture, and history (older kids will find it enjoyable and educational, but this is not for the young set). The pavilion's **Gallery of Arts and History** contains an ever-changing exhibit of Moroccan art, while the Center of Tourism offers a continuous three-screen slide show.

Norway
Frommer's Rating: B+
Recommended Ages: 10–adult

This pavilion is centered on a picturesque cobblestone courtyard. A *stavekirke* (stave church), styled after the 13th-century Gol Church of Hallingdal, has changing exhibits. A replica of Oslo's 14th-century **Akershus Castle,** next to a cascading woodland waterfall, is the setting for the featured restaurant (p. 139). Other buildings simulate the red-roofed cottages of Bergen and the timber-sided farm buildings of the Nordic woodlands.

Maelstrom, a boat ride in a dragon-headed Viking vessel, traverses Norway's fjords and mythical forests to the music of *Peer Gynt.* Along the way, you'll see images of polar bears prowling the shore; then trolls cast a spell on the boat. The watercraft crashes through a narrow gorge and spins into the North Sea, where a storm is in progress. (This is a relatively calm ride that's fine for all but the littlest kids, though it's not recommended for expectant mothers or folks with heart, neck, or back problems.) The storm abates, and passengers disembark safely to a 10th-century Viking village to view the 5-minute 70mm film *Norway,* which documents 1,000 years of history. **Spelmanns Gledje** entertains with Norwegian folk music.

Shops here sell hand-knit wool hats and sweaters, troll dolls, toys (kids can play at the LEGO table), wood carvings, Scandinavian foods, and jewelry.

United Kingdom
Frommer's Rating: B
Recommended Ages: 8–adult

This pavilion takes you to Merry Olde England through **Britannia Square,** a London-style park with a copper-roof gazebo bandstand, a stereotypical red phone booth, and a statue of the Bard. Four centuries of architecture are represented along quaint cobblestone streets, including a traditional British pub. A formal garden with low box hedges in geometric patterns, flagstone paths, and a stone fountain replicates the land-scaping of 16th- and 17th-century palaces. Of special interest for the kids is a small, traditional hedge maze that features topiaries shaped like Disney characters at the back of the pavilion. *Note:* Characters, especially from British stories such as *Winnie the Pooh* and *Alice in Wonderland,* tend to show up here quite often.

Entertainment is provided by the **British Invasion,** a group that impersonates the Beatles (Mon–Sat); pub pianist **Pam Brody** (Thurs and Sun); pub magician **Jason Wethington** (Fri); and the comedic acting troupe the **World Showcase Players** (daily).

High Street and Tudor Lane shops display a broad sampling of British merchandise, including toy soldiers, Paddington bears, personalized coats of arms, Scottish clothing (cashmere and Shetland sweaters, golfwear, tams, and tartans), English china, Water-ford crystal, and pub items such as tankards, dartboards, and the like. A tea shop occu-pies a replica of Anne Hathaway's thatched-roof 16th-century cottage in Stratford-on-Avon. Other emporia represent the Georgian, Victorian, Queen Anne, and Tudor periods. Background music ranges from "Greensleeves" to the Beatles.

U.S.A.—The American Adventure
Frommer's Rating: A
Recommended Ages: 8–adult
Housed in a vast Georgian-style structure, **The American Adventure** is a 29-minute dramatization of U.S. history, utilizing a 72-foot rear-projection screen; rousing music; and a large cast of lifelike audio-Animatronic figures, including narrators Mark Twain and Ben Franklin. The adventure begins with the voyage of the *Mayflower* and encom-passes major historic events. You'll view Jefferson writing the Declaration of Indepen-dence, Matthew Brady photographing a family about to be divided by the Civil War, the stock-market crash of 1929, Pearl Harbor, and the *Eagle* heading toward the moon. Teddy Roosevelt discusses the need for national parks. Susan B. Anthony speaks out on women's rights; Frederick Douglass, on slavery; and Chief Joseph, on the plight of Native Americans. Scenes added in 2007 include September 11th, the victories of Lance Armstrong, and Oprah Winfrey's work with African children. It's one of Disney's best historical productions and offers great entertainment for the entire family.

National Treasures, a new exhibit added in 2007, features a rare collection of trin-kets, treasures, and personal items from prominent figures in American history includ-ing Abraham Lincoln, George Washington Carver, Rosa Parks, and Jackie Robinson. Items displayed will rotate and change from time to time. Entertainment in this pavil-ion includes the **Spirit of America Fife & Drum Corps;** the **Voices of Liberty,** an a cappella group that sings patriotic songs; and **American Vybe,** which features the sounds of swing, jazz, and gospel.

Formal gardens shaded by live oaks, sycamores, elms, and holly complement the 18th-century architecture. **Heritage Manor Gifts** sells autographed presidential pho-tographs, needlepoint samplers, quilts, pottery, candles, Davy Crockett hats, history books, historically costumed dolls, classic political campaign buttons, and vintage newspapers with banner headlines such as "Nixon Resigns!"

A NIGHTTIME SPECTACLE
IllumiNations *(Moments)*
Frommer's Rating: A+
Recommended Ages: 3–adult
Little has changed since Epcot's millennium version of IllumiNations ended on Janu-ary 1, 2001. This 13-minute grand nightcap continues to be a blend of fireworks,

Tips **Cruise Control**

There are two cruise-style options for watching Epcot's IllumiNations fireworks display (below) from the World Showcase Lagoon. You can charter the 1930s vintage speedboat *Breathless* ($180 for up to seven people) or catch the show aboard a less romantic but less expensive **pontoon boat** ($235 for up to 10 people). Both rides last 45 to 50 minutes, and you must rent the entire boat for your family or find your own boatmates. For information or to make reservations, call ℂ **407/939-7529.**

---

lasers, and fountains in a display that's signature Disney. The show is worth dealing with the crowds that flock to the parking lot when it's over (just be sure to keep a firm grip on young kids). *Tip:* Stake your claim to your favorite viewing area a half hour before showtime (listed in your entertainment schedule). The ones near Showcase Plaza have a head start for the exits. Another good viewing spot is the terrace at the Rose & Crown Pub in the United Kingdom (p. 140).

Ryan's Rating: "That was cool—better than the Magic Kingdom's fireworks." Thanks to its added dimensions—lasers and fountains—my older kids found it more interesting than the Wishes fireworks display (p. 207).

5 Disney's Hollywood Studios

You'll probably see the Tower of Terror and the Earrfel Tower, the water tank with mouse ears, before you enter Disney's Hollywood Studios (formerly Disney–MGM Studios). Once inside, you'll find pulse-quickening rides such as **Rock 'n' Roller Coaster,** movie- and TV-themed shows such as **Jim Henson's Muppet*Vision 3-D,** and a spectacular laser-light show called **Fantasmic!** The main streets include Hollywood and Sunset boulevards, where movie sets recall the golden age of Hollywood. New York Street is lined with miniature renditions of Gotham's landmarks (the Empire State, Flatiron, and Chrysler buildings), and there are mock-ups of San Francisco, Chinatown, and other places. You'll find some of the best street performing in the Disney parks here. More important, it's a working movie and TV studio where shows are occasionally in production.

Arrive early. Unlike Epcot, Hollywood Studios' 154 acres of attractions are easier to see in 1 day. If you don't get a *Hollywood Studios Guide Map* and *Times Guide* (or entertainment schedule) as you enter the park, you can pick one up at Guest Relations or in most shops. Straight off, check showtimes and work out a schedule based on attractions and geographical proximity. My favorite Studios restaurants are described in chapter 5, "Family-Friendly Dining." There's a tip board listing the day's shows, ride closings, and other information at the corner of Hollywood and Sunset boulevards.

ARRIVING   The parking lot reaches to the gate, but trams serve most areas. Pay attention to your parking location; this lot isn't as well marked as the Magic Kingdom's. Again, write your lot and row number on something you can find at day's end.

HOURS   The park is usually open from 9am to at least 6 or 7pm, with extended hours sometimes as late as midnight during holidays and summer.

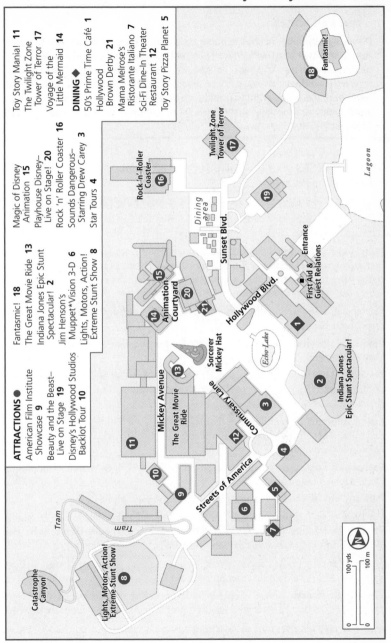

ATTRACTIONS ●

American Film Institute Showcase **9**

Beauty and the Beast— Live on Stage **19**

Disney's Hollywood Studios Backlot Tour **10**

Fantasmic! **18**

The Great Movie Ride **13**

Indiana Jones Epic Stunt Spectacular! **2**

Jim Henson's Muppet*Vision 3-D **6**

Lights, Motors, Action! Extreme Stunt Show **8**

Magic of Disney Animation **15**

Playhouse Disney— Live on Stage! **20**

Rock 'n' Roller Coaster **16**

Sounds Dangerous— Starring Drew Carey **3**

Star Tours **4**

Toy Story Mania! **11**

The Twilight Zone Tower of Terror **17**

Voyage of the Little Mermaid **14**

DINING ◆

50's Prime Time Café **1**

Hollywood Brown Derby **21**

Mama Melrose's Ristorante Italiano **7**

Sci-Fi Dine-In Theater Restaurant **12**

Toy Story Pizza Planet **5**

Tips **Call Ahead**

Disney's Hollywood Studios is home to some of Disney World's most unique restaurants (see chapter 5, "Family-Friendly Dining," for more details). If you plan to dine in any of them, be sure to make **Advance Dining Reservations** (preferably before you leave home, but if not, the minute you arrive at your hotel or in the park). Waiting until lunch or dinnertime will almost ensure that you'll miss out, especially at the Sci-Fi Dine-In Theater Restaurant and the 50's Prime Time Café.

TICKET PRICES   A 1-day park ticket is $71 for adults and $60 for children 3 to 9. Kids under 3 get in free.

SERVICES & FACILITIES IN DISNEY'S HOLLYWOOD STUDIOS

ATMs   ATMs accepting cards from banks using the Cirrus, Honor, and PLUS systems are to the right of the entrance and near Toy Story Pizza Planet.

Baby Care   Hollywood Studios has a small Baby Care Center to the left of the entrance, where you'll find facilities for nursing and changing. Disposable diapers, formula, baby food, and pacifiers are for sale. Changing tables are in all women's restrooms and some men's restrooms.

Cameras & Film   Film, disposable cameras, and limited digital supplies are available throughout the park.

First Aid   It's located in the Entrance Plaza, adjoining Guest Relations and the Baby Care Center, and staffed by registered nurses.

Lockers   Lockers are located alongside Oscar's Classic Car Souvenirs, to the right of the Entrance Plaza after you pass through the turnstiles. The cost is $5, plus a $2 deposit.

Lost Children   Lost children at Disney's Hollywood Studios are taken to Guest Relations, where lost-children logbooks are kept. *Children under 7 should wear name tags* inside their clothing.

Package Pickup   Any purchase can be sent to Oscar's Super Service in the Entrance Plaza. Allow 3 hours for delivery.

Parking   It's $11 a day for cars, light trucks, and vans, and $12 for RVs.

Pet Care   Day accommodations for $10 are offered at kennels to the left and just outside the entrance (© **407/824-6568**). There are also four other kennels in the WDW complex. Proof of vaccination is required.

Stroller Rental   Oscar's Super Service, inside the main entrance, charges $10 for a single and $18 for a double. Discounts are available for length-of-stay rentals.

Wheelchair Rental   Oscar's Super Service, inside the main entrance, rents regular chairs for $10 a day. Electric wheelchairs go for $35, plus a $5 refundable deposit.

MAJOR ATTRACTIONS & SHOWS
American Film Institute Showcase
Frommer's Rating: C
Recommended Ages: 10–adult

This shop and exhibit area is the final stop on the Backlot Tour (see below) and looks at the efforts of the editors, cinematographers, producers, and directors whose names roll by in the blur of credits. It also showcases the work of the American Film Institute's Lifetime Achievement Award winners, including Bette Davis, Jack Nicholson, and Elizabeth Taylor. A special exhibit here, **Villains: Movie Characters You Love to Hate,** features the costumes and props of several notable bad guys, including Darth Vader.

Beauty and the Beast–Live on Stage
Frommer's Rating: B+
Recommended Ages: All ages
A 1,500-seat covered amphitheater is the home of this 30-minute, live Broadway-style production of *Beauty and the Beast* (adapted from the movie). Musical highlights from the show include the rousing "Be Our Guest" opening number and the poignant title song featured in the romantic waltz-scene finale. The sets and costumes are lavish, and the production numbers are pretty spectacular. It's a treat for the whole family and a great place to rest your feet. There are usually four or five shows a day.

Disney's Hollywood Studios Backlot Tour
Frommer's Rating: B+
Recommended Ages: 6–adult
This 35-minute tram tour takes you behind the scenes for a close-up look at the vehicles, props, costumes, sets, and special effects used in movies and TV shows. On many days, you'll see costume makers at work in the wardrobe department (Disney has around 2 million garments here). But the real fun begins when the tram heads for **Catastrophe Canyon,** where an earthquake in the heart of oil country causes canyon walls to rumble. A raging oil fire, massive explosions, torrents of rain, and flash floods threaten you and other riders before you're taken behind the scenes to see how filmmakers use special effects to make such disasters (little kids may get a little intimidated if they aren't warned in advance). The preshow is almost as interesting. While waiting in line, you can watch entertaining videos hosted by several TV and movie stars. The Backlot Tour is a solid ride that's of the same type as Universal Studios Florida's Earthquake (p. 264).

   Hailey's Rating: "How'd they do that? That was cool." **Nicolas's Rating:** He thought it worth a second ride later that day.

Fantasmic! *(Moments*
Frommer's Rating: A+
Recommended Ages: All ages
Disney mixes heroes, villains, stunt performers, choreography, laser lights, and fireworks into a spectacular end-of-the-day extravaganza. This is a 25-minute visual feast

---

Tips Out of the Warmth & into the Cold

Over at soundstage four, on Mickey Avenue, the frozen world of Narnia comes alive. At **Journey into Narnia: Creating the Lion, the Witch, and the Wardrobe,** visitors can walk through a gigantic wardrobe and into an elaborate wintry landscape much like the set from the hit blockbuster movie. They'll be treated to a behind-the-scenes look at movie-making magic a la Disney. Filling the gallery just beyond the set are elaborate creatures, along with actual costumes, armory, and props used in the making of the film.

Tips **Dinner & a Show**

At press time, Disney was offering preferred seating at the end-of-the-day spectacular, **Fantasmic!,** along with a fixed-price dinner at one of the sit-down restaurants in Hollywood Studios. All you need to do is make Advance Dining Reservations ((©) **407/939-3463**) and request the Fantasmic! package for the Hollywood Brown Derby ($47 adults, $12 kids 3–9), Mama Melrose's Ristorante Italiano ($33 adults, $12 kids), or Hollywood & Vine ($25 adults, $12 kids). Packages must be guaranteed with a credit card at the time of booking. You'll get your line pass at the restaurant and instructions on getting to the special entrance for the preferred-seating area of the show.

---

where the Magic Mickey comes to life in a show featuring shooting comets, great balls of fire (our apologies to Jerry Lee), and animated fountains that really charge the audience. The cast includes 50 performers, a giant dragon, a king cobra, and 1 million gallons of water, just about all of which are orchestrated by a sorcerer mouse that looks more than remotely familiar. You'll probably recognize other characters as well as musical scores from Disney movie classics such as *Fantasia, Pinocchio, Snow White and the Seven Dwarfs, The Little Mermaid,* and *The Lion King.* You'll also shudder at the animated villainy of Jafar, Cruella de Vil, and Maleficent in the battle of good versus evil, part of which is projected onto huge water-mist screens. The amphitheater holds 9,000 souls, and during holidays and summers, it's often standing-room only, so arrive early. (There is sometimes an additional show earlier in the evening.)

Nicolas's Rating: He was wide-eyed and smiling but silent. This isn't a good show for those with sensitive ears, including adults. If anyone in your family has that problem, bring earplugs or cotton balls to deaden the sound effects. Be aware as well that the show can be frightening for younger kids, thanks to the occasional eerie music, loud pyrotechnics, lighting, after-dark setting, and scary characters.

Note: The rates above are for a fixed-price meal and do not include tax, tip, or alcoholic beverages; if you order off the menu, you'll pay more. They also don't include a reserved seat at Fantasmic!—only a pass that will get you into the preferred-seating area (you must arrive at least 30 min. in advance—a much shorter wait than usual and a boon if you have restless kids).

The Great Movie Ride
Frommer's Rating: C for most, B+ for adults who love classics
Recommended Ages: 8–adult
Film footage and 50 audio-Animatronic replicas of movie stars are used to re-create some of the most famous scenes in filmdom on this 22-minute ride through movie history. You'll relive magic moments from the 1930s through the present, starring Gene Kelly, Jimmy Cagney, John Wayne, Julie Andrews, Marlon Brando, and arguably the best Tarzan, Johnny Weissmuller, giving his trademark yell while swinging across the jungle. The action is enhanced by special effects, and outlaws hijack your tram en route—so pay attention when the conductor warns, "Fasten your seat belts. It's going to be a bumpy night." The ride appeals mostly to adults and film buffs (younger kids and teens may not recognize some of the classic movies depicted), but it's a great place to rest your feet with tired toddlers while your older kids are off riding the Tower of Terror. The setting is a full-scale reproduction of Hollywood's famous

Mann's Chinese Theatre, complete with handprints of the stars out front. *Tip:* Some of the movie scenes, especially the ones from *Alien,* can frighten young kids.

Honey, I Shrunk the Kids Movie Set Adventure
Frommer's Rating: B+
Recommended Ages: 3–10
Let the kids catch up to you in the exhaustion category as they ride talking ants, slide through a film canister, get slimed by a giant dog's sinuses, crawl through LEGO-ville, and get chilled by a sneaky hose. It's a fabulous larger-than-life playground that young kids will love.

Indiana Jones Epic Stunt Spectacular!
Frommer's Rating: A+
Recommended Ages: 6–adult
Visitors get a peek into the world of movie stunts in this dramatic 30-minute show, which re-creates major scenes from the Indiana Jones series. The show opens on an elaborate Mayan temple backdrop. Indy crashes onto the set via a rope, and as he searches with a torch for the golden idol, he runs into booby traps. Then a boulder straight out of *Raiders of the Lost Ark* chases him! The set is dismantled to reveal a colorful Cairo marketplace where a swordfight ensues; the action includes virtuoso bullwhip maneuvers, gunfire, and a truck bursting into flames. An explosive finale takes place in a desert scenario. Music and a narrative enhance the action. Throughout the production, guests get to see how elaborate stunts are pulled off. Arrive early and sit near the stage if you want a shot at being picked as an audience participant. Alas, it's a job for *adults only.*

Austin's Rating: "The airplane scene is so great with all the explosions!" This show definitely keeps you on the edge of your seat at times.

Jim Henson's Muppet*Vision 3-D
Frommer's Rating: A+
Recommended Ages: All ages
This must-see film stars Kermit and Miss Piggy in a delightful marriage of Jim Henson's puppets and Disney audio-Animatronics, special-effects wizardry, 70mm film, and cutting-edge 3-D technology. The action includes flying Muppets, cream pies, and cannonballs, plus high winds, fiber-optic fireworks, bubble showers, and even an actual spray of water. Kermit is the host; Miss Piggy sings "Dream a Little Dream of Me"; Statler and Waldorf critique the action (which includes numerous mishaps and disasters); and Nicki Napoleon and his Emperor Penguins (a full Muppet orchestra) provide music from the pit. In the preshow area, guests view an entertaining video on overhead monitors. Note the Muppet fountain out front and the Muppet version of a Rousseau painting inside. The 25-minute show (including the 12-min. video

---

Tips Go Wildcats!

With the popularity of the Disney Channel's hit movies *High School Musical* and *High School Musical 2,* it shouldn't surprise anyone that a bit of Disney's movie magic has made its way to the streets of Hollywood Studios. Everyone's catching Wildcat fever as guests are invited to join in on all the dancing and singing at the high-energy **High School Musical 2: School's Out!** street show.

Finds Find the Hidden Mickeys

Hidden Mickeys (HM, for short) started as an inside joke among early Disney Imagineers and soon became a park tradition. Today, dozens of subtle Mickey images—usually silhouettes of his world-famous ears, profile, or full figure—are hidden (more or less) in attractions and resorts throughout the Walt Disney empire. No one knows how many, because sometimes, they exist only in the eye of the beholder. See how many Hidden Mickeys you can locate during your visit (keeping track of them is a cool game for kids and will keep them entertained throughout their visit). And be sharp-eyed about it. Those bubbles on your souvenir mug might be forming one. Here are a few to get you started:

In the Magic Kingdom:
- In the Haunted Mansion banquet scene, check out the arrangement of the plate and adjoining saucers on the table.
- In the Africa scene of It's a Small World, note the purple flowers on a vine on the elephant's left side.
- While riding Splash Mountain, look for Mickey lying on his back in the pink clouds to the right of the *Zip-A-Dee Lady* paddle-wheeler.

In Epcot:
- In Imagination!, check out the little girl's dress in the lobby film of *Honey, I Shrunk the Audience,* one of five HMs in this pavilion.
- In the Land Pavilion, don't miss the small stones in front of the Native American man on a horse and the baseball cap of the man driving a harvester in the *Circle of Life* film.
- In Maelstrom in the Norway Pavilion, a Viking wears Mickey ears in the wall mural facing the loading dock.

---

preshow) runs continuously. *Tip:* Sweetums, the giant but friendly Muppet monster, usually interacts with a few kids sitting in the front rows during the show.

Hailey's Rating: "I thought I could reach out and touch stuff." That's how realistic the in-your-face, 3-D action is! **Davis's Rating:** While he giggled all the way through the show, he took off his 3-D glasses—something that kids may find helpful if they don't like the 3-D effects.

Lights, Motors, Action! Extreme Stunt Show
Frommer's Rating: A
Recommended Ages: 6–adult
This attraction debuted at Hollywood Studios in mid-2005—and it's a biggie. Taking its cue from the original show at Disneyland Paris, this version features high-flying, high-speed movie stunts full of pyrotechnic effects and more. Like the **Indiana Jones Epic Stunt Spectacular!** (p. 231), the storyline has the audience following the filming of an action-packed movie (in this case, a spy thriller set in a Mediterranean village). Over 40 vehicles are used in the show, including cars, motorcycles, and watercraft—each modified to perform the rather spectacular stunts. It's entertaining and certainly

- There are four HMs inside Spaceship Earth, one of them in the Renaissance scene, on the page of a book behind the sleeping monk. Try to find the other three.

In Disney's Hollywood Studios:
- On the Great Movie Ride, there's an HM on the window above the bank in the gangster scene.
- At Jim Henson's Muppet*Vision 3-D, take a good look at the top of the sign listing five reasons for turning in your 3-D glasses, and note the balloons in the film's final scene.
- In the Twilight Zone Tower of Terror, note the bell for the elevator behind Rod Serling in the film. There are at least five other HMs in this attraction.
- Outside Rock 'n' Roller Coaster, look for two in the rotunda's tile floor.
- By the way, the park's least Hidden Mickey is what's called the Earrfel Tower, Hollywood Studios' tall water tower, which is fitted with a huge pair of Mouseket-EARS.

In Disney's Animal Kingdom:
- Look at the Boneyard in Dinoland U.S.A., where a fan and two hard hats form an HM.
- There are 25 Hidden Mickeys at Rafiki's Planet Watch, where Mickey lurks in the murals, tree trunks, and paintings of animals.

In the Resort Areas:
- HMs are on the weather vane atop the Grand Floridian Resort & Spa's convention center and in the interactive fountains at the entrance to Downtown Disney Marketplace. One forms a giant sand trap next to the green at the Magnolia Golf Course's sixth hole.

You can learn more at **www.hiddenmickeys.org**.

---

offers its share of thrills, but it's not as engaging as the Indiana Jones production unless you're a family of car buffs. The show is part of the redevelopment of the Studios backlot area that's also seen the addition of new cityscapes of San Francisco and Chicago, among others. Check the entertainment schedule for showtimes.

Magic of Disney Animation
Frommer's Rating: B
Recommended Ages: 8–adult

Once hosted by Walter Cronkite and Robin Williams, the new version of Magic of Disney Animation features Mushu the dragon from Disney's *Mulan* as he co-hosts a theater presentation in which some of Disney's animation secrets are revealed. The Q & A session that follows allows guests to ask questions about the animation process before attempting their own Disney character drawings under the supervision of a working animator. Joining in on the fun for a meet-and-greet opportunity are an array of Disney-Pixar film favorites.

Tips Midway Mayhem

Slated to make its debut in 2008, **Toy Story Mania!** is the newest family attraction to grace the stage at Disney's Hollywood Studios. This interactive carnival-inspired ride, based on the popular Disney-Pixar *Toy Story* movies, has guests sporting 3-D glasses, shrinking to the size of a toy, and traveling along a *Toy Story*–themed midway—think Honey, I Shrunk the Audience meets Buzz Lightyear's Space Ranger Spin. Shooting at animated targets to earn points, you'll move from one game to the next (the details of which have yet to be released) with Woody, Buzz, Hamm, Bo Peep, and the Little Green Men cheering you on. Hidden targets, while adding extra points to your score, lead to different levels of play (and a different experience each time you ride).

Playhouse Disney–Live on Stage!

Frommer's Rating: B
Recommended Ages: 2–5

Younger audiences love this 20-minute show, in which they meet characters from Mickey Mouse Clubhouse, Little Einsteins, Handy Manny, and other stories. The show encourages preschoolers to dance, sing, and play along with the cast. If your kids are the right age, don't miss it. The action happens several times a day; check your show schedule. Character meet and greets are held in the nearby Animation Courtyard daily.

Rock 'n' Roller Coaster *Moments*

Frommer's Rating: A+
Recommended Ages: 10–adult

Some say this is one of Disney's attempts to go head to head with Universal Orlando's Islands of Adventure. True or not, this inverted roller coaster is one of the best thrill rides at WDW. Kids looking for an adrenaline rush will demand to ride it. It's a fast-and-furious indoor ride in semidarkness. You sit in a 24-passenger "stretch limo" outfitted with 120 speakers that blare Aerosmith at 32,000 watts! Flashing lights deliver a variety of messages and warnings, including "Prepare to merge as you've never merged before." Then, faster than you can scream "I want to live!" (2.8 sec., actually), you shoot from 0 to 60 mph and into the first gut-tightening inversion at 5Gs. It's a real launch (sometimes of lunch), followed by a wild ride through a make-believe California freeway system. One of three inversions cuts through an O in the Hollywood sign. The ride lasts 3 minutes, 12 seconds—the running time of Aerosmith's hit "Sweet Emotion." ***Note:*** Riders must be at least 48 inches tall. Expectant moms, people prone to motion sickness, and those with heart, neck, or back problems shouldn't try this ride.

   Nicolas's Rating: "Wow!" That was the last thing he said as he headed back to the end of the line.

Sounds Dangerous–Starring Drew Carey

Frommer's Rating: C+
Recommended Ages: All ages

Drew Carey provides laughs while dual audio technology provides some hair-raising effects during this 12-minute show at ABC Sound Studios. You'll feel like you're right in the middle of the action of a TV pilot featuring undercover police work and plenty of mishaps. Even when the picture disappears, and the theater is plunged into darkness, you continue on Detective Charlie Foster's chase via headphones that show off "3-D" sound effects. Most of this attraction takes place in total darkness, which will likely disturb young kids.

Tip: After the show is over, check out **Sound Works,** which offers interactive activities that allow you and your kids to experiment with different sound effects.

Star Tours
Frommer's Rating: B+
Recommended Ages: 8–adult

Cutting-edge when it opened, this galactic journey, based on the original *Star Wars* trilogy (George Lucas collaborated on the ride), is now a couple of rungs below the latest technology but is still fun. The preshow, which should eventually be updated with characters from *Episode II: Attack of the Clones,* now has R2-D2 and C-3PO running an intergalactic travel agency (it offers some of the best detailing of any preshow at Disney World). Once inside, you board a 40-seat spacecraft for a journey that greets you with sudden drops, crashes, and oncoming laser blasts as it careens out of control. This is another of those virtual-simulator rides where you go nowhere, but feel like you do. If you or your kids have sensitive stomachs, try to ride up front, where you won't get tossed around as much. *Note:* Riders must be at least 40 inches tall. Expectant mothers, those prone to motion sickness, and people with neck, back, and heart problems shouldn't ride.

Tip: The **Jedi Training Academy,** a popular interactive event normally held only during Star Wars Weekends, is now part of the permanent lineup at Disney's Hollywood Studios. Check the park's *Times Guide* for showtimes.

The Twilight Zone Tower of Terror *(Moments*
Frommer's Rating: A+
Recommended Ages: 10–adult

This is a truly stomach-lifting (and dropping) ride, and Disney continues to fine-tune it to make it even better: A 2003 upgrade added random drop sequences with individual features, meaning that you might get a different fright from ride to ride. The legend says that during a violent storm on Halloween night of 1939, lightning struck the Hollywood Tower Hotel, causing an entire wing and an elevator full of people to

---

Moments You Want Characters?

Characters and hot spots change, but as of this writing, the best bets at Disney's Hollywood Studios are the following (see the handout *Times Guide* for exact schedules and lineups):

Cars: Near Sounds Dangerous–Starring Drew Carey.

The Incredibles: Near the Magic of Disney Animation.

Mickey Mouse, JoJo's Circus Friends & Kim Possible: Mickey Avenue between the Backlot Tour and Toy Story Mania!

Monsters, Inc.: On Commissary Lane.

Power Rangers: On the Streets of America.

Toy Story Friends: At Al's Toy Barn.

disappear. And you're about to meet them as you become the star in a special episode of . . . *The Twilight Zone.* En route to this formerly grand hotel, guests walk past overgrown landscaping and faded signs that once pointed the way to stables and tennis courts; the vines over the entrance trellis are dead; and the hotel is a crumbling ruin (it's some of Disney's best theme work). Eerie corridors lead to a dimly lit library, where you can hear a storm raging outside. After various spooky adventures, the ride ends in a dramatic climax: a 13-story free fall in stages. Some believe this rivals Rock 'n' Roller Coaster in the thrill department (one of the Imagineers who helped design the tower admitted that he's too scared to ride his own creation). At 199 feet, it's the tallest ride in the World, and it's a grade above Doctor Doom's Fearfall at Islands of Adventure. *Note:* You must be at least 40 inches tall to ride. Expectant moms, people prone to motion sickness, and those with heart, neck, or back problems shouldn't try to tackle it. If you're scared of heights or darkness, this one isn't for you, either. ***And one final amusing tidbit:*** If you decide to back out before taking the plunge, there is an escape route from the hotel—via an elevator.

Austin's Rating: "Wow! This is definitely the best ride at Disney!" This one definitely impressed Austin—he headed back five times in a row. **Ryan's Rating:** In contrast, Ryan wouldn't go within 10 feet of this one.

Voyage of the Little Mermaid
Frommer's Rating: B+
Recommended Ages: 4–adult

Hazy lighting creates an underwater effect in a reef-walled theater and helps set the mood for this musical based on the Disney feature film, which charms even older kids and adults. The show combines live performers with more than 100 puppets, movie clips, and innovative special effects. Sebastian sings the movie's Academy Award–winning song, "Under the Sea"; the ethereal Ariel shares her dream of becoming human in a live performance of "Part of Your World"; and the evil Ursula, 12 feet tall and 10 feet wide, belts out "Poor Unfortunate Soul." It has a happy ending, as most of the young audience knows it will; they've seen the movie. This 17-minute show is a great place to rest your feet on a hot day, and you get misted inside the theater to further cool you off.

PARADES, PLAYGROUNDS & MORE
Disney's **Block Party Bash** (replacing the Disney Stars and Motor Cars Parade) is an interactive dance party/parade through the streets. Guests are invited to sing and dance along to the retro-style tunes playing throughout the park's streets as high-flying acrobats dazzle and amaze those watching from below. Fan favorites from Disney-Pixar flicks including *Finding Nemo, Toy Story 2, Monsters, Inc., The Incredibles, A Bug's Life,* and others all join in on the family-style fun. The parade is popular enough that if you decide to skip it, you'll find shorter lines at the park's primo rides (check the parade schedule in your park map).

6 Disney's Animal Kingdom

Disney's fourth major park opened in 1998 and combines exotic animals, the elaborate landscapes of Asia and Africa, and the prehistoric lands of the dinosaur. Animals, architecture, and lush surroundings take center stage here, with a handful of rides thrown in for good measure.

Although it's 500 acres, the park can easily be toured in a single day, usually less. A conservation venue as much as an attraction, you won't find animals blatantly

Disney's Animal Kingdom

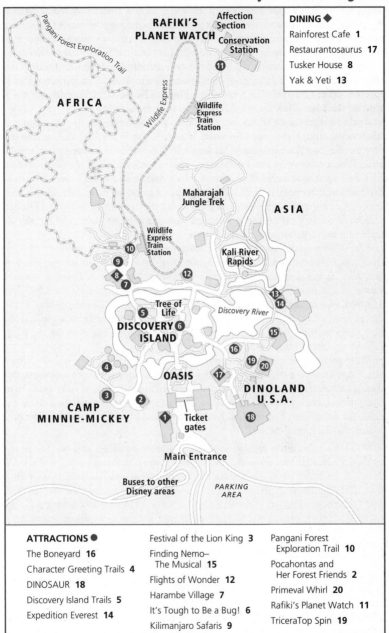

DINING ◆
Rainforest Cafe **1**
Restaurantosaurus **17**
Tusker House **8**
Yak & Yeti **13**

AFRICA

RAFIKI'S PLANET WATCH

Affection Section

Conservation Station **11**

Pangani Forest Exploration Trail

Wildlife Express

Wildlife Express Train Station

Maharajah Jungle Trek

ASIA

Wildlife Express Train Station

Kali River Rapids

10
9
8
7
12
13
14

Tree of Life

Discovery River

5
DISCOVERY **6**
ISLAND

15

16
19 **20**
17

OASIS

DINOLAND U.S.A.

4

3
2

CAMP MINNIE-MICKEY

1 Ticket gates

18

Main Entrance

Buses to other Disney areas

PARKING AREA

ATTRACTIONS ●
The Boneyard **16**
Character Greeting Trails **4**
DINOSAUR **18**
Discovery Island Trails **5**
Expedition Everest **14**

Festival of the Lion King **3**
Finding Nemo– The Musical **15**
Flights of Wonder **12**
Harambe Village **7**
It's Tough to Be a Bug! **6**
Kilimanjaro Safaris **9**

Pangani Forest Exploration Trail **10**
Pocahontas and Her Forest Friends **2**
Primeval Whirl **20**
Rafiki's Planet Watch **11**
TriceraTop Spin **19**

displayed throughout the park as in other venues such as **Busch Gardens Tampa Bay** (p. 341). Animal habitats at Disney's Animal Kingdom are re-created in a natural manner, which unfortunately means that at times, you'll have to search a bit to find the wildlife. Most of the animals can be found around the Kilimanjaro Safari and the Pangani Forest Exploration Trail. The exotic animal theme does, however, carry throughout the park in its rides, shows, and architecture. As an added bonus, the best shows in all of Disney can be found here: **Finding Nemo–The Musical** and the **Festival of the Lion King** should definitely be on your to-do list.

Animal Kingdom is divided into the **Oasis,** a shopping area near the entrance that has limited animal viewing; **Discovery Island,** home of the Tree of Life, the park's very unique icon; **Camp Minnie-Mickey,** which is mainly a character meet-and-greet area; **Africa,** where you can wander the village streets and head out on safari (you'll find the largest concentration of animals here); **Asia,** with Mount Everest looming on the horizon (the newest thrill ride in the park), a raging river ride, exotic animal exhibits (including Bengal tigers and giant fruit bats), and a bird show; and **Dinoland U.S.A.,** filled with carnival-style rides and games, a large play area, and a herky-jerky thrill ride that transports you back in time.

The 145-foot-tall **Tree of Life** is in the center of the park. It's an intricately carved free-form representation of animals, handcrafted by a team of artists over the period of a year. It's not nearly as tall or imposing as Spaceship Earth at Epcot or Cinderella Castle in the Magic Kingdom. The tree is impressive, though, with 8,000 limbs; 103,000 leaves; and 325 mammals, reptiles, bugs, birds, dinosaurs, and Mickeys carved in its trunk, limbs, and roots. (One cool game to play with young kids is to see how many animals they can find represented in the trunk.) For more on the tree, see "Discovery Island Trails," below.

Note: Most of the rides are accessible to guests with disabilities, but the hilly terrain, large crowds, narrow passages, and long hikes can make for a strenuous day if there's a wheelchair user in your party or you're schlepping lots of baby gear. Anyone with neck or back problems, as well as pregnant women, may not be able to enjoy rides like Expedition Everest, Kali River Rapids, and Dinosaur (even the Kilimanjaro Safaris may be questionable).

ARRIVING From the parking lot, walk or (where available) ride one of the trams to the entrance. If you do walk, watch out for the trams and autos, as the lot isn't designed for pedestrians. Also, make certain to note where you parked (section and row). Lot signs aren't as prominent as in the Magic Kingdom, and the rows look alike when you come back out; I've gotten a bit confused on more than one occasion. Upon entering the park, consult the handout guide map for special events or entertainment. If you have questions, ask park staffers.

HOURS Disney's Animal Kingdom is open at least from 8 or 9am to 5pm, but it sometimes stays open an hour or so later.

TICKET PRICES The ticket prices are $71 for adults and $60 for children 3 to 9. See "Tickets & Passes," earlier in this chapter, for information on multiday options.

SERVICES & FACILITIES IN DISNEY'S ANIMAL KINGDOM

ATMs Animal Kingdom has an ATM near Garden Gate Gifts to the right of the entrance as well as in Dinoland across from the Primeval Whirl. It accepts cards from banks using the Cirrus, Honor, and PLUS systems.

> **Tips Animal Kingdom Tip Sheet**
>
> 1. Arrive at the park's opening, or stay until near closing for the best view of the animals.
> 2. **Kilimanjaro Safaris** is one of the most popular rides and the best place to see a lot of animals in one sitting. But in summer, the animals can be scarce except near park opening and closing times. If you can hoof it there first thing, do so. If not, try late in the day. The same applies to viewing the gorillas on the **Pangani Forest Exploration Trail.**
> 3. **Finding Nemo–The Musical** and the **Festival of the Lion King** shows are a must.
> 4. Looking for Disney characters? Head for the Character Greeting Trails in **Camp Minnie-Mickey.**

Baby Care   The Baby Care Center is located near Creature Comforts gift shop on the west side of the Tree of Life, but as in the other Disney parks, you'll find changing tables in both women's and men's restrooms. You can buy disposable diapers at Guest Relations.

Cameras & Film   You can drop film off for same-day developing at the Kodak Kiosk in Africa or Garden Gate Gifts near the park entrances. Cameras and film are available in Disney Outfitters in Safari Village; at the Kodak Kiosk in Africa, near the entrance to the Kilimanjaro Safari; and in Garden Gate Gifts.

First Aid   It's located near the Creature Comforts gift shop, on the west side of the Tree of Life, and staffed by registered nurses.

Lockers   Lockers ($5, plus a $2 deposit) are located in Garden Gate Gifts to your right as you enter the park. They're also located to the left, near the Rainforest Cafe.

Lost Children   A center for lost children is near Creature Comforts at the Baby Care Center on the west side of the Tree of Life. At the risk of rehashing, *make your younger kids wear name tags* inside their clothing.

Package Pickup   Purchases can be sent to the front of the park at Garden Gate Gifts. Allow 3 hours for delivery.

Parking   The cost is $11 a day for cars, light trucks, and vans, and $12 for RVs.

Pet Care   Pet facilities are located outside the park entrance ($10 per day; ✆ **407/ 824-6568**). There are four other kennels located in the WDW complex. Proof of vaccination is required.

Stroller Rental   Stroller rentals are available at Garden Gate Gifts to the right as you enter the park ($10 for a single, $18 for a double; discounts available for length-of-stay rentals). There are also satellite locations deeper into the park; ask a Disney employee to steer you in the right direction.

Wheelchair Rental   You can rent wheelchairs at Garden Gate Gifts, to the right as you enter the park. Rentals are $10 for a standard wheelchair and $35 for an electric wheelchair, plus a $5 refundable deposit. Ask Disney employees for other rental locations scattered throughout the park.

Tips **Dehydration Alert!**

Disney's Animal Kingdom can get very hot, especially during summer. Bring bottled water (unless you want to pay 2½ times the free-world price), and get refills at fountains inside the park. Don't forget sunscreen and wide-brimmed hats *for the whole family,* and plan to ride Kali River Rapids during the hottest part of the day (bring a change of clothes as well, because you'll likely get soaked).

THE OASIS

This painstakingly designed landscape of streams, grottoes, and miniwaterfalls sets the tone for the rest of the park. This is a good place to see wallabies, tiny deer, giant anteaters, sloths, iguanas, tree kangaroos, otters, and macaws (*if,* as I remind you ad nauseum, you get here early or stay late). But thick cover provides a jungle tone and sometimes makes seeing the animals difficult. There are no rides in this area, and aside from the animals, it's mainly a pass-through zone. Those guests traveling with eager children will probably have more time to enjoy these exhibits on the way out—if everyone isn't too pooped.

DISCOVERY ISLAND

Like Cinderella Castle in the Magic Kingdom and Spaceship Earth in Epcot, the 14-story **Tree of Life** located here has been designed to be the park's central landmark. The man-made tree and its carved animals are the work of Disney artists, who spent a full year creating the various sculptures. It's worth a stroll on the walks around its roots, but most folks are smart to save it for the end of the day. (Much of it can be seen while you're in line for **It's Tough to Be a Bug!** or on the **Discovery Island Trails.**) The intricate design makes it seem as though a different animal appears from every angle. One of the creators says he expects it to become one of the most-photographed works of art in the world. (He's probably a Disney shareholder.) There's a wading pond directly in front of the tree that often has flamingos.

Discovery Island Trails
Frommer's Rating: B
Recommended Ages: All ages
The old, pre-FASTPASS queue for It's Tough to Be a Bug! provides a leisurely path through the root system of the Tree of Life and a chance to see real, not-so-rare critters, such as axis deer, red kangaroos, otters, flamingos, lemurs, Galapagos tortoises, ducks, storks, and cockatoos. Again, the best viewing times are early or late in the day.

It's Tough to Be a Bug!
Frommer's Rating: A, C for young ones scared silly from sensory effects
Recommended Ages: 5–adult
This show's cuteness quotient is enough to earn it a B+. But it goes a rung higher thanks to the preshow: To get to the theater, you have to wind around the Tree of Life's 50-foot base, giving you a front-row look at this man-made marvel. After you've passed that, grab your 3-D glasses and settle into a sometimes-creepy-crawly seat. Based on the film *A Bug's Life,* the special effects in this multimedia show are pretty impressive. It's *not a good one for very young kids* (it's dark and loud, and I've even seen 6- and 7-year-olds reduced to hysteria by the effects) or bug haters of any age, but for

others, it's a fun, sometimes poignant look at life from a smaller perspective. Flick, Hopper, and the rest of the cast—ants, beetles, and spiders—literally deliver some in-your-face action. And the show's finale always leaves the crowd buzzing.

DINOLAND U.S.A.

Enter by passing under Olden Gate Bridge, a 40-foot brachiosaurus reassembled from excavated fossils. Speaking of which, until late summer 1999, this land had three pale-ontologists working on the very real skeleton of Sue, a monstrously big *Tyrannosaurus rex* unearthed 9 years earlier in the Black Hills of South Dakota. They patched and assembled the bones here because Disney helped pay for the work. Alas, Sue's perma-nent home is at Chicago's Field Museum, but Dinoland U.S.A. has a replica cast from her 67-million-year-old bones. It's marked as **Dino-Sue** on park guide maps.

The Boneyard
Frommer's Rating: B
Recommended Ages: All ages

The Boneyard is a great place for parents to catch a second wind. Kids absolutely love the prehistoric playground, where they can discover the life-like remains of triceratops, T. rex, and other vanished giants. They can slide and climb over a paleontological dig site and squeeze through the fossils and skeletons of a triceratops and a brontosaurus. They can even search the sands for skeletal remains and play music on a "xylobone." There are plenty of unique activities to keep them quite occupied.

Note: Although the Boneyard is contained within a latticework of metal bars and netting, you still have to be vigilant about keeping track of your kids here. It's a large area, and although Disney staff monitors them at both ends, kids play in a multilevel arena where tube slides can take them from one level to the next in a heartbeat. *Tip:* The later in the afternoon, the hotter this area can get. Make sure the kids keep hydrated with plenty of cold water.

DINOSAUR
Frommer's Rating: B
Recommended Ages: 8–adult

This ride hurls you through the darkness in CTX Rover "time machines" back to the era when dinosaurs ruled the Earth. The expedition takes you past an array of snarling and particularly ferocious-looking dinosaurs, one of which decides you would make a great munchie. What started out as a journey back through time becomes a race to escape the jaws of an irritated and rather ugly Carnotaurus. Young children may find the large lizards and the darkness a bit frightening, and the ride a bit jarring. *Note:* You must be 40 inches or taller to climb aboard. Expectant mothers, those prone to motion sickness, and people with neck, back, and heart problems shouldn't ride.

Tips Pin Mania

Pin buying, collecting, and trading can reach frenzied proportions among Dis-ney fans, including many cast members. All of the theme parks have special locations set aside for the fun—they're marked on the handout guide maps. You can learn more about the madness (and the rules of pin-trading etiquette) at **www.dizpins.com** and **www.officialdisneypintrading.com**.

Fun Fact Did You Know?

Tobacco products aren't the only things unavailable in the theme parks. You can't buy chewing or bubble gum, either. It seems that too many guests stuck it under tables, benches, and chairs—or tossed it on sidewalks, where it often hitched a ride on the soles of the unsuspecting.

Ryan's Rating: "That was pretty cool. I liked all the bumps, but we look really goofy in that photo." If you have the presence of mind to smile (or even pretend to be frightened) when you hear the T. rex roar, your souvenir photo (it's snapped on the sly) will look a lot better. The cost of one: Ouch! ($18 for an 8×10). *Tip:* Using Disney's Photopass will alleviate the trouble of carrying it around all day.

Primeval Whirl
Frommer's Rating: B+
Recommended Ages: 8–adult
Disney introduced this spinning, freestyle twin roller coaster in 2002 in an effort to broaden the park's appeal to young kids (odd, as this ride has a pretty tall height minimum). You control the action through its wacky maze of curves, peaks, and dippity-do-dahs, encountering faux asteroids and hokey cutouts of dinosaurs. This is a cross between those old carnival coasters of the '50s and '60s, and a more daring version of **The Barnstormer at Goofy's Wiseacre Farm** (p. 202). *Note:* The ride carries a 48-inch height minimum. Expectant moms, as well as those with neck, back, or heart problems and folks prone to motion sickness, should stay planted on firm ground.

TriceraTop Spin
Frommer's Rating: B+ for tykes and parents
Recommended Ages: 2–7
Cut from the same cloth as the **Magic Carpets of Aladdin** (p. 192), this is another minithrill for youngsters (and another ride with long lines). In this case, cars that look like cartoon dinosaurs are attached to arms that circle a hub while moving up and down and all around. This ride, Primeval Whirl, and an arcade-game area make up a Dinoland U.S.A. mini land called Chester & Hester's Dino-Rama. It's a great spot to take little ones.

CAMP MINNIE-MICKEY
Disney characters are the main attraction in this land, designed in the same vein as an Adirondack resort. Aside from those characters, however, this zone for the younger set *isn't as kid-friendly* as rivals **Mickey's Toontown Fair in the Magic Kingdom** (p. 202) or **Woody Woodpecker's KidZone** in Universal Studios Florida (p. 268).

Character Greeting Trails *Moments*
Frommer's Rating: A for younger kids, D for waiting parents
Recommended Ages: 2–8
Some say this is a must-do for people traveling with children; I say run the other way—quickly. If, however, your kids are hooked on getting every character autograph possible, this is the place to go. A variety of Disney characters, from Winnie the Pooh and Pocahontas to Timon and Baloo, have separate trails where you can meet and mingle, snap photos, and get those autographs. Mickey, Minnie, Goofy, and Pluto

even make periodic appearances. Be aware, however, that the lines for these meet-and-greet opportunities are at times excruciatingly long, so unless your kids are really gung-ho on collecting the characters' signatures, don't even think of coming here.

Festival of the Lion King *Finds*
Frommer's Rating: A+
Recommended Ages: All ages

Almost everyone in the audience comes alive when the music starts in this rousing 28-minute show in the Lion King Theater. It's one of the top three theme-park shows in Central Florida, and it thrills young and old alike. The production celebrates nature's diversity with a talented, colorfully attired cast of singers, dancers, and life-size critters leading the way to an inspiring singalong that gets the entire audience caught up in the fun. Based loosely on the animated film, this show blends the pageantry of a parade with a tribal celebration. The action takes place both on stage and around the audience. Even though the pavilion has 1,000 seats, it's best to arrive at least 20 minutes early.

Pocahontas and Her Forest Friends
Frommer's Rating: C
Recommended Ages: All ages

The wait can be nightmarish, and the 15-minute show isn't close to the caliber of Festival of the Lion King. In this one, Pocahontas, Grandmother Willow, and some forest creatures (a raccoon, turkey, porcupine, snake, and some rats) hammer home the importance of treating nature with respect. If you must, go early. The theater has only 350 seats, but it allows standing-room crowds.

AFRICA

Enter through the town of Harambe, a worn and weathered African coastal village poised on the edge of the 21st century. (It actually took a great deal of effort to create the run-down appearance.) Costumed employees will greet you as you enter the buildings. The whitewashed structures, built of coral stone and thatched with reed by African craftspeople, surround a central marketplace rich with local wares and colors.

Kilimanjaro Safaris
Frommer's Rating: A+ early or late, B+ other times
Recommended Ages: All ages

Disney's Animal Kingdom doesn't have an abundance of rides, but the animals you'll see on this one make it a winner as long as your timing is right; they're scarce at midday during most times of year (cooler months the exception), so I recommend that you ride as close to park opening or closing as possible. If you don't make it in time for one of the first or last journeys, the lines can be horrific, so a FASTPASS may be in order.

A large, rugged truck takes you through the African landscape (though just a few years ago, it was a cow pasture). The animals usually spotted along the way include giraffe, black rhinos, hippos, antelopes, Nile crocodiles, zebras, wildebeests, cheetahs, and a pair of lions that may offer half-hearted roars toward some gazelles that are safely out of reach. Early on, a shifting bridge gives riders a brief thrill; later, there's a bit of drama (a la Disney) as you help catch some poachers. While everyone has a good view, photographers may get a few more shots when sitting on the left side of their row.

Hailey's Rating: "Where'd they all go?" An afternoon safari ride on a summer day has its disadvantages, but my kids are far from early risers. **Davis's Rating:** Davis, on the other hand, was thrilled as several giraffe came practically within arm's length.

Pangani Forest Exploration Trail *(Finds*

Frommer's Rating: B+, A if you're lucky enough to see the gorillas

Recommended Ages: All ages

The hippos put on quite a display (and draw a riotous crowd reaction) when they do what comes naturally and use their tails to scatter it over everything above and below the surface. There are other animals here, including ever-active mole rats, but the **lowland gorillas** are the main event. The trail has two gorilla-viewing areas: One sports a family, including a 500-pound silverback, his ladies, and his children; the other has bachelors. Guests who are unaware of the treasures that lie herein often skip or rush through it, missing a chance to see the magnificent creatures. That said, they're not always cooperative, especially in hot weather, when they spend most of the day in shady areas out of view. There's also an **Endangered Animal Rehabilitation Center** with Colobus and Mona monkeys. Most children are usually delighted if they catch a glimpse of the playful meerkats, which young kids will recognize as the models for Timon in *The Lion King*. *Note:* The walk and frequent dearth of animal sightings can make this the wrong choice for families with restless little ones.

Rafiki's Planet Watch *(Overrated*

Frommer's Rating: C

Recommended Ages: All ages

This land, located just above Africa and accessible only by boarding the open-sided train (the Wildlife Express; the station is located near Pangani Forest Exploration Trail), includes **Conservation Station,** which offers a behind-the-scenes look at how Disney cares for animals inside the park as you walk past a series of nurseries and veterinary stations. The problem is that these facilities need staff members present to make them interesting, and that isn't always the case. **Affection Section** gives you a chance to cuddle some friendly animals (including goats and potbellied pigs but not much more), while **Habitat Habit!** has a trail that's home to some smaller animals, such as cotton-topped tamarins. *Note:* Take heed of the signs in the Affection Section that instruct you to put all paper, including maps, away. Goats love paper and will cause a stampede in an attempt to snatch your paper products from you.

ASIA

Disney's Imagineers completely outdid themselves when creating the mythical kingdom of Anandapur (place of delight). The exotic atmosphere is further enhanced by the crumbling ruins of an ancient village, its temples, streaming prayer flags, and even a maharajah's palace, all decorated with intricate and ornate carvings and artwork.

Expedition Everest–Legend of the Forbidden Mountain

Frommer's Rating: A+

Recommended Ages: 8–adult

Your journey begins in the mythical Himalayan village of Serka Zong, where guests board the Anandapur Rail Service for a seemingly casual trek to the snowcapped peak of Mount Everest (and one of Florida's highest peaks). Upon departing, you'll pass dense bamboo forests, glacier fields, and thundering waterfalls as the train ascends higher and higher to the top of the mountain. But your journey will quickly get off track (almost literally), suddenly becoming an out-of-control high-speed train ride that sends you careening along rough and rugged terrain, the cars hitting tracks that are mangled and twisted, moving backward and forward along icy mountain ledges and through darkened caverns—only to end up in a confrontation with the legendary

Yeti, guardian and protector of the mysterious mountain. Our adrenaline is racing already.

Touted as a family thrill ride, don't be fooled—it packs quite a punch. The feeling that you may plummet down the side of the mountain as you hit the tangled and severed tracks before suddenly thrusting backward into the darkness . . . yikes! This ride is more intense than **Big Thunder Mountain Railroad** in the Magic Kingdom (p. 195), but a step or two down from the twists, turns, loops, and inversions of the **Rock 'n' Roller Coaster** at Disney's Hollywood Studios (p. 234).

Note: The meticulous and painstaking detail is some of the most impressive in all of WDW. Prayer flags are strung between the aged and distressed buildings, while intricately carved totems, stone carvings, and some 2,000 authentic handcrafted Asian objects are scattered throughout the village.

Nicolas's Rating: "Wow! We were staring straight down the mountain—for a second I thought we were really going to fall right off." This comes from a true coaster crazy, and this ride's at the top of his list of favorites. **Ryan's Rating:** "No way, you're not getting me on that!"—especially after watching (and hearing the screams) from below.

Flights of Wonder
Frommer's Rating: B
Recommended Ages: All ages

This live-animal action show has undergone several transformations since the park opened. It's a low-key break from the madness and has a few laughs, including Groucho the African yellow-nape, which entertains the audience with op-*parrot*-ic a cappella solos, and the just-above-your-head soaring of a Harris hawk and a Eurasian eagle owl. To entertain guests waiting in line for the show to begin, trainers often bring out an owl or hawk, allowing for an up-close look and the opportunity to learn about the stars of the show. Young kids will especially enjoy it; parents will appreciate the brief reprieve from walking.

Kali River Rapids
Frommer's Rating: B+
Recommended Ages: 6–adult

Its churning water mimics real rapids, and optical illusions have you wondering whether you're about to go over the falls. The ride begins with a peaceful tour of lush

---

Moments Finding Nemo, Take 2

Making a splashy debut in 2007, **Finding Nemo–The Musical** is, in a word, enchanting. In this visually stunning undersea production ("re-imagined" as a musical), Nemo, Marlin, Dory, Crush, and Bruce come to life before your eyes as live actors work in combination with spectacular puppet-like costumes to recreate the adventure made popular by the Disney-Pixar film. The story line, for those who don't already know it, has the ever-curious Nemo becoming separated from his overly protective father, who then goes to great lengths traveling through the big blue to be reunited with his son. Spectacular special effects and a moving musical score complete and complement the experience. Even the squirmiest toddler will sit mesmerized through this 30-minute show—it's a must-see for the entire family.

foliage, but soon you're dipping and dripping as your tiny craft is tossed and turned. You *will* get wet—just how wet depends on where you're seated. (Bring a plastic garbage bag for your valuables or store them in a locker before riding. The rafts' center storage areas, while helpful, likely won't keep them dry.) The lines can be long, but keep your head up and take in the magnificent artwork overhead and on the spectacular murals. *Note:* There's a 38-inch height minimum. Expectant moms, people prone to motion sickness, and those with neck, back, and heart problems shouldn't ride it.

Ryan's and **Nicolas's Rating:** "Wow, the water is *c-c-c-cold!* But the ride is a blast." The experience was made better, post-ride, when he and his brothers manned the water cannons near the exit and fired at other raft riders (yet another reason you'll emerge soaked after this one). **Austin's Rating:** He thought it a bit tame by comparison—he preferred the wilder ride on **Popeye & Bluto's Bilge-Rat Barges** at Islands of Adventure (p. 280), but enjoyed it nonetheless.

Maharajah Jungle Trek
Frommer's Rating: B
Recommended Ages: 6–adults

Disney keeps its promise to provide up-close views of animals with this exhibit, the setting of which is almost an attraction in its own right. Lush tropical foliage and bamboo grow amidst the ruins, architecture, and carvings of Nepal, India, Thailand, and Indonesia. It's some of Disney's best thematic work. If you don't show up in the midday heat, you may see Bengal tigers through a wall of thick glass, while nothing but air separates you from dozens of giant fruit bats hanging in what appears to be a courtyard. Some have wingspans of 6 feet. (If you or your kids have a phobia, you can bypass this, though the bats are harmless.) There are lots of spots for your kids to get good views of the animals. Guides are on hand to answer questions, and you can also check a brochure that lists the animals you may spot; it's available on your right as you enter. You'll be asked to turn it back in as you exit.

PARADES
Mickey's Jammin' Jungle Parade at Disney's Animal Kingdom is an interactive street party featuring whimsical, colorful animals and characters on expedition. The music and overall atmosphere are lively, and the one-of-a-kind visuals are some of the best in all of the parks.

7 Disney Water Parks

Walt Disney World has two renowned water parks where guests can retreat to cool off: **Typhoon Lagoon** and **Blizzard Beach.** Attracting well over 50 million people since they opened, both offer a slate of cool rides and slides, swimming areas, and plenty for pint-sized park-goers, too.

Tips Closed for the Winter

Both Disney water parks are refurbished on a rotating basis for a month or more each winter. So if a water park is on your itinerary, check the schedules in advance.

All of the attractions mentioned in this section can be found on the "Walt Disney World Parks & Attractions" map (p. 177).

TYPHOON LAGOON ✯✯✯

Ahoy swimmers, floaters, run-aground boaters!

A furious storm once roared 'cross the sea

Catching ships in its path, helpless to flee . . .

Instead of a certain and watery doom

The winds swept them here to TYPHOON LAGOON.

Such is the Disney legend relating to Typhoon Lagoon, which you'll see posted on consecutive signs as you enter the park. Located off Buena Vista Drive between the Downtown Disney Marketplace and Disney's Hollywood Studios, this is the ultimate in water-theme parks. Its fantasy setting is a palm-fringed island village of ramshackle, tin-roofed structures, strewn with cargo, surfboards, and other marine wreckage left by the "great typhoon." A storm-stranded fishing boat (the *Miss Tilly*) dangles precariously atop 95-foot Mount Mayday, the steep setting for several attractions. Every half-hour, the boat's smokestack erupts, shooting a 50-foot geyser of water into the air.

ESSENTIALS

HOURS The park is open daily from at least 10am to 5pm, with extended hours during some holiday periods and summer (© **407/560-4141;** www.disneyworld.com).

ENTRANCE FEES A 1-day ticket to Typhoon Lagoon is $39 for adults and $33 for kids 3 to 9, plus 6.5% tax. See p. 176 for details on packages that include admission to several WDW attractions.

HELPFUL HINTS In summer, arrive no later than 9am to avoid long lines. The park is often filled to capacity by 10am and then is closed to later arrivals. Beach towels ($2) and lockers ($5 and $8) can be rented, and beachwear can be purchased at **Singapore Sal's.** Light fare is available at two eateries: **Leaning Palms** and **Typhoon Tilly's.** A beach bar called **Let's Go Slurpin'** sells beer and soft drinks. There are picnic tables (consider bringing picnic fare; you can keep it in your locker until lunch). Guests aren't permitted to bring their own flotation devices, and glass bottles are prohibited.

ATTRACTIONS IN THE PARK
Castaway Creek
Hop onto a raft or an inner tube, and meander along this 2,100-foot lazy river that circles most of the park. It tumbles through a misty rainforest, by caves and secluded grottoes, and on into the sunshine, all the while passing along some of Disney's meticulously maintained tropical foliage. Tubes are included in the admission price.

Crush 'n' Gusher
The newest thrill to splash onto the scene is a first-of-its-kind water coaster, featuring three separate experiences to choose from. The **Banana Blaster, Coconut Crusher,** and **Pineapple Plunger** offer steep drops, twists, and turns of varying degrees as you're sent careening through an old rusted-out fruit factory. Intense jets of water actually propel riders back uphill at one point. *Note:* This ride carries a 48-inch height requirement.

Ketchakiddee Creek

Many of the park's other attractions require guests to be older children, teens, or adults, but this section is a kiddie area *exclusively for 2- to 5-year-olds* (under 48 in. tall). An innovative water playground, it has bubbling fountains to frolic in, mini–water slides, a pint-size "whitewater" tubing run, spouting whales and squirting seals, rubbery crocodiles to climb on, grottoes to explore, and waterfalls to loll under. It's also small enough for you to take good home videos or photographs.

Shark Reef

Guests are given free equipment (and instruction) for a 15-minute swim through this very small snorkeling area, which includes a simulated coral reef populated by about 4,000 parrotfish, angelfish, yellowtail damselfish, and other cuties, including small rays and sharks. If you don't want to get in, you can observe the fish via portholes in a walk-through viewing area.

Surf Pool *Moments*

This large (2.75-million gal.) and lovely lagoon is the size of two football fields and is surrounded by a white sandy beach. It's the park's main swimming area. The chlorinated water has a turquoise hue much like the Caribbean. **Large waves** (about 6 ft.) roll through the deeper areas every 90 seconds; a foghorn sounds to warn you when one is coming. Young children can wade in the lagoon's more peaceful tidal pools— **Blustery Bay** or **Whitecap Cove**—but don't let little ones near the main pool without direct supervision, as a wave can easily knock a child over. The lagoon is also home to a special weekly **surfing program** (p. 306).

Nicolas's, Austin's, and **Ryan's Rating:** "I'm not getting out!" (Well, they did, but not without a fuss. If your kids love the water, you may have the same problem.)

Water Slides

Humunga Kowabunga consists of three 214-foot Mount Mayday slides that propel you down the mountain on a serpentine route through waterfalls and bat caves and past nautical wreckage before depositing you in a bubbling catch pool; each offers slightly different views and 30-mph thrills. There's seating for non-Kowabunga folks whose braver kids have commissioned them to "Watch me." *Note:* You must be 48 inches or taller to ride this. **Storm Slides** offers a tamer course through the park's manmade caves. Kids not quite ready for the bigger slides (and those under 60 in. tall) can catch a mini-thrill body sliding on the **Bay Slides.**

Whitewater Rides

Mount Mayday is the setting for three whitewater rafting adventures: **Keelhaul Falls, Mayday Falls,** and **Gang Plank Falls,** all offering steep drops coursing through caves and passing lush scenery. Keelhaul Falls has the most winding route, Mayday Falls has the steepest drops and fastest water, and the slightly tamer Gang Plank Falls uses large tubes so that the whole family can pile on.

BLIZZARD BEACH 🎿🎿🎿

Blizzard Beach, arguably the most popular water park in North America, is the younger of Disney's water parks, a 66-acre "ski resort" in the midst of a tropical lagoon centering on the 90-foot, uh-oh, Mount Gushmore. There's a legend for this one as well. Apparently, a freak snowstorm dumped tons of snow on Walt Disney World, leading to the creation of Florida's first—and, so far, only—mountain ski resort (complete with Ice Gator, the park's mascot). Naturally, when temperatures returned to their normal broiling range, the snow bunnies prepared to close up shop, when they

Tips Water Park Dos & Don'ts

1. Go in the afternoon, about 2pm, even in summer, if you can stand the heat that long and want to avoid crowds. The early birds usually are gone by then.

2. If you have to rise with the sun, and you're staying at a WDW resort, and holding a ticket with the Water Parks Fun & More option, take advantage of the Extra Magic Hours and beat the crowds by at least an hour.

3. Go early in the week, when most of the weeklong guests are filling the lines at the theme parks.

4. Kids can get lost just as easily at a water park as at the other parks, and the consequences can be tragic. All Disney parks have lifeguards, usually wearing bright red suits, but to be safe, make yourself the first line of safety for the kids in your crew (children 10 and under must be accompanied by an adult to get into the parks).

5. Women should wear a securely attached one-piece bathing suit (minus the belt buckles, studs, and other doodads) unless they want to put on a show for the rest of the crowd. And all bathers should remember **the "wedgie" rule** on the more extreme rides, such as Summit Plummet (at Blizzard Beach, below). *What's the wedgie rule?* It's a principle of physics that says you may start out wearing baggies, but you'll end up in a thong.

6. Use waterproof sunscreen with an SPF of at least 30 (preferably 50), and drink plenty of fluids. Despite all that water, it's easy to get dehydrated in summer.

realized—this is Disney; happy endings are a must—that what remained of their snow resort could be turned into a water park featuring the fastest and tallest waterlogged "ski" runs in the country. The base of Mount Gushmore has a sand beach with several other attractions, including a wave pool and a smaller version of the mount for younger children. The park is located off World Drive, just north of the All-Star Movies, Music, and Sports resorts.

ESSENTIALS

HOURS   It's open daily from at least 10am to 5pm, with extended hours during holiday periods and summer (© **407/560-3400;** www.disneyworld.com).

ENTRANCE FEES   A 1-day ticket to Blizzard Beach is $39 for adults and $33 for children 3 to 9, plus the 6.5% tax. See p. 176 for details on packages that include admission to several WDW attractions.

HELPFUL HINTS   Arrive at or before opening to avoid long lines and to be sure you get in. Beach towels ($2) and lockers ($5 and $8) are available, and you can buy the beachwear you forgot to bring at the **Beach Haus.** You can grab something to eat at **Avalunch** and **Lottawatta Lodge** (burgers, hot dogs, nachos, pizza, and sandwiches).

MAJOR ATTRACTIONS IN THE PARK

Cross Country Creek

Inner-tubers can float lazily along this park-circling, 2,900-foot creek, but beware of the mysterious cave, where you'll get splashed with melting ice. It's a good ride for the entire family.

Melt-Away Bay

Waterfalls of melting "snow" feed this 1-acre bobbing wave pool, which features relatively calm waves.

Runoff Rapids

Another tube job, this one lets you careen down any of three twisting-turning runs, one of which sends you through darkness.

Ski Patrol Training Camp

Designed for preteens, it features a rope swing, a T-bar drop over water, slides like the wet and slippery **Mogul Mania** from the mount, and a challenging ice-floe walk along slippery floating icebergs. It's a good spot for kids not up to the more adrenaline-pumping slides in the park.

Slush Gusher

This super-speedy slide travels along a snow-banked gully. *Note:* It has a 48-inch height minimum.

Snow Stormers

These three flumes descend from the top of Mount Gushmore and follow a switch-back course through ski-type slalom gates.

Summit Plummet *Moments*

Read *every* speed, motion, vertical-dip, wedgie, and hold-onto-your-breastplate warning in this guide. Then test your bravado in a bullring, a space shuttle, or dozens of other death-defying hobbies as a warmup. This one starts pretty slow, with a lift ride to the 120-foot summit (and it's only one way). Then . . . well . . . kiss any kids or religious medal you may be carrying, because if you board, you *will enter* Disney World's fastest body slide, a test of your courage and swimsuit that virtually goes straight down and has you moving sans vehicle at 60 mph to the catch pool (aka stop zone). *Note:* It has a 48-inch height minimum. Expectant mothers and people with neck, back, and heart problems shouldn't ride.

   Ryan's Rating: "Uh. No way!" (I don't blame him. Even the hardiest rider may find this one hard to handle; a veteran thrill-seeker I know described the experience as "15 seconds of paralyzing fear.")

Teamboat Springs

One of Disney World's longest whitewater raft rides, your six-passenger raft twists down a 1,200-foot series of rushing waterfalls.

Tike's Peak

This kid-size version of Mount Gushmore offers short water slides, rideable animals, a snow castle, a squirting ice pond, and a fountain play area for young guests. If you have kids under 48 inches in height, this is the place to take them.

Toboggan Racers

Here's an eight-lane slide that sends you racing head first over exhilarating dips into a snowy slope. The **Downhill Double Dipper** sends you racing side by side, too, but it (unlike the Toboggan Racers) carries a 48-inch height requirement to ride.

8 Other WDW Attractions

Note: All of the attractions mentioned in this section can be found on the "Walt Disney World Parks & Attractions" map (p. 176).

FANTASIA GARDENS & WINTER SUMMERLAND

Fantasia Gardens Miniature Golf ★★, located off Buena Vista Drive across from Disney's Hollywood Studios, offers two 18-hole miniature courses drawing inspiration from the Walt Disney classic cartoon of the same name. You'll find hippos, ostriches, and alligators on the **Fantasia Gardens** course, where the Sorcerer's Apprentice presides over the final hole. It's a good bet for beginners and kids. Seasoned minigolfers will probably prefer **Fantasia Fairways,** a scaled-down golf course complete with sand traps, water hazards, tricky putting greens, and holes ranging from 40 to 75 feet.

Santa Claus and his elves provide the theme for **Winter Summerland** ★★ (Disney reports that Santa built it as a vacation resort for his off-duty elves), which has two 18-hole miniature golf courses across from Blizzard Beach on Buena Vista Drive. The **Winter** course takes you from an ice castle to a snowman to the North Pole (it's reportedly the easier of the two courses and the best one for young kids and beginners). The **Summer** course is pure Florida, from sandcastles to surfboards to a visit with Santa on the "Winternet."

Tickets at both venues are $11 for adults and $9.05 for children 3 to 9. Both are open daily from 10am to 10 or 11pm. For information, call © **407/560-4582** for Fantasia Gardens, © **407/560-3000** for Winter Summerland. You can find both online at **www.disneyworld.com**.

DISNEY'S WIDE WORLD OF SPORTS

The 200-acre Disney's Wide World of Sports complex has a 7,500-seat professional baseball stadium, 10 other baseball and softball fields, six basketball courts, 12 lighted tennis courts, a track-and-field complex, a golf driving range, and six sand volleyball courts. It's a haven for sports fans and wannabe athletes.

Note: The **Hess Sports Field North** opened in the spring of 2005, the first expansion of the Wide World of Sports venue since its opening in 1997. The addition features 20 acres of playing fields, with space for four football/soccer fields and four baseball/softball diamonds.

The complex is located on Victory Way, just north of U.S. 192 (west of I-4; © **407/939-1500;** www.disneyworldsports.com). It's open daily from 10am to 5pm; the cost is $11 for adults and $8 for kids 3 to 9. Organized programs and events include:

- The **Multi-Sports Experience,** which challenges guests with a variety of activities, covering many sports: football, baseball, basketball, hockey, soccer, and volleyball. It's open on select days.
- The **Atlanta Braves** play 16 spring-training games during a 1-month season that begins in early March. For tickets, which cost $14 to $23, call Ticketmaster (© **407/939-4263**). In addition to the Braves, the facility hosts the **Tampa Bay Buccaneers'** spring training camp.
- The **NFL, NBA, NCAA, PGA,** and **Harlem Globetrotters** also host events at the complex, sometimes annually and sometimes more frequently. Admission varies by event.

(Finds DisneyQuest

The minute you step inside, you'll realize this is no ordinary arcade—throughout the five levels are some of the most cutting-edge games you'll find anywhere. Disney has taken the state-of-the-art technology of virtual reality, added a spirit of adventure, and shaken it all up with some of that magical pixie dust for good measure. The result is the World's most interactive game complex. From kids just old enough to work the controls to jaded teens, reactions to DisneyQuest are pretty much the same: "Awesome!" And although adults may enter the arcade thinking that they're only going to find kids' stuff, many bite the hook as hard as their offspring when they get a gander at the electronic wizardry—everything from old-fashioned pinball with a newfangled twist to virtual-reality adventure rides. Want appetizers?

Aladdin's Magic Carpet Ride puts you astride a motorcycle-type seat and flies through the 3-D Cave of Wonders. **Invasion! An ExtraTERRORestrial Alien Encounter** has the same kind of intensity. Your mission is to save colonists from intergalactic bad guys. One player flies the virtual module, while others fire weapons.

Pirates of the Caribbean: Battle for Buccaneer Gold puts you and three mates in 3-D helmets so that you can battle pirate ships virtual-reality style. One plays captain, steering your ship, while the others assume positions behind cannons to blast the blackhearts into oblivion. Each time you do, you're rewarded with some doubloons, but beware of the sea monsters that can gobble you and your treasure. In the final moments, you come face to face with a ghost ship, which can send you to Davy Jones's Locker.

Songmaker has short lines, perhaps for a reason: It involves karaoke. Step into a phone-booth-size recording studio to make your own CD (the CD costs extra). If you're a pinball fan, try the **Mighty Ducks Pinball Slam,** an interactive life-size game in which you ride platforms and use body English to score points.

If you have an inventive mind, stop by **CyberSpace Mountain** 🎢🎢, where Bill Nye the Science-Turned-Roller-Coaster-Guy helps you create the ultimate loop-and-dipster, which you can then ride in a simulator. It's a major hit with the coaster-crazy crowd.

Finally, if you need some quiet time, sign up at **Animation Academy** for a minicourse in Disney cartooning. There are also snack and food areas for those who need something more tangible than virtual refreshment.

DisneyQuest (✆ **407/828-4600;** www.disneyquest.com) is located in Downtown Disney West Side, on Buena Vista Drive. The admission ($37 for adults, $31 for kids 3–9, plus 6.5% sales tax) allows you unlimited play from 11:30am to 11pm (until midnight Fri–Sat). Unfortunately, heavy crowds tend to gather here after 1pm, which can cut into your fun and patience.

What Kids Like to See & Do Beyond Disney

Younger members of your party may not draw battle lines in so many words, but still, kids may boldly declare they like one ride, show, or theme park far better than another.

Veteran vacationers call it the Great Theme-Park War—the ongoing, "anything-you-can-do-we-can-do-better," knock-down-drag-out battle between the Magic Mouse and top-ranked challenger Universal Orlando, which each year since 1999 has chipped away at what was once Walt Disney World's virtual monopoly. Still, make no mistake: Disney is king, leading in theme parks (4–2) and smaller attractions (9–1). It has a two-to-one edge in nightclub venues, a huge lead in restaurants, and, when it comes to hotel rooms, its lead is simply insurmountable.

Nevertheless, Universal is making a stand. Its substantial growth spurt in 1999 bolstered its original theme park, **Universal Studios Florida (USF),** with a second one, **Islands of Adventure,** that's the top park in town for teens and offers the city's largest single collection of thrill rides. Universal also added **CityWalk,** an entertainment and dining complex, along with three uniquely themed luxury resorts: **Portofino Bay,** the **Hard Rock Hotel,** and the **Royal Pacific Resort.**

USF opened two new kid-friendly rides in 2003—**Jimmy Neutron's Nicktoon Blast** and **Shrek 4-D**—and it replaced Kongfrontation (much to my disappointment) in 2004 with **Revenge of the Mummy,** an indoor roller coaster with more than just thrills in store. There's also the **Fear Factor Live** stunt show—featuring reality TV a la Universal Studios—which began running in 2005. Alas, 2007 saw Back to the Future: The Ride replaced by a ride (similar in nature to its previous tenant) based on the popular animated television series *The Simpsons.* And to bolster Universal's lineup of live entertainment, the **Blue Man Group** joined the ranks as a permanent (though separately ticketed) show. Keep in mind that Universal Orlando still has plenty of room for expansion. Plans are already in place to re-create the **Wizarding World of Harry Potter** at Islands, and while the company's lips are tightly sealed, the future could bring at least two more hotels, a golf course, and even 300 acres of additional rides and attractions in upcoming years.

A few miles south, **SeaWorld** and its sister parks, **Discovery Cove** and **Aquatica,** also grab a share of the Orlando action (especially with the kid set). With what seems like an explosive expansion, SeaWorld has created new shows (*Odyssea* in 2003, *Mistify* in 2004, *Blue Horizons* in 2005, and *Believe* in 2006); added the **Waterfront,** a 5-acre shopping, dining, and entertainment area; and expanded **Shamu's Happy Harbor** (doubling the number of child-friendly rides within the popular play area). **Aquatica,** an eco-edutainment–themed water park (and the first new park—theme, water, or otherwise—to be built since 1999), splashed onto the scene in 2008, allowing SeaWorld to lay claim to a shark-sized share of the area's water parks.

Aside from greater variety, these players mean more multiday packages and special deals for you. To compete with Disney, SeaWorld and Universal Orlando teamed up on multiday pass options a few years back. They offer a **FlexTicket** (see below) that also includes admission to **Wet 'n Wild** (a Universal-owned water park) and **Busch Gardens** in Tampa. (Unfortunately for you, Universal rivals Disney with single-day tickets that, without tax, cost $71 for adults and $60 for children 3–9, while SeaWorld, at a cost of $65 for adults and $54 for kids, and Busch Gardens, at a cost of $62 for adults and $52 for kids, aren't far behind.)

Meanwhile, as the wars rage on in the traditional tourist areas, it has finally dawned on the rest of Orlando that Central Florida is one of the world's favorite vacation destinations.

Since the early 1990s, downtown Orlando has gotten a makeover that woos hundreds of thousands to its attractions, nightclubs, and restaurants. Recent expansions at the **Orlando Museum of Art** and the **Orlando Science Center** show that the city is trying to grab its share of the tourist pie. This expansion means visitors can enjoy the spoils: more variety, greater opportunities, and a world beyond the theme parks.

THE FLEXTICKET   The most economical way to see the various non-Disney parks is with these passes, which counter Disney's Magic Your Way Park Hopper tickets. With the FlexTicket, you pay one price to visit any of the participating parks as many times as you want during a 14-day period. At press time, a four-park pass to Universal Studios Florida, Islands of Adventure, Wet 'n Wild, and SeaWorld costs $195 for adults and $161 for children 3 to 9. A five-park pass, which adds Busch Gardens in Tampa, is $240 for adults and $200 for kids. The FlexTicket can be ordered through **Universal** (© **800/711-0080** or 407/363-8000; www.universalorlando.com), **SeaWorld** (© **800/327-2424** or 407/351-3600; www.seaworld.com), or **Wet 'n Wild** (© **800/992-9453** or 407/351-9453; www.wetnwild.com).

Note: There's a round-trip shuttle (© **800/221-1339**) available to Busch Gardens Tampa Bay (p. 341) that's free for FlexTicket buyers (it's $10 for other guests).

UNIVERSAL EXPRESS   This is Universal's answer to Disney's FASTPASS; however, at Universal, you'll pay a price (literally) to skip the long lines. Single- and multiday ticket buyers not staying at a Universal resort can purchase an **Express Plus Pass** that's good for either 1 day at one park ($20–$46) or 1 day at two parks ($26–$56). The plus in Express Plus: Waits are usually 15 minutes or less. The downside (other than having to fork out the extra cash): Express Plus Passes are good only on select dates during the year (for a complete list, see Universal's website), and they are valid only for a single entry to each ride featuring an express line. In other words, you can only wait in the express line for the Hulk once; if you want to ride a second (or third, or fourth) time, you'll have to head to the regular line with everyone else. And if you're a multiday ticket holder, the Express Plus Pass is good only for a single day—you'll have to purchase an additional pass if you want to skip the long lines for more than just a day. Also note that passes are not unlimited and can run out during busier times.

If you're at the parks during peak season, really can't stand waiting in line, and have plenty of cash to spare, the Express Plus Pass may be worth your while; otherwise, don't bother. A family of four

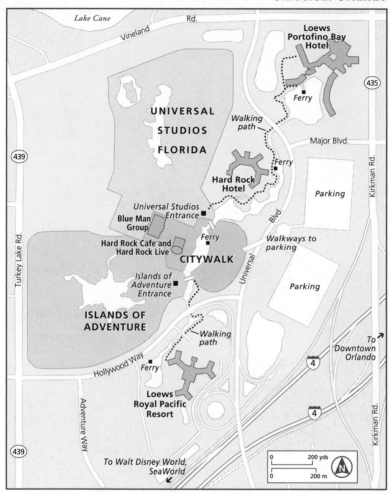

would be far better off spending the extra bucks ($60–$200) to stay at one of Universal's resorts. Guests of the **Portofino Bay, Hard Rock,** and **Royal Pacific** hotels need only show their room key to skip the long lines. And the best part:

Resort guests are allowed unlimited express-line access for the length of their stay. Call ℂ **407/363-8000** or go to **www.universalorlando.com** for more information.

1 Universal Studios Florida

Even with fast-paced grown-up rides based on blockbusters such as *The Mummy, Twister, Terminator, Men in Black,* and *The Simpsons,* Universal Studios Florida is a ton of fun for kids. As a plus, it's a working motion-picture and TV production studio, so occasionally you may catch some live filming being done. Even if there isn't a film or

Universal Studios Florida

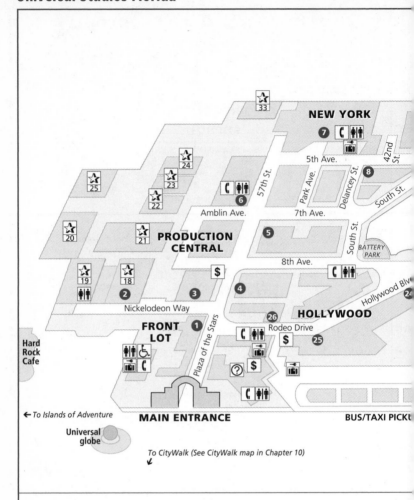

FRONT LOT
Universal Studios Store **1**

PRODUCTION CENTRAL
Blue Man Group **2**
Classic Monsters Cafe **5**
Jimmy Neutron's
  Nicktoon Blast **3**
Shrek 4-D **4**

NEW YORK
Blues Brothers **8**
Revenge of the Mummy **7**
Twister . . . Ride It Out **6**

SAN FRANCISCO/AMITY
Beetlejuice's Graveyard Revue **9**
Earthquake **10**
Fear Factor Live **13**
Jaws **12**
Lombard's Seafood Grille **11**

WORLD EXPO
International Food and Film
  Festival **16**
Men in Black Alien Attack
The Simpsons **15**

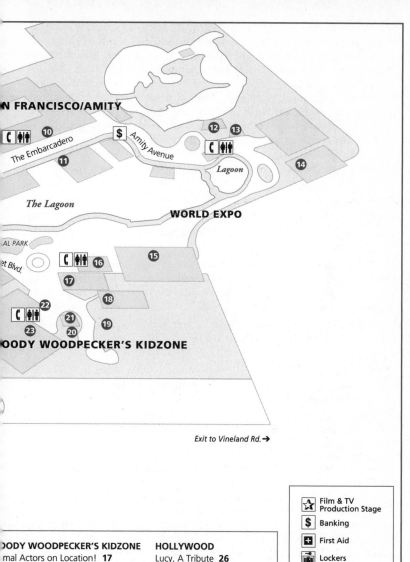

N FRANCISCO/AMITY

The Embarcadero 10
11

$ Amity Avenue
12 13
C 🚻

Lagoon

14

The Lagoon

WORLD EXPO

AL PARK
et Blvd.

C 🚻 16
15
17
18
22
C 🚻
21 19
23 20

OODY WOODPECKER'S KIDZONE

Exit to Vineland Rd. →

OODY WOODPECKER'S KIDZONE
mal Actors on Location! **17**
rious George Goes to Town **19**
)ay in the Park with Barney **18**
. Adventure **23**
el's Playland **21**
Zone Characters Meet & Greet **22**
'ody Woodpecker's Nuthouse
oaster **20**

HOLLYWOOD
Lucy, A Tribute **26**
Terminator 2:
  3-D Battle Across Time **25**
Universal Horror Make-Up
  Show **24**

⭐	Film & TV Production Stage
$	Banking
➕	First Aid
🔒	Lockers
🚻	Restrooms
C	Telephones
❓	Guest Services
♿	Wheelchair & Stroller Rental

show in production, you can see reel history displayed in the form of some 40 actual sets exhibited along Hollywood Boulevard and Rodeo Drive. And there are plenty of action shows and rides, including **Twister . . . Ride It Out, Men in Black Alien Attack, Jaws, Terminator 2: 3-D Battle Across Time, Fear Factor Live,** and **Blue Man Group** (a separately ticketed show, and the park's most recent addition).

After a period of quiet on the expansion front, 2003 saw Universal add two new attractions—**Jimmy Neutron's Nicktoon Blast** and **Shrek 4-D**—while 2004 saw the debut of **Revenge of the Mummy,** a ride based on the hit films *The Mummy* and *The Mummy Returns.* In 2008, the park will debut a ride based on the hit TV series *The Simpsons.* Universal also replaced some stale shows and characters with fresh ones (see "Universal Has New Characters & Shows," p. 261). As a result, the park is better than it's ever been as a place to bring the kids.

ESSENTIALS

GETTING THERE   Universal Orlando is a half mile north of I-4 Exit 75B, Kirkman Road/Highway 435. There may be construction in the area, so follow the signs directing you to the parks.

PARKING   If you park in the multilevel garage, write down the theme and row in your area to help you find your car later. Parking costs $11 for cars, light trucks, and vans. Valet parking is $18. Universal's garages are connected to its parks and have moving sidewalks, but it's still a long walk.

HOURS   The park is open 365 days a year, usually at least from 9am to 6pm, though later in summer and around holidays. Call before you go so you're not caught by surprise.

TICKETS, PASSES & TOURS   At press time, a **1-day ticket** costs $71 for adults and $60 for children 3 to 9. A **1-day, two-park pass** runs $83 for adults, $73 for children. A **two-park, unlimited-admission pass** (allowing unlimited admission with park-hopping privileges for 7 consecutive days starting on the first day of use) costs $86 for all ages if purchased at least 2 days in advance, or $96 if purchased for immediate use.

A **two-park Annual Power Pass** is good for an entire year except for about 30 or so blackout dates, mainly during summer and around the December holidays. It costs $130, regardless of age. A **two-park Preferred Annual Pass** has no blackout dates, includes free parking and discounts on dining and merchandise, and costs $190 per person. A **two-park Premier Annual Pass** costs $280 and provides unlimited admission to the parks with no blackout dates, free valet or self-parking, unlimited Universal Express Plus access, on-site hotel discounts and offers, free CityWalk club access, and more. A 6.5% sales tax is added to all of the above prices.

Tips **Shorter Days**

Like Disney, Universal juggles park hours to adjust for varying attendance due to seasonal shifts and holidays. The hours listed in this chapter are generally accurate, but sometimes the parks close earlier, or some rides or shows may open later. To avoid disappointment, check www.universalorlando.com or call ℂ 407/363-8000 for up-to-the-minute schedules.

Moments   Universal Has a Few 'Toons, Too

While the options pale in comparison with Disney, Universal does have character meet-and-greets on a rotating basis. At Universal Studios Florida, you may run into Woody Woodpecker, SpongeBob SquarePants, Shrek and Donkey, Jimmy Neutron, and others. At Islands of Adventure, the cast may include Spider-Man, Popeye and Olive Oyl, Beetle Bailey, the Cat in the Hat, Betty Boop, or Boris and Natasha.

All multiday passes let you move between Universal Studios Florida and Islands of Adventure. Multiday passes also give you *free access to CityWalk clubs* at night. See p. 254 for information on the **FlexTicket,** which provides multiple-day admission to Universal Studios Florida, Islands of Adventure, SeaWorld, and Wet 'n Wild.

Note: Because Universal Studios Florida and Islands of Adventure are within walking distance of each other, you won't lose much time jockeying back and forth, which is not the case at Disney. Nevertheless, it's a long walk for tykes and people with limited mobility, so consider a stroller or wheelchair.

Both Universal parks offer 5-hour **VIP Tours,** which include a guided tour and line-cutting privileges at a number of high-profile attractions, for $100 to $120 per person. A 7-hour, two-park VIP tour covers both parks and costs $125 to $150 per person. Perks include refreshments, discounts on dining and merchandise, and free valet parking. Prices for both tours do not include the 6.5% tax and *do not cover admission to the parks!* For more information, call © **407/363-8295** or e-mail viptours@universal orlando.com. Tours start at 10am and noon daily. If you plan on visiting during peak season, money isn't an issue, and you aren't staying at one of the Universal resorts, this is a good way to experience the best of the park without having to spend most of your day in lines.

MAKING YOUR VISIT MORE ENJOYABLE
HOW WE'VE MADE THIS CHAPTER USEFUL TO PARENTS
As in chapter 6, "What Kids Like to See & Do in Walt Disney World," before every listing in the major parks, you'll note the **Recommended Ages** entry that tells which ages will most appreciate that ride or show. This guideline can be helpful in planning your daily itinerary. In the ride ratings, I've indicated whether a ride will be more enjoyable for kids than for adults. Fewer of Universal Orlando's rides and shows appeal to very young kids than at some of the Disney parks, and one bad experience can spook your small fry for a long time. You'll also find any **height** and **health restrictions** noted in the listings that follow.

For the Universal and SeaWorld parks, I also rely on my kids—**Ryan** (age 14), **Austin** (age 12), **Nicolas** (age 10), **Hailey** (age 8), and **Davis** (age 6)—for ratings. They have happily shared their opinions, good and bad, after tackling the parks with me on more than a few occasions. On select rides, I'll give you their views and reviews.

BEST TIME OF YEAR TO VISIT
As at Walt Disney World, there's really no off season for Universal, but the week after Labor Day until mid-December (excluding Thanksgiving week) and January to mid-May (excluding spring break) are known for smaller crowds, cooler weather, and less-humid air. The summer months, when the masses throng to the parks, are the worst

time for crowds and hot, sticky days. During cooler months, you also won't have to worry about daily thunderstorms.

If you're planning a trip from mid-February to mid-April, keep in mind that a raucous **Mardi Gras** celebration goes on in the evenings. Schedules have varied over the years, including only weekends at first and then daily celebrations during the last 2 weeks, so check with Universal for the most up-to-date info. It's a very grownup event, with lots of alcohol flowing and a separate ticket price—definitely not suitable for younger children. The park is still open to all during the day, but generally closes earlier than usual. The same is true in October at Universal's Islands of Adventure, which hosts the very grownup, not to mention frightening, **Halloween Horror Nights.**

BEST DAYS TO VISIT

Go near the end of the week, on a Thursday or Friday. The pace is somewhat fast Monday through Wednesday, with the heaviest crowds on weekends and during summers and holidays.

PLANNING YOUR VISIT

Get information before you leave home by calling **Universal Orlando Guest Services** at ✆ **407/224-4233**, 407/363-8000, or 877/801-9720. Ask about travel packages as well as theme-park information. You can also write to Guest Services, 1000 Universal Studios Plaza, Orlando, FL 32819-7601.

On the Internet, go to **www.universalorlando.com**. The *Orlando Sentinel* operates **www.orlandosentinel.com**. Additionally, there's a lot of information on the parks, hotels, restaurants, and more at the Orlando/Orange County Convention & Visitors Bureau site at **www.orlandoinfo.com**.

As you plan your trip, check the listings that follow to research **height restrictions** and suggested ages for the various attractions. Here, as in Disney World, the rules won't be bent to accommodate a screaming child. Even where restrictions don't exist, some shows have loud music and pyrotechnics that can scare little ones. Review this chapter's descriptions to make sure your child won't be unduly disappointed or frightened. *Note:* Some of the park's best attractions are action-based thrill rides, which means your options are limited if you are pregnant, are prone to motion sickness, or have heart, neck, or back problems. Review the rides and restrictions in this book or when you enter the park so that you don't stand in line for something you're unable to experience. (There are stationary areas available at some moving rides. Check your park guide for information, as well as the boards in front of each ride; then ask the attendants for help as you enter.) A child-swap program (allowing parents to switch off on rides without having to stand in line twice) is available at the rides as well.

Overall, Universal Studios does a much better job in the way of entertaining its guests while they wait in line for the attractions. Many have preshows or TV screens with previews. Universal has also got it all over the House of Mouse when it comes to beating the sun—many attractions have waiting areas under some sort of cover or, in some cases, indoors (unless the line is so long that it extends beyond these areas).

It is also exponentially easier to get from your car (or resort) to the parks. From the parking lot, if you have kids and all of the gear that comes with them, pack your stroller and bring it along—you will be able to walk directly to the parks, though it can be a long haul for small feet (and there are no trams from the parking decks to the theme parks). Elevators, moving sidewalks, and covered walkways will take you up to the entrance of CityWalk. And, if you're staying at a Universal resort, you'll be glad to

---

Tips **Universal Has New Characters & Shows**

Universal Studios Florida has replaced some of its old (read: stale, if you've been here a few times) street characters and shows in favor of new ones. The occasionally changing lineup includes Lucy and Ricky Ricardo; Fiona, Shrek, and Donkey; SpongeBob SquarePants; the Men in Black agents; and the Madagascar menagerie. Note that characters rotate or appear seasonally.

---

know that all three resorts are relatively close by (the Hard Rock Hotel is within walking distance) and are served by water taxi that will drop you off in CityWalk. We're not saying that you will not have to wait at all—it can take several minutes—but not nearly as long as some trips at Disney can.

FOR VISITORS WITH SPECIAL NEEDS

Guests with disabilities should go to **Guest Services,** located just inside the main entrance, for a *Rider's Guide for Rider Safety & Guests with Disabilities,* a Telecommunications Device for the Deaf (TDD), or other special assistance. You can rent a standard wheelchair for $12 or an electric one for $40 (both require a signed contract and a $50 deposit). Reserve them 24 hours or more in advance by calling ✆ **407/224-4233.** You can arrange for sign-language interpreting services at no charge by calling ✆ **888/ 519-4899** (toll-free TDD), 407/224-4414 (local TDD), or 407/224-5929 (voice). Make arrangements for an appointment with an interpreter 1 to 2 weeks in advance. Information is also available at www.universalorlando.com.

Tip: The *Rider's Guide* is also a great tool for parents, as it describes in great detail the various rides' special effects, warnings, height requirements, and information on general guest services at both Universal parks.

CREATING AN ITINERARY

Pick three or four things that you must see or do, and plan your day along a rough geographical guide. Universal Studios Florida is relatively small, so walking from one end of the park to the other isn't as daunting as it is in some of the Disney parks. Still, the sometimes-long lines dictate that you should remain flexible.

SUGGESTED ITINERARIES

For Families with Young Kids

Waste no time: Hoof it to Woody Woodpecker's KidZone, where you and your heirs can spend most of the day. If they're 36 inches or taller, don't miss multiple rides on **Woody Woodpecker's Nuthouse Coaster.** Try to make an early pit stop at **Fievel's Playland** (especially its water slide, which is slow-moving and has longer lines after 10:30am). Then take a leisurely pace to see **E.T. Adventure, A Day in the Park with Barney,** and **Animal Actors on Location!**

Take a lunch break, but don't leave before visiting the wet-and-wild **Curious George Goes to Town.** Round out the day with a stop at **Jimmy Neutron's Nicktoon Blast** and **Shrek 4-D.**

For Families with Older Kids & Teens

A single day to see the park is usually sufficient if you arrive early and keep a fairly brisk pace. Skip the city sidewalks of the main gate and Terminator 2 until later. Go to the right, and tackle **Men in Black Alien Attack,** the new **Simpsons** ride, and the **Fear Factor Live** stunt show. Then make a counterclockwise loop, visiting **Jaws, Earthquake, Revenge of the Mummy,** and **Twister . . . Ride It Out.** Break for lunch somewhere in that bunch; tackle the 'toons in the new **Jimmy Neutron's Nicktoon Blast** and the **Shrek 4-D** adventure; then catch the fun in **Terminator 2: 3-D Battle Across Time.**

A second day lets you revisit some of your favorites or see those you missed. With the pressure to hit all the major rides lessened, you can get to the **Universal Horror Make-Up Show** and **Beetlejuice's Graveyard Revue,** and then head back to the rides you liked most for a second go-round.

SERVICES & FACILITIES AT UNIVERSAL STUDIOS FLORIDA

ATMs   Cash machines accepting cards on the Cirrus, Honor, and PLUS systems can be found to the right of the main entrance (outside and inside the park), in New York near Revenge of the Mummy, and in San Francisco/Amity near Lombard's Seafood Grille restaurant.

Baby Care   Changing tables are in men's and women's restrooms; there are nursing facilities at Family Services, just inside the main entrance and to the right. Diapers, food, formula, and infant supplies are not sold at the parks.

Cameras & Film   Film, disposable cameras, and limited digital supplies are available at the On Location shop in the Front Lot, just inside the main entrance. One-hour photo developing is available, though I don't recommend paying park prices.

Car Assistance   Battery jumps are provided. If you need assistance with your car, raise the hood and press the blue button at one of the guest-assistance stations located throughout the garage to call for security.

First Aid   Go to the station located between New York and San Francisco, next to Louie's Italian Restaurant on Canal Street. There's also a station just inside the main entrance next to Vacation Services.

Lockers   Lockers are across from Guest Services, near the main entrance, and cost $8 and $10 a day. Lockers are also available at select rides.

Lost Children   If you lose a child, go to Guest Services near the main entrance, or contact any park employee for assistance. *Children under 7 should wear name tags* inside their clothing.

Package Pickup   Purchases made at park stores (though not at kiosks and carts) can be sent to It's A Wrap near the entrance to be picked up on your way out. If you're a guest at one of the three Universal hotels, you can have your purchases delivered to your room (though delivery will be the following day).

Pet Care   You can board pets at the kennel located inside the parking garages for $10 a day (no overnight stays). Ask the parking attendant for directions upon entering the toll plaza. You must provide food, show proof of vaccination, and return to walk your

---

Value **Money Saver**

You can save 10% off your purchase at many Universal Orlando gift shops and eateries by showing your AAA card. However, the discount isn't available at food and merchandise carts or on tobacco, candy, film, collectibles, and sundry items.

pet periodically. Note that all Universal resorts allow small pets to stay with you in your room.

Stroller Rental   Strollers can be rented in Amity and at Guest Services, just inside the entrance to the right. The cost is $11 for a single and $17 for a double.

Wheelchair Rental   Regular wheelchairs can be rented for $12 in Amity and at Guest Services, just inside the main gate. Electric wheelchairs are $40. Both require a signed agreement and a $50 deposit.

MAJOR ATTRACTIONS IN THE PARK

Rides and attractions use cutting-edge technology to create spectacular special effects. While waiting in line, you'll be entertained by excellent preshows—far better than those at the Disney parks (some as entertaining as the attractions themselves). Universal, as a whole, takes itself less seriously than the Mouse, and the atmosphere is peppered by subtle reminders that in the competitive theme-park industry, it's really not such a small world after all.

Animal Actors on Location!

Frommer's Rating: B+ for kids and parents
Recommended Ages: All ages

Get an up-close look at Hollywood's hottest animal actors as they entertain audience members in a 20-minute multimedia show that combines video clips and lots of live action. Members of the audience occasionally get to participate in the fun. If your kids love animals, it's a must.

Beetlejuice's Graveyard Revue

Frommer's Rating: C+ for classic-rock fans, C for others
Recommended Ages: 10–adult

Dracula, Wolfman, the Phantom of the Opera, Frankenstein and his bride, and Beetlejuice show up to scare you silly. Their funky rock-musical includes pyrotechnic special effects, some adult jokes, and MTV-style choreography. It's loud and lively

---

Frommer's Rates the Rides

As I do for the Disney parks in chapter 6, I've used a grading system to score the Universal Orlando and SeaWorld rides in this chapter. (I'll return to the star-rating system toward the end of the chapter, when I explore some of Orlando's smaller attractions.) Most of the grades below are *As, Bs,* and *Cs.* That's because the major parks' designers have done a pretty good job on the attractions. But you'll also find a few *Ds* for Duds.

Here's what the **Frommer's Ratings** mean:

A+	=	Your trip wouldn't be complete without it.
A	=	Put it at the top of your to-do list.
B+	=	Make a real effort to see or do it.
B	=	It's fun but not a must-see.
C+	=	A nice diversion; see it if you have time.
C	=	Go if it appeals to you but not if there's a wait.
D	=	Don't waste your time.

enough to aggravate adults and scare smaller children. *Note:* It's carries Universal's PG-13 rating, meaning that it may not be suitable for preteens—though young teens seem to like it the most.

A Day in the Park with Barney

Frommer's Rating: A+ for tiny tots and their parents, D for everyone else
Recommended Ages: 2–6

Set in a parklike theater-in-the-round, this 25-minute musical stars the Purple One, Baby Bop, and BJ. It uses song, dance, special effects, and interactive play to entertain the kids. This could be the highlight of the day for preschoolers (parents can console themselves with their kids' happiness). The playground adjacent to the theater is unique, with chimes to ring, treehouses to explore, and lots more to intrigue wee ones.

Davis's Rating: His big, goofy smile said it all: He adored the entire experience as he sang and danced right along with Barney and his pals. But my over-8 set couldn't stand having to hang around any longer than was required of them. The theater is air-conditioned, but even in the hottest months, that's not enough to entice me to spend another minute around Barney; the smile on my son's face, however, was.

Earthquake

Frommer's Rating: A
Recommended Ages: 6–adult

After a short preshow, you climb on a BART train in San Francisco for a peaceful subway ride, but just as you pull into the Embarcadero Station, there's an earthquake—a big one, 8.3 on the Richter scale! As you sit helplessly trapped, slabs of concrete collapse around you; a propane truck bursts into flames; a runaway train hurtles your way; and the station floods—65,000 gallons of water cascade down the steps. *Note:* Universal says expectant moms should skip this one.

Ryan's, Austin's, and **Nicolas's Rating:** "That was way cool." (Surprisingly, the noise, flames, and other special effects didn't bother the youngest of the three.)

E.T. Adventure

Frommer's Rating: B for preteens and their families
Recommended Ages: All ages

You'll soar with E.T. on a mission to save his ailing planet, through the forest and into space aboard an intergalactic bicycle. You'll also meet some characters created by Steven Spielberg for the ride, including Botanicus, Tickli Moot Moot, Horn Flowers, and Tympani Tremblies. This family favorite (young kids especially adore it) is definitely a charmer. If there is a knock, it's that there are two waiting areas: inside and outside. And wait you will. *Note:* No lap riders here, so you'll have to take advantage of the child swap if you have very small children.

Fear Factor Live

Frommer's Rating: B for most, D for those who can't stomach the stunts
Recommended Ages: 8 and up

One of the latest additions to USF's lineup of shows is Fear Factor Live. Having debuted in the spring of 2005, it's the first reality show (based on NBC's blockbuster hit *Fear Factor*) to become a theme-park attraction. Audience members—the ones who are willing to sign up, that is—perform stunts that test their courage, strength, and at times their stomach. It's similar to the stuff seen on the hit TV show, but live in Orlando. You can catch the show in the venue set between Jaws and Men in Black, where the park's Wild, Wild, Wild West Stunt Show once reigned supreme.

ⓘ Tips Quiet on the Set!

The comedy, music, and multimedia theatrics of Blue Man Group have found a new home—and it's in Orlando. This highly dynamic and unique group of wild and at times wacky performers is now wowing audiences at Universal Studios in a newly re-created theater (previously Nickelodeon Studios) accessible from both Universal Studios and CityWalk. Park admission is not required for this separately ticketed show (which has two daily performances). Tickets (for the show only) run between $45 and $69 for adults, and between $39 and $59 for children ages 3 to 9, depending on the showtime. Combination tickets (including theme-park admission and a single show, at a discounted price) are available and range from $108 to $140 for adults and $98 to $140 for children. The price is dependent upon showtimes and the type of park ticket chosen; options currently include either a 1-day, two-park pass or an unlimited-admission ticket.

Jaws

Frommer's Rating: B+

Recommended Ages: 6–adult

As your boat heads into the 7-acre, 5-million-gallon lagoon, a dorsal fin appears on the surface. Then what goes with the fin—a 3-ton, 32-foot, mechanical great white shark—tries to sink its urethane teeth right into your hide (or at least your boat's). A 30-foot wall of flame that surrounds the vessel truly causes you to feel the heat in this $45-million attraction. I won't tell you exactly how it ends, but in spite of a captain who can't hit the broad side of a dock with his grenade launcher, some lucky Orlando restaurant will be serving blackened shark tonight. *Tip:* The effects of this ride are far more spectacular after dark. *Note:* While it lacks a height requirement, the shark may be too intense for kids younger than 6, and Universal recommends that expectant mothers avoid it.

Warning: Universal has put Jaws on a limited operational schedule—it's open only during peak seasons and select times—so if it's on your to-do list, check ahead of time to see if it will be running when you're visiting.

Jimmy Neutron's Nicktoon Blast

Frommer's Rating: A

Recommended Ages: 6–adult

Buckle up for one of the park's newer rides. In this one, you climb aboard Jimmy's Rocket Pod, which hurtles you through hyperspace thanks to a motion simulator, sophisticated computer graphics, state-of-the-art ride technology, animation, and programmable motion-based seats. Your task: Defeat the evil Yokians, egg-shaped aliens that have stolen Jimmy's latest invention, the Mark IV rocket, and are threatening to take over Universal Orlando and the rest of the world. The attraction also features Jimmy's robot dog, Goddard; his nemesis, Cindy Vortex; and popular characters from other cartoons, including SpongeBob SquarePants, Rugrats, Wild Thornberrys, and Fairly Odd Parents. *Note:* You must be 40 inches or taller to join Jimmy's Air Force.

Hailey's Rating: "Wow, it's the best ride here!" (Arguably, for kids it is, though the fact that she's a huge Nickelodeon fan may have something to do with it, too.)

Fun Fact **Goodbye Kong, Hello Mummy**

Kongfrontation, one of the original rides at Universal Studios (dating back to the park's opening in 1990), closed in 2002 and was replaced in 2004 with Revenge of the Mummy. (I guess they didn't know they'd be releasing Oscar-winner Peter Jackson's Kong movie soon after.) This is, of course, not the first time that Universal has replaced a popular attraction, claiming that its relevance has long since past (but remind me again—what year did Earthquake, E.T., Twister, and even The Terminator come out?). While there's plenty of room, Production Central has gotten pretty sparse, as has the World Expo. What once made this studio-themed park so inviting (other than its amazing streetscapes) was its wide range of offerings, spanning the early days of movie-making to the present. The mysterious disappearance of classics like the house from Alfred Hitchcock's Psycho; the Wild, Wild, Wild West Stunt Show; Kongfrontation; and now Back to the Future: The Ride simply eludes me.

Men in Black Alien Attack

Frommer's Rating: A+

Recommended Ages: 6–adult

Armageddon may be upon us, unless you and your mates fly to the rescue and destroy the alien menace. Once aboard your six-passenger cruiser, you'll buzz the streets of New York, using your "zapper" to splatter up to 120 bug-eyed targets. You have to contend with return fire and distractions such as light, noise, and clouds of liquid nitrogen (aka fog), any of which can spin you out of control. Earn a bonus by hitting Frank the Pug (to the right, just past the alien shipwreck). The 4-minute ride relies on 360-degree spins rather than speed for its thrill factor. At the conclusion, you're swallowed by a giant roach (it's 30 ft. tall, with 8-ft. fangs and 20-ft. claws) that explodes, dousing you with bug guts as you blast your way to safety and into the pest-control hall of fame—maybe. When you exit, Will Smith rates you anywhere from galaxy defender to bug bait. (There are 38 possible scores; those assigned to less than full cars suffer the scoring consequences.) *Note:* Guests must be at least 42 inches tall to climb aboard this $70-million ride. *Note #2:* Men in Black often has a *much* shorter line for single riders. Even if you're not alone but have older kids and are willing to be split up, get in this line, and hop right on a vehicle that has fewer than six passengers.

Ryan's, Austin's, Nicolas's, and even **Hailey's Rating:** "Very cool! Gross, but very cool." "I loved blasting those gigantic bugs, and the spinning made it even more fun." (Of course, we immediately had to head back to the end of the line to ride again . . . and again.)

Revenge of the Mummy

Frommer's Ratings: A+

Recommended Ages: 10 and up

Ten years in the making, the $40-million Revenge of the Mummy, billed as a "psychological thrill ride," made its debut in 2004. The indoor roller coaster uses a sophisticated propulsion system to hurtle riders through the shadowy, darkened tombs of ancient Egypt (all spectacularly re-created) while trying to escape the curse of the mummy. The sound system (enhanced by 200 speakers and surround-sound technology in the coaster cars) will spook you, too. Highly advanced robotics are used to bring to life some pretty scary-looking skeletal warriors, one of whom jumps aboard your car; even Imhotep himself makes an appearance. Overhead flames, fireballs, and creepy creatures combine with surprising twists, turns, stops, and starts to make for a thrill like no other in the park. And just when you think it's over . . . well, I have to leave some surprises for you. *Note:* Guests must be 48 inches tall to ride, and the normal back, neck, motion-sickness, and pregnancy warnings apply. I would also add phobia warnings for darkness, bugs, pyrotechnic effects, and special effects that jump out at you.

Austin's Rating: "What a cool coaster! First you go forward, then backward, and it's so smooth—scary, too!" (Riding the movies takes on a whole new meaning here!)

Shrek 4-D
Frommer's Rating: B+
Recommended Ages: All ages

This amusing and entertaining 20-minute show can be seen, heard, felt, and smelled thanks to film, motion simulators, OgreVision glasses, and other special effects, such as water spritzers. The attraction picks up where the movie left off—allowing you to join Shrek and Princess Fiona on their honeymoon (at least, the G-rated portions of it). After one of the most amusing preshows in the park (featuring a ghostly Lord Farquaad, the Three Little Pigs, Pinocchio, and the Magic Mirror), you're settled in specially designed seats in the main auditorium and then transported to the fairy-tale realm of Duloc. The screen comes alive as you help Shrek and Donkey rescue Fiona from her kidnappers: Lord Farquaad and his knights. Along the way, spiders will scamper about your feet, and you'll ride a dragon that spritzes you when she clears her sinuses. The theater's seats are pneumatic air-propulsion nodules that are capable of turning and tilting (though not dramatically). Again, if your kids don't like touchy-feely special effects, they may get upset at certain points during this attraction. *Note:* The line can stretch for miles (made worse with the recent release of *Shrek the Third*), though thankfully you can use Express Plus Passes here. If you didn't shell out the extra cash, at least you can wait under cover from the sun.

Tips The Simpsons Are Coming

In 2007, Back to the Future: The Ride became part of Universal Studios past. Even though this wild ride through time was one of the best in the park, it was edited out of the picture to make way for a more updated attraction based on the very popular, and the longest-running, animated television sitcom: *The Simpsons*. At press time, the ride was yet unnamed. The attraction (similar in nature to the previous tenant) will feature sitcom sensations Bart, Homer, Marge, Maggie, and Lisa Simpson on a wildly amusing adventure—and you'll be right smack in the middle of it. According to Universal, riders will be rocketed off through Springfield (though a side that's never before been seen) as they explore and experience a fantasy amusement park filled with dark rides, live shows, and other assorted attractions—all dreamed up by Krusty the Clown. Promising to be a hysterical high-speed adventure, it's likely that this, like the previous ride, will have more warnings than a centipede has legs.

Terminator 2: 3-D Battle Across Time
Frommer's Rating: A
Recommended Ages: 10–adult
This is billed as "the quintessential sight and sound experience for the 21st century!" The same director who made the movie, James Cameron, supervised this $60-million production. After a slow start, it builds into an impressive experience featuring the *Ahnud* (on film), along with other original cast members. It combines 70mm 3-D film (utilizing three 23-ft.-x-50-ft. screens) with thrilling technical effects and live stage action that includes a custom-built Harley-Davidson "Fat Boy." *Note:* The crisp 3-D effects are among the best in any Orlando park, but Universal has given this show a PG-13 rating, meaning that the violence and loud noise may be too intense for preteens. That may be a little too cautious, but some kids under 10 may be frightened. The rest may proclaim that they want to go back.

    Ryan's Rating: "The action, the motorcycle—what a cool show."

Twister . . . Ride It Out
Frommer's Rating: A
Recommended Ages: 8–adult
Visitors from the twister-prone Midwest may find this re-creation a little too close to the real thing. An ominous funnel cloud, five stories tall, is created by swirling 2 million cubic feet of air per minute (that's enough to fill four full-size blimps). The sensory elements are pretty incredible. Power lines spark and fall, an oak tree splits, and the storm rumbles at rock-concert level as cars, trucks, and a cow fly about while the audience watches from only 20 feet away. In the finale, the floor begins to buckle at your feet. It's the windy version of Earthquake and packs quite a wallop. Crowds have been known to applaud when it's over.

    Note: This show, too, comes with a PG-13 rating. Its loudness and intensity certainly can be too much for children under 8. Also, readers who have visited Universal Studios Hollywood in California will find Twister similar in theme to that park's Backdraft attraction, although (sacrilege!) the one in California offers a better overall experience.

Woody Woodpecker's Nuthouse Coaster
Frommer's Rating: A+ for kids and parents, B+ for others
Recommended Ages: 5–adult
This is the top attraction in Woody Woodpecker's KidZone, an 8-acre concession Universal Studios made several years ago after being criticized for having too little for younger visitors. This kiddie coaster will thrill some moms and dads, too. While only 30 feet at its peak, it offers quick, spiraling turns as you sit in a miniature steam train. The ride lasts only 55 seconds, and waits can be 30 minutes or more, but few kids will want to miss it. It's very much like The Barnstormer at Goofy's Wiseacre Farm in the Magic Kingdom (p. 202). *Note:* Its height minimum is 36 inches.

    Hailey's and **Nicolas's Rating:** "We're going again . . . !" They finally quit after four trips. I have to say I enjoyed sitting down while I waited for them to run out of steam.

ADDITIONAL ATTRACTIONS
The somewhat corny **Universal Horror Make-Up Show** gives a behind-the-scene look at what goes into (and oozes out of) some of Hollywood's most frightening monsters. It has a PG-13 rating and may frighten young kids. **Lucy, A Tribute** is a remembrance of America's queen of comedy (kids will most likely be ready to move on after

Tips **Universal Cuisine**

The best food here is just outside the main gates at CityWalk, Universal's restaurant and nightclub venue. But there are more than a dozen places to eat inside the park. Here are some favorites:

Best Sit-Down Meal: The menu at **Lombard's Seafood Grille** offers a hearty fried-shrimp basket, as well as a selection of seafood, pasta, salads, and sandwiches ($10–$16), served in slightly more upscale surroundings. It's located across from Earthquake.

Best Counter Service: The **Universal Studios' Classic Monsters Cafe** serves salads, pizza, pasta, and rotisserie chicken ($7–$9), with a side of classic and creepy creatures. It's off 7th Avenue near the Shrek 4-D.

Best Place for Hungry Families: Similar to a food court, the **International Food and Film Festival** offers options ranging from stir-fry to chicken Parmesan, so families can please all palates (even the pickier ones) under one roof. There are some kids' meals for under $6. The fare is far from gourmet, but a cut above fast food ($7–$10). It's near the back of Animal Actors on Location!

Best Snack Stops: Grab a malt ($4) and enjoy the classic atmosphere of **Mel's Drive-In,** across from the Universal Horror Make-Up Show. The **San Francisco Pastry Co.,** across from Earthquake, has a case full of sweets, including a decadent brownie. **Boardwalk Snacks,** in San Francisco, and **Schwab's Pharmacy,** about halfway along Hollywood Boulevard, both offer ice-cream treats to cool you off on a hot day.

only a few minutes here), and the **Blues Brothers** launch their foot-stomping revue several times a day on Delancy Street (most kids will find it entertaining).

Back at Woody Woodpecker's KidZone, **Fievel's Playland** is a wet, Western-themed playground with a house to climb and a water slide for small fry (the ride lines can get long, but most little kids love it). **Curious George Goes to Town** is filled with whimsical watery fun, from fountains to ball-shooting cannons. Bring a change of clothes; you and your kids will get wet.

SHOPPING IN THE PARK

Every major attraction has a theme store attached, many of them selling some unique merchandise. The **Hard Rock Cafe** shop in adjacent CityWalk is extremely popular and has a small but diverse selection of Hard Rock everything (including memorabilia with astronomical sticker prices). For just about everything else a la Universal, the **Universal Studios Store,** near the entrance, carries a rather decent selection of toys, T-shirts, and souvenirs.

More than two dozen other shops in the park sell collectibles. Be warned, though, that unlike Walt Disney World, where Mickey is everywhere, Universal's shops are specific to individual attractions. If you see something you like, buy it; you probably won't find it in another store. There is a Universal store at Orlando International Airport, but

Tips **Great Buys at Universal Studios Florida**

Here's a sampling of the more unusual gifts available at some of the Universal stores. Of course, you can find the standard tourist fare, with a staggering array of mugs, key chains, T-shirts, and the like. I've tried to include things you wouldn't find (or consider buying) anywhere else:

E.T.'s Toy Closet and Photo Spot   This is the place for plush stuffed animals, including a replica of the alien namesake.

MIB Gear   If you find yourself in need of a ray gun or alien blaster, this is the place to buy everything out of this world.

Quint's Surf Shack   Stop by Quint's for a different kind of T-shirt. Tropical colors, with subtle Universal logos, are the thing here.

it mainly carries the usual souvenirs. *Tip:* If you did forget to pick something up, there's a shop-by-phone service. Just call © **407/224-5800,** describe the item and where you think you saw it, and the phone rep will likely be able to help you out.

Note: Universal has a service similar to Disney's in which you can have your store purchases delivered to It's A Wrap near the entrance of the park, to be picked up on your way out; allow 3 hours. If you're a guest at one of the Universal hotels, you can have your purchases delivered to your room the following day.

A NIGHT AT THE MOVIES

Universal 360–A Cinesphere Spectacular, Universal Orlando's newest seasonal show, made its debut in the summer of 2006. This spectacular nighttime show (albeit seasonal) immerses guests in the movie experience, projecting images from Hollywood's hottest hits across four tremendous "cinespheres" in the park's central lagoon. The scenes and images appear and change throughout the show, while 300 outdoor speakers ensure that the accompanying music is heard by everyone who's even remotely nearby. Lasers and pyrotechnic effects add to the already spectacular visuals.

2 Islands of Adventure

Universal's second theme park opened in 1999 with a colorful and cleverly themed collection of fast and sometimes furious rides. At 110 acres, it's the same size as its big sister, Universal Studios Florida, but it seems larger, and it's definitely *the* Orlando destination for thrill-ride junkies. Roller coasters roar above pedestrian walkways, while water rides slice through the park. The trade-off: There are few shows. If you have teens in tow, this is unquestionably the top park in town for them. If you have little children, the options aren't as extensive, but Islands does offer plenty of places to play for young kids.

Expect total immersion in the park's various "islands." From the wobbly angles and Day-Glo colors in **Seuss Landing** to the lush foliage of **Jurassic Park,** Universal has done a good job of differentiating various sections of this billion-dollar park (unlike Universal Studios Florida, where the cityscapes tend to blend together, making it hard to tell whether you're in San Francisco or New York). It's also done an outstanding job

Islands of Adventure

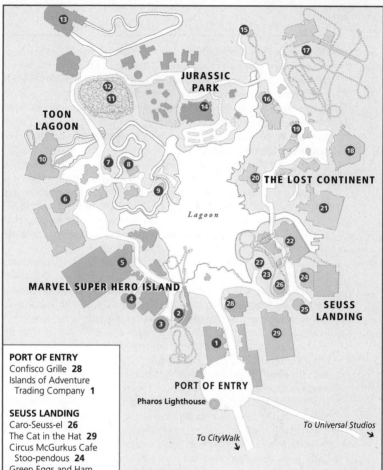

JURASSIC PARK

TOON LAGOON

THE LOST CONTINENT

MARVEL SUPER HERO ISLAND

Lagoon

SEUSS LANDING

PORT OF ENTRY
Pharos Lighthouse

To Universal Studios ↗

To CityWalk ↓

PORT OF ENTRY
Confisco Grille **28**
Islands of Adventure
  Trading Company **1**

SEUSS LANDING
Caro-Seuss-el **26**
The Cat in the Hat **29**
Circus McGurkus Cafe
  Stoo-pendous **24**
Green Eggs and Ham
  Cafe **27**
High in the Sky Seuss
  Trolley Train Ride **22**
If I Ran the Zoo **23**
One Fish, Two Fish, Red
  Fish, Blue Fish **25**

**MARVEL SUPER HERO
ISLAND**
The Amazing Adventures
  of Spider-Man **5**
Doctor Doom's Fearfall **4**
Incredible Hulk Coaster **2**
Storm Force Accelatron **3**

TOON LAGOON
Comic Strip Cafe **6**
Dudley Do-Right's Ripsaw Falls **10**
King's Row & Comic Strip Lane **7**
Me Ship, *The Olive* **9**
Popeye & Bluto's Bilge-Rat Barges **8**

JURASSIC PARK
Camp Jurassic **12**
Jurassic Park Discovery Center **14**
Jurassic Park River Adventure **13**
Pteranodon Flyers **11**
Thunder Falls Terrace **13**

THE LOST CONTINENT
Dueling Dragons **17**
Eighth Voyage of
  Sindbad **18**
Enchanted Oak Tavern
  & Alchemy Bar **16**
Flying Unicorn **15**
Mystic Fountain **19**
Mythos **20**
Poseidon's Fury **21**

Tips Some Practical Advice for Island Adventurers

1. **The Shorter They Are . . . :** Note that *13* of the 14 major rides at Islands of Adventure have height restrictions. Dueling Dragons and the Incredible Hulk Coaster, for instance, deny access to anyone under 54 inches. For those who want to ride but come with little kids, there's a child-swap station at all major attractions, allowing one parent to ride while the other watches the tykes. But sitting in a waiting room isn't much fun for the little ones, so take your child's height into consideration before coming to the park.

2. **Cruising the Islands:** If you hauled your stroller along on your trip, bring it with you to the park. It's a very long walk from your car, through the massive parking garage and the CityWalk nighttime entertainment district, before you get to the fun. Carrying a young child and the accompanying paraphernalia, even with a series of moving sidewalks, can make the long trek seem even longer—especially at the end of the day.

3. **The Faint of Heart:** Even adults need to heed all the ride restrictions. Expectant mothers, people prone to motion sickness, and those with heart, neck, or back trouble will be discouraged—with good reason—from riding most primo attractions. There's still plenty to see and do, but without the roller coasters, Islands of Adventure isn't nearly as adventurous. Also, beer, wine, and liquor are more available at the Universal parks than at the Disney ones, but booze, roller coasters, and hot weather can make for a messy mix.

4. **Beat the Heat:** Several rides require that you wait outside; though most lines are covered to protect you from the sizzling Florida sun, the heat is a different matter. Bring some bottled water (freeze it the night before) for the long waits (a 99¢ free-world bottle costs $2.50 or more if you buy it here), or use the fountains smartly placed in the queues. Make sure your kids wear hats and sunscreen.

5. **Cash in on Your Card:** You can save 10% on meals and gift-shop purchases by showing your AAA card. This discount isn't available at food or merchandise carts, or on tobacco, candy, film, collectibles, and sundry items.

of differentiating Islands from Disney or any other Orlando park. The closest competitor in Florida is Busch Gardens in Tampa, but this attraction clearly has the edge on the ride front—at least when it comes to diversity.

The park is divided into six islands, beginning with the **Port of Entry,** a marketplace filled with shops, bazaars, and eateries all occupying a street designed to recall ancient far-off lands and exotic ports of call. The remaining islands include: **Seuss Landing,** where you'll feel as if you've jumped into the pages of the good doctor's whimsical classic tales; **The Lost Continent,** which combines mythical and mystical enchantments; **Jurassic Park,** where you enter through a massive stone gateway, are surrounded by towering dense foliage, and can hear the rumblings of gigantic prehistoric beasts off in the distance; **Toon Lagoon,** which takes you on an amusing, lighthearted stroll through the classic Sunday comic strips of the past; and **Marvel Super Hero Island,** where super heroes and their arch nemeses jump off the pages of comic books to entertain and impress with their super powers.

ESSENTIALS
GETTING THERE   Universal Orlando is a half mile north of I-4 Exit 75B, Kirkman Road/Highway 435. There may be construction in the area, so follow the signs directing you to the park.

PARKING   If you park in the multilevel garage, make a note of the row and theme in your area to help you find your car later. Parking costs $11 for cars, light trucks, and vans. Valet parking is available for $18.

HOURS   The park is open 365 days a year, generally from 9am to 6pm, though often later, especially in summer and around holidays, when it's sometimes open until 9pm or later. During Halloween Horror Nights, the park closes around 5pm, reopens at 7pm (with a new admission), and remains open until at least midnight. Call before you go so you're not caught by surprise.

TICKETS, PASSES & TOURS   A **1-day ticket** costs $71 for adults and $60 for children 3 to 9. A **two-park, unlimited-admission pass** (with park-hopping privileges for 7 consecutive days starting on the first day of use) runs $86 for all ages. A 6.5% sales tax is added to these prices.

All multiday passes let you move between Universal Studios Florida and Islands of Adventure. Multiday passes also give you *free access to CityWalk clubs at night.* Because the parks are within walking distance of each other, you won't lose much time jockeying back and forth, unlike the situation at Disney. Nevertheless, it's a long walk for tykes and people with limited mobility, so consider a stroller or wheelchair.

For more information on multiday pass options and VIP Tours, see "Tickets, Passes & Tours" in the Universal Studios Florida section, earlier in this chapter.

MAKING YOUR VISIT MORE ENJOYABLE
BEST DAYS TO VISIT
Like Universal Studios Florida, it's best to visit Islands near the end of the week, on a Thursday or Friday. The pace is somewhat fast Monday through Wednesday, with the heaviest crowds on weekends and during summer and holidays.

PLANNING YOUR VISIT
Before you leave home, you can get information on the theme parks and travel packages by calling ✆ **407/224-4233** or 407/363-8000. You can also write to Guest Services, 1000 Universal Studios Plaza, Orlando, FL 32819-7601. For online information, see "Planning Your Visit" in the Universal Studios Florida section, earlier in this chapter.

Note that many of the park's attractions have minimum **height requirements,** described in the listings that follow. Universal also recommends that expectant mothers steer clear of some rides (also noted in the listings).

FOR VISITORS WITH SPECIAL NEEDS
Guests with disabilities should go to **Guest Services,** located just inside the main entrance, for a *Rider's Guide for Rider Safety & Guests with Disabilities,* a Telecommunications Device for the Deaf (TDD), or other special assistance. You can rent a standard wheelchair for $12 or an electric one for $40 (both require a $50 deposit and a

signed contract). Reserve them 24 hours or more in advance by calling © **407/224-6350.** You can arrange for sign-language interpreting services at no charge by calling © **888/519-4899** (toll-free TDD), 407/224-4414 (local TDD), or 407/224-5929 (voice). Make arrangements for an appointment with an interpreter 1 to 2 weeks in advance. Check www.universalorlando.com for more information.

Tip: The *Rider's Guide* is also a great tool for parents, as it describes in great detail the various rides' special effects, warnings, height requirements, and information on general guest services at both Universal parks.

SERVICES & FACILITIES AT ISLANDS OF ADVENTURE

ATMs   Cash machines accepting cards from the Cirrus, Honor, and PLUS systems are located outside and to the right of the main entrance, in the Lost Continent near Mythos, near the bridge between the Lost Continent and Jurassic Park, and in Marvel Super Hero Island near the Amazing Adventures of Spider-Man.

Baby Care   Nursing facilities are located in the Guest Services building in the Port of Entry. Look for the FAMILY SERVICES sign. There are no infant supplies sold anywhere in the park, so come prepared with diapers, food, and other necessities.

Cameras & Film   Film, disposable cameras, and digital supplies are available at De Foto's Expedition Photography, to the right just inside the main entrance.

Car Assistance   Battery jumps are provided. If you need assistance with your car, raise the hood and press the blue button at one of the guest-assistance stations located throughout the garage to call for security.

First Aid   There's one station just inside and to the right of the main entrance, and another in the Lost Continent, across from Oasis Coolers.

Lockers   Lockers are across from Guest Services near the main entrance and cost $8 or $10 a day. There are also lockers near the Incredible Hulk Coaster in Marvel Super Hero Island, the Jurassic Park River Adventure in Jurassic Park, and Dueling Dragons in the Lost Continent. The lockers at Dueling Dragons and the Incredible Hulk Coaster are free for the first 45 minutes. Thereafter, or at the Jurassic Park River Adventure, they're $2 per hour, to a maximum of $14 per day. You're not supposed to—and shouldn't—take things on these rides, so put them in a locker or give them to a nonrider for safekeeping.

Lost Children   If you lose a child, go to Guest Services, near the main entrance, or talk to the first park employee you see. *Children under 7 should wear name tags* inside their clothing.

Pet Care   You can board pets at the kennel located inside the parking garages for $10 a day (no overnight stays). Ask the parking attendant for directions upon entering the toll plaza. You must provide food, show proof of vaccination, and return to walk your pet periodically. Note that all Universal resorts allow small pets to stay with you in your room.

Stroller Rental   Look to the left as you enter through the turnstiles. The cost is $11 for a single and $17 for a double.

Wheelchair Rental   Regular wheelchairs can be rented for $12 in the center concourse of the parking garage or to your left as you enter the turnstiles of the main entrance. Electric wheelchairs are $40. Both require a signed rental agreement and a $50 deposit.

Tips Finding Your Way

Park maps are available at Guest Services in the Port of Entry in English, French, German, Japanese, Portuguese, and Spanish.

SUGGESTED ITINERARIES

For Families with Young Kids

If you have kids under 10, enter and go to the right to **Seuss Landing,** an island where everything is geared to the young and young at heart. You'll easily spend the morning or longer exploring real-life interpretations of the wacky, colorful world of Dr. Seuss. (The wild colors make for some good photographs.) Be sure to ride **The Cat in the Hat; One Fish, Two Fish, Red Fish, Blue Fish;** and **Caro-Seuss-el.** After all that waiting in line, let the little ones burn some energy playing in **If I Ran the Zoo.** Grab lunch at the **Green Eggs and Ham Cafe** (yes, they really are green).

Next, head to the **Lost Continent** to ride the **Flying Unicorn** (36-in. height minimum) and talk to the **Mystic Fountain;** then let them play in **Camp Jurassic** or watch a "hatching" at the **Discovery Center** in **Jurassic Park.** They can have some more interactive fun in **Toon Lagoon** aboard **Me Ship, The Olive,** and meet characters at King's Row and Comic Strip Lane.

Those 40 inches or taller can end the day in **Marvel Super Hero Island** by riding the **Amazing Adventures of Spider-Man.**

For Families with Older Kids & Teens

Head left from Port of Entry to **Marvel Super Hero Island** and ride the **Incredible Hulk Coaster,** the **Amazing Adventures of Spider-Man,** and **Doctor Doom's Fearfall.** (If you arrive early, the line will be short for your first choice, but you'll have to wait or use Universal Express Plus for the others.) There should be time to squeeze in **Dudley Do-Right's Ripsaw Falls** in **Toon Lagoon** before you break for lunch at **Comic Strip Cafe** or **Blondie's: Home of the Dagwood.**

Now that you're fully refueled, ride **Popeye & Bluto's Bilge-Rat Barges;** then move to **Jurassic Park,** where you can ride **Jurassic Park River Adventure** and visit the **Discovery Center.** End your day in the **Lost Continent,** where you can catch the show in **Poseidon's Fury** and test your courage aboard **Dueling Dragons.**

PORT OF ENTRY

Beyond the gigantic, crumbling-stone archway, you'll find the Port of Entry's numerous souvenir shops, bazaars, and eateries lining the exotic streetscape. Save this area for last (unless you're in need of nourishment to start you on your way), spending only a few minutes now to take in your surroundings—the architecture and attention to detail are striking. If you plan to save shopping for the end of the day, return to **Islands of Adventure Trading Company,** where you'll find almost everything from T-shirts to trinkets that relate to the various attractions at the park.

SEUSS LANDING

This 10-acre island, inspired by the works of the late Theodor Seuss Geisel, is awash in Day-Glo colors, whimsical architecture, and curved trees (the latter were downed and bent by Hurricane Andrew before the park acquired them). Needless to say, the main attractions here are aimed at the younger set, though anyone who loved the good Doctor as a child will enjoy some nostalgic fun. Those who aren't familiar with his work will enjoy the visuals: Seussian art is like Dalí for kids.

Caro-Seuss-el
Frommer's Rating: A+ for young kids, parents, and carousel lovers
Recommended Ages: All ages
Forget tradition. This not-so-average carousel gives you a chance to ride seven whimsical characters of Dr. Seuss (a total of 54 mounts), including cowfish, elephant birds, and mulligatawnies. They move up and down as well as in and out. Their eyes blink and their heads bob as you twirl through the riot of color surrounding the ride. *Note:* A special ride platform lets guests in wheelchairs experience the up-and-down motion of the ride, making this a great stop for visitors with disabilities.

The Cat in the Hat
Frommer's Rating: A for preteens, C+ for teens and adults
Recommended Ages: All ages
Any Seuss fan will recognize the giant candy-striped hat looming over the entrance to this ride and probably the chaotic journey. Comparable to but spunkier than It's a Small World at Magic Kingdom (p. 199), the Cat in the Hat is among the signature children's experiences at Islands of Adventure. Love or hate the idea, *do it,* and earn your stripes. Your couch travels through 18 scenes retelling *The Cat in the Hat*'s tale of a day gone very much awry. You, meanwhile, spin about, meeting Thing 1 and Thing 2, in addition to other colorful characters. The highlight is a revolving 24-foot tunnel that alters your perceptions and leaves your head with a feeling oddly reminiscent of a hangover. While a bit herky and jerky at times, that's all part of the fun. *Note:* Pop-up characters may be scary for riders under 5, but it's usually a hit with the 4-to-7 crowd. Expectant moms are discouraged from riding.

   Nicolas's Rating: "Are you kidding? It's not fast at all, and *The Cat in the Hat*—it's a little-kids' story." **Hailey's** and **Davis's Rating:** In contrast, they thought otherwise.

If I Ran the Zoo
Frommer's Rating: A for the very young
Recommended Ages: 2–7
This small interactive play area is where kids can dodge flying water snakes and tickle the toes of a Seussian creature. It's filled with 19 play stations that include slides, wheels to spin, caves to explore, and other things geared to burning off some of the

---

Tips A Late Debut

After 7 years of klonking, bonking, jerking, and berking, the mini monorail hanging high over Seuss Landing (which has gone rider-less until now) is once again in operation. Running along two tiny train tracks, the High in the Sky Seuss Trolley Train Ride takes riders on a whimsical journey through several classic Seussian stories. Lines for this one can be excruciatingly long (and well hidden from sight), but high-power fans help keep you cool while you wait. Note: Though a rather tame ride, kids (and parents) who are afraid of heights may find it slightly unnerving.

excited energy of tinier tots. Just plan on them getting wet—that's half the fun! It's perfect for the preschool set.

One Fish, Two Fish, Red Fish, Blue Fish
Frommer's Rating: B+ for kids and parents
Recommended Ages: 2–7

This kiddie charmer will move "up, up, up" and "down, down, down" as you ride in a funky flying fish whose controls enable you to ascend or descend 15 feet while you spin around on an arm attached to a hub (much like Magic Kingdom's Magic Carpets of Aladdin—including the ridiculously long line). Watch out for squirt posts, which spray unsuspecting riders who don't follow along with the ride's little rhyme (and sometimes even the ones who *do* follow it).

MARVEL SUPER HERO ISLAND

Thrill junkies love the twisting, turning, stomach-churning rides on this island filled with building-tall murals of super heroes. Fans can **meet the Marvel Super Heroes** in front of the Amazing Adventures of Spider-Man (for times, check the guide map you get when you enter the park, or grab a copy at Guest Services). The munch crowd can dig into sandwiches and burgers at **Captain America Diner** ($6–$10) or pizza, pasta, and sandwiches at **Cafe 4** ($4–$12).

The Amazing Adventures of Spider-Man *Finds*
Frommer's Rating: A+
Recommended Ages: 8–adult

The original Web master stars in this exceptional show/ride (arguably the best in town), which features 3-D action and special effects. The story line: You're on a tour of the *Daily Bugle* when—yikes!—something goes horribly wrong. Peter Parker suddenly encounters evil villains and becomes Spider-Man. This high-tech ride isn't stationary, but travels—similar to the way you move through Men in Black Alien Attack at Universal Studios (p. 266), but here the cars twist and spin, plunge and soar through a comic-book universe. Passengers wearing 3-D glasses squeal as computer-generated objects fly at their 12-person cars. There's even a simulated 400-foot drop—and it feels an awful lot like the real thing. *Note:* There's a 40-inch height minimum. Expectant mothers and those with heart, neck, or back problems shouldn't ride.

Tip: Waits can be 45 minutes even on an off day (and sometimes a whole lot longer), so if you've paid for Universal Express Plus, this is definitely the place to use it. The ride also offers a single-rider line that can drastically reduce waiting times. If you've got older kids or teens who won't mind splitting up, take advantage of it.

Ryan's Rating: "I think I left my stomach back there." (He wasn't the only one. This ride is unsuitable for young children and squeamish adults—though closing your eyes at just the right time can help immensely. If you are neither, it's an absolute must.)
Austin's and **Nicolas's Rating:** "You gotta do this one a couple times at least!"

Doctor Doom's Fearfall
Frommer's Rating: C+
Recommended Ages: 8–adult

Look! Up in the sky! It's a bird, it's a plane . . . uh, it's you falling 150 feet, if you're courageous enough to climb aboard this towering metal skeleton. The screams can be heard at the ride's entrance, adding to the anticipation of a big plunge followed by smaller ones (even the initial upward surge catches some by surprise). The plot? You're touring a lab when—are you sensing a recurring theme here?—something goes wrong as Doctor Doom tries to cure you of fear. You're fired to the top, with feet dangling, and dropped in intervals, feet first, leaving your stomach at several levels. The experience isn't nearly up to the Tower of Terror's at Disney's Hollywood Studios (most of the velocity moves in the "up" direction, not the down one), but it's still frightful (and you do get a neat view of the entire park). The waiting times can also be scary, but the teens who flock here don't seem to mind. *Note:* If you or your kids are scared of heights, don't even think about getting on this one. Minimum height is 52 inches. Expectant mothers and those with heart, neck, or back problems shouldn't ride.

Incredible Hulk Coaster (Finds

Frommer's Rating: A+
Recommended Ages: 10–adult
Bruce Banner is working in his lab when—yes, again—something goes wrong. But this rocking rocket of a ride makes everything oh so right, except maybe your heart and stomach. From a dark tunnel, you burst into the sunlight while accelerating from 0 to 40 mph in 2 seconds. While that's only two-thirds the speed of the Rock 'n' Roller Coaster at Disney's Hollywood Studios, this is in broad daylight; there's a lot more motion still to come; and you can *see* the asphalt! From there, you spin upside down 128 feet from the ground, feel weightless, and careen through the center of the park over the heads of other visitors. Coaster-lovers will be pleased to know that this ride, which lasts 2 minutes and 15 seconds, includes seven inversions and two deep drops. It's extremely smooth, however, making it one of the better coaster experiences for all types of riders. Sunglasses, change, and an occasional set of car keys lie in a mesh net beneath the ride—proof of its motion and the fact that most folks don't heed the warnings to stash their stuff in the nearby lockers. As a nice touch, the 32-passenger metal coaster glows green at night (riders who ignore all the warnings occasionally turn green as well). *Note:* Riders must be at least 54 inches tall. Expectant mothers and those with heart, neck, or back problems shouldn't ride.

Austin's Rating: "That was sooooooo smooooooth, and you shot off like a rocket." (Adrenaline-seeking teens not only love this ride, but also often wait in an even longer line to get a front-row seat for all the action.)

Storm Force Accelatron

Frommer's Rating: C+
Recommended Ages: 4–adult
Despite the exotic name, this ride is little more than a spinoff (no pun intended) of the Magic Kingdom's Mad Tea Party (p. 200)—spinning teacups that, in this case, have a 22nd-century design. While aboard, you and the X-Men's super heroine, Storm, try to defeat the evil Magneto by converting human energy into electrical

---

(Tips Out of Sight . . .

If your kids are at the age where they are just starting to test the more intense thrill rides, they may overreach once or twice. To be on the safe side, tell your kids that if they find a ride a little too intense, they should hang on and close their eyes. A lot of the thrills at many of the parks are visually driven, and the intensity will come down a notch or two if you can't see what's coming. The only exception to this is Epcot's Mission: Space (p. 215), where shutting your eyes may actually cause even more disorientation.

forces. To do that, you need to spin faster and faster. In addition to some upset stomachs (your kids will be happy to give you one), the spiraling creates a thunderstorm of sound and light that gives Storm all the power she needs to blast Magneto into the ever-after (or until the next riders arrive). This ride is sometimes closed during off-peak periods. *Note:* Expectant moms are advised not to ride.

TOON LAGOON

More than 150 life-size sculpted cartoon images—characters range from Betty Boop and Flash Gordon to Bullwinkle and Cathy—let you know you've entered an island dedicated to your favorites from the Sunday funnies. Many of the selected characters will probably be more familiar to parents than to children, but Popeye is present, and the cool rides mean your kids will be happy anyway.

Dudley Do-Right's Ripsaw Falls
Frommer's Rating: A
Recommended Ages: 7–adult
The setting and effects at Disney's Splash Mountain (p. 196) are better, but the adrenaline rush here is higher. The staid red hat of the heroic Dudley can be deceiving: The ride that lies under it has a lot more speed and drop than onlookers suspect. Six-passenger logs take you around a 400,000-gallon lagoon before launching you into a 75-foot drop at 50 mph. At one point, you're 15 feet below the surface. Though the water is contained on either side, you *will* get wet. Younger kids may be a bit intimidated by the whole experience, but most children who make the height requirements like it. *Note:* Once again, expectant mothers and folks with heart, neck, or back problems should do something else. Riders must be at least 44 inches tall.

   Austin's Rating: "I'm soaked . . . but what a rush! Just when you think you're done, it makes another dip and dive." (It may not, however, be as much of a rush for the taller members of your family: One of the ride's biggest knocks is that its passenger logs are pretty cramped, especially if you have long legs.)

King's Row & Comic Strip Lane
Frommer's Rating: C+
Recommended Ages: All ages
Dudley Do-Right, Woody Woodpecker, Popeye, and other favorites from the Sunday comics will have you rockin' and rollin' in the streets as they sing and make you laugh during this several-times-a-day show.

Me Ship, *The Olive*
Frommer's Rating: B+
Recommended Ages: 4–adult
This three-story boat is a family-friendly play land with dozens of interactive activities from bow to stern. Kids can toot whistles, clang bells, or play the organ. Sweet Pea's Playpen is a favorite of younger guests. Kids 6 and up will love Cargo Crane (adults will like it, too), where they can drench riders on Popeye & Bluto's Bilge-Rat Barges (see below). *Note:* If you or your kids are shutterbugs, the second and third deck of the good ship offer great views and **photo ops** of the Incredible Hulk Coaster and some of the rest of Islands of Adventure.

Popeye & Bluto's Bilge-Rat Barges
Frommer's Rating: A
Recommended Ages: 6–adult

This is the same kind of ride with the same kind of raft as Kali River Rapids at Disney's Animal Kingdom (p. 245), but it's a bit faster and bouncier. You'll be squirted by mechanical devices as well as the water cannons fired by guests at Me Ship, *The Olive* (see above). The 12-passenger rafts bump, churn, and dip (14 ft. at one point) along a whitewater course lined with Bluto, Sea Hag, and other villains. You will get soaked—and then drenched for good measure. Kids find this a whole lot less intimidating than some of the other rides at Islands. *Note:* Yes, once again, expectant mothers and people with heart, neck, or back problems shouldn't ride this one. Riders must be at least 42 inches tall.

Austin's Rating: "The water is *c-c-cold*"—a blessing on hot summer days but less so in January.

JURASSIC PARK

All the basics and some of the high-tech wizardry from Steven Spielberg's wildly successful films are incorporated into this lushly landscaped tropical locale that includes a replica of the visitor center from the movie. There's something here for every child, from teens to toddlers. Expect long lines at the River Adventure and pleasant surprises at the Discovery Center.

Camp Jurassic
Frommer's Rating: A+ for young children
Recommended Ages: 2–7

This play area, similar in theme to (but even better than) the Boneyard in Disney's Animal Kingdom, has everything from lava pits with dinosaur bones to a rainforest to amber mines. Watch out for the spitters that lurk in dark caves. The multilevel play area has plenty of places for kids to crawl, slide, climb, explore, and expend their excess energy. Little kids need close supervision, though: It's easy to get turned around inside the caverns, and some of the areas enhanced with sound effects may be a bit too frightening for the very young. Be prepared for your kids to get soaked—you will be, too, if you have to retrieve them (very likely).

Jurassic Park Discovery Center
Frommer's Rating: B+
Recommended Ages: All ages

Here's an amusing, educational pit stop with life-size dinosaur replicas and some interactive games, including a sequencer that pretends to combine your DNA with a dinosaur's. The "Beasaur" exhibit allows you to see and hear as the huge reptiles did. You can play the game show *You Bet Jurassic* (grin) and scan the walls for fossils. The highlight is watching a velociraptor "hatch" in the lab. Because there are a limited number of interactive stations, this can consume a lot of time on busy days. Be sure to enter from the lower level—the view is spectacular and there's an elaborate stone plaza—which is far more impressive than the doors upstairs.

Jurassic Park River Adventure
Frommer's Rating: A
Recommended Ages: 7–adult

A leisurely raft tour along a river is interrupted when some raptors, who could hop aboard your boat at any moment, escape. The ride lets you literally come face-to-face

---

> **Tips Up, Up & Away**
>
> Strength and fitness folks can get a little extra workout at the small rock-climbing venue (for an additional fee) outside the Thunder Falls Terrace restaurant in Jurassic Park. If you or the kids are looking for a more economical and less strenuous option, try walking the elevated trails and climbing the net ladders beneath the Pteranodon Flyers attraction, also in Jurassic Park.

---

with "breathing" inhabitants of Jurassic Park. At one point, a *Tyrannosaurus rex* decides you look like a tasty morsel, and at another point, spitters launch venomous saliva your way. The only way out: an 85-foot plunge in your log-style life raft that will leave you dripping. If your stomach can take only one flume ride, this one's a lot more comfortable than Dudley Do-Right (see above), and the atmosphere is better. ***Note:*** Expectant mothers and those with heart, neck, or back problems shouldn't ride. Guests must be at least 42 inches tall.

Austin's and **Nicolas's Rating:** "The drop was definitely scary . . . in a fun sort of way, but definitely scary." (It's steep and quick enough to lift your fanny out of the seat. Fact is, when Spielberg rode it, he made them stop the ride and let him out before the plunge.)

Pteranodon Flyers
Frommer's Rating: C+
Recommended Ages: All ages (sort of—see restrictions below)
The 10-foot metal frames and simple seats seem flimsy, but this quick spin around Jurassic Park offers a great bird's-eye view. The landing is bumpy, and you'll swing side to side throughout, which makes some riders queasy. Unlike the traditional gondolas in sky rides, on this one, your feet hang free from the two-seat skeletal flyer, and there's little but a restraining belt between you and the ground. ***Note:*** That said, this is a child's ride. Single passengers must be between 36 and 56 inches tall; adults can climb aboard *only* when accompanying someone that size. And because this ride launches only two passengers every 30 to 40 seconds, it can consume an hour of your day, even in the off season. So although it is nice, and your little ones will love it, pass it up if you're pressed for time.

Nicolas's Rating: "That was cool. It was like flying, but the wait was horrible." The swaying adds a little thrill to the equation, but we waited over an hour for this one, and it wasn't even a particularly crowded day.

THE LOST CONTINENT
Although it's mixed its millennia—ancient Greece with a medieval forest—Universal has done a good job of creating a foreboding mood in this section of the park, whose entrance is marked by menacing stone griffins. This is another section that offers at least one attraction that every child in your party will find to his or her liking.

Dueling Dragons *(Moments*
Frommer's Rating: A+
Recommended Ages: 10–adult
Maniacal minds created this thrill ride, sending two roller coasters right at each other at high speeds (when both are running, which isn't always the case). True coaster crazies will love the intertwined set of leg-dangling racers that climb to 125 feet, invert

---

Tips   Universal's Conjuring Up a Bit of Its Own Magic

Soon the witchcraft and wizardry of Harry Potter will cast its spell on Universal Orlando's Islands of Adventure. Slated to debut in late 2009, the Wizarding World of Harry Potter (based on the wildly popular books written by J. K. Rowling as well as the Warner Bros. blockbuster movies) will bring to life the adventures of the young wizard. Immersive rides and interactive attractions—including meticulous re-creations of the Hogwarts castle, the village of Hogsmeade, and the Forbidden Forest—plus an array of shops and restaurants (think Diagon Alley) will be created from areas within the Lost Continent, extending beyond to land that's yet to be developed. The estimated budget for this 20-acre park-within-a-park is said to be somewhere between $230 and $265 million.

---

five times, and three times come within 12 inches of each other as the two dragons battle and you prove your bravery by tagging along. A couple of thrill junkies (after riding this one for the third time in a day) revealed that this is where they head in Orlando when they want the ultimate adrenaline rush (though it's not as smooth a ride as the Hulk Coaster). Teens flock here in droves. For the best ride, try to get one of the two outside seats in each of the eight rows. If you want to get into the front seat, there's a special (yes, longer!) line near the loading dock for daredevils. *Note:* Expectant mothers and those with heart, neck, or back problems shouldn't ride. (Why aren't you surprised?) Riders must be at least 54 inches tall.

Eighth Voyage of Sindbad *Overrated*
Frommer's Rating: C+
Recommended Ages: 6–adult
The mythical sailor is the star of a stunt demonstration that takes place in a 1,700-seat theater decorated with blue stalagmites and eerie, gloomy shipwrecks. The show has water explosions and dozens of pyrotechnic effects, including a 10-foot circle of flames. Younger kids may find some of the characters too scary, so a seat in the back may be in order if you have tots in tow. Although it offers a rest for park-weary feet, it doesn't come close to the quality of the Indiana Jones stunt show in Disney's Hollywood Studios (p. 231). *Note:* This show is closed from time to time, including during the run of Halloween Horror Nights (p. 260).

Flying Unicorn
Frommer's Rating: A+ for kids and parents, B+ for others
Recommended Ages: 5–adult
The Flying Unicorn is a small roller coaster that travels through a mythical forest in the Lost Continent, next to Dueling Dragons. It's very much like Woody Woodpecker's Nuthouse Coaster at Universal Studios Florida (p. 268) and The Barnstormer at Goofy's Wiseacre Farm in the Magic Kingdom (p. 202). That means a fast corkscrew run that is sure to earn squeals, but probably not at the risk of someone's losing his lunch. It's the perfect introductory coaster for the young set. *Note:* Here's another one that expectant moms are warned not to ride. The Unicorn has a 36-inch height minimum.

(Tips Adventures in Dining

Islands has dozens of sit-down restaurants, eateries, and snack carts. There are also several restaurants just a short walk from the park in Universal's entertainment complex, CityWalk (see chapter 5, "Family-Friendly Dining").

To save money, look for kiddie menus, offering a children's meal and a small beverage for $6 to $8. Also consider combo meals, which usually offer a slight price break. For instance, **Thunder Falls Terrace**, in Jurassic Park, offers a rib-and-chicken combo as well as other options in the $9-to-$14 range.

The park's creators have taken some extra care to tie in restaurant offerings with the theme. The **Green Eggs and Ham Cafe** may be one of the few places on earth where you'd be willing to eat tinted huevos. (An egg-and-ham sandwich goes for about $7.)

Best Sit-Down Meal: At **Mythos** (p. 162), in the Lost Continent, enjoy cedar-planked salmon, chicken a la Oscar, or sandwiches and pastas. The undersea cavelike atmosphere makes a pleasant setting for a grown-up dinner, best suited to adults and kids over 10. Entrees cost $11 to $16; Mythos is usually open from 11:30am to 3:30pm and again at 5pm for dinner.

Best Atmosphere for Adults & Teens: The **Enchanted Oak Tavern** (and **Alchemy Bar**), also in the Lost Continent, has a cavelike interior that looks like a mammoth tree from the outside and is brightened by an azure skylight with a celestial theme. The tables and chairs are thick planks, and the servers are clad in "wench wear." Try the chicken/rib combo with waffle fries for about $13. Mom and Dad can sample from the 45 types of beer on the menu.

Best Atmosphere for Kids: The fun never stops under the big top at **Circus McGurkus Cafe Stoo-pendous**, in Seuss Landing, where animated trapeze artists swing from the ceiling. Kids' meals, including a souvenir cup, are $6 to $8. The adult menu features fried chicken, chicken sandwiches, cheeseburgers, spaghetti, and pizza ($7–$12).

Best Diversity: The **Comic Strip Cafe**, located in Toon Lagoon, is a four-in-one, counter-service-style eatery offering burgers, pizza and pasta, chicken and fish, and even Chinese. Entrees run $6 to $9.

Mystic Fountain

Frommer's Rating: B+ for kids
Recommended Ages: 3–8

Located just outside Sindbad's theater, this interactive "smart" fountain delights younger guests (and usually provides a cool photo op or two for parents). It can see and hear, leading to a lot of kibitzing with those who stand before it. If you want to stay dry, don't get too close when it starts "spouting" its wet wisdom. On the other hand, if you need a quick cool-off, go for it.

Tips **Great Buys at Islands of Adventure**

Here's a sampling of some of the more unusual wares available at Islands of Adventure. It represents a cross-section of tastes:

Jurassic Outfitters There are plenty of T-shirts with slogans like "I Survived [the whatever ride]."

Spider-Man Shop This shop specializes in its namesake's paraphernalia, including red Spidey caps covered with black webs and denim jackets with logos.

Toon Extra Where else can you buy a miniature stuffed Mr. Peanut bean-bag, a frame with Olive Oyl and Popeye, or a stuffed Beetle Bailey? Life doesn't get any better for some of us.

Treasures of Poseidon Located in the Lost Continent, it carries an array of blue glassware, including tumblers, stuffed animals, and toys.

Poseidon's Fury
Frommer's Rating: B+
Recommended Ages: 6–adult

This is the park's best show—though with a lack of competition (there are only two productions at Islands), that's something of a backhanded compliment. The story line revolves around a battle between Poseidon, god of the sea, and the evil Darkenon. The highlight is when you pass through a small room with a 42-foot vortex where 17,500 gallons of water swirl around you, barrel-roll style. (If you wear glasses, note that they will fog up completely when passing through the vortex—take them off if you can.) In the battle royale, the gods hurl 25-foot fireballs at each other. It's more interesting than frightening, but it's not worth the long lines that often plague it, so if you're on a tight schedule, skip it unless you have Universal Express privileges. *Note:* The fireballs, explosive sounds, and rushing water (not to mention the dark and eerie passageways of the queue area) may be too intense for children under 6.

SHOPPING IN THE PARK

There are more than 20 shops within the park, offering a variety of theme merchandise. You may want to check out **Cats, Hats & Things** for special Seussian souvenirs, books, and T-shirts. **Jurassic Outfitters** and **Dinostore** feature a variety of stuffed and plastic dinosaurs, plus safari-themed clothing. Superhero fans should check out the **Marvel Alterniverse Store** and the **Spider-Man Shop.** In Toon Lagoon, **Toon Extra** has the largest selection of souvenirs. **Islands of Adventure Trading Company** is a good stop on the way out if you're still searching for something that will help you or the folks back home remember your visit.

   Note: Universal has a service similar to Disney's in which you can have your purchases delivered to the front of the park; allow 3 hours. If you get home and realize you can't live without a certain something, use the shop-by-phone service: Just call © 407/224-5800, describe the item and where you think you saw it, and the phone rep will likely be able to help you out.

3 SeaWorld

Cleverly disguised as a theme park—or, as SeaWorld likes to call itself, an adventure park—this popular 200-acre marine park lets visitors explore the mysteries of the deep and learn about the oceans and their inhabitants, all while having tons of fun. Recently rated by *Parents* magazine as one of the top 10 U.S. aquariums for kids, Sea-World combines wildlife-conservation awareness (otherwise known as edutainment), actual marine-life care, and plain old fun all in one fell swoop. While that's what Disney is attempting with its latest park, Animal Kingdom, the message here is subtle and a more inherent part of the experience.

SeaWorld's beautifully landscaped grounds center on a 17-acre lagoon and include flamingo and pelican ponds and a lush tropical rainforest. **Shamu,** a killer whale, is the star of the park, along with his expanding family, which includes baby whales. The pace is much more laid-back than at either Universal or Disney, and it's a good way to break up a long week trudging through the other parks. Close encounters at feeding pools are among the real attractions (so be sure to budget a few extra dollars to buy fishy hand-outs for the sea lions and dolphins, who've turned begging into an art form).

SeaWorld manages a few thrills and chills. **Journey to Atlantis** is a high-tech water ride similar to Splash Mountain at Disney's Magic Kingdom (p. 196) and Jurassic Park River Adventure at Universal Orlando's Islands of Adventure (p. 280). And **Kraken** is a floorless roller coaster that sports seven inversions, much like coasters such as Montu and Kumba at SeaWorld's sister, Busch Gardens Tampa Bay (p. 341). But this park doesn't try to compete with the wonders of WDW or Universal. Instead, it lets you discover the crushed-velvet texture of a stingray or the song of the seals. And your children will enjoy that every bit as much as the techno wonders elsewhere.

ESSENTIALS

GETTING THERE The marine park is south of Orlando and Universal, north of Disney. From I-4, take Exit 72, Beachline Expressway/Highway 528, and follow the signs.

PARKING Parking costs $10 for cars, light trucks, and vans. The lots aren't huge, and most folks can walk to the entrance (if you prefer a very short walk, preferred parking is available for $15). Trams also run. Write down the location of your car so you can find it later; SeaWorld characters such as Wally Walrus mark the sections, but at the end of a long day, it's easy to forget where you parked.

HOURS The park is usually open from 9am to 6pm and sometimes later, 365 days a year. Call ✆ **800/327-2424** or 407/351-3600 for more information.

TICKET PRICES At press time, a **1-day ticket** costs $65 for ages 10 and over, $54 for children 3 to 9, plus 6.5% sales tax (a relative bargain). SeaWorld often offers promotions that net you a second day, or more, for free. The park's new online ticketing allows you buy and print out tickets at **www.seaworld.com.**

See p. 254 for information on the **FlexTicket,** multiday admission tickets for Sea-World, Universal Orlando, Wet 'n Wild, and Busch Gardens.

The **Adventure Express Tour** ($90 adults, $80 kids, *plus park admission*) is a 7-hour guided excursion that includes front-of-the-line access to Journey to Atlantis, Kraken, and Wild Arctic; reserved seating at select shows; lunch; and a chance to touch or feed penguins, dolphins, stingrays, and sea lions. It's the only way to dodge

---

Tips **Shuttle Service**

SeaWorld Orlando and Busch Gardens Tampa Bay, both owned by Anheuser-Busch, have a shuttle service that charges $10 round-trip to get you from Orlando to Tampa and back. The 1½- to 2-hour (one-way) shuttle runs daily and has several pickup locations in Orlando, including at Universal and on I-Drive (© 800/221-1339). The schedule allows about 7 hours at Busch Gardens. The service is free if you have a FlexTicket (p. 254).

---

park lines, though these aren't as long as Disney's or Universal's. Call © **800/406-2244** or 407/363-2380 to book.

MAKING YOUR VISIT MORE ENJOYABLE
BEST TIME OF YEAR TO VISIT
SeaWorld has smaller crowds from January through April and from just after Labor Day until just before Thanksgiving. Because this is a mostly outdoor, water-related park, however, you may want to keep in mind that even Florida gets a tad nippy during January and February.

BEST DAYS TO VISIT
Thursday through Sunday are busy days at this park. Monday through Wednesday are usually better days to visit, because tourists coming for a week go to the Disney and Universal parks early in their stays, saving SeaWorld for the end, if at all.

PLANNING YOUR VISIT
Get information before you leave by writing to **SeaWorld Guest Services** at 7007 SeaWorld Dr., Orlando, FL 32801, by calling © **800/327-2424** or 407/351-3600, or by going online to **www.seaworld.com**. The *Orlando Sentinel* newspaper produces **www.orlandosentinel.com**. You can also get a ton of information from the Orlando/Orange County Convention & Visitors Bureau website at **www.orlandoinfo.com**.

Because it has few thrill rides, SeaWorld has few restrictions, but you may want to check out the special tour programs offered through the education department. SeaWorld lives up to its reputation for making education fun, and these wonderful experiences will entertain both you and your kids—and are well worth the extra expense. The 1-hour options include a **Polar Expedition Tour** (touch a penguin), **Predators Tour** (touch a shark), and **Saving a Species Tour** (see manatees and sea turtles). All cost $12 to $18 for adults and $10 to $12 for children 3 to 9, *plus park admission.* A **Dolphin Nursery Close-up** is available as well ($40 for ages 10 and up). Call © **407/363-2380** for information or © **800/406-2244** for reservations.

FOR VISITORS WITH SPECIAL NEEDS
The park publishes an accessibility guide for guests with disabilities, although most of its attractions are easily accessible to those in wheelchairs. (The guide is also available at www.seaworld.com in the "Park Information" section.) SeaWorld also provides a Braille guide for the visually impaired. For the hearing-impaired, there's a very brief synopsis of shows. Assisted-listening devices are available at select attractions for a $20 refundable deposit. Sign-language interpreting services are available at no charge, but must be reserved by calling © **407/363-2414** at least a week in advance of your visit.

SeaWorld

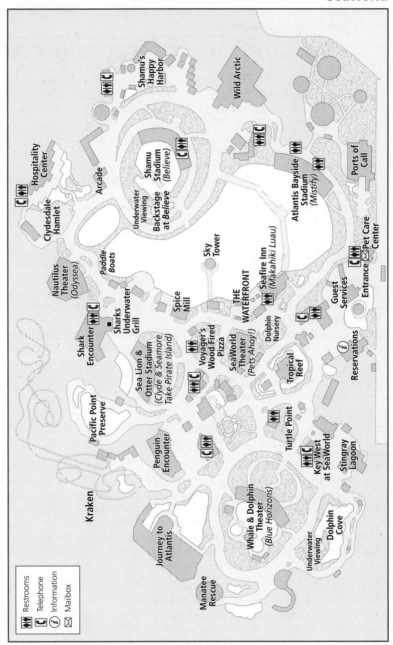

Legend:
- Restrooms
- Telephone
- Information
- Mailbox

Map labels:

Shamu's Happy Harbor

Wild Arctic

Hospitality Center

Arcade

Clydesdale Hamlet

Ports of Call

Nautilus Theater (Odyssea)

Shamu Stadium (Believe)

Underwater Viewing

Backstage at Believe

Atlantis Bayside Stadium (Mistify)

Pet Care Center

Paddle Boats

Sky Tower

Sharks Underwater Grill

Shark Encounter

Spice Mill

THE WATERFRONT

Seafire Inn (Makahiki Luau)

Guest Services

Entrance

Sea Lion & Otter Stadium (Clyde & Seamore Take Pirate Island)

Voyager's Wood Fired Pizza

SeaWorld Theater (Pets Ahoy!)

Dolphin Nursery

Tropical Reef

Reservations

Pacific Point Preserve

Penguin Encounter

Turtle Point

Kraken

Key West at SeaWorld

Stingray Lagoon

Journey to Atlantis

Whale & Dolphin Theater (Blue Horizons)

Underwater Viewing

Dolphin Cove

Manatee Rescue

287

Tips **Dining with the Fishes**

SeaWorld is diving deeper into the restaurant game with **Backstage at Believe** (✆ **800/327-2424** or 407/351-3600; www.seaworld.com), a reservations-only seafood buffet served poolside, with Shamu as a special guest. While eating, guests can mingle and question SeaWorld trainers. The menu includes seafood Creole, sliced turkey, roast chicken, pasta shrimp Alfredo, an array of sides, rolls, and desserts (children can choose from their own buffet of kid-friendly favorites). The cost is $37 for adults and $19 for kids 3 to 9, in addition to park admission. Reserving a spot 2 to 3 weeks in advance is usually sufficient, unless you're coming in one of the crunch periods (summer or holidays), when you should call as soon as your travel plans are firm.

Additional up-close or unique dining experiences (including the Shamu Rocks Buffet, a Spooktacular Breakfast, and others) are offered seasonally. Check online for details and dates.

Sharks Underwater Grill is an underwater venue with floor-to-ceiling windows where diners can dig into Florida and Caribbean treats while watching denizens of the Shark Encounter exhibit swim by. Menu prices are $22 to $28 for adults, $6 to $12 for kids 3 to 9 (pasta, hot dogs, chicken breast, steak, and popcorn shrimp). Theme-park admission is required. Call ✆ **800/327-2420** for reservations.

Other dining options once you're inside the park include the **Seafire Inn** (stir-fry, burgers, coconut shrimp, chicken, and salads) and **Voyager's Wood Fired Pizza** (pizza, grilled salmon, smoked chicken, and focaccia club sandwiches).

For a complete rundown of all of your options, head to Guest Services when you enter the park; you can also call ✆ **407/351-3600** for more information.

BUDGETING YOUR TIME

Don't be in a rush: SeaWorld has a leisurely pace because its biggest attractions are up-close encounters with the animals. This park can easily be enjoyed in a day, and its layout and the many outdoor exhibits give it an open feel. Because of the large capacity and walk-through nature of many of the attractions, crowds generally aren't a concern except at Journey to Atlantis and Kraken. Wild Arctic also draws a sizable crowd, and you'll need to arrive at Shamu Stadium in plenty of time for the show. But the lines here don't reach Disney's proportions even at peak times, so relax. Isn't that what a vacation is supposed to be about?

SERVICES & FACILITIES AT SEAWORLD

ATMs ATMs are located at the front of the park, near Dolphin Cove in Key West, across from Mama's Kitchen, near the paddle boats, in Shamu's Happy Harbour, and behind Mango Joe's Cafe. They accept cards affiliated with Cirrus, Honor, and PLUS.

Baby Care Changing tables are in or near most women's restrooms and in the men's restroom at the front entrance near Shamu's Emporium. You can buy diapers and select baby supplies at the gift shop near Guest Services at the entrance. There's a special area for nursing mothers near the women's restroom at Friends of the Wild gift shop, near the Penguin Encounter, at the Guest Assistance Center, and at Shamu's Happy Harbor Baby Care Center.

Cameras & Film   Film, disposable cameras, and limited digital supplies are available at stores throughout the park.

First Aid   Stations staffed with registered nurses are behind Stingray Lagoon and in Shamu's Happy Harbor.

Lockers   Lockers are located next to Shamu's Emporium, just inside the park entrance. The cost is $1 per entry for small lockers, $1.50 per entry for larger ones.

Lost Children   Lost children are taken to the Information Center. A parkwide paging system and a Parent Contact Wristband (available at Guest Services) helps reunite guests. *Children under 7 should wear name tags* inside their clothes.

Pet Care   A kennel is available between the parking lot and the main gate. The cost is $6 a day (no overnight stays).

Stroller Rental   Fabric joggerlike strollers (replacing the old hard-plastic dolphin-shaped ones) can be rented at the Information Center near the entrance. The cost is $10 for a single, $17 for a double. You can even reserve one ahead of time online. If you prefer to purchase a stroller, umbrella strollers are available for $20.

Wheelchair Rental   Regular wheelchairs are available at the Information Center for $10; electric chairs are $38. A signed rental agreement and ID are required for both.

MAJOR ATTRACTIONS IN THE PARK

Believe *(Moments*
Frommer's Rating: A+
Recommended Ages: All ages
Believe, an all-new killer-whale show (replacing the Shamu Adventure, though still taking place at the Shamu Stadium), made its debut in the summer of 2006. Spectacular ballet-like choreography, a new three-story-high set design (featuring a gigantic whale tail, fountains, and video screens), and an exciting musical score combine to create an impressive and splashy show. And don't worry: Shamu remains in the starring role. Adjoining the exhibit is an **underwater-viewing area** that lets you get a close-up view of the killer whales.

   Ryan's, Austin's, and **Nicolas's Ratings** (in unison): "That's *f-f-freezing!*" (I warned them, but they insisted on sitting in the splash zone. Bring extra clothes and shoes!)

Blue Horizons
Frommer's Rating: A
Recommended Ages: All ages
This isn't your run-of-the-mill aquatic animal act. Inside the park's partially covered, open-air stadium, Atlantic bottlenose dolphins, false killer whales, exotic and colorful birds, divers, and elaborately costumed aerialists perform in this new Broadway-style show. A young girl's image of the sea and sky sets the story line as acts are performed both high above and below the water. The spectacular stage is filled with clouds, bubbles, and waves, making for an impressive backdrop. The animals and actors alike impress with spectacular and graceful stunts as they perform to an original musical score (recorded by the Seattle Symphony Orchestra).

Clyde & Seamore Take Pirate Island
Frommer's Rating: A
Recommended Ages: All ages
A lovable and amusing sea-lion-and-otter duo, with a supporting cast of walruses and harbor seals, stars in this fish-breathed comedy that comes with a swashbuckling series of stunts. The show, staged inside the aptly named Sea Lion & Otter Stadium, is corny, but don't hold that against the animal actors, who are predictably adorable. The performance serves as a welcome change from all the high-tech rides and shows at the other theme parks. Be sure to arrive early enough to catch the mime as he pokes fun at the guests who arrive a bit late, much to the amusement of the entire audience.

Clydesdale Hamlet
Frommer's Rating: C+ (A for horse lovers)
Recommended Ages: All ages
Here is where you will find all the famous Clydesdale horses. Guests can walk through, see the grand beasts, and, in some instances, watch them being hitched up for the occasional parade through the park.

Journey to Atlantis
Frommer's Rating: A
Recommended Ages: 8–adult
Taking a cue from Disney's Imagineers, SeaWorld has created a story line to go with this $30-million water ride. It has to do with a Greek fisherman and ancient Sirens in a battle between good and evil. But what really matters is the drop: a wild plunge from an altitude of 60 feet, in addition to lugelike curves and a shorter drop. Journey to Atlantis breaks from SeaWorld's edutainment formula and offers good old-fashioned fun. There's no hidden lesson—just a splashy thrill when you least expect it. And yes, you will get wet. *Note:* Riders must be at least 42 inches tall. Expectant moms, as well as folks with heart, neck, or back problems, should find some other way to pass the time.

Austin's Rating: "I like that better than Splash Mountain." (I agree that this one has a slight edge over that Magic Kingdom ride, but the Jurassic Park River Adventure, p. 280, wins the battle of Orlando's water coasters—for now—though it's also the scariest.)

Key West at SeaWorld
Frommer's Rating: A+ for kids, B+ for adults
Recommended Ages: All ages
This Caribbean-style village has island food, entertainers, and street vendors. But the big attractions are the hands-on encounters with harmless Southern diamond and cownose rays; Sea Turtle Point, the home of threatened and endangered species; and Dolphin Cove, where you can feed smelt to the namesakes. *Warning:* If you have a soft heart (and little kids are major softies for these animal encounters), it's easy to spend $20 feeding the critters.

Davis's and **Hailey's Rating:** "They're so soft and tickly!" (Indeed, those brave enough to feed the toothless rays likely will find one of their funny bones brushed—and their arms and shirts quite wet.)

Kraken
Frommer's Rating: A+
Recommended Ages: 10–adult
SeaWorld's deepest venture onto the field of thrill-ride battle starts slow, like many coasters, but it ends with pure speed. Kraken is named for a massive, mythological,

---

Tips   Nighttime Fun

Summers bring extended hours—and extended hours bring nighttime entertainment. In addition to its regular productions, SeaWorld stages a few shows only seasonally, including **Shamu Rocks,** an all-new nighttime killer-whale show set to a rock-'n'-roll remix of the hottest hits on the airwaves from Jennifer Lopez, Savage Garden, Lifehouse, and Shakira; and **Mistify,** a spectacular combination of fireworks and fountains on the lagoon (if you're dining at the Spice Mill, you can enjoy dinner and a show). Even **Blue Horizons** (thanks to theatrical lighting) and **Clyde & Seamore** (in Clyde & Seamore Present–Sea Lions Tonight) spiff up their shows after nightfall.

---

underwater beast kept caged by Poseidon. This 21st-century version offers floorless and open-sided 32-passenger trains (the better for you to see what awaits you) that plant you on a pedestal high above the track. When the monster breaks loose, you climb 151 feet, fall 144 feet, hit speeds of 65 mph, go underground three times (spraying bystanders with water), and make seven loops during a 4,177-foot course. It may be the longest 3 minutes, 39 seconds of your life. For adventurous teens, this is *the* top attraction in the park, and the lines can get very long. *Note:* Kraken carries a 54-inch height minimum. Expectant moms, as well as folks with heart, neck, or back problems, should skip this one.

Manatee Rescue
Frommer's Rating: B+
Recommended Ages: All ages

Today, the West Indian manatee is an endangered species, with as few as 3,200 remaining in Florida's wild. Underwater viewing stations, innovative cinema techniques, and interactive displays combine here for a tribute to these gentle marine mammals. While this isn't as good as seeing them in the great outdoors, it's as close as most folks get, and it's a much roomier habitat than the tight quarters their kin have at the Seas with Nemo & Friends in Epcot.

Odyssea
Frommer's Rating: B+
Recommended Ages: All ages

This 30-minute, Cirque du Soleil–style stage show opened at SeaWorld's Nautilus Theater in 2003. The show combines circus acrobatics, comedy, colorful costumes, music, and special effects to create a mythical underwater atmosphere. The special effects are good, and the aerial stunts are even better. You and your kids will be entranced.

Penguin Encounter (Overrated
Frommer's Rating: C; B for young kids
Recommended Ages: All ages

Guests are transported by moving sidewalk through Arctic and Antarctic displays. You'll get a glimpse of penguins as they preen, socialize, and swim at bullet speed in their 22°F (–5°C) habitat. You'll also see puffins and murres in a similar, separate area. While it gives you a nice view of the penguins (and they are always a hit with the kids), the surroundings in the viewing area leave a bit to be desired, especially among so many other elaborate and well-done exhibits.

Pets Ahoy!

Frommer's Rating: B
Recommended Ages: All ages

A veritable menagerie of cats, dogs, pot-bellied pigs, skunks, and a horse are joined by birds and rats (nearly 100 animals in all) to perform comic relief in a 25-minute show held several times a day inside the SeaWorld Theater. Almost all the performers were rescued from animal shelters. It's a charmer that appeals to young and old.

Shamu's Happy Harbor

Frommer's Rating: A for kids
Recommended Ages: 3–12

This 3-acre play area has a four-story net tower with a 35-foot crow's-nest lookout, water cannons, remote-controlled vehicles, a life-size ship, and a water maze. It's one of the most extensive play areas at any park and a great place for kids to unwind. Recent additions that will assuredly entertain little ones include the **Shamu Express,** a kid-friendly coaster with Shamu seats; **Jazzy Jellies,** a ride that lifts and spins kids in jellyfish-like seats; **Swishy Fishies,** a Mad Tea Party–style ride, where kids spin around in buckets that surround a gigantic sand castle; **Ocean Commotion,** a swinging tug boat that gently rocks back and forth and whirls from side to side with up to 24 passengers aboard; the **Flying Fiddler,** a gigantic red Fiddler crab that gently lifts its 12 passengers up into the air and then in a series of very short drops begins his decent; and the **Sea Carrousel,** a whimsical ride with an ocean full of colorful sea creatures including dolphins, fishes, sharks, otters, and sea lions gently going round and round, up and down, to the sounds of the sea. *Note:* Because of the size of Shamu's Happy Harbor, smaller kids can easily get lost—and while there's only one escape, it's still possible to get out to other areas of the park if parents are not paying close attention. Bring extra clothes for the tots (or for yourself) because much of the Harbor isn't designed to keep you dry.

Shark Encounter

Frommer's Rating: B
Recommended Ages: 3–adult

SeaWorld has added other species to this formerly shark-exclusive attraction—about 220 specimens in all. Pools out front have small sharks and rays (feeding isn't allowed here). The interior aquariums have big eels, beautiful but poisonous lionfish, hauntingly still barracudas, and bug-eyed pufferfish. This isn't a tour for the claustrophobic because you have to walk through an acrylic tube, beneath hundreds of millions of gallons of water. Also, small fry may find the swimming sharks a little too much to handle. *Note:* Part of this exhibit has given way to **Sharks Underwater Grill** (p. 288).

Sizzlin' Pianos

Frommer's Rating: C
Recommended Ages: All

This amusing 25-minute show takes place several times a day at the Waterfront's Seafire Inn. Guests are entertained with many a merry musical tune, a dash of comedy, a tall tale or two, and a little interactive participation. Though you can see the show without eating at the inn, it makes for a very entertaining dining experience, especially with younger kids who at times may require a diversion to make it through a meal.

⌒Moments More Active Fun

SeaWorld offers three other hands-on programs. The 9-hour **Marine Mammal Keeper Experience** (starting bright and early at 6:30am) allows guests to work side by side with a trainer, preparing meals and feeding the animals, and learning how to care for and interact with dolphins, beluga whales, sea lions, and walruses. The cost is $399 (with tax), which includes 7 days of consecutive park admission, lunch, a career book, and a T-shirt. Participants must be at least 13 years old.

Sharks Deep Dive gives guests a chance to have limited, hands-off contact with over 30 sharks, including a nearly 9-foot sand tiger, in the Shark Encounter area. Two at a time, guests don a wet suit and special underwater helmet (it lets you breathe and communicate with others) for a 30-minute encounter inside a cage that rides a 125-foot track. Part of the cage is above water, but participants can dive up to 8 feet underwater for a close-up look at the denizens. The cost is $150 (minimum age 10). The price includes a souvenir booklet, T-shirt, and souvenir photo, but *does not include the required park admission fee.*

The 2-hour **Beluga Interaction Program** gives an up-close, hands-on encounter (about 30 min.) with these mammoth whales (minimum age 10; participants must know how to swim). The $179 price includes a book on whales and a souvenir photo but *does not include the required park admission fee.*

The programs are not open to expectant mothers. Call ℰ **407/370-1382** or visit **www.seaworld.com** for more information. *Note:* If you're willing to splurge on only one program, opt for Discovery Cove (see below) over these options—it's much more hands-on.

Wild Arctic
Frommer's Rating: B+
Recommended Ages: All ages for exhibit; 6–adult for ride

Enveloping guests in the beauty, exhilaration, and danger of a polar expedition, Wild Arctic combines a high-definition adventure film with flight-simulator technology to display breathtaking Arctic panoramas. After a hazardous flight over the frozen north, you emerge into an exhibit where you can see a playful polar bear or two, beautiful beluga whales, and walruses performing aquatic ballets (on different levels, you can see them both above and below the surface). Small kids and those prone to motion sickness may find the ride bumpy. There's a separate line if you want to skip the flight and just see the critters.

ADDITIONAL ATTRACTIONS

The park's other attractions include **Pacific Point Preserve,** a 2½-acre natural setting that duplicates the rocky home of California sea lions and harbor seals. Tropical fish and sea creatures at the **Tidepool** offer a hands-on experience for all ages. The **Tropical Reef** surrounds guests with aquariums filled with a variety of sea creatures to look

---

Tips **On the Waterfront**

SeaWorld's 5-acre **Waterfront** area, which debuted in late spring 2003, added a seaport-themed village to the park's landscape. On High Street, look for a blend of shops; street shows; and the Seafire Inn restaurant, where lunch includes a musical revue. At Harbor Square, the Groove Chefs make musical mayhem with pots, pans, trays, and cans. The park also added street performers, including a crusty old captain who tells fish tales and makes music with bottles and brandy glasses. The array of Waterfront eateries includes the Spice Mill, Voyager's Wood Fired Pizza, and the Seafire Inn.

---

at—and you can touch the sea urchins, starfish, and anemones. **Tropical Rain Forest,** a bamboo-and-banyan-tree habitat, is the home of cockatoos and other birds. And **Turtle Point** showcases sea turtles swimming in the lagoon or lounging on the beach and sand dunes. The **Hospitality Center** lets you indulge in free samples of Anheuser-Busch beers and then stroll through the stables to watch the famous Budweiser Clydesdale horses being groomed. The **Xtreme Zone** tests your climbing and jumping skills with a rock wall and trampoline jump (both for an additional fee). Even shopping is an experience at SeaWorld; at **Oyster's Secret,** guests can watch as pearl divers dive in search of just the right oyster, which will be pried open for the pearl inside. Guests can then have the pearls made into jewelry.

The **Makahiki Luau** is a full-scale dinner show featuring South Seas–style food (mahimahi in piña-colada sauce, Hawaiian chicken, and sweet-and-sour pork) while guests are entertained by music and dance of the Pacific Islands. It's hardly haute cuisine or Broadway, but is very much on par with Disney's Spirit of Aloha Dinner Show (p. 324). It's held daily at 6:30pm; park admission is not required. The cost is $46 for adults and $30 for children 3 to 9. *Note:* A special holiday-themed luau is offered from late November to the end of December. Reservations are required; call ✆ **800/327-2420** or go to www.seaworldorlando.com.

SHOPPING IN THE PARK

SeaWorld doesn't have nearly as many shops as Walt Disney World and Universal Orlando, but with the opening of the Waterfront, it has added some rather unique boutiques, including **Allura's Treasure Trove,** featuring fanciful dolls, mermaids, fairies, jewelry, and more. The **Tropical Trading Company** is filled with handcrafted gifts made by artisans from exotic ports all over the world. At **Oyster's Secret,** guests can watch as pearl divers dive in search of just the right oyster, which will be pried open for the pearl inside. Guests can then have the pearls made into jewelry.

There are, of course, also lots of cuddly toys for sale around the park. Where else can you get a stuffed manatee but at **Manatee Gifts?** The **Friends of the Wild** gift shop (near Penguin Encounter) has one of the larger and more varied selections in the park. The shop attached to **Wild Arctic** is good for plush toys as well. **Shamu's Emporium,** near the entrance, is one of the largest stores in the park featuring an array of souvenirs, from T-shirts to toys.

And, because of the Anheuser-Busch connection, the gift shop outside the entrance to the park offers a staggering array of **Budweiser**-related items.

DISCOVERY COVE: A DOLPHIN ENCOUNTER

Anheuser-Busch spent $100 million building SeaWorld's sister park, which debuted in 2000. The price is $269 to $289 per person (plus 6.5% sales tax) for ages 6 and up if you want to swim with the dolphins. It's $169 to $189 if you just want to enjoy the fishes and other sea life without having the dolphin experience. In order to make the experience a bit more tolerable in the cost department, admission includes a 7-day consecutive pass to either SeaWorld or Busch Gardens Tampa Bay. You can upgrade this feature to a 14-day combination pass for all three parks (including Aquatica) for an additional $50.

If you've never gone for a dip with a dolphin, words hardly do it justice. It's exhilarating and exciting—exactly the kind of thing that can make for a most memorable vacation. The actual dolphin encounter deserves an **A+ rating.** It's open only to those ages 6 and older (younger guests or those who don't want to participate in the dolphin swim can take part in other activities).

The park has a cast of more than 2 dozen dolphins, and each of them works 2 to 4 hours a day. Many of them are mature critters that have spent their lives in captivity, around people. They love having their bellies, flukes, and backs rubbed. They also have an impressive bag of tricks. Given the proper hand signals, they can make sounds much like a human passing gas, chatter in dolphin talk, and do seemingly effortless 1½ gainers in 12 feet of water. They take willing guests for rides in the piggyback or missionary position. They also wave "hello" and "goodbye" with their flippers, and take great pleasure in roaring by guests at top speed, creating waves that drench them.

The dolphin experience lasts 90 minutes, about 35 to 40 minutes of which is spent in the lagoon with one of them. Trainers use the rest of the time to teach visitors about these remarkable mammals.

The rest of the day isn't nearly as exciting, but it is wonderfully relaxing. Discovery Cove doesn't deliver thrill rides, water slides, or acrobatic animal shows; that's what SeaWorld, Disney, and Universal are for. This is where you come to get away from all that.

Here's what you get for your money, with or without the dolphin encounter:

- A limit of *no more than 1,000 other guests a day.* (The average daily attendance at Disney's Magic Kingdom is 41,000.) This ensures that your experience will be more relaxing and private, which is part of what you are paying for in the first place anyway.
- A continental breakfast, lunch, snacks, beverages (throughout the day), a towel, a locker, sunscreen, snorkeling gear including a flotation vest, a souvenir photo, and free self-parking are also part of the deal.
- Other 9am-to-5:30pm activities include a chance to swim near (but on the other side of the Plexiglas from) **barracudas** and **black-tip sharks.** There are no barriers between you and the gentle rays and brightly colored tropical fish in a new 12,000-square-foot lagoon, where some of the rays are 4 feet in diameter. The 3,300-foot **Tropical River** is a great place to swim or float in a mild current; it goes through a cave, two waterfalls, and a large aviary where you can also take a stroll, becoming a human perch for some of the 30 exotic bird species. There are also beach areas for catching a tan.
- As mentioned above, 7 days of **unlimited admission** to SeaWorld and/or Busch Gardens Tampa Bay (park admission normally costs $65 a day for adults and $54 for children 3–9).

For a more intimate experience, try **Twilight Discovery** (limited to 150 guests; running from 3–9pm), available only in the summer (usually June–Aug). The package includes an upscale dinner, snacks and beverages, a dolphin wade, snorkeling and gear, access to the various swim facilities, critter interaction, and a 7-day consecutive pass to SeaWorld or Busch Gardens. The cost is $269 if you want to wade with dolphins (at least one person in your party must take this option), or $169 if you skip the dolphins.

One other option is Discovery Cove's **Trainer for a Day,** which for $468 to $488 allows guests 6 and older to ride a dolphin, take a behind-the-scenes tour, spend the day with a trainer (learning how to care for the inhabitants of the park), have a private photo session, and interact with critters including tropical birds, sloths, and anteaters. Included is a waterproof disposable camera and trainer T-shirt. A paying adult must accompany guests ages 6 to 12.

You can drive to Discovery Cove by following the above directions to SeaWorld and then following the signs. Unlike other parks, Discovery Cove doesn't have a parking charge. For up-to-the-minute information, call ℂ **877/434-7268** or go to **www.discoverycove.com.**

If you plan on trying this adventure, make reservations far, far in advance. With the limited number of guests admitted and the number of people who want a chance to swim with the fishes, this park gets booked very quickly. *Note:* There is an ever-so-small chance of getting in as a walk-up customer. The park reserves a small number of tickets daily for folks whose earlier dolphin sessions were canceled due to bad weather. The best chance for last-minute guests comes during any extended period of good weather.

4 Other Area Attractions

There are—surprise!—a number of cool things in Orlando for families that don't revolve around Mickey, the Hulk, or Shamu. Now that I've covered the monster parks, let's explore some of Central Florida's best smaller attractions.

IN KISSIMMEE

Kissimmee's tourist strip is on Walt Disney World's southern border and extends about 2 miles west and 8 to 10 miles east. Irlo Bronson Memorial Highway (U.S. 192), the highway linking the town to WDW and points west, is under perpetual construction, and the development clutter can make it hard to see some smaller destinations. Check with your hotel's front desk or the attractions themselves for updates that might make finding them a little easier.

Note: The following prices don't include the 6.5% to 7% sales tax, unless otherwise noted.

Gatorland 𝔊 *(Finds* **All ages**   It's hard to miss the gigantic green jaws—a perfect photo op, by the way—marking this park's entrance. Founded in 1949, with just a handful of alligators living in huts and pens, Gatorland, still privately owned and operated, now houses thousands of alligators (including a rare blue one) and crocodiles on its 110-acre grounds that do dual duty as a wildlife preserve and theme park.

Gatorland has survived the arrival of Disney, Universal, and SeaWorld in part because of its old-Florida charm and resistance to becoming overly commercialized (though it hasn't escaped entirely—additional parking, a whole new façade and gift shop, and additional landscaping have all been added thanks to an extensive million-dollar renovation).

Orlando Area Attractions

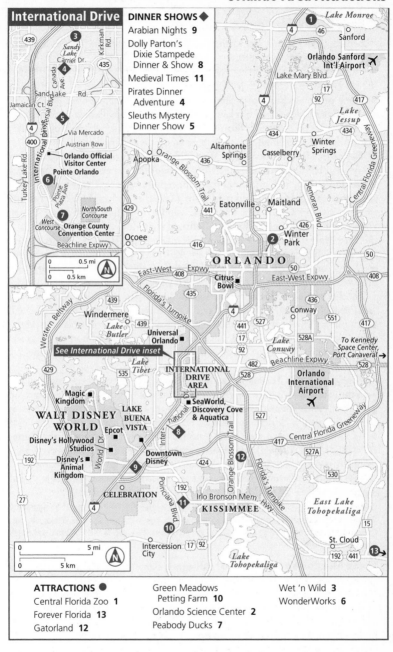

International Drive

DINNER SHOWS ◆

Arabian Nights **9**

Dolly Parton's Dixie Stampede Dinner & Show **8**

Medieval Times **11**

Pirates Dinner Adventure **4**

Sleuths Mystery Dinner Show **5**

Sandy Lake
Carrier Dr.
Kirkman Rd.

Canada Ave.

Sand Lake Rd.
Jamaican Ct.
Via Mercado
Austrian Row
Orlando Official Visitor Center
Pointe Orlando
Pointe Plaza Ave.
North/South Concourse
West Concourse
Orange County Convention Center
Beachline Expwy.
Turkey Lake Rd.
International Blvd.

0   0.5 mi
0   0.5 km

Lake Monroe
Sanford
Orlando Sanford Int'l Airport ✈
Lake Mary Blvd.
Lake Jessup
Altamonte Springs
Apopka
Orange Blossom Trail
Casselberry
Winter Springs
Semoran Blvd.
Central Florida Greeneway
Eatonville
Maitland
Ocoee
Winter Park
ORLANDO
East-West Expwy.
Citrus Bowl
Conway
Windermere
Lake Butler
Universal Orlando
See International Drive inset
Lake Tibet
INTERNATIONAL DRIVE AREA
Lake Conway
To Kennedy Space Center, Port Canaveral →
Beachline Expwy.
Orlando International Airport ✈
Magic Kingdom
WALT DISNEY WORLD
LAKE BUENA VISTA
Epcot
SeaWorld, Discovery Cove & Aquatica
Disney's Hollywood Studios
World Dr.
Downtown Disney
Disney's Animal Kingdom
CELEBRATION
Poinciana Blvd.
Irlo Bronson Mem. Hwy.
KISSIMMEE
Central Florida Greeneway
Florida's Turnpike
Intercession City
Lake Tohopekaliga
East Lake Tohopekaliga
St. Cloud

0   5 mi
0   5 km

ATTRACTIONS ●

Central Florida Zoo **1**

Forever Florida **13**

Gatorland **12**

Green Meadows Petting Farm **10**

Orlando Science Center **2**

Peabody Ducks **7**

Wet 'n Wild **3**

WonderWorks **6**

Tips **Out With the Old . . .**

In 2005, Water Mania, the Kissimmee water park that drew families to its doors by the thousands, was sold.

Breeding pens, nurseries, and rearing ponds are scattered throughout the densely land-scaped property, which also displays monkeys, snakes, birds, Florida turtles, and a Gala-pagos tortoise. Its 2,000-foot boardwalk winds through a cypress swamp and breeding marsh with an observation tower for those who prefer an overhead view.

The park's shows include **Gator Wrestlin',** in which wrestlers simultaneously wran-gle the reptilians and educate the audience about their opponents and how they live; **Gator Jumparoo,** which features the giant reptiles lunging 4 to 5 feet up out of the water to snatch a dead chicken right from a trainer's hand; and **Upclose Encounters,** which showcases a variety of the park's wildlife, including some venomous snakes. Younger kids will enjoy the **Express Railroad** train ride ($2 a ride) through the park; the **Very Merry Aviary** with its colorful Lorikeets; and **Allie's Barnyard,** a small pet-ting zoo. While you're here, try the smoked gator ribs or nuggets in the open-air restaurant, or grab a gator-skin souvenir in the gift shop. Allow 4 to 5 hours to explore the park—this one's a huge hit with all of my kids (and me, too!).

The **Gator Gully Splash Park,** a splashy $1-million expansion within the existing park, opened in 2007. This quarter-acre water-based (and loosely bayou-themed) play area is filled with plenty of wet and watery fun as gigantic gators (this kind won't bite), armed with water guns, stand (okay, sit) ready to squirt, enormous Egrets spew streams of water from their beaks, and a bucket tree spills over onto anyone standing (or running) within reach.

Note: Gatorland's **Trainer for a Day** lets up to five guests get up close and personal with the gators. The 2-hour experience puts you side by side with trainers and includes a chance to wrangle some alligators (minimum age 12). The $100 price includes admis-sion to the park; a 20 percent discount off a regular admission ticket is also extended to up to six members of your party. Another option is the 1-hour **Night Shine Tour** ($19 adults, $17 children), which takes you along the wooden walkways with only a flashlight and a guide. Advance reservations are required for both programs.

Tip: Printable discount coupons and special Internet ticket prices are available at the park's website. Be sure to check it out before you leave home.

14501 S. Orange Blossom Trail (U.S. 441; between Osceola Pkwy. and Hunter's Creek Blvd.). © 800/393-5297 or 407/855-5496. www.gatorland.com. Admission $23 adults, $15 kids 3–12. Daily 9am–5 or 6pm usually, but closing times vary by season. Free parking. From I-4, take Exit 65/Osceola Pkwy. east to U.S. 17/92/441, and go left/north. Gatorland is 1½ miles on the right.

Green Meadows Petting Farm   All ages   Families can take a break from the raz-zle-dazzle and get a taste of the country at this 300-critter farm that features pigs, chickens, ducks, geese, donkeys, and more. The 2-hour guided tour includes a chance to milk a cow; the farm also has pony rides, train rides, and hayrides. The emphasis is on teaching children and their tagalongs about life on a farm. Allow about 3 to 4 hours. *Tip:* Check out the farm's website for discount admission coupons.

1368 S. Poinciana Blvd. (5 miles south of U.S. 192). © 407/846-0770. www.greenmeadowsfarm.com. Admission $19 adults and children, free for kids 2 and under. Daily 9:30am–5:30pm, tours 9:30am–4pm. From I-4, take Exit 64A/U.S. 192 east about 5 miles; then go south on Poinciana.

IN THE INTERNATIONAL DRIVE AREA

These attractions are a 10- to 15-minute drive from the Disney area and a 5- to 10-minute drive from Universal Orlando. Most appeal to special interests, but one is free (the Peabody Ducks' show), and another, Wet 'n Wild, is in the same class as Disney's water parks.

Peabody Ducks *(Moments)*   **All ages**   One of the best shows in town is short but sweet and, most important, *free.* Your children, especially young kids, will love it. The Peabody Orlando hotel's five mallards march into the lobby each morning, accompanied by John Philip Sousa's "King Cotton March" and their own red-coated duck master. They get to spend the day splashing in a marble fountain. Then, in the afternoon, they march back to the elevator and up to their fourth-floor "penthouse." Donald Duck never had it this good. There are multiple crews, so every couple of months, they get to rotate back to the farm for some extra R&R. Allow 1 hour.

9801 International Dr. (between Beachline Expwy. and Sand Lake Rd.). *(C)* **800/732-2639** or 407/352-4000. Free admission. Daily at 11am and 5pm. Free self-parking, valet parking $10 for day visitors. From I-4, take Exit 74A, Sand Lake Rd./Hwy. 528, east to International Dr., and then south. Hotel is on the left across from the Convention Center.

Wet 'n Wild   **All ages**   Who knew people came in so many shapes and sizes? Stacked or stubby, terribly tan or not, all kinds come here, so there's no reason to be bashful about squeezing into a bathing suit and going out in public. This 25-acre Universal-owned water park is in the same league as **Typhoon Lagoon** and **Blizzard Beach** with regard to its rides (though not, in my opinion, with regard to atmosphere). In terms of popularity, it ranks third in the country, right behind the two Disney parks.

It has several first-rate water rides, including the **Flyer,** a six-story, four-passenger toboggan ride packing 450 feet of banked curves; the **Surge,** which offers 600 feet of greased curves and is billed as the fastest tube ride in the Southeast; the **Black Hole,** in which two-person rafts shoot through 500 feet of twisting, sometimes dark passages; the **Bomb Bay,** where the floor drops right out from under you like a bomb being dropped from high in the sky, plunging down a 76-foot vertical (almost) slide; and the **Disco H$_2$O,** which takes riders back in time on a four-person raft through an enclosed and rather wild flume ride. Riders eventually end up floating about in the **Aqua Club,** giving a whole new meaning to the phrase *Disco Duck.* Laser lights and disco balls flash as you move and groove to the sounds of the '70s. Finally, there's the all-new **Brain Wash,** a two- or four-person tube ride that sends you careening down a 53-foot vertical drop inside an enclosed tunnel—and if that doesn't make you lose your grip on reality, the 65-foot domed funnel you spiral down afterward might.

You can also ride **Mach 5,** which consists of a trio of twisting, turning flumes; the **Blast,** a tube ride that sends you winding along a ruptured pipeline; the **Storm,** where you drop from an elevated chute into a gigantic open bowl; the **Bubba Tube,** a family-sized tube ride down a six-story triple-dip slide; and **Der Stuka,** a six-story slide built for speed. The park has a large kids' area with miniature versions of some of the grown-up rides, a lazy river, and a surf lagoon. The **Knee Ski,** a cable-operated kneeboarding course (56-in. height minimum); the **Wild One,** a wild two-person tube ride across an open lake; and **Wakeboarding** are available at the **Wake Zone** in warm weather only.

If you enjoy the water, plan on spending a full day here. You can rent tubes ($4), towels ($2), and lockers ($5), or a combination of all three ($9); each rental requires a $2 refundable deposit. Life vests are free. *Note:* All multiperson rides require that kids 36 to 48 inches tall have an adult with them.

Tip: In addition to the admission prices below, Wet 'n Wild is part of the multiday **FlexTicket,** which includes admission to Universal Orlando (which owns this attraction), SeaWorld, and Busch Gardens in Tampa. See p. 254 for more information.

6200 International Dr. (at Universal Blvd.). 🅒 800/992-9453 or 407/351-1800. www.wetnwild.com. Admission $37 adults, $31 kids 3–9. Hours vary seasonally, but the park is usually open at least 10am–5pm daily, weather permitting (it's one of the few water parks open year-round). Parking $7 for cars, light trucks, and vans. From I-4, take Exit 75A/Hwy. 435 south and follow the signs.

WonderWorks *Finds* **All ages**   On an uncharted island somewhere in the Bermuda Triangle, a tornado was inadvertently created by scientists experimenting with some seriously weird science. In the midst of the storm, the gigantic building where they were working was swept up and carried off, dropping right in the middle of Orlando—amazingly, the building is fully intact, but it's now upside down. This attraction is educational and fun; just don't show up here expecting things to be as glitzy as they are in some of the major parks. Throughout the three levels, you'll feel the tremble of an earthquake, experience the rush of hurricane-force winds, create massive bubbles, lie on a bed of nails, walk across the bridge of fire—a hair-raising, electrical experience—and even ride the rails via a simulator on a create-your-own-coaster ride. You'll learn dozens of fun and interesting facts (Where are a cricket's ears? On its knees!) and experience plenty of mind-boggling visual effects. More than 100 exhibits are included, but if you're not a good shot, steer clear of the Lazer Tag game: It costs $4.95 above regular admission and can make for a frustrating few minutes. While you're at it, skip the arcade extras as well.

The attraction also features a nightly combination of magic and comedy in the **Outta Control Magic Comedy Dinner Show.** The 90-minute show features magic and improvisational comedy, as well as unlimited pizza, popcorn, soft drinks, and beer. It's a fun time for the kids and not too bad for adults, either. Call to reserve a spot.

Tip: Combination tickets are available for discounted admission to WonderWorks, Lazer Tag, and the dinner show; these are a good buy. Discount coupons are also available on the attraction's website, so check it out beforehand.

9067 International Dr. 🅒 407-351-8800. www.wonderworksonline.com. Admission $20 adults, $15 kids 4–12; Outta Control Dinner Show $22 adults, $15 kids; combination tickets to WonderWorks, Lazer Tag, and Outta Control Dinner Show $40 adults, $30 kids. Parking $2 an hour next door at the Pointe Orlando parking garage. Daily 9am–midnight. Dinner show nightly at 6 and 8pm. From I-4, take Exit 74A, Sand Lake Rd./Hwy. 528, east to International Dr., and then go south. WonderWorks is on the left.

ELSEWHERE IN CENTRAL FLORIDA

The listings that follow are out of the mainstream tourist areas, meaning that you won't have to battle heavy crowds. The Central Florida Zoo and Orlando Science Center are close enough to incorporate a visit to Winter Park if you choose to make a day of it.

Central Florida Zoo *Finds* **All ages**   This community zoo has come a long way since it was born in 1923, when a circus came to town, leaving a monkey and a goat behind. The monkey rode the goat in the earliest show. Today, the animal collection includes beautiful clouded leopards, cheetahs, and black-footed cats, all of which are endangered. You'll also meet a ham of a hippo named Geraldine, as well as black howler monkeys, siamangs, American crocodiles, a banded Egyptian cobra, a Gila monster, hyacinth macaws, barred owls, bald eagles, and dozens of other species. The zoo has half-price admission for everyone Thursdays from 9 to 10am and all day Tuesdays for seniors 60 and over. Allow 2 to 3 hours.

⸨Tips⸩ **Back in Action (For Now)**

After closing its doors in 2003, **Cypress Gardens Adventure Park** (© 863/324-2111; www.cypressgardens.com) has reopened and now features 41 thrill rides, an all-new water-ski show, and the beautiful botanical gardens that started it all. A water park, **Splash Island,** has also opened just next door and features plenty of wild raft rides, a children's play area, and other aquatic fun. Call or visit the website for up-to-date details. The only downside is the hour-long drive to get to the park from the Disney area.

Tip: A 1-year membership includes additional perks and admission to this and 100 other participating zoos and aquariums across the country. A family membership is $60, which, depending on your family's size, may be more economical than purchasing individual tickets.

3755 NW U.S. 17/92, Sanford. © 407/323-4450. www.centralfloridazoo.org. Admission $9.95 adults, $7.95 seniors, $5.95 kids 3–12. Daily 9am–5pm. Free parking. From I-4, take Exit 104 right onto Orange Ave., turn left at the traffic light on Lake Monroe Rd., and then right on U.S. 17/92. The zoo is on the right.

Forever Florida   **All ages**   The 4,700-acre Crescent J Ranch is a nature preserve that offers a chance to see native wildlife, Florida flora, and a working cattle ranch by guided tour. Options include touring by horseback, bike, covered wagon, and Cracker coach, a funky buggy that puts riders on a perch 10 feet above ground level. Allow a half day or longer to get here, take the tour, and see the grounds, which also include a pony-riding ring (there are ponies set aside for young kids to ride), hiking trails, and a petting zoo.

4755 N. Kenansville Rd., St. Cloud (southeast of Kissimmee). © 866/854-3837. www.foreverflorida.com. Tours and rides from $25 adults, $20 kids on up to $89 per person (higher for overnights). Daily tours at 10am and 1pm. Free parking. From I-4, take Exit 64A/U.S. 192 east about 15 miles to U.S. 441; then go south 7½ miles to Forever Florida on the left.

Orlando Science Center 𝄞𝄞 ⸨Finds⸩   **All ages**   The four-story center, the largest of its kind in the Southeast, provides 10 exhibit halls that allow visitors to explore everything from Florida swamps to the arid plains of Mars to the human body. There's also a **Weird Science** hall (hosted by Dr. Dare and his creation, Frankenboy), featuring a number of interactive sound, graphics, animation, and video kiosks. One of the big attractions is the **Dr. Phillips CineDome,** a 310-seat theater that presents large-format films, planetarium shows, and laser-light extravaganzas. In **KidsTown,** little folks wander in exhibits representing a miniature version of the big world around them. In one section, there's a pint-size community that includes a construction site, park, and wellness center. Children of all ages will find at least one or two (and often more) memorable experiences waiting for them. Additional kid-friendly exhibits include **Dr. Dare's Laboratory, Body Zone, DinoDigs,** and **Natureworks.** Allow 3 to 4 hours, or more if your family has inquiring minds.

777 E. Princeton St. (between Orange and Mills aves.), in Loch Haven Park. © 888/672-4386 or 407/514-2000. www.osc.org. Admission (includes exhibits, CineDome film, and planetarium show) $15 adults, $14 seniors 55 and older, $9.95 kids 3–11. Sun–Thurs 10am–6pm; Fri–Sat 10am–9pm. Parking $4 in a garage across the street. From I-4, take Exit 85/Princeton St. east and cross Orange Ave.

8

Orlando for Active Families

The majority of Orlando's visitors often overlook the fact that there are plenty of fun and exciting things to do beyond the boundaries of the theme parks. Activities range from relaxing to adventurous and even outrageous, with many far more laid-back in pace and price than the theme parks.

Championship golf courses, lakes for boating and fishing, hot-air ballooning, and even hang gliding and surfing are all available in and around Orlando. If you and your kids are looking for a little four-legged fun, you can giddy-up on horseback or stretch out and sing along on an old-fashioned hayride. Central Florida's rather lengthy menu of indoor and outdoor recreation venues ensures that everyone in the family, no matter what their age or interests, will find something fun (and often unique) to do.

Those of you staying with the Mouse will certainly find plenty to do without having to stray too far; however, even the Mickster can't top some of Central Florida's true treasures. Orlando's many parks, preserves, and waterways offer those willing to venture beyond theme-park boundaries a chance to explore Florida's more natural side. To get to most of these, you'll need a car (or you'll face a costly taxi or limo ride), as they're out of the mainstream tourist areas.

Note: Two additional treasures worth noting, the Canaveral National Seashore and Merritt Island National Wildlife Refuge, are within a reasonable driving distance of Walt Disney World, so be sure to check out chapter 11, "Side Trips from Orlando," for all the details.

1 Outdoor Activities

Walt Disney World and the surrounding areas have plenty of recreational options for those who believe the theme parks aren't the be-all and end-all of a trip to Orlando. Most of those mentioned below are open to everyone, no matter where you're staying. The prices listed don't include tax unless otherwise noted. For further information about WDW recreational facilities, call © 407/939-7529 or go to **www.disneyworld. com** (click the "Other Recreation" link).

AIRBOATING   You can glide across the surface of local waters at **Boggy Creek Airboat Rides,** in Kissimmee (© 407/344-9550; www.bcairboats.com), where you'll pay $22 per adult and $16 per child for half-hour tours. Other choices include **Old Fashioned Airboat Rides** (© 407/568-4307; www.airboatrides.com), which charges $40 per adult and $25 per child 12 and under for 90 minutes; and **A-Awesome Airboat Rides** (© 407/568-7601; www.airboatride.com), which charges $40 per adult and $25 per child for a 90-minute ride along the St. Johns River, in Christmas, east of Orlando. Both of the latter require reservations.

BALLOONING   There are several places in the area to experience an early-morning hot-air balloon flight, including **Orange Blossom Balloons,** in Lake Buena Vista (© 407/239-7677; www.orangeblossomballoons.com), and **Blue Water Balloons** (© 800/586-1884 or 407/894-5040; www.bluewaterballoons.com). Sunrise flights are available daily. All flights, which last approximately 1 hour, are followed by a champagne toast (sorry, kids) and a breakfast buffet or picnic. Children who make the age grade will probably be delighted with the view and the unique sensation, unless they (or you) don't see eye to eye with heights. Blue Water offers hotel pickup at no extra charge. Rates for both run approximately $175 per adult and $95 per child under 10.

BICYCLING   Bike rentals (single and multi-speed adult bikes, tandems, baby seats, and children's bikes—including those with training wheels) are available from the **Bike Barn,** at Disney's Fort Wilderness Resort & Campground (© 407/824-2742). Rates for each bike are $8 per hour, $22 per day (surrey bikes run $18–$22 per half-hour), regardless of age. Fort Wilderness offers a lot of good bike trails. Many of the other Disney resorts also offer rentals at similar rates. Either call your hotel in advance or inquire upon check-in.

BOATING   With the many manmade lakes and lagoons dotting the WDW landscape, it's no surprise that Disney owns a navy of pleasure boats. **Capt. Jack's,** at Downtown Disney, rents sailboats ($20 per half-hour, including tax), Sea Raycers by Sea Ray ($25 per hour, including tax), and pontoons ($42 per half-hour, including tax). For information, call © 407/828-2204. The **Bike Barn,** at Disney's Fort Wilderness Resort & Campground (© 407/824-2742), rents canoes, pedal boats, and kayaks ($6.50 per half-hour). At both sites, kids must be at least 12 to rent a boat, and those under 18 cannot rent without a signed parental waiver.

FISHING   There are several fishing excursions offered on Disney waterways, including Bay Lake and Seven Seas Lagoon. The lakes are stocked, so you may catch something, but true anglers probably won't find it much of a challenge. The excursions can be arranged 2 to 90 days in advance by calling © 407/939-2277. A license isn't required. The fee is $200 to $235 for up to five people for 2 hours, $405 for 4 hours ($100 for each additional hour), including refreshments, gear, guide, bait, and tax. Children above the toddler stage are permitted on these tours when accompanied by an adult; however, a 1-hour excursion just for kids ages 6 to 12 is available for $28.

A less-expensive alternative: Rent fishing poles at the **Bike Barn** (© 407/ 824-2742) to fish in the Fort Wilderness canals. Pole rentals cost $6 per hour, $10 per day (not including tax). Bait is $3.50 to $3.65. A license isn't necessary.

Outside the realm, **A Pro Bass Guide Service** (© 800/771-9676 or 407/877-9676; www.probassguideservice.com) offers guided bass-fishing trips along some of Central Florida's most picturesque rivers and lakes. Hotel pickup is available; the cost is $250 for one or two people per half-day, $400 for a full day. A license costs $17.

HANG GLIDING   Flying from 2,000 feet in the air, you'll get the chance to glide through the sky—with a little help from your instructors. If you're a thrill-ride junkie, this is the real deal. Pricing depends upon the number of lessons and type of flight you want (starting at $95). The **Wallaby Ranch** (© 863/424-0070; www.wallaby.com) is located in Davenport, just south of Kissimmee.

HAYRIDES   The hay wagon departs **Pioneer Hall** at Disney's Fort Wilderness nightly at 7 and 9:30pm for old-fashioned 45-minute hayrides with singing, jokes, and games. Most kids will find it enjoyable, though some teens may think it corny.

Hitting the Links

Walt Disney World operates five 18-hole, par-72 golf courses and one 9-hole, par-36 walking course, so if you want to work on your putting and need some time away from the kids (who will most likely prefer an outing to one of Disney's miniature golf courses—see p. 251), you'll have plenty of options. All are open to the public and offer pro shops, equipment rentals, and instruction. The rates are $79 to $165 per 18-hole round for resort guests ($10 more if you're not staying at a WDW property). Twilight and Price Slice specials are often available at a greatly reduced rate. For tee times and information, call ℂ 407/939-4653 up to 7 days in advance (up to 30 days for Disney resort and "official" property guests). Call ℂ 407/934-7639 for information about golf packages.

Beyond Mickey's shadow, try **Celebration Golf Club** (ℂ 888/275-2918 or 407/566-4653; www.celebrationgolf.com), which has an 18-hole regulation course (greens fees: $55–$95 depending on the day and season) that kids under 17 are eligible to play; there's a 3-hole junior course for 5- to 9-year-olds. Note that the club has a dress code, so be sure to ask ahead so that your kids are decked out in suitable attire. **Champions Gate** (ℂ 888/554-9301 or 407/787-4653; www.championsgategolf.com) offers 36 holes designed by Greg Norman, where greens fees will set you back $55 to $175, and the **David Leadbetter Golf Academy** (ℂ 407/787-3330; www.davidleadbetter.com).

Golf magazine recognized the 45 holes designed by Jack Nicklaus at the **Villas of Grand Cypress** ★★★ (p. 111) as among the best in the nation. Tee times begin at 8am daily. Special rates are available for children under 17, and the resort even runs a 5-day summer golf program for kids interested in the game. For information, call ℂ 407/239-1909. The course is generally

The ride is $8 for adults, $5 for children 3 to 9, and free for kids 2 and under. An adult must accompany children under 12. No reservations are necessary. Call ℂ 407/824-2832 for more information.

HIKING   The **Nature Conservancy's Disney Wilderness Preserve** (ℂ 407/682-3664; www.nature.org/florida) is a 12,000-acre, little-discovered getaway from the theme-park madness. It has 7 miles of trails at the headwaters of the Everglades ecosystem, just south of Orlando. Self-guided options range from a half-mile interpretive trail, good for younger kids, to a 4.5-mile hiking trail for adults and teens. Picnic facilities are available along the trails. Admission is $3 adults, $2 for kids 6 to 17 and Nature Conservancy members. It's open Monday through Friday from 9am to 5pm. The preserve also features Sunday-afternoon **buggy rides** ($12 adults, $6 kids).

HOOPS & MORE   The **Multi-Sports Experience** at Disney's Wide World of Sports (ℂ 407/939-1500; www.disneyworldsports.com; p. 251) lets you and the kids try your hand at basketball, football, soccer, and more. Admission is $11 for adults and $8.25 for children 3 to 9. It's open on select days.

HORSEBACK RIDING   **Disney's Fort Wilderness Resort & Campground** offers 45-minute guided trail rides several times a day. The cost is $42 per person. Children

restricted to guests or guests of guests (rates run approximately $120–$175 per round), but there's limited play available to those not staying at the resort. Fees run approximately $150 to $250. Lessons are available for $135 to $175 per hour.

With more than 150 courses located throughout the Orlando area, it's simply impossible to list them all. There are, however, several additional courses and academies worth noting: The **Shingle Creek Golf Club,** including the **Brad Brewer Golf Academy** (✆ 866/966-9933 or 407/966-9933; www.shinglecreek golf.com), located at the Rosen Shingle Creek Resort; **Hawk's Landing Golf Club and Academy** (✆ 407/238-8660), at the Marriott World Center; the **Legacy, Independence,** and **Tradition** golf courses, as well as the **Annika Academy,** all located at Ginn Reunion Resort at Orlando (✆ 888/418-9610, or 407/662-1000); and the **Ritz-Carlton Golf Club** and **Grande Pines Golf Club,** both located at the Grande Lakes Orlando (✆ 407/393-4814), where the only golf-caddie concierge program around is available to make your game all it can be. The program offers advice, helpful hints, caddie services, food and beverage service, and much more.

Also consider **Golfpac Florida** (✆ 888/471-4712 or 407/260-8989; www. golfpacflorida.com), an organization that packages golf vacations with accommodations and other features, and also prearranges tee times at more than 40 Orlando-area courses. The earlier you call (months, if possible), the better your options. **Advanced Tee Times USA** (✆ 888/465-3356; www.tee timesusa.com) and **Golforlando** (✆ 866/342-4782; www.golforlando.com) are two other reservations services that offer packages and course information.

must be at least 9 years old. Maximum rider weight is 250 pounds. If you or your kids have never ridden before, the tame horses and gentle terrain make this ride a good introductory experience. Call ✆ **407/824-2832** for information and reservations up to 30 days in advance.

The **Villas of Grand Cypress** (✆ **800/835-7377** or 407/239-1938; www.grand cypress.com) opens its equestrian center to outsiders, offering programs and options for riders of all ages and skill levels. You can go on a 45-minute walk-trot trail ride—offered four times daily—for $45, though your children must be at least 10 years old to participate. A 30-minute private lesson is $55; a 1-hour lesson goes for $100. A private junior lesson (15 min.) is available for riders ages 2 to 9 for $30. A host of other package options is offered as well.

Another choice outside the world of Walt Disney is the **Horse World Riding Stables,** 3705 Poinciana Blvd. (✆ **407/847-4343;** www.horseworldstables.com), in Kissimmee. The stables offer nature trail rides and individual riding lessons. Rates for a 1-hour ride start at $39 for ages 4 and up; the cost is $17 for kids under 40 pounds who ride with an adult. Reserve in advance.

HORSE-DRAWN CARRIAGE RIDES   Disney offers evening carriage rides at two of its resort locations: **Fort Wilderness Resort & Campground** and the **Port Orleans Resort.** The 30-minute rides cost $35 for up to four people. Most kids will enjoy the ride and the sightseeing opportunity. For information, call © **407/824-2832.**

JOGGING   Many of the Disney resorts have scenic jogging trails. For instance, the **Yacht Club** and **Beach Club** resorts share a 2-mile trail; the **Caribbean Beach Resort** has a 1.4-mile promenade circling a lake; **Port Orleans** has a 1.7-mile riverfront trail; and **Fort Wilderness** has a tree-shaded 2.3-mile jogging path with exercise stations about every quarter mile. Pick up a jogging-trail map at any Disney property's concierge desk.

PARASAILING   The **Sammy Duvall Watersports Centre** (© 407/939-0754; www.sammyduvall.com) at Disney's Contemporary Resort will take you up to 600 feet above Seven Seas Lagoon and Bay Lake on a flight that lasts 8 to 12 minutes. The cost runs approximately $50 for one rider and $160 for two riders. Kids over 2 are eligible if they fly in tandem with someone else (minimum weight 115 lb.), though you'll have to judge whether your child is up to such an experience. While older kids and teens would probably fare well, younger children likely wouldn't. Everyone who goes up has to sign a waiver, and parents have to sign off on their kids' participation. You can reserve a spot up to 90 days in advance.

SCUBA DIVING & SNORKELING   Believe it or not, even inland you can scuba and snorkel in the Florida waterways. **Fun 2 Dive Scuba & Snorkeling Tours** (© 407/322-9696; www.fun2dive.com) and **Orlando Dive & Snorkel Tours** (© 407/466-1668; www.floridamanateetours.com) both offer the chance to swim and snorkel with manatees (and other wildlife), as well as other eco-tour opportunities. Prices at Fun 2 Dive (which also offers scuba lessons and deep-sea fishing excursions) run approximately $85 per person (with a maximum of six people) to swim and snorkel; at Orlando Dive & Snorkel, the fun starts at $28 per person, plus $12 for rental gear.

SKATING   On the occasional rainy afternoon (or even on a good day), **Vans Skatepark** (© 407/351-3881; www.vans.com) offers both beginner and advanced skateboarders the chance to ride the day away on the ramps, bowls, street courses, and more. Safety equipment is required (and available for rent if you don't have your own), and those under 18 are required to have a parent or guardian sign a waiver (in front of a Vans employee or a notary). Rates run approximately $12 per session for non-members and $5 for members (requiring a 1-year commitment) on weekdays; $15 and $7, respectively, on weekends and holidays. Sessions are 2 hours long and run at scheduled times. Equipment is available for rent, from boards to helmets and pads (cost runs about $2 to $5). Private lessons, camps, and birthday parties are also offered. The park is located in the Festival Bay Mall at the far north end of International Drive.

SURFING   It's true. The creative minds at Disney have added a way for you to learn how to catch a wave and "hang ten" at the Typhoon Lagoon water park (p. 247). On Tuesdays and Fridays, instructors from the **Ron Jon Surf School by Craig Carroll** (© 407/939-7529; www.ronjonsurfschool.com) show up for an early-bird session in the namesake lagoon, which has a wave machine capable of 8-footers. The 2½-hour sessions are held before the park opens to the general public and are limited to 14 people. Minimum age is 8. The $140-per-person cost (including tax) doesn't include park admission, which you'll have to pay if you want to hang around after the lesson. You'll also need alternative transportation to get here if you're staying in Walt's world, because the WDW Transportation System doesn't service Typhoon Lagoon until official park-opening time.

SWIMMING   Almost all of Orlando's resorts have their own pools, some of which are rather unique or rather extensive (and discussed in more detail in "Coolest Pools," p. 111, and in the rest of chapter 4, "Family-Friendly Accommodations"), but if you're not satisfied with the one at your hotel, the **YMCA Aquatic Center,** 8422 International Dr. (© **407/363-1911**), has a full fitness center, racquetball courts, an Olympic-size indoor pool, and a heated 25-meter pool for kids. All pools have lifeguards. Admission is $10 per person or $25 for families.

TENNIS   There are several lighted tennis courts scattered throughout the Disney properties and the Wide World of Sports complex. Most are free and open to resort guests on a first-come, first-served basis. Call © **407/621-1991** for more information.

Playing on the clay courts at **Disney's Grand Floridian Resort & Spa,** however, will cost you $8.52 per hour; reservations are required. Private lessons are available at a rate of $75 per hour, group clinics at a rate of $15 per hour.

The **Grand Cypress Racquet Club** (© **407/239-1944**; www.grandcypress.com) features 12 courts, five of which are lit for night play. Racquetball courts, a clubhouse, and pro shop are available as well. Clinics are offered daily, as are both private lessons ($70 per hour, $40 per half-hour) and semiprivate lessons ($85 per hour).

WATER-SKIING & WAKEBOARDING   Water-skiing trips (including boats, drivers, equipment, and instruction) can be arranged Tuesday through Saturday at Walt Disney World by calling the **Sammy Duvall Watersports Centre** (© **407/939-0754**; www.sammyduvall.com) at Disney's Contemporary Resort. Make reservations up to 14 days in advance. The cost for skiing is $155 per hour for up to five people. You also can arrange for wakeboarding for up to four people; rates run $155 for an hour. There's no minimum age, although I wouldn't recommend this for children under 8 and definitely not for those at all uncomfortable in the water.

Outside Disney, you can get some time behind a boat or at the end of an overhead cable at the **Orlando Watersports Complex,** 8615 Florida Rock Rd. (© **407/251-3100**; www.orlandowatersports.com), near Orlando International Airport. The complex has lights for nighttime thrill-seekers—a feature teens will likely find cool—but kids under 8 and those not completely comfortable in the water aren't the best candidates for this activity. Prices for wakeboarding and water-skiing, including lessons, runs about $45 a half-hour, $180 for all you can ride. If you want to ride with a cable, it will cost $21 for an hour, $39 for the day. Call or check the website to find out about the various specials and discounts aimed at kids and families.

Another good option is **Buena Vista Water Sports** (© **407/239-6939**; www.bv watersports.com), located closer to all the action at Lake Bryan in Lake Buena Vista. It offers Sea-Doo rentals ($50 per half-hour, $90 per hour) and water-ski, wakeboard, and tube rides ($70 per half-hour, $130 per hour).

The **Ron Jon Surfpark** (© **321/799-8880**; www.ronjons.com) has opened at the Festival Bay Mall on International Drive. It features wave pools for intermediate- and pro-level surfers and bodyboarders, as well as wave pools for novice wave riders. Lessons and clinics are available, too.

2 Spectator Sports

Orlando is not a sporting town of the same caliber as, say, New York or Chicago, but it still is home to one major franchise and a number of other athletic teams. If you and your kids are sports nuts, you won't have to forgo your fix while in town.

BASEBALL

The **Atlanta Braves** (www.braves.com) call the 7,500-seat baseball stadium at Wide World of Sports (p. 251)—dubbed Cracker Jack Stadium in 2002—their spring-training home. They play 16 games during a 1-month season that begins in March. The smaller setting makes for a far more intimate experience for kids than a regular-stadium game would, and the atmosphere is usually a lot more relaxed. Tickets are $14 to $23. For information, call © **407/828-3267.** You can get tickets through **Ticketmaster** (© **407/839-3900**).

The **Houston Astros** (www.astros.com) train at Osceola County Stadium, 1000 Bill Beck Blvd., Kissimmee. Tickets are $17 and $20. Get them through Ticketmaster (© **407/839-3900**).

BASKETBALL

The 17,500-seat Amway Arena—known in a previous life as the TD Waterhouse Centre (and before that the Orlando Arena)—is the home court of the NBA's **Orlando Magic** (© **407/896-2442;** www.nba.com/magic), which plays 41 of its regular-season games here from October to April. To get here, take I-4 east to Exit 83B, Highway 50/U.S. 17/92 (Amelia St.), turn left at the traffic light at the bottom of the off-ramp, and follow the signs. Single-game tickets ($10–$115) can be hard to find. The team schedules special theme nights and promotions throughout the season, many of them family-related; and its mascot, Stuff (that really is his name) the Dragon, is a hit with kids. For up-to-the-minute parking information, tune your car radio to 1620 AM.

3 Parks & Playgrounds

After several days of barnstorming through the theme parks and other tourist attractions, a day in the area's nature parks can be a refreshing break. Need I also mention that it will help you recover from the sticker shock of digging deeply into your wallet day after day?

CITY PARKS

Lake Eola Park   More than a million people visit this 20-acre park each year. The 0.9-mile sidewalk that circles the downtown lake offers a good course for hikers and

---

Moments The Multi-Sports Experience

In 2002, Disney replaced its NFL Experience at the Wide World of Sports complex with the expanded **Multi-Sports Experience,** a venue that lets you test your skills not only at football, but also at baseball, basketball, hockey, soccer, and volleyball. Admission is $11 for adults and $8.25 for kids 3 to 9. It's open on select days. For information and event schedules, call © **407/939-1500** or head online to **www.disneyworldsports.com.**

joggers. Visitors can feed the live birds that inhabit the park, catch a tan on the lawn, or burn some calories cruising the lake in swan-shaped paddleboats ($12 per half-hour) or gondolas ($15 per half-hour). You'll find a playground for kids and toddlers, plus several concessions, picnic areas, and restrooms. Musical and theatrical performances are often held at the Walt Disney Amphitheater. This park is also the home of several annual events, including the Fourth of July fireworks blast.

195 N. Rosalind Ave. ⓒ 407/246-2827. Free admission. Daily 6am–midnight. Take I-4 to Anderson St. in downtown Orlando, go east past City Hall, cross Orange and Magnolia aves., and turn left at Rosalind Ave. and into the park.

Turkey Lake Park   This 36-acre city park, originally a citrus grove, has one of the most natural settings of all Orlando's parks. The park—last renovated in December 2002—has a swimming pool; picnic pavilions; a lake stocked with fish (you can fish off the pier or from a boat, with rentals available Thurs–Sun for $15); a large children's playground and two smaller ones; nature, jogging, and biking trails; a farm-animal petting zoo; a boardwalk running through a scrub-pine habitat; and an ecology center.

3401 S. Hiawassee Rd. ⓒ 407/299-5581. Daily 8am–5pm, sometimes later. Admission $4 per vehicle. Take I-4 to Kirkman Rd., go north to Conroy; turn west/left to Hiawassee, and then go north to the park, which is just past the Florida Turnpike.

STATE PARKS & PRESERVES
Wekiwa Springs State Park   The namesake springs and river provide a fertile habitat for white-tailed deer, gray foxes, bobcats, raccoons, and (careful here) black bears. The waters also offer some of the best paddling venues in Central Florida. Canoe rentals are $14 for 2 hours and $2 per hour thereafter. There are biking and hiking trails, as well as picnic, grilling, volleyball, and camping areas.

1800 Wekiwa Springs Rd., Sanford. ⓒ 407/884-2008. www.floridaparks.com/stprks/centralstateparks.htm. Daily 8am–sundown. Admission $5 per vehicle. Take I-4 to Exit 94; then take S.R. 434 west to Wekiwa Springs Rd. or S.R. 436 to Wekiwa Springs Rd. near Apopka.

4 Kids' Camps & Classes

It's hard to imagine, but this mecca of theme parks also has some of the coolest kids' camps around. **SeaWorld** (p. 285) features a few that could even qualify for extra credit. (Keep in mind, however, that these are summer camps, and as your kids are likely between teachers, it's best to check with your school's guidance counselor to find out whether extra credit for attending camp is agreeable.)

SeaWorld offers the following resident camps during the summer:

- **Ocean Explorers:** Designed for grades 5 and 6, this program allows kids to interact with dolphins, snorkel in a shark cage, check out the rehabilitation facilities, play at the park, and sleep next to the beluga whales and dolphins. Duration: 6 days. Price: $975 per child.
- **Career Camp:** This option covers three separate camps designed by grade: Career Camp for grades 7 through 9, Advanced Career Camp for grades 10 through 12, and Coastal Career Camp for grades 10 through 12. The programs include lessons on what it takes to train and work with the park's animals, as well as to maintain and enrich the animal exhibits. Kids train with animal experts and learn about animal rescue and rehabilitation. The Coastal program includes snorkeling in the Florida National Marine Sanctuary (in the Florida Keys), touring Key West, airboating through the Everglades, canoeing along the waterways, and more. All the

career camps include plenty of fun at the theme park, including a day with the dolphins, sharks, stingrays, and other critters at Discovery Cove (p. 295), as well as at SeaWorld. Duration: 6 days. Price: $1,350 per child for the Career and Advanced Career camps. The Coastal camp runs 10 days at a cost of $2,200 per child.

The cost of the above camps includes meals, lodging, equipment, and more. For more information, call © **800/327-2424** or check out **www.seaworld.org**. Due to the camps' popularity, SeaWorld recommends making reservations between the preceding December and February.

Day camps (both half-day and full-day) for younger kids (preschool through 8th grade) include behind-the-scenes tours; enrichment sessions on training, animal care, rescue, and rehabilitation; and plenty of time at the parks to play. Weeklong camps run throughout the summer, with 1-day camps running at select times throughout the year (generally around a holiday). Prices for summer weeklong preschool camps are approximately $199, for both your child and the participating (required) adult. Prices for the summer camps (grades K through 8) are approximately $229 to $269 for the half-day option and $329 to $369 for the full-day option (prices vary, depending upon the week). Special 1-day holiday camps cost $49 per child. All rates include up-close animal encounters, activities, crafts, a T-shirt and water bottle, lunch, and a snack. (The exception: Single-day seasonal camps and preschool camps do not include lunch or a T-shirt.)

A variety of other kids' camps are held throughout Central Florida, including the **Ron Jon Surf School by Craig Carroll,** over in Cocoa Beach (© **321/868-1980;** www.ronjonsurfschool.com), offered by the same folks who hang ten at Disney's Typhoon Lagoon (p. 247). Kids ages 8 and over can learn to ride the waves under the watchful eye of the surf school's instructors—and there's never more than four kids per instructor, allowing for plenty of personal attention. Schools are offered from late May through mid-August (Mon–Fri 9am–3pm). Make sure to reserve a spot several months ahead, as they book up quickly. Both group and private lessons are offered at an hourly rate as well.

Skate camps are offered at **Vans Skatepark** (p. 306). You'll also find plenty of great (though often far less unique) camps at the area's better resorts, including select WDW properties (see the listings in chapter 4, "Family-Friendly Accommodations," for more details).

9

Shopping for the Whole Family

Except for mouse ears and other tourist trinkets, Orlando has few products to call its own. Generally speaking, the merchandise and the malls won't be all that different from those you have back home. Still, many of you need some kind of shopping fix, and goofy souvenirs often are among your priorities—especially for the kids. After all, what else says "theme park" better than a pair of Mickey Mouse ears? (Except perhaps a blinking Buzz Lightyear, a Cinderella glass slipper, a Spider-Man suit . . . you get the idea.)

But before revving your credit cards into high gear, consider these words to the wise: If you're going to ring registers in the theme parks, you're going to pay top dollar. Alas, most official Disney and Universal merchandise is available only in on-site stores. But when it comes to other goods, plan a day away from tourist central, and be as savvy here as you are at home. You can find a lot of what you want, and at the best possible prices, by knowing what is and isn't a bargain.

1 The Shopping Scene

SHOPPING HOURS & SALES TAXES

Generally speaking, neighborhood stores in Orlando open daily at around 9 or 10am and don't close before 5pm at the very earliest. An exception would be some of the stores in downtown Orlando, which are usually closed on Sundays. Malls and major shopping centers tend to open around 10am, often not closing before 9 or 10pm, except on Sundays, when they usually close around 5 or 6pm. Stores in all Orlando theme parks generally stay open from the official park-opening time until just after the official park-closing time (giving you a last-minute opportunity to buy your child that stuffed Mickey or Cat in the Hat that she suddenly decided she can't live without).

At all the Disney resorts, you'll usually find at least one shop that's open by 8am and keeps going until 10 or 11pm. Stores in the Downtown Disney Marketplace are usually open daily from 9:30am until around 11 or 11:30pm; those in Downtown Disney West Side usually stay open from around 10:30am until 11pm, or midnight on Friday and Saturday. The shops at Pleasure Island open at 10:30am and close at 1am.

The shops at Universal Orlando's CityWalk open at 11am and don't close until 2am.

Sales tax in Osceola County, which includes Kissimmee, the U.S. 192 corridor, and *all* of Disney's All-Star resorts, is 7%. In Orange County, which includes the International Drive area, SeaWorld, Universal Orlando, most (but not all) of Disney World, and most of the lesser attractions, it's 6.5%. The tax is charged on every purchase except most edible grocery items and medicines.

GREAT SHOPPING AREAS

CELEBRATION Though not the best place to head if you're the shop-till-you-drop type, Celebration (© **407/566-2200**) is a rather pleasant spot to stroll leisurely along

Tips Setting Limits

The theme parks are filled one end to the other with shops of every sort, and unless they've been properly prepared, your kids could catch a serious case of the "buy me" flu. (You might also, but that's a whole different ballgame.) And nothing will sour a vacation faster than your kids whining at the sight of every storefront (again, there are plenty of them) that they want Mickey this and Mickey that.

Depending on your child's age, you'll need to set buying limits and make sure that he or she knows them in advance. Souvenirs aren't cheap in Disney or Universal, and if you give your kids a set spending limit and stick to it, they may even learn a lesson or two about value shopping and getting their money's worth (my own spend far more wisely—and much less quickly—with only their own money in hand). Personally, I set a total vacation allowance and then remind the kids several times along the way of how many parks and attractions they will need to allot for in their budget. If your kids seem overanxious to spend early on, you may need to jog their memory. Or you might find that setting a fixed allowance per park works better for your family; it all depends on your kids. Older kids (and even some younger ones) might be persuaded to set aside portions of their allowance for use as souvenir money, with a few subtle reminders tossed in well ahead of time, of course. Special chores that pay more than the going rate can help out as well.

Another suggestion: Set specific shopping times so your kids won't be continually bugging you every time you pass a souvenir store (keeping in mind that almost every ride will dump you into stores filled with shelves of them). If Susie and Timmy know ahead of time that they'll be getting their toy at the end of the day, they won't worry so much about passing up that store at the end of the ride. (It will also save you the trouble of having to carry around that gigantic stuffed Mickey or fragile glass slipper all day long if you're not staying on park property; guests at Disney's and Universal's on-site resorts can have their purchases delivered to where they're staying.) There are times an exception may be necessary, however, as some of the shops inside WDW, and many stores at Universal and SeaWorld, carry ride- or area-specific merchandise that may not be found elsewhere in the park. So if you promised a Spider-Man shirt to your budding web-slinger or a Cat in the Hat to your young Seuss fan, you'll need to pay up after you ride, or you'll be heading back to the store before you leave for the day.

quaint streets filled with upscale shops, coffeehouses, and restaurants. This is, after all, a Disney-designed community, making it practically the perfect little town. It's a throwback to mid-20th-century mainstream America, when Main Street shopping was in style. Market Street and the area just surrounding it are home to a dozen or so shops, a couple of art galleries, a handful of restaurants, and a three-screen theater. The storefronts, especially the galleries and gift shops, offer interesting and unique merchandise. The high prices, however, may make for more window-shopping than actual

Orlando Shopping

Antiques Row & Ivanhoe Row **3**	Festival Bay Mall **7**	Orlando Premium Outlets **9**	Prime Outlets International **7**
Bass Pro Shops Outdoor World **7**	Florida Mall **5**	Orlando Science Center **1**	Ron Jon Surf Shop **7**
Celebration **10**	Mall at Millenia **6**	Pointe Orlando **8**	Sunday Eola Market **4**
	Orlando Museum of Art **2**		

Tips Getting Your Fill

The neatest new way to buy toys at several Downtown Disney stores (especially Once Upon a Toy) is in bulk . . . sort of. Toys such as pirate treasure, Lincoln Logs, and Mr. Potato Head, as well as several others, can be purchased by the piece. Here's how it works: You pick out a box (there are usually two sizes to choose from) and fill it with as many (or few) pieces as you can fit inside. The only stipulation: You have to be able to close the lid properly. No matter how many pieces you've stuffed inside, the price of the box remains the same. If you've got good space-saving skills, buying your toys this way may net you a very good deal. (Here's a hint to get you started: Mr. Potato Head has a hole in his back, so fill it up, and you'll fit more pieces in your box.)

---

spending. The real attraction here is the relaxing, picture-perfect atmosphere. If, by chance, Celebration reminds you of the movie *The Truman Show,* you're not alone. The movie was filmed in Seaside, a Florida Panhandle community that inspired the builders of this burg. This would be a far better place to head for an afternoon without the kids in tow.

DOWNTOWN DISNEY   With three distinct areas—the Marketplace, West Side, and Pleasure Island—Downtown Disney (© **407/939-2648;** www.downtowndisney. com) is chock full of some of the most unique shops in Orlando, as well as many restaurants and entertainment venues.

The best shops in the Marketplace include the 50,000-square-foot **World of Disney** (p. 322), the largest store in Downtown Disney. There are rooms and more rooms filled with everything Disney, from toys and trading pins to clothes and collectibles—and everything (and I mean everything) in between. In the **Adventure Room,** kids can create their own pirate hat, play video games, and check out the latest space explorer, cowboy, and pirate gear. The **Princess Room** is filled with everything imaginable for little girls—they can play dress up, create their own crowns, and pick up the latest princess paraphernalia. The **Bibbidi Bobbidi Boutique,** also located within the World of Disney, arrived in 2006; it's where little girls can have their hair styled, their faces made up with sparkly makeup, and their nails done so when they emerge, they look just like a princess. I always stop by the **LEGO Imagination Center** (p. 322) when I'm in town. The play area keeps little ones thoroughly entertained, and the shelves are filled with LEGO blocks designed for everyone from toddlers to tweens, including hard-to-find sets, Bionicles, T-shirts, and trinkets. Check out the really neat display behind the counter—it's filled top to bottom with little LEGO people (their faces visible thanks to a nifty magnifying glass that runs back and forth on a wire). **Once Upon a Toy** (p. 322) is one of the best stores in the Marketplace and the best toy store I've ever been in. It's stocked from floor to ceiling with games and toys, many of them classics—you know, the ones you played with while growing up. Its 16,000 square feet are divided into three separate sections: the first is filled with board games; the second is loaded with stuffed animals, building sets, and Playskool toys; and the third features action figures, vehicles, and videos. There's even a "Build Your Own Light Saber" station. **Team Mickey's Athletic Club** is filled with character clothing with a sporty spin. Other smaller but similarly interesting shops include **Summer Sands,** featuring the hottest in beachwear from top names such as Quicksilver and

Calvin Klein; **Pooh Corner,** which offers everything Pooh; and the **Art of Disney,** where you can buy limited-edition animation cels and other collectibles.

Notable stores at West Side include **Magic Masters,** where you can load up on magic tricks for your budding Harry Houdini; **Magnetron,** which sells a huge variety of magnets (though, strangely enough, no Disney ones); and **Pop Gallery,** filled with colorful artwork and gifts with an artsy flair. *Note:* For details on the **Virgin Megastore,** see "Music," later in this chapter.

INTERNATIONAL DRIVE AREA   (*Note:* Locally, this road is always referred to as **I-Drive.**) Extending 8 or so miles northeast of Disney between Highway 535 and the Florida Turnpike, this busy thoroughfare is one of the most popular tourist districts in the area, in part because it is filled with so many restaurants, shops, hotels, and attractions. From surfing and glow-in-the-dark golf to dozens of themed restaurants and shopping spots, this is *the* tourist strip in Central Florida. The area's main shopping draws include the **Orlando Premium Outlets,** just off the southern end of I-Drive (see below), and **Prime Outlets,** just off the northern end (see below). Another I-Drive shopping spot, **Pointe Orlando** (© **407/248-2838;** www.pointe orlandofl.com), features a collection of upscale restaurants, clubs, and specialty shops. Thanks to a major overhaul (including the addition of several new high-end eateries and boutiques), tree-lined walkways, courtyards, and fountains now create an especially inviting atmosphere. The **Square** (under construction at press time) stands where the Mercado (now leveled) once stood. The area is slated to include an open plaza filled with landscaping and fountains, a mix of upscale shops and eateries, and eventually a hotel.

KISSIMMEE   Skirting the south side of Walt Disney World, Kissimmee centers on U.S. 192/Irlo Bronson Memorial Highway, as archetypal of modern American cities as Disney's Main Street is of America's yesteryear. U.S. 192 is lined end to end with budget motels, smaller attractions, and almost every fast-food restaurant known to humankind (though a handful of decent eateries can be found here as well). Kissimmee does not offer the fabulous array of shopping options found elsewhere in Orlando. The shopping here is notable for the quantity, not necessarily the quality, but it's a good place to pick up some knickknacks, a cheap souvenir, or white-elephant gifts.

WINTER PARK   Just north of downtown Orlando, Winter Park (© **407/644-8281;** www.winterpark.org) is the place many of Central Florida's old-money families call home. It began as a haven for Yankees trying to escape the cold. Today, its centerpiece is cobblestone Park Avenue, which has quite a collection of upscale shops—Ann

---

⌐Tips   Build Your Own

Another craze of late is to "build your own" toys. Star Wars fans will appreciate the "Build Your Own Light Saber" at Downtown Disney's Once Upon a Toy. Similar to the way you fill specially created containers with pirate booty, Lincoln Logs, and Mr. Potato Head parts, here you can pick and choose from bins filled with doodads, blades, switches, and trinkets in order to create your very own custom light saber (or, if you prefer, re-create that of your favorite characters—instructions are provided). Batteries are handed out upon checkout. The bonus: The cost, no matter how elaborate the design, remains the same (currently $20).

Tips **Forget Something?**

If you arrived home (or even to your hotel room) only to realize that you forgot to buy that special souvenir, you're in luck. If you were at any of the Disney
theme parks at the time you saw the item, call © **407/363-6200;** if you were
anywhere at Universal Orlando, call © **407/224-5800.** Tell the customer-service
representative which park you were in and describe the item; you'll likely be
able to order it by phone and have it sent to your home.

Taylor, Williams-Sonoma, Restoration Hardware, and Crabtree & Evelyn, among
others—with many an upscale restaurant and occasional art gallery as well. The quaint
atmosphere and boutique-style shops make for a great place to spend a relaxing afternoon, just not with the kids along (though there are plenty of shops that sell something to take back to them). To get here, take I-4 to Exit 87, Fairbanks Avenue/
Highway 426, east past U.S. 17/92 to Park Avenue, and turn left.

SHOPPING AT DISNEY'S THEME PARKS

You'll find dozens of places to buy everything from trinkets to treasures at the WDW
parks, many of which have shops bearing themes and merchandise from specific rides
and lands. Most of the stores carry merchandise that will appeal to both kids and
adults, so everyone can shop together without getting bored. And if you're staying at
a Disney resort, the stores will happily send your purchase there (you can pick it up
from the resort's main gift shop), so you won't have to lug everything around with you.
(If you're not staying on Disney property, you can have shops send your purchases to
the package pickup stations at each park, where you can get them before you leave,
but you'll have to allot at least 3 hr. for them to get there.)

Below are just a few favorites from each of the parks. Also, keep in mind that
although they're not inside the Big Four theme parks, the shops at **Blizzard Beach** and
Typhoon Lagoon sell loads of bathing suits, towels, beach toys, and more. Kids into
skateboarding and surfing will appreciate the selection of branded merchandise at
both water parks as well.

MAGIC KINGDOM   The **Emporium** on Main Street has a huge collection of
everything Disney, from clothing to collectibles. You won't have to stop there, however; the entire row of shops, each filled with clothing, toys, memorabilia, and more,
is interconnected. The **Pirates Bazaar** in Adventureland peddles pirate hats, Captain
Jack T-shirts, toy muskets, and loads of other yo-ho-ho buccaneer booty. The **Toontown Hall of Fame Tent,** in Mickey's Toontown Fair, has an avalanche of things
(including a large selection of sweets) kids under 7 will beg you to buy.

EPCOT   *Careful:* With all the cultural products (edible and otherwise), a stroll
around the World Showcase can break your bank unless you keep your wits about you.
The headliners include China's **Yong Feng Shangdian Shopping Gallery,** which features silk robes, lacquer and inlaid mother-of-pearl furniture, jade figures, cloisonné
vases, brocade pajamas, silk rugs and embroideries, wind chimes, and Chinese clothing. Artisans occasionally demonstrate calligraphy. **Mitsukoshi Department Store**
(Japan's answer to Macy's) sells lacquerware, kimonos, kites, fans, dolls in traditional
costumes, origami books, samurai swords, Japanese Disneyana, bonsai trees, Japanese
foods, netsuke carvings, pottery, modern electronics, and Pokémon cards (your kids

will be thrilled). Shops in and around Mexico's **Plaza de Los Amigos** are where you'll find an array of silver jewelry, leather goods, baskets, sombreros, piñatas, pottery, embroidered dresses, maracas, serapes, colorful papier-mâché birds, and blown-glass trinkets; an artisan occasionally gives demonstrations. The **Norway** shops sell hand-knitted wool hats and sweaters (including a collection by Dale of Norway), toys, and trolls, among other Scandinavian and Christmas items. And Canada's **Northwest Mercantile** carries sandstone and soapstone carvings, fringed leather vests, duck decoys, moccasins, stuffed animals, Native American dolls, Native American spirit stones, rabbit-skin caps, heavy knitted sweaters, and maple syrup. If you have little ones in tow, don't miss a stop at **MouseGear** in Future World's Innoventions East; it's loaded with toys and stuffed animals for the young set, and some of the best Epcot and Disney merchandise in all WDW.

DISNEY'S HOLLYWOOD STUDIOS The best shopping at this park is aimed more at older kids and teens than very young kids. **Animation Courtyard Shops** carry collectible cels, plus costumes from Disney classic films, plush toys, and pins for the younger set. **Sid Cahuenga's One-of-a-Kind** sells autographed photos of the stars, original movie posters, and star-touched items such as canceled checks signed by Judy Garland and others. Parents will be suitably impressed. **Celebrity 5 & 10,** modeled after a 1940s Woolworth's, has stocked its shelves with housewares a la Mickey. If you're with little ones, your best bet is the **Stage One Company Store,** which carries Muppet-themed souvenirs; **Legends of Hollywood,** which sells Pooh-and-friends clothing; and **L.A. Cinema Storage,** with its Mr. Potato Head station.

DISNEY'S ANIMAL KINGDOM **Creature Comforts** on Discovery Island focuses on kids' things, including themed toys and clothing. **Mombasa Marketplace** in Africa has a nice selection of safari clothing and African-themed gifts. **Chester & Hester's Dinosaur Treasures,** off to the side of the TriceraTop Spin, has tons of really unique little trinkets I didn't spot anywhere else in WDW, much of it for under $5 (though there are plenty of higher-priced items as well). In Asia, **Serka Zong** is the place to shop for stuffed Yetis, T-shirts, and everything Expedition Everest. **Mandala Gifts** offers a small assortment of Asian-themed items such as ornate wind chimes, colorful kites, and stuffed tigers. The **Island Merchantile** sells merchandise from throughout each of the lands.

Tips **Ship It**

Because Orlando is geared to travelers, many retailers offer to ship packages home for a few dollars more (Disney definitely does). So if you're pondering an extra-large or rather fragile purchase, or even just one you'd rather not have to carry, ask about shipping. If a retailer doesn't offer such a service, check with your hotel. Many a concierge or business-center staffer can arrange a pickup by UPS, the U.S. Postal Service, or other carrier. If you prefer to do it yourself (of if your hotel can't arrange for a pickup), there are UPS stores and post offices located throughout the tourist districts (all listed in the Yellow Pages). Anything's better than dragging that 6-foot stuffed Goofy through the friendly skies.

SHOPPING AT UNIVERSAL'S THEME PARKS

At **Universal Studios Florida,** the **Men in Black Gear Shop** is filled floor to ceiling with alien blasters of every kind; **Quint's Surf Shack** features island-inspired beach wear; kids will find plenty of plush toys at **ET's Toy Closet;** and the **Universal Studios Store,** near the park entrance, appeals to all ages and sells just about everything when it comes to Universal apparel.

Next door at **Islands of Adventure,** there are more than 20 shops within the park, offering a variety of themed merchandise. You may want to check out **Cats, Hats & Things** for special Seussian storybooks and souvenirs, especially with little kids in tow. **Jurassic Outfitters** and **Dinostore** feature enough plush and plastic dinosaurs to populate a geologic period, as well as safari-style clothing and souvenir T-shirts. Superhero fans should check out the **Spider-Man Shop.** If your kids are into comic books, the **Comic Shop** offers a great selection of titles (Marvel comics only, of course). **Islands of Adventure Trading Company** is a good stop on the way out if you're still searching for something to help your kids remember their visit. The store carries a wide variety of themed merchandise geared to visitors of all ages.

FACTORY OUTLETS

Sure, you probably have one of these in (or at least near) your hometown, and you won't get appreciatively better savings here. But if you're seeking school clothes, summer clothes, or just something to wear while you're in town, the two outlet malls below are some of the best in Orlando (and among the few places on the planet where you can get official theme-park merchandise at discounted prices).

Orlando Premium Outlets *(Finds* Opened in June 2000, this 440,000-square-foot outlet center offers shoppers the atmosphere of a beautiful open-air mall filled with lush landscaping and natural lighting. It's inviting instead of outlet-ish thanks to its chic Mediterranean styling. It's billed as Orlando's only upscale outlet mall (for now) and is by far the best choice for a great outlet-shopping experience in Orlando. Some of its 110 tenants include Armani, Banana Republic, BCBG, Coach, DKNY, Fendi, Hugo Boss, Kenneth Cole, Lacoste, MaxMara, Nautica, Nike, Polo Ralph Lauren, Salvatore Ferragamo, and Tommy Hilfiger. The selection at all of the stores is fabulous. Set just between S.R. 535 and I-Drive, it's easily accessible from either location. 8200 Vineland Ave. © 407/238-7787. www.premiumoutlets.com. From I-4, take Exit 68, Apopka-Vineland Rd./Hwy. 535 right/south to the first light; then go left at the first light to the outlet. It's near SeaWorld.

Prime Outlets International *(* This mall was formerly Belz Factory Outlet World, the granddaddy of all Orlando outlets. Located at the northern end of International Drive, it sports hundreds of stores including its newest anchor—Neiman Marcus Last Call. Thanks to a multimillion-dollar makeover (currently in the works at press time), the entire center's layout has been dramatically redesigned. Phase 1, completed in 2007, brought with it an all-new open-air complex with an upscale Mediterranean style, as evidenced by the Tuscan hues and Spanish tiles that run throughout, palm-lined semi-sheltered walkways, inviting plazas, fountains, and even a canal. Phase 2, slated for completion in 2008, ensures that shoppers, who once had to contend with having to drive between several buildings (but who can now take advantage of the free trolley service running during the construction), will find a far more inviting atmosphere with the completion of its second center (yet to be named). Currently the outlet offers more than a dozen shoe stores (including Vans, Cole Haan,

Tips **Homegrown Souvenirs**

Oranges, grapefruit, and other citrus products rank high on the list of local products. **Orange Blossom Indian River Citrus,** 5151 S. Orange Blossom Trail, Orlando (© **800/624-8835** or 407/855-2837; www.orange-blossom.com), is one of the top sellers during the late-fall-to-late-spring season. If your kids are fruit lovers, it's a great place to get a tasty souvenir. For something entirely different, alligator-skin leather goods are a specialty in the gift shop at **Gatorland,** 14501 S. Orange Blossom Trail, Orlando (© **407/855-5496;** www.gatorland.com).

and Nine West), housewares stores, and more than 60 clothing stores (Adidas, Calvin Klein, Geoffrey Beene, Gap, Guess?, Izod, Liz Claiborne, Nautica, Polo Ralph Lauren, and Tommy Hilfiger, among many others). You'll also find records, electronics, sporting goods, health and beauty aids, jewelry, toys, gifts, accessories, lingerie, hosiery, and so on. 5401 W. Oak Ridge Rd. © **407/352-9600.** www.primeoutlets.com. From I-4, take Exit 74B and turn north on I-Drive, continuing to the mall. It's near Universal Orlando.

THE MALLS

Festival Bay Mall   One of the newest additions to the local shopping scene, Festival Bay's tenants include a Ron Jon Surf Shop, Hilo Hattie, Bass Pro Shops, and several other specialty stores. Restaurants include a handful of fast-food eateries as well as Bergamo's Italian Restaurant, Cricketers Arms Pub & Eatery, Monkey Joes, Fuddruckers, Dixie Crossroads, and a Cold Stone Creamery to top off your meal. Some of the area's more unique recreational venues can be found here as well, including Vans Skatepark (which is indoors); the Putting Edge, a glow-in-the-dark miniature golf park; and a 20-screen Cinemark Theater. The Ron Jon Surf Park, where beginners and experts alike can ride the waves and hang ten all day long, splashed onto the scene in 2007. 5250 International Dr. © **407/351-7718.** www.shopfestivalbaymall.com. From I-4, take Exit 74B and turn north on I-Drive, continuing to the mall. It's near Universal Orlando.

Florida Mall   Anchors here include Nordstrom, Macy's, Dillard's, JCPenney, Sears, and Saks to go along with the Florida Hotel and more than 250 specialty stores (Abercrombie & Fitch, Banana Republic, Coach, Club Libby Lu, Crabtree & Evelyn, and Sharper Image, to name a few), restaurants (the Salsa Taqueria and Tequila Bar, California Pizza Kitchen, Le Jardin, Buca Di Beppo), and entertainment venues. No fewer than 10 stores offer children's clothing, and there are three toy stores as well. Strollers can be rented at several locations inside the mall. If you have young children, this is definitely your best bet for a mall excursion. 8001 S. Orange Blossom Trail. © **407/851-6255.** www.simon.com. Take I-4 to Exit 74A, Sand Lake Rd./Hwy. 482, and look for the mall on the corner of Orange Blossom and Sand Lake.

Mall at Millenia   This 1.3-million-square-foot upscale center made quite a splash when it debuted in 2002 with anchors that include Bloomingdale's, Macy's, and Neiman Marcus. In addition to the heavyweights, Millenia offers 200 specialty stores such as Burberry, Chanel, Charles David, Crate & Barrel, Godiva, Gucci, Juicy Couture, Lladro, Swarovski, and Tiffany & Co. Restaurants include the Cheesecake Factory, P. F. Chang's China Bistro, Brio Tuscan Grill, McCormick & Schmick's Seafood, and Panera Bread. The Blue Martini, an upscale bar, has a tapas menu and 29 designer martinis. Your label-conscious teens will find the rarified air here to their liking, though you, like me, may find it a bit too nose-in-the-air snooty. The mall is 5 miles from downtown Orlando and offers shuttle service to some hotels. 4200 Conroy Rd. (at I-4 near Universal Orlando). ✆ **407/363-3555**. www.mallatmillenia.com. Take I-4 to Exit 74A, Sand Lake Rd./Hwy. 482 east to the John Young Pkwy./Hwy. 423, and go north to Conroy and then west to the mall.

2 Shopping A to Z

Most visitors to Orlando will spend their time—and money—shopping in the theme parks. That's what the city is renowned for, after all. But if you aren't happy confining your credit card purchases to Disney, Universal, and SeaWorld, there are a few other opportunities for family spending in the Orlando area.

ANTIQUES

If you can think of nothing better than a relaxing afternoon of bargain-hunting or scouring thrift and antiques shops, check out **Antiques Row** and **Ivanhoe Row** on North Orange Avenue (stretching from Colonial Dr./Hwy. 50 to Lake Ivanhoe), in downtown Orlando. The shops are an interesting assortment of the old, the new, and the unusual—and a long way from the manufactured fun of Disney. **Flo's Attic,** 1800 N. Orange Ave. (✆ **407/895-1800**), and **A. J. Lillun,** 1913 N. Orange Ave. (✆ **407/ 895-6111**), sell traditional antiques. Kids who like perusing cool old stuff will enjoy the experience, but if your children aren't into that sort of experience, they'll likely be bored stiff.

To get here, take I-4 to Exit 85/Princeton Street, and turn right on Orange Avenue. Parking is limited, so stop wherever you find a space along the street.

BOOKS

All the major bookstore chains have stores in the Orlando area, though there are one or two local shops as well. This is a city that caters to kids, so almost all bookstores have well-stocked children's sections.

Barnes & Noble   This branch of the nationwide chain offers a wide selection of books for all ages. It's open daily from 9am to 11pm. 7900 W. Sand Lake Rd. ✆ 407/345-0900.

B. Dalton   This store has a large selection of children's books, as well as bestsellers and magazines. It's open from 10am to 10pm Monday through Saturday, 11am to 9pm on Sunday. 9101 International Dr. ✆ 407/363-0500.

Borders   A cafe is a welcome addition to this store's collection of books, appealing to all ages. It's open from 10am to 10pm Monday through Thursday, until 11pm Friday and Saturday, and from 10am to 9pm on Sunday. 1051 W. Sand Lake Rd. ✆ **407/826-8912.**

Brandywine Books   This local bookstore specializes in rare, out-of-print, and used hardbacks. It's open from 10:30am to 5pm Monday through Saturday. 114 S. Park Ave., Winter Park. ✆ 407/644-1711.

Long's Christian Book & Music Store   Families looking for Christian-oriented reading material should head for this local shop. It sells cassettes, CDs, videos, church supplies, and cards, in addition to a large selection of books and Bibles. Long's is open from 9am to 9pm Monday through Saturday. 1610 Edgewater Dr. ✆ 407/422-6934.

Waldenbooks   This member of the popular chain features a large selection of children's books, as well as bestsellers and other titles that appeal to all ages. It's open from 10:30am to 9pm Monday through Saturday, noon to 6pm on Sunday. In the Florida Mall, 8001 S. Orange Blossom Trail. ✆ 407/859-8787.

COMICS

Coliseum of Comics   This regional chain has three locations around Central Florida, including this Orlando store. It is a large purveyor of new and used comics (X-Men, Spider-Man, Superman, and more), as well as toys, games, videos, and collectible cards. If your kids are comics-crazed, it's a sure bet they'll love this store. There's also a branch in Kissimmee at 22 Broadway St. (© **407/870-5322**). The stores are usually open Monday through Thursday from 10am to 6pm, Friday from 10am to 11pm, Saturday from 10am to 9pm, and Sunday from noon to 6pm. 4722 S. Orange Blossom Trail. © **407/240-7882**. www.coliseumofcomics.com.

FARMERS' MARKETS

You can shop for fresh produce, plants, baked goods, and crafts every Sunday beginning at 9am at downtown's **Sunday Eola Market.** It's located at the intersection of North Magnolia and East Central. For more information, go to www.downtown orlando.com.

HAIRCUTS

The **Harmony Barber Shop,** on Main Street in Disney's Magic Kingdom, is a real scissor shop (with an atmospheric old-fashioned decor) where you can get your hair cut from 9am to 5pm daily. The barbers are incredibly friendly, give a good cut, and are an absolute marvel with kids. Haircuts are $17 for adults, $14 for kids. If it's your child's first haircut, Disney barbers will throw in a certificate, pixie dust, bubbles, and a set of special mouse ears. Colored gel runs $5 a pop. The shop is near the beginning of Main Street, set back by the firehouse. If you're lucky, Disney's barbershop quartet, the Dapper Dans, will serenade you and your kids as you get your locks shorn.

There are also beauty shops located at Disney's Contemporary, Coronado Springs, Beach Club, and Yacht Club resorts, as well as at the Grand Floridian.

MUSEUM STORES

Orlando Museum of Art   The museum has not only some exciting exhibits for kids and their caretakers, but also a wonderful shop featuring jewelry, books, videos, posters, and Dale Chihuly glass art. You can access the store without having to pay admission to the museum. It's open from 10am to 4pm Tuesday through Friday, noon to 4pm Saturday and Sunday. 2416 N. Mills Ave., in Loch Haven Park. © **407/896-4231**. www.omart.org.

MUSIC

Virgin Megastore   This 49,000-square-foot Virgin Megastore stocks more than 150,000 titles on CDs and cassettes; has 2,000 CD-ROM and video-game titles; and also sells books, magazines, and graphic novels. Preteens and teens will be in music heaven. The store has listening stations, video stations, game demo stations, a cafe with indoor and outdoor seating, and an outdoor stage for concerts. It's open from 11am to midnight Sunday through Thursday, until 1am Friday and Saturday. 1494 Buena Vista Dr., in Downtown Disney West Side. © **407/828-0222**.

SCIENCE STORES

Orlando Science Center   The store at the Science Center (p. 301) has a fun selection of mind-bending puzzles, interactive games, theme clothing, and jewelry that will appeal to kids of all ages. You can access the shop without having to pay admission to the museum. It's open from 10am to 6:15pm Sunday through Thursday, 10am to 10pm Friday and Saturday. 777 E. Princeton St., between Orange and Mills aves., in Loch Haven Park. © **407/514-2230**. www.osc.org.

SPORTS STUFF

Bass Pro Shops Outdoor World   This is the retail version of fishing and hunting (including archery) heaven. Located in the Festival Bay Mall, this store also features areas for watersports equipment, camping gear, and outdoor apparel, as well as a golf pro shop and an aquarium. If your family interests tend toward the outdoors, this is a worthy stop. The store is open daily, usually from 9am to 6pm, except Christmas. 5156 International Dr. © 407/563-5200. www.basspro.com.

Ron Jon Surf Shop   Also located in Festival Bay, this is a mini version of the wild and wacky Ron Jon's in Cocoa Beach. That means if you're looking for legitimate surfboards and gear, swimwear, T-shirts, or Ron Jon bumper stickers, this is one place to find it. It's open from 9am to 10pm Monday through Saturday, 10am to 7pm on Sunday. 5156 International Dr. © 407/481-2555. www.ronjons.com.

SWEETS

Downtown Disney has two favorite spots for sweet satisfaction in Orlando:

Candy Cauldron (© 407/828-1470), in Disney's West Side, will satisfy your and your kids' sweet tooth with 200 temptations, such as fudge, caramel apples, cotton candy, chocolate candies and fruit, and truffles. This candy-coated heaven is open from 10:30am to 11pm daily.

At the Marketplace, the **Ghirardelli Soda Fountain & Chocolate Shop** (© 407/934-8855), a branch of the famous San Francisco institution, sells truffles, double-chocolate mocha bars, and more. But Ghirardelli's is famous for its ice-cream concoctions, and if you've promised your kids fountain drinks, this is the place to come. There's a tantalizing selection of cones, floats, shakes, malts, and ice-cream sodas. The hot-fudge sundae here is a classic. Hours are 9:30am to 11pm daily.

TOYS

Need a way to keep the kids distracted while you shop for toys in peace? In the Downtown Disney Marketplace, the **LEGO Imagination Center** (© 407/828-0065) has a nifty outdoor play area where kids can build monster robots, race cars, and other creations. There are LEGO pirate ships, cowboy towns, and high-rise dollhouses, as well as the traditional LEGO buckets of building blocks. It's open from 9:30am to 11pm daily.

Also in the Downtown Disney Marketplace, **Once Upon a Toy** (© 407/934-7775) is a 16,000-square-foot store created by Disney and the Hasbro toy company. It's a toy-lover's nirvana. You can buy a Mr. Potato Head with Disney parts (or build your own on one of five touch screens), a Clue board game based on WDW's *Haunted Mansion* attraction, a Disney theme-park version of Monopoly, and a Play-Doh play set based on Disney's It's a Small World attraction. There are also Disney character dolls and miniature versions of Disney's monorail system. Other toys include Lincoln Logs (adults will marvel at the miniature replica of Disney's Wilderness Lodge), Tinker Toys, and *Star Wars* memorabilia. The store is open from 9:30am to 11pm daily. *Tip:* This is a great place for taking snapshots of the kids, as the store is loaded with backdrops, including a child-size version of the WDW Railroad and a Peter Pan–themed castle.

Kids, especially those 12 and under, and their parents can browse for hours in the mammoth **World of Disney** (© 407/828-1451), a Downtown Disney Marketplace store with a dozen themed rooms, featuring toys, dolls, and other trinkets a la Disney. You'll also find Disney art, clocks, and clothing in sizes ranging from infant to adult. Just keep an eye on the kids: The store is so big (about half a million sq. ft.), it's easy for the little shoppers to wander off.

10

Entertainment for the Whole Family

Most visitors, after a week of pounding the theme-park pavement, are desperately in need of yet another week off just to recover from the experience. This, however, may not include the kids, who are allowed the luxury of sleeping at times when the adults are otherwise occupied driving back to the hotel, scurrying about organizing for the next day's activities, packing for the trip home, or simply keeping watch over their children. A lot of vacationers, especially first-timers, burn the candle at both ends, completely wearing themselves out. The result: They'll likely need a vacation from their vacation. (Your kids, however, will likely bemoan the fact that the vacation is over.)

Some of you know the feeling. You're simply not willing to miss a beat even after a long day at the parks, or perhaps you have older kids and teens whose interest won't be flagging at the end of the day. You want after-hours adventure, and in the last decade, Orlando's tourism czars have built a bundle of entertainment options to satisfy your family's cravings.

The success of Central Florida's dinner shows, video arcades, cultural-arts programs, and adult nightclub districts—including Universal's **CityWalk, Downtown Disney West Side,** and **Pleasure Island**—shows that many visitors have the pizzazz to pick up the pace even after a day of toting their toddlers and teens around Mickeyville and Universal.

Check the "Calendar" section of Friday's *Orlando Sentinel* for up-to-the-minute details on local clubs, visiting performers, concerts, movies, and events. It has hundreds of listings, many of which are online at **www.orlandosentinel.com**. The *Orlando Weekly* is a free magazine found in red boxes throughout Central Florida. It highlights the more offbeat and often more of-the-minute performances. You can see it online at **www.orlandoweekly.com**. Another good source on the Internet is **www.orlandoinfo.com**, operated by the Orlando/Orange County Convention & Visitors Bureau.

Note: In addition to the places listed in this chapter, there are several other nighttime options for families, including end-of-evening productions in the theme parks (see chapters 6 and 7 for more information), sporting events at Disney's Wide World of Sports (p. 251), and after-dark miniature golf at Disney's courses (p. 251).

1 Dinner Shows

IN WALT DISNEY WORLD

The Magic Mickster offers tons of nighttime entertainment aimed at the whole family, including laser-light shows, fireworks, and IllumiNations (p. 225). There are also three dinner shows worthy of special note: the Spirit of Aloha Dinner Show, the Hoop-Dee-Doo Musical Revue, and a third production that's an occasional player.

While they offer entertainment, don't expect haute cuisine. The food, though good, takes a back seat to the show.

Note: If you intend on experiencing the Walt Disney World dinner shows, always, always, *always,* make **Advance Dining Reservations** (© **407/939-3463**). Disney's shows fill up fast, often months in advance, during peak vacation seasons and around holidays of any kind. Also note that all three dinner shows require that you *pay in full with a credit card at the time of booking.* If you find that you have to cancel your dinner plans, do so at least 48 hours in advance to ensure a full refund.

Disney's Spirit of Aloha Dinner Show *(Moments* **All ages** While not quite as much in demand as the Hoop-Dee-Doo, the Polynesian Resort's delightful 2-hour show is like a big neighborhood party. The Spirit of Aloha features Tahitian, Samoan, Hawaiian, and Polynesian singers, drummers, and dancers who entertain while you feast on a menu that includes tropical appetizers, Lanai-roasted chicken, pork ribs, sliced pineapple, Polynesian wild rice, Polynesian-style bread, South Seas vegetables, dessert, wine, beer, and other beverages. Kids can eat mac and cheese, hot dogs, chicken nuggets, or PB&J if they prefer. It all takes place in an open-air theater (dress for nighttime weather, and bring sweaters) with candlelit tables, red-flame lanterns, and tapa-bark paintings on the walls.

Reservations should be made 60 to 90 days in advance (but can be made up to 180 days in advance), especially during peak periods such as summer and holidays. Showtimes are 5:15 and 8pm Tuesday through Saturday. *Note:* A new tiered pricing system is now in place—meaning the closer you sit to the action, the higher the price. Not all seats are created equal in this venue: The further you sit from the stage (and the less expensive the ticket), the less you'll see of the show. At Disney's Polynesian Resort, 1600 Seven Seas Dr. © 407/939-3463. www.disneyworld.com. Reservations required. $51–$59 adults, $26–$30 kids 3–9, including tax and tip. Free parking.

Hoop-Dee-Doo Musical Revue ★★★ *(Moments* **All ages** This is Disney's most popular show, so make reservations *early.* The reward: You'll feast on a down-home, all-you-can-eat barbecue: fried chicken, smoked ribs, salad, corn on the cob, baked beans, bread, strawberry shortcake, and your choice of coffee, tea, beer, wine, sangria,

---

⟨ *Tips* **If You're Lucky . . .**

Mickey's Backyard BBQ (© **407/939-3463**; www.disneyworld.com) is a seasonal offering at Pioneer Hall at Disney's Fort Wilderness Resort & Campground, where Tom Sawyer and Huck Finn host a thigh-slapping feast in a covered outdoor pavilion. Mickey and his pals join you for a meal that includes barbecued pork ribs and chicken, hot dogs, corn on the cob, baked beans, mac and cheese, watermelon, beer, wine, lemonade, iced tea, and dessert. (There's no menu for kids, but plenty of options on the regular menu will satisfy them.) The storytelling, games, and character appearances make this a huge thrill for most young kids. The 3-hour meal starts at 6:30pm and costs $45 for adults, $27 for kids 3 to 9, including tax and tip. It's held only on Tuesdays and Thursdays, but weather plays a big factor and shows can be cancelled at times, so call ahead. As with Disney's other dinner shows, payment in full is expected at the time of booking.

Tips **You Are Cordially Invited . . .**

To the longest running off-Broadway comedy in history: *Tony n' Tina's Wedding.*
Witness Tony and Tina's side-splitting ceremony, then join the relatives for the
fun and festivities afterward—it's guaranteed to be the most hilarious reception
you've ever attended. You'll dine on a full Italian dinner (chicken Parmesan,
pasta, homemade bread, and tossed salad), enjoy a champagne toast, and even
get a slice of wedding cake. The price (including tip and tax) is $69 for adults
and $49 for kids 12 and under. Appropriate attire ranges from wedding formal
to business casual. The show takes place Thursday through Saturday from 7 to
about 9:30pm. It's now located at the Glo Lounge (8967 International Dr., next
to WonderWorks). Call (*C*) **407/390-7400** or go to www.tonyandtinaorlando.com
or www.tonylovestina.com for reservations.

---

or soda. (There's no kids' menu, but your kids shouldn't have much of a problem finding something to their liking.) While you stuff yourself silly in Pioneer Hall, performers in 1890s garb lead you in a foot-stomping, hand-clapping, and high-energy 2-hour
show that includes a lot of corny jokes you haven't heard since second grade. Kids of
all ages love it (and some may be selected to participate in the proceedings). *Note:* Be
prepared to join in on the fun, or else the singers and dancers, along with the rest of
the crowd, may humiliate you until you do. It's easy to get caught up in this lively and
entertaining family show.

Reservations should be made 60 to 90 days in advance or earlier (you can make them
up to 180 days in advance), especially during peak periods. Showtimes are 5, 7:15, and
9:30pm nightly. *Note:* A new tiered pricing system is now in place—meaning the closer
you sit to the action, the higher the price you'll pay. Seating in tier one is located on the
first floor nearest the stage, seating in tier two is in the back half of the first floor and in
the center of the balcony, and seating in tier three is to the right and left sides on the balcony level. To be honest, there's really not a bad seat in the house. At Disney's Fort Wilderness
Resort & Campground, 3520 N. Fort Wilderness Trail. (*C*) **407/939-3463.** www.disneyworld.com. Reservations required. $51–$59 adults, $26–$30 kids 3–9, including tax and tip. Free parking.

ELSEWHERE IN ORLANDO

Outside Mickey's kingdom, Orlando has an active dinner-theater scene, but keep in
mind that the city is a family destination—and the dinner shows are very reflective of
that. You won't find sophisticated offerings like those in major cultural centers such as
New York, London, or Paris. Most of the local dinner shows focus on pleasing the
kids, so if you're looking for fun, you'll find it, but if you want critically acclaimed
entertainment, look elsewhere. You also won't find four-star food, but the meals are
certainly palatable enough, with some a bit better than others. Attending a show is
considered by many to be a quintessential Orlando experience, and if you arrive with
the right attitude, you'll most likely have an enjoyable evening. Your children certainly
will.

Note: Discount coupons to the following dinner shows can often be found in the
tourist magazines that are distributed in gas stations and visitor centers; you'll also find
them in many non-Disney hotel lobbies and sometimes on the listed websites. Trust
me—you'll appreciate having them when you add up your bill.

(Tips   Supper at SeaWorld

While it may not appeal to some children (the 8-and-older squad should be okay), **SeaWorld's Makahiki Luau,** 7007 SeaWorld Dr. (© **800/327-2424** or 407/363-2559; www.seaworld.com), starts with the arrival of the tribal chief via boat, with a ceremonial progression leading the audience into a theater located in the Seafire Inn at the park's Waterfront district. You'll experience ancient customs, music and dance, authentic costumes, and family-style dining on Polynesian-influenced cuisine that includes tropical fruit, mahimahi in piña-colada sauce, sweet-and-sour pork, Hawaiian chicken, stir-fried island vegetables, fried rice, lava cake with chocolate fudge and peanut-butter drizzle, and beverages, including one free cocktail. The kids' menu has chicken fingers and hot dogs (and even select Gerber baby foods) for those whose tastes are less exotic. A holiday version runs during the Christmas season. The price is $46 for adults and $30 for children 3 to 9; reservations are necessary. Park admission is *not* required.

Arabian Nights   Age 5 and up   If you're a horse fancier, this is *the* attraction to see in Central Florida, and your kids will be impressed by the equestrian acrobatics even if you aren't hoof-happy. Arabian Nights is one of the classier dinner-show experiences. It stars many of the most popular breeds, from chiseled Arabians to hard-driving Andalusians to beefcake Belgians. They giddy-up through performances that include Wild West trick riding, chariot races, slapstick comedy, and bareback bravado. On most nights, the performance opens with a ground trainer working one-on-one with a black stallion. Though locals rate it number one among local dinner shows, do note that my kids preferred the action of some of Orlando's other offerings. The dinner served during the 2-hour show includes salad; a choice of New York strip steak, grilled chicken, Black Angus chopped steak, chicken tenders, or primavera penne pasta (all of which are served with steamed vegetables); mashed potatoes; rolls; wedding cake for dessert; and wine, beer, and unlimited soda. Special diets can be accommodated with advance notice. Showtimes vary, but there is at least one performance nightly. *Tip:* Book your tickets online to save about $10 to $15 per person off the regular price. 6225 W. Irlo Bronson Memorial Hwy. (U.S. 192), Kissimmee. © **800/553-6116** or 407/239-9223. www.arabian-nights.com. Reservations recommended. $53–$72 adults, $29–$45 kids 3–11. Free parking.

Dolly Parton's Dixie Stampede Dinner & Show   Age 4 and up   Here's a hootin'-and-hollerin' good time. This $28-million venture is similar to the ones the actress and country singer has in other Southern locations, although the venue is slightly larger. While horses have less of a role here than at Arabian Nights (see above), the Quarter Horses, Appaloosas, Belgians, and others that perform help put on a "God Bless the U.S.A." show that opens with a herd of bison charging around the arena. Any weaknesses in the early themes and songs are forgotten when the fun and games begin, including a rivalry that pits half the audience (the North) against the other half (the South) in a who-can-cheer-and-stomp-the-loudest battle. The blue-versus-gray competition continues in a number of offbeat events, including a chicken chase using four kids from the audience, pig races, a game of toilet-seat horseshoes, and more. Some may blink at the Civil War theme, but your kids will have a great time. The vittles (plan to eat with your fingers; you don't get utensils) include a small rotisserie chicken (whole), barbecued pork tenderloin, a potato wedge, corn on the cob, creamy vegetable soup, apple pastry, and unlimited coffee, tea, or soda—and beer and wine are now served, with a two-drink limit. Vegetarians have a choice of lasagna and a fruit bowl (in addition to the other fixin's). There's no specific menu for kids, and be advised that *children 3 and under are free only if they sit on a parent's lap.* Showtimes vary, but there is at least one performance nightly, and during the Christmas season, you can enjoy a special holiday version of the show. As Dolly said at the opening, "It's fun for families, and I'm gettin' rich on it." 8251 Vineland Ave. (across from Orlando Premium Outlets), Orlando. *C* 866/443-4943 or 407/238-4455. www.dixiestampede.com. Reservations recommended. $50 adults, $22 kids 4–11. Free parking. From I-4, take Exit 68, Apopka–Vineland Rd./Hwy. 535 right/south to the first light, and then go left at the first light to the outlets.

Medieval Times   Age 5 and up   Orlando has one of the eight Medieval Times in North America, and this is the show my kids rate tops in town. Guests gorge on barbecued spare ribs, herb-roasted chicken, tomato bisque, potatoes, dessert, and beverages (including beer). But because this is the 11th century, you eat with your fingers while knights mounted on Andalusian horses run around the arena, jousting and clanging to please the fair ladies. A new storyline, "Knights of the Realm," introduced in 2004, adds to the action a touch of romance between one of the knights and the princess. Arrive 90 minutes early for good seats and to see the Medieval Village, a re-created Middle Ages settlement. Recent renovations have doubled the size of the Hall of Arms (where you gather prior to showtime, and where you'll find the gift shop) and added landscaping, a moat and drawbridge, and an enclosed ticketing area. Showtimes vary, but there is at least one performance nightly. While I recommend it for kids over 5, mine have all been to the show at varying ages from 9 months on up. They have always appreciated the chance to scream and yell as loud as they can while stomping their feet during dinner, as this is not so well received at home. The biggest concern when bringing very young kids is definitely the noise level. 4510 W. Irlo Bronson Memorial Hwy. (U.S. 192), Kissimmee. *C* 800/229-8300 or 407/396-1518. www.medievaltimes.com. Reservations recommended. $45–$55 adults, $30–$35 kids 3–11. Free parking.

Pirates Dinner Adventure   Age 5 and up   The special-effects show at this theater includes a full-size ship in a 300,000-gallon lagoon, circus-style aerial acts, a lot of music, and a little drama. It's a big hit with pirate-happy kids—especially when they're invited to join in on the fun. Dinner features "The King's Festival" with live entertainment, a complimentary appetizer buffet, face painting, and family photo ops before

---

Tips **A Universal Luau**

Universal Orlando's Royal Pacific Resort offers its own South Seas–style luau on Tuesday and Saturday nights. The **Wantilan Luau** features entertainment from various Polynesian islands, including drum performances, dancing, and music. Dinner features a variety of island cuisines (including the ubiquitous roast pig); a special kids' menu; and unlimited wine, beer, mai tais, and nonalcoholic drinks. The price (including tip, but not tax) is $50 for adults and $29 for kids 12 and under. A new pavilion, built just for the event, guarantees that you'll enjoy the luau rain or shine. Call *C* 407/503-3463 to make reservations.

(Moments Prime Rib & a Side of Murder

Ever dream of being Sherlock Holmes? **Sleuths Mystery Dinner Show** ⟨★★★⟩, 8267 International Dr. (© **800/393-1985** or 407/363-1985; www.sleuths.com), is an interactive dinner show staged in an intimate theater setting where guests play detective and try to solve a whodunit murder mystery.

A roster of suspects and impending victims (OK, they're really actors) interact with guests throughout the experience, which includes a preshow where you're introduced to the characters as they serve appetizers and salad. When the actual performance begins, the actors both entrance and, at times, reduce you to hysterical laughter. Then it's time for dinner, which includes a choice of Cornish game hen, prime rib (for $3 more), or lasagna. While eating, you discuss clues with the other detectives at your table (the round tables seat eight). Each table is given the opportunity to interrogate the suspects (which can get quite hilarious, depending on the amount of alcohol consumed—adults get unlimited wine and beer). A mystery dessert is served, and then the murderer is revealed. It makes for a very entertaining yet relaxing evening out.

Thirteen different productions (each about 2–2½ hr. long) are offered throughout the year, so you can keep coming back for more. Admission is $49 for adults and $24 for kids 3 to 11. Reservations are recommended.

To get here from I-4, take Exit 75A; at the light, turn right onto International Drive and then left at Universal Boulevard; it's 1 mile down on the right at the Gooding's Plaza. Parking is free.

---

the main event. The meal includes tossed salad, roast chicken, a choice of pork loin or garlic lobster and shrimp, mixed vegetables, West Indies rice or red potatoes, dessert, and beverages. Vegetarian meals are available upon request, as are kids' meals (chicken fingers). After the show, you're invited to the Buccaneer Bash dance party, where you can mingle with cast members. Showtimes vary, but there is at least one performance nightly (with a holiday version that runs from November to the first week in January). Be sure to check out the Pirate's Maritime Museum (created with the help of the famed Mel Fisher). This is the only dinner show I've come across that has highchairs for young kids. *Note:* While many of the dinner shows have violent scenes, this one in particular features a great deal of fistfighting. 6400 Carrier Dr. © **800/866-2469** or 407/248-0590. www.piratesdinneradventure.com. Reservations recommended. $56 adults, $36 kids 3–11. Free parking. Take I-4 to Exit 74A, Sand Lake Rd./Hwy. 482, north to Carrier; turn right.

2 Arcades & Fun Centers

DisneyQuest   **Age 7 and up**   This five-level arcade usually inspires awe in children just reaching the video-game stage, firmly hooked teens, and nostalgic adults who never outgrew Pac-Man. While you will find a few things for the younger set—such as video and pinball games—this high-tech arcade is really geared more to older children, teens, and adults. Options include **Aladdin's Magic Carpet Ride,** a virtual-reality adventure that puts you astride a motorcycle-like seat for a journey into the 3-D Cave of Wonders;

Invasion! An ExtraTERRORestrial Alien Encounter, in which you and three others in your space module try to save colonists from intergalactic bad guys; **Pirates of the Caribbean: Battle for Buccaneer Gold,** another 3-D virtual-reality adventure that has you and your shipmates fighting blackhearts; the **Mighty Ducks Pinball Slam,** a life-size pinball game in which body English and reflexes help you score; and **CyberSpace Mountain,** in which you build, and then ride, your own simulated roller coaster. For more on this attraction, see the "DisneyQuest" box (p. 252). *Warning:* Heavy crowds after 1pm can significantly cut into your game time. Downtown Disney West Side. ℂ 407/828-4600. www.disneyquest.com. $37 adults, $31 kids 3–9. Mon–Thurs 11:30am–11pm, Fri–Sat until midnight.

Fun Spot Action Park **Age 4 and up** This throwback amusement park on the north end of International Drive, near Universal Orlando, has something for just about everyone. There are bumper cars, bumper boats, a carousel, kiddie rides, spinning teacups, a Ferris wheel, go-kart tracks, and a lift-and-drop ride that's a tame version of Universal's Doctor Doom's Fearfall (p. 277). General admission is free; you can pay as you ride or purchase an armband good for unlimited rides and games. An unlimited play-all-day band for the arcade (where you'll find simulators, video games, and pinball) costs $4.95, single-ride tickets are $3, single go-kart tickets run $6 per ride, and there is an array of multiride armbands available ($15 kids 2–6, $25 ages 6 to adult and 46–51 in. tall, including the beginner go-kart track; $35 age 10 and up and 52 in. and taller, including all go-kart tracks). 5551 Del Verde Way. ℂ 407/363-3867. www.fun-spot.com. Mon–Fri 2–11pm (10am–midnight in summer); Sat–Sun 10am–midnight.

Note: Fun Spot's baby sister, **Fun Spot USA,** recently opened in Kissimmee. 5720 U.S. 192. ℂ 407/397-2509. www.fun-spotusa.com. Mon–Fri 2pm–midnight; Sat–Sun 10am–midnight.

3 Movies

There are several theaters scattered through tourist and high-traffic areas in Central Florida, many of them conveniently located to those staying near the theme parks. Most theaters offer discounted ticket pricing for children under 12 and discounted matinees (though, really, who's going to choose the movies over the theme parks?); some also offer discounts to students with ID. I definitely recommend that you head for those theaters that offer stadium seating (available at the ones recommended below), so that even the shortest members of your party will get to see the picture.

AMC Pleasure Island 24 (ℂ 407/298-4488) is a 24-screen complex—the largest in the southeast—in Downtown Disney. It seats 6,000 and has stadium seating and digital sound systems in most of its theaters. **AMC Universal Cineplex 20** at CityWalk (ℂ 407/354-5998; www.citywalk.com) has 20 screens, stadium seating, and a state-of-the-art projection system. **Muvico Pointe 21** has 21 screens in the Pointe Orlando shopping center on International Drive (ℂ 407/926-6843; www.pointeorlandofl.com), including an IMAX screen that's nearly six-and-a-half stories high. All of its theaters have stadium seating and top-of-the-line sound systems. You can find other theaters and showtimes in the *Orlando Sentinel* or at **www.orlandosentinel.com/entertainment/movies**.

4 Theater

Orlando Youth Theatre **Age 4 and up** Here's a nifty way for families to keep the "kid" theme going outside the parks. This theater by the young includes 6- to 18-year-olds presenting shows such as *Little Women, Footloose,* and *Alice in Wonderland,* as

Tips **Ghostly Experience**

Orlando Ghost Tours (📞 407/423-5600; www.hauntedorlando.com) puts a different spin on the city's nightlife with 2-hour walking tours that explore downtown's spookier side. The tours include narratives (some funnier than others) on Florida history and folklore, followed by a chance to use "ghost-finding" equipment in a haunted building. If your kids are over 8, aren't easily spooked, and are into the supernatural and ghost stories, it's good fun. The cost is $25 for adults, $15 for kids 7 to 12. Tours run Monday through Saturday at 8pm.

well as drama and improv in fall and spring, plus during summer camps. 128 W. Church St. 📞 407/254-4930. www.orlandoyouththeatre.com. Tickets $10.

5 Concert Venues

Amway Arena   Formerly the TD Waterhouse Center, this 17,500-seat venue has a resume that includes the NBA's Orlando Magic (see "Spectator Sports," in chapter 8); big-name concert performers such as Garth Brooks, Elton John, and Bruce Springsteen; and family-oriented entertainment like the Ringling Bros. Barnum & Bailey Circus in January. There's also a slate of cultural offerings such as Broadway-style shows, ballets, plays, and symphony performances. 600 W. Amelia St. (between I-4 and Parramore Ave.). 📞 407/849-2001 for event information, 407/849-2020 for box-office information, 877/803-7073 or 407/839-3900 for tickets via Ticketmaster. www.orlandocentroplex.com. Parking $5–$8.

Florida Citrus Bowl   With 70,000 seats, the bowl is the largest venue in the area for rock concerts, which in the past have featured such heavyweights as Elton John and the Rolling Stones. It's also home of the Capital One Florida Citrus Bowl (see "Kids' Favorite Orlando Events," p. 19). 1610 W. Church St. (at Tampa St.). 📞 407/849-2001 for event information, 407/849-2020 for box-office information, 877/803-7073 or 407/839-3900 for tickets via Ticketmaster. www.orlandocentroplex.com. Parking $10.

6 Dance

Orlando Ballet   *Age 7 and up*   Formerly called the Southern Ballet Theatre, this troupe stages productions such as *The Pirates of Penzance* and *Sleeping Beauty*, along with a family series that includes *Rumpelstiltskin* and *Fairytale Princes and Princesses*. Both *The Nutcracker* and a children's version of the cherished classic are annual events. Performances are held in the Bob Carr Performing Arts Centre. One cool holiday program offers a character brunch that lets families dine with characters from *The Nutcracker*. Call for details if you'll be visiting in December. 401 W. Livingston St. 📞 407/426-1739 for information, 877/803-7073 or 407/839-3900 for tickets via Ticketmaster. www.orlandoballet.org. Tickets $15–$65. Parking $5–$8.

7 A Night Out for Mom & Dad

If you're so inclined, take advantage of the various babysitting services and kids' clubs mentioned in the listings in chapter 4, "Family-Friendly Accommodations," and step out for at least one night of fun *sans* the kids.

Tips   On the BoardWalk

Disney's BoardWalk can be a cheap night out if you enjoy strolling and people-watching (and if you stay out of the restaurants and clubs). The whole area has a midway atmosphere reminiscent of Atlantic City's heyday. Street performers sing, dance, and do a little juggling and magic on the outdoor promenade. There are also a few options for folks searching for off-the-field nightlife:

Atlantic Dance (© 407/939-2444 for recorded information) features Top 40 and '80s dance hits Tuesday through Thursday, with live bands on Friday and Saturday. It's open to ages 21 and over. Hours are 9pm to 2am; no cover.

The saloon-style **Jellyrolls** (© 407/939-5100) offers dueling pianos and a boisterous crowd. Strictly for the over-21 set, it's popular with business travelers and is usually packed to the rafters on weekends. There's a $10 cover after 7pm.

If you're looking to hoist a pint, the **Big River Grille & Brewing Works** (© 407/939-5100) serves microbrewed beer, as well as steaks, ribs, chicken, fish, sandwiches, and salads. Prices range from $9 to $25, and there's no cover. It's located near Atlantic Dance and is open Monday through Thursday from 11:30am to 1am, Friday through Sunday from 11:30am to 2am.

Sports nuts, look no farther than **ESPN Club** (© 407/939-3463), where 100 screens—there are even a few in the bathroom—broadcast sporting events from around the world. There's a full-service bar, but you'll also find a restaurant and a small arcade, so if you're stuck for the night with the kids, you all will have something to do.

The places described here can be located on the "Downtown Disney" map (p. 333). For information on nighttime activities throughout Downtown Disney, call © 407/939-2648.

PLEASURE ISLAND

This 6-acre complex of nightclubs, restaurants, and shops, not to mention a multi-screen movie theater, will not disappoint those in search of an exciting night on the town. Visitors can walk the grounds and enjoy the sights, sounds, and surroundings free of charge, but if you want to enter the clubs, admission is required. A single admission price—$23 plus tax—allows you to club-hop into the wee hours every night of the week. If you prefer to head to a single club, admission is $12 (though the Comedy Club and the Adventurers Club don't offer single-club admission prices, so it's all or nothing if you want to hang at either of them—and you do). If you have a **Water Park Fun & More** admission ticket (see p. 176 for more on Disney's ticket options), you can use one of your Plus options for a 1-night admission to all clubs on Pleasure Island. Pay special attention to **Mannequins Dance Palace** (listed a little later). This club is the cream of Pleasure Island's crop and fills quickly, so late arrivals may be left standing at the door.

Pleasure Island is designed to look like an abandoned waterfront industrial district with clubs in its lofts and warehouses—but the streets are decorated with brightly colored lights and balloons. Dozens of searchlights play overhead, with rock music emanating from the bushes. You'll be given a map and show schedule when you enter the park. Take a look at it, and plan your evening around the shows that interest you. The mood is always festive, both inside the clubs and out, no matter where you choose to party the night away. In addition to the clubs, there are shops and eateries (some with outdoor umbrella tables) on the island—the most notable of which is **Raglan Road** (p. 334). Just a few steps away is **Planet Hollywood** (p. 157), adjacent to Disney's West Side. (You don't need an admission ticket to eat at any of the Pleasure Island restaurants.)

For more information on Pleasure Island's clubs and events, call ✆ **407/939-2648** or surf over to **www.disneyworld.com**. Clubs are open daily from 7pm to 2am; shops open at 10:30am, and some don't close until 1am. There's free self-parking, but as the night wears on, spots can become very hard to find.

Although this is Disney, Pleasure Island is essentially a bar district where liquor is served both in the clubs and on the street—making it, in my opinion, an inappropriate destination for anyone under the age of 21. Also note that six of the eight clubs now require that you be at least 21 to get in (the only exceptions being the Comedy Warehouse and the Adventurers Club, where you must be at least 18 unless accompanied by a parent or legal guardian).

Here's the club lineup:

Adventurers Club The most unique of Pleasure Island's clubs occupies a multistory building that, according to legend, was designed to house the library and archaeological-trophy collection of island founder and compulsive explorer Merriweather Adam Pleasure, a figment of Disney's imagination. It's also the global headquarters of the Adventurers Club, which Pleasure headed until he vanished at sea in 1941. The plush club is chock full of artifacts: early aviation photos, hunting trophies, shrunken heads, Buddhas, and a mounted "yakoose," a half yak, half moose that occasionally speaks, whether you've been drinking or not. In the eerie Mask Room, more strange sounds are heard as the 100 or so masks move their eyes and make odd pronouncements. Also on hand are Pleasure's zany band of globetrotting friends and servants, played by actors who interact with guests. Comedy, cabaret, and other shows run in various rooms. It's easy to see why it's the most popular place on the island; it's a hoot. This one's an especially good choice for those who may find dancing the night away at the other clubs a bit more than they bargained for. You can easily hang out here all night, sipping potent tropical drinks in the library or the bar, where elephant-foot barstools rise and sink mysteriously.

BET Soundstage Club This club grooves—loudly—to the sounds of reggae, R&B, and hip-hop. If you like the BET cable network, you'll love it. You can boogie on an expansive dance floor or kick back on the terrace. The club also serves Caribbean-style finger food and periodically has concerts for a separate charge (✆ **407/934-7666**). You must be 21 to enter (and they will check!).

Comedy Warehouse Housed in the island's former power plant, the Comedy Warehouse has tiered seating. A troupe of comics performs 45-minute improvisational shows based on audience suggestions. This is Disney, so the shows are neither as risqué as those at other improv clubs nor candidates for anyone's top 10, but if you like your

Downtown Disney

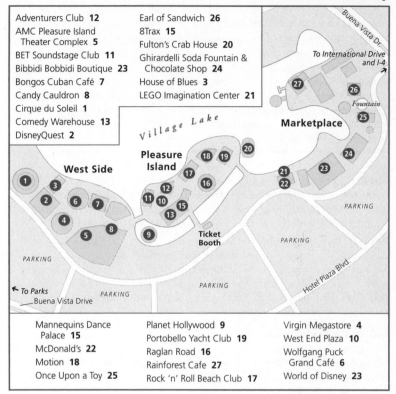

Adventurers Club **12**
AMC Pleasure Island Theater Complex **5**
BET Soundstage Club **11**
Bibbidi Bobbidi Boutique **23**
Bongos Cuban Café **7**
Candy Cauldron **8**
Cirque du Soleil **1**
Comedy Warehouse **13**
DisneyQuest **2**

Earl of Sandwich **26**
8Trax **15**
Fulton's Crab House **20**
Ghirardelli Soda Fountain & Chocolate Shop **24**
House of Blues **3**
LEGO Imagination Center **21**

Village Lake

West Side

Pleasure Island

Marketplace

Fountain

To International Drive and I-4

Buena Vista Dr.

Ticket Booth

PARKING

PARKING

PARKING

PARKING

PARKING

← To Parks
Buena Vista Drive

Hotel Plaza Blvd.

Mannequins Dance Palace **15**
McDonald's **22**
Motion **18**
Once Upon a Toy **25**

Planet Hollywood **9**
Portobello Yacht Club **19**
Raglan Road **16**
Rainforest Cafe **27**
Rock 'n' Roll Beach Club **17**

Virgin Megastore **4**
West End Plaza **10**
Wolfgang Puck Grand Café **6**
World of Disney **23**

comedy relatively clean, you're in luck. There are several shows nightly, and drinks are served. Arrive early.

8Trax   Disco and bell bottoms rule in this 1970s-style club, where some 50 TV screens air shows and videos over the dance floor. A DJ plays everything from "YMCA" to "The Hustle" while the disco ball spins. All you need to bring are your polyester and patent leather. If you grew up during the Reagan years, you can relive your musical past on Thursday nights, when the tunes fast-forward to the '80s. You must be 21 to enter.

Mannequins Dance Palace   Housed in a vast dance hall with a small-town movie-house facade, Mannequins is supposed to be a converted mannequin warehouse (remember, you're still in Disney World). This high-energy club has a big rotating dance floor, and it's a local favorite—thus it's one of the toughest clubs to get into, so arrive early. Those who get in will find three levels of bars festooned with elaborately costumed mannequins and moving scenery. A DJ plays contemporary tunes filtered through speakers powerful enough to wake Sleeping Beauty. You must be 21 to get in, and they're very serious about it. Have your ID ready, even if you learned to dance to the Beatles live.

Tips **The Luck of the Irish**

The Great Irish Pubs of Florida, Inc. (the company that created the Nine Fine Irishmen pub in Las Vegas's New York–New York Hotel & Casino), brought the luck of the Irish to Downtown Disney in 2005 with the opening of **Raglan Road.** The pub immerses guests in a wholly Irish environment that includes custom-made furnishings direct from the Emerald Isle. Entertainment includes story-telling, dance, and music. Guests can dine on a menu of traditional fare created by well-known Irish chef Kevin Dundon. Pleasure Island admission is not required to eat here.

Motion   This hyperactive joint features Top 40 tunes and alternative rock, appeal-ing to younger or young-at-heart partyers. It uses moody blue lighting, but the outer-space idea eluded me; it just looks like a cool, high-tech dance club. The place usually doesn't heat up until later in the evening. You must be 21 to enter.

Rock 'n' Roll Beach Club   This three-story structure houses an always-crowded dance club where live bands play classic rock from the '60s through the '90s. There are bars on all three floors, including one that serves international brews. The first level contains the dance floor. The second and third levels offer air hockey, pool tables, basketball machines, pinball, video games, darts, and a pizza-and-beer stand. You must be 21 to enter.

DISNEY'S WEST SIDE

This area adjoins Pleasure Island and offers additional shops, restaurants, and a 24-screen AMC movie theater (see "Movies," earlier in this chapter). Older kids and teens will find DisneyQuest (p. 252) an alluring, if crowded, enticement. The two most popular adult entries are:

Bongos Cuban Café *(Overrated*   Created by singer Gloria Estefan and her husband, Emilio, this is Disney's version of old Havana. There are leopard-spotted chairs and bar stools shaped like bongo drums (and a Desi Arnaz impersonator every night). There's no dance floor to speak of, though you could cha-cha on the upstairs patio, which overlooks the rest of Disney's West Side. It's a great place to sit back and bask in the Latin rhythms. While the mood is good, the food is a little lacking. Open daily from 11am to 2am. (**407/828-0999.** www.bongoscubancafe.com. No reservations or cover. Free self-parking.

House of Blues   Several well-known artists have performed here, including Jethro Tull, Cyndi Lauper, Duran Duran, and others. The barnlike building may be a little difficult for those with disabilities to maneuver, but there isn't a bad seat in the house. The atmosphere is dark and boozy, perfect for the bluesy sounds that raise the rafters. The dance floor is big enough to boogie without doing the Bump with a stranger. You can dine in the adjoining restaurant (p. 158) on baby back ribs, jambalaya, and Cajun meatloaf. You have to see it to believe the voodooish atmosphere and extremely ornate decor. There's also a Sunday gospel brunch (see p. 158 for details). (**407/934-2583.** www.hob.com. Cover varies by event/artist. Free self-parking.

Finds   Not Your Ordinary Circus

Lions and tigers and bears? Oh, no. But don't worry—you won't feel cheated.

This Disney partnership with **Cirque du Soleil,** the famous Montréal-based, no-animals circus, is located in Disney's West Side. The eye-popping *La Nouba* (derived from the French for "to live it up"), set in a custom-built, state-of-the-art theater, is a Fellini-style amalgam of live music, dance, theater, and acrobatics that will make your jaw drop. Highlights include a cyclist who does things with a bicycle that would make an X-Gamer jealous, a spectacular coordinated trampoline performance, and a pint-sized troupe of Chinese acrobats whose tricks with *diabolos* (Chinese yo-yos) bring the house down. I rank this one just beneath Las Vegas's *Mystère*, though the comedic interludes in this production are the best of all the permanent Cirque shows.

That said, though *La Nouba* is a ton of fun, it's also one of the priciest shows in town. Ticket prices vary according to seat location (though nearly every spot in the theater offers a good view) and range from $63 to $112 for adults, $50 to $90 for children 3 to 9 (plus 6.5% tax). Yes, it's an expensive 90 minutes, but keep in mind that tickets here are the cheapest of all the permanent Cirque productions in the U.S. Shows are at 6 and 9pm Tuesday through Saturday, though the show is dark 6 weeks each year. There are occasional matinees, so call ahead (© **407/939-7600**) or check the show's website (**www.cirquedusoleil.com**) for information.

CITYWALK

Located between the Islands of Adventure and Universal Studios Florida theme parks, this nightclub, restaurant, and shopping district competes nose to nose with Disney's Pleasure Island. It's open daily from 11am, but the hours of many clubs and restaurants vary, so call in advance if you're interested in a specific venue. Most clubs stay open until 2am and will not allow anyone under 21 to enter after a certain time (see listings below for details).

At 30 acres, CityWalk (© **407/363-8000** or 407/224-9255; www.citywalk.com or www.universalorlando.com) is five times larger than Pleasure Island. Alcohol is prominently featured here, and the nights can get pretty wild, so an adult should accompany all teens, young children, and party-hearty peers. Better yet: Don't bring the kids at all unless you're heading to the movies or one of the theme restaurants for dinner.

Just like at Pleasure Island, you can walk the district for free, hitting individual clubs and paying a cover at each. If you prefer to club-hop, CityWalk also offers two **party passes.** For $12 plus tax, you get a pass to all clubs. For $15 plus tax, you get a club pass and a movie at AMC Universal Cineplex 20 (© **407/354-3374**). Universal also offers free club access to those who buy multiday theme-park tickets (see chapter 7). If all you want on your night out is dinner and a movie, CityWalk's **Meal & Movie Deal** nets you dinner (an entree and a soft drink from a limited menu) at one of the district's participating restaurants and a movie ticket for $22, including tax and gratuity. Kids get no special price or meals; CityWalk is aimed at parents taking the night

off. To get your tickets, ask at the CityWalk Guest Services ticket window or call
℃ **407/224-CITY.**

Daytime parking in the Universal Orlando garages costs $11, but parking is free
after 6pm. To get to CityWalk, take I-4 to Exit 74B (westbound) or 75A (eastbound),
and follow the signs to the parks.

Bob Marley—A Tribute to Freedom   This bar/restaurant has a party atmosphere
that will make the food more appealing as the night wears on. The clapboard building is said to be a replica of Marley's home in Kingston. Jamaican vittles—meat pat-
ties, jerk snapper, and Red Stripe beer—are served under patio umbrellas, while reggae
bands perform on a microdot stage. Open daily from 4pm to 2am. ℃ 407/224-2262.
www.bobmarley.com. Cover $7 after 8pm, more for special acts. Must be 21 or over to get in after 9pm.

CityJazz   The cover at this club includes the **Downbeat Jazz Hall of Fame** (with
memorabilia from Louis Armstrong, Ella Fitzgerald, and other greats). The two-story,
10,500-square-foot building houses more than 500 pieces of memorabilia representing Dixieland, swing, bebop, and modern jazz. It also has a state-of-the-art sound system and stage. Acts of national renown perform frequently. It's a real treat for jazz fans,
who can sip cocktails while browsing. On Thursday through Saturday nights, the
theme gives way to comedy as **BONKERZ Comedy Club** invites you in for a good
laugh. Open Sunday through Thursday from 8pm to 1am, Friday and Saturday from
7pm to 2am. ℃ 407/224-2189. Cover $7 (more for special events). Must be 18 to get in.

the groove   This crowded multilevel club features a huge dance floor and a number
of bars and lounges. Three unique themed lounges are outfitted in blue, green, and red;
each features its own decor, style of music, bar, and specialty drink to fit its ambience.
The high-tech sound system will blow you away; try the upper-level patio for a brief
reprieve. Most nights, a DJ spins the latest in hip-hop, jazz fusion, techno, and alternative rock. Bands occasionally play, too. Open daily from 9pm to 2am. ℃ 407/363-
8000. Cover $7. Must be 21 to get in.

Hard Rock Cafe/Hard Rock Live   The first concert hall to bear the Hard Rock
name is next door to the largest Hard Rock Cafe in the world (p. 161). This building,
fashioned to look like an ancient coliseum, has a 2,500-seat concert venue. Tickets for
big names sell fast. A lot of bands only your teens will know play the venue, but oldies
such as Bob Dylan and the Moody Blues have performed here, too. Concerts generally begin about 8pm. The sound system is loud, and the sightlines are pretty decent.
The Hard Rock Cafe is open daily from 11am to midnight. ℃ 407/351-7655. www.
hardrock.com. Tickets $6–$150, depending on concert.

Jimmy Buffett's Margaritaville   Flip-flops and flowered shirts are the proper
attire here. Music from the maestro is piped throughout the building, with live tunes
performed on a small stage inside later in the evening. Barwise, there are three options:

(Tips **Free Ride**

A free public transportation system called **Lymmo** (℃ **407/841-2279**; www.
golynx.com) runs in a designated lane through the downtown area. But
because Lymmo stops running at 10pm (midnight on Fri–Sat), it may stop moving before you do. So stash enough cash for a taxi if you're going to party late
into the night.

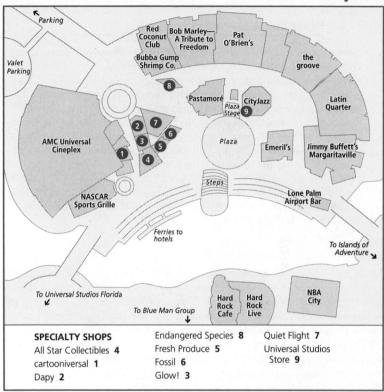

The Volcano erupts margarita mix; the Land Shark has fins hanging from the ceiling; and the 12 Volt, is . . . well, a little electrifying—we'll leave it at that. If you opt for a meal among the palm trees, go for a cheeseburger in paradise, conch fritters, one of many kinds of fish (pompano, sea bass, dolphin), and Key lime pie. See p. 161 for more on the food here. Open daily from 11:30am to 2am. ℭ **407/224-2155.** Cover $7 after 10pm.

Latin Quarter   This two-level restaurant/club features the salsa-and-samba culture of 21 Latin nations. It's filled with the music of the merengue, the mambo, and the tango, along with a bit of Latin rock thrown in for good measure. The surprisingly intimate atmosphere features mountainous architecture and waterfalls surrounding the dance floor; you'll feel like you're dancing in a Mayan temple. Open daily from 4 to 10pm. ℭ **407/224-3663.**

NASCAR Sports Grille   This recently revamped (and renamed) NASCAR-licensed eatery is a must for race-car and sports enthusiasts alike. Tableside screens (you pick the programming), high-tech simulators and games, and a huge plasma wall create what Universal calls an "outdoor tailgating experience." An upgraded menu features favorites such as ribs, pasta, sandwiches, and more. Open daily from 11am to 11pm or later. ℭ **407/224-3663.**

> ## *Tips* Other Places to Party
>
> In addition to the clubs listed in this chapter, downtown hot spots include **Chillers**, the **Big Belly Brewery**, and **Lattitudes**, 33 W. Church St. (② 407/939-4270)—three separate clubs located in a single tri-level building. All are geared to the young-adult crowd, with a very casual atmosphere. Another nighttime complex lined with clubs and bars is **Wall Street Plaza** (www.wallstplaza.net), a "meet market" on Wall Street that's home to the **Globe** (② 407/849-9904), a European patio cafe; **Slingapours** (② 407/849-9904), a dance club with an indoor and outdoor patio; **Waitiki** (② 407/849-0471), a retro tiki lounge and restaurant; the **Monkey Bar** (② 407/849-0471), a hip martini lounge and cocktail bar; **One-Eyed Jacks** (② 407/648-2050) and the **Loaded Hog** (② 407/649-1918), both party bars; the **Tuk Tuk Room** (② 407/849-9904), a cocktail-and-sushi lounge; and the **Wall Street Cantina** (② 407/420-1515), a bar that serves mean margaritas.

NBA City   Hoops and memorabilia hang from the walls, while TV screens play seemingly every game on the airwaves. The menu ($5–$20) ranges from steaks and chicken to fish, pasta, and sandwiches. The kids' menu ($6) has burgers, hot dogs, grilled cheese, and chicken nuggets. Fans young and old will like it, but if you seek better-than-average food, look elsewhere. Open daily from 11am to midnight (last seating at 10:30pm), later on Friday and Saturday (last seating at 11:30pm). ② 407/363-5919.

Pat O'Brien's   Just like the French Quarter, which is home to the original Patty O's, drinking, drinking, and more drinking are the highlights here. Enjoy the piano bar or the flame-throwing fountain while you suck down the drink of the Big Easy: the Hurricane. No one under 21 is permitted after 9pm (a kids' menu is available until then, but this is *not* the place to take them!). If your plans for the evening fall anything short of full intoxication, this may not be the place for you. There's a limited menu of sandwiches and treats like jambalaya and shrimp Creole ($8–$10). Open daily from 4pm to 2am. ② 407/363-8000. www.patobriens.com.

Red Coconut Club   Replacing the Decades Cafe is this two-story cocktail lounge, where you can sip exotic concoctions on an outdoor balcony, or head indoors for a more intimate (though somewhat louder) setting. The chic interior, signature martinis, gourmet appetizers, and live music draw a hip crowd—something the previous tenant couldn't manage. Open Sunday through Wednesday from 7pm to 2am, Friday and Saturday from 6pm to 2am. ② 407/224-3663. Cover $7 after 9pm.

ELSEWHERE IN ORLANDO

Pleasure Island, Downtown Disney, and CityWalk are the biggest nighttime draws for most visitors and some locals. However, the dozens of clubs and bars on International Drive, along Orange Avenue, and in the rest of downtown Orlando attract most home-grown night owls, business travelers who want to avoid the Mickey madness, and a small number of enterprising tourists who venture north at night. If Mom and Dad are truly looking to avoid kids on their evening out, heading to one of these areas is their best bet.

Cricketers Arms Pub & Eatery   Whether you're British or just a sympathizer, this pub is a fun place to party. As the name implies, cricket (and soccer) matches are featured on the telly. Nightly entertainment ranges from karaoke to live bands (usually blues or soft rock). The revelry offers a good excuse to try a pint or two of any of the 17 beers and ales on tap, such as Boddingtons and Old Speckled Hen. A fun menu offers English standards such as cottage pie, bangers and mash, and fish and chips ($4–$19, most under $10). Open daily from noon to 2am. At the Festival Bay Mall, 5250 International Dr. ✆ 407/354-0686. www.cricketersarmspub.com. Free parking.

11

Side Trips from Orlando

Although many visitors to Orlando never venture outside the city, an excursion away from the theme parks can allow you and your kids time to recharge your batteries while enjoying some of Central Florida's other unique and sometimes more natural offerings.

Many families who vacation in Orlando (especially those using the FlexTicket pass; see p. 254) eventually drive or shuttle it an hour and a half west on I-4 to visit another major theme park, **Busch Gardens,** as well as some of Tampa's big-league spectator sports and smaller attractions, including the **Museum of Science and Industry.** Others—especially those with space-crazed kids—head an hour east on Highway 528 to the Space Coast, where "having a blast" takes on new meaning. Rockets really do blast off from the **John F. Kennedy Space Center** at Cape Canaveral, which is also the home of **Canaveral National Seashore** and, nearby, some of the finest surfing spots in Florida. The coastal areas offer a combination of entertainment and education (be it astronomy or the natural sciences) that the whole family will enjoy.

1 Tampa

84 miles W of Orlando

The Busch Gardens theme park, with its wild animals and even wilder rides, is Tampa Bay's biggest draw for families. While you're in town, you can also visit the much less frantic exhibits at the Lowry Park Zoo; educate the kids (and yourself) at the Florida Aquarium; and, in warmer months, take a refreshing plunge at the Adventure Island water park. You can do Tampa as a day trip from Orlando, or you can spend a day or two exploring the city with your kids (I've provided accommodations and dining options below for those of you who choose to go that route); your choice will depend on your family's interests, your remaining stamina (after hitting all of Orlando's offerings), and how much vacation time you have. Most people with only a week off won't do more than travel to Busch Gardens before heading back to Mickeyville. If you've got more time, a day or two in Tampa is a fun and slightly less frenetic place to wind down your vacation.

GETTING THERE

BY CAR From Orlando, take Interstate 4 west (it's really southwest) to the downtown Tampa area. From downtown, Interstate 275 north goes to Busch Gardens.

BY SHUTTLE SeaWorld Orlando and **Busch Gardens Tampa Bay,** both owned by Anheuser-Busch, offer daily shuttle service between those parks for $10. The 1½- to 2-hour run (each way) has seven pickup locations in Orlando, including SeaWorld, International Drive, U.S. 192 in Kissimmee, and Universal Orlando (© **800/221-**

1339). The schedule allows about 5 to 7 hours at Busch Gardens, and the service is free if you buy a FlexTicket (p. 254).

VISITOR INFORMATION   Contact the **Tampa Bay Convention & Visitors Bureau** (aka **Tampa Bay & Company**), 400 N. Tampa St., Tampa, FL 33602-4706 (© **800/448-2672,** 800/368-2672, or 813/223-2752; www.visittampabay.com), for advance information. Once you're downtown, head to the bureau's **visitor information center** at the Channelside Entertainment Complex, 615 Channelside Dr. Suite 108A (© **813/223-2752**). It's open Monday through Saturday from 9:30am to 5:30pm.

EXPLORING THE PARKS & MORE

Adventure Island   If the summer heat gets to you before one of Tampa's famous thunderstorms brings late-afternoon relief, your family can take a break at this 25-acre outdoor water park near Busch Gardens Tampa Bay (see below). You can also frolic here during the cooler days of spring and fall, when the water is heated. Adults and teens enjoy Key West Rapids, RipTide, Gulf Scream, Wahoo Run, and other exciting water rides (there are height requirements on many of these thrill rides, usually starting at 48 in.). Young children can have a ton of fun in the miniature wave pool, water jets, bubbling springs, and aqua gym at Fabian's Funport. Lifeguards are there to supervise. There are also places to picnic and sunbathe, a games arcade, a volleyball complex, and an outdoor cafe. If you forget to bring your own, a surf shop sells bathing suits, towels, and suntan lotion.

10001 Malcolm McKinley Dr. (between Busch Blvd. and Bougainvillea Ave.). © 813/987-5600. www.4adventure.com. Admission $36 adults, $34 kids 3–9, plus tax. 2-day combination tickets with Busch Gardens Tampa Bay (1 day each) $76 adults, $66 kids 3–9. Website sometimes offers discounts. Parking $6. Mid-Mar–Labor Day daily 10am–5pm; Sept–Oct Fri–Sun 10am–5pm (extended hours in summer and on holidays). Closed Nov–mid-Mar. From I-275, take Exit 50 and go east on Busch Blvd. for 2 miles. Turn left onto McKinley Dr. (N. 40th St.); entry is on right.

Busch Gardens Tampa Bay ★★★   If you have time for a day trip, this venerable theme park is a don't-miss attraction for children and adults, who can see, in person, all those wild beasts from shows like *Animal Planet*—and you'll get better views of them here than at Disney's Animal Kingdom in Orlando (p. 236). Busch Gardens has several thousand animals living in naturalistic environments that help carry out the park's overall African theme, including an 80-acre plain that's reminiscent of the real Serengeti of Tanzania and Kenya, upon which zebras, giraffes, and other animals graze. Unlike the animals on the real Serengeti, however, the grazing animals have nothing to fear from lions, hyenas, crocodiles, and other predators, which are confined to enclosures— as are hippos and elephants. *Tip:* Before you leave home, spend some time with your kids on the park's website (www.buschgardens.com), which offers some wonderful educational information about the animals and environments in the park.

Timbuktu, near the center of the park, is a great place for smaller kids to enjoy the miniature train and rides including the **Busch Flyers, Pigmy Vines** and **Pigmy Glyders,**

(*Tips* **Flexing Your Muscle**

Busch Gardens is part of the Orlando–Tampa **FlexTicket,** which also includes Universal Studios Florida, Islands of Adventure, SeaWorld, and Wet 'n Wild. The ticket, which allows unlimited admission to the five parks over a 14-day period, costs $240 for adults and $200 for children 3 to 9.

Tampa

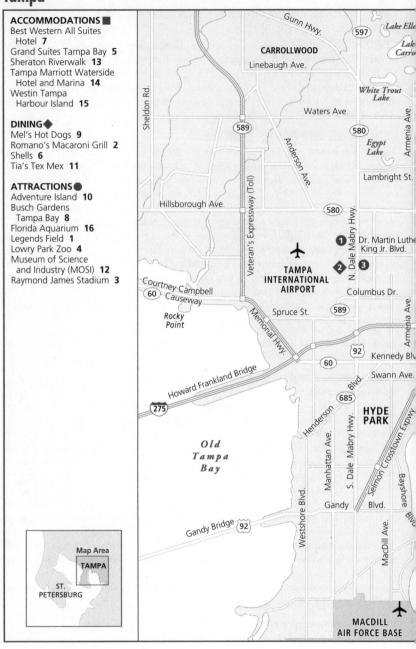

ACCOMMODATIONS ■
Best Western All Suites
  Hotel **7**
Grand Suites Tampa Bay **5**
Sheraton Riverwalk **13**
Tampa Marriott Waterside
  Hotel and Marina **14**
Westin Tampa
  Harbour Island **15**

DINING ◆
Mel's Hot Dogs **9**
Romano's Macaroni Grill **2**
Shells **6**
Tia's Tex Mex **11**

ATTRACTIONS ●
Adventure Island **10**
Busch Gardens
  Tampa Bay **8**
Florida Aquarium **16**
Legends Field **1**
Lowry Park Zoo **4**
Museum of Science
  and Industry (MOSI) **12**
Raymond James Stadium **3**

Gunn Hwy.

597 Lake Elle

Lake
Carro

CARROLLWOOD
Linebaugh Ave.

White Trout
Lake

Waters Ave.

Sheldon Rd.

589

Anderson Ave.

580

Egypt
Lake

Armenia Ave.

Lambright St.

Hillsborough Ave.

Veteran's Expressway (Toll)

580

N. Dale Mabry Hwy.

❶

Dr. Martin Luthe
King Jr. Blvd.

❷ ❸

**TAMPA
INTERNATIONAL
AIRPORT**

Columbus Dr.

Courtney Campbell
60 Causeway

Spruce St. 589

*Rocky
Point*

Memorial Hwy.

92 Kennedy Blv

60

Armenia Ave.

Swann Ave.

Howard Frankland Bridge

685

Blvd.

**HYDE
PARK**

275

Henderson

Manhattan Ave.

S. Dale Mabry Hwy.

Selmon Crosstown Expw

Bayshore Blv

*Old
Tampa
Bay*

Westshore Blvd.

Gandy Blvd.

MacDill Ave.

Gandy Bridge 92

Map Area
TAMPA

ST.
PETERSBURG

**MACDILL
AIR FORCE BASE**

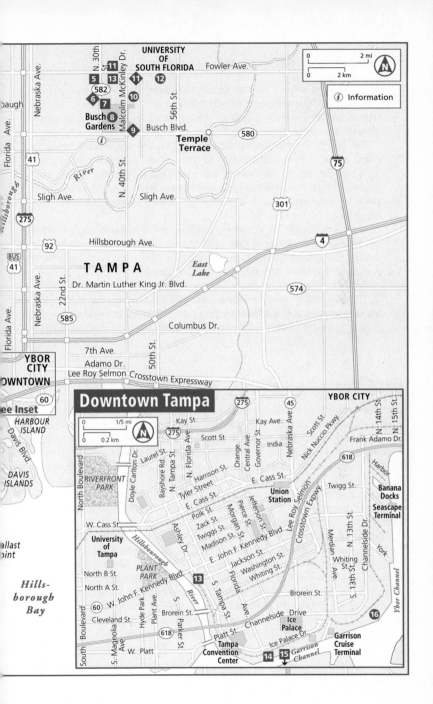

Busch Gardens

Temple Terrace

UNIVERSITY OF SOUTH FLORIDA

Fowler Ave.

N. 30th St.

Malcolm McKinley Dr.

56th St.

Nebraska Ave.

582

Busch Blvd.

580

River

Florida Ave.

41

N. 40th St.

Sligh Ave.

Sligh Ave.

75

301

275

92

Hillsborough Ave.

4

BUS 41

TAMPA

East Lake

Dr. Martin Luther King Jr. Blvd.

574

Nebraska Ave.

22nd St.

585

Columbus Dr.

50th St.

7th Ave.
Adamo Dr.
Lee Roy Selmon Crosstown Expressway

Florida Ave.

YBOR CITY
DOWNTOWN

See Inset

60

HARBOUR ISLAND

Davis Blvd

DAVIS ISLANDS

Ballast Point

Hills-borough Bay

Downtown Tampa

YBOR CITY

275

45

Kay St.

Kay Ave.

Nick Nuccio Pkwy.

N. 14th St.

N. 15th St.

275

Scott St.

India

Frank Adamo Dr.

Scott St.

Orange

Central Ave.

Governor St.

Nebraska Ave.

Scott St.

618

Harbor

North Boulevard

RIVERFRONT PARK

Doyle Carlton Dr.

Bayshore Rd.

Laurel St.

N. Tampa St.

N. Florida Ave.

Harrison St.

E. Cass St.

Tyler Street

E. Cass St.

Polk St.

Zack St.

Twiggs St.

Madison St.

Ashley Dr.

Pierce St.

Morgan St.

Jefferson St.

E. Cass St.

Union Station

Lee Roy Selmon Crosstown Expwy

Twigg St.

Banana Docks

Seascape Terminal

S. 13th St.

Meridian Ave.

Channelside Dr.

W. Cass St.

University of Tampa

Hillsborough

E. John F. Kennedy Blvd.

Jackson St.

Washington St.

Whiting St.

S. 13th St.

Whiting St.

York

PLANT PARK

North B St.

North A St.

W. John F. Kennedy Blvd.

13

Hyde Park Ave.

Plant Ave.

S. Tampa St.

River

S. Florida Ave.

Brorein St.

Ybor Channel

60

South Boulevard

S. Magnolia Ave.

Cleveland St.

Brorein St.

618

W. Platt

S. Parker St.

Platt St.

Tampa Convention Center

Channelside Drive

Ice Palace Dr.

14

15

Ice Palace

Garrison Channel

Garrison Cruise Terminal

16

2 mi
2 km

N

ⓘ Information

0   1/5 mi
0   0.2 km

N

Moments **Special Tours at Busch Gardens**

Busch Gardens offers a number of special options that are geared to families. Although you and your kids will get close to Busch Gardens' predators, hippos, and elephants in their glass-walled enclosures, the only way to mingle with the grazers is on a tour.

The best is the VIP **Animal Adventure Tour,** on which you'll roam the plains in the company of a zoologist. These 2-hour excursions cost a pricey $120 per person (in addition to the park's entry fee) and usually leave around 1:30pm daily. The park provides bottled water but advises all participants to wear hats and lots of sunscreen. Be sure to reserve ahead—tours fill up fast.

Another (though less attractive) alternative is the 30-minute, zoologist-led **Serengeti Safari Special Tour,** in which you and 19 other people ride out among the grazers on the back of a flatbed truck. Five tours are offered daily, and they are worth the extra $34 per person.

Reserve a space on the above tours or ask about other options by calling ⓒ 813/984-4043 or going to **www.buschgardens.com**. You can pick up tickets for the tours at the Adventure Tour Center, located in the Moroccan Village at the main entrance. *Children under 5 are not permitted on tours.*

Dessert Runners, and the **Cheetah Chase.** The **Friends Forever** show, at the Dragon's Tale Theater, and the entire **Land of the Dragons,** with its treehouse, slides, and miniature rides, make this pint-size play area another high point for younger guests.

The entire family can enjoy the **Skyride** cable cars that glide high above the park; the **Clydesdale** barn, where these large horses are groomed several times daily; the **bumper cars;** and the arcade area, though the games here can significantly dent your budget. A baby-animal nursery, petting zoo, and elephant and hippo exhibits are other family favorites. Ditto for **Curiosity Caverns,** where bats, reptiles, and small mammals that are active in the dark are kept in cages. Note that the latter is housed in one of those faux tunnels made of concrete and stucco, and the area is kept dark, so it could be frightening for some kids under 5.

Older thrill-ride fans find an enterprising mix of six roller coasters. The newest and by far the scariest is **SheiKra,** America's first and only dive coaster (and one of only three in the world)—and now floorless, along with the **Montu, Kumba, Gwazi, Python,** and **Scorpion,** all with minimum height requirements of 42 to 54 inches. The park also has a pair of water rides: **Tanganyika Tidal Wave** (48-in. minimum height) and the **Stanley Falls Flume** (an aqua version of a roller coaster that's tame enough for most kids 7 or 8 and older). Near the back of the park, **Rhino Rally** puts you in a Land Rover for a bouncy ride through habitat that includes white rhinos, gazelles, and wildebeests. A "flash flood" turns the Rovers into rafts that float down a short manmade river. While not particularly scary, the frantic feeling of a narrow escape combined with the rough ride may not be suitable for those under 6. **Pirates 4-D** offers fun and surprises for adults and older kids.

The park also offers exotic architecture, crafts demonstrations, an alligator-and-turtle exhibit, a hospitality house with free beer for adults, and the **Ka Tonga** and **Mirage Canteen** song-and-dance shows.

The new 4-acre **Jungala** is slated to debut in mid-2008. Located in the Congo area, it will allow guests to explore the jungles of the world as they make their way through a lush setting filled with exotic animal experiences and jungle villages. Multi-story play areas, a children's water play area, two new rides, two new restaurants, and live entertainment will add to the fun.

Note: You can get to Busch Gardens from Orlando via shuttle buses, which pick up at area hotels between 8 and 10:15am for the 1½- to 2-hour ride, with return trips starting at 5pm and continuing until the park closes. Round-trip fares are $10 per person (free if you have a FlexTicket). Call © **800/221-1339** for schedules, pickup locations, and reservations.

3000 E. Busch Blvd. (at McKinley Dr./N. 40th St.). © **888/800-5447** or 813/987-5283. www.buschgardens.com. Admission $62 adults, $52 kids 3–9, plus tax. Website offers discounts. Daily 10am–6pm (extended to 7 or 8pm in summer and on holidays). Parking $9. From downtown Tampa, take I-275 north to Busch Blvd. (Exit 50) and go east 2 miles. From I-75, take Fowler Ave. (Exit 54) and follow the signs west.

Florida Aquarium 𝒜𝒜   See more than 5,000 aquatic animals and plants that call Florida home at this entertaining and informative attraction, which appeals to all ages. The exhibits follow a drop of water from the pristine springs of the **Florida Wetlands Gallery;** through a mangrove forest in the **Bays and Beaches Gallery;** and out onto the **Coral Reefs,** where an impressive 43-foot-wide, 14-foot-tall panoramic window lets you look out on schools of fish and lots of sharks and stingrays. The **No Bone Zone** is an exhibit on invertebrate sea life that features a child-pleasing touch tank with sea stars and crabs. Also worth visiting is the **Explore a Shore** aquatic discovery zone, where kids can explore the pirate ship, scale the coral-reef rock, crawl through the wave tunnel, or slide down the water slide (with water cannons, jet sprays, and more). Lockers and a changing area are nearby (you will get wet). You can also go out on the bay to look for birds and sea life on 90-minute Dolphin Quest cruises in the *Bay Spirit,* a 64-foot catamaran.

Note: For kids 8 and older, a cool Behind the Scenes eco-tour program gives an inside look at how the aquarium feeds and houses its marine residents and also offers up-close encounters with some of the animals. Older kids (and those certified to dive) can dive with the sharks for $150. Kids 6 and up can swim with the fishes for $75 (if the kids are under 9 years old, you'll be swimming, too).

701 Channelside Dr. © 813/273-4000. www.flaquarium.net. Admission $18 adults, $15 seniors, $13 kids 3–11. Dolphin Quest $20 adults, $18 seniors, $15 kids 2–13. Combination aquarium admission and eco-tour $33 adults, $30 seniors, $23 kids 3–11. Eco-tours only $20 adults, $19 seniors, $15 kids 3–11. Premium Pass including admission, eco-tour, and behind-the-scenes tour $38 adult, $35 seniors, $28 kids 3–11. Website sometimes offers discounts. Parking $5. Daily 9:30am–5pm. Closed Thanksgiving and Christmas. Take I-4 west to Exit 1E (22nd and 21st sts.); head down 21st St. to Hwy. 60; make a right off Hwy. 60 onto Channelside Dr.

Lowry Park Zoo 𝒜   The opportunity to view 3,000-pound manatees, Komodo dragons, Persian leopards, and rare red pandas makes this a worthwhile excursion. With lots of greenery, bubbling brooks, and cascading waterfalls, this 24-acre zoo displays animals in settings similar to their natural habitats. Other major exhibits include a Florida wildlife display, Primate World, an Aquatic Center, a free-flight aviary with a birds-of-prey show, a hands-on Discovery Center, and an endangered-species carousel ride that's a real hit for children. **Wallaroo Station** has kids' rides, a small water park, a kangaroo walkabout, and a petting zoo. In 2004, a **Safari-Africa** exhibit opened, featuring elephants, meerkats, and reticulated giraffes. The **Treetop Skyfari** offers guests a bird's-eye view of the animal habitats below. The **River Odyssey Eco Tour** allows guests a glimpse of the manatees, hawks, herons, and other inhabitants that live along the river. Kids will have fun feeding the giraffes, and camel rides are available as well. Lowry Park has one of Florida's three manatee hospitals and rehabilitation centers. It's also a sanctuary for Florida panthers and red wolves. The zoo occasionally offers fun and educational classes and programs that allow up-close encounters with some animals. Call the zoo or consult its website (an excellent and entertaining resource for kids) for more information.

Tip: If you're a member of your local zoo, you may be eligible for discounted or free admission to the Lowry Park Zoo. Call ahead and ask.

1101 W. Sligh Ave. ©️ 813/935-8552, or 813/932-0245 for recorded information. www.lowryparkzoo.com. Admission $17 adults, $16 seniors, $13 kids 3–11. Ecotour $14 adults, $13 seniors, $10 kids 3–11. Unlimited-ride wristbands $18. Free parking. Daily 9:30am–5pm. Closed Thanksgiving and Christmas. Take I-275 to Sligh Ave. (Exit 48) and follow the signs.

Museum of Science & Industry (MOSI) 🎯🎯   A great place to take the kids on a rainy day, MOSI is the largest science center in the Southeast and has more than 450 interactive exhibits. You can step into the **Gulf Hurricane** and experience 74-mile-per-hour winds, take flight in the unique **Max Flight Jet fighter** simulator experience, and explore the human body in the **Amazing You.** If your heart is up to it, you can ride a bicycle across a 98-foot-long cable suspended 30 feet above the lobby (don't worry; you'll be harnessed to the bike). Your kids will likely find the dinosaurs in the lobby awe-inspiring. The new **Kids in Charge,** a 45,000-square-foot space dedicated entirely to kids and the largest children's science center in the country, is filled with four unique interactive exhibits that will stimulate curiosity and encourage learning. You can also watch stunning movies in Florida's first IMAX dome theater (free with admission) or take a 5-minute ride in a flight simulator. Outside, trails wind through a 47-acre nature preserve with a butterfly garden. The museum also has a planetarium.

4801 E. Fowler Ave. (at N. 50th St.). ©️ 813/987-6100. www.mosi.org. Admission $21 adults, $19 seniors, $17 kids, free for children under 2. Regular admission includes IMAX movies. Admission w/special exhibits $26 adults, $23 seniors, $21 kids. Mon–Fri 9am–5pm. Sat–Sun 9am–6pm. From downtown, take I-275 north to the Fowler Ave. E. exit (Exit 51). Take this 2 miles east to the museum, on the right.

SPECTATOR SPORTS

From August through December, NFL fans can catch the **Tampa Bay Buccaneers** at the modern 66,000-seat Raymond James Stadium, 4201 N. Dale Mabry Hwy., at Dr. Martin Luther King, Jr. Boulevard (©️ **813/879-2827;** www.buccaneers.com). Single-game tickets (starting at $30) are *very* hard to come by.

The National Hockey League's **Tampa Bay Lightning** play in the St. Pete Times Forum (©️ **813/301-6500;** www.tampabaylightning.com). The season begins in October. You can usually get single-game tickets ($8–$155) on game day.

New York Yankees fans can watch the Bronx Bombers during baseball spring training, from mid-February to the end of March at Legends Field (©️ **813/879-2244** or 813/875-7753; www.legendsfieldtampa.com), opposite Raymond James Stadium. This scaled-down replica of Yankee Stadium is the largest spring-training facility in Florida, with a 10,000-seat capacity. Tickets are $10 to $20. The club's minor-league team, the **Tampa Yankees** (same phone and website), plays at Legends Field from April through August.

> ## *Value* Discount Packages
>
> Many Tampa hotels combine tickets to major attractions such as Busch Gardens in their packages, so always ask about special deals.

WHERE TO STAY

If you're going to Busch Gardens, Adventure Island, Lowry Park Zoo, or MOSI, the motels listed in the "Near Busch Gardens" section are much more convenient than those downtown, about 7 to 12 miles to the south (and about a 20- to 30-min. drive in traffic). Most of these are also geared to families, so you're more likely to find kid-friendly amenities. The downtown Tampa hotels are geared to business travelers, but staying there will put you near the Florida Aquarium and reasonably close to the sports venues listed above. You can also check with your favorite chain, many of which have places in the Westshore area, a few miles west of downtown.

Rates at most hotels in Tampa vary little from season to season. This is especially true downtown, where the hotels do a brisk convention business all year. Hillsborough County adds 12% tax to your hotel-room bill.

NEAR BUSCH GARDENS

In addition to the hotels listed below, a good option in the area is the **Grand Suites Tampa Bay,** 11310 N. 30th St. (© **813/971-7690;** www.grandsuitestampa.com), which offers all the comforts of home (including a kitchenette), spacious accommodations, and free high-speed Internet access.

Best Western All Suites Hotel 🏖️🏖️ *Value*   This three-story, all-suite hotel is the most beachlike vacation venue you'll find close to the park, and it's an attractive spot for families. Whimsical signs lead you around a lush tropical courtyard with a heated freshwater pool (popular with kids and adults alike), a hot tub, and a lively, sports-oriented tiki bar. The bar can get noisy before closing at 9pm, and ground-level units are musty, so ask for an upstairs suite away from the action if you have little ones with early bedtimes. Suite living rooms are well equipped with fridges and microwaves, and separate bedrooms have narrow screened patios or balconies. The 11 family suites have VCRs, bunk beds, and a queen-size bed for parents. The hotel restaurant has a good kids' menu.

3001 University Center Dr. (faces N. 30th St. between Busch Blvd. and Fowler Ave.; behind Busch Gardens), Tampa, FL 33612. © 800/786-7446 or 813/971-8930. Fax 813/971-8935. www.bestwesternflorida.com. 150 units. $89–$119 suite for 2. Children under 17 stay free in parent's room. Rollaway beds not available, cribs free. Rates include hot breakfast buffet. AE, DC, DISC, MC, V. **Amenities:** Restaurant (breakfast and dinner only); bar; heated outdoor pool; access to nearby health club; Jacuzzi; game room; limited room service; laundry service; coin-op washers and dryers. *In room:* A/C, TV, dataport, fridge, coffeemaker, hair dryer, iron, microwave.

DOWNTOWN TAMPA

If the hotels listed below are sold out, another good option is the **Sheraton Riverwalk,** 200 N. Ashley St. (© **800/325-3535** or 813/223-2222; www.starwoodhotels.com). Set on the east bank of the Hillsborough River, this former Radisson hotel underwent extensive renovations before reopening in 2005 as a Sheraton. Half the comfortable rooms face west and have views from their balconies of the arabesque minarets atop the University of Tampa campus across the river—quite a scene at sunset (your kids should be suitably impressed). There isn't much here that's especially

---

Tips **On the Go with Babies in Tow**

If you're headed to Tampa for an overnight and don't want to have to schlep all the baby gear along—or if you decide last minute to stay and have left all yours in Orlando—**Baby's Away** (© 800/252-0254 or 813/933-0035; www.babys away.com) will come to the rescue. It rents strollers, cribs (though most hotels have them), beach equipment, and plenty more. If you're in need of other necessities, the **University Mall** (© 813/971-3456; www.universitymall tampa.com) is just a minute or two away from the Busch Gardens area hotels listed above, and there's a **Walgreens** nearby as well.

---

aimed at the younger set, but they should find no fault with the pool that overlooks the riverfront.

Tampa Marriott Waterside Hotel & Marina 🌟🌟 This luxurious 22-story hotel occupies downtown's most strategic location—beside the river and between the Tampa Convention Center and the St. Pete Times Forum—and was built for the business set, though it's not a bad choice for families. Opening onto a riverfront promenade, the towering three-story lobby (look out for those palm trees) should suitably impress. The third floor has a fully equipped spa, modern exercise facility, and outdoor heated pool where kids and parents can relax. About half the guest quarters have balconies overlooking the bay or city (choice views are high up on the south side). The regular rooms are spacious enough and can easily fit a family of four (you can ask for a refrigerator), though they're dwarfed by the 720-square-foot suites.

700 S. Florida Ave. (at St. Pete Times Forum Dr.), Tampa, FL 33602. © 800/228-9290 or 813/221-4900. Fax 813/221-0923. www.tampawaterside.com. 717 units. $129–$254 double; $450–$1,800 suite. AE, DC, DISC, MC, V. Weekend rates available. No self-parking, valet parking $18. **Amenities:** 3 restaurants; 3 bars; heated outdoor pool; health club; spa; Jacuzzi; concierge; activities desk; car-rental desk; business center; salon; limited room service; massage; babysitting; laundry service; coin-op washers and dryers; boat dock; concierge-level rooms. *In room:* A/C, TV, fax, dataport (with high-speed Internet), fridge, coffeemaker, hair dryer, iron, video games (fee).

Westin Tampa Harbour Island 🌟🌟🌟 Close enough to downtown but still worlds away on its own 177-acre island, this stylishly contemporary Westin insists that you're here on vacation and not stuck in some insipid downtown convention hotel. Rooms overlook the harbor and are hypercomfortable, with Heavenly amenities (including mattresses, cribs, showers—and even dog beds), oversized bathrooms, and conveniences like refrigerators. The hotel's main restaurant, 725 South, overlooks the water and offers Continental cuisine in an upscale atmosphere. Guest privileges include use of the nearby Harbour Island Athletic club, with its full workout facilities, tennis courts, racquetball courts, and full-service spa (additional fees apply). Stroll the boardwalk to fully appreciate your surroundings.

725 S. Harbour Island Blvd., Tampa, FL 33602. © 888/625-5144 or 813/229-5000. Fax 813/229-5322. www.starwood hotels.com. 299 units. $199–$289 double; $495–$895 suite. AE, DC, DISC, MC, V. Weekend rates available. No self-parking, valet parking $12. **Amenities:** 2 restaurants; 3 bars; heated outdoor pool; access to nearby health club; access to spa; Jacuzzi; concierge; activities desk; car-rental desk; business center; salon; limited room service; massage; babysitting; laundry service. *In room:* A/C, TV, fax, high-speed Internet (fee), coffeemaker, hair dryer, iron, video games (fee), VCR (fee).

WHERE TO DINE

In addition to the following options, you can find a number of fast-food and chain eateries on Kennedy Boulevard, west of Dale Mabry.

IN & NEAR BUSCH GARDENS

You'll find several national chains and family restaurants east of I-275 on Busch Boulevard and Fowler Avenue.

Mel's Hot Dogs ★★ *Value* AMERICAN   Catering to everyone from businesspeople on a lunch break to hungry families craving inexpensive all-beef hot dogs, Mel Lohn's red-and-white cottage offers everything from "bagel-dogs" to bacon/cheddar Reuben-style hot dogs. All options are served on a poppyseed bun and can be ordered with fries and a choice of coleslaw or baked beans. The decor highlights all things hot dog, and the pictures, articles, and memorabilia that line the walls highlight the restaurant's history; there's also an eye-catching red wienermobile usually parked out front. Your kids will love it—and so will you. But just in case hot-dog mania hasn't won you over, there are a few alternatives (chicken, beef, and veggie burgers, and terrific onion rings). Children's meals include hot dogs, corn dogs, hamburgers, or chicken nuggets, all of which come with fries, dessert, and a toy. Be sure to say hello to Mel; he usually greets everyone with a smile and a story.

4136 E. Busch Blvd., at 42nd St. © 813/985-8000. Kids' menu, highchairs, boosters. Reservations not accepted. Most items $4–$12; kids $4–$4.50. No credit cards. Sun–Thurs 11am–8pm; Fri–Sat 11am–9pm.

Shells ★ *Value* SEAFOOD   You'll see Shells restaurants in many parts of Florida, and with good reason, for this casual chain consistently provides excellent value for families. Each branch has virtually identical menus, prices, and hours. Particularly good for adults are the spicy Jack Daniel's buffalo shrimp and scallop appetizers. Main courses range from the usual fried-seafood platters to pastas and charcoal-grilled shrimp, fish, steaks, and chicken. Kids can dig into chicken tenders, shrimp, fish, mini burgers, or macaroni and cheese while they color on their placemats and sip their Shark Attack specialty drinks.

11010 N. 30th St. © 813/977-8456. www.shellsseafood.com. Kids' menu, highchairs, boosters, placemats w/crayons. Reservations not accepted. Main courses $9–$28; kids $4–$7. AE, DISC, MC, V. Sun–Thurs 4–10pm; Fri–Sat 4–11pm.

Tia's Tex Mex *Value* SOUTHWEST   Create your own combination platter from a list that includes tamales, chicken flautas, chalupas, tacos, and enchiladas (all the taco shells here are made with vegetable oil). Or dig into one of the menu standards, such as mesquite-grilled shrimp with chipotle glaze. The younger set's menu offers corn dogs, chicken fingers, tacos, and grilled cheese.

2815 Fowler Ave. (between I-275 and Bruce B. Downs Blvd.). © 813/972-7737. www.tiastexmex.com. Kids' menu, highchairs, boosters, placemats w/crayons and word games. Reservations recommended. Main courses $7–$15; kids $4–$5. AE, DC, DISC, MC, V. Daily 11am–10pm, except Thanksgiving and Christmas.

WEST OF DOWNTOWN

You'll find the usual chain restaurants in town, including T.G.I. Friday's, Carrabba's, and Chili's, along North Dale Mabry, near Raymond James Stadium.

Romano's Macaroni Grill ★ *Value* ITALIAN   Romano's is a small chain with a nice family atmosphere (you can definitely hear the buzz of conversation), and unlike most of Tampa's better restaurants, it's not oriented toward the business crowd. The staff will put jug wine on your table and deliver entrees such as veal piccata, chicken Marsala, shrimp scampi, and a meaty lasagna, which are reasonably priced and pretty tasty. Kids can feast on a grilled macaroni-and-cheese sandwich, a corn dog, pizza, or chicken fingers, which all come with refillable soft drinks and dessert. This place also offers stuff to keep the young ones busy while Mom and Dad eat their meals.

14904 N. Dale Mabry Hwy. ℂ 813/264-6676. www.macaronigrill.com. Kids' menu, highchairs, boosters, placemats w/crayons and word games. Reservations recommended. Main courses $6–$15 lunch, $8–$19 dinner; kids $4. AE, MC, V. Daily 11am–10pm.

2 Cocoa Beach, Cape Canaveral & Kennedy Space Center ⊙★

46 miles SE of Orlando

Today, this once-sleepy region, known to many as the imaginary home of *I Dream of Jeannie,* now welcomes crowds attracted primarily by Kennedy Space Center, which is not only the launching pad for the U.S. space program, but also a tourist attraction that thrills hundreds of thousands of visitors each year. A visit to the space center is usually an awe-inspiring experience for even the most jaded kids (and has launched many dreams of becoming an astronaut). If your kids' interests tend more toward natural life on earth, the area is also home to 72 miles of sandy beaches (the closest beach to Orlando's attractions); some of the best surfing anywhere around; and wildlife, at the zoo (the Brevard Zoo, which offers exhibits on par with Tampa's Lowry Park Zoo, listed earlier in this chapter) or in its more natural state—in the wild.

GETTING THERE

BY CAR   From Orlando, take Highway 528 (a toll road), exit on Highway 407, and go to Highway 405/NASA Parkway; then follow the signs east to the space center.

BY SHUTTLE   Mears Transportation (ℂ 407/423-5566; www.mearstransportation. com) runs Kennedy Space Center shuttles Monday, Wednesday, and Friday from Lake Buena Vista and U.S. 192 (near Disney) and International Drive (near Universal). The cost is $30 per person round-trip (free for kids 3 and under), and the trip allows for 7 hours at the center.

VISITOR INFORMATION   For area information, contact **Florida's Space Coast Office of Tourism/Brevard County Tourist Development Council,** 8810 Astronaut Blvd., Suite 102, Cape Canaveral, FL 32920 (ℂ 800/872-1969 or 321/868-1126; www.space-coast.com). The office is in the Sheldon Cove building, on Florida A1A a block north of Central Boulevard, and is open Monday through Friday from 8am to 5pm. It also operates an information booth at the Kennedy Space Center Visitor Complex (see below).

EXPLORING THE ATTRACTIONS

Brevard Zoo   At this small-town zoo, you'll find over 550 exotic animals. In addition to a pair of rare white rhinos, lemurs, gazelles, antelopes, and a variety of primates, the Expedition Africa exhibit is home to ostriches and giraffes (you and your kids can hand-feed the latter, whose 18-in. tongues usually startle when they snake out to grab a snack!). Other residents include dingoes, red kangaroos, wallabies, cottontop tamarins, crocodiles, howler monkeys, bald eagles, red wolves, and river otters. Kayak rides (for an additional fee of $5 per person per adventure) allow for up close views of the park's inhabitants. Choices include a 20-minute excursion through Africa or through the wetlands of Wild Florida (where the gators, crocs, and river otters roam). A hands-on petting zoo features a miniature horse, miniature donkey, fallow deer, and goats. The zoo also offers a 10-minute train tour of the grounds ($3 for ages

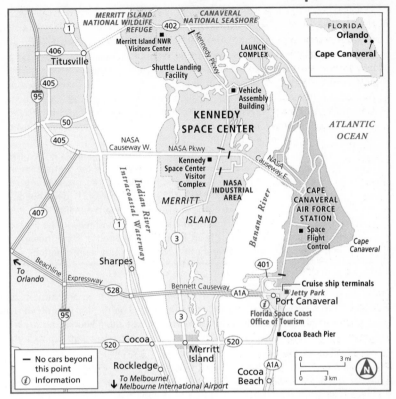

2 and up), educational kayak trips ($5; kids must be at least 5), a tropical garden inhabited by flying fox bats and muntjac deer, a free-flight aviary, and alligator feedings usually 3 days a week (check the schedule or website below for days and times). **Note:** The Paws on Play area is slated to reopen in the summer of 2008 after undergoing extensive renovations.

8225 N. Wickham Rd., Melbourne (just east of I-95, Exit 73/Wickham Rd.). ☎ **321/254-9453**. www.brevardzoo.org. Admission $11 adults, $9.50 seniors, $7.50 kids 2–12. Daily 9:30am–5pm (last entrance 4:15pm). Closed Thanksgiving and Christmas.

John F. Kennedy Space Center ★★★ Whether you and your kids are space buffs or not, you'll appreciate the sheer grandeur of the facilities and technological achievements displayed at NASA's primary space-launch facility, which is rich in history. This is where Alan Shepard, America's first man in space, and Neil Armstrong, the first human on the moon, started their memorable journeys.

Because all roads other than S.R. 405 and S.R. 3 are closed to the public in the space center, you must begin your visit at the **Kennedy Space Center Visitor Complex.** A bit like a themed amusement park, this privately run complex has had an ambitious $130-million renovation and expansion, and operators continue to tweak its offerings (which includes the new $60-million Space Shuttle Experience)—so

---

Tips Out to Launch

If you'd like to see a shuttle launch at the **Kennedy Space Center,** first call
(℃ **321/867-5000** or check NASA's official website (www.ksc.nasa.gov) for a
schedule of upcoming takeoffs. You can buy special launch-day viewing tickets
by calling (℃ **321/449-4444** or going online to www.ksctickets.com. *A word of
caution:* Shuttle launches are frequently delayed due to weather, equipment
malfunctions, or other factors, so you might have to make multiple visits to see
one. If you don't have that flexibility, the launch window may be delayed
beyond your going-home date.

If you can't get into the space center, other good viewing spots are on the
causeways leading to the islands and on U.S. 1 as it skirts the waterfront in
Titusville. The **Holiday Inn Riverside–Kennedy Space Center,** on Washington
Avenue (U.S. 1) in Titusville (℃ **800/465-4329** or 321/269-2121; www.holiday
innksc.com), also has a clear view of the launch pads across the Indian River. I've
watched from the beach at the Holiday Inn, and hearing and feeling the distant
rumbles of the shuttle at takeoff is an incredible experience. Note, however,
that area motels raise their rates and often book up during launch periods.

---

check the complex's website or call in advance to see whether tours and exhibits have
changed. Also check beforehand to see what's happening on the day you intend to be
here, and arrive early to plan your visit. You'll need at least 2 to 3 hours to see the highlights on the bus tour through the center (which I highly recommend), up to 5 hours
if you linger at the stops along the way (or if you've got small kids and end up making lots of stops), and an additional 2 to 4 hours to see the Visitor Complex attractions. All in all, plan on a full day to see and do everything here.

The Visitor Complex has real NASA rockets and the actual Mercury Mission Control Room from the 1960s. Exhibits look at early space exploration and where it's
going in the new millennium. There are a rocket garden, where kids of all ages can
explore spacecraft, including a shuttle; a realistic and thrilling new Shuttle Launch
Experience, where astronauts in training can travel into space several times a day; an
opportunity to dine with a real astronaut; several dining venues; and a shop selling a
variety of memorabilia and souvenirs. Two space-related IMAX movies (one in 3-D)
shown on five-and-a-half-story-high screens are informative and entertaining.

While you could spend your entire day at the Visitor Complex, you must take a
KSC Tour to see the actual space center, where rockets and shuttles are prepared and
launched. Plan to take the bus tour early in your visit, and be sure to hit the restrooms
before boarding the bus. The buses depart every 10 minutes or so, and you can
reboard as you wish. They stop at the **LC-39 Observation Gantry,** with a dramatic
360-degree view over launch pads where space shuttles blast off; the **International
Space Station Center,** where scientists and engineers prepare additions to the space
station now in orbit; and the impressive **Apollo/Saturn V Center,** which includes artifacts, photos, interactive exhibits, and the 363-foot **Saturn V,** the most powerful
rocket ever launched by the United States.

Kids will appreciate the **Mad Mission to Mars,** where they can explore the cosmos
via a combination of live action, 3-D animation, and theatrical effects.

Don't miss the **Astronaut Memorial,** a moving black-granite monument that bears the names of the U.S. astronauts who have died on missions or while in training (including those who perished in the 2003 *Columbia* tragedy). The 60-ton structure rotates on a track that follows the movement of the sun (on clear days, of course), causing the names to stand out above a brilliant reflection of the sky.

The **U.S. Astronaut Hall of Fame** (located on S.R. 405 just west of the center) features displays, exhibits, and tributes to the heroes of the Mercury, Gemini, and Apollo space programs. There's also a collection of spacecraft, including a Mercury 7 capsule, a Gemini training capsule, and an Apollo 14 command module. In the Simulator Station, guests can experience the pressure of four times the force of gravity, ride a rover across Mars, and land the space shuttle. Kids around age 7 and up will think the experience out of this world; adults will be suitably impressed as well.

Note: Pay an extra $23 per adult and $16 per child 3 to 11 over the cost of regular admission, and you and your kids can **have lunch with a real-life astronaut.** It's usually a thrilling treat for kids old enough to appreciate it. The schedule of astronauts changes frequently, and you'll need to book in advance (call or go online to check availability and make reservations). Lunch is included in the price, though there's no kids' menu.

Future space explorers ages 14 and up (though those under 18 must be accompanied by a parent) can see and feel what space flight is really like at the **ATX,** or **Astronaut Training Experience.** It's an out-of-this-world experience that includes a full day of hands-on training, mission simulations, and exploration (as well as a T-shirt and VIP tour of the Kennedy Space Center). At $250 per astronaut, space flight can, however, get rather expensive. Call © **321/449-4400** to reserve a space.

A $160-million, 10-year development plan is currently on the books (and in the works). Included in the plan, and one of the most notable additions to date, is the new **Shuttle Launch Experience**—a thrilling (though simulated) ride into space that mimics an actual launch (and the first of many new additions to come at the complex). Custom-designed motion platforms, special simulator seating, multiple video screens, and audio and visual effects will combine to re-create the feeling of blasting off into space (think Mission: Space at Epcot; p. 215).

NASA Pkwy. (S.R. 405), 6 miles east of Titusville, ½ mile west of S.R. 3. © 321/449-4444 for general information, or 321/449-4444 for guided bus tours and launch reservations. www.kennedyspacecenter.com. Admission $38 adults, $28 kids 3–11. Astronaut Hall of Fame (only) passes $17 adults, $13 kids 3–11. Guided tours $21 adults, $15 kids 3–11. All tours and movies free for children under 3. Daily 9am–5:30pm. Shuttle-bus tours daily 10am–2:15pm. Closed Christmas and some launch days.

BEACHES & WILDLIFE REFUGES

To the north of the Kennedy Space Center, **Canaveral National Seashore** ✹✹ is a protected 13-mile barrier island backed by cabbage palms, sea grapes, palmettos, marshes, and Mosquito Lagoon. This is a great area for watching herons, egrets, ibises, willets, terns, and other birds. You might also glimpse dolphins and manatees in the lagoon. It's a nice, quiet spot for a family picnic. The beaches near parking lots 1 and 2 have lifeguards, in case you want to take a swim. Note that the park runs special Junior Ranger programs for children 6 to 12; ask at the visitor center or check the park's website. The main visitor center is at 7611 S. Atlantic Ave., New Smyrna Beach (© **321/867-4077,** or 321/867-0677 for recorded information; www.nps.gov/cana), on Apollo Beach, at the north end of the island. The southern-access gate to the island is 8 miles east of Titusville on S.R. 402, just east of S.R. 3.

Its neighbor to the south and west is the 140,000-acre **Merritt Island National Wildlife Refuge** ☆☆, home to hundreds of species of shorebirds, waterfowl, reptiles, alligators, and mammals, many of them endangered. Pick up a map and other information at the visitor center, on Highway 402 about 4 miles east of Titusville. The center has a quarter-mile-long boardwalk along the edge of the marsh and displays showing the animals you may see here. You can spot them from the 7-mile-long Black Point Wildlife Drive or one of the nature trails through the hammocks and marshes. The visitor center is open Monday through Friday from 8am to 4:30pm, Saturday and Sunday from 9am to 5pm (closed Sun Apr–Oct). Admission is free. For more information and a schedule of interpretive programs, contact the refuge at P.O. Box 6504, Titusville, FL 32782 (© **321/861-0667;** www.nbbd.com/godo/minwr).

Note: Those parts of the national seashore near the Kennedy Space Center and all of the refuge close 72 hours before a shuttle launch and usually reopen the day after a launch.

OUTDOOR ACTIVITIES

FISHING   If you and your kids like to fish, head to Port Canaveral for catches such as snapper and grouper. **Jetty Park** (© **321/783-7111**), at the south entry to the port, has a fishing pier equipped with a bait shop (see "Beaches & Wildlife Refuges," above). The south bank of the port is lined with charter boats, and you can go deep-sea fishing on the *Miss Cape Canaveral* (© **321/783-5274,** or 321/648-2211 in Orlando; www.misscape.com), one of the party boats based here. All-day voyages (including all gear, bait, breakfast, lunch, and unlimited soft drinks) depart daily at 8am and cost $50 to $65 for adults, $45 to $60 for seniors, $40 to $55 for students 11 to 17, and $30 to $45 for kids 6 to 10. Be sure to bring hats, sunscreen, and shoes with good traction.

SURFING   Rip through some occasionally awesome waves (by Florida's standards, not California's or Hawaii's) at the **Cocoa Beach Pier** area or down south at **Sebastian Inlet.** Get outfitted at Ron Jon Surf Shop, and learn how to hang ten at the **Ron Jon Surf School** ☆, 150 E. Columbia Lane (© **321/868-1980;** www.cocoabeach surfingschool.com). It offers equipment and lessons for beginners and pros at area beaches (kids must be at least 8 and able to swim in order to participate). Private lessons run approximately $60 for 1 hour, $90 for 2, and $130 for 3; semiprivate (two kids only) and group lessons are offered at slightly discounted prices ($45, $60, and $80 per person respectively). Be sure to bring along a towel, flip-flops, sunscreen (including some zinc oxide), and a lot of nerve. The school also offers 5-day surfing camps that cover water safety, instruction, and plenty of surfing for kids ages 8 to 16 from May to August. The cost is $325 per child (you'll pay an extra $50 for lunches). To ensure a spot in surf camp (they're limited), sign up early. My three oldest boys learned to surf just this past summer at the Ron Jon surf camp, and before week's end were asking to sign up again!

WHERE TO STAY

The hotels listed below are all in Cocoa Beach, the closest resort area to Kennedy Space Center, about a 30-minute drive to the north. If they're booked up, or if you're traveling with older kids (and don't require tot-friendly accommodations and amenities), head to the hip new **Four Points by Sheraton,** 4001 N. Atlantic Ave. (© **800/ 368-7764;** www.starwoodhotels.com), which opened in December 2005. Though small (even boutique-ish), its 75 rooms and suites have surf-chic themes and are located just a block from the beach. Corner rooms and those on higher floors are larger. The lobby opens directly into the Cocoa Beach Surf Company as well as an intimate and trendy sea-themed eatery. Another often overlooked choice is the **Courtyard by Marriott,** 3435 N. Atlantic Ave. (© 321/784-4800; www.marriott.com), which has spacious and well-appointed rooms, casual dining, a nicely landscaped pool area (with giant overhanging oaks), thoughtful little extras (like a laptop pillow and free high-speed Internet), and a location that's just a short walk to the beach.

Note: You'll pay a 4% hotel tax on top of the Florida 6% sales tax here.

DoubleTree Hotel Cocoa Beach Oceanfront ✿   This six-story hotel, a good choice for families, was extensively renovated in late 2004 after suffering some damage from Hurricane Frances. Your kids should be suitably thrilled with the chain's signature chocolate-chip cookies upon check-in. All rooms have balconies with ocean views and easy chairs, and 10 suites have living rooms with sleeper sofas and separate bedrooms. A charming dining room facing the beach serves decent Mediterranean fare (a kids' menu and highchairs are available) and opens to a bilevel brick patio with water cascading between two heated pools. The beach is a short walk away.

2080 N. Atlantic Ave., Cocoa Beach, FL 32931. © **800/552-3224** or 321/783-9222. Fax 321/799-3234. www.cocoa beachdoubletree.com. 148 units. $89–$207 double; $126–$441 suite. Children under 18 stay free in parent's or grandparent's room. Rollaway beds $15, cribs free. AE, DC, DISC, MC, V. **Amenities:** Restaurant; bar; 2 heated outdoor pools; exercise room; game room; limited room service; laundry service; coin-op washers and dryers; concierge-level rooms. *In room:* A/C, TV, dataport, coffeemaker, hair dryer, iron.

Holiday Inn Cocoa Beach Oceanfront Resort ✿✿   Set on 27 beachside acres, this sprawling family-oriented complex, last renovated in 2004 (after that year's flurry of hurricanes had taken their toll), offers a variety of rooms, efficiencies, suites, and two-level lofts, and is the best bet in town for families with young kids. A few of the suites are themed KidSuites with bunk beds, VCRs, and video games; other suites feature sitting rooms with pullout couches. All suites come with refrigerators and microwaves. Most accommodations are in 1960s-style motel buildings flanking the meticulously landscaped central courtyard, where you'll find tropical foliage surrounding the tennis courts, a small playground area, an oversized pool, and plenty more. The pirate-themed kids' pool is popular with little ones, and adults can relax in the tropical-themed Olympic-size pool or the hot tub. Only those rooms directly facing the beach or pool have patios or balconies; the rest are entered from exterior corridors. There's direct access to the beach.

1300 N. Atlantic Ave. (Hwy. A1A, at Holiday Lane), Cocoa Beach, FL 32931. © **800/206-2747** or 321/783-2271. www.hicocoabeachhotelsite.com. Fax 321/783-8878. 500 units. $89–$199 double; $179–$399 suite and loft. Resort fee $4.95. Children under 18 stay free in parent's room. Rollaway beds $11, cribs free. AE, DC, DISC, MC, V. **Amenities:** 2 restaurants; 2 bars; heated outdoor pool; kids' pool; 2 tennis courts; exercise room; Jacuzzi; watersports equipment; game room; concierge; limited room service; laundry service; coin-op washers and dryers. *In room:* A/C, TV, dataport, coffeemaker, hair dryer, iron.

WHERE TO DINE

On the **Cocoa Beach Pier,** at the beach end of Meade Avenue, you'll get a fine view down the coast to accompany the seafood offerings at **Atlantic Ocean Grill** (© 321/783-7549) and the fairly good pub fare at adjacent **Marlins Good Times Bar & Grill** (same phone). Another good casual option is **Grills Restaurant & Tiki Bar,** 505 Glen Cheek Dr. (© **321/868-2226;** www.visitgrills.com), an open-air waterfront eatery

Chowing Down in Nearby Titusville

Dixie Crossroads, 1475 Garden St. (© **321/268-5000;** www.dixiecrossroads. com), in nearby Titusville, is a must-stop for families. Well worth the 20-minute drive from the Cape, this unpretentious, family-owned eatery earns high marks for its hospitality and service—oh, and the food's pretty good, too. Rock shrimp is the specialty, but seafood of any sort is worth trying. Landlubbers can dine on chicken, steaks, and ribs. Kids can choose items from their own menu or share a plate for $3 (a deal unheard of anywhere else). Prices are easy on the pocketbook, with a good portion of the menu costing under $12 (all-you-can-eat entrees run up to $34). Hand-painted murals adorn the walls, while fish ponds (kids can feed the fish for a quarter), a butterfly garden, walking trails, and fountains make it an experience, not just a meal. Be prepared for a wait—this very popular spot can get quite crowded.

that's friendly enough to bring the kids along. Your children will likely get a kick out of watching the fishing boats come in with the catch of the day, and when there's live entertainment out on the deck, the occasional squeak or squeal easily goes unnoticed. Main courses on the immense menu (chicken, beef, pasta, seafood galore, and more) run $7 to $19.

Note: All of the restaurants listed below provide crayons or other activities to keep kids busy during mealtimes.

Bernard's Surf ⊛ SEAFOOD/STEAKS   Photos on the walls testify that many astronauts—and Russian cosmonauts, too—have come to Bernard's and the adjoining Fischer's (below) to celebrate their landings. It all started as Bernard's Surf, which has been serving standard steak-and-seafood fare in a nautical setting since 1948. The menu offers specials such as stone-crab claws, Florida lobster tails stuffed with crab, char-grilled red snapper, and a belly-busting platter of shrimp, scallops, grouper, crab cakes, lobster, and oysters. Little mates can choose fried flounder, shrimp, chicken fingers, clams, burgers, or pasta marinara. All kids' meals include fries and ice cream.

2 S. Atlantic Ave. (at Minuteman Causeway Rd.), Cocoa Beach. © **321/783-2401.** Reservations recommended. Kids' menu, highchairs, boosters, placemats w/crayons. Main courses $14–$55; kids $6. AE, DC, DISC, MC, V. Mon–Thurs 4–10pm; Fri–Sat 4–11pm. Closed Christmas.

Fischer's Seafood Bar & Grill ⊛ *(Value* SEAFOOD/STEAKS   Fresh seafood finds its way into this bar and grill, a friendly, *Cheers*-like lounge popular with the locals and right next to Bernard's (above). Fischer's features fried combo platters, shrimp and crab-claw meat sautéed in herb butter, and mussels with wine sauce over pasta. The menu also lists sandwiches, burgers, and other pub fare, and it has the same 25¢ happy-hour oysters and spicy wings as Rusty's Seafood & Oyster Bar (see below), which also has a branch in this complex. The kiddie menu has most of the same options as Bernard's (though cheaper), plus a grilled-cheese sandwich.

2 S. Atlantic Ave. (at Minuteman Causeway Rd.), Cocoa Beach. © **321/783-2401.** Reservations not accepted. Kids' menu, highchairs, boosters, placemats w/crayons. Main courses $9–$16; sandwiches and salads $4–$9; kids $3. AE, DC, DISC, MC, V. Mon–Thurs 11am–10pm; Fri–Sat 11am–11pm. Closed Christmas.

Rusty's Seafood & Oyster Bar *(Value* SEAFOOD   This lively sports bar, beside Port Canaveral's manmade harbor, offers inexpensive chow ranging from very spicy seafood gumbo to a pot of seafood that includes steamed oysters, clams, shrimp, crab legs, potatoes, and corn on the cob. Raw or steamed fresh oysters and clams from the raw bar are first rate and a very good value, as is the lunch buffet on weekdays. Seating is available indoors or out, but the inside tables have the best view of fishing boats and cruise liners going in and out of the port (which should keep kids entertained). The kids' menu offers chicken nuggets, fried shrimp, burgers, grilled cheese, and spaghetti.

Note: Daily happy hours, from 3 to 6pm, see beer drafted at 60¢ a mug, and tons of raw or steamed oysters and spicy buffalo wings go for 25¢ each. As a result, lots of couples and adults congregate here. It's a busy and sometimes-noisy joint, especially on weekend afternoons, but the clientele tends to be somewhat older and better behaved than at some other pubs along the banks of Port Canaveral. So it's unlikely that you'll encounter a problem by bringing your kids here (and any noise they make will likely get lost in the din).

There's another **Rusty's** in the Bernard's Surf/Fischer's Seafood Bar & Grill restaurant complex in Cocoa Beach (see above), with the same menu.

628 Glen Cheek Dr. (south side of the harbor), Port Canaveral. © 321/783-2033. Kids' menu, highchairs, boosters, placemats w/crayons. Main courses $7–$25; sandwiches and salads $4–$7; kids $3–$9; lunch buffet $6 adults, $3 kids. AE, DC, DISC, MC, V. Sun–Thurs 11am–11:30pm; Fri–Sat 11am–12:30am (lunch buffet Mon–Fri 11am–2pm).

Appendix:
Useful Toll-Free Numbers
& Websites

AIRLINES

Aer Lingus
℃ 800/474-7424 in the U.S.
℃ 0818/365-000 in Ireland
www.aerlingus.com

Aero Mexico
℃ 800/237-6639
℃ 01/800/021-4010 in Mexico
www.aeromexico.com

Air Canada
℃ 888/247-2262
www.aircanada.ca

Air New Zealand
℃ 800/262-1234 or 800/262-2468
in the U.S.
℃ 800/663-5494 in Canada
℃ 0800/737-767 in New Zealand
www.airnewzealand.com

Air Tran Airlines
℃ 800/247-8726
www.airtran.com

Alaska Airlines
℃ 800/426-0333
www.alaskaair.com

American Airlines
℃ 800/433-7300
www.aa.com

American Trans Air
℃ 800/225-2995
www.ata.com

British Airways
℃ 800/247-9297
℃ 0345/222-111 or 0845/773-3377
in the U.K.
www.british-airways.com

Continental Airlines
℃ 800/525-0280
www.continental.com

Delta Air Lines
℃ 800/221-1212
www.delta.com

Frontier Airlines
℃ 800/432-1359
www.frontierairlines.com

JetBlue Airways
℃ 800/538-2583
www.jetblue.com

Midwest Express
℃ 800/452-2022
www.midwestexpress.com

Northwest Airlines
℃ 800/225-2525
www.nwa.com

Quantas
℃ 800/227-4500 in the US
℃ 612/9691-3636 in Australia
www.quantas.com.au

Southwest Airlines
℃ 800/435-9792
www.southwest.com

Spirit Airlines
℃ 800/772-7117
www.spiritair.com

Ted
℃ 800/225-5833
www.flyted.com

United Airlines
℃ 800/241-6522
www.united.com

US Airways
✆ 800/428-4322
www.usairways.com

CAR-RENTAL AGENCIES
Alamo
✆ 800/327-9633
www.goalamo.com

Avis
✆ 800/331-1212 in the continental U.S.
✆ 800/TRY-AVIS (800/879-2847) in
Canada
www.avis.com

Budget
✆ 800/527-0700
www.budget.com

Dollar
✆ 800/800-4000
www.dollar.com

Enterprise
✆ 800/325-8007
www.enterprise.com

SHUTTLE SERVICES
Mears Transportation Group
✆ 407/423-5566
www.mearstransportation.com

Quicksilver Tours & Transportation
✆ 888/GO-TO-WDW
✆ 407/299-1431
www.quicksilver-tours.com

Virgin Atlantic Airways
✆ 800/862-8621 in the continental U.S.
✆ 0293/747-747 in the U.K.
www.virgin-atlantic.com

Hertz
✆ 800/654-3131
www.hertz.com

Luxury Rental Cars of Orlando
✆ 888/641-9221
✆ 407/641-9221
www.luxrentals.com

National
✆ 800/CAR-RENT (800/227-7368)
www.nationalcar.com

Payless
✆ 800/PAYLESS (800/729-5377)
www.paylesscarrental.com

Thrifty
✆ 800/367-2277
www.thrifty.com

Tiffany Towncar Service
✆ 888/838-2161
✆ 407/251-5431
www.tiffanytowncar.com

Index

See also Accommodations and Restaurant indexes, below.

RESTAURANTS

FROMMER'S® PORTABLE GUIDES

Acapulco, Ixtapa & Zihuatanejo
Amsterdam
Aruba, Bonaire & Curacao
Australia's Great Barrier Reef
Bahamas
Big Island of Hawaii
Boston
California Wine Country
Cancún
Cayman Islands
Charleston
Chicago
Dominican Republic

Florence
Las Vegas
Las Vegas for Non-Gamblers
London
Maui
Nantucket & Martha's Vineyard
New Orleans
New York City
Paris
Portland
Puerto Rico
Puerto Vallarta, Manzanillo &
    Guadalajara

Rio de Janeiro
San Diego
San Francisco
Savannah
St. Martin, Sint Maarten, Anguil
    St. Bart's
Turks & Caicos
Vancouver
Venice
Virgin Islands
Washington, D.C.
Whistler

FROMMER'S® CRUISE GUIDES

Alaska Cruises & Ports of Call

Cruises & Ports of Call

European Cruises & Ports of Cal

FROMMER'S® NATIONAL PARK GUIDES

Algonquin Provincial Park
Banff & Jasper
Grand Canyon

National Parks of the American West
Rocky Mountain
Yellowstone & Grand Teton

Yosemite and Sequoia & Kings
    Canyon
Zion & Bryce Canyon

FROMMER'S® WITH KIDS GUIDES

Chicago
Hawaii
Las Vegas
London

National Parks
New York City
San Francisco

Toronto
Walt Disney World® & Orlando
Washington, D.C.

FROMMER'S® PHRASEFINDER DICTIONARY GUIDES

Chinese
French

German
Italian

Japanese
Spanish

SUZY GERSHMAN'S BORN TO SHOP GUIDES

France
Hong Kong, Shanghai & Beijing
Italy

London
New York
Paris

San Francisco
Where to Buy the Best of Everyth

FROMMER'S® BEST-LOVED DRIVING TOURS

Britain
California
France
Germany

Ireland
Italy
New England
Northern Italy

Scotland
Spain
Tuscany & Umbria

THE UNOFFICIAL GUIDES®

Adventure Travel in Alaska
Beyond Disney
California with Kids
Central Italy
Chicago
Cruises
Disneyland®
England
Hawaii

Ireland
Las Vegas
London
Maui
Mexico's Best Beach Resorts
Mini Mickey
New Orleans
New York City
Paris

San Francisco
South Florida including Miami &
    the Keys
Walt Disney World®
Walt Disney World® for
    Grown-ups
Walt Disney World® with Kids
Washington, D.C.

SPECIAL-INTEREST TITLES

Athens Past & Present
Best Places to Raise Your Family
Cities Ranked & Rated
500 Places to Take Your Kids Before They Grow Up
Frommer's Best Day Trips from London
Frommer's Best RV & Tent Campgrounds in the U.S.A.

Frommer's Exploring America by RV
Frommer's NYC Free & Dirt Cheap
Frommer's Road Atlas Europe
Frommer's Road Atlas Ireland
Retirement Places Rated

CLOSED
due to
accidental demolition

WEGEN BISSIGEN
EICHHÖRNCHEN GESCHLOSSEN

CERRADO

CABRAS

Κλειστό
Μετεωρίτες

プール POOL CLOSED 閉
も 鎖
ELECTRIC EELS 中

Hotel
closed for
facelifting

FERMÉ POUR
RAISON
DE GRÈVE
DES BONNES

FECHADO!
POR CAUSA DE
ATAQUES DOS CROCODILOS

I don't speak sign language.

A hotel can close for all kinds of reasons.

Our Guarantee ensures that if your hotel's undergoing construction, we'll let you know in advance. In fact, we cover your entire travel experience. See www.travelocity.com/guarantee for details.

travelocity
You'll never roam alone.

There's a parking lot where my ocean view should be.

 À la place de la vue sur l'océan, me voilà avec une vue sur un parking.

 Anstatt Meerblick habe ich Sicht auf einen Parkplatz.

 Al posto della vista sull'oceano c'è un parcheggio.

 No tengo vista al mar porque hay un parque de estacionamiento.

 Há um parque de estacionamento onde deveria estar a minha vista do oce

 Ett parkeringsområde har byggts på den plats där min utsikt över ocean
borde vara.

 Er ligt een parkeerterrein waar mijn zee-uitzicht zou moeten zijn.

 ك موقف للسيارات مكان ما وجب ان يكون المنظر الخلاب المطل على المحيط .

 眼前に広がる紺碧の海・・・じゃない。窓の外は駐車均

 停车场的位置应该是我的海景所在。

I'm fluent in pig latin.

Hotel mishaps aren't bound by geography.
Neither is our Guarantee. It covers your entire travel experience
including the price. So if you don't get the ocean view you booked
we'll work with our travel partners to make it right, right away. See
www.travelocity.com/guarantee for details.

You'll never roam alone